WORLD WAR II

WORLD WAR II

H.P. WILLMOTT · CHARLES MESSENGER · ROBIN CROSS

Introduction by RICHARD OVERY

With contributions from

MICHAEL BARRETT · MARK GRANDSTAFF
MICHAEL PAUL · DAVID WELCH

DK

LONDON, NEW YORK, MELBOURNE,
MUNICH, AND DELHI

Senior Designer Juliette Norsworthy
Designers Victoria Clark, Jerry Udall, Phil Gamble
Senior Editors Jane Edmonds, Ferdie McDonald
Editorial Consultants Haruo Tohmatsu, Winfried Heinemann
Editors Michelle Crane, Elizabeth Wyse
Picture Researcher Franziska Marking
Special Photography Gary Ombler
Digital maps created by Advanced Illustration
Project Cartographers Rob Stokes, Iowerth Watkins
DTP John Goldsmid
Production Joanna Bull

Editorial Direction Andrew Heritage
Art Director Bryn Walls
Managing Editor Debra Wolter
Managing Art Editor Louise Dick

AT BROWN REFERENCE GROUP
Art editor Stefan Morris
Designers Thor Fairchild, Alison Gardiner,
Colin Tilley-Loughrey
Editors Dennis Cove, James Murphy, Henry Russell
Picture Researcher Susy Forbes
Art Director Dave Goodman
Managing Editor Tim Cooke
Editorial Director Lindsey Lowe

First American Edition 2004
This edition published 2007

Published in the United States by
DK Publishing
375 Hudson Street
New York, New York 10014

07 08 09 10 11   10 9 8 7 6 5 4 3 2

WD109—08/07

Published in Great Britain by Dorling Kindersley Limited.

Library of Congress Cataloging-in-Publication Data
Willmott, H.P.
World War II / H.P. Willmott, Robin Cross, Charles Messenger.
p. cm.
Includes index.
ISBN 978-0-7566-2968-7 (alk. Paper)
1. World War, 1939-1945. I. Title: World War Two. II. Title: World War 2.
III. Cross, Robin. IV. Messernger, Charles, 1941 – V. Title.
D743.W525 2004
940.54'002'2--dc22
2004049351

ISBN 978-0-7566-2968-7
Color reproduction by GRB, Italy
Printed and bound in China by L.Rex Printing Co. Ltd

For our complete catalog visit
www.dk.com

US artillery bombardment
US Marines of the 4th Division shell concealed Japanese
positions from the beach on Iwo Jima. The Americans
landed in strength on the tiny volcanic island in February
1945 and secured it after four weeks' fighting.

CONTENTS

1 THE PATH TO WAR 8
1919–39

Postwar Europe 14
Japanese Imperialism 20
Rearmament and Expansion 28

2 WAR BEGINS IN EUROPE 36
1939–40

First Conquests 42
German Invasion of the West 52
Britain in Peril 58
The Home Front in Western Europe 66

3 GERMANY TRIUMPHANT 74
1940–41

The War at Sea 80
Campaigns in Africa and the Middle East 84
The Balkan Campaign 92
Operation Barbarossa 98

4 THE WAR BECOME GLOBAL 104
1941–42

The US Joins the War 110
Japanese Onslaught 116
The Home Front in the US and Japan 124
Wartime Cinema 130
From Moscow to Stalingrad 132

5 THE INITIATIVE CHANGES HANDS 142
1942–43

Changing Fortunes on the Eastern Front 148
The Holocaust 156
The Axis Defeated in North Africa 160
The U-boat Campaign in the Atlantic 168
The Pacific War in the Balance 174

6 THE AXIS ON THE DEFENSIVE 180
1943–44

Recapture of the Western Soviet Union 186
The Invasion of Italy 194
War in the Air 202
American Offensives in the Pacific 208

7 THE ALLIES' GREAT OFFENSIVES 214
1944–45

Advance into Northwest Europe 220
Balkan Resistance 238
Advance into Poland 242
Japan Near the Brink 248

8 THE FINAL BATTLES 256
1945

The Road To Berlin 262
The End of the Reich 272
Japan Surrenders 282

9 A NEW WORLD 294
1945–49

The Legacy of War 300

Glossary 312
Index 313
Acknowledgments 320

INTRODUCTION

WORLD WAR II was the largest and costliest war in human history. The deaths directly and indirectly caused by the war may have reached 60 million; the war, or more properly the wars, fought between 1939 and 1945 involved literally the entire globe. At its peak more than 50 million men and women were serving in the armed services; two-thirds of the national product of the major combatants was devoted to waging war. War was the product not only of a profound disequilibrium in world affairs; it reflected deep hatreds and powerful imperial ambitions inherited from the Great War of 1914–18, where lay the seeds of the second, and larger conflict.

The attempt to produce a stable world order in 1919 was undermined from the start. In East Asia, China collapsed politically and Japan slowly expanded at Chinese expense. In the Mediterranean and Middle East, the end of Ottoman rule provoked a nationalist Italy under Mussolini to carve out a new "Roman Empire". In Europe the

Bolshevik Revolution of 1917 created a permanent sense of social crisis, while the Versailles Treaty created festering political sores which contributed to the rise of Hitler and the breakdown of the balance of power in the late 1930s.

The new war was the last fling of the wars for empire that had been the hallmark of the rise of Europe since the 17th century. Britain and France wished to preserve their world empires. Italy, Japan, and Germany all wanted empires of their own. These imperial ambitions led to the largest and most destructive conflicts of World War II: the German war against the Soviet Union and Japan's war against China.

Britain and France declared war over the German invasion of Poland in September 1939, but Anglo-French efforts on their own to stem the tide of violent imperialism were futile. They were swept aside by German forces in a matter of weeks in the summer of 1940 thanks largely to a revolution in warfare made possible by the aeroplane and the tank— weapons whose potential had been apparent at the end of the war of 1914–18.

The desolation of war
A Japanese soldier surveys the destruction of Hiroshima in an area near the centre of the atomic blast in September 1945.

In combination with radio communication, they gave armies a mobile striking power that could win sudden, annihilating victories. Slowly, ways were found to contain or limit the effectiveness of the tank, aircraft, and radio attack system, but it proved irreversible when the Germans first used it, and when German armies were in turn pushed back by reorganized and heavily-armed Soviet, British, and American forces.

By September 1940 the three new imperial powers, Germany, Italy, and Japan, signed the Tripartite Pact, which divided the world into new spheres of imperial interest. Over the next year they each embarked on vast imperial wars: Italy attacked Greece and tried to drive Britain from North Africa and the Middle East; Germany launched war against the Soviet Union in June 1941; by January 1942 Japan had seized control of most of Southeast Asia and the Western Pacific. The effect of these wars of conquest was to unite the rest of the world against the violent revision of the globe. Britain, undefeated but powerless on its own to reverse the tide of conquest, was joined by the Soviet Union and, in December 1941, by the United States. This proved an alliance just powerful enough to stem the imperial wars after four years of bitter, costly, and massively destructive warfare.

Victory was won for many reasons. The Soviet Union won the war on land by learning to organize its forces in the same way as the Germans, and by channeling its entire society and economy into the waging of "total war". Britain and the United States focussed on winning the war at sea and in the air in order to be able to fight a global war at lower cost. Bombing was central to Western strategy and hundreds of thousands of Germans and Japanese were killed by bombing attacks. Naval power gave the west exceptional flexibility in moving forces and supplies and strangling the economic lifelines to the enemy. By the time Britain and the United States assaulted Europe on land the defeat of Italy and Germany was already assured. Japan was not even invaded. The first and only use of nuclear weapons in war ended Japanese resistance in August 1945.

The final defeat of imperialism produced a reconfiguration of the world and a stabilization of the international order. Britain and France had to give up the global empires they had fought to defend. Communism came to control much of Asia and eastern Europe, while the United States used its economic and military power to preserve its interests in the non-communist world. The war had brought a precarious peace, but only at the price of misery for the hundreds of millions caught in its merciless crossfire.

Richard Overy
May 2004

THE PATH TO WAR
1919–39

THE CAUSES OF WORLD WAR II LAY IN THE AFTERMATH OF WORLD WAR I AND THE GLOBAL ECONOMIC CRISIS OF THE 1930s. IN THE 1920s AND EARLY 1930s, RIGHT-WING DICTATORS ROSE TO POWER IN A NUMBER OF EUROPEAN COUNTRIES BY OFFERING MILITARISTIC SOLUTIONS TO ECONOMIC AND SOCIAL PROBLEMS. IN EAST ASIA JAPAN'S GROWING IMPERIAL AMBITIONS EVENTUALLY LED TO THE OUTBREAK OF FULL-SCALE WAR WITH CHINA. FROM 1934 ADOLF HITLER'S GERMANY DEFIED EUROPE TO REARM AND EXPAND EASTWARD. THIS COURSE OF ACTION LED IN SEPTEMBER 1939 TO A WAR THAT MANY SAW AS A CONTINUATION OF THE EARLIER CONFLICT.

1

Warm welcome
Joyful Austrians welcome German troops to the city of Salzburg on March 13, 1938. The *Anschluss*, the German annexation of Austria, was widely popular in both countries and encouraged German leader Adolf Hitler's territorial ambitions.

THE RISE OF EXTREMISM

THE SEEDS OF WORLD WAR II WERE SOWN IN THE 1920S, WHEN ECONOMIC HARDSHIP AND NATIONAL HUMILIATION DROVE THE GERMAN PEOPLE TO ADOLF HITLER, WHO PROMISED TO RESTORE NATIONAL PRIDE AND PROSPERITY.

WORLD WAR I, fought between 1914 and 1918, resulted in over 10 million deaths and traumatized a generation. When peace came in November 1918 it brought few solutions and many new problems. The European economy was left in ruins and the social structure severely disrupted. The peace settlements failed to resolve the tensions that had caused the conflict and gave rise to such resentment that it soon became clear that they would not provide the framework for a lasting peace. Indeed, they contributed significantly to the outbreak of World War II in Europe in September 1939.

THE TREATY OF VERSAILLES, 1919

Although the "peacemakers" who met at Versailles, near Paris, France, in January 1919, reconstructed the map of the Middle East, Africa, and Asia, they saw these areas as being relatively unimportant. The so-called "war to end all wars" had been, despite its geographical range, a struggle for mastery of Europe. The three leading statesmen at Versailles—French prime minister Georges Clémenceau, British prime minister David Lloyd George, and US president Woodrow Wilson—had to establish immediate and lasting peace in a continent still in turmoil. The conflict was Europe's first experience of "total war," in which whole economies had been geared to the war effort, with profound effects on society. The challenge of restoring political and economic stability was correspondingly huge.

The Treaty of Versailles was by far the most important of a number of settlements at the end of the war. It saw Wilson's vision of a better world, in which rights and freedoms were guaranteed, enshrined in a swathe of new democracies across Europe—from the Baltic to the Balkans—all with new, liberal constitutions. Yet the triumph of idealism and liberalism would prove short-lived.

One problem confronting the new democracies related to territory and population. Newly independent states such as Poland, Czechoslovakia, Yugoslavia, and Hungary were created under the principle of national self-determination. However, 30 million people still found themselves as national and racial minorities. The long-term consequences of incorporating minority populations into new states would be a source of tension and discontent into the 1930s.

Versailles failed to satisfy victors and vanquished alike. In Germany, dissatisfaction stemmed from a widespread belief that, although the Germans had signed an armistice, they had not actually been defeated on the field of battle. The Germans were not invited to participate in the discussions at Versailles. When the terms of the treaty were announced, even political moderates saw them as being harsh and vindictive.

The treaty—which the Germans condemned as a *diktat*, or dictated peace—fixed the blame for the war solely on Germany and its allies, and demanded reparations. Germany, moreover, was forced to disarm and its African colonies were taken away. The fledgling Weimar Republic was thus tainted from its inception with the humiliation of having accepted the imposed terms of Versailles.

One of the noblest features of the Treaty of Versailles was the establishment of the League of Nations as an agency for maintaining international peace and for protecting the new democracies. However, the League was fatally weakened by the failure of the United States to join it or to ratify the Versailles Treaty. The League was also damaged by initially excluding Germany and the Soviet Union, and its authority was further undermined by the preference of many states to sign peace agreements independently. In Asia, Japan, which had profited economically from the war, was unhappy with attempts to impose limitations on naval and arms development. Not surprisingly, when challenges did occur, notably in the 1930s, the League of Nations was found wanting.

EUROPE IN TURMOIL

The political and economic impact of the war contributed to the fragility of democracy. It sharpened class tension which, in turn, was fueled by the triumph of Bolshevism in Russia. Moreover,

The new world order
Nazi storm troopers and Berliners gather around a bonfire at a book-burning ceremony in May 1933. More than 20,000 volumes were destroyed. Hitler came to power determined to wipe out "degenerate" culture, which included many pillars of the liberal European tradition and the works of Jewish and other writers.

the disappointment of ex-servicemen with the conduct of their politicians, and their perception that they had been betrayed at the conference table, fed widespread discontent. In Germany and Italy, government reliance on right-wing paramilitary groups to neutralize the threat of Soviet-style revolution legitimized political violence. The very real fear of revolution among Europe's middle

"Germany is not a warlike nation. It is a soldierly one, which means it does not want a war, but does not fear it. It loves peace, but also loves its honor and freedom."

ADOLF HITLER
ADDRESSING THE REICHSTAG IN 1938

classes and the inability of some of the Western democracies to defuse class warfare contributed substantially to the collapse of liberal democracy and the meteoric rise of fascism.

The Versailles Treaty's failure to support Italy's territorial claims on its northeastern borders only exacerbated the country's political and economic problems. Between 1919 and 1922 five governments failed to take decisive action that might have helped to resolve Italy's developing crisis. In an atmosphere of tension, characterized by strikes and riots, there seemed to be a real danger of a left-wing revolution. Amid the turmoil, the founder of the Italian Fascist Party, former socialist Benito Mussolini, posed as the savior of the state against communism. By 1922 he felt confident enough to seize power.

The abandonment of parliamentary democracy for right-wing fascism was repeated in Germany and later in Spain. Like Italy, both countries had comparatively little experience of operating a democratic parliamentary system. In Germany, the Weimar Republic was plagued by economic crises, which the government failed to solve permanently. Adolf Hitler's National Socialist German Workers' Party (or Nazi Party) started life as a radical group opposed to Versailles and the parliamentary system. The rise of the Nazis, fostered by economic crisis, helped bring the downfall of the republic.

Japan, like Germany, had a long tradition of militarism and weak democratic roots. World War I had seen an increase in Japanese influence in Asia, especially in China, and in industrial growth at home. However, the trading boom of the war years lasted only until 1921, when Europe was able to recover lost markets. Thereafter unemployment and industrial unrest grew. Democratically elected governments seemed unable to solve the problems, and as the fragile

prestige of parliament suffered, conservative and military groups, attracted by fascism, reasserted themselves. In 1930 a strong nationalist government controlled by the army seized power.

THE LEAGUE FAILS

By the early 1930s the idealistic hope that the League of Nations would preserve the peace by arbitration or conciliation was challenged by fascist regimes

intent on pursuing imperialistic ambitions by aggressive means. Collective security gave way to old-style bilateral diplomacy. The continued policy of isolationism in the United States encouraged the drift to extremism. In 1931 Japan seized Manchuria, an important economic region in China. In 1935 Italy invaded Abyssinia (Ethiopia), and in Germany Hitler embarked on an extensive rearmament program and also introduced conscription.

Pride of a nation
The Japanese battleship *Fuso* nears the completion of its refit in dry dock in April 1933. The Imperial Navy of Japan saw strengthening the fleet as vital to national pride after the limitations imposed by the Washington and London naval treaties were cast aside.

The failure of the League to respond to any of these violations of international treaties significantly undermined its authority and persuaded Hitler to take a calculated risk. In March 1936 he ordered his troops to reoccupy the Rhineland, which under the peace treaties had been demilitarized since 1919. Again the League and the Western powers failed to

act. Emboldened, Hitler signed the Rome–Berlin Axis with Mussolini in October 1936, and the following month Germany and Japan agreed to an Anti-Comintern Pact. By 1937 Germany, Italy, and Japan had all withdrawn from the League of Nations.

In July 1936 Spanish right-wing nationalists led by General Francisco Franco rose in an attempt to overthrow the democratically elected republican government. The Spanish conflict rapidly assumed international significance when Hitler and Mussolini sent military help to Franco, while the republicans received aid from the Soviet Union. The resolutions that the League passed in response showed it to be sympathetic to the plight of the legitimate Spanish government but largely ineffectual.

By supporting the League's principle of non-intervention, Britain and France—still Europe's major powers—revealed the timidity and moral indifference of the parliamentary democracies when challenged from both the left and the right. Moreover, the ideological issues of the Spanish war polarized public opinion in Britain and France and helped shape their policy of appeasement, under which concessions were granted to Hitler and Mussolini. With Europe preoccupied with events in Spain, in July 1937 the Japanese embarked upon a full-scale invasion of northern China, precipitating a war that was to last until 1945. The United States, the only power that was capable of effectively resisting Japan, continued its policy of isolationism.

GERMAN EXPANSION

The Rome–Berlin Axis had changed the balance of power in Europe, and in March 1938 Hitler fulfilled a long-cherished ambition by annexing Austria and proclaiming *Anschluss* (union) with Germany. Britain and France continued to believe that appeasement was the only way to deal with successive crises. In Munich in September 1938 they

Peace in our time
British prime minister Neville Chamberlain brandishes Hitler's promise that Germany has no territorial ambitions in Europe after its claims on Czechoslovakia. In fact, the Munich Pact of September 30, 1938, failed to halt German rearmament or expansion.

acceded to Hitler's claims on the Sudetenland, a German-speaking region of Czechoslovakia, on the understanding that this would be Hitler's final territorial demand. The agreement, acclaimed as guaranteeing "peace in our time," was soon broken.

The German invasion of Czechoslovakia in March 1939 gave rise to a new resolve in the British and French governments to confront aggression and guarantee Poland's independence. The controversial signing of the Nazi–Soviet Non-Aggression Pact on August 23, 1939, was widely seen as a cynical reversal of ideological allegiances by Hitler and Stalin. Hitler believed that the pact would show the British and French the futility of the promises they had made to Poland in the wake of the invasion of Czechoslovakia. When, however, Germany invaded Poland on September 1, the British and French declared war two days later, and World War II began in Europe. Twenty-one years after the war to end all wars, Europe was to be torn apart again.

> "Provided China perseveres in the war of resistance and in the united front, the old Japan will surely be transformed into a new Japan and the old China into a new China, and people and everything else in both China and Japan will be transformed."
>
> MAO ZEDONG, CHINESE COMMUNIST LEADER, LECTURE ON THE SINO-JAPANESE WAR, MAY 1938

DEVELOPMENTS IN EUROPE

JUNE 28, 1919–AUGUST 2, 1934

The failure of the Treaty of Versailles and the League of Nations to resolve the social, political, and economic problems after World War I brought radical politics to center stage throughout Europe. The Wall Street Crash and the Great Depression plunged the continent into an economic crisis that allowed fascism to flourish in Germany.

1919

MARCH 23, 1919
Mussolini among those who form the Fascist Fighting Corps

JUNE 28, 1919
Germany signs Treaty of Versailles with the Allies

NOVEMBER 19, 1919
US Senate refuses to ratify Treaty of Versailles

1920

APRIL 1, 1920
German Workers' Party, with program drafted by Hitler, renamed Nazi Party

APRIL 25, 1920
Poland invades Russia

NOVEMBER 15, 1920
First session of League of Nations Assembly is held

MARCH 18, 1921
Russia and Poland sign Treaty of Riga, giving Poland most of the land seized in 1920

MAY 15, 1921
Fascists win 35 seats in elections

APRIL 16, 1922
Germany and Russia sign Treaty of Rapallo, enabling Germans to establish arms factories in Russia

OCTOBER 28, 1922
50,000 fascist Blackshirts begin their march from Milan to Rome

OCTOBER 30, 1922
Mussolini is invited by King Victor Emmanuel to form a government

JANUARY 11, 1923
French and Belgian troops begin occupation of the Ruhr following German failure to maintain reparations payments

NOVEMBER 9, 1923
As chairman of the infant National Socialist Workers' (Nazi) Party, Hitler launches an unsuccessful armed coup in Munich

1925

DECEMBER 1, 1925
Locarno Pact, signed by Germany with Britain, France, Belgium, and Italy, confirms Germany's western borders with France and Belgium as established by the Treaty of Versailles

SEPTEMBER 10, 1926
Germany joins League of Nations

AUGUST 27, 1928
Kellogg-Briand Pact is drawn up, renouncing war as a means of settling international disputes; it is eventually signed by nearly all of the world's nations

OCTOBER 29, 1929
Collapse of US stock market in the Wall Street Crash heralds the start of the Great Depression

APRIL 22, 1930
US, Britain, and Japan sign London Naval Treaty, in which they agree to restrict tonnages of warships

1930

SEPTEMBER 14, 1930
With unemployment at 3 million, Nazi Party makes first electoral breakthrough in Reichstag elections, winning 107 seats

MARCH 13, 1932
Hitler comes second after Hindenburg in presidential elections, gaining 30 percent of the vote

JULY 31, 1932
Nazis win 230 of 609 seats in national elections, but Hitler refuses to join a coalition

JANUARY 30, 1933
President Hindenburg appoints Hitler as chancellor

MARCH 5, 1933
Nazis secure 44 percent of the vote

MARCH 23, 1933
Enabling Act passed, giving Hitler dictatorial powers

AUGUST 2, 1934
Hitler merges offices of president and chancellor to become Führer and Supreme Commander

OCTOBER 14, 1933
Germany leaves League of Nations

Mussolini's rise to power Mar 23, 1919–Oct 30, 1922

Other events

Hitler's rise to power Apr 1, 1920–Aug 2, 1934

POSTWAR EUROPE

THE TREATY OF VERSAILLES achieved two things: it imposed peace terms on Germany—terms even some of the victors considered harsh—and established an international organization, the League of Nations, to preserve the peace and settle disputes by arbitration and conciliation. However, Versailles was fatally weakened by the failure of the United States to either ratify the treaty or join the League. Germany was not allowed to join until 1926, and the Allies were so determined to isolate the Bolshevik regime that they barred the Soviet Union until 1934. Consequently, for the first few years of its existence the League was deprived of the involvement of three of the world's most important powers.

Germany was excluded from the discussions at Versailles; it was simply presented with the terms and told to sign. German grievances were further fueled by the War Guilt Clause (Article 231), which stated that Germany took responsibility for starting the war, and the subsequent reparations. The Reparations Commission established by the treaty agreed in May 1921 on a total of $26 billion to be paid by Germany and its allies. Germany's promise to pay reparations, together with its very reluctant

acceptance of an unfavorable territorial settlement, had a profound effect on postwar politics. The decision to exclude Germany from the League only reinforced the complaints of right-wing German nationalists, who condemned Versailles as a dictated peace that should not have been signed.

POLITICAL UPHEAVAL

Following the abdication of Kaiser Wilhelm II in November 1918, Germany experienced mounting instability and violence. In February 1919 the National Assembly met and set up the Weimar Republic, named after the city where it first met. The new republic was immediately beset by challenges. Communist movements, such as the Spartacists led by Karl Liebknecht and Rosa Luxemburg, attempted to overthrow the government. However, a poorly organized uprising in 1919 was crushed by the army and independent groups formed by ex-servicemen, known as the *Freikorps*. Similar uprisings in Bremen and Munich were also crushed. At the other political extreme, right-wing monarchists such as Wolfgang Kapp, together with other *Freikorps* units, engineered a successful military *putsch*, or seizure of power, in March 1920. It was eventually defeated by a general strike, but not before armed conflict between left and right had broken out in a number of German cities.

POSTWAR REVOLT

Grievances with the postwar peace settlements and fear of communism were not confined to Germany. The rise of fascism in Italy was a direct result of the strains produced by World War I and the postwar economic fluctuations that a succession of liberal governments failed to resolve. The failure of the Versailles Treaty to support Italy's territorial claims served only to exacerbate the country's political and economic problems. The subsequent rise to power of Benito Mussolini was aided by the breakdown of the existing political system and the rise of political extremism. Mussolini, who had begun his political career as a socialist, founded the Fascist Party in 1919 with a radical program and a promise of establishing strong government and restoring national pride. By focusing on the threat that communism posed, the fascists tapped into a latent fear on the

Revolution in Berlin
A group of armed communists patrol Berlin in November 1919. Many former soldiers were among the recruits to the extreme right- and left-wing groups who clashed in pitched battles in the streets of postwar Germany.

After Versailles
Germany was split in two, as East Prussia and Upper Silesia went to a restored Poland. The treaty also created new states in the Baltic region and in central and eastern Europe.

part of many sections of Italian society. Above all, fascism offered the prospect of dynamic action and leadership in contrast to the inertia of parliamentary politics. By the end of 1921 Mussolini had gained the support of property owners who saw him as a guarantor of law and order. He also gave up his republican ambitions, thus allowing the king to support him. The Italian socialists, for their part, were in disarray.

Posing as the saviors of the state from the threat of communism, Mussolini and 50,000 Blackshirts launched their famous "March on Rome" in October 1922. Although Italian prime minister Luigi Facta was prepared to resist, King Victor Emmanuel III refused to declare a state of emergency and instead addressed the crisis by summoning Mussolini to form a new government. Once in power, Mussolini moved quickly to suppress all opposition to his rule and to establish laws that removed any need for parliamentary approval of legislation. In December 1928 he replaced the parliamentary system with the

MUSSOLINI AND THE FASCISTS

School for fascists
Young blackshirts are drilled in Batilla, Italy. Modeled on Mussolini's Fascist Party Blackshirts, this organization was similar to the Hitler Youth movement in Germany, but not as successful.

Italian propaganda
In this propaganda poster in support of Mussolini, every soldier looks like the fascist dictator.

BENITO MUSSOLINI (1883–1945) was the first fascist dictator in Europe. Born the son of a blacksmith and schoolteacher, he turned to politics and joined the Socialist Party in 1910. Mussolini's rise inside the party was meteoric and following the Libyan War of 1912 he was elected editor of *Avanti!*, the party's official newspaper. However, in October 1914 he was expelled from the party for attacking its neutralist position, an experience he never forgot nor forgave. During World War I he was wounded at Isonzo and returned to Milan as editor of a new daily newspaper *Il Popolo d'Italia*. He also formed groups *(fasci)* of working men in order to agitate for revolutionary social changes. These groups, including the black-shirted Arditi, were merged into a Fascist Party *(Fascio di Combattimento)*.

Fascism varied from nation to nation—it emerged in different forms in Germany, Portugal, and Spain. In essence, it was a doctrine that sanctified the interests of the nation-state and minimized the rights of the individual. In Italy, fascism began to transform itself into a mass-movement when it took on a paramilitary edge, exemplified by Mussolini's Blackshirt supporters. Assuming dictatorial powers upon forming a government in November 1922, Mussolini established a Fascist Grand Council, carried out an extensive program of public works at home, and embarked upon a foreign policy designed to restore Italian prestige abroad.

Departing army
French soldiers garrisoned in the Ruhr in Germany march out of Essen on their way home. In 1925, when this photograph was taken, all Allied forces were ordered home and withdrawn from the Ruhr.

Fascist Grand Council. This put the finishing touches to the dictatorship and effectively gave Mussolini and the Fascist Party total political control in Italy.

DEATH OF A NATION

In Germany the period 1919–23 brought uprisings, political assassinations, and economic collapse. The fledgling Weimar Republic was experiencing a series of financial problems that caused the government to fall behind with reparations. Disagreements about whether Germany could afford the reparations caused tensions between Britain and France. Meanwhile in 1922 Russia and Germany signed a treaty of mutual respect—the Treaty of Rapallo. This canceled any reparations between the two states and demonstrated the recovery of both from isolation. The French, who needed the income from reparations in order to balance their own budget and pay their debts to the United States, decided in January 1923 to send troops into the Ruhr—the industrial heartland of Germany— to seize factories and mines. The occupation paralyzed the Ruhr and the effect on the whole

German economy was catastrophic. It led to the collapse of the German mark and hyperinflation. In December 1922 the exchange rate stood at 8,000 marks to the US dollar; by November 1923 it had reached 4,200 million marks to the dollar.

Throughout the Ruhr crisis a little-known agitator by the name of Adolf Hitler, leader of the National Socialist German Workers' Party, had kept up a barrage of criticism against the Republic. On November 8, 1923 Hitler and his right-wing supporters attempted a *putsch* in Munich, the capital of Bavaria. The intention was to take control of the state government and then lead a revolution to overthrow the national government in Berlin. The uprising was easily crushed, but the subsequent trial of Hitler for high treason gave him a nationwide platform from which to launch an attack on the Weimar Republic. The trial had the effect of turning the farce into a propaganda coup. Hitler was sentenced to five years' imprisonment in the fortress

Money to burn
A housewife uses German currency to light a stove during the period of hyperinflation in Germany, 1922–23. So low was the value of the German mark that it was worth more as fuel than as a method of payment.

of Landsberg in February 1924, but he was set free after only nine months. In prison, he dictated the first volume of his autobiographical manifesto *Mein Kampf* (*My Struggle*) to his loyal follower, Rudolf Hess.

EMERGING FROM DEFEAT

In August 1923 a new German government, led by the liberal politician Gustav Stresemann, began to take measures to stabilize the financial situation and to improve Germany's diplomatic position. Stresemann developed a close working relationship with the French foreign minister, Aristide Briand, which began in 1924 with the Dawes Plan. The plan eased reparations, allowing Germany to pay what it could afford. The relationship culminated in the signing of the Locarno Pact in December 1925. This confirmed the inviolability of the Franco-German and Belgo-German frontiers, and the demilitarized Rhineland, and repudiated the use of force to revise Germany's western border. The measures gave rise to international optimism known as the "spirit of Locarno" and cleared the way for Germany's entry into the League of Nations the following year. Two years later, in 1928, 65 nations signed the Kellogg-Briand Pact renouncing war, and in 1929 the Young Plan further reduced German reparations. Europe seemed set for a peaceful future. The fragile harmony of Locarno was destroyed, however, by the death of Stresemann in 1929 and by the Wall Street Crash that same year. In the subsequent world economic crisis, the Nazi Party began to flourish.

HITLER'S RISE TO POWER

With unemployment exceeding 6 million and the Weimar Republic entering its final death throes, the elections of 1932 were fought in a growing atmosphere of political violence and disorder. After the July Reichstag elections, the Nazis emerged as the largest party, but in the November 1932 elections the Nazi vote fell by 2 million, with their Reichstag seats reduced from 230 to 196. While the Nazi vote appeared to be in decline and the party's tactics in disarray, an increase in support for Germany's communists persuaded many industrialists and bankers to transfer their backing from the ineffectual conservatives and liberals to the Nazis. They were seen as the only bulwark against the growth of communism. In December 1932, after a series of further political intrigues, Kurt von Schleicher succeeded Franz von Papen as chancellor. However, in January 1933 Papen acted as a power-broker between business interests and landowners in political maneuvers that were intended to oust Schleicher. The ensuing negotiations eventually resulted in Hitler becoming chancellor. The fatal miscalculation made by Papen—indeed by the conservative right and the German establishment in general—was to believe that Hitler and the Nazis could be "tamed" once in power. The establishment tried to use Hitler and his party to give itself legitimacy for a new authoritarianism. In reality it served only to legitimize Nazism. Out of a labyrinth of intrigues, Hitler emerged the victor.

The Ehrhardt Brigade in Berlin

After World War I Hitler was sent by the German Army to observe right-wing groups. In this capacity he witnessed the short-lived Kapp *Putsch* of March 1920 by the Freikorps Ehrhardt Brigade in Berlin.

HITLER AND NAZISM

ADOLF HITLER (1889–1945) was born in Braunau am Inn, Austria, on April 20, 1889. He left home for Vienna in 1907 to pursue a career as an artist, only to be rejected by the Viennese Academy of Fine Arts. Living as a virtual "down and out" in the capital, Hitler developed a pathological hatred of Jews and Marxists, liberalism, democracy, and the cosmopolitan Habsburg monarchy. On the outbreak of World War I in August 1914 he enlisted in the 16th Bavarian Infantry Regiment, and twice won the Iron Cross for bravery in the war.

After the war the army sent Hitler to spy on the new radical groups emerging in Germany, giving him his first taste of politics. In September 1919 he joined a small nationalist group that grew into the Nazi Party. The failure of the Munich Beer-Hall *putsch* in 1923 and his subsequent imprisonment gained Hitler national fame. When *Mein Kampf (My Struggle)* was published in 1925, it laid out the fundamental principles of Nazism: totalitarian government, militarized society, the racial superiority of Germanic peoples, and loyalty to Hitler himself.

Over the next decade Hitler rose through the political system. In 1933 he was appointed chancellor, and laid the foundations of a one-party state. In August 1934 Hitler further strengthened his own position by merging the offices of president and chancellor into the new office of Führer (leader).

Hitler's Old Guard

The founders of the National Socialists were known as the Old Guard. After coming to power, Hitler purged many of these early supporters in the "Night of the Long Knives" on June 30, 1934. More than 70 Nazis were murdered to protect Hitler's authority.

ANTI-SEMITISM IN GERMANY

AS ELSEWHERE IN EUROPE, anti-Semitism grew during the 19th century in Germany, where Jews were prominent in culture and business. Conservatives and radical nationalists feared that the assimilation of Jews would only increase their influence and strengthen the left. After World War I the Jews became the scapegoats for Germany's defeat; later they were similarly blamed for the political and economic chaos of the Weimar Republic.

Anti-Semitism was a main theme of Nazi ideology. Between taking power in 1933 and 1939 the Nazis waged three main campaigns against the Jewish population. In March 1933 rank-and-file party activists went on the rampage, assaulting Jews, damaging Jewish shops, and demanding a boycott of Jewish businesses. In April 1933 Jews were banned from the civil service and the legal and medical professions. Despite continued local harassment, there were no further official moves against Jews until September 1935, when Hitler announced the Nuremberg Laws. These deprived Jews of German citizenship and political rights, and forbade marriage and sexual relations between Jews and non-Jewish Germans.

The position of Jews deteriorated further with the *Kristallnacht* ("Crystal Night") of November 1938, when Nazis burned down synagogues and placed 20,000 Jews in concentration camps. However, the unpopularity of *Kristallnacht* with the German public convinced the Nazi leadership that the solution to the so-called "Jewish Question" would be implemented outside Germany and well away from public sight. *Kristallnacht* was a crucial junction on the road to Auschwitz.

Public torment
Jews and gentiles who associated with each other were publicly humiliated by the SA and the SS.

The Eternal Jew
A poster for an anti-Semitic documentary commissioned by Josef Goebbels plays on a Jewish stereotype that had been common in Europe for many decades before the rise of the Nazis.

Covered in shame
A woman hides her face from the photographer in an anonymous German town in 1938. The sign on the bench reads "For Jews only."

Swastikas on parade
German soldiers carry swastika flags styled in the same manner as the standards of the Roman legions. The swastika symbol is over 3,000 years old, and the term is derived from two Sanskrit words; *su asti*—"well-being."

Despite the political intrigue and machinations that led to his appointment, Hitler became chancellor constitutionally; the suggestion that he somehow "seized" power is misleading. On February 27, 1933, shortly after he gained power, an arson attack destroyed the Reichstag, the German parliament. A communist sympathizer was blamed, although his guilt remains a matter of controversy. The Nazis used the fire as a pretext for suspending civil liberties and conducting an election campaign in circumstances highly favorable to themselves.

LIFE UNDER THE NAZIS

Hitler's rise to power had exploited the weaknesses of the political establishment, but the Nazis also enjoyed popular support, particularly for their promise to tackle unemployment. They introduced public works programs, such as building a system of *autobahns* (highways), and used tax concessions to encourage industrial growth. By the summer of 1934 unemployment had fallen to 2.4 million, and many Germans had renewed hope for the future, despite their loss of the right to unionize or strike. Inflation was low, wages stable, and public satisfaction high.

Economic success was not as strong as it seemed, however, and may not have been sustainable into the 1940s if war had not broken out. Government expenditure from 1933 to 1939 was 101.5 billion marks, but government revenue was only 62 billion marks. Some 60 percent of public expenditure went on rearmament. Business profited, but it was at the price of increased control by central government over what and how much it could produce.

Nazi control extended to German society. By the end of 1933 all youth organizations had been banned except the Hitler Youth and a few Catholic groups. Many boys were in the Hitler Youth, which was

> "The primitive simplicity of their minds renders them a more easy prey to a big lie than a small one, for they themselves often tell little lies but would be ashamed to tell a big one."

ADOLF HITLER ON WINNING THE SUPPORT OF THE GERMAN PEOPLE, *MEIN KAMPF*, 1925

initially popular for providing opportunities for leisure activities. The *Kraft durch Freude* (Strength through Joy) movement extended the opportunity for vacations to ordinary Germans. Meanwhile, women's organizations summed up the role of the ideal mother in the Third Reich in the slogan *"Kinder, Küche, Kirche"* ("Children, Kitchen, Church").

Nazi influence spread to culture and the arts. While party rallies and parades became common, Nazi propaganda minister Josef Goebbels staged exhibitions of art designed to reinforce "German" values and young Nazis burned thousands of books condemned as being "un-German."

For many Germans the 1930s were a period of order, calm, and prosperity. For others, however, they brought terror and repression. A number of artists and intellectuals fled abroad. Anti-Semitism was enshrined in law; the first concentration camps for political prisoners opened in 1933. In June 1934 it was the turn of some of Hitler's allies to feel the

force of repression, when the SS—Hitler's elite bodyguard—executed around 150 senior members of the Brownshirts, the Nazi paramilitaries who had aided Hitler's rise to power, including their leader Erich Röhm. Now that he had control, the Führer was taking no chances of any opposition to his rule.

Nazi poster
The slogan of this Nazi poster—"Our Last Hope: Hitler"—appealed to the despair that many Germans felt.

Women Hitlerites
Enthusiastic female supporters of Adolf Hitler give the Nazi salute during a military parade through Berlin. Hitler enjoyed widespread support among German women who appreciated his oratorical skills.

JAPANESE EXPANSION IN CHINA
1930–1939

The 1930s saw Japan, suffering under the Great Depression, embark on an increasingly assertive policy in East Asia. Militant nationalism was tied to a perceived need to secure raw materials, markets, and areas of settlement. The natural focus of Japanese attention was China, particularly Manchuria.

1930

JANUARY–APRIL
London Treaty limiting size of all the major navies

NOVEMBER 14
Prime minister Hamaguchi Osachi shot by a nationalist fanatic, possibly as a result of Japanese accession to the London Treaty

1931

SEPTEMBER 18
Japanese-staged Mukden incident: start of Japanese campaign of conquest of Manchuria, completed with capture of Harbin in February 1932

1932

JANUARY
Japan sends troops to Shanghai, where the Imperial Navy has provoked a fight with local Chinese forces

FEBRUARY 18
Japanese proclamation of independence of Manchukuo (the State of the Manchus) in Manchuria

MAY 15
Prime minister Inukai Tsuyoshi assassinated during attempted military coup

1933

FEBRUARY 24–25
League of Nations condemns Japan and calls for end to occupation of Manchuria: Japanese delegation walks out

JANUARY–FEBRUARY
Japanese conquest of Jehol province in Manchuria

MAY 31
Tangku Truce effectively eliminates Chinese military presence in northern China and Inner Mongrolia

MARCH 27
Japan announces its intention to withdraw from League of Nations

1934

OCTOBER 1934
Start of Long March. Chinese communists break through nationalist lines, then set out on march of almost 6,000 miles (10,000 km)

MARCH 1
Coronation of P'u Yi as K'ang-te, Emperor of the Manchus

DECEMBER 19
Japan announces refusal to be bound by future naval limitation treaties

1935

OCTOBER
Chinese communist forces reach temporary safety in Shansi province after the Long March

1936

JANUARY 15
Japan withdraws from Second London Naval Conference after request that its fleet be granted parity with fleets of Britain and the US is refused

FEBRUARY 26–29
Attempted coup; army effectively prevents re-forming of civilian government

NOVEMBER 25
Japan concludes the Anti-Comintern Pact with Germany

DECEMBER
"Sian Incident." Chiang Kai-shek obliged to curtail war against communists in order to oppose Japanese aggression

1937

JULY 7
Marco Polo Bridge incident outside Peking: start of Japan's "special undeclared war" throughout China

DECEMBER 13
Japanese occupy Nanking; widespread atrocities against civilian population follow

1938

APRIL
Japan's National Mobilization Law and start of comprehensive wartime mobilization

OCTOBER
Chinese Nationalist government withdraws to Chungking

OCTOBER 21
Japanese capture Canton

1939

MAY
Japanese launch long-range bombing raids against Chungking

MAY
Japanese and Soviet troops clash in Nomonhan region

AUGUST–SEPTEMBER
Comprehensive Japanese defeat at Nomonhan

SEPTEMBER 16
Soviet–Japanese armistice

■ Events in Japan 1930–1939 ■ Events in China and Manchuria 1930–1939 ■ Other events

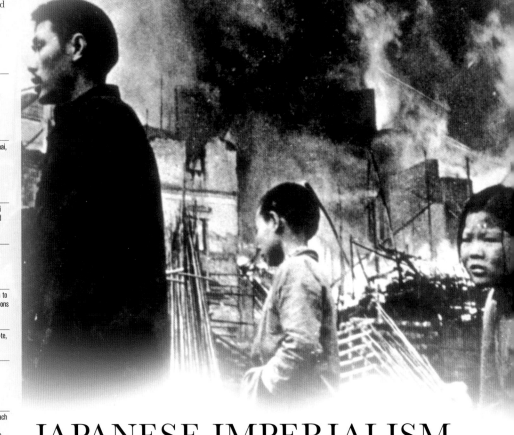

JAPANESE IMPERIALISM

ALTHOUGH THE TIDE of conflict barely washed its shores, East Asia was profoundly affected by the events of World War I. Decades of Western, primarily European, predominance in the area and in the Western Pacific was over. The presence of certain powers was ended, permanently in the case of Germany and Austria-Hungary, and temporarily in the case of Russia. Even the victorious powers found their status and power weakened, partly because the war had meant a withdrawal of forces from the area and partly because Japan had been immensely strengthened as a result of the conflict.

For Japan, World War I was "an opportunity that comes once in a thousand years." Prior to 1914 Japan had only limited industrial and financial resources; by the war's end the cessation of European imports

had guaranteed profitability for Japanese industry. The disappearance of Western shipping left Japanese lines free to dominate the Pacific and Indian oceans. Japan also ended the war holding possession of all Germany's Pacific islands north of the equator and its trading concessions in China, such as Tsingtao. Moreover, although allied to Britain, and thus

Japanese naval power
The Japanese battleship *Yamashiro*, which was commissioned in 1917, opens fire. The *Yamashiro* and its class were among the leading battleships in the world.

associated with France and the United States, Japan was free to take as much or as little part in the war as it chose. Its contribution consisted of sending destroyer formations to the eastern Mediterranean and heavier units and formations to Australia, and consequently, its casualties were light.

JAPAN AFTER WORLD WAR I

Japan's position at the end of the war was not, however, entirely advantageous. Japan faced two significant problems. The first stemmed from the "Twenty-one Demands," its clumsy 1915 attempt to ensure itself a position of dominance in China. The Japanese sought financial, trading, and other

Chungking in flames
Chinese refugees flee through the wrecked streets of Chungking after it was bombed by the Japanese during the Sino-Japanese War that began in 1937.

economic concessions that would leave China in a position of dependence. The action aroused deep suspicion and resentment among the Chinese and, more importantly, the opposition of both Japan's wartime associates and the United States. Under pressure, Japan abandoned its claims. However, over the next three years it secured local but far-reaching gains that in effect gave it possession of Germany's prewar concessions, which legally should have been returned to China.

At the same time Japan's relations with the United States grew more difficult. The sting was temporarily drawn from the China question by the Lansing–Ishii agreement of November 1917, which included recognition of Japan's right to protect its special interests in areas of China bordering on Japanese territory. The fact remained, however, that the United States reserved for itself a special position in China and, by virtue of its possession of the Philippines, the Western Pacific. Meanwhile, Japan's wartime domination of shipping in the Pacific prompted a determination in the United

States to develop naval yards and national shipping on the west coast. This determination was made all the greater by increasingly strident nationalism that in the western states in particular took the form of opposition to Chinese and Japanese immigration.

Even in the first decade of the 20th century, Japan and the United States had begun to measure themselves against one another in terms of naval programs. With the declaration in 1916 of the American determination to acquire a navy "second to none," the two countries found themselves committed to construction programs specifically

directed against the other. Involvement in World War I temporarily curbed American ambition, but it revived at the war's end to pose diplomatic dangers. In any case, the sheer financial cost of an arms race was enough to lead the representatives of the major powers to meet in November 1921, in Washington, D.C., to hammer out a comprehensive series of treaties governing China, the Western and Central Pacific, and naval building programs.

The next four months produced seven accords, including the Naval Limitation Treaty of February 6, 1922. This treaty dealt primarily with battle

JAPANESE SOCIETY

THE TRANSFORMATION OF JAPANESE SOCIETY from feudal to modern was accelerated after victory in the Russo–Japanese War of 1904–05. Japanese liberals wanted to copy Western democracy and ways of life, while traditionalists resented Western influence. After the Allied victory in World War I, the popularity of Western sports, music, and fashion soared. The people enjoyed greater freedoms throughout the 1920s than at any time previously, and the standard of living in Japan was the highest anywhere in Asia.

The accession of Emperor Hirohito in 1926 initially seemed to signal a continuation of the liberal period, but the Great Depression hit Japan very hard and, just as in Europe, the failure of economic liberalism discredited its political counterpart. The collapse of parliamentary rule, right-wing nationalism, the increasingly aggressive attitude of the army in China, and increasing conformity were the hallmarks of Japan in the Thirties. The most famous, or infamous, part of this process involved the idea of *Kokutai*—"the Body of the Nation"—which held that Japan's divine's origins meant that modern political definitions and ideas were not merely irrelevant but deeply offensive and tantamount to blasphemy. After 1935 the worship of the emperor and imperial family became state and personal obligations.

Japanese suffragettes
Wearing Western dress, Japanese women bring petitions calling for female suffrage to the Japanese parliament in the 1920s.

Emperor Hirohito
Hirohito's 1926 coronation used specially devised rituals that were falsely claimed to have been handed down over generations— a reflection of Japan's increasing obsession with historical example and values.

The rise of baseball
Members of the Waseda University Baseball Team toured the United States in 1925. The growing popularity of baseball in Japan was one of a number of signs of the Westernization of the country.

forces, and set down the 5:5:3 ratio by which Britain and the United States were afforded 500,000 tons of capital ships, while Japan was allotted 300,000 tons, and France and Italy 175,000 tons. The treaties, plus Japan's agreement to return a number of concessions to China, resolved immediate disputes among the Great Powers and avoided the dangers of a naval race. Within a decade, however, the arrangements had begun to unravel.

JAPANESE MILITARISM GROWS

As the Washington treaties unraveled and general war in East Asia seemed increasingly likely, events were largely shaped by Japanese actions. These were influenced by a number of factors, of which the widespread distress caused by the Great Depression—particularly in the countryside—was the most significant.

Just as the Depression brought in its wake the upheavals that resulted in the demise of liberal democracy in much of Europe, so it closed a decade of unprecedented prosperity within Japan. That prosperity, however, had been flawed in three long-term ways. Most notably, while the 1920s in Japan were marked by "Constitutionalism at home,

Patriotism on parade
Members of the Young Women's Patriotic Association celebrate the first birthday of Japan's crown prince in January 1935. Such groups were typical of the increasing militarization of Japanese society.

Imperialism abroad,"—the phrase did not actually imply an unbridled, aggressive form of imperialism—the Imperial Army found itself involved in the Russian Civil War and its aftermath, and then China's civil wars. These conflicts saw forces on the ground obliged to decide policy and operational priorities without reference to superior civil and military authorities. The habit, once acquired, was not lost.

This development came in parallel with an unforeseen consequence of the 1924 reduction of the Imperial Army by four divisions. Many of the officers released from service were directed into the state

education service to supervise a newly introduced program of compulsory military training for children. Retired officers and noncommissioned officers were heavily represented in the *seinengakko* (youth school) system, which provided vocational training for youths with relatively poor educational records. This system was especially strong in the countryside and played an important role in the provision of job opportunities for its students. Meanwhile, a growing population meant that more people were subject to conscription. The result of these factors was that ex-soldier associations became increasingly powerful pressure groups during the 1920s and 1930s, while the emergence of the *seinengakko* system pointed in

Winter campaign
Japanese infantry warm themselves beside a fire during the campaign for Jehol in February 1933. Once Jehol was secured, the Japanese set about encroaching on Chinese positions astride the Great Wall.

THE CHINESE CIVIL WARS

AFTER 1916 CHINA WAS WRACKED by power struggles between local warlords, but by the mid-Twenties one political party, the Kuomintang under Chiang Kai-shek, was the leading single grouping in southern and central China. A real civil war, about the nature of society, developed after 1926, when Chiang set about purging the Kuomintang's communist associates: the communists established themselves in provinces in central China, specifically Kiangsi, and sought to overthrow the Kuomintang in a largely urban-based struggle. By 1934 Kuomintang offensives forced the communists to abandon their existing base areas. Thus in October 1934 began the Long March, a journey by some 100,000 communists, soldiers, and civilians that ended a year and 6,000 miles (9,600 km) later in Shansi province. The Kuomintang sought a final effort that would have brought the communists' defeat, but the Sian Incident in December 1936 brought an end to conflict and the creation of a common front by the Kuomintang and the communists in the face of Japanese aggression.

The Long March
Chinese communists cross a mountain in 1935 on the arduous retreat to Shansi province. Of the 100,000 who began the journey, only around 10,000 reached the destination.

Nationalists on patrol
Kuomintang troops patrol through the city of Canton in late 1925 as part of a nationalist campaign to wrest power from China's numerous warlords.

Communist masterminds
Mao Zedong (left) and Zhou Enlai led the combination of rural insurgency and people's war that ultimately brought the Chinese communists to power in 1949.

the direction of the gradual imposition of military values on the countryside and the process of general low-key militarization of Japanese society.

This phenomenon developed in association with the process whereby, when universal suffrage was introduced in 1925, it was in association with the *Chian ijiho* (the National Security Act), which provided for the suppression of communist, socialist, anarchist, or any other political movement thought to pose a threat to the imperial system. In many ways such a provision amounted to a mandate for the *Tokubetsu Koto Keisatsu* (Special High Police)—or more commonly the *Tokko* (Thought Police—which had been established in Tokyo and certain prefectures in 1911. After 1928 the *Tokko*, which was already notorious for its manipulation of policial parties, intervention in legitimate party activities, and controlling the press, was established in every prefecture.

THE CAMPAIGN IN MANCHURIA

Such was the background against which the Kwantung Army, the Japanese garrison formation in southern Manchuria, a northern region of China, deliberately initiated a process in 1931 whereby it was able to overrun three of Manchuria's four provinces. The onset of the Depression and an increasingly volatile nationalism within Japan were

the basis of a Kwantung calculation that Tokyo would be unable to repudiate its action. The growing success of Chiang Kai-shek's nationalist Kuomintang suggested that China's civil wars might be drawing to a close, which could harm Japanese aspirations in China. Kwantung commanders suspected too that the great powers were indifferent to Manchuria: in 1928 a Soviet intervention provoked by local authorities there had gone unchecked. Consequently, in 1931 the Kwantung Army enjoyed maximum opportunity and minimal risk.

The campaign in Manchuria was the first of three Japanese offensive efforts north of and across the Great Wall: within Manchuria, in Inner Mongolia, and in northern China. These successive campaigns lasted until early 1937, by which time Japan had secured Manchuria and largely neutralized Chinese influence in Inner Mongolia and northern China, specifically Shansi, Hupei, and Shantung provinces.

Events north of the Great Wall had three phases. The main effort, from September 1931 to March 1932, saw the conquest of Heilungkiang, Kirin, and Fengtien, although mopping-up operations went on until November 1932. Next, between January and March 1933 the Japanese occupied Jehol, although fighting in the area of the Great Wall continued into the summer of 1932. Finally, from November

1932 to December 1935 the Japanese forces in effect established the basis of a move into Inner Mongolia. Much of this last phase was, in fact, not military but involved direct negotiations in which blandishments were combined with implied threats. Nevertheless, it resulted in Japan being the power with the greatest influence in Inner Mongolia.

SOUTH OF MANCHURIA

The Japanese constituted their gains as the puppet state of Manchukuo (the State of the Manchus) on March 1. Its president was the last emperor of the Qing (Manchu) dynasty, P'u Yi, who became the Emperor K'ang-te when Manchutikuo (the Empire of the Manchus) was proclaimed on March 1, 1934, amid what the Japanese official communiqué was to describe as "wild scenes of high nostalgia."

While the Manchurian campaign continued, the greatest single Japanese military effort had come farther south in China. In January 1932 Imperial Navy personnel in Shanghai provoked fighting that drew in the Imperial Army. Local Chinese forces resisted for a month, but a local truce was not concluded until May 5, by which time Japanese attention was directed toward Jehol province and Inner Mongolia. The completion of the conquest of Jehol in early 1933 proved to be merely the start

Noble tradition
Recruits in the Chinese Army learn to use traditional swords in this image from the late 1930s. The military in both China and Japan professed to follow ancient and honorable codes of warfare: the reality was often different.

Gas drill
Japanese troops practice putting on their gas masks during a training drill shortly before the outbreak of the Sino–Japanese War in 1937.

> "The Japanese are a disease of the skin. The Communists are a disease of the heart."

CHIANG KAI-SHEK, CHINESE NATIONALIST LEADER, DECEMBER 1941

of a continuing process of incidents, truces, and imposed agreements that resulted in successive Chinese surrenders to Japanese demands.

Kwantung Army encroachments upon Chinese positions north of the Great Wall went hand-in-hand with Japanese sponsorship of local collaborationist regimes and with what was dubbed "government-by-assassination" in Tokyo. In September 1931 the government led by Wakatsuki Reijiro, confronted by the refusal of the Army Ministry and Korean and Manchurian commands to obey its instructions, and outmaneuvered by a military with public opinion on its side, capitulated to army intransigence. The Wakatsuki cabinet remained in office, but not in power, until December 11, when it was replaced by

the government of Inukai Tsuyoshi. Inukai was prime minister until May 15, 1932, when he was killed by a group of naval officers and army cadets.

The military increasingly dominated the political process within Japan. After Inukai's assassination, an attempt to secure a government of national unity foundered because an administration could only be formed with the assent of the military—and only if it granted military demands. When a government was formed in 1936 under Hirota Koki, the new prime minister found that effectively the army minister had the power of veto over all appointments.

In these same years Japan associated itself with Germany in the Anti-Comintern Pact of November 25, 1936, but by the spring of 1937 it was isolated

and largely friendless. Japan had not helped itself by a refusal to engage in any serious discussion about naval limitation. The Imperial Navy had accepted the 1930 London Treaty—imposing new limits on shipbuilding—only because financial and economic considerations precluded opposition, but was determined that the treaty would be the last. The navy had its way between December 1934 and January 1936 and was freed from treaty limitation thereafter, but by the year's end a development within China had heralded general war in July 1937.

Within China, Kuomintang head Chiang Kai-shek had emerged as national leader. His priority was the pacification of Chinese communists rather than resistance to Japan in the north. Kuomintang forces conducted five major offensives in 1936 that brought the communists to the verge of defeat. However, a sixth offensive was conducted by Chiang's Manchurian allies, who had no interest in civil war while the Japanese occupied their homeland. When Chiang went to Sian in central China in December to enforce his orders, he was taken into custody and forced to bargain with the Manchurians and the communists. The price of release was an end to the civil wars and an undertaking to form a united front to oppose Japanese aggression.

The significance of these events was not lost on the Japanese. Their gains in Manchuria and northern China had been made possible because of Chinese weakness and internal divisions. The Sian Incident, in which Chiang Kai-shek was held hostage, served notice that China would attempt to resolve its internal disputes in order to present Japan with a united front. Such a development was nothing short of incitement to Japanese militarists and hard-liners to move quickly before China had a chance to make something of its intent.

Japan's puppet
P'u Yi, the last emperor of China, was installed as first chief executive and then emperor in the Manchurian states established by the Japanese between 1932 and 1934. He was a mere figurehead; real political, economic, and military power lay in Japanese hands.

THE CAMPAIGN IN CHINA

On July 7, 1937 a Japanese patrol and Chinese troops skirmished at the Marco Polo Bridge in Wanping, just outside Peking. Such events had often been used by the Japanese as a pretext to browbeat Chinese authorities into local concessions. The Marco Polo Bridge incident, however, proved the first step to full-scale war. In late July 1937 there was a massacre of Japanese soldiers, police, and civilians in Tungchow. Then, as a result of provocation by the Imperial Navy, fighting broke out in Shanghai on August 13. As in 1932, the Japanese Navy was unable to win the fight it had started; the army had to send reinforcements to help, which made mobilization necessary. Once ordered, on August 17, 1937, mobilization ensured full-scale war in China.

Thus began the Sino–Japanese War, which lasted until August 1945. Its first phase, between summer 1937 and October 1938, saw the Japanese gain the upper hand. Two initial advances, in northern and central China, came together on May 19, 1938,

THE RAPE OF NANKING

ALSO KNOWN AS THE NANKING MASSACRE, the Rape of Nanking ranks as one of the most infamous episodes in the history of modern warfare. The city in Kiangsu province had been the capital of the Nationalist Chinese from 1928 to 1937. Chiang Kai-shek's troops had already left the city when it was captured by the Japanese Central China Front Army on December 13, 1937. The destruction of Nanking was ordered by the Japanese commanding officer, General Matsui Iwane, and in the weeks that followed, some 50,000 Japanese troops went on a spree of mass killing and violence. Brutality was not uncommon from either side in the Sino–Japanese War, but even by these standards the events in Nanking were breathtaking. The soldiers bayoneted, shot, burned, buried alive, and decapitated their victims, and, according to eyewitness accounts, mutilated corpses lined the streets of the city.

The total number of Chinese killed in the Nanking massacre has been the subject of much debate, with most estimates ranging from around 100,000 to more than 300,000. It is almost certain that the accurate figure will never be known. In addition, it is thought that a total of 20,000 Chinese women and girls were raped before being murdered. As well as the mass human slaughter, the Japanese army looted and burned the city and surrounding towns, destroying more than one-third of the buildings in the process. In 1940 the Japanese made Nanking the capital of a Chinese client regime headed, until 1944, by Wang Ching-wei, the most senior member of the Kuomintang to have defected. Japan officially surrendered to China in Nanking on September 9, 1945. At the end of World War II Matsui and Tani Hisao, a lieutenant who had participated in murder and rape in Nanking, were tried for war crimes. They were found guilty and executed.

The conqueror's spoils
A Japanese soldier holding the national flag looks over the ruins of Nanking after the city's occupation in December 1937.

Buried alive
Japanese troops herd Chinese prisoners into a pit where they will be buried alive. The Japanese also committed other atrocities, including using live prisoners for bayonet practice.

with the capture of Suchow, which gave the Japanese possession of overland communications between Peking and the port of Shanghai. The Japanese effort then divided against the cites that lay in central China between the Yellow River in the north and the Yangtze River to the south. The first phase of the war ended when the Japanese drove along the Yangtze to capture the Wuhan cities—Wuchang, Hanyang, and Hangkou. The campaign was notable

for a number of reasons: the deliberate Japanese bombing of British and American warships at Shanghai, the Japanese atrocities at Nanking, and the breaching by the Chinese of dikes along the Yellow River in order to slow the Japanese advance. The Japanese incurred some defeats, mainly in the early weeks of the air war, when it became all too apparent that their bombers, without adequate fighter cover, were vulnerable to Soviet-supplied Chinese fighters.

Such defeats were, however, minor. The Japanese met with no real, sustained resistance as they conquered large areas of northern and central China.

Onward to victory
Japanese troops speed past a railroad sign during the March 1939 occupation of the strategically vital city of Nanchang, the capital of Kiangsi province in southeast China. By the time the Japanese arrived, retreating Chinese forces had destroyed most of the city's infrastructure.

Children of war
A famous—and possibly staged—photograph of the China conflict: Shanghai station after a bombing raid in August 1937. The Sino-Japanese conflict saw the first sustained employment of air power against civilian targets.

JAPAN'S FURTHER PLANS

The Japanese faced an age-old military truism: conquering territory was one thing, but holding on to it was quite another. They might be able to defeat Kuomintang forces, but they could not defeat the Kuomintang. What was more, there was no political option. On December 26, 1937 Chiang Kai-shek announced a policy of protracted resistance that precluded negotiations. Likewise, the Japanese would not deal with Chiang. They thus faced a dilemma. They had not conquered vast territories in order to set up client regimes that possessed real power, which might then be used against themselves. Yet without establishing popularly-based government in occupied China, they had no chance of securing support from the Chinese population.

Members of the Japanese military who were prepared to acknowledge the dilemma proposed genuine cooperation with a properly constituted alternative to Chiang and the Kuomintang. Some figures, such as Ishihara Kanji (the main architect of the Manchurian Incident in 1931), helped found the *Toa Remmei* (East Asian League) in October 1938. The league promoted war in East Asia as the means of creating a united continent in which Japan would be the equal partner of other Asian nations. Such a goal was opposed by Lieutenant-General Tojo Hideki, the Kwantung Army's chief of staff and the founder of the governmental *Koa Domei* (Agency for Developing Asia). The agency argued for the military conquest of Asia, and absolute Japanese domination of conquered areas in preparation for a "final war" with the Western races. Tojo and like-minded officers increasingly came to dominate political and military life.

While the war in China could not be won by political or military means, the effort of conquest worsened the international trading position on which the overpopulated, under-resourced Home Islands depended. Exploitation of the natural resources of Manchuria and northern and central China demanded capital investment that could only be secured at the expense of domestic programs. Similarly, the massive rise in state spending and concentration on military production imposed cuts on domestic consumption that were severe even by 1940. Moreover, with the outbreak of war in Europe in 1939, Western commercial shipping in the Pacific and international credits all but disappeared, with obvious implications for a Japan that lacked sufficient

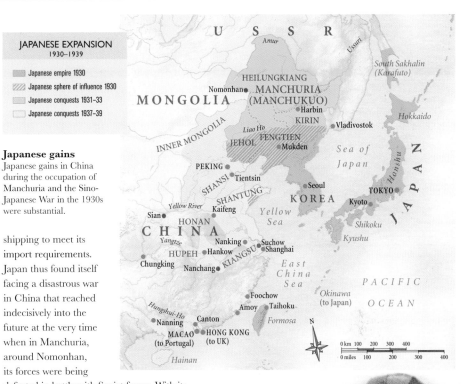

Japanese gains
Japanese gains in China during the occupation of Manchuria and the Sino-Japanese War in the 1930s were substantial.

shipping to meet its import requirements. Japan thus found itself facing a disastrous war in China that reached indecisively into the future at the very time when in Manchuria, around Nomonhan, its forces were being defeated in battle with Soviet forces. With its German ally signing a non-aggression treaty with the Soviet Union even as this defeat took shape, Japan chose caution and waited upon events to unfold before deciding its next course of action.

The start of battle
Soviet tankmen prepare to attack Japanese forces and their local allies at Nomonhan, in Manchuria, in July 1939. The clash was the most significant Soviet military action before the outbreak of the war itself.

BUILD-UP TO WAR IN EUROPE

OCTOBER 1, 1934–SEPTEMBER 1, 1939

On attaining power in 1933, Adolf Hitler set about rearming Germany in preparation for military conquests abroad. His expansion of the Reich met with little initial resistance from Britain and France, and Hitler acquired Austria and Czechoslovakia with little difficulty. However, when he sent German troops into Poland in 1939, the course for war was set.

1934

OCTOBER 1
Hitler orders creation of air force and expansion of army and navy

DECEMBER 30
Mussolini orders preparations for fall attack on Abyssinia

1935

MARCH 7
Saarland restored to Germany

MAY 2
France and USSR sign Mutual Assistance Pact

SEPTEMBER 15
Nuremberg Laws passed, depriving Jews of full German citizenship

JUNE 26
Mussolini rejects British suggestion for compromise over Italian claims on Abyssinia

SEPTEMBER 18
USSR joins League of Nations

OCTOBER 3
Italy invades Abyssinia

1936

MARCH 7
Germany reoccupies Rhineland

MARCH 23
Italy, Austria, and Hungary sign Rome Pact

MAY 9
Italy proclaims its annexation of Abyssinia

JULY 18
Spanish Civil War begins between republicans and nationalists led by Francisco Franco

OCTOBER 14
Belgium ends military alliance with France

NOVEMBER 1
Hitler and Mussolini sign Berlin-Rome Axis

NOVEMBER 25
Germany signs Anti-Comintern pact with Japan

1937

NOVEMBER 18
Germany and Italy recognize Franco's regime in Spain

FEBRUARY 8
In southern Spain, Franco's forces take Malaga

APRIL 26
Axis powers bomb Basque town of Guernica in Spain

NOVEMBER 25
Italy joins German–Japanese Anti-Comintern Pact

1938

MARCH 12
German troops march into Austria and *Anschluss* is proclaimed

APRIL 23
Sudeten Germans in Czechoslovakia demand full autonomy

SEPTEMBER 29
Munich Pact signed with Britain, France, and Italy, agreeing to the transfer of Sudetenland to Germany

1939

JANUARY 27
Britain and France recognize Franco's government

MARCH 15
Germans begin occupation of rest of Czechoslovakia

MARCH 21
Hitler demands that Poland return Danzig to Germany

MARCH 23
Germany and USSR sign Nazi–Soviet Pact, with agreement about partition of Poland

MARCH 23
Germans occupy Memel, Lithuania

APRIL 7
Italy invades Albania

MAY 22
Germany and Italy sign Pact of Steel, a military alliance

AUGUST 23
Germany and USSR sign Non-Aggression Pact

AUGUST 25
Britain signs Mutual Assistance Pact with Poland

SEPTEMBER 1
Germany invades Poland

German actions Oct 1934– Sept 1939	Other events	Italian actions Dec 1934– Apr 1939	German-Italian actions Nov 1936–May 1939

REARMAMENT AND EXPANSION

WITHIN 18 MONTHS of becoming chancellor of Germany on January 30, 1933, Adolf Hitler turned his attention to three foreign policy goals that were central to his avowed goal of restoring national prestige. First, the military restrictions imposed by the Versailles Treaty of 1919 should be lifted. Second, Germany should be restored to its rightful place as the strongest European power, and a "Greater Germany" should be created, to include German-speaking Austria, the Czech Sudetenland, and regions lost after World War I. Third, the German empire should be expanded to encompass Poland and European Russia.

Hitler had no concrete plan for attaining his ambitions. Instead, he would take what opportunities presented themselves. As his success grew, however, so did his appetite for conquest and his recklessness.

Defending the homeland
Mussolini's invasion of Abyssinia on October 3, 1935, was designed to acquire a glorious Italian empire. It was fiercely resisted by Abyssinian soldiers.

Hitler's rhetoric during the 1920s had made it clear that, should he come to power, Germany would set about rearming. For Europe, sapped by the effects of the Depression, the timing could not have been worse. Both Britain and France lacked the military means to oppose Hitler with force, and the economic resources to fund military programs.

In March 1933 Hitler argued that only Germany had disarmed in accordance with the Versailles Treaty, and that either other nations should disarm or Germany should be allowed to raise its own level of armaments. Later that year he threatened to quit the League of Nations if Germany was not granted parity. On October 19, he duly ordered his delegation to walk out of the League. The move shocked Europeans, but many Germans saw it as a sign that their national honor was at last being restored.

Hitler among his people
Admiring Germans surround Adolf Hitler at a meeting in Munich. Capable of great charm, Hitler had the ability to inspire strong personal loyalty in his followers.

DEVELOPMENTS IN AUSTRIA

A natural prize in the quest for a Greater Germany was Hitler's homeland, Austria, where in May 1932 Engelbert Dollfuss became chancellor. He began economic reforms and sought allies, especially Mussolini's Italy, to help him oppose a union with Germany. In May 1933 he dissolved parliament and banned the major political parties. Putting down an armed uprising in May 1934, Dollfuss proclaimed a new constitution modeled on that of fascist Italy, to the anger of German and Austrian Nazis. In July 1934 Austrian Nazis killed Dollfuss in a failed coup.

In response Mussolini, who saw Austria as a useful buffer between Italy and Hitler's Germany, sent three divisions of troops toward the Brenner Pass. The gesture made it clear that, if Germany came to the aid of the Nazi conspirators, war would ensue. Not yet in a position to fight such a war, Hitler could only watch as the new government banned the Austrian Nazi Party and executed the conspirators. Hitler's foreign policy was at its nadir.

GERMAN REARMAMENT

In early 1935 Hitler announced that Germany would build what military forces it chose. He also staged a lavish ceremony to reveal the existence of a new German Air Force, the 2,500-plane Luftwaffe, which he had been secretly building for two years. The Germans celebrated wildly, but Germany's neighbors were not so enthusiastic. Italy, France, and Britain forged the "Stresa Front" to resist German violations of the Versailles Treaty. Hitler saw the gesture for what it was: an empty show of strength, disguising the Allies' true weakness.

Versailles had also limited Germany's navy, but Hitler now sensed that he could increase it without reprisal. He forced Britain to allow him a surface navy equivalent to one-third of the tonnage of the British surface fleet and an equal tonnage of submarines. The British accepted that Germany would expand its navy with or without a treaty, and reluctantly signed an agreement to Hitler's naval expansion on June 18, 1935. Similar German agreements with France and the Soviet Union followed. The Versailles Treaty was dead.

ITALY'S INVASION OF ABYSSINIA

Mussolini, meanwhile, decided that if Hitler could flout treaties, so could he. He needed an overseas adventure to distract from the domestic troubles caused by the Depression. His target was Abyssinia (now Ethiopia) in East Africa, where on a previous colonial adventure in 1898 Italy had suffered a humiliating defeat at the hands of African troops.

EUROPEAN REARMAMENT

THE TREATY OF VERSAILLES specified the need for general disarmament in Europe. Germany was forced to disarm, but by 1933 talks among the other nations had failed. Hitler argued for rearmament on the grounds that he feared the superior forces of Germany's neighbors, but France would not agree. In 1933 Hitler withdrew Germany from the League of Nations and embarked on a program of unilateral rearmament. By late 1935 he had reintroduced conscription and created a new air force, the Luftwaffe. In addition, the Anglo-German Naval Agreement of 1935 allowed for expansion of Germany's navy.

German rearmament went hand-in-hand with territorial expansion, as Hitler sent forces into the Rhineland, Austria, and Czechoslovakia. At first France and Britain, weakened by the effects of the Depression and reluctant to plunge their countries into war, practiced a policy of appeasement. Both increased their armed forces as the decade went on, but the delay allowed Germany to gain a decisive lead.

By September 1939 Germany had amassed a fighting force of 86 infantry divisions (1,500,000 men) together with 6 tank (panzer) divisions, 3,000 planes, 5 battleships, and 55 submarines. While Britain had built up the Royal Air Force to over 2,000 planes, and retained the world's largest navy, its army had only 17 infantry divisions. Even with the French Army of 66 divisions, the main Allies' combined military might was still smaller than that of Nazi Germany.

Versailles in shreds
Adolf Hitler, along with naval chief Admiral Erich Raeder, inspects the new warship *Scharnhorst* in October 1936. The Führer ignored the Versailles Treaty limitations on shipbuilding.

Stockpiling shells
British munitions workers stack shells in a factory late in 1938. German rearmament triggered a reciprocal arms build-up in Britain and France.

Soviet defiance
"We will respond to this war-mongering" declares a 1934 Soviet propaganda poster.

SPANISH CIVIL WAR

THE SPANISH CIVIL WAR (1936–39) was a full-scale military revolt by conservative nationalists against the leftist republican government. Under the leadership of General Francisco Franco, the rebel forces coalesced around the policies of the fascist Falange Party. Adolf Hitler despatched Luftwaffe transports and fighters to assist Franco, and allowed his own forces to go to Spain as "volunteers" in the Condor Legion. Hitler used the conflict as a test-bed for equipment and new military doctrines—the introduction of area or carpet-bombing techniques in the attack on Guernica in 1937 was an innovation that reemerged in World War II—but the Führer's motives were more generally concerned with spreading fascism and sowing the seeds of disunity among the Western powers. Likewise, Mussolini also sent men and equipment, seeing the nationalist cause as an opportunity to bolster Italy's international standing and to gain respect for its armed forces.

The republicans asked for help from the Western democracies and the Soviet Union. In France and Britain, divided public opinion prevented official involvement, while Stalin offered limited support. However, Western neutrality could not stop volunteers from joining the war. Thousands of young men flocked to Spain to fight fascism. Most served in the republican International Brigade, but some

Women snipers
Female republican fighters take cover in the early stages of the Spanish Civil War. Control of Spain's cities, where much of the fighting took place, was vital to the eventual victory of Franco's nationalists in March 1939.

formed their own national units. From the United States, for example, came the Abraham Lincoln and George Washington Brigades; refugees from Germany formed the Ernst Thälmann Brigade. Nonetheless, by 1938 the fighting had clearly tilted in Franco's favor. In March 1939 the Spanish fascists achieved final victory. In May the German troops returned home to a heroes' welcome, and the "volunteers" rejoined their units.

In addition to dividing the Western powers, the Spanish Civil War cemented Benito Mussolini's relationship with Adolf Hitler, culminating in the Rome–Berlin Axis Agreement of September 1937, a fascist alliance that would have profound effects on the course of World War II.

Spanish propaganda
The cover of this right-wing magazine reflects the influence of Spanish artist Salvador Dalí. Both sides were quick to exploit graphic art such as posters to drum up support.

Symbolic city
A lone dog stands in a ruined street in the city of Guernica, in northern Spain, destroyed by a German bombing raid on April 26, 1937.

Fleeing for their lives
Uncertainty marks the faces of women and children fleeing Spain's capital, Madrid, in December 1936. Thousands of civilians were caught up in the fighting.

Isolated and poor, Abyssinia lay within easy reach of Italy's colonies in Eritrea and Somaliland. Starting a campaign, however, would leave Italy vulnerable to any punitive sanctions imposed by the League of Nations. Mussolini gambled that he could eliminate Abyssinia before the League of Nations had time to react and thus present it with a *fait accompli*.

Accordingly, Italian troops invaded Abyssinia on October 3, 1935. Abyssinian emperor Haile Selassie pleaded with the League to react. The League realized, however, that any form of military intervention would come too late to affect events and that any economic sanctions might drive Mussolini into alliances with non-League members such as the Soviet Union or Germany. The League made a hopeless compromise: it imposed minimal sanctions that caused no harm but succeeded in angering the Italians. On the ground, the Italians routed the Abyssinians. By the time the "dispute" came to the top of the League's agenda, Abyssinia had ceased to exist as an independent nation.

Nazism on display
Hitler Youth parade in the form of a stylized swastika during the Berlin Olympic games in 1936. Hitler tried to turn the event into a publicity coup for Aryan ideals, but German athletes failed to achieve the success he craved.

HITLER AND THE RHINELAND

Hitler, in turn, reasoned that if Italy could get away with such naked aggression, so could Germany. In March 1936 the major European powers watched helplessly as he ordered troops into the German Rhineland, in defiance of the Versailles Treaty.

An effective reaction to the remilitarization of the Rhineland was partly prevented by political paralysis within France, where a Popular Front—an alliance of socialists and communists—expected to win a parliamentary majority in elections in April 1936. By May 1936, when the Popular Front finally came to power, the German Army had been stationed in the Rhineland for more than two months.

Among those who were most alarmed by the German move into the Rhineland were Hitler's own generals, who knew that their forces' training and equipment were inadequate. German troops had no modern artillery or tanks. The infantry had no transport. The generals wrung a concession from Hitler: if the French mobilized their troops, Hitler would order the German forces back.

However, Hitler had read the French well. The Maginot Line along the German border revealed a mentality more suited to defense than attack. Hitler was also right that the French would not fight alone, and that Britain, the most important ally of France, would not go to war over the Rhineland. His gamble succeeded, and his popularity at home rose to unprecedented levels.

On November 5, 1937 Hitler told his defense staff that his focus lay on creating a Greater Germany, involving the amalgamation into the Reich of German-speaking Austrians, the Germans of the Czech Sudetenland, the areas lost in post-World War I plebiscites, and the coastal city of Danzig at the head of the Polish Corridor. He also indicated that he would turn east in a bid to establish *Lebensraum*, or "living space," for the expanded German populace.

The implications were clear: unless Poland and the Soviet Union agreed to surrender territory, only war could bring about Hitler's goals. The Führer told his audience to be ready for war by late 1942 or early 1943. But he also warned them to prepare to take advantage of any earlier opportunities that might arise.

After firing those ministers and generals who were clearly less than enthusiastic about his plans, Hitler took his first step toward creating an expanded Germany—the *Anschluss*, or annexation of Austria. Using as a pretext the refusal of Chancellor Kurt von Schuschnigg to lift the ban on the Austrian Nazi Party, illegal since the attempted coup in 1934, Hitler presented the Austrian leader with a document that essentially imposed Nazi control on the country. Browbeaten and shattered, Schuschnigg signed. On March 12, 1938, German troops marched into Austria, which was rapidly and fully incorporated into Germany as the Ostmark province.

DEMANDS FOR THE SUDETENLAND

Hitler now looked to the region of Czechoslovakia bordering Germany. Known as the Sudetenland, it was home to some 3 million ethnic Germans. Hitler instructed the local Nazi leader, Konrad Henlein, to begin a campaign for greater autonomy for Sudeten Germans. Throughout the summer of 1938, no sooner did the Czech government offer a concession than Henlein would make new demands.

Dictators in tandem
Hitler and Mussolini take the salute during Il Duce's state visit to Berlin in September 1937. The visit cemented the military alliance between Germany and Italy, which would have long-term consequences for the fate of Europe.

> "…the lost land will never be won back by solemn appeals to God, nor by hopes in any League of Nations, but only by the force of arms."
>
> ADOLF HITLER, SPEAKING OUTSIDE THE REICHSTAG IN 1936

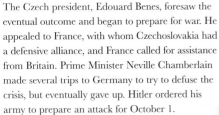

EXPANSION OF NAZI GERMANY
MAR 1935–MAR 1939

- Germany 1933
- Area of German expansion Mar 1935–Mar 1939
- --- German defensive lines

The quest for "living space"
German expansion from 1936 to 1939 concentrated on territories with large German minorities—but further eastern expansion seemed inevitable.

Accordingly, Germany invited France and Britain to a meeting to discuss the crisis. The Czechs were not asked to attend. In Munich in September 1938 Hitler offered France and Britain a pledge that the Sudetenland marked the end of his quest to create a Greater Germany. To Chamberlain and French premier Edouard Daladier this offered the chance of an honorable exit. Daladier told the Czechs that Hitler's forces would occupy their country within 48 hours, and no opposition would be voiced by Britain or France. Appeasement had reached its zenith. On October 1, 1938, Czech border guards stood aside as German troops occupied the Sudetenland.

THE FALL OF CZECHOSLOVAKIA

Hitler, however, remained unsatisfied. He was no closer to his goal of "living space" for the German people than before the Czech crisis had arisen, a situation he was determined to rectify by invading the remainder of Czechoslovakia. With winter approaching, the earliest feasible date for such an action was March 1939. As the moment neared, the new Czech president Emil Hacha visited Berlin. Aged 67, and a diabetic in poor health, Hacha was harangued until at 4:00 am on March 15, 1939, he agreed to invite the Germans to enter

The Czech president, Edouard Benes, foresaw the eventual outcome and began to prepare for war. He appealed to France, with whom Czechoslovakia had a defensive alliance, and France called for assistance from Britain. Prime Minister Neville Chamberlain made several trips to Germany to try to defuse the crisis, but eventually gave up. Hitler ordered his army to prepare an attack for October 1.

Faced with certain defeat in the event of a German mobilization, in September 1938 Benes agreed to cede the Sudetenland in six months' time. Hitler increased the stakes. The Czechs must hand over the Sudetenland immediately, he said. Chamberlain mobilized British forces in anticipation of a military conflict that appeared to be inevitable. The French took similar measures, and Europe prepared for war.

Some of Hitler's generals were as unhappy as Europe's leaders. Led by Army chief of staff General Ludwig Beck, they regarded Hitler's ultimatums with horror. Beck wanted to expose Hitler's recklessness so that the army might be able to act against him. Risking the death penalty for treason, he approached the British political maverick Winston Churchill, urging him to tell the British government to stand up to Hitler. Chamberlain ignored Churchill's pleas for action.

Meanwhile, German military units moved to the Czech border in readiness for the invasion. Hitler had counted on popular support, but the Germans looked on sullenly. As he rethought the situation, intervention came from an unexpected source: Mussolini, fearing a European-wide conflagration, urged Hitler to give peace one more chance.

Bohemia and Moravia and establish a "protectorate." Unopposed, German troops crossed the border later that day, to remain there for the next six years.

Chamberlain and Daladier had been duped. Knowing what Hitler's next target would be, they extended promises to Poland to protect its territorial integrity if Germany invaded. Hitler's response was to set his sights on the Polish Corridor.

INVASION OF POLAND

The Polish Corridor, which separated East Prussia from Germany, was a daily reminder for Germans of the humiliation of the Versailles Treaty. The Poles had expelled most Germans from the area, but at the top of the corridor was Danzig, whose German inhabitants made growing demands for autonomy. In a familiar pattern, any concessions by the Poles were met only with more demands. France and Britain now sought assistance from the Soviet Union in the belief that if Stalin would give support to Poland, Hitler could not attack.

Hitler sent his foreign minister, Joachim von Ribbentrop, to Moscow to broker a deal with Stalin. Ribbentrop offered what the Allies

THE FREE CITY OF DANZIG

UNDER THE TERMS of the Treaty of Versailles, the port of Danzig, on the Vistula River at the top of the corridor through Germany that gave Poland access to the Baltic Sea, became a "free city." The former capital of the German province of West Prussia, Danzig was under the protection of the League of Nations, but had special administrative ties

Staking a claim
"Danzig is German": this propaganda postcard printed by the Nazis in 1938 shows the imperial eagle above a stylized view of the free city.

with Poland. Poland could use the harbor without paying duty, and was in charge of foreign policy. The arrangement irked both the city's 96 percent German majority and Germans everywhere. Economic and political developments in Danzig mirrored those in Germany. In late 1930 the Nazis emerged as the second-largest political party in the city. After taking power in elections in 1933, they outlawed opposing parties and introduced racial laws that led to an exodus of Jewish inhabitants.

Throughout the 1930s Danzig's Germans lobbied for increased autonomy, and in March 1939 Hitler demanded the cession of Danzig to Germany and the restoration of a land link with East Prussia. Poland rejected these demands and obtained French and British guarantees against German aggression.

On the march
Hitler Youth march past Danzig harbor in June 1930. That same year the Nazi Party emerged from nowhere to become one of the major powers in the city.

could not: the eastern half of Poland and non-intervention should Stalin try to repossess Finland and states on the Baltic which had broken away from the Soviet Union. Not yet ready for war, Stalin accepted. On August 23, 1939, Europe learned that Hitler and Stalin had signed a Non-Aggression Pact.

The Poles mobilized their armed forces. Hitler still expected Britain and France to back off from any military action, as they had done previously over Czechoslovakia. To give them a means of doing so without losing face, he staged a "border outrage" in order to make it appear that the Poles were the aggressors. Responding to this "provocation," German troops crossed the border into Poland at 4:30 am on September 1. Britain and France presented an ultimatum. When Hitler failed to halt the German invasion, to his surprise the allies honored their guarantees to Poland by quickly declaring war on Germany. On September 3, 1939, World War II in Europe began.

Military on the move
German-speaking inhabitants of the Czech village of Waldheusel welcome Nazi troops during Hitler's occupation of the Sudetenland in October 1938.

Politics as spectacle
Thousands of Nazi supporters crowd an arena at Buckeberge to mark Thanksgiving Day, January 1, 1937. The Nazis used mass rallies, particularly at Nuremberg, to reinforce the impression of power and discipline.

WAR BEGINS IN EUROPE
1939–40

DURING THE FIRST PHASE OF THE WAR IN EUROPE
THERE WAS ACTION AT SEA AND FOUR CAMPAIGNS
ON LAND: THE GERMAN AND SOVIET INVASION OF
POLAND, A WINTER WAR BETWEEN THE SOVIET UNION
AND FINLAND, THE GERMAN INVASION OF DENMARK AND
NORWAY, AND FINALLY, AFTER MANY MONTHS IN WHICH
LITTLE HAPPENED IN WESTERN EUROPE, THE GERMAN
ASSAULT ON FRANCE AND THE LOW COUNTRIES.
THIS ATTACK WAS A DEVASTATING DEMONSTRATION
OF THE NEW GERMAN HIGH-SPEED WARFARE AND,
AT THE END OF IT, BRITAIN STOOD ALONE.

Germans marching in Warsaw
The Germans unleashed their attack on
Poland on September 1, 1939. The Polish
army, with its largely obsolescent weapons,
was no match for them, and Warsaw was
forced to surrender on September 27.

2

BLITZKRIEG AND TOTAL WAR

EUROPE WENT TO WAR IN SEPTEMBER 1939 IN A MOOD OF GRIM ACCEPTANCE THAT THE EFFORTS OF THE PEACEMAKERS IN 1919 TO CREATE A EUROPE AT PEACE WITH ITSELF HAD FAILED. THE TECHNOLOGICAL ADVANCES OF THE PREVIOUS 25 YEARS WOULD RESULT IN A CONFLICT VERY MUCH MORE TOTAL THAN WORLD WAR I, WITH CIVILIANS IN THE FIRING LINE AS NEVER BEFORE.

A WIDELY HELD BELIEF had grown up between the two world wars that any future war would open with mass attacks by bombers, armed with gas bombs, on cities. It had been argued that air power was now the decisive weapon of war since it had the ability to strike at the heart of a nation and destroy its will to fight, thus making armies and navies virtually superfluous. Incidents such as the bombing of Guernica during the Spanish Civil War and Japanese air attacks in China appeared to confirm that the aircraft was now the dominant weapon, although in no instance was poison gas actually used. Consequently, in the months leading up to the outbreak of war, the belligerent nations had begun to prepare their citizens for such an event, even to the extent of issuing them with gasmasks and arranging for the evacuation of children from cities.

USE OF AIR POWER

The fact that massed air attacks on cities did not immediately take place was largely through fear of instant retaliation in kind. The air forces of both sides were under strict instructions to confine themselves to military targets. By the same token, while some nations held stocks of poison gas, governments laid down that it would only be employed if the other side used gas warfare first. Consequently, air power was employed primarily in support of ground forces, both on the battlefield itself and to the rear in attacks on communications. There was a need to gain air superiority over the battlefield, which for the German Luftwaffe meant that the first priority in any campaign was to destroy the opposing air force, ideally by attacking its aircraft on its airfields. The Luftwaffe did, in fact, stray beyond military targets when it attacked Warsaw in September 1939, Rotterdam in May 1940, and refugees in the Low Countries and

France. Its defense was that the two cities refused demands to surrender, hence making themselves military targets. As for attacks on refugees, the justification was that creating panic would hamper the movement of enemy military forces.

An adjunct to air power was the employment by the Germans of a new form of warfare in the campaigns in both Norway and the west. They used paratroops and airlanded forces to secure key points, enabling the troops on the ground to advance quickly. The success enjoyed by the German airborne forces prompted both the British and the Americans to establish their own.

BLITZKRIEG TACTICS

On land the fighting would be dominated by the new German style of warfare—blitzkrieg ("lightning war")—that made great use of tanks and aircraft. The Poles were the first victims in September 1939, when they paid the penalty for their lack of modern equipment. The French and British might have hoped to cope better in May 1940, especially since they had had nine months in which to prepare for the German attack. Their armies, however, were suffering from prewar parsimony. In France much of the defense budget had gone into constructing the Maginot Line, while in Britain greater priority had been given to rearming the navy and air force. Cooperation between both the British and French air force and army was not nearly as close as that between the German Army and the Luftwaffe. Furthermore, it was only late in the day that the French began to concentrate their tanks into armored divisions, while the one British armored formation was only ready to be deployed in late May. Finally, Allied communications, especially at the higer levels of command, were too cumbersome to enable commanders to react sufficiently quickly to rapidly changing situations.

Dunkirk evacuation
A total of 340,000 British, Belgian, and French troops were rescued from Dunkirk by the Royal Navy after being driven back to the English Channel coast.

The result of these deficiencies in the French and British armies was that neutral Belgium and the Netherlands were quickly overrun and France was forced to sign a humiliating armistice. Much of the British Army in France did manage to escape, largely thanks to the Royal Navy, which rescued it from the beaches of Dunkirk. It was not the first time, since the navy had also had to carry out evacuations of Allied forces from Norway. This was in parallel with a grim campaign that it had been waging from the outbreak of war—the defense of Britain's maritime communications.

"We must be very careful not to assign to this deliverance the attributes of a victory. Wars are not won by evacuations."

WINSTON CHURCHILL ADDRESSING THE HOUSE OF COMMONS ON JUNE 4, 1940
AFTER THE END OF THE DUNKIRK EVACUATION

WAR AT SEA

At sea the main focus was on the Atlantic, as it had been during World War I. Indeed, the second Battle of the Atlantic would be the longest running campaign of World War II, the first victim being on September 3, 1939 (the liner *Athenia*), and the last in May 1945 during the dying days of the war in Europe. The French and British had agreed that the Royal Navy, still the most powerful in the world, would be responsible for the Atlantic and North Sea, while the French took care of the Mediterranean, which did not become a theater of war until June 1940, when Italy finally entered the conflict. The British imposed a maritime blockade on Germany, as they had during World War I. Otherwise, the Royal Navy's main task was keeping Britain's sea communications open.

Hitler, with his fleet in the midst of an expansion plan when war broke out, recognized that, although modern, it lacked the strength to meet the Royal Navy head on. Instead, the German Navy would concentrate on throttling Britain's maritime communications, something it had very nearly succeeded in doing in 1917. In September 1939, the German U-boat arm was still comparatively small, and from the outset the British limited the amount of damage it could inflict on merchant vessels by instituting a convoy system. This was despite a grave shortage of escort ships. Consequently, most of the U-boat victims were ships sailing on their own. On the other hand, few

French refugees
Possibly as many as 5 million French civilians took part in a vast southward exodus ahead of the advancing Germans, sometimes greatly hampering the movements of Allied troops. Here, refugees arrive by train in an area of France not yet occupied by the Germans.

U-boats were sunk and they did cause two major embarrassments. One sunk the aircraft carrier *Courageous* in the North Sea in September 1939 and another managed to penetrate the British Home Fleet anchorage in Scapa Flow in the Orkneys and sink the battleship *Royal Oak*. More serious were the German surface raiders, the fast and heavily armed pocket battleships. Most notable of these was the *Graf Spee*, which had sailed from Germany before the outbreak of war and caused havoc in the Indian Ocean and South Atlantic. At one point as many as five Allied naval task forces were attempting to hunt her down. Eventually she was brought to bay and trapped by three British cruisers off the South American coast in December 1939. Her captain scuttled her rather than face the disgrace of surrender. It was one of the few bright spots for the Allies during the lengthy period of waiting and relative inactivity in the west, between September 1939 and May 1940, known as the "Phoney War."

"The final German victory over England is now only a question of time. Enemy offensive operations on a large scale are no longer possible."

GENERAL ALFRED JODL, CHIEF OF STAFF GERMAN ARMED FORCES HQ, DIARY ENTRY, JUNE 30, 1940

were conscripted. They not only worked in the factories to produce the weapons, but also helped to operate them. Strict food rationing, too, was a fact of life in the belligerent nations and those under Axis occupation. An even grimmer aspect of total war was what is today termed "ethnic cleansing." Hitler's persecution of Jews had, of course, begun almost as soon as he gained power in Germany. After the outbreak of war the policy was expanded to include the entire Jewish population of Europe. By the fall of 1940 all Jews in German-occupied Europe were under threat. In Poland they were already being confined to ghettoes, but it was to be another year before the Nazis adopted a policy of wholesale extermination.

In the meantime, Britain was being nightly hammered by the Luftwaffe. Yet while Churchill was certain that the British people would remain steadfast and that the danger of a German invasion was receding, he accepted that his country lacked the resources to defeat the fascist powers on its own, even with the British Empire taken into account. Only the entry of the United States into the war could achieve victory. Thus, from the summer of 1940, he began to woo President Franklin Roosevelt. But while Roosevelt had every sympathy for Britain's plight and admired the way in which the British were fighting on, he knew that the vast majority of Americans were still isolationist and had no wish to become involved in what they saw as yet another European squabble. In the months to come the US president would give Britain what help he could, as well as preparing his own country for what he believed was ultimately inevitable. The United States' actual entry into the war was, however, still a long way off.

Fleeing civilians
As the Germans advanced rapidly through the Netherlands, Belgium, and France in May–June 1940, literally millions of civilians took to the roads to flee from the fighting. Often in columns, they were an easy target for German machine-gun fire from the air.

One other aspect of the war at sea that grew in significance was maritime air power. The British had aircraft carriers, while the Germans did not, but initially they saw little action, aside from off Norway in April 1940, when they provided some air support to the forces ashore. Norway, however, also revealed the threat of land-based aircraft to ships. This would become even more apparent in the Mediterranean, as would the carrier's ability to strike at the enemy from long range, something that would be employed to great effect in the Pacific war.

Another type of warfare that would come to dominate much of the conflict—but was used only tentatively in the first phase of the war—was amphibious warfare. The events at Gallipoli during World War I had made many believe that landings on a hostile coast were no longer viable. As a result, little specialized shipping, such as landing craft, was available to either side when they executed landings in Norway. Faced with the prospect of a cross-Channel invasion of Britain, the Germans did realize that air superiority over the landing area was essential, but when they failed to achieve this during the Battle of Britain, Hitler postponed the invasion indefinitely. By then he had turned on Britain's cities, hoping to bomb the country into submission.

TOTAL WAR

"City busting," as it came to be known, helped to make World War II a total war, in which civilian populations were not only in the firing line, but were also mobilized as never before to support the war effort. In particular, and notably in Britain, women

A factory in occupied France
The Germans expected the civilians in the countries they occupied to contribute to the German war effort. Some factory workers were forced to leave their homes and go to work in Germany where, by 1943, foreigners made up 20 percent of the workforce.

INVASION OF POLAND AND SCANDINAVIA

SEPTEMBER 1, 1939–JUNE 9, 1940

While Germany and the Soviet Union dismembered Poland, little happened in the west. The British and French only became actively involved on the gound with the German invasion of Norway in April 1940 and then of the Low Countries and France in May.

1939

SEPTEMBER 3
Britain, France, Australia, and New Zealand declare war on Germany

SEPTEMBER 9
British troops depart for France to be deployed on Belgian border

SEPTEMBER 17
Soviet troops invade eastern Poland

OCTOBER 6
Fighting in Poland comes to an end

NOVEMBER 30
Soviet troops invade Finland

DECEMBER 7
Denmark, Norway, and Sweden declare their neutrality

DECEMBER 30
Finns inflict humiliating defeat on Russians at Suommusalmi

1940

FEBRUARY 1
Russians launch offensive in Karelia

FEBRUARY 11
Russians break through Mannerheim Line

MARCH 6
Hitler adopts "Plan Sickle" for invasion of west, with main thrust to be made through Ardennes

APRIL 6
Allied forces set sail to lay mines in Norwegian waters

APRIL 10
Denmark surrenders. Two German destroyers are sunk in Narvik Fjord

APRIL 18
British and French troops join Norwegian forces in Trondheim

MAY 10
Germans launch invasion of Low Countries and France

MAY 26
British evacuation from beaches of Dunkirk begins

JUNE 8
Allied forces and Norwegian king and government are evacuated from Narvik. Armistice is signed

SEPTEMBER 1
Germans cross border into Poland and annex Danzig

SEPTEMBER 5
US affirms its neutrality

SEPTEMBER 15
German armies surround Warsaw

SEPTEMBER 27
Warsaw surrenders

OCTOBER 1
French begin withdrawal in Saarland to behind Maginot Line

DECEMBER 3
Finns withdraw to Mannerheim Line in Karelia

DECEMBER 15
5th British Regular Division arrives in France

JANUARY 15
Belgium refuses Allied request to advance through its territory

MARCH 3
Major Russian offensive launched against Viipuri

MARCH 12
Treaty of Moscow signed, ending the war in Finland

APRIL 9
Germans invade Denmark and Norway. Copenhagen is occupied within 12 hours

APRIL 13
Seven German destroyers sunk in Narvik Fjord

APRIL 14
British and French make first landings at Narvik

MAY 2
Following fierce fighting around Trondheim, Allied troops are forced to begin evacuation

MAY 17
Germans take Brussels

JUNE 9, 1940
Quisling is installed by Germany as puppet ruler of Norway

■ Campaign in Poland
Sept 1–Oct 6, 1939

■ Campaign in Finland Nov 30, 1940–Mar 12, 1940

■ Campaign in Denmark and Norway
Apr 9–June 8, 1940

■ Other events

FIRST CONQUESTS

THE GERMAN PLAN for the assault on Poland had been drawn up by a small team headed by the Prussian Gerd von Rundstedt, who was nominally in retirement. In essence, General Fedor von Bock's Army Group North was to seal the base of the hated Polish Corridor and drive south from East Prussia to cut off the withdrawal of the Polish forces defending the German frontier. Rundstedt himself was to take command of Army Group South and advance rapidly on the Polish capital Warsaw.

The Poles, who had not begun serious planning until spring 1939, faced a dilemma. They had a number of well placed river lines, notably the Warthe and the Vistula, on which to anchor their defenses. However, to do so would mean abandoning the most heavily populated and economically developed part of the country in the west. In addition, with Slovakia now under Nazi thrall, they had to worry about their southern border. There was also the threat from the German Third Army in East Prussia. Consequently, they felt forced to adopt a linear defense along their borders. This left them with just one army in reserve

Polish cavalry
The Poles considered the cavalry to be the cream of their army. It was, however, ill-equipped to combat blitzkrieg, and claims that it charged German tanks were baseless.

German motorcyclists in Warsaw
German troops poured into Warsaw after its surrender on September 27. For the Poles this day was to mark the end of 20 years as an independent state and the beginning of nearly six years of intense suffering.

and placed to guard the approaches to Warsaw from the west. The Poles hoped, however, that a German attack would immediately precipitate an assault by the French and the British on Germany.

THE INVASION OF POLAND

Hitler's original intention was to launch his invasion on August 26, but the Anglo-Polish Alliance signed the previous day, together with Mussolini's declaration that he was not yet ready for war, caused him to delay at the last moment. He finally ordered that the attack should begin in the early hours of September 1. The invasion opened at 4:45 am with the guns of the elderly battleship *Schleswig-Holstein*, which was on a goodwill visit to the Polish port of Danzig (Gdansk), pounding the Polish garrison at nearby Westerplatte. Minutes later, the skies thundered to the sound of German aircraft, their main target Polish airfields. The Poles, however, had taken the precaution of dispersing many of their aircraft to satellite airfields, so frustrating the German goal of destroying the air force on the ground in one blow. Then, as dawn broke, the ground forces, spearheaded by the panzer divisions and supported by artillery, crossed the border. The Poles fought bravely, with the Westerplatte garrison not surrendering for a week, but they lacked the mobility to counter the new form of blitzkrieg warfare. Even so, the Germans

were not without their problems. Most had never been under fire before and maneuvers that had worked like clockwork on the training ground were now marked by a hesitancy, but it was not enough to halt the advance. By the end of two days' fighting the Polish Corridor was sealed and on September 5 Army Group South had broken through the Poznan and Lodz Armies in the center (see map page 47). Having destroyed the infrastructure of the main Polish airfields, the Luftwaffe now turned its attention to communications and this soon began to affect the Polish supply lines.

The British and French declarations of war on September 3 may have boosted Polish morale, but they did nothing to impede the German advance. The Pomorze Army, now trapped in the Corridor was totally destroyed, while the Modlin Army was forced to withdraw. The Polish Air Force was being shot out of the skies and was running out of fuel due

to the disruption to its logistics. Indeed, by September 9 it was virtually grounded. With the German Third Army now advancing south from East Prussia, and the Eighth and Tenth Armies from the west, the threat to Warsaw was growing by the day. To restore the situation, on the 9th the Poznan Army counterattacked from Kutno into the flank of the Eighth Army. In the three-day battle that followed, the Poles decimated one German infantry division.

The Poles were courageous, but they could not halt the remorseless advance of the German panzer divisions. Polish communications were breaking down and it proved impossible to establish a coherent defense on the Vistula and San Rivers. The Poznan Army was trapped and destroyed, and by September 15 Warsaw was surrounded.

WARSAW BESIEGED

Demands that the Poles surrender their capital were met with defiance. Not wishing to become embroiled in costly street fighting, the Germans subjected Warsaw to a prolonged artillery and air bombardment. To outside observers it seemed that

STALIN AND THE SOVIET UNION

JOSEF VISSARIONOVICH DZHUGASHVILI (1879–1953) was born in Tiflis, the son of a cobbler, and in his youth was a candidate for the priesthood in the Russian Orthodox Church. He changed his name to Stalin, meaning "Man of Steel," on becoming involved in revolutionary politics in 1903. Stalin became a close associate of Lenin during the Bolshevik Revolution of 1917 and later a member of the Revolutionary Military Council. By 1928 he had emerged from a bitter leadership struggle as the dictator of the Soviet Union, and he then launched a Five-Year Plan to develop heavy industry and collectivize agriculture. The plan was ruthlessly implemented, transforming the economy at the cost of millions of lives.

In the 1930s Stalin responded to opposition to his reforms by instituting a wholesale purge of the ruling hierarchy in which most of his former Bolshevik comrades were sentenced to death. The purges spread downward into every stratum of society and hundreds of thousands were shot or sent to the rapidly expanding network of

labor camps in the far north. Subsequent purges of the Soviet armed forces cut a swathe through the officer corps, destroying morale and throwing into reverse the reforms introduced by Marshal Tukhachevsky, a proponent of armored warfare.

In the weeks leading up to Germany's invasion of Poland, Stalin was only too aware that his country was not ready for war. He signed a nonaggression pact with his archenemy, Hitler, in the belief that being allowed half of Poland and a free rein in the Baltic States would provide him with a land buffer against a possible future German invasion.

State propaganda
Throughout the 1930s Stalin was portrayed in state propaganda as a benign leader committed to the good of the Soviet people.

Stalin
A ruthless dictator, Stalin's driving ambition was to turn the Soviet Union into a modern industrial state in just 10 years.

MILITARY STRENGTH OF THE COMBATANTS IN 1939

IN THE WEHRMACHT (German Armed Forces), a new philosophy of high-speed warfare had been adopted. However, the instruments of this new style of warfare were not perfected by 1939. The navy's expansion plan was not due for completion until 1942, and much of the army was still reliant on its feet and horsedrawn transportation. Only the Luftwaffe, with its imposing fleet of modern aircraft, was ready for war.

The French had strong armed forces on paper, but they had developed a wholly defensive mentality. The British placed their faith, as always, in the Royal Navy, still the strongest navy in the world. The Royal Air Force had modernized, but was still small when compared to the Luftwaffe, while the army had serious equipment deficiencies. On the sidelines, for the moment, stood Italy and the Soviet Union. Mussolini had created a

modern navy, which rivaled the British in the Mediterranean. His air force, too, appeared capable, but the army had much still to do to prepare itself. In terms of numbers, the forces of the Soviet Union, especially the Red Army, dwarfed those of other countries, but morale had suffered as a result of the purges, which had also snuffed out any vestige of individual initiative.

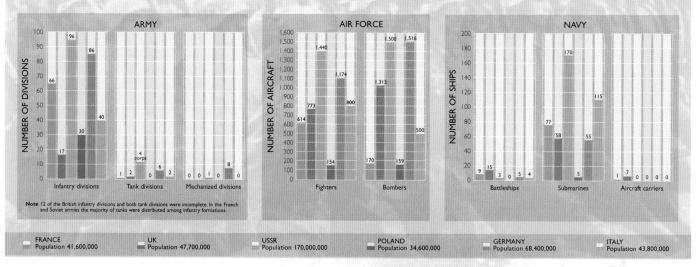

ARMY

NUMBER OF DIVISIONS

Infantry divisions: 66, 96, 86, 40, 17, 30
Tank divisions: 1, 2, 0, 6, 2, 4 corps
Mechanized divisions: 0, 0, 1, 0, 0, 8

Note 12 of the British infantry divisions and both tank divisions were incomplete. In the French and Soviet armies the majority of tanks were distributed among infantry formations.

AIR FORCE

NUMBER OF AIRCRAFT

Fighters: 614, 773, 1,440, 1,174, 800, 154
Bombers: 170, 1,313, 1,500, 1,516, 500, 159

NAVY

NUMBER OF SHIPS

Battleships: 9, 15, 3, 0, 5, 4
Submarines: 77, 58, 170, 115, 5, 55
Aircraft carriers: 1, 7, 0, 0, 0, 0

FRANCE Population 41,600,000
UK Population 47,700,000
USSR Population 170,000,000
POLAND Population 34,600,000
GERMANY Population 68,400,000
ITALY Population 43,800,000

the Luftwaffe was repeating what had happened at Guernica in the Spanish Civil War, but Hitler had ordered that indiscriminate attacks were not to be made on urban areas and in this instance it was mainly the public utilities that were bombed.

Throughout the siege of Warsaw the Poles lived in hope that the Western Allies would attack Germany. True, the French did make a limited advance into the Saarland, but they halted before getting beyond the range of the guns in the Maginot Line. The British, still deploying troops to France and under the overall control of the French, were in no position to do anything. The Poles, however, would continue to fight as long as they still possessed territory. Their

determination to do so was shaken on September 17, when the Soviet Union suddenly attacked from the east. Stalin, surprised by the rapid German advance, decided that he should act before the Germans occupied the whole of Poland and placed themselves on the Soviet border. With the bulk of their forces engaged with the Germans, the Poles were in no position to counter the Red Army, despite its huge deficiencies. Thus, after just two days the Soviet troops met German troops at Brest-Litovsk on the Bug River.

The ultimate outcome was now in no doubt. Polish troops began to fight their way into neutral Romania and Hungary in the hopes of evading capture by either of their two most bitter enemies. Yet, in spite of the battering it was receiving, Warsaw continued

Soviet and German troops near Brest-Litovsk
There was much mutual suspicion when German and Soviet troops met in Poland, a reflection of the hatred their countries had recently borne for each other.

to hold out, as did the fortress of Modlin to its north, where 10 divisions had been trapped since September 10. The suffering of the citizens in the capital increased by the day and, with the city's utilities almost destroyed, the military commander decided, on the 27th, that it was time to surrender. Modlin fell the next day. Isolated pockets of Polish troops remained, but by October 6 all resistance had ended.

This first demonstration of the German blitzkrieg, with its rapidly moving armored formations, closely supported by air power, making pincerlike moves to trap opposing forces in pockets that were then reduced by the follow-up infantry, deeply impressed the world at large. It was in stark contrast to the trench-bound warfare of World War I. The casualties suffered by both sides demonstrated its effectiveness. The German losses were some 40,000 killed, wounded, and missing, while the Poles had some 200,000 killed and wounded, with very many more being made prisoner. Soviet losses were just

over 3,000, an indication of the paucity of Polish forces in the east. Poland itself was now split in two. The Soviet Union took possession of the eastern part of the country up to the line of the Bug River, which had been Russian territory until the war with Poland in 1919–20. The remainder fell under German rule. The agendas of the two occupying powers differed, however. The Soviet government was determined that Poland should never regain its independence

German propaganda
This photograph of German troops feeding Polish children disguised the fact that the Germans treated the Poles very much as a subject people.

and, to this end, it incarcerated all the members of the intelligentsia it could find. Many officers were placed in camps in Russia, while others, together with their men, were transported to Siberia. In 1940 up to 4,500 officers were massacred at Katyn near Smolensk. The Nazis, on the other hand, targeted the Polish Jews, who represented a sizeable minority of the population. Initially, they were forced into ghettos and virtually starved, but ultimately a grimmer fate awaited most of them—the extermination camps.

Hitler at the Warsaw victory parade
Many of the triumphant troops in Poland would soon be sent across Germany to prepare for the planned invasion of the Low Countries and France.

Despite the dismemberment of their country, the Polish spirit of resistance had not been extinguished. In Poland itself an underground organization, the Home Army, was set up. Abroad, General Wladyslaw Sikorski formed a government-in-exile, the first of many, in Paris, and some 90,000 of his countrymen, including many who managed to escape from Poland itself, flocked to his banner, placing themselves under French command so as to continue the fight. As for Hitler, he was now looking westward and was determined to strike at the French and British as soon as possible. Circumstances would conspire against him and it would be many months before this could be done.

FINLAND INVADED

In the immediate aftermath of the Polish campaign, attention switched to Finland, a country that had broken away from the Russian Empire during the revolution of 1917. Finland was, however, strategically significant in Soviet eyes. Its border was only 20 miles (32 km) from Leningrad (St. Petersburg) and the northern coast of the Gulf of Finland—the sea approach to the city—was Finnish. The entrance to the vital Soviet northern port of Murmansk was also guarded by Finnish territory. Stalin, fearful that Finland would come under German influence, proposed an exchange of territory. If the Finns would cede territory on the shores of Lake Ladoga and the Gulf of Finland, as well as leasing ports, notably Viipuri in the south and Petsamo in the extreme north, they would gain some desolate terrain in southern Karelia. Negotiations dragged on through much of October and November 1939, but the Finns refused to agree. Stalin decided that force was the only answer. He attacked on November 30.

Captured Soviet soldier
Ill-equipped and poorly led, Soviet prisoners had little idea why they were fighting the Finns and were often just pleased to be out of the fighting.

On paper, the Finns stood little chance. They could call only 150,000 men to arms and their one set of fixed defenses covering their long border with the Soviet Union was the Mannerheim Line, which ran between the Gulf of Finland and Lake Ladoga. In contrast, the Leningrad Military District of the Red Army, which was to conduct the campaign, had some 700,000 men. In the far north the Soviet 14th Army quickly seized Petsamo and cut off Finnish access to the Barents Sea, while the Eighth and Ninth Armies attacking from Karelia also made rapid progress. In the extreme south it was a different matter. The Finns conducted a fighting withdrawal back to the Mannerheim Line and when the Soviet troops attempted to storm it they were bloodily repulsed. By mid-December there was stalemate. The condition of the postpurge Red Army was starkly revealed. Incompetent officers and a poor supply system, with many men still wearing summer uniform, resulted in numerous unnecessary casualties, a significant proportion from frostbite.

The reactions of other nations to this David versus Goliath contest were mixed. Denmark, Sweden, and Norway had no wish to see the fighting spill over into their territory and reaffirmed their neutrality. The League of Nations expelled the Soviet Union and called on member states to give

Finnish ski troops moving up for an attack
The ability of the Finnish ski troops to infiltrate the Soviet positions noiselessly and strike unsuspecting units to the rear did much to enable the Finns to hold out for so long against numerically superior forces.

Finland all possible support. The United States, although not a League member, launched strong protests to Moscow. The British and the French went even further and began to draw up plans to send munitions and troops to Finland.

FINNISH COUNTERATTACKS

In late December the Finns launched a series of counterattacks on the Karelian front. Their highly skilled ski troops came into their own, penetrating deep into the Soviet lines. At Suomussalmi they destroyed two Soviet divisions and captured much equipment. Stalin had already realized that all was not well with his high command, and at the beginning of January he appointed one of the few competent generals to have survived the purges, Semyon Timoshenko, to take over command. Timoshenko began to build up his forces for a major assault, but his first attempt, across the ice-bound Viipuri Bay, failed at the beginning of February, when the few remaining Finnish bombers attacked his troops as they were crossing the ice. By now, Anglo-French plans for sending troops to help the Finns had been finalized. They necessitated ignoring Norwegian neutrality by sending troops through the north of the country. At this juncture

Antitank rifle
All the belligerent nations used antitank rifles, such as this Finnish model, early in the war. But they were only effective up to 330 yd (300 m) and soon gave way to more powerful antitank guns.

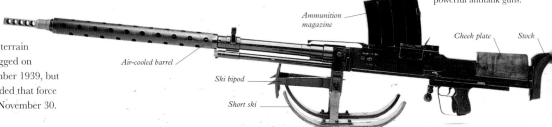

Ammunition magazine

Cheek plate   Stock

Air-cooled barrel

Ski bipod

Short ski

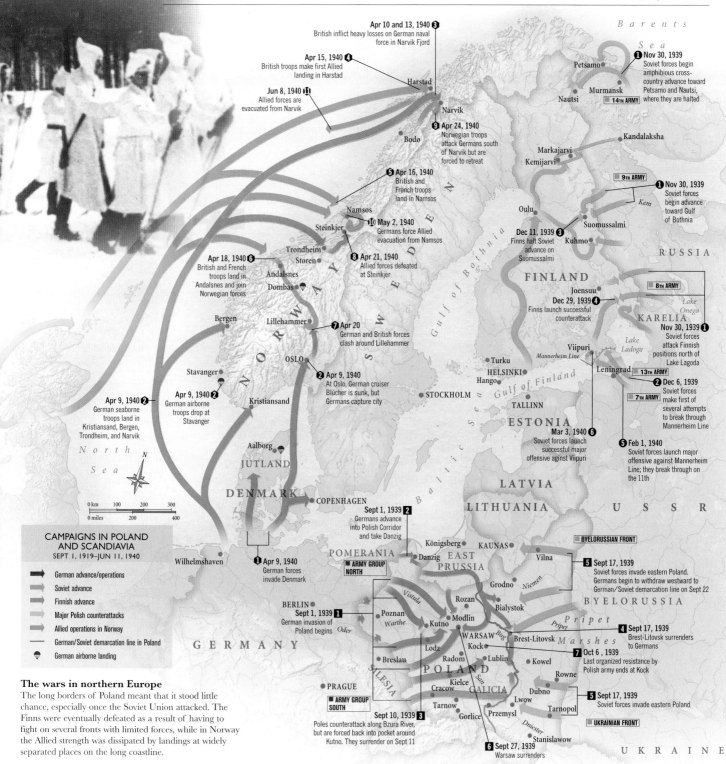

Apr 10 and 13, 1940 ❸
British inflict heavy losses on German naval force in Narvik Fjord

Apr 15, 1940 ❹
British troops make first Allied landing in Harstad

Jun 8, 1940 ⓫
Allied forces are evacuated from Narvik

Apr 24, 1940 ❾
Norwegian troops attack Germans south of Narvik but are forced to retreat

Apr 16, 1940 ❺
British and French troops land in Namsos

May 2, 1940 ❿
Germans force Allied evacuation from Namsos

Apr 21, 1940 ❽
Allied forces defeated at Steinkjer

Apr 18, 1940 ❻
British and French troops land in Andalsnes and join Norwegian forces

Apr 20 ❼
German and British forces clash around Lillehammer

Apr 9, 1940 ❷
At Oslo, German cruiser Blücher is sunk, but Germans capture city

Apr 9, 1940 ❷
German seaborne troops land in Kristiansand, Bergen, Trondheim, and Narvik

Apr 9, 1940 ❷
German airborne troops drop at Stavanger

Apr 9, 1940 ❶
German forces invade Denmark

Nov 30, 1939 ❶
Soviet forces begin amphibious cross-country advance toward Petsamo and Nautsi, where they are halted
14TH ARMY

Nov 30, 1939 ❶
Soviet forces begin advance toward Gulf of Bothnia
9TH ARMY

Dec 11, 1939 ❸
Finns halt Soviet advance on Suomussalmi

Dec 29, 1939 ❹
Finns launch successful counterattack
8TH ARMY

Nov 30, 1939 ❶
Soviet forces attack Finnish positions north of Lake Lagoda
13TH ARMY

Dec 6, 1939 ❷
Soviet forces make first of several attempts to break through Mannerheim Line
7TH ARMY

Mar 3, 1940 ❻
Soviet forces launch successful major offensive aginst Viipuri

Feb 1, 1940 ❺
Soviet forces launch major offensive against Mannerheim Line; they break through on the 11th

Sept 1, 1939 ❷
Germans advance into Polish Corridor and take Danzig

Sept 17, 1939 ❺
Soviet forces invade eastern Poland. Germans begin to withdraw westward to German/Soviet demarcation line on Sept 22
BYELORUSSIAN FRONT

Apr 9, 1940 ❶
German forces invade Denmark
ARMY GROUP NORTH

Sept 1, 1939 ❶
German invasion of Poland begins

Sept 17, 1939 ❹
Brest-Litovsk surrenders to Germans

Oct 6, 1939 ❼
Last organized resistance by Polish army ends at Kock

Sept 17, 1939 ❺
Soviet forces invade eastern Poland
UKRAINIAN FRONT

Sept 27, 1939 ❻
Warsaw surrenders

Sept 10, 1939 ❸
Poles counterattack along Bzura River, but are forced back into pocket around Kutno. They surrender on Sept 11

ARMY GROUP SOUTH

CAMPAIGNS IN POLAND AND SCANDIAVIA
SEPT 1, 1919–JUN 11, 1940

➤ German advance/operations
➤ Soviet advance
➤ Finnish advance
➤ Major Polish counterattacks
➤ Allied operations in Norway
— German/Soviet demarcation line in Poland
⛛ German airborne landing

The wars in northern Europe

The long borders of Poland meant that it stood little chance, especially once the Soviet Union attacked. The Finns were eventually defeated as a result of having to fight on several fronts with limited forces, while in Norway the Allied strength was dissipated by landings at widely separated places on the long coastline.

Timoshenko attacked again and finally breached the Mannerheim Line, forcing the Finns to retire to a second line of defenses. Moscow now broadcast its final conditions for peace. Finland was to cede territory in the south, while the Soviet Union would hand back Petsamo. Again, the Finns refused and, at the end of February, Soviet forces broke through

the second defense line on the Karelian isthmus. Viipuri then came under direct attack and the Finns, realizing that they could not resist much longer, sent a peace delegation to Moscow. On March 12 a peace treaty was signed. The terms were harsh, requiring the Finns to hand over the whole of the Karelian isthmus, including Viipuri,

other parts of Karelia, including Lake Ladoga, and Petsamo. The Soviet Union also extracted a 30-year lease on the Hango peninsula at the entrance to the Gulf of Finland. Stalin had thus gotten everything he wanted, but at the cost of 85,000 Soviet troops killed or missing, and 186,000 wounded.

In constrast, the Finnish casualties were 25,000 killed and 45,000 wounded. Clearly the Soviet armed forces were in particularly urgent need of reorganization. The campaign left Finland embittered, but it would have the chance for revenge. As for the Western Allies, they had for a second time been powerless to provide timely help to a distant ally. The conflict, though, would continue to focus on Scandanavia.

THE PHONEY WAR

Prior to the outbreak of war, the British and French, seemingly secure behing the Maginot Line, had agreed to adopt a strictly defensive strategy and to wait. The only positive action on the ground was the advance by the French into the Saarland, but they quickly withdrew. In the air, fear that inflicting civilian casualties might bring about German retaliation in the form of aerial bombardments of Allied cities resulted in attacks being restricted to warships in port. Allied bombers were also used to drop propaganda leaflets over Germany. The only real activity took place at sea, with the beginning of the Battle of the Atlantic (see pages 80–83).

Parisians with gas masks
The French practiced protecting themselves against the gas bombs that they feared would be used against them by the Germans.

Child's gas mask
In Britain colorful "Mickey Mouse" gas masks were issued to young children, who were taught to carry their masks with them at all times.

Hitler wanted to attack west as soon as possible after the Polish campaign, and he issued orders to this effect on October 9, 1939. The intention was to avoid the Maginot Line and attack through the neutral Low Countries, thus destroying the northern Allied armies and securing the North Sea and English Channel coasts. Bases from which to wage an air and sea campaign against Britain could then be established. Hitler wanted to attack in November, but his commanders argued that they needed time to put into effect the lessons from Poland. They were also well aware of the apparent strength of the French Army, which, on paper at least, was equal to that of the German Army. The onset of a particularly severe winter caused further postponement.

ALLIED PREPARATIONS

The Allies, too, had been planning. They anticipated a German attack through the Low Countries, but there were few natural obstacles close to the Belgian border on which to base a defense. Consequently, they decided that they would have to advance into Belgium once the Germans had invaded, and take up positions based on the Meuse and Dyle rivers and the Albert Canal. This "Plan D," as it was called, would be executed by the northern Allied armies under General Pierre Billotte's First Army Group, comprising the best of the French and the British Expeditionary Force (BEF). But the Allied chain of command was cumbersome. Immediately above Billotte was General Alphonse Georges, commanding the northeast of France, while in overall charge was General Maurice Gamelin, who envisaged Georges controlling the whole battle, but according to Gamelin's plan. The problem was that there was mutual antipathy between Georges and Gamelin. Furthermore, there was a plethora of headquarters with inadequate communications, which relied on an imperfect telephone system and despatch riders. It was hardly the infrastructure with which to combat high-speed warfare. Meanwhile, the troops on the ground spent some time training and the remainder in attempting to improve the Belgian border defenses.

On January 10 Hitler commanded that the invasion take place in a week's time. However, that same day a German light aircraft carrying a Luftwaffe liaison officer made a forced landing inside Belgium. He was carrying details of the German plan and although he and the pilot set the plane on fire, they could not be sure that the Belgians remained in ignorance. Furthermore, there had been rumblings among the German high command over the plan itself. Rundstedt and, more especially, his chief of staff, Erich von Manstein, argued that the emphasis should be on completely cutting off the Allied forces in the north and then turning on the remainder of France. In the circumstances, Hitler decided that the invasion should be postponed until the spring. He then approved the Manstein plan under which Army Group B in the north

Digging a British air-raid shelter
During the Phoney War British civilians continued to make preparations for a German attack. With the encouragement of the government, many constructed air raid shelters in their backyards.

would advance into the Netherlands and Belgium to draw the British and French forward, while Army Group A, with the bulk of the panzer divisions, would thrust through the Ardennes and make for the English Channel. Army Group C would remain opposite the Maginot Line to tie down the forces manning it. Meanwhile, Hitler received reassurance from Mussolini that Italy would join in the invasion.

In the Allied camp the long months of inactivity had done little for morale. True, the BEF had been able to double its strength during the early months of 1940, but many of the British divisions now arriving in France lacked essential equipment and were poorly trained. The French had begun to concentrate some of their tanks into armored divisions in the German style, but they had not yet developed cohesion among these formations. Many were beginning to hope and, indeed, believe that Hitler might have had second thoughts. Both sides, however, now became distracted by Norway.

PLANS FOR NORWAY

Allied attention had been drawn to Norway as a means of sending troops and supplies to the Finns. Indeed, just before the Finnish surrender the British and French finalized their plans for landing at Narvik and Trondheim—the former a port that handled the Swedish exports of iron-ore that were vital to the German war industry.

Patrolling the line
Thirteen divisions were committed to manning the line in 1939.

Location of the line
The main Maginot Line covered the Franco-German border. There was, however, another belt of defenses protecting the border with Italy.

THE MAGINOT LINE

PLANS TO PROTECT France's eastern frontier were drawn up following the huge losses suffered in World War I. Serious construction began in 1929 under war minister André Maginot with the goal of providing an impenetrable wall.

A complication was added in 1936, when Belgium renounced its military alliance with France in favor of neutrality. An extension of the main Maginot Line began to be established, but this was by no means continuous, especially since the general view was that the hilly and wooded Ardennes region of southern Belgium and Luxembourg was impassable to invading troops. With their

subterranean forts topped by armored cupolas mounting a wide range of guns, the fortifications were sufficiently impressive to deter invaders. However, they lulled the French into a false sense of security, and the money spent on them, which was twice the original estimate, meant that modernization of the armed forces was held back.

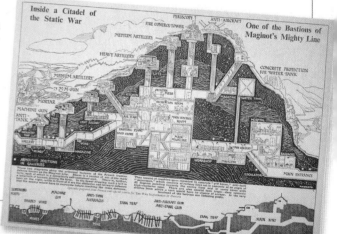

Section through the line
The gun cupolas above the ground concealed a web of passages, living quarters, and command bunkers.

British destroyer HMS *Bittern* in Namsos Fjord
Even though the Royal Navy enjoyed domination of the North Sea, it was unable to prevent the Germans from making several landings in Norway. While it sank several warships during the campaign, it also suffered losses.

German troops in northern Jutland
Denmark's armed forces were too small to offer anything other than a very token resistance to the forces that invaded on April 9, and by the end of the day the country was in German hands.

There was, too, in February 1940 the affair of the *Altmark*, a German vessel carrying crews of British merchant vessels sunk by the *Graf Spee* battleship during her rampage in the Indian Ocean and South Atlantic. The Norwegians gave sanctuary to the *Altmark* in their waters and, when she was boarded by the crew of a British destroyer, they complained that their neutrality had been violated. The British countered that Norway had allowed its neutrality to be abused by the Germans.

The Germans had been considering establishing bases in Norway for waging the maritime war against Britain since October 1939. Hitler was so attracted to the idea that at the end of January 1940 he took over personal control of Weser Exercise, as the invasion of Norway was codenamed. This would also embrace the occupation of Denmark. On February 20 General Niklaus von Falkenhorst was appointed to command the invasion force and the final plan took shape. A number of simultaneous landings would be made, from Narvik in the north to Oslo Fjord, and airborne forces would be used for the first time to secure airfields at Oslo and Stavanger.

ACTION IN NORWEGIAN WATERS

The Allies did not believe that the Germans could invade Norway because of the dominance of the North Sea by Britain's navy. At the end of March they agreed to mine Norwegian territorial waters so as to force the iron-ore ships leaving Narvik into the open sea, where the Royal Navy could deal with them. Anticipating German attempts to interfere with the mining, they also began to reconstitute the forces that had been earlier assembled for securing the routes through Norway to Finland.

German paratroopers landing at Narvik
The use of paratroops in support of land forces had not been tried by either side before the German campaign in Denmark and Norway.

On April 2 Hitler gave orders that the landings were to take place in seven days' time, and German merchant vessels carrying troops set sail for Narvik, Trondheim, and Bergen. On April 6, British minelayers, with a powerful escort, set sail, and the following day the landing forces boarded their vessels. Simultaneously, an RAF aircraft spotted German warships. Bombers were sent to attack them but did no damage. That evening, the British Home Fleet set sail to intercept the invasion force. On April 8 the British laid mines at the entrance of Vertsj Fjord, north of Bodo. Bad weather prevented the Home Fleet from locating the Germans, except for one straggling British destroyer, which rammed a German cruiser and was sunk.

DENMARK AND NORWAY INVADED

The following day the invasion began. Both the Danish mainland (Jutland) and islands were overrun within 24 hours, with the Danes offering little or no resistance. By this time, the Norwegian government had ordered a partial mobilization and it enjoyed an early success when coastal batteries sank the German cruiser *Blücher* in Oslo Fjord and seriously

French Chasseurs Alpins near Narvik
Unlike the British troops who landed at Narvik and elsewhere in Norway, the Chasseurs Alpins were well trained in mountain and winter warfare.

damaged another cruiser off Bergen. They were unable, however, to prevent the Germans from getting ashore in all their landing areas. The Germans also secured the airfields at Stavanger and Oslo. This provided them with immediate air superiority. They soon entered Oslo and then began to advance northward and westward. The Norwegians themselves initially considered that the cause was hopeless, but a failed coup by right-wing extremist Vidkun Quisling on the day of the invasion and a British assurance that help was on its way gave them the resolve to fight on.

The first positive Allied response came on April 10, when British destroyers entered Narvik Fjord and sank two German destroyers and some transport ships. They returned three days later to sink the remainder of the German naval force, thus leaving the troops on shore isolated. In the meantime, an Allied landing force set sail for Narvik, while during April 13–18 other troops landed in the Namsos area and in Andalsnes with the intention of isolating the German force in Trondheim. They also began to land in Harstad close to Narvik.

British prisoners in Norway
The losses of the Allies, including Norwegians, during the campaign in Norway were 4,000 dead, missing, or taken prisoner. The Germans lost 5,300 men and subsequently required up to 350,000 troops to occupy the country.

The Allied forces labored under a number of major disadvantages. Rapid changes of plan and a cumbersome command structure caused confusion. In the haste to mount the expedition, the ships had been loaded in a totally haphazard fashion and on landing in Norway the troops often found there was a lack of essential items such as radios and mortar ammunition, and sometimes even artillery and antiaircraft guns. This put them at a serious disadvantage from which they never recovered.

The Norwegians also had their problems. Because there had been no general mobilization before the invasion, the Norwegian Army had to try to organize its forces and fight the Germans at the same time. The scattered Norwegian units did their best, but could not slow the German advance northward. The decisive factor was German airpower, to which the Allies had no answer aside from some RAF Gloster Gladiator biplanes that were unable to make much of an impression.

The remorseless German advance from the south and successful link-up with their troops in Trondheim necessitated the evacuation of the Allied forces in Namsos and Andalsnes in early May. The focus then switched to Narvik. The Allies landed further forces, including French and Poles, and on May 28 they drove the isolated German garrison out of Narvik. It was a short-lived triumph. By this time King Haakon and his government had been taken by the Royal Navy to Britain. Worse, far to the south in France, the Allied situation was becoming desperate. In consequence, the Allies had no option but to evacuate Narvik. The whole of Norway was now in German hands, with a puppet government established under Quisling. The Germans had totally outwitted the Allies.

FIGHTING IN THE SNOW

THE IMPORTANCE OF TROOPS well equipped for winter warfare was demonstrated during the Soviet-Finnish War. In particular, it was the skill of the Finnish ski troops that was a significant fact in enabling Finland to hold out for so long. The German mountain troops were also well trained for winter warfare, as were the French Chasseurs Alpins. The "lowland" countries, like Britain, had paid little or no attention to this art before the war, although one British battalion was hastily trained as ski troops for possible use in Finland.

In Norway, with the advent of spring, expertise in fighting in the snow was not really a factor, even though snow was still on the ground in the northern part of the country. Indeed, after Finland, the ability to operate in the extremes of winter would not be fully tested until late 1941 in the Soviet Union. The Red Army was used to these conditions, but the Germans were initially taken by surprise over the effect of a plummeting thermometer on weapons and equipment, and many of their soliders were to suffer from the lack of adequate winter clothing.

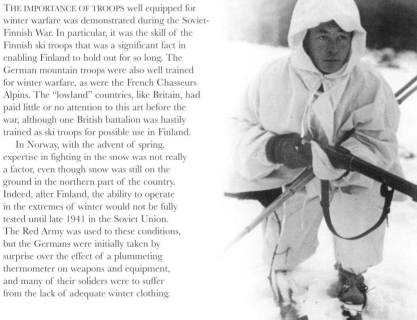

Finnish ski soldier
Many Finns were brought up on skis and were at home in the snow. The white smocks and trousers worn by the ski troops provided ideal camouflage.

INVASION OF THE LOW COUNTRIES AND FRANCE

MAY 10–JUNE 25, 1940

The campaign in the west consisted of two phases. In the first the Germans overran the Netherlands, Belgium, and northern France, forcing the Allied evacuation from Dunkirk on the English Channel coast. In the second the Germans turned south and conquered a lot more of France, forcing the French to seek an armistice.

MAY 10
Germany launches invasion of Belgium and Netherlands

MAY 10
Chamberlain resigns as British prime minister, and Churchill forms coalition government

MAY 11
Belgian army begins to fall back to Dyle River, where French and British have arrived

MAY 12
Leading panzer troops begin advance into France

MAY 13
Dutch troops begin to withdraw to Amsterdam-Rotterdam area

MAY 14
German bombing raid causes massive damage in Rotterdam

MAY 15
The Netherlands surrenders. Germans break through Allied positions south of Namur

MAY 15
French army is defeated at Sedan on Meuse River

MAY 17
Germans take Brussels

MAY 17
French 4th Armored Division under de Gaulle attacks panzers in Laon area with little success

MAY 18
Germans take Antwerp

MAY 19
Pétain becomes French deputy prime minister

MAY 22
German tanks advance toward Channel ports

MAY 23
Panzer divisions advancing to coast are ordered to halt

MAY 25
German attack separates Belgian army from BEF

MAY 25
Boulogne falls

MAY 27
Calais falls

MAY 27
Operation Dynamo–the evacuation of British, French, and Belgian troops from the beaches of Dunkirk–begins

MAY 28
Belgium surrenders

JUNE 3
Last night of evacuation from Dunkirk, bringing the total number of men rescued to 220,000 British and 120,000 French and Belgians

JUNE 5
Germans attack southward in area of Amiens

JUNE 9
Germans launch attack southward in area of Reims

JUNE 10
Italy declares war on Britain and France; US promises help to Allies

JUNE 14
French government under Weygand established in Bordeaux

JUNE 14
Germans enter Paris; also advance toward Dijon and Lyons

JUNE 16
Pétain becomes prime minister and seeks armistice the next day

JUNE 18
De Gaulle makes broadcast from London establishing a "Free France" to continue the fight

JUNE 20
Italians attack along French border in south but make little headway against stubborn French resistance

JUNE 22
France signs armistice with Germany. It signs armistice with Italy on 24th

JUNE 25
Hostilities end in France

■ Invasion of the Low Countries May 10–28

■ Invasion of France May 12–Jun 25, 1940

■ Other events

GERMAN INVASION OF THE WEST

At DAWN ON MAY 10, 1940, the Luftwaffe attacked airfields in the Netherlands, Belgium, and France, aiming, as they had done in Poland, to establish immediate air superiority. A second wave then took off to attack known headquarters, communications centers, railroads, and military camps. Paratroops were dropped over the Netherlands, their objectives an airfield in Rotterdam, three in The Hague, and crossings over major river defense lines. Not all went according to plan, especially since the Dutch had learned lessons from Norway and were prepared for airborne operations. In Belgium further airborne troops seized crossings over the Meuse River in the Maastricht area, while a small glider-borne force was used to deal with the key fortress of Eben Emael, near the junction of the Meuse with the Albert Canal (see map page 54).

ADVANCE IN THE LOW COUNTRIES

As Rundstedt's Army Group A and Bock's Army Group B crossed the Belgian and Dutch borders, the northern Allied armies—three French and the British Expeditionary Force (BEF)—began to move into

Belgium to establish themselves on the defense line along the Dyle River. The Dutch made life difficult for the German airborne troops. But after many years of strict neutrality they were no match for the Germans, who within 48 hours had penetrated deep into the country. The Dutch withdrew to the protection of some fortifications in the south, and German attention now focused on Rotterdam. Its capture would signal the end for the Dutch, and they fought fiercely to protect it. The city had, however, already surrendered when the Germans launched a wave of bombers against it. Radio orders for the bombers to abort the mission did not get through, and over 1,000 civilians lost their lives as Rotterdam was devastated. It was too much for the Dutch, who had already begun to run low on ammunition. On May 15 they surrendered.

In Belgium the Germans thrust toward Brussels, while panzer spearheads forced their way through the Ardennes, brushing the Belgian forces aside. Luftwaffe attacks against airfields and other targets continued. There were fierce battles in which the Germans gradually wore down the Allied fighter

WINSTON CHURCHILL

WINSTON SPENCER CHURCHILL (1874–1965) was one of the greatest
war leaders of all time. He spent his early career as a soldier and war
correspondent before entering politics. In 1911 he was appointed First
Lord of the Admiralty, with ministerial responsibility for the Royal
Navy. His support for the ultimately disastrous 1915 Dardanelles
campaign caused his fall from office and he then spent time on
the Western Front. In 1917 he became minister of munitions
and subsequently served as minister of war and air, and
chancellor of the exchequer. He fell from grace in 1929
and spent the next 10 years in the political wilderness.
His dire warnings on German rearmament did not
accord with the general policy of appeasing Hitler. On
the outbreak of war in 1939, he was reappointed First
Lord of the Admiralty and then became prime minister
on the day the German invasion of the west opened. While
Churchill's hands-on approach to the conduct of the war
often put severe pressure on military staff, his inspirational
speeches fired all in the Allied camp, and he was single-
minded in his determination to secure ultimate victory.

German troops in action
The speed of the German advance into
the Low Countries and France took the
Allies by surprise. They had no answer
to the Germans' blitzkrieg tactics.

strength. In desperation, the French called on
Britain to send more fighters across the Channel.
Against the advice of Sir Hugh Dowding, in charge
of RAF Fighter Command, Churchill ordered the
despatch of further Hurricanes, but to no avail.
RAF and Belgian fighter-bombers also tried to
destroy the Maastricht bridges, across which

German forces continued to pour. Most were shot
down and the bridges remained intact.

On May 12 the German tanks reached the east
bank of the Meuse to the consternation of the
French. The following day the tanks crossed, broke
through the defenses on the other bank, and began
to sweep westward toward the English Channel.
To their north, elements of Army Group B closed
up to the Dyle Line, which initially held them. As
the panzers rampaged westward, the Allies realized
that their armies in Belgium were under increasing
threat of being cut off. Accordingly, on May 16 they
began to withdraw from Belgium. On the following
day Brussels fell. Simultaneously, a French armored
division, commanded by General Charles de Gaulle,
attacked the southern flank of the German panzers,
but made little impression. Hitler, however, was
concerned that the panzer divisions were becoming
overextended and ordered a temporary halt to allow
the infantry to catch up.

For the Allied armies in the north it was a
bewildering period. Aside from the French Seventh
Army, which had been unable to extend the Dyle
Line to the North Sea coast because of the rapid
Dutch collapse, the Allied troops felt that they had
given a good account of themselves in keeping
Bock's Army Group B at bay and were perplexed
by the orders to withdraw. Nevertheless, they pulled
back in an orderly fashion. One major problem they
did face was that of refugees. They had come across
them on the move up to the Dyle, but now life was
made much more difficult by the fact that civilians
were fleeing in the same direction and clogging up
the roads that the troops wanted to use. The
situation was made even worse when the Luftwaffe
instilled panic among the refugees by machine-
gunning them from the air. It was just as well for
the Allies that the troops of Army Group B were
advancing with a degree of caution. This was out
of recognition that the decisive blow was being
struck by Rundstedt's Army Group A to their south.

On May 19 Gamelin was replaced as the French
commander-in-chief by Maxime Weygand. At the
same time, Marshal Henri Pétain, the great
French hero of 1914–18, was appointed deputy
prime minister. The changes came too late.
Rundstedt's tanks were on the move once
more and on May 20 they reached the
mouth of the Somme. The Allied
armies were now totally split. The
following day it was the British
turn to counterattack, but all

French defenders
This light machine-gun team
was among the French troops
who struggled to withstand the
German onslaught. Many were
demoralized from the outset.

that was available were two battalions of slow-moving infantry tanks and some infantry. At Arras they struck at the 7th Panzer Division, under Erwin Rommel, and briefly knocked it off balance, causing Hitler further concern over the vulnerability of the flanks of his panzer formations. The British force was, however, too weak to cause any lasting damage and the German thrusts continued.

ALLIED RETREAT TO THE COAST

The northern Allied forces, now comprising the remnants of the Belgian Army, the French First Army, and the BEF, were being squeezed into an ever tighter pocket by Army Group B pressing from the north and Army Group A from the south and west. The Allied troops were also becoming increasingly

Attack in the west
German Army Group A thrust through the Ardennes and cut off the Allied forces in northern France, while Army Group B dealt with the Netherlands and the remainder of Belgium. Both army groups then turned south and cut swathes through the rest of France.

exhausted by the seemingly endless cycle of withdrawal, followed by preparing fresh defensive positions and then receiving orders to abandon them. The skies above appeared dominated by the Luftwaffe and movement on the roads during daylight hours became ever more dangerous. Yet, they still largely maintained their cohesion. The German troops, too, especially those in Army Group A, were beginning to suffer from the rapidity of their advance. In particular, Rundstedt was conscious of the increasing wear and tear on Army Group A's armor after almost two weeks of constant action. Indeed, some panzer divisions had only a third of their tanks still running. Knowing that the remainder of France still had to be conquered, on May 23 he ordered the bulk of them to halt,

believing that Army Group B and his own infantry could deal with the Allied pocket. The following day, Hitler approved his halt order. Rundstedt's forces were now seeking to overrun the Channel ports so as to cut off the BEF, especially, from its homeland. In spite of last-minute reinforcement, Boulogne fell on May 25 and Calais, after a brave defense, two days later. Meanwhile, worse had befallen the Allies.

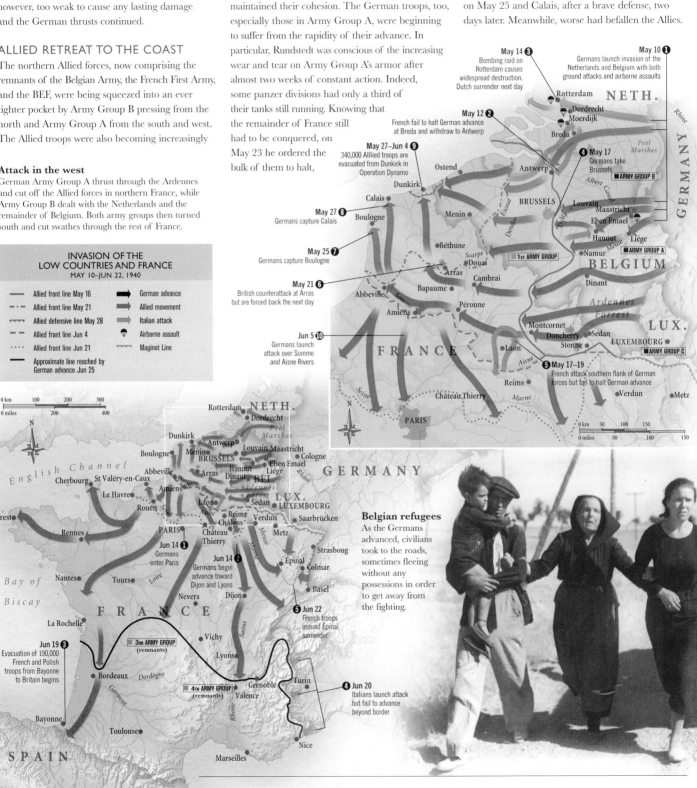

INVASION OF THE LOW COUNTRIES AND FRANCE
MAY 10–JUN 22, 1940

- —— Allied front line May 16
- - - Allied front line May 21
- ⌐⌐⌐ Allied defensive line May 28
- – – Allied front line Jun 4
- ···· Allied front line Jun 21
- —— Approximate line reached by German advance Jun 25
- ➡ German advance
- ➡ Allied movement
- ➡ Italian attack
- ▼ Airborne assault
- ⫟ Maginot Line

May 10 ❶ Germans launch invasion of the Netherlands and Belgium with both ground attacks and airborne assaults

May 14 ❸ Bombing raid on Rotterdam causes widespread destruction. Dutch surrender next day

May 12 ❷ French fail to halt German advance at Breda and withdraw to Antwerp

May 17 ❹ Germans take Brussels

May 27–Jun 4 ❾ 340,000 Allied troops are evacuated from Dunkirk in Operation Dynamo

May 27 ❽ Germans capture Calais

May 25 ❼ Germans capture Boulogne

May 21 ❻ British counterattack at Arras but are forced back the next day

Jun 5 ❿ Germans launch attack over Somme and Aisne Rivers

May 17–19 ❺ French attack southern flank of German forces but fail to halt German advance

Jun 14 ❶ Germans enter Paris

Jun 14 ❷ Germans begin advance toward Dijon and Lyons

Jun 22 ❺ French troops around Épinal surrender

Jun 19 ❸ Evacuation of 190,000 French and Polish troops from Bayonne to Britain begins

Jun 20 ❹ Italians launch attack but fail to advance beyond border

Belgian refugees
As the Germans advanced, civilians took to the roads, sometimes fleeing without any possessions in order to get away from the fighting.

To the northeast the withdrawal of the now cut-off northern Allied armies continued. For the remains of the Belgian Army on the coast, it was a repeat of August 1914, when the Belgians had found themselves left holding just one strip of their country. Hopes of achieving even this were now fading. The BEF and the French First Army still maintained their cohesion, but the endless retreats were sapping morale and their exhaustion was growing. Matters were not helped by growing rumors of fifth columnists and disguised German paratroops, some apparently dressed as nuns, operating in their rear. These added to the increasing sense of confusion and the stark truth was that the northern Allied forces were being progressively squeezed into a pocket from which there appeared to be no escape.

Weygand, who had taken over command from Gamelin on May 20, had proposed an ambitious plan to extricate the forces in northern France from the trap in which they now found themselves. The BEF and French First Army would attack out of the pocket, while the French Seventh and 10th Armies did so from the south, with the goal of cutting off the German armor. Given the German pressure and poor communications, this proved impossible to accomplish. Then, on May 25 the Belgian high command warned the French and British that its remaining forces, which were on the left flank of those troops facing Army Group B, could not hold on for much longer. Lord Gort, commanding the BEF, now decided that his duty lay in saving as much as he could of his force rather than continuing to fight on and lose it all. Without telling his allies, he ordered the BEF to withdraw to Dunkirk, on the English Channel coast, and asked the British government to evacuate it by sea. This proved fortuitous since the Belgians decided to surrender on May 28. That night the evacuation of the BEF from Dunkirk began. The Germans, rather than using their ground forces to destroy the shrinking pocket, decided to rely on airpower after Reichsmarschall Hermann Göring had boasted that his Luftwaffe could do the task on its own.

SOUTHWARD ADVANCE

On May 29, with the Dunkirk evacuation gathering momentum, Hitler ordered his forces to turn south to deal with the remainder of France. The new offensive was launched on June 5, the day after German troops finally entered Dunkirk. On the same day, de Gaulle was appointed the French deputy war minister, but like the earlier changes, it was too late to make any difference. The Germans quickly secured crossings over the Somme River and once again the panzer divisions were on

BLITZKRIEG TACTICS

THE CONCEPT OF BLITZKRIEG or "lightning war" was born out of the infiltration tactics practiced by the German storm troops in 1917–18 and the development of mechanized warfare, especially the tank. Rather than the bludgeonlike tactics that had dominated much of World War I, blitzkrieg was more like the thrust of a rapier and was designed not to destroy the opposing forces *per se*, but to fatally degrade the ability to command and control them through sheer pace of operations. A key to the secret of the success of blitzkrieg during the early part of the war was radio. This enabled the quick passing of orders, and the immediate response of aircraft providing close support—especially the Junkers Ju 87 dive-bombers—to calls for assistance from the ground. Commanders were encouraged to position themselves well forward and to identify the *Schwerpunkt*, or critical point on the battlefield. The Germans did, however, have a major problem in that in any advance the great majority of their infantry relied on their feet and horsedrawn forms of transportation. Furthermore, there was always the danger that the tip of the blade, represented by the fast-moving panzer and panzergrenadier formations, would advance too far in front of the main body and thus put itself in danger of being cut off.

Stuka dive-bomber
The Ju 87 was a key element of blitzkrieg, with its ability to attack pinpoint targets. Its siren had a terrifying effect.

Panzer Mark II
Armed with a 20-mm gun and a 7.92-mm machine-gun, this tank had a crew of three and was generally used for reconnaissance.

Sidecar with panniers and spare wheel

Pannier for gear or ammunition

Zündapp KS750
A light machine-gun was often mounted in the sidecar of this motorcycle combination that was largely used by reconnaissance troops.

Gas tank

Unit symbol

Half-track vehicle
The Sd Kfz 251 became the main vehicle of the Panzer Grenadiers, many of whom were still truck-borne in May 1940. The tracks enabled it to accompany tanks when moving cross-country.

Allied troops line up for evacuation
The Allied troops awaiting rescue on the beaches were very vulnerable to attack by the Luftwaffe, which also wrought havoc among the rescue ships.

EVACUATION FROM DUNKIRK

AS EARLY AS MAY 20 preparations had begun for a possible evacuation of at least part of the BEF in France. Thus when the order came, on May 26, to mount Operation Dynamo, as it was codenamed, there were ships available. No one believed, however, that more than a small proportion of the BEF could be rescued before Dunkirk fell. During May 27–28 some 25,000 troops were evacuated from the port, but there were problems. Because Calais was in German hands, ships had to use an indirect route that first ran parallel to the Belgian coast, and because the Luftwaffe

Some who got away
Exhaustion, relief, and bewilderment are etched on the faces of these British troops waiting to be picked up from a pontoon.

had put Dunkirk's port facilities out of action, the troops had to be rescued from the beaches. The privately-owned craft from the navy's "small vessels pool" were pressed into service to take the troops to the ships waiting offshore, and they were joined by other volunteer private vessels. Collectively, they became known as the Little Ships.

For the men waiting in Dunkirk it was a terrible experience to huddle on the sandy beach as the Luftwaffe's bombs exploded all around them. Many were required to march into the sea up to their necks again and again before finally getting into a boat. During most of the evacuation, French troops held much of the perimeter and bought valuable time. However, only British troops were allowed to leave, causing French bitterness. RAF Fighter Command was increasingly unable to provide the ships with full protection from the Luftwaffe, making it necessary on June 1 to restrict the evacuation to the hours of darkness. By now the alternative route along the Belgian coast had become too vulnerable to German torpedo-boats, and another route had

The aftermath
When the Germans finally entered Dunkirk on June 4, 1940, they found many corpses. Among those who had died in the fighting in and around the town were the largely French rearguard.

to be opened. It was only at this point that French and Belgian troops were taken off. With the Germans on the outskirts of Dunkirk, the night of June 3 was to be the last of the evacuation. In all, 220,000 British and 120,000 French and Belgian troops were taken to England, though almost all the French quickly returned to France to continue the fight. Some 200 ships and 177 Allied aircraft were lost. Yet the fact that so many men were brought home did much to stiffen British resolve to fight on.

The smallest ship
Tamzine—14 ft (4.4 m) long—was the smallest of more than 900 "Little Ships" that ferried men from the beaches to deep-water vessels.

the rampage, spreading panic among French civilians who began to flee from their homes in huge numbers. Perhaps over 5 million took to the roads that went southward; about 2 million fled from the Paris region alone. Even the government joined the exodus, leaving Paris for Tours on June 10.

Fearing that their capital might suffer the same fate as Warsaw and Rotterdam, the French declared Paris an open city and the Germans entered it in triumph on June 14. Pleas were sent for the British to send more RAF fighters to France, but this time Churchill heeded the advice of Dowding, who was now certain that the fighters would be needed to defend Britain, and refused. Even so, two British divisions were still fighting with the French. One had been gaining combat experience on the Maginot Line when the Germans invaded and the other was the only British armored division, which had not crossed to France until late May. Churchill now decided to send a second BEF to Cherbourg to help the French form a redoubt in Brittany. But in view of the rapidly deteriorating situation, the force was recalled just as it was about to land. The 51st Highland Division and four French divisions were trapped by Rommel's tanks, but the British 1st Armoured Division did get back to England.

FRENCH-GERMAN ARMISTICE

On June 16 the French prime minister, Paul Reynaud, whose government had fled to Bordeaux, resigned. He was replaced by Marshal Pétain, who decided to seek an armistice.

Slowly they came, bewildered and shocked, yet the faces of hundreds showed the great joy of once again being on dry land, above all their homeland. Even the troops of other nations accepted thankfully the greeting and helping hand from those waiting on the quayside... Sodden and bloodstained uniforms were gratefully exchanged for trousers, jackets, shirts and dressing gowns.

W. E. WILLIAMSON, RAILWAY CLERK, ON THE ARRIVAL IN WEYMOUTH OF TROOPS RESCUED FROM DUNKIRK

De Gaulle got himself flown to Britain and, once there, broadcast to the French people. He told them that he would continue the struggle and called for volunteers to join him. While an armistice meeting was being set up, there was a development in southeastern France. On June 10 Mussolini had declared that his country would be at war with Britain and France from the following day. Ten days later, his troops invaded France. While the main Maginot Line had now been enveloped from the rear and penetrated by the Germans, the Alpine extension kept the Italians out. But it made no difference. The French signed an armistice with the Germans on June 22 in the same railroad car that had been used to bring World War I to an end in November 1918. Two days later, they also signed with the Italians. The campaign in the west officially came to an end on June 25. Allied losses were 100,000 killed and—as a result of the surrender of the Dutch, Belgians, and French—the huge figure of 2,200,000 taken prisoner. German losses were 45,000 killed and missing.

In just six weeks Hitler had achieved what Imperial Germany had failed to do during the whole of 1914–18. France and the Low Countries were now under Nazi occupation, although the southern half of France was given a degree of limited autonomy under Pétain's Vichy government, which was prepared to bow to Germany's every command. Just a few rallied to de Gaulle, now seen as a traitor in his own land. Dutch and Belgians also joined the various "free" forces being formed in Britain to one day liberate their countries. Yet, for Britain itself, shorn as it was of European allies and with only its far-flung empire still on its side, the future looked bleak. Few outside observers gave the country any chance of holding out against a now triumphant and seemingly invincible Hitler.

Germans occupy Paris
The Germans' triumphant march down the Champs Elysées marked a high point in their conquest of France.

THE BATTLE OF BRITAIN AND THE BLITZ

MARCH 1940–JULY 1941

In the summer of 1940, while Germany prepared to invade Britain, the Luftwaffe was ordered to gain control of the skies. In the ensuing Battle of Britain it failed to do this, but by a very narrow margin. German strategy then switched to a bombing campaign aimed at London and other major industrial cities—the Blitz.

1940

MARCH 16
German bombers attack British Grand Fleet at Scapa Flow in Orkney Islands

MARCH 19
British air raid on German seaplane base on island of Sylt in retaliation for raid on Scapa Flow

APRIL 15
British raid on German port of Wilhelmshaven

MAY 22
British break Luftwaffe's Enigma code

JUNE 3
Germans launch 300-bomber raid on Paris

JULY 10
Germans attack Channel convoys and launch raid on Swansea docks and arms factory in Wales

AUGUST 11
Numerous air battles over English Channel and south coast of England. Attacks directed at ports, airfields, and radar stations

AUGUST 13
Adlertag (Eagle Day). Official start of Göring's offensive to gain control of the skies over Britain prior to invasion (Operation Sea Lion)

AUGUST 15
Greatest German effort to date with more than 1,000 German planes in action

AUGUST 25
Night raid on Berlin–in retaliation for accidental bombing of London the night before

SEPTEMBER 7
Start of London Blitz. Luftwaffe directs bombing offensive at London and other major cities

SEPTEMBER 17
Hitler calls off invasion of Britain (planned for September 21)

SEPTEMBER 30
Last large daylight raid on Britain. Total civilian air-raid casualties for September are 6,954 killed and 10,615 injured

OCTOBER 3
Over 170,000 people spend night in London Underground stations

NOVEMBER 14
Night raid by 449 bombers virtually destroys city of Coventry

DECEMBER 16
Largest air raid on Germany to date. 134 bombers attack Mannheim

DECEMBER 29
Massive incendiary raid on City of London, but winter weather now restricts number and size of raids until March

1941

JANUARY 20
Compulsory fire-watching introduced in Britain

FEBRUARY 10
RAF raid on oil-storage tanks in Rotterdam

MARCH 2
RAF raid on Cologne

MARCH 13
Raid on Clydebank near Glasgow leaves 35,000 homeless

MARCH 31
After let-up in bombing over winter, German raids intensify. Civilian casualties for March total 4,259 killed and 5,557 injured

MAY 1
First of seven consecutive raids on Liverpool

MAY 10
1,436 killed in largest ever raid on London

MAY 16
Heavy raid on Birmingham. Blitz now comes to an end as Luftwaffe transfers bombers from France and Low Countries for invasion of USSR

JUNE 8
RAF sends 360 aircraft on largest raid yet on Germany

JULY 27
German raid on London is first for 10 weeks. July casualty figures: 501 civilians killed in raids on Britain

---

Battle of Britain
Jul 10–Sept 6, 1940

The Blitz
Sept 7, 1940–
May 16, 1941

Other events

BRITAIN IN PERIL

V ICTORY IN FRANCE had brought the German army to the Channel coast. While German officers viewed the white cliffs of Dover through the warm summer haze, Hitler pondered his options, weighing the advantages of a cross-Channel operation against his evolving plan for an invasion of the Soviet Union. On July 16, 1940, he issued Führer Directive No 16, stating, "I have decided to prepare a landing operation against England, and, if necessary, to carry it out." Preparations for the invasion of Britain, codenamed *Seelöwe* (Sea Lion), were to be completed by the middle of August.

THE OPPOSING FORCES

An essential precondition of Sea L.ion was the securing of air control over the English Channel. The commander of the Luftwaffe, Hermann Göring, was brimming with confidence. He estimated that a mere four days would be sufficient to eliminate the RAF from southern England. At the Luftwaffe's disposal were three *Luftflotten* (air fleets). The largest, Luftflotte 2, was based in Belgium and northern France, facing England from the east. Luftflotte 3 was stationed in Normandy and poised to strike at the southwest and south coasts. The smaller Luftflotte 5, based in Denmark and Norway, was tasked with attacking targets in the north of England and Scotland.

RAF Fighter Command, led by Sir Hugh Dowding, faced the German threat with its squadrons organized into four Groups. In the critical southeastern sector, 11 Group was commanded by Air Vice-Marshal Keith Park; in the Midlands and East Anglia, 12 Group was led by Air Vice-Marshal Trafford Leigh-Mallory. In mid-July, 10 Group became operational in the west of England; the rest of the UK—the

Heinkel He 111 over London
Photographed on the first day of the Blitz, September 7, 1940, a Heinkel bomber flies over the Thames River in the East End of London, where the capital's docks and factories were concentrated.

north of England, Scotland, and Northern Ireland was covered by 13 Group. Group areas were divided into sectors, each consisting of a main airfield (sector station) and several satellite stations.

HEAVY LOSSES

On the eve of battle, both sides were licking the wounds sustained in the Battle of France. Between May 10 and June 20, the British had lost 944 aircraft, including 386 Hurricanes and 67 Spitfires. Not counting losses over Dunkirk, they had also lost 350 fighter pilots killed, missing, wounded, or taken prisoner. Nor had the Luftwaffe escaped lightly. In the fighting of May–June 1940, it had lost some 1,100 aircraft on operations, plus 200 more in accidents and 145 damaged. By July 20, RAF Fighter Command could field just 531 operational aircraft compared with the 725 operational fighters and 1,280 combat-ready bombers of Luftflotten 2, 3, and 5. The British, however, enjoyed a significant advantage in the "Chain Home" system of 30 radar stations established on the coastline from Land's End in the southwest to Newcastle in the northeast.

With hindsight the Battle of Britain can be seen as the prelude to a battle that was never fought— the invasion of England. It passed through a number of phases, each triggered by the Luftwaffe's decisions to switch targets. The first phase opened in early July as the Luftwaffe launched a series of attacks on coastal targets and convoys, seeking to draw Fighter Command out over the Channel.

EAGLE DAY

At the end of July Hitler ordered Göring to prepare "immediately and with the greatest haste … the great battle of the German air force against England." On August 2 Göring issued the final order for *Adlertag* (Eagle Day) on which the destruction of Fighter

RADAR

AN ACRONYM FOR "Radio Direction and Ranging," radar was originally known as "RDF" (Radio Direction Finding) by the British. Its principle is that of sending out a pulse of radio energy to strike a target and then detecting the energy reflected back. As the speed of the pulse is known, measuring the time between transmission and reception enables radar operators to calculate the target range. In the 1930s the concept was developed independently in Britain, France, Germany, and the United States.

In Britain, radar was first developed for defensive purposes, and by 1939 a chain of 30 radar stations had been established around the southwest, southern, and eastern British coastlines. Reports from radar stations were fed back to Fighter Command headquarters along with information

Operations room
Members of the Women's Auxiliary Air Force (WAAF) track incoming German aircraft. One of the Luftwaffe's greatest blunders in 1940 was its failure to appreciate the effectiveness of Britain's radar.

Cierva C-30 autogiro
In the years immediately preceding the war Cierva autogiros were used by the RAF to test and calibrate Britain's chain of coastal radar stations.

from observation posts. The cross-checked results were then transmitted to the relevant Fighter Command Group and sector stations, where controllers would scramble interceptor aircraft to meet the incoming enemy bombers. Radar avoided the wasteful system of flying standing patrols and was a vital element in the narrow margin of victory secured by Fighter Command in the Battle of Britain.

Command was to be accomplished. This was set for August 10, but bad weather caused its postponement for three days while the air fighting intensified. On August 12 Luftflotte 2 struck at England's central south coast. Targets included the docks and war industries in Portsmouth and Southampton, and the radar station in Ventnor on the Isle of Wight. This last target, with its tall, latticed masts, was assigned to 15 Ju 88s, operating in their dive-bomber role. The station was put out of action but within three days was replaced by a mobile station. The Luftwaffe then decided, fatally, not to press home its attack on the radar stations.

Scramble
RAF pilots always raced to their fighters when they were "scrambled." Time was precious and a few extra seconds allowed them to gain height before engaging the enemy.

Luftwaffe operations on August 13—the rescheduled Eagle Day—were disrupted by bad weather and it was on August 15 that the most intensive phase of the Battle of Britain began. For the first and last time, all three Luftflotten took part in the attack, throwing five successive waves of aircraft against Britain—over 2,000 sorties, some two-thirds of them by fighters. The Luftwaffe was unable to coordinate operations against southern England with those in the north, and Luftflotte 5 was withdrawn from the battle after suffering heavy losses. It also failed to coordinate the operations of Luftflotten 2 and 3. At no point were attacks timed to catch the British fighters on the ground refueling and rearming. Thus, when Luftflotte 3 launched its main attack in the west with some 200 aircraft, 10 and 11 Groups were able to concentrate 170 fighters against them, a move that would have been impossible an hour earlier. In the evening, Luftflotte 2 had the opportunity to launch a series of raids at full strength, but sent barely 100 aircraft over southeast England.

Loading a Heinkel 111 with bombs
In the short-range missions of the Battle of Britain the He 111 operated reasonably efficiently as a bomber, but for the longer-range missions of the Blitz, its bombload had to be reduced by half to 2,200 lb (1,000 kg).

At the end of the day's fighting, both sides claimed success, but the Luftwaffe had lost 69 aircraft and 190 aircrew while Fighter Command had lost only 34 aircraft and 13 pilots. On what the Germans called "Black Thursday," the Luftwaffe had sustained its worst losses in a single day of the Battle of Britain. The vulnerable Ju 87 (Stuka) dive-bomber was pulled out of the battle on August 18.

CHANGES IN STRATEGY

The Luftwaffe now narrowed its goal to the destruction of 11 Group's seven sector stations—Biggin Hill, Debden, Hornchurch, Kenley, Northolt, North Weald, and Tangmere. On August 30 Biggin Hill suffered the first of six major attacks. Littered with wreckage, with most its buildings destroyed and much of its vital equipment being worked in the open, the airfield nevertheless remained operational.

Both sides were now feeling the strain. In the first six days of September, the Luftwaffe lost 125 aircraft. The twin-engined Me 110s had proved no match for Spitfires and Hurricanes. In the same period Fighter Command lost 119 aircraft, and its reserve of experienced aircrew was running low. The rate of fighter production was impressive—476 were delivered in August—but the aircraft were of no use without trained pilots to fly them.

The weight of the Luftwaffe's attacks had fallen most heavily on 11 Group—12 Group lay beyond the range of Me 109 escorts—and Park's tactics were aimed at engaging the enemy as early as possible, often despatching single unsupported squadrons against formations of 100 or more enemy aircraft. Park's tactics attracted criticism, not least from Leigh-Mallory, commander of 12 Group, who argued for the use of wings of up to five squadrons. But these so-called "Big Wings" took time to assemble, and Park believed that the short time available for interception, and the need to protect vital airfields and factories, should be the key determinants in this desperate phase of the battle.

My nerves were in ribbons and I was scared stiff that one day I would pull out and avoid combat. That frightened me more than the Germans and I pleaded with my CO for a rest. He was sympathetic but quite adamant that until he got replacements I would have to carry on. I am glad now that he was unable to let me go. If I had been allowed to leave the squadron, feeling as I did, I am sure that I would never have flown again.

PILOT OFFICER J.H. "GINGER" LACEY, 501 SQUADRON

Ju 88 bombsight
German bombsights were more sophisticated than British ones and allowed for ground speed, wind speed and direction, and drift.

Turn and drift knob

The Luftwaffe's main problem was fighter escort. From mid-August the fighters had been pulled in to fly above, ahead, and on the flank of bomber formations, reducing both their combat efficiency and endurance. The short range of the Me 109 became an increasing handicap.

At this point the Luftwaffe's strategy took a new turn. Late in the afternoon of September 7, it launched its first daylight raid on London, ordered by Hitler in retaliation for an RAF raid on Berlin on the night of August 25/26. A total of 348 bombers, escorted by 617 fighters bombed the oil tanks at Thameshaven and the London docks. Throughout the night a steady procession of 318 Heinkels and Dorniers added 300 tons of high-explosive and 13,000 incendiary bombs to the flames below. The city's antiaircraft defenses downed just one bomber.

On the basis of German intelligence estimates that Fighter Command could now muster only 100 aircraft, a new pattern of bombing was adopted. The Luftwaffe would continue to bomb London by night, while smaller daylight raids—escorted in overwhelming strength—would clear the sky of the remnants of Fighter Command. The pressure was taken off the battered sector stations, allowing them to attack in larger formations—the moment of vindication for Leigh-Mallory's Big Wing tactics.

THE OPPOSING AIR FORCES

THE LUFTWAFFE went into the Battle of Britain with a significant numerical advantage over the RAF. Britain's aircraft, however, were probably better equipped for the roles they had to play in the battle—in particular the two single-seater fighters, the Hurricane and the Spitfire. Even so, these had to land frequently to rearm. On the German side, the Ju 87 Stuka dive-bomber, proved far too vulnerable, while the Ju 88, He 111, and Do 17 medium bombers were limited in their range and had to reduce their bombloads in order to carry sufficient fuel. The principal German fighter, the Messerschmitt Bf 109 was the equal of the Spitfire, but was crucially hampered by its limited range.

Dornier 17Z-2

Nicknamed the "Flying Pencil" because of its long, thin fuselage, the Dornier medium bomber, like the Heinkel 111, started life as a commercial airplane in the 1930s. Production ceased in 1940 as it became clear that the Junkers 88 was a much better aircraft, but large numbers of Dorniers were used during the Battle of Britain and as night bombers during the Blitz.

Engines 2 × 1,000 hp Bramo 323P Fafnir	
Wingspan 59 ft (18 m)	Length 52 ft 6 in (15.95 m)
Max Speed 265 mph (426 kph)	Crew 4 or 5
Armament 6 × 7.92-mm machine-guns; bombload 2,200 lb (1,000 kg)	

Junkers Ju 88A-1

Over 15,000 Ju 88s, of which 9,000 were bombers, were produced in 1939–45. Arguably the most versatile aircraft of the war, the Ju 88 was heavily armored against stern and quarter attacks, but unprotected against head-on attack. Pilots used the dive as an evasive maneuver—the plane had been designed to perform as a dive bomber.

Engines 2 × 1,200 hp Junkers Jumo 211B-1	
Wingspan 65 ft 8 in (19.8 m)	Length 51 ft (15.6 m)
Max Speed 286 mph (460 kph)	Crew 4
Armament 6 × 7.92-mm machine-guns; maximum bombload 5,510 lb (2,500 kg)	

Heinkel He 111H-3

Designed ostensibly as a civil airliner, the He 111 made its combat debut in the Spanish Civil War. It proved vulnerable in daylight raids without heavy fighter escort and was switched to night bombing, mine-laying, and torpedo-bombing. The ventral gondola, dubbed "the Death Bed," was a favorite target for RAF fighter pilots.

Engines 2 × 1,340 hp Junkers Jumo 211F-1	
Wingspan 74 ft 2 in (22.6 m)	Length 54 ft 6in (16.6 m)
Max Speed 258 mph (415 kph)	Crew 5
Armament 7 × 7.92-mm machine guns; maximum bombload 4,400 lb (2,000 kg)	

Light metal alloy monocoque (weight-bearing) fuselage

Liquid-cooled V-12 Rolls Royce Merlin engine

Elliptical-section wing, housing machine-guns and the retracted undercarriage

Messerschmitt Bf 109E-3

As a weapon of blitzkrieg, operating at the forward point of contact with the enemy, the Me 109 (seen here in desert markings) was a formidable aircraft. But range was less important in France than it was in the skies over southern England. The Me 109 had wooden drop tanks to extend its range, but these had degraded in northern France and were not used in the Battle of Britain.

Engine 1,350 hp Daimler Benz DB 601 E	
Wingspan 32 ft 4 in (9.87 m)	Length 28 ft 2 in (8.64 m)
Max Speed 348 mph (560 kph)	Crew 1
Armament 2 × 20-mm cannon, 2 × 7.9-mm machine-guns	

Supermarine Spitfire I

The Spitfire became synonymous with the success of the British fighters in the Battle of Britain, although Hurricanes were more numerous and shot down more enemy planes. But the Spitfire had a certain mystique and won the affection of all the pilots that flew it. In combat the Spitfire had the edge on the Messerschmitt Bf 109 in speed and climb and in turning circle. The Me 109, however, outperformed the Spitfire over 20,000 ft (6,000 m), a height at which the prewar RAF had not expected dogfighting. When flown to its limits a Spitfire could shake off a pursuer by means of a flick and half roll and a quick pull out of the subsequent dive. However, at the start of the Battle of Britain the Me 109 had the advantage in a steep dive because its direct-injection engine kept running under negative gravity while the Spitfire's Merlin cut out as the Spitfire tried to follow.

Engine 1,030 hp Rolls Royce Merlin III	
Wingspan 36 ft 10 in (11.23 m)	Length 29 ft 11 in (9.12 m)
Max speed 357 mph (575 kph)	Crew 1
Armament 8 × .303-in Browning machine-guns	

Boulton Paul Defiant

The Defiant had no fixed forward firing armament but featured instead a power-operated revolving turret immediately behind the pilot. Designed as a bomber destroyer, which could fly alongside enemy aircraft, pouring fire into their unprotected flanks, the Defiant was no match for enemy fighters, but had some success against bombers as a night fighter during the Blitz.

Engine 1,030 hp Rolls Royce Merlin III	
Wingspan 39 ft 4 in (10.77 m)	Length 35 ft 4 in (11.99 m)
Max Speed 304 mph (489 kph)	Crew 2
Armament 4 × .303-in Browning machine-guns	

Hawker Hurricane I

The Hurricane was the RAF's first monoplane fighter, entering service in 1937. The principal fighter in the Battle of Britain, it was a rock-solid gun platform, immensely maneuverable, and capable of absorbing a huge amount of battle damage. Its roomy cockpit, excellent all-around visibility, responsive handling, and reliable engine made it a true pilot's aircraft.

Engine 1,030 hp Rolls Royce Merlin II or III	
Wingspan 40 ft (12.1 m)	Length 32 ft 2 in (9.8 m)
Max Speed 329 mph (529 kph)	Crew 1
Armament 8 × .303-in Browning machine-guns	

On the morning of September 15, 100 Do 17s crossed the English coastline, battling into a strong headwind. Their slow approach forced their escorts to turn back as their fuel ran low and also gave Fighter Command time to deploy. The Dorniers were harried all the way to the outskirts of London, where they were met by five squadrons of the Duxford Big Wing—60 fighters attacking in close formation—which shot down six Dorniers as the raiders jettisoned their bombs and turned for home.

In the afternoon, British radar operators picked up the slow assembly, over their airfields in France, of another large formation. The raiders flew in over Kent to be met by over 160 fighters of 11 Group. By the end of the day nearly 300 British fighters were operating over London. The Luftwaffe lost 55 aircraft and at least 25 percent of the remainder suffered severe damage. Hitler ordered the indefinite postponement of Sealion and the He 111s and Do 17s were switched to night operations.

THE BLITZ

Between September 7 and November 12 London was spared bombing on a mere 10 nights. Some 13,000 tons of high explosive and almost one million incendiaries fell on the city, killing 13,000 people and injuring 20,000 more. At this stage in the war, the RAF's night defenses were little more than a collection of hasty improvisations. Only a handful of fighters were equipped with a primitive form of airborne radar. Nor had the Luftwaffe's bombers much to fear from antiaircraft guns. In September 1940 an expenditure of some 20,000 shells was needed to down one plane.

The Germans, moreover, had a secret weapon, described by Churchill as "a radio beam which, like an invisible searchlight, would guide bombers… to their target." Dubbed *Knickebein* (crooked leg), it consisted of two radio beams directed from stations in Europe. Aircraft would fly along one beam and release their bombs when the first beam was intersected by the second. The Luftwaffe had foolishly tested the system over Britain in March 1940, at a time when it was not contemplating large-scale night-bombing operations. The examination of an He 111 shot down by a night fighter enabled scientists to work out how to jam the beams. A more sophisticated version of this system—X-Verfahren—used four beams and a clockwork timer linked to the beams and bomb release. A crack unit, Kampfgruppe (KGr) 100, was formed early in 1940 to test this system. By mid-October a regular pattern of night raids had emerged: KGr 100 acted as a pathfinding force, marking targets for the main force flying in behind.

The bombing of Coventry
In an 11-hour attack, 554 people were killed and over 1,200 injured. Some 60,000 buildings were destroyed or damaged, including the city's medieval cathedral, which was completely gutted.

① Mar 16, 1940
Luftwaffe attacks Scapa Flow naval base. First British civilian casualty of the war

⑥ Mar 13/14, 1941
Luftwaffe attacks Clydebank in attempt to destroy its shipyards. Homes, factories, and a munitions plant are obliterated

Apr 1941 ⑧
Belfast, an important ship-building center, suffers two heavy raids

⑪ May 15, 1941
111 German bombers carry out a massive assault against Birmingham

May 31, 1941 ⑫
Bomb falls on Dublin. Neutral Ireland occasionally bombed in error

⑤ Nov 14/15, 1940
449 German bombers devastate Coventry, leaving one-third of its inhabitants homeless

③ Sept 7, 1940 – Nov 12, 1941
Raids kill over 15,000 in London and make more than 250,000 homeless

May 1–7, 1941 ⑨
Luftwaffe targets Liverpool for second time, subjecting it to seven successive nights of bombing

Jul 10, 1940 ②
In first major attack, Luftwaffe bombs Swansea docks and Royal Ordnance factory in Pembrey

Apr 1941 ⑦
Five relentless bombing raids virtually reduce Plymouth to rubble

Sept 30, 1940 ④
Luftwaffe pounds Westland aircraft factory

⑩ May 10, 1941
London suffers largest raid so far. Thousands left without electricity, gas, or water

Orkney Islands · Scapa Flow · Outer Hebrides · Inner Hebrides · SCOTLAND · Aberdeen · Dundee · Clydebank · Glasgow · EDINBURGH · NORTHERN IRELAND · BELFAST · Newcastle-upon-Tyne · Tyne · Workington · Isle of Man · Middlesbrough · 13 GROUP · Catterick · IRELAND · Irish Sea · Church Fenton · Manchester · Liverpool · Hull · Humber · Sheffield · Kirton in Lindsey · Digby · DUBLIN · Stoke-on-Trent · Nottingham · Wittering · Norwich · Birmingham · Coventry · Duxford · 12 GROUP · WALES · ENGLAND · Pembrey · Swansea · Filton · North Weald · Oxford · Northolt · Debden · Hornchurch · Chatham · CARDIFF · Bristol · Thames · LONDON · Kenley · Dover · 10 GROUP · Yeovil · Middle Wallop · 11 GROUP · Lympne · Calais · Exeter · Hastings · Weymouth · Brighton · Biggin Hill · Portland · Isle of Wight · Tangmere · Portsmouth · Southampton · English Channel · Cherbourg · Rouen/Rennes · Laon · Caen · Evreux · Seine · PARIS · St André-de-l'Eure · Orly · Melun · Dreux · Chartres · Etampes · Brest · Dinard · Châteaudun · LUFTFLOTTE 3 · Vannes · FRANCE · NETH. · AMSTERDAM · Soesterberg · Nijmegen · Gilze-Rijen · Eindhoven · Antwerp · BRUSSELS · St Trond · Lille · BELGIUM · LUFTFLOTTE 2 · North Sea

0 km 50 100 150
0 miles 50 100 150

GERMAN BOMBING OF BRITISH CITIES
MAR 1940–MAY 1941

☀ Major air raids or towns suffering repeated bombing
☼ Other important air raids
▪ Main British industrial areas
⊙ British fighter base
⊙ German air base

The war in the air over Britain
When Hitler called off his planned invasion of Britain from northern France, he ordered the Luftwaffe to bomb the country into submission instead. The most intense period of bombing (the Blitz) lasted from September 1940 to May 1941.

Late in the afternoon of November 14 an X-beam was detected crossing the Midlands, an area as yet largely unscathed by heavy night raids. This confirmed reports that the Germans were planning a major night offensive, code-named *Mondscheinserenade* (Moonlight Serenade), timed to take advantage of the full moon.

Less than two hours later the first of 13 He 11s of KGr 100 arrived over Coventry. The aiming point was to the east of the city center and when the last of the Heinkels flew away, numerous fires had been started. These lit the way for 449 bombers which dropped 1,500 high-explosive bombs, 50 huge parachute and land mines, and some 30,000 incendiaries. The city was

London firefighters
On the first night of the Blitz 25,000 auxiliary firefighters rushed to assist the London Fire Brigade. On many nights there were over 2,000 major fires in the city, as well as countless minor spot fires.

devastated and 21 factories—12 of them connected with the aircraft industry— severely damaged. Yet Coventry quickly recovered. Just over a month of industrial output was lost but most of the factories were back in production within days. Nor had civilian morale collapsed. After the initial shock there was no mass panic.

Throughout January and February, in the face of winter weather, the Luftwaffe fought to maintain the pressure on London, the industrial centers of

the Midlands, and Britain's western ports, the last links in the Atlantic supply chain. However, air defenses were now making life more difficult for the German bombers. By March, improved radar equipment was reaching the night fighter squadrons. In March, night fighters shot down 22 bombers and AA guns claimed another 17. In April, the figures rose to 48 and 39 respectively and reached a peak in May, with 96 fighter victories and 32 claimed by the guns.

The final phase of the Blitz began in mid-April 1941 and concluded with a heavy raid on London on the night of May 10/11 in which some 1,436 civilians were killed and 16 aircraft were brought down by the air defenses, the highest total in a single night. These losses were not sufficient in themselves to bring a halt to the Blitz. Rather it was the transfer to the East of units earmarked for the invasion of the Soviet Union, which Hitler launched on June 22, 1941. By the end of June two-thirds of the Luftwaffe had been removed from the bombing operations against Britain.

"The whole sky to the east was blazing red… it seemed as though half of London must be burning… In Shaftesbury Avenue, five miles from the blaze, it was possible to read an evening paper."

AIR RAID WARDEN BARBARA NIXON
ON SEPTEMBER 7, 1940

BASS

Rescuing a victim of the Blitz
A Heavy Rescue Squad pulls a survivor from the remains of a bombed building. Some 40,000 civilians were killed in the Blitz, in which London and other British cities were bombed over a nine-month period. The Blitz failed, however, to affect British morale.

THE BRITISH, FRENCH, AND GERMAN HOME FRONTS

SEPTEMBER 1939–JUNE 1943

World War II was a "total war" in which civilians were mobilized to contribute to their countries' war effort more fully than ever before. This was particularly the case in Britain and Germany, where rationing was introduced almost immediately and the government took control of the economy. Women played a major part in military hardware production, to which resources were increasingly diverted.

1939

SEPTEMBER 1
Nationwide blackout and mass evacuation of children from cities to countryside begins

SEPTEMBER 4
War Economy decree published, under which rationing is introduced on a wide range of products.

1940

JANUARY 8
Ration books for sugar, butter, ham, and bacon are introduced

MARCH 1
Some rationing of food and drink is introduced

MAY 14
Recruitment of Local Defence Volunteers (to be renamed Home Guard on July 23) begins

JUNE 3
First major German bomber raid on Paris

JULY
Economic New Order–bringing trade and financial affairs of Europe into single system–is launched

JUNE 22
Armistice with Germany divides France into occupied and unoccupied zones

JULY 28
All movement between occupied and unoccupied zones is banned

SEPTEMBER 7
Start of Blitz on London and other major British cities

OCTOBER 14
In Vichy France marrried women are banned from jobs in public services

1941

MARCH 17
Announcement of plans for mobilization of women to perform essential jobs in industry

MAY 10
Final heavy raid of Blitz is directed at London

JUNE 1
Clothes rationing is introduced

JUNE 13
12,000 Jews are "interned" in camps in France

AUGUST 8
Wine consumption limited to 2 liters (4 pints) per person per week

SEPTEMBER 24
Tobacco ration in Paris reduced to four cigarettes per day for men and one for women

DECEMBER 2
Beginning of registration for service of women up to 40

DECEMBER 20
War production committees are set up

1942

FEBRUARY 9
Speer is appointed Minister of Weapons and Munitions

FEBRUARY 23
German bomber raids on Britain's cathedral cities begin

MARCH 29
Much of old city of Lübeck is bombed and destroyed by British; followed by further bombing raids on German cities

MAY 29
Jews in occupied zone required to wear yellow star

AUGUST 25
Germans introduce conscription in Alsace-Lorraine, from which they have expelled 23,000 French citizens

NOVEMBER 11
Germans begin their occupation of Vichy France

JANUARY 27
Civil conscription of women is introduced

1943

FEBRUARY 4
Inessential businesses are ordered to close

APRIL 20
Recruitment of women into the Home Guard is announced

JUNE 26
Speer takes over all war production except aircraft

JULY 1
Ban placed on gasoline for anyone but essential users

■ Events in Britain ■ Events in France ■ Events in Germany

THE HOME FRONT IN WESTERN EUROPE

WORLD WAR II involved civilians on a scale never experienced before, both as contributors to the war effort and as victims. The number of civilian casualties in western Europe did not approach the number reached in eastern Europe. Even so, as many as 2 million were killed in Germany, 170,000 in France, and 65,000 in Britain.

The single greatest cause of civilian casualties in western Europe—apart from the Nazi death camps—was aerial bombardment. An early warning of the massive destruction that could be inflicted on cities by bomber planes came during the German invasion of Poland in September 1939, when Warsaw was bombed into submission. The following May the bombing of Rotterdam, which resulted in the death of over 1,000 civilians and 78,000 being made homeless, was followed by the Blitz on British cities between September 1940 and May 1941, in which some 40,000 people lost their lives.

Training for the British Home Guard
In 1940, when volunteers to the Home Guard were first recruited, the training was patchy and equipment either nonexistent or outdated. Both improved greatly in 1941.

CIVILIAN EVACUATIONS

IN 1932 THE WARNING of the British politician, Stanley Baldwin, that "the bomber will always get through" made a deep impression in Britain, the only state to make serious plans to evacuate civilians from large towns before the war started. The Germans did not expect to be bombed, but when they were, the *Kinder Land Verschickung* was set up to evacuate children from the north and west to the south. Child casualties of the bombing in cities in the south were possibly one-third of those in the north and west. In France, between the outbreak of war and defeat in June 1940, many parents in the cities sent children to stay with relatives in the country. Others were taken in by Catholic schools and orphanages.

In Britain, plans to evacuate 4 million children, mothers, and expectant mothers were put into effect as soon as the war began. About 1.5 million actually went, plus another 2 million privately. But the bombers did not come, and about half the evacuees returned home within four months. Air raids during the Blitz of 1940 prompted a new evacuation, although patchy and unplanned. In the summer of 1944, the arrival of the V-1 and V-2 was to prompt the evacuation of another 1.5 million Londoners.

Children went first to "reception areas," where they were allotted to households judged able to take them. Billeting was compulsory if sufficient volunteers were not forthcoming. Such close contact between city slums and rural prosperity caused problems. Evacuees, especially poor Roman Catholics from the Liverpool and Glasgow slums, were often resented. Some mothers never returned to reclaim their children, and there were cases of physical and sexual abuse. There were also benefits—greater social awareness on both sides and, more tangibly, good country food for poor city children.

Encouraging evacuation
Only a minority of children were evacuated from London and other cities, despite the authorities' efforts.

LEAVE THIS TO US SONNY—YOU OUGHT TO BE OUT OF LONDON

MINISTRY OF HEALTH EVACUATION SCHEME

Sheltering in a subway station
London's underground stations were not always as safe as people supposed them to be. In October 1940 a bomb falling on Balham station killed or injured 600 people.

Evacuees
For many city children, evacuation to the countryside was a frightening experience. Sometimes it involved having to live with a family that clearly did not want them.

The German bombs were a combination of high-explosive, ranging from several pounds to 2.5 tons, and incendiaries of various types. The incendiaries were far more effective. A high-explosive bomb might destroy a building but an incendiary could set fire to a huge area. Although it only caused a small explosion, it ignited chemicals that burned for a few minutes at very high temperature, long enough to set fire to the surroundings.

Scenes of destruction were horrific. In some cases whole families were wiped out, and from a high vantage point most of east London on a bad night in the Blitz seemed to be on fire. London Transport lost so many buses it had to borrow 500 from other cities. In the notorious raids on Coventry in November 1940 and April 1941, when most of the city center was destroyed, 50,000 houses were rendered uninhabitable. Rehousing the homeless caused severe difficulties here and elsewhere: prefabricated houses were not built until 1944. Yet paradoxically the "Blitz," which was expressly designed to break British morale, actually raised it. Large-scale bombardment of civilian targets in Germany did not begin until 1943, when Hamburg was the chief victim, with 40,000 of its citizens dying in one night. Even this huge figure was to be far exceeded by the casualties in German cities during the massive Allied raids of 1944–45.

CIVIL DEFENSE

In Britain plans had been laid for rationing, evacuation, and aspects of civil defense before the war began. The Anderson air-raid shelter, which could be dug into any backyard, was widely distributed from February 1939. It was followed by the indoors Morrison shelter, a reinforced iron cage that doubled as a table. Both required scarce steel and provided inadequate protection against direct hits. Public shelters, usually brick, also proved inadequate. People preferred their own barricaded homes or, against the initial resistance of the authorities, impregnable underground railroad stations. Better, deeper shelters were then built, too late for the Blitz but useful when the V-1s and V-2s arrived toward the end of the war.

Gas masks were issued to all citizens, who were urged to carry them at all times, though they proved an unnecessary precaution. Considerable chaos was caused by a nationwide blackout: the road accident rate doubled in the first month of its operation but later fell with less stringent lighting restrictions and the rationing of gasoline (later withdrawn entirely for private use). In Germany the blackout began the day before war started, and flashlights soon joined the growing number of articles unobtainable in stores. Buses crawled along darkened Berlin streets bearing a single, ghostly, blue light. Pedestrians wore a phosphorescent button on their coats.

Windows had to be blacked out, too, and were usually also crisscrossed with gummed newspaper strips as protection against splinters. Blackout discipline was maintained in Britain by ARP (Air Raid Protection) wardens, volunteers who had generally done a day's work first. The cry "Put out that light!" became another wartime watchword.

The call in Britain for ARP wardens—made in 1937—had met with a big response. This was repeated in May 1940 with the Local Defence Volunteers, soon to be renamed the Home Guard. Within one month of the government's appeal, 1.5 million men had volunteered. They included men of every age and class, though perhaps the core was made up of World War I veterans, now too old for the army. Their main task was to guard factories, airfields, and other sensitive places, and to man coastal defenses. In such a role they were immensely valuable, but few people put much faith in their ability to resist a German invasion.

The fear of imminent invasion led to a plethora of security measures—such as barricades, camouflage, and obstacles against enemy tanks—of which some were of doubtful utility. The removal of signposts from road junctions, for example, overlooked the fact that the Germans had maps. Encouraged by official urging to avoid careless talk ("you never know who is listening"), fantasies about German agents, even German paratroopers, being everywhere, proliferated during the Phoney War. They largely subsided when the situation became more serious.

Women in war work
In Britain women were recruited to the industrial workforce on a huge scale. By 1943 all those under 40 were in war work unless they had particularly heavy domestic responsibilities. They were employed in all forms of industry and acquired a wide range of skills, including welding.

LIFE UNDER GERMAN OCCUPATION

The wartime experience of civilians naturally varied greatly from one country to another, even in those under German occupation. Moreover, conditions changed, invariably for the worse, as time went on.

Reactions to occupation varied widely, while the German attitude toward conquered peoples depended on Nazi racial prejudices. In the Netherlands the German regime was, to begin with, comparatively mild, since the Dutch were regarded as racially akin to Germans and potential members of a future Greater Reich. Scandinavians were also acceptable. The Nazi hope of enlisting Norwegians, Danes, and Dutch in support of the war against

INTERNMENT OF CIVILIANS

AT THE OUTBREAK OF WAR most combatant nations arrested and held without trial "enemy aliens"—residents who were citizens of enemy states, had been born there, or in some cases were merely descended from people born there. Initially, Britain and Germany allowed some aliens to return home, whereas in France all German males were interned. When the Germans invaded, many more were arrested in Belgium and the Netherlands as well as France, where they were sent to camps in the far south. In Britain only those people considered "high-risk" were held in camps in 1939, but during the spy scare of May 1940 more were interned, including refugees from Naziism. The sinking of a ship carrying 600 internees to Canada provoked popular protest, leading to the majority being freed by mid-1941.

Camp in Huyton, near Liverpool
In the summer of 1940 around 27,000 men, women, and children were interned in camps in Britain, often in very poor conditions.

communism, to which, after the attack on the Soviet Union in June 1941, a hefty propaganda effort was directed, induced Hitler initially to avoid putting native Nazi sympathizers in power. However, apart from a small minority of collaborationists on the one hand and resistance members on the other, the great majority of civilians in the occupied countries opted for a policy of pragmatism, cooperating nenthusiastically with the German authorities and only so far as necessary to avoid trouble. After all, until 1943, German dominance looked likely to be long-lasting, if not permanent.

The extent to which the Germans took direct control of civil administration reflected their racial attitude, with the Netherlands, and still more Denmark, retaining a large measure of authority for the first two years. But the economies of all occupied countries rapidly became wholly subservient to the German war effort. Foreign workers were encouraged, and later compelled, to take work in Germany, where by 1943 they made up nearly 20 percent of the workforce. Sometimes factories were dismantled and their machinery transported to the Fatherland.

Checking papers
The Germans used checkpoints to help regulate the movement of people into and out of France's occupied zone.

A wide variety of raw materials, food, and other goods was earmarked for German consumption. Banks, including their gold reserves, were taken over, and the foreign exchange rate was rigged to favor the mark. The costs of the occupation were borne by its victims, a burden exacerbated, particularly in Belgium and France, by runaway inflation.

France was an unusual case because the Germans did not occupy the whole country between May 1940 and November 1942, and left the Vichy government headed by Pétain in sole charge of the center and south. The veneer of French national unity at the outbreak of war soon cracked as old animosities resurfaced. The Vichy regime represented the reactionary, anti-republican Right, as much anti-British as anti-German, and hostile to the liberal Left, reflecting a profound division in French society dating from the 1789 Revolution.

CONNAISSEZ-VOUS MIEUX QUE LUI LES PROBLÈMES DE L'HEURE ?

Promotion of a personality cult
"Do you know more than he does about the problems of the moment?," asked this poster featuring Marshal Pétain.

" I collaborate: therefore I have the right to contribute my own thought and individual effort to the common cause."

THE BISHOP OF ARRAS, MGR. HENRI-ÉDOUARD DUTOÎT, ATTEMPTING TO JUSTIFY THE DECISION OF PÉTAIN AND HIS FOLLOWERS TO COLLABORATE WITH THE GERMANS

Germans in Paris
From June 1940 Paris was the seat of the German Military Administration that governed the occupied section of France.

The old watchwords, Liberté, Egalité, Fraternité, were replaced by Travail, Famille, Patrie (Work, Family, Fatherland), and the government was increasingly dominated by fascist collaborators.

In both zones of France, as elsewhere, most people settled for minimal cooperation if not tacit collaboration. However, despite the extra difficulties imposed by the division of the country, viable resistance —to both Germans and the Vichy government— was active in the north within weeks of the armistice and developed later with equal strength in the south.

THE ROLE OF WOMEN

Women were recruited to the labor force throughout Europe. In Britain, for example, about 80 percent of the workers added to the British labor force in 1939–43 were women who had not formerly figured in the labor market, the majority having been housewives. Later, certain categories of women were

Vichy propaganda poster
The Vichy government was both authoritarian and patriarchal, and it cooperated with the Germans on a major scale. Its people were exhorted to work in support of the German war effort.

conscripted for work in war industries, learning hitherto masculine trades such as carpentry or welding. By 1943, when workers in the munitions industry had expanded from 1.25 million (1939) to 8.5 million even grandmothers were being recruited. Women workers were not always popular, sometimes because the admission of women to a factory freed men for military service, and there was considerable discrimination. In a team assembling Lancasters, men and women did the same work side by side, but the women's pay was half that of the men.

Women were also required to take the place of absent farmworkers. In Britain the Women's Land Army, popularly known as Land Girls, eventually numbered over 80,000. It attracted office girls yearning for an outdoor life, though working long hours in all weather for £1.40 ($5.60) a week plus room and board dented some illusions. It was perfectly possible to join the Land Girls to get away

from the Blitz, only to find oneself on a farm near an airfield that was a regular target of German air raids.

At the beginning of the war, Germany made less use of women workers. Hitler believed that to remove women from family life was bad for morale, and the Nazi concept of the woman as a Nordic domestic goddess devoted exclusively to husband and children continued to prevail. Women were theoretically subject to civil conscription under prewar legislation, but in June 1940 only 250,000 had been recruited and they did not affect the workforce total because all had previously been employed. Generous family allowances, nearly three times their equivalent in Britain, discouraged soldiers' wives from taking jobs.

Ministers who, as time went on, urged greater employment of women, came up against Hitler's prejudices. When the Soviet Union was cited as an example, Hitler replied that "slim, long-legged German women" could not be compared with "dumpy, primitive . . . Russian women." He even disliked mobilizing domestic servants, who decreased in numbers in 1939–45 by only 15 percent, while in Britain they virtually disappeared. However, in a

RADIO PROPAGANDA

PROPAGANDA IN ALL FORMS was a vital force in raising public morale, and all governments established a ministry of propaganda. Paper shortages notwithstanding, posters and leaflets urged people to contribute to their country's war effort. Slogans, such as the British "Dig for Victory" and "Mend and Make-do," assaulted both eye and ear. While sometimes being criticized for putting too much emphasis on exhortation and not supplying enough facts, radio was particularly effective. In Germany it was largely responsible for continued confidence in the government after defeat had become inevitable. Churchill and Hitler, in rather different styles, exploited radio with skill.

Broadcasts to occupied Europe by the British Broadcasting Corporation (BBC), which was independent though supportive of the British government, reached eager listeners who risked death if caught. In general it broadcast what it believed to be the truth, though not necessarily the whole truth. The BBC's German service had perhaps 1 million listeners in Germany in 1943. Josef Goebbels, appointed the German minister of propaganda in 1933, recognized the advantages of truthfulness in propaganda, though he was often overruled. Radio Suisse could also be relied on for relative accuracy.

Listening to Churchill
Through speeches broadcast on the radio, Churchill did much to raise public morale in Britain.

"Black" propaganda aimed at the enemy or, by the Germans, at the people of occupied countries, was less successful, though under the guidance of Goebbels it played a part in damaging French morale before June 1940. The broadcasts of "Lord Haw-Haw," from Germany to Britain, by a British traitor, William Joyce, who had a very upper-class accent, met with general derision. Similarly, British broadcasts pretending to emanate from Germany and aiming to undermine morale in the German army and U-boat crews apparently had little effect.

Earpiece

Secret radio
Owning a radio was forbidden in many countries. This radio hidden in a tin was used by a Dutch family to listen to BBC broadcasts.

German aircraft factory, 1940
Resources were diverted from the civilian to the military economy on an even greater scale in Germany than elsewhere. However, there was not a corresponding increase in the production of weapons and aircraft until 1942.

country where 6.6 million men were recruited to the armed services during the first two years of the war, it was inevitable that women should be required to join the workforce, whether on a paid or voluntary basis. In the countryside, from which many of the army recruits were drawn, women had to take on a greater share of the work on often unmechanized farms, while in the towns they took over from men in transportation, commerce, and administration. They also worked in the armaments industry, though not on as great a scale as would have been necessary if Germany had not begun to use foreign workers.

Hitler refused to contemplate equal pay for women, and sexist discrimination was common everywhere. For example, the huge contribution of women to the Resistance in France, as well as to French society generally under the occupation, is now well known, yet the attitude toward women of the male-dominated Resistance, even the Communist Party, was not much different from the paternalistic attitude of the Vichy regime, which banned married women from jobs in public services. Women were highly praised, but as defenders of their families and supporters of those "actively engaged" in the fight against the Nazis.

RATIONING AND FOOD

Rationing was introduced everywhere at the beginning of the war, or as soon as a program could be set up. Such programs were so extensive that they amounted to near-total government control of food. In Britain the only basic food items not rationed were bread and potatoes, while other, nonessential foods were "rationed" by simple nonavailability. When a supply of something scarce appeared in a local store, large lines quickly formed. In prosperous western Europe, there was scope for reducing consumption without severe hardship. Although some people had to make sacrifices, the overall effect of rationing in Britain, assisted by subsidies, price controls, and higher wages, was,

ironically, an overall improvement in the national diet. Child mortality rates and developmental diseases such as rickets registered a marked fall, whereas in France and other occupied countries, health and diet deteriorated. Even in Britain, the wartime diet was far from ideal, however, being short on protein and Vitamins A and D.

The rationing system adopted in Britain was to allocate a minimum quantity—for example, 2 oz (60 grams) of butter per week—to each individual, obtainable only with coupons from a ration book. Although rigid, this ensured that no one was undernourished. A more flexible system, which gave some choice, operated for clothes and consumer goods. In Germany citizens needed seven ration books, each color-coded for a specific type of food.

Britain imported nearly two-thirds of its food in 1939, hence the importance of the Battle of the Atlantic. More needed to be produced at home.

THE TREATMENT OF JEWS IN EUROPE 1939–41

BEFORE 1939 GERMANY had passed a series of measures against the Jews that included their effective exclusion from all economic life. The next step was to push them out of Germany. Various plans for expulsion were considered, Madagascar being one favored destination. Some Jews in eastern Germany were deported across the border to Poland as early as 1938. The question became more pressing for the German authorities with the conquest of Poland and, in 1941, the invasion of the Soviet Union, which resulted in a huge increase in the number of Jews under German rule. Some massacres of Jews and other "undesirables" were carried out by mass shootings. Elsewhere the Jews were rounded up and forced into ghettos with the intention of starving them to death. The numbers were, however, too large for this generally to be a practicable course of action. Consequently, in the fall of 1941 preparations began for the extermination of Jews in eastern Europe by gassing.

In the occupied countries of western Europe, measures against the Jews were not introduced as quickly as in the east and initially were less extreme. This was partly due to the decision not to permit the SS carte blanche, but also because the Jews were proportionately fewer and more integrated. Jews were expelled from public life, not allowed

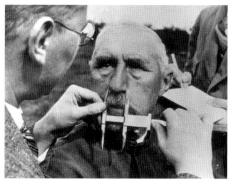

Anti-Semitic poster
Jews were often portrayed as being in an alliance with the communist Soviet Union against Europe.

Determining Jewishness
German officials could go to extreme lengths—such as measuring the length and width of a person's nose—to establish whether he or she was a true "Aryan" or had Jewish blood.

to use public transportation and were encouraged to emigrate. Their property was frequently confiscated.

Nazi racial policy often contradicted other goals of German policy. For instance, the Germans were hopeful of gaining the cooperation of the Dutch people, but an attack on the Jewish district in Amsterdam provoked a 48-hour strike by Dutch workers. By contrast, the Vichy regime in France cooperated fully with the Nazis. It introduced anti-Semitic laws of its own. As early as July 1940 it deprived naturalized Jews of French citizenship and one year later interned 12,000 in camps.

The country most successful in thwarting Nazi destruction of its Jews was Denmark, where a large majority of the 8,000 Danish Jews were safely smuggled to Sweden and the king boldly wore a star of David.

The yellow star
Jews in the occupied countries were ordered to wear a yellow star of David as a way of making them feel like outcasts and to facilitate rounding them up into ghettos and camps.

> "I saw German soldiers dragging Jewish men from their houses, and kicking and beating them in the street…"
>
> AREK HERSH, AGED 11, AT THE OUTBREAK OF WAR IN SIERADZ, POLAND

Jews in Warsaw
The Jews in Poland were treated with great brutality as soon as the Germans took over. In 1940 they were rounded up in the cities and herded into sealed-off ghettos.

Everywhere in Britain, unproductive land was cultivated. Even elegant Greenwich Park in London was dug up for gardens, and the government urged people to "Dig for Victory" while bombarding them with "economy" recipes. Some schools and other groups raised a communal pig on kitchen scraps. (In France, Parisians took to keeping rabbits on their balconies.) Along with the National Wheatmeal Loaf, the Woolton Pie (named after the minister of food) appeared, its ingredients infinitely variable, but excluding meat.

Circumstances varied from country to country and district to district, but in general, and unsurprisingly, people everywhere ate better if they lived in the country rather than an urban environment—especially in occupied countries where townspeople were more closely watched—and if they had the means to take advantage of the black market. This was ubiquitous though illegal, and also expensive. In France the official price of butter in 1942 was 66 francs per kilo (30 francs per lb);

on the black market it was 175 francs. In some occupied countries, such as Belgium, the turnover of the black market was possibly greater than that of the official food outlets.

In Germany, where rationing was introduced for a wide range of foodstuffs following the publication of the War Economy Decree in September 1939, civilians were probably worse off than in Britain even in the early years of the war. With the exception of workers in heavy industry who received extra rations, they were certainly less well fed—and this despite the additional food resources drawn from the conquered countries. Supplies of meat and fresh foods were reserved for the armed forces, with the result that most people's diet consisted of potatoes, black bread, and *ersatz* (substitute) foods of the type produced during World War I, such as "meat" made of vegetable flour, barley, and mushrooms. Real meat and eggs were occasional luxuries. The supply of manufactured clothing was little better, with over 40 percent being diverted to the armed forces. In 1939–40 a man's clothing allowance was 100 coupons, but he needed 80 coupons for a suit (*ersatz* cloth at that). In the occupied countries, official rations were even lower. The meat ration of an industrial worker in

German family collecting metal
As part of the drive to help the German war effort, families collected metal for use in the production of armaments and other goods for the armed forces. By 1941 between 40 and 50 percent of consumer goods went to the military, leaving little for civilians.

France was only one-third that of his or her German equivalent, while the bread ration was one-half.

There were shortages in virtually all kinds of consumer goods throughout Europe, including—though to a lesser degree—neutral countries such as Sweden. Some industries disappeared altogether, or were diverted to different purposes, for the course of the war. Children's toys were just one example of goods that soon became almost unobtainable.

THE WAR ECONOMY

The governments of the combatant nations adopted extensive powers that enabled them to impose tight controls on virtually all aspects of the economy and society and divert resources to where they were needed. In Germany they were transferred from the civilian to the military economy on a greater scale than elsewhere. This did not mean, however, that Germany's requirements for armaments were met from the outset. The armed forces established a system of inspectorates to oversee armaments production, but attempting to do the same job were the Economics and Labor Ministries. The resulting lack of centralization meant that the war economy was extemely inefficient, a situation that Hitler sought to rectify by appointing Albert Speer as minister for armaments and munitions in February 1942. By rationalizing the whole system, Speer succeeded in trebling armaments production. Only in 1944, when the Allied bombing of German cities and industrial installations caused major devastation, did Speer begin to struggle to maintain the output of the war economy.

German air-raid poster
Germans were warned to observe the blackout during bombing raids with the words "The Enemy Sees Your Light."

GERMANY TRIUMPHANT
1940–41

THE EVACUATION OF THE BRITISH EXPEDITIONARY FORCE (BEF) FROM DUNKIRK AND THE FALL OF FRANCE IN JUNE 1940 OPENED NEW STRATEGIC HORIZONS FOR HITLER. WHILE THE BRITISH REFUSED TO BEND TO HIS WILL, HE WAS NOW IN A POSITION TO MULTIPLY THE FRONTS ON WHICH THEY WOULD BE FORCED TO FIGHT—IN THE ATLANTIC, THE MEDITERRANEAN, AND NORTH AFRICA. ABOVE ALL, HE COULD NOW GIVE HIS ATTENTION TO A LONG-CHERISHED CAMPAIGN—THE INVASION AND CONQUEST OF THE SOVIET UNION.

Military pride
Hitler gives the Nazi salute to the Wehrmacht guard of honor at a march past in Unter den Linden, Berlin, on March 16, 1941. In Nazi Germany the day commemorated national heroes.

THE FÜHRER IN COMMAND

HITLER HAD SECURED A STUNNING VICTORY IN THE BATTLE OF FRANCE, WHICH NOW ALLOWED HIM TO DOMINATE GERMAN DECISION MAKING ON THE STRATEGIC COURSE OF THE WAR. WHILE BEING CONVINCED OF HIS OWN MILITARY GENIUS, HITLER WAS IN FACT A POOR STRATEGIST, AND HE COMMITTED GERMANY TO FIGHTING ON AN EVER-WIDENING NUMBER OF FRONTS. THIS WAS TO LEAD TO A FATEFUL DECISION.

O N JULY 19, 1940, in the first flush of the victory won in France, and in a conscious echo of Napoleon, Hitler created 12 new field marshals and elevated Hermann Göring, chief of the Luftwaffe, to the rank of Reichsmarschall. He also made an hour-long speech in which, as "the victor speaking in the name of reason," he appealed to the British to come to terms. He "could see no reason why this war should go on." Almost a month later he told his new field marshals that Germany "was not striving to smash Britain" because the ultimate beneficiaries of its destruction would not be Germany, but rather Japan in the east, Russia in India, Italy in the Mediterranean, and the United States in world trade. He still hoped for peace with Britain—indeed, he considered it inevitable that Britain would have no alternative but to capitulate.

THE FIRST "HAPPY TIME"

The capture of naval bases on the Norwegian and French Atlantic coasts gave Germany the chance to starve the British into submission by deploying its U-boat fleet, commerce raiders, heavy units of its surface fleet, and long-range patrol aircraft. The British had adopted the convoy system in 1939, but they were hamstrung by a shortage of escorts, many of which were retained in home waters until the fear of invasion passed. This left the field free for Admiral Karl Dönitz's U-boats to operate in "wolf packs," attacking the U-boats at night. The U-boat crews were to remember this period as the "Happy Time," and between July and October 1940 they sank 217 ships for the loss of only two U-boats.

The commander-in-chief of the German Navy, Grand Admiral Erich Raeder, urged Hitler to strike at Britain in the Mediterranean Sea by capturing Gibraltar at the western end, in the so-called Felix Plan, and to apply pressure at the eastern end in the Balkans. He also advocated the seizure of French North Africa—as a means of supporting Italy in Libya and threatening the British in Egypt—and the capture of the Spanish and Portuguese possessions of the Azores, Canaries, and Cape Verde islands, so severing Britain's supply lines in the western and mid-Atlantic. This prospect appealed to Hitler, but would also further exacerbate Germany's relations with the United States. At this stage, Hitler did not rate the United States as a military power. Nevertheless, he was an unqualified admirer of its industrial might and was reluctant to add it to his growing list of enemies.

CAMPAIGNS IN THE BALKANS

On October 4, 1940, Hitler met Mussolini at the Brenner Pass, on the border between Germany and Italy. Here it was decided to enlist the support of a third dictator, the Spanish General Franco, in the Felix Plan by offering him part of French North Africa. Vichy France would be compensated with a chunk of British West Africa. However, neither Franco nor Marshal Pétain, the leader of Vichy France who impressed Hitler with his hostility to Britain, would entertain the plan. Hitler's calculations were thrown into further disarray when, on October 28, Mussolini—piqued at not being consulted about the movement of German troops into Romania earlier in the month—launched an invasion of Greece from Albania. There was, perhaps, a sound strategic reason for Mussolini to deprive the British of naval and air bases in the Adriatic, but the principal driving force for his Greek adventure was an overweening desire to emulate Hitler, a former admirer whose power now far outstripped his own.

The immediate effect of the Italian invasion of Greece was to torpedo Hitler's attempts to secure the Balkans as a compliant satellite zone by peaceful diplomacy. Hard on its heels came the British decision to occupy the islands of Crete and Lemnos, placing the Romanian oilfields—the principal source of German oil—within the range of British bombers. The invasion foundered as soon as it ran into determined Greek resistance, which steadily pushed the Italians back beyond the Albanian border. Hitler watched with growing

"We've already reached our first objective, which we weren't supposed to get to until the end of May. The British are falling over each other to get away. Our casualties small. Booty can't be estimated."

GENERAL ERWIN ROMMEL IN A LETTER TO HIS WIFE, DESCRIBING
THE GERMAN OFFENSIVE IN NORTH AFRICA IN APRIL 1941

Tank battle in Libya
Panzer Mark IIs of Rommel's Afrika Korps block the progress of the British offensive, Operation Crusader, in November 1941. A grim two-week tank battle was fought around the airfield at Sidi Rezegh as the British tried to break through to Tobruk.

> "The fight will be very different from the fight in the west; in the east harshness is kindness toward the future. The leaders must force themselves to sacrifice their scruples."

FROM THE DIARY OF FRANZ HALDER, GERMAN ARMY CHIEF OF STAFF, AFTER A SPEECH BY HITLER TO SENIOR OFFICERS, MARCH 30, 1941

concern before deciding to intervene. In March 1941 he successfully pressured Bulgaria into joining Germany and Italy in the Axis and then did the same to a reluctant Yugoslavia, which subsequently agreed to permit the transit of German troops.

OPERATIONS IN AFRICA

Mussolini, who was fast becoming a strategic embarrassment, also needed propping up. Luftwaffe formations were despatched to Sicily and, in February 1941, General Rommel was appointed commander of the German force sent to support the Italian troops in Libya, where in the previous three months a large Italian army under Marshal Rodolfo Graziani had been forced to retreat by the much smaller British Western Desert Force under General Sir Richard O'Connor. A month later, O'Connor was taken prisoner during Rommel's first offensive in North Africa. Between March and June 1941 Rommel was to recapture all of the territory taken by the British since December 1940.

On March 27, 1941 the government of Yugoslavia was overthrown (just two days after the country had joined the Axis), and the regent, Prince Paul, was forced into exile. The new government immediately made friendly overtures to the Soviet Union and Britain. Hitler's response was to go on the offensive in the Balkans in Operation Marita, which was launched on April 6, 1941. Yugoslavia was overrun in ten days, and the conquest of Greece took just over two weeks. The British evacuated some 18,000 troops from Greece to Crete, which was captured by the Germans at the end of May after an airborne invasion. Nine British warships were sunk and a total of 17 badly damaged in a second evacuation.

The German victory in Crete was gained at a cost of nearly 10,000 casualties. Alarmed by the scale of these losses, Hitler canceled a proposed airborne seizure of the strategically crucial British colony of Malta, in the central Mediterranean, which was supplied by regular naval convoys from Gibraltar. Both the convoys and the island continued to suffer constant attacks from the Luftwaffe and the Italian air force, but the island remained an Allied stronghold, serving as the vital link in the supply line between Gibraltar and Alexandria.

RELATIONS WITH THE SOVIET UNION

In early November 1940 Hitler had conferred with the Soviet foreign minister, Molotov, in Berlin, but their talks had been unproductive. Molotov was unimpressed by an offer to share with Germany the spoils of a dismembered British Empire and insisted on the full implementation of the terms of the Nazi-Soviet Pact. He also demanded that the Soviet Union should be free to annex Finland and should have freedom of access to the North Sea via the Baltic—a matter of extreme sensitivity to Germany. In addition, he wanted Bulgaria's borders to be guaranteed. When he finally departed, an enraged Hitler was convinced that the final confrontation with Bolshevism could be delayed no longer.

Since October 1940, when Hitler had canceled Operation Sea Lion—the projected invasion of England—his overriding strategic preoccupation had been the invasion of the Soviet Union. He was

German troops at the Parthenon
The Germans entered Athens almost unopposed on April 27, 1941, while Greek troops helped cover the evacuation of the British expeditionary force. The Germans had conquered Yugoslavia and Greece in less than three weeks.

driven by the conviction that German hegemony in Europe could be secured only by the seizing of *Lebensraum* (living space) in the east and, with it, the industry and agricultural land that would ensure Germany's survival as a world power. A new German empire would reach a line stretching south from Archangel to Astrakhan, the so-called "A-A line," some 2,000 miles (3,200 km) east of Berlin.

In July 1940 Hitler informed Field Marshal Walther von Brauchitsch, commander-in-chief of the German Army, and General Franz Halder, his chief of staff, that the transfer of divisions from western Europe to the east was to be accelerated. By the spring of 1941, 120 German divisions would be massed on the border of the Soviet Union, ostensibly as a response to the Soviet occupation of the Baltic states of Latvia, Lithuania, and Estonia in June 1940, and the annexation of Bessarabia and Bukovina from Romania in the same month.

PLANNING THE INVASION

From the summer of 1940 both OKW (the German armed forces high command) and OKH (the German Army high command) were preoccupied with drafting plans for the invasion of the Soviet Union. The evolution of the operation went through three distinct phases. In August 1940 the initial plans placed the principal thrusts in the north, through Byelorussia and toward Moscow, and in the south toward Kiev. In December, Halder proposed a variant, adding a third thrust in the direction of Leningrad and strengthening the drive on Moscow, where Soviet political authority was concentrated, at the expense of the advance on Kiev. To this Hitler added his own variant, in which the emphasis shifted north, with Leningrad as the main objective, while the operation in the south was reduced to the occupation of the western Ukraine.

At joint staff discussions held in Berlin on December 5, the specter of Napoleon's retreat from Moscow in 1812 was a nagging reminder of the perils inherent in an invasion of the Soviet Union. The sheer scale of the country's interior threatened to swallow the armies of the Third Reich just as it

had devoured Napoleon's Grande Armée in 1812. However, Hitler believed that the Red Army could be destroyed close to the frontier in a series of "cauldron battles" in which fast-moving German armor would encircle the Red Army's major elements in huge pockets before they were ground to bits by the follow-up infantry.

The joint staff deliberations of early December 1940 were embodied in Führer Directive 21, which was issued on December 18. At Hitler's insistence the directive emphasized the destruction of the Red Army in the Baltic region and the capture of Leningrad at the expense of the drive on Moscow in the central sector. The directive also gave the operation a codename, Barbarossa, after the medieval Holy Roman Emperor, and laid down that planning was to be completed by mid-May 1941.

German treatment of Soviet partisans
Members of a German army execution squad force Soviet partisans to dig their own graves. The German troops who invaded the Soviet Union in June 1941 often treated civilians in the conquered territories with great cruelty.

Hitler's intervention in the Balkans in the spring of 1941 was to delay the launch of Operation Barbarossa by approximately a month, to June 22, 1941. The extent to which this affected the operation's outcome is debatable. What is certain is that the delay had less of an impact than the confusion about the operation's precise goals, which had been introduced by Hitler at the planning stage in December 1940. Combined with the unforgiving Soviet climate, this confusion was fatally to undermine Hitler's greatest strategic gamble.

NAVAL WAR IN EUROPEAN AND ATLANTIC WATERS

SEPTEMBER 1939–SEPTEMBER 1941

Despite losses to U-boats, bombers, and mines and the failure of the Allied expedition to Norway, up until June 1940 Britain was able to contain the German threat at sea. The fall of France in June 1940 altered everything. From their new bases in western France U-boats began to wreak havoc on British convoys.

1939

SEPTEMBER 3
U 30 sinks British liner Athenia sailing from Glasgow to Montreal

SEPTEMBER 3
Britain and France declare war on Germany

SEPTEMBER 15
First sinking of ship in North Atlantic convoy by U-boat

SEPTEMBER 30
Pocket battleship Graf Spee starts campaign against shipping in South Atlantic and Indian Ocean

OCTOBER 14
Battleship Royal Oak sunk by U 47 in Scapa Flow

NOVEMBER
German magnetic mines inflict serious losses on British east coast shipping

DECEMBER 13–17
Battle of the River Plate; Admiral Graf Spee scuttled off Montevideo, Uruguay, on 17th

1940

FEBRUARY 16
British destroyer rescues prisoners from German ship Altmark in Norwegian waters

APRIL 9
German occupation of Denmark and landings in Norway between Oslo and Narvik

MAY 5
Germans capture British submarine Seal with complete set of naval ciphers

APRIL 10 & 13
Naval battles at Narvik

JUNE 17
Lancastria, Cunard liner serving as troopship, sunk off St. Nazaire

JUNE 4–8
Allied evacuation of northern Norway

JUNE 22
Fall of France

JULY 6
First U-boat base in France established in Lorient

JULY 3
British bombard French warships in North African ports of Oran and Mers el-Kebir

AUGUST 17
Hitler announces "total blockade" of Britain

SEPTEMBER
First use of wolfpack tactics devised by Admiral Dönitz

SEPTEMBER 28
First of 50 old destroyers, sent by US in exchange for bases, reaches Britain

OCTOBER 16–20
U-boat wolfpack attacks two Atlantic convoys, sinking 32 ships. No U-boats lost

OCTOBER 23
Sortie by heavy cruiser Admiral Scheer. Start of major German warship campaign against shipping

1941

NOVEMBER 5
Admiral Scheer sinks cruiser Jervis Bay in attack on convoy HX-84

JANUARY 21
German battleships Scharnhorst and Gneisenau sail from Kiel

FEBRUARY 1
German heavy cruiser Admiral Hipper sails from Brest

MAY 9
British capture Enigma cipher machine and codebooks after boarding U 110 south of Iceland

MAY 18
Sortie of German battleship Bismarck and heavy cruiser Prinz Eugen into North Atlantic. British battlecruiser Hood sunk on 24th

MAY 27
Bismarck hunted down and sunk. End of German warship operations in Atlantic

JULY
U-boat effort concentrated in mid-Atlantic

JULY 7
Arrival of US garrison forces in Iceland

AUGUST 21
First Arctic convoy leaves Iceland for Archangel

SEPTEMBER 27
First Liberty ship launched

SEPTEMBER 15
US Navy provides escorts for British ships as far as Iceland

North Atlantic
Jun 22–Dec 6, 1941

Naval actions in other theaters
Jun 22–Dec 6, 1941

Other events

THE WAR AT SEA

At the outbreak of war in September 1939, Britain and France enjoyed a major strategic advantage over Germany at sea. Their geographical position allowed them to cut off German lines of communication with the world beyond Europe, and their command of ports, coaling stations, and narrows throughout the world meant that German oceanic trade all but ended with the start of war. A total of 76 ships returned to Germany, evading Allied patrols, but the greater part of German shipping outside Europe sought the safety of neutral ports.

Britain and France also had a huge advantage in terms of numbers. For most of the interwar period the size of the Kriegsmarine (the German Navy) and of individual warships was limited by treaty, and the coming of war in 1939 found Germany massively outnumbered in every type of warship. In September 1939 it had just four battleships, three armoured, one heavy, and three light cruisers, 34 destroyers, and 57 submarines. It also had no air arm of its own, and in the early part of the war the Luftwaffe proved uncooperative. Jealous of its independence and primarily committed to air support of the army, the Luftwaffe had little interest in naval operations. At any rate, it had very few long-range aircraft suitable for operations over the sea.

Coastal U-boat
In 1939 Germany had more Class II coastal U-boats than any other kind. These were only suitable for operations in the Baltic or North Sea, not for long-range missions.

British minesweepers in the North Sea
At the start of the war the greatest danger to British shipping was not the U-boat, but mines. The danger was contained, but only at the expense of a heavy defensive commitment. In May 1945 the British had over 700 minesweepers and auxiliaries.

submerged submarines—would be enough to defeat the U-boat menace. With the outbreak of war the British intention was to close the Dover Strait by defensive mining and to mine and patrol northern waters, while RAF Coastal Command covered the North Sea. Any threat outside these waters, it was believed, would be small and short-lived.

FIRST U-BOAT CAMPAIGN

The first seven months of war more or less bore out these British calculations. Without a balanced fleet and supporting air arm, German naval effectiveness was limited. At the outbreak of war Germany had only 27 ocean-going U-boats, of which 17 were at sea. There were striking successes by individual U-boats against warships, such as the sinking of the aircraft carrier *Courageous* while on antisubmarine duty in the Western Approaches and of the battleship *Royal Oak* at Scapa Flow. The U-boat campaign against merchant shipping, however, did not give Britain cause for serious alarm. In 1939 German submarines sank 114 merchantmen, but only 12 of these were sailing in convoy. The cycle of operations, with U-boats returning to port for refitting, meant that the rate of monthly sinkings actually declined in November–December 1939.

SURFACE RAIDERS AND MINES

For the first six months of the war most German surface warships remained in port. The armored cruiser (or "pocket battleship") *Admiral Graf Spee* made a menacing sortie and succeeded in sinking nine merchantmen in the South Atlantic and the Indian Ocean. She was eventually intercepted by three cruisers in December at the Battle of the Plate River. The captain scuttled the ship after seeking refuge in Montevideo. The first German auxiliary cruisers sailed in March 1940. In all, six of these raiders—converted merchantmen with concealed guns and torpedo tubes, equipped for long voyages—sailed in the spring of 1940. It was not until July, however, that these raiders managed to sink 10 merchantmen in a single month.

In many ways the most effective German weapon in the early months of the war was the mine. Between September 1939 and April 1940 a total of 128 merchantmen of 429,899 tons were sunk by mines

Torpedo room
The standard German torpedo was electrically driven. Armed with a warhead of 617 lb (280 kg), it was 21 in (53.3 cm) in diameter.

This latter part of the action has attracted many spectators and, unfortunately, their cars. Headlights along the shore with other illuminations possibly allow Graf Spee to detect our stealthy approach, and at 20:48 when we race past, guns in her huge turrets wave like a robot's arms elevating whilst training on to our blurred outline. And then she lurches under her own heavy recoil, thunder rolls across a grey sky to quicken the heartbeats of excited Uruguayans watching her vivid gunflashes through enveloping bursts of cordite smoke.

FROM *HMNZS ACHILLES* BY JACK HARKER, WIRELESS TELEGRAPHIST ON THE *ACHILLES* AT THE BATTLE OF THE PLATE RIVER

laid by German U-boats, destroyers, and aircraft. This was about a third of all Allied and neutral losses to mines in the course of the whole war. The reason for this success was the use of a magnetic firing mechanism that detonated as a ship passed over the mine. Fortunately for the British merchant fleet, metal hulls could be demagnetized and new methods of minesweeping were soon developed to counter the threat. Even so, mines continued to cause serious delays and disruption to shipping.

In the interwar period the German Navy, despite the failure of its submarine campaign against shipping in World War I, convinced itself that the war at sea was an economic, not a military struggle. The seeking of battle at sea was a distraction to be avoided. German naval staff argued that if they could sink 750,000 tons of shipping every month for a year Britain would be defeated. This was exactly the same "tonnage war" argument that it had used in 1916, the necessary tonnage having increased slightly in the intervening years.

BRITISH ASSUMPTIONS

Throughout the interwar period Britain had paid little attention to the defense of shipping. There was a general confidence that use of convoys—along with ASDIC, the sonar system for locating

ENIGMA AND ULTRA

ENIGMA, THE GERMAN ENCODING MACHINE developed in the 1920s and 1930s, was a portable electromechanical device resembling a typewriter. Each keystroke set in motion a series of rotors and electrical circuits. The Germans believed that the system was totally secure. Even with a captured machine, the enemy needed to know the current code and settings for the day. The German services each had different codes: the Luftwaffe's were relatively simple, those of the navy the most complex. The Poles had managed to read some Enigma messages during the 1930s and their assistance was of great value to the British decryption unit set up in Bletchley Park in 1939.

Intelligence gathered from Enigma intercepts was highly sensitive. The Allies could not let the Germans know that they were able to read coded radio signals. Intelligence gathered in this way was code-named Ultra and was used with extreme caution. The Germans never realized that their Enigma codes had been cracked.

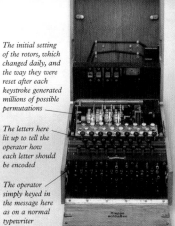

The initial setting of the rotors, which changed daily, and the way they were reset after each keystroke generated millions of possible permutations

The letters here lit up to tell the operator how each letter should be encoded

The operator simply keyed in the message here as on a normal typewriter

Enigma machine
As the machine spelled out the coded message, this was copied down letter by letter, then transmitted in Morse code.

U-boat surfacing
Enigma gave a fairly constant picture of U-boat positions, often allowing convoys to be rerouted.

The war at sea was completely transformed in spring 1940 with the German occupation of Norway and northern and western France. At a stroke German warships, submarines, and bombers could reach far out into the North Atlantic to strike directly at Allied shipping. At the same time the threat of invasion meant that the British navy had to keep large numbers of warships in home waters even at the expense of the shipping and trade on which Britain depended. In addition, Italy's entry into the war meant a greater naval commitment in the Mediterranean and also forced shipping to make

the lengthy diversion around the Cape of Good Hope. Such were the circumstances that made for what the Germans came to call their first *Glückliche Zeit* (Happy Time), when their submarines began to inflict serious losses on Allied and neutral shipping.

A TRIPLE ASSAULT ON SHIPPING

Between September 1939 and July 1941 German U-boats sank 848 British, Allied, and neutral merchantmen of 4,058,909 tons, for the loss of just 43 of their number. U-boats, however, were not the only threat to Britain's vital trade. In the first five months of 1941, when Allied shipping losses averaged 490,456 tons a month, the Luftwaffe accounted for about 30 percent of the total. The Luftwaffe did not begin operations in the Atlantic under the control of the U-boat arm until February 1941. Many of its successes in this period, however, were obtained not in the Atlantic, but in the eastern Mediterranean by short-range bombers during the German conquest of Greece in April 1941.

These results were complemented by four sorties into the Atlantic by warships between October 1940 and May 1941,

which accounted for 47 merchantmen of 254,759 tons and caused massive disruption in convoy sailings. The most successful cruise was that of the pocket battleship *Admiral Scheer*, which sailed on October 27, 1940, sank 16 ships, including three in the Indian Ocean, evaded all her pursuers, and returned to Bergen on March 30, 1941. The battleships *Scharnhorst* and *Gneisenau* enjoyed similar success, together sinking or capturing 22 ships between January and March 1941.

Perhaps the main weakness of the German war against shipping was the fact that for most of the war it was pursued primarily by the U-boat service with very little support from the Luftwaffe or from the rest of the navy. In this period, however, with major contributions from the Luftwaffe and from warships, the combined effort achieved a level of success that seemed to augur very badly for Britain.

REVERSING THE TREND

By spring 1941, however, various factors were combining to bring this period of easy German success to an end. The brief, ill-fated sortie of the battleship *Bismarck* in May spelled the end of raiding operations by major warships. After her sinking on May 27, 1941, the German naval staff concluded that, with Britain's air search and carrier strike capabilities in the North Atlantic, such operations were now too risky. This was followed by the German attack on the Soviet Union in June 1941, which led to a long-term commitment of air power to the Eastern Front. The Luftwaffe's contribution to the German effort at sea declined sharply after

Dining aboard a U-boat
Living conditions on a U-boat, with its cramped berths and limited sanitary arrangements, were not good. The men, however, were well fed. When fresh food ran out, there were hams and sausages, and canned vegetables and fruit.

The apparatus was powered by rechargeable battery

The telephone was used principally by the captain for issuing orders and receiving status reports

Portable telephone from *U 219*
Telephones were used for communication between the various parts of a U-boat, for example the boiler room, the torpedo rooms, and even the conning tower.

May 1941. In 1941 the Luftwaffe accounted for 23.5 percent of Allied losses, but this was reduced to a mere 9 percent in 1942.

STRENGTHENING THE CONVOYS

The most important British countermeasure was the introduction in July 1941 of continuous two-way escort across the North Atlantic. Despite the loss of 55 destroyers and eight escorts, Britain now had 395 escorts with another 306 under construction. It was slowly acquiring sufficient numbers to establish a comprehensive convoy system throughout and beyond the North Atlantic. Since January 1941 escorts had been equipped with radar, the first step in stripping U-boats of their invisibility when conducting attacks on the surface under cover of darkness. This was backed up by new, more powerful depth charges and more effective firing patterns.

Convoys could now count on reconnaissance and support provided by increasing numbers of aircraft, equipped with effective airborne radar and improved weapons, including airborne depth charges. Aircraft were deployed to Iceland in April 1941 and the first escort carrier accompanied a convoy in September.

For the first 18 months of the war the German Navy had held a clear intelligence advantage over the British. B-Dienst (Beobachtungs-Dienst, the

U-boats in dry dock
German U-boats *U 106* and *U 124* undergo repairs in the French port of Brest. Only a small fraction of total U-boat strength was operational at any one time.

German intelligence service) had broken British naval codes and could quickly decipher radio traffic. In the course of 1941, however, the British managed to crack the German Navy's Enigma code. Messages took time to decipher, but the two sides were now competing on more equal terms. The British had also developed better means of locating and tracking broadcasting U-boats.

In April 1941 the United States claimed that its defense zone extended as far as 26° West, almost to Iceland. After July all US shipping was escorted to and from Iceland and after September US ships also escorted British shipping in the Western Atlantic. Hitler, seeking to avoid a clash with the United States, scaled back German operations in

the North Atlantic. U-boats now operated chiefly in waters where British escorts were at their most numerous. Construction programs, meanwhile, lagged behind the German Navy's requirements. In February 1941 just 21 U-boats were operational. There were simply not enough to take advantage of British vulnerability. Between June and December 1941 monthly Allied shipping losses fell to an average of 268,039 tons, a decrease of 5.4 percent from the average over the previous five months.

THE SINKING OF THE BISMARCK

AT 42,000 TONS AND ARMED with eight 15-in (38-cm) guns, the *Bismarck* and her sister ship the *Tirpitz* were Germany's two most powerful battleships. The British had been awaiting their completion with some trepidation. First to be commisssioned was the *Bismarck* in August 1940. After trials in the Baltic she sailed from Gotenhafen in the Gulf of Danzig in May 1941. Then, accompanied by the heavy cruiser *Prinz Eugen*, she left the Baltic for the North Sea.

The British knew the ships were heading for the Atlantic and despatched patrols to hunt for them. On May 23 the two ships were spotted in the Denmark Strait between Iceland and Greenland and the following day the battleship *Prince of Wales* and the battlecruiser *Hood* intercepted them. Both the *Bismarck* and the *Prinz Eugen* concentrated their fire on the *Hood*. A shell struck the British ship's magazine, causing a massive explosion, and she split in two. Only three of her crew of 1,421 survived.

The *Bismarck* had been damaged in the encounter and received minor damage that night when hit by a Swordfish torpedo-bomber from the carrier *Victorious*. Her admiral then decided to make for Brest, but on May 26 she was spotted by a Catalina flying boat, then crippled in an attack by Swordfish from the carrier *Ark Royal*. The next day, as British warships from across the Atalantic closed in for the kill, she was sunk by the battleships *King George V* and *Rodney*.

The fortunate few
Survivors from the *Bismarck* struggle to climb aboard the cruiser *Dorsetshire*. Only 115 of the 2,222 officers and men in the *Bismarck* were rescued.

The *Bismarck* in action
This picture of the *Bismarck* firing on the *Prince of Wales*, after the sinking of the *Hood*, was taken from the *Prinz Eugen* on the morning of May 24.

AFRICA, THE MIDDLE EAST, AND THE MEDITERRANEAN
JUNE 1940–FEBRUARY 1942

Italy aimed to challenge Britain for control of the Mediterranean and to move on Egypt and the Suez Canal, and the British colonies in East Africa. In addition to these threats, the British had to fight to counter German influence in the Middle East. Early in 1941, as Italian offensives collapsed, Germany was forced to come to the aid of its weaker ally.

1940

JUNE 11
Italian planes bomb Malta, following a declaration of war on Britain and France the previous day

JULY 4
Italians capture British border posts in Sudan

AUGUST 4
Italian invasion of British Somaliland from Ethiopia

SEPTEMBER 13
Italian troops invade Egypt from Libya

NOVEMBER 11/12
Successful British air attack on Italian fleet in Taranto harbor

DECEMBER 9
Start of British campaign (Operation Compass) to drive Italians back across Libya

JANUARY 10
First Luftwaffe action in Mediterranean. Carrier *Illustrious* badly damaged

1941

JANUARY 21
Haile Selassie and troops enter Abyssinia from Sudan

JANUARY 24
British invasion of Italian Somaliland from Kenya

FEBRUARY 12
Rommel lands in Tripoli to assume command of Axis forces in North Africa

MARCH 6
German aircraft mine Suez Canal. It remains blocked for three weeks

MARCH 24
Rommel starts to drive British out of Libya

APRIL 3
Pro-Axis coup by Rashid Ali in Iraq

APRIL 11
Rommel attacks Tobruk, but defense holds

APRIL 25
British driven back to defensive positions in western Egypt

MAY 5
Triumphal entry of Haile Selassie into Addis Ababa

MAY 27
British forces enter Iraq; Rashid Ali flees to Iran on May 30

JUNE 8
British and Free French invasion of Syria and Lebanon

JUNE 15
Disastrous Operation Battleaxe fails to break through Axis lines on Egyptian-Libyan border

JULY 14
Armistice signed in Syria

JULY 31–AUGUST 2
Malta garrison reinforced by "Style" convoy

AUGUST 25
British and Russian troops invade Iran

SEPTEMBER 16
Reza Shah, ruler of Iran, abdicates in favor of his son

SEPTEMBER 4
Heavy bombing raid by Germans and Italians on Malta

NOVEMBER
Reconquest of Abyssinia completed

NOVEMBER 18
British offensive, Operation Crusader, launched. Rommel initially caught by surprise

NOVEMBER 24
Rommel's "Dash to the Wire." Tanks push eastward in attempt to cut off British 8th Army from supply routes

DECEMBER 15
Rommel orders withdrawal from Cyrenaica

1942

JANUARY 21
Rommel begins spectacular attack across Cyrenaica

JANUARY 29
Germans take Benghazi

FEBRUARY 6
Rommel's offensive comes to halt in front of Gazala-Bir Hacheim Line

■ Mediterranean Jun 1940–Feb 1942   ■ East Africa Jul 1940–Nov 1941
■ North Africa Sept 1940–Feb 1942   ■ Middle East Jun–Sept 1941

CAMPAIGNS IN AFRICA AND THE MIDDLE EAST

Mussolini's decision to bring Italy into the war immediately opened another theater—the Mediterranean and North Africa. With France rapidly collapsing, the initial phase would be fought just between an Italy determined to make the Mediterranean its own and expand its African empire and a Britain desperate to maintain its lines of communication through the Mediterranean and the Suez Canal. While the British Mediterranean Fleet and Force H based in Gibraltar could match the Italian Navy, on land and in the air British forces faced overwhelmingly superior numbers. Including those based on the mainland, the Italians had some 1,700 aircraft; the British had a mere 205 serviceable planes in Egypt and a further 163 in East Africa. Most were obsolete or obsolescent and, with the Battle of Britain about to begin, there was little prospect of any reinforcement. On the ground the situation appeared even more desperate. To protect Egypt and police Palestine and Iraq, the British had just 63,000 troops. The main threat came from Libya, which had 250,000 Italian and indigenous troops, while to the south 300,000 more Italian and native troops in Abyssinia and Eritrea faced a mere 10,000 British troops in Sudan, British Somaliland, and Kenya. At sea the British were determined to bring the Italians into battle, but elsewhere they naturally opted for the defensive.

FIRST CLASHES

There were minor bombing raids by both sides during the first few weeks. A naval clash took place off the Calabrian coast on July 9, 1940. The Italian fleet withdrew to port after its flagship was damaged. On the ground, the British were expecting the Italians to invade Egypt from Libya. To keep them off balance, they adopted a policy of aggressive patrolling on the Libyan side of the border. The first Italian move, however, came on July 4, when they seized a number of frontier posts on Sudan's borders with Abyssinia and Eritrea. This was followed in early August by an invasion of British Somaliland from Abyssinia. After two weeks' fighting, the small British garrison was withdrawn to Aden. Churchill now took the brave step, in view of Britain's parlous position, of sending further ships to reinforce the

German reinforcements, April 1941

Airplanes and tanks made operations in Libya extremely mobile, as the two sides took turns pursuing the other across the desert. Here, German light tanks, recently arrived in Tripoli, are marshaled in preparation for Rommel's first offensive in March 1941.

Mediterranean Fleet and a troop convoy, which included 150 tanks. This, however, had to be routed around the Cape of Good Hope and did not reach Egypt until late September. By this time, the Italians had entered Egypt from Libya. After advancing a mere 60 miles (100 km), they halted and established a network of fortified camps. The arrival of the additional British tanks deterred them from pressing toward the Suez Canal.

BRITISH SUCCESS

General Sir Archibald Wavell, the British commander in the Middle East, now set in motion preparations for a counteroffensive in Egypt and for the conquest of Italian East Africa. At sea, the British adopted the policy of using supply convoys to Malta to tempt the Italian fleet out of the port. This was unsuccessful and so Admiral Sir Andrew Cunningham conceived a daring plan. On the night of November 11–12, 1940, carrier-borne torpedo-armed Swordfish aircraft attacked the naval base at

Taranto, severely damaging three of Italy's six battleships, and forcing its fleet to withdraw to more distant bases on Italy's west coast.

Wavell's attack on the Italians in Egypt was launched in the early hours of December 9. The troops

The Swordfish had a top speed of 138 mph (222 kph) and just one rear machine-gun for protection

The normal bombload was a single 1,610-lb (730-kg) torpedo carried under the fuselage

Fixed undercarriage

Aircraft carriers

British aircraft carriers, such as the *Ark Royal* (above), played a vital role in the protection of Mediterranean convoys. The main offensive carrier aircraft was the obsolete torpedo-bomber, the Fairey Swordfish (left).

taking part thought that it was merely an exercise until shortly before H-hour. This tight security worked, since the Italians were taken totally by surprise. Within two days their camps had been overrun and after a further 24 hours they were left with just three small toeholds in Egypt. At this juncture, Wavell replaced the 4th Indian Division, which was sent to Sudan in preparation for the offensive against East Africa, with the newly arrived

6th Australian Division. The Australians took the port of Bardia on January 5 and advanced along the coast, reaching Tobruk two days later. The port was besieged, but the British needed to pause since their rapid advance was overstretching their supply lines, a problem that was to characterize the Desert War. However, the fall of Tobruk on January 22 did much to ease the supply situation. Wavell now gave orders to push on to Benghazi.

THE ISLAND OF MALTA UNDER SIEGE

MALTA'S KEY STRATEGIC POSITION made it the traditional base of the British Mediterranean Fleet. When Italy declared war in June 1940, one of its first acts was an air attack on the island, which lies just 60 miles (100 km) from Sicily. The Italians knew that if they could seize it, they would deny the British the central Mediterranean and remove a major threat to their supply lines to North Africa. The air offensive against Malta intensified when Luftwaffe units were deployed to Sicily at the beginning of 1941. Even though they had moved their main fleet base to Alexandria, the British were determined to hang on to Malta, but the cost would be high. Every supply convoy had to have a heavy naval escort and during the two years beginning August 1940 over one-third of the merchant vessels sent out never reached the island. Food became desperately short and the Maltese had to endure starvation rations, as well as the destruction of much of the island's infrastructure.

Valletta under bombardment

During March and April 1942 alone, Axis aircraft dropped twice the bomb tonnage on Malta that London had endured in the Blitz.

The bombing did ease in June 1941, when many Luftwaffe units were redeployed for the invasion of the Soviet Union, but at the end of the year it

resumed in intensity. Even so, Malta-based aircraft and submarines continued to disrupt the Axis supply lines. The German commander-in-chief in the Mediterranean, Field Marshal Albert Kesselring, was determined to break Malta's resistance. The Axis had laid so many minefields in the waters around Malta that it was almost impossible for a ship to get in or out and by early May Kesselring was convinced that Malta had been neutralized. He therefore diverted many of his Luftwaffe units to other missions. The arrival, however, of some much needed replacement fighters restored morale on the island, as did the clearance of lanes in some of the minefields. But the crisis was not yet over.

In June a crucial convoy failed to get through and rations on the island were cut to 1,500 calories per day. Kesselring then launched a further air assault in October, but Montgomery's victory at El Alamein and the subsequent capture of the Axis airfields in Libya eased the situation once more. The siege was not yet over, but food and other essentials now got through on a regular basis.

George Cross

In recognition of the steadfast resistance of the islanders, King George VI awarded Malta the George Cross, Britain's highest decoration for civilian bravery.

While the Australians pursued the Italian 10th Army along the coast road, the 7th Armoured Division was sent inland to the base of the Cyrenaican "bulge," which is dominated by the semimountainous Jebel el Akhdar. The Australians were temporarily stalled by a strong Italian position just to the west of Derna. Simultaneously, RAF reconnaissance reported that the Italians were evacuating the port of Benghazi. General Dick O'Connor, the operational commander, decided to send the 7th Armoured Division to cut the coast road south of Benghazi. The tanks drove 150 miles (240 km) in 33 hours over rock-strewn terrain and arrived at the road, 70 miles (110 km) south of Benghazi, late on February 5. They were just in time to establish a blocking position.

During the next two days, as the Australians secured Benghazi, the 7th Armoured Division fended off repeated Italian attempts to break through. Eventually, the Italians decided that they had had enough and 20,000 surrendered, adding to the total of 100,000 prisoners already netted during the campaign. The Battle of Beda Fomm marked the final destruction of the Italian 10th Army and the capture of the whole of the eastern Libyan province of Cyrenaica. It was also the British Army's first significant victory of the war. The triumph would, however, be short-lived.

ERITREA AND ABYSSINIA

Meanwhile, Wavell had launched another offensive, this time into Italian East Africa. His plan was for General William Platt, with two Indian divisions, to attack into Eritrea from Sudan. At much the same time, three divisions under General Alan Cunningham, brother of the Admiral, were to advance into Abyssinia from the south. Emperor Haile Selassie and his small force would enter from the west. Sensing what was about to happen and demoralized because of the increasingly grim news from Libya, the Italians withdrew from the outposts they had captured in Sudan just before the offensive opened. Platt crossed into Eritrea on January 19, 1941. The subsequent campaign was to be no walk-over, however. After a fierce battle for Agordat, the Italians withdrew to the mountain fortress of Keren, which guarded the only approach to Asmara, the Eritrean capital. Platt closed up to this position on

The battle for Keren
Indian troops survey the debris of a skirmish near the fortified town of Keren. An Italian truck lies beside the road. Keren proved the critical battle in the British campaign in the Italian colony of Eritrea.

February 3, but, with the Italians holding all the high ground, it proved impossible to force. He therefore decided to pause in order to strengthen his forces and improve his logistics.

In contrast, Cunningham made good progress in the more open country of southern Abyssinia. On February 25, he captured the port of Mogadishu and his forces then turned northward in two separate prongs, one aimed at the western part of the country and the other the center. A further element was added on March 16, when troops from Aden landed at Berbera and, within a week, had liberated British Somaliland. By now, Platt had resumed his attacks on Keren and, after two weeks' tough fighting, the fortress finally fell on March 27. This broke the back of the Italian resistance and within two weeks both Asmara and the port of Massawa were in British hands. Simultaneously, 11th African

THE RETURN OF THE EMPEROR

IN SPITE OF THEIR CONQUEST of Abyssinia in 1935, the Italians were unable to subdue the more remote mountainous areas. But, while the British gave Emperor Haile Selassie sanctuary, they were not prepared to provide open support for any resistance.

The situation changed once Italy entered the war. In June 1940 the emperor was flown out to Sudan and settled near Khartoum under the alias of Mr. Smith. Word soon got around that he had come to reclaim his throne. British plans included an offensive from the west, which the emperor would accompany. The principal element of this offensive was Gideon Force, under the command of Orde Wingate, a British officer who had established a reputation for irregular warfare in Palestine. Haile Selassie raised his standard inside Abyssinian territory on January 21, 1941. Gideon Force then began its advance. Wingate relied on bluff and daring. All forage and food was paid for in Maria Theresa silver thalers dated 1764, which had been specially minted in Britain and was the one currency the locals respected.

Wingate's first major action came at the end of February, when, with 450 men, he surprised and routed a force of 7,000. Gideon Force then drove the Italians out of Debra Markos. Abyssinians had flocked to join their emperor and the Italians thought a whole British division was advancing against them. General Cunningham's troops had already taken Addis Ababa, but Haile Selassie, accompanied by Gideon Force, did enter his capital in triumph at the beginning of May.

Haile Selassie reviews his troops
Gideon Force, the irregular force that accompanied Haile Selassie, was made up of a Sudanese battalion and one of Abyssinian refugees known as the Patriots.

German and Italian cooperation
This propaganda photograph from the German *Signal* magazine shows German troops helping Italians manhandle a gun into position in the Libyan desert.

Division entered Addis Ababa on April 6. Yet, even with the Abyssinian capital in British hands, the campaign was not over. The Italian commander-in-chief, the Duke d'Aosta, had decided to make a stand in the fortress of Amba Alagi. It took 18 days to reduce the defenses in the hills surrounding the fortress, which finally surrendered on May 18, with the duke the last to leave it. Four days later, the fall of Soddu marked the end of the campaign in the south. The Italians continued to hold out in the mountains around Lake Tana in the northwest of Abyssinia and it would not be until the end of November 1941 that the last stronghold, Gondar, finally surrendered.

GERMAN SUPPORT FOR ITALY

Mussolini may have lost his East African empire, but in Egypt and Libya the situation changed dramatically during spring 1941. Hitler decided to give his ally some material support. He had, at the beginning of 1941, deployed elements of the Luftwaffe to Sicily to help in the air assault on Malta and an early victim was the carrier *Illustrious*, which was attacked by Stukas on January 10 and badly damaged. He also decided to send two mechanized divisions, as well as further aircraft, to Libya. Their commander, Erwin Rommel, arrived in Tripoli on February 12

and two days later his Deutsches Afrika Korps (DAK) began to unload its vehicles at the quayside. On the British side, the victors of the overrunning of Cyrenaica, 7th Armoured and 6th Australian Divisions, were sent back to the Nile Delta to reequip. Their places were taken by the newly arrived 2nd Armoured and 9th Australian Divisions, but part of the former was then diverted to Greece, where Churchill had ordered Wavell to send troops. Because there were insufficient fit British tanks available, part of the new division had to be equipped with inferior captured Italian models. At the time, though, it was not believed that the Axis would make an early attempt to regain Cyrenaica.

As early as February 24, DAK reconnaissance elements clashed with their British opposite numbers between Sirte and El Agheila. It was an indication that Rommel was impatient for action. By March 11, the first of his two divisions, the 5th Light, had deployed close to the border with Cyrenaica, but he himself was then ordered by his German superiors to await the arrival of the other division, which

was not due until the end of May, before attacking. Rommel was not, however, prepared to sit on his hands. On March 24 he drove the British out of El Agheila with comparative ease and was encouraged by this success to press on further. A week later he seized Mersa Brega and decided to clear the whole of Cyrenaica. The British were so taken by surprise that they decided on a voluntary withdrawal, but it was almost too late. Sending an Italian division up the coast road to Benghazi, Rommel took his own 5th Light Division and the Ariete Armored Division south of the Jebel el Akhdar, thus mirroring in reverse the British clearance of Cyrenaica at the beginning of the year.

Bersaglieri offroading
The Bersaglieri were a crack Italian corps of sharpshooters, who traditionally rode to the front on bicycles. In North Africa the more fortunate were issued with motorcycles.

By April 7, Rommel had cleared the Cyrenaican bulge and such was the British confusion that the new commander in Libya, General Philip Neame, and General O'Connor, who had been asked by Wavell to give him advice, were both captured. Some of their men were evacuated by sea from Tobruk, which was now to be held by 9th Australian Division with an additional brigade sent by sea from Egypt. The remainder withdrew back into Egypt. Given the disintegration of his opponent, Rommel would have liked to continue as far as the Suez Canal, but was ordered to halt on the Egyptian border and concentrate on capturing Tobruk, which had already resisted his initial attacks.

WAVELL UNDER PRESSURE

April 1941 was indeed a time of trouble for Wavell. The forces he had sent to Greece had to be withdrawn after another German blitzkrieg campaign. Then there was a revolt in Iraq led by Rashid Ali, who was in the pay of the Germans. An Indian brigade en route for Malaya had to be

The tank's main armament was
a 2-pounder (40-mm), most
effective as an antitank weapon

The Matilda's strength was its
armor. At the front of the hull,
it was 3 in (78 mm) thick

This form of camouflage—sand,
blue, and gray—was widely used
in the desert campaign

Matilda II
The British Matilda tank performed well in the opening exchanges in North Africa against antitank guns, but its armor was no match for the mighty German 88-mm gun.

The overrunning of Crete was another disaster, but no sooner had this occurred than Wavell was further distracted. Concern had been growing that the Vichy French in Syria were preparing to allow the Germans use of their airfields. This would have presented a grave threat to the British position in the Middle East. Therefore, on June 8, 1941, on Churchill's orders, Wavell invaded Syria. He had hoped that the Vichy French would offer only token resistance, but this was not to be. Not until mid-July did hostilities come to an end. By this time, Wavell had been relieved of his command.

Churchill had been determined that he strike once more at Rommel and lift the siege of Tobruk and had agreed to sending a reinforcement of tanks through the Mediterranean. This duly arrived and Wavell mounted another attack, code-named Battleaxe, on June 15. It was a disaster. Capuzzo was regained for a short time, but within 48 hours Rommel had driven the British back to their start line, with the loss of over 90 tanks. It was the last straw, as far as Churchill was concerned. Wavell was replaced by General Sir Claude Auchinleck.

THE GERMAN THREAT IN IRAN

Despite pressure from Churchill to resume the offensive against Rommel, Auchinleck wanted to wait until he had rebuilt his forces. He remained confident, however, that Tobruk would hold out. But before he could start preparing for a fresh attack, he was faced with another problem. The spectacular success the Germans were enjoying

Australian troops in Syria
The Syrian campaign was fought by Australian, Indian, British, and Free French forces. The Australians, advancing from Palestine, had nearly reached Beirut when the Vichy French requested an armistice on July 10, 1941.

in the Soviet Union created the possibility that they might launch an assault on the Middle East from the Caucasus. The Shah of Iran had adopted an anti-British stance and there were fears that he might allow the Germans free passage through his country. The Russians were equally concerned and both they and the British demanded access to Iran. When the Shah refused, they had no option but to invade, which they did on August 25. After two days, the Iranians asked for a ceasefire and installed a government more sympathetic to the Allies. Later, the Allies demanded that the Shah expel all Axis nationals and, when he was slow to do so, their troops occupied Tehran. The Shah promptly abdicated in favor of his son. Allied troops remained in Iran for the rest of the war and it became one of the routes used to keep the Soviet Union supplied with munitions from the West.

German supply planes in Libya
German and Italian forces often had to rely on aircraft for supplies. Most of planes here are Junkers Ju 52s, the three-engined transport plane that was the workhorse of the Luftwaffe throughout the war. In the right foreground is a Messerschmitt Bf 110 fighter.

hastily diverted and landed at Basra to protect the RAF airfield in Shaibah, but this did not deter Rashid Ali from laying siege to the other British air base in the country, Habbaniyah. Two more Indian brigades were landed during May, but Habbaniyah could only be relieved from the west and so Wavell had to organize a force in Palestine for this purpose. Not until the end of May was the revolt crushed.

FURTHER SUCCESS FOR ROMMEL

In the meantime, Wavell had suffered further reverses. On May 15 he launched Operation Brevity against the Axis positions on the frontier with Libya. His troops succeeded in regaining Capuzzo, Sollum, and the Halfaya Pass. But Rommel counterattacked the following day and recaptured the first two. Before the end of the month, and now finally joined by 15th Panzer Division, he also drove the British out of the Halfaya Pass. These battles brought the British up against the German 88-mm gun for the first time. Although essentially an antiaircraft weapon, it proved highly effective against armor, completely outranging the guns of the British tanks.

ERWIN ROMMEL

ERWIN ROMMEL (1891–1944) made his mark as a young officer during World War 1. He came to Hitler's attention after he had written a book on infantry tactics and commanded the Führer's security detachment during the Polish campaign. Hitler rewarded him with command of a panzer division for the campaign in the West, then in 1941 with command of the Afrika Korps. Rommel soon became a national hero, also gaining the respect of the British. He always liked to lead from the front and had an ability to sense the critical point on the battlefield. In summer 1942 he became the youngest German Field Marshal, but, after being stalled at El Alamein, was forced onto the defensive, conducting a skillful withdrawal into Tunisia. By March 1943 he was a sick man and left North Africa, but was then appointed to command Army Group B, responsible for the defense of northern Italy. He later conducted the battle for Normandy before being badly wounded. His name was linked with the July 1944 Bomb Plot and he was forced to commit suicide to save his wife and son from the Gestapo.

The siege of Tobruk
The first siege of the port lasted from April to December 1941. The Italians had built strong defenses around the town, to which the Australian and British troops added trenches, foxholes, and gun emplacements.

Auchinleck now turned his attention to his forthcoming offensive. Given the reinforcements that he was receiving, which included a sizeable quantity of American tanks, he decided that not only would he relieve Tobruk, but once more seize the whole of Cyrenaica. This would also deny the Axis airfields from which to attack Malta and supply convoys sailing to it. At the end of September, the British and Dominion troops in the Western Desert were formed into the Eighth Army under Sir Alan Cunningham, one of the victors of the Abyssinian campaign. A week later Cunningham presented his final plan for Operation Crusader. In essence, his XXX Corps, which contained the bulk of his tanks, was to tie down Rommel's armor, while XIII Corps advanced on Tobruk, whose garrison would break out and link up with it. Rommel himself was to be the target of a raid by Commandos, who would be landed by submarine and attack his suspected headquarters in the Jebel el Akhdar. Another Special Forces operation would involve the newly created L Detachment of the Special Air Service (SAS), which was to be dropped behind enemy lines to destroy aircraft on the ground.

OPERATION CRUSADER

Crusader got off to a bad start, with the failure of both special operations, which were launched the night before the main attack. The Commandos' target turned out to be merely a logistics HQ and almost all of them were killed or captured. At any rate, Rommel was in Rome at the time. The aircraft carrying the SAS were blown off course in a

Antiaircraft gun defending Tobruk
Not only did the defenders of Tobruk have to withstand attacks on three sides on land, but they also had to fight off night raids by Axis bombers.

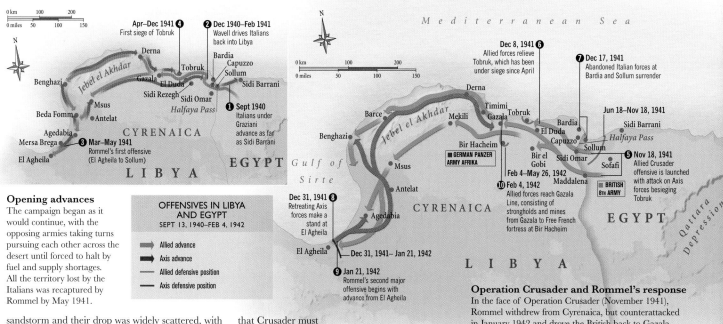

Opening advances
The campaign began as it would continue, with the opposing armies taking turns pursuing each other across the desert until forced to halt by fuel and supply shortages. All the territory lost by the Italians was recaptured by Rommel by May 1941.

OFFENSIVES IN LIBYA AND EGYPT
SEPT 13, 1940–FEB 4, 1942

➡ Allied advance
➡ Axis advance
— Allied defensive position
— Axis defensive position

Apr–Dec 1941 ❹
First siege of Tobruk

Dec 1940–Feb 1941 ❷
Wavell drives Italians back into Libya

Sept 1940 ❶
Italians under Graziani advance as far as Sidi Barrani

Mar–May 1941 ❸
Rommel's first offensive (El Agheila to Sollum)

Dec 8, 1941 ❻
Allied forces relieve Tobruk, which has been under siege since April

Dec 17, 1941 ❼
Abandoned Italian forces at Bardia and Sollum surrender

Nov 18, 1941 ❺
Allied Crusader offensive is launched with attack on Axis forces besieging Tobruk

Dec 31, 1941 ❽
Retreating Axis forces make a stand at El Agheila

Jan 21, 1942 ❾
Rommel's second major offensive begins with advance from El Agheila

Feb 4, 1942 ❿
Allied forces reach Gazala Line, consisting of strongholds and mines from Gazala to Free French fortress at Bir Hacheim

GERMAN PANZER ARMY AFRIKA

BRITISH 8TH ARMY

Operation Crusader and Rommel's response
In the face of Operation Crusader (November 1941), Rommel withdrew from Cyrenaica, but counterattacked in January 1942 and drove the British back to Gazala.

sandstorm and their drop was widely scattered, with many of them also being lost. Crusader itself was launched at 6:00 am on November 18. It initially caught the Axis by surprise and the tanks of XXX Corps reached the airfield at Sidi Rezegh, just 10 miles (16 km) southeast of Tobruk. XIII Corps also made good progress, capturing Sidi Omar and Capuzzo. Rommel, now returned from Rome, sent the DAK against XXX Corps. After two days of bitter struggle in Sidi Rezegh, the British armor was brought to a grinding halt and the Tobruk garrison break-out had to be postponed. XIII Corps, however, continued its advance.

THE DASH TO THE WIRE
Rommel now seized the initiative. He took his tanks on a dash across the frontier into Egypt with the goal of cutting off the Eighth Army from its supply lines. This caused such confusion that Cunningham wanted to withdraw. Auchinleck refused to countenance this. He immediately replaced Cunningham, with his own deputy chief of staff, Neil Ritchie, telling him

that Crusader must continue. What encouraged him was the fact that the New Zealand Division in XIII Corps had managed to link up with the Tobruk garrison in El Duda. Rommel had hoped to capture a British fuel dump, but failed to find one and was running short of fuel. The DAK was also being harried by the Desert Air Force. Aware, too, of the situation in El Duda, Rommel was forced to turn back. On December 5 he gave orders for the eastern part of the perimeter around Tobruk to be evacuated and mounted another attack on XXX Corps. When this failed, Rommel withdrew from Tobruk, which was relieved on December 7.

Eight days later, Ritchie attacked Rommel in Gazala. The Axis position here had an exposed desert flank that could be easily turned. Rommel therefore decided on a further withdrawal across Cyrenaica and by early January 1942 he was back in El Agheila in Tripolitania. The Eighth Army, exhausted after six weeks of continuous fighting, was in no position to advance farther westward.

The final act of Crusader was the capture of Bardia, the port close to the Egyptian border, which had been bypassed at the beginning of the offensive.

The situation in Libya was now more or less what it had been 11 months earlier. Not believing that the Axis forces were in a fit state to launch another offensive, Ritchie withdrew some of his divisions to reequip in preparation for continuing the advance. Rommel, however, encouraged by the arrival of two ships' worth of replacement tanks and learning through lax radio security that the British had few serviceable tanks, decided not to allow his adversary time to draw breath.

Without informing his more cautious Italian masters or Kesselring, his immediate German superior, Rommel launched his attack on January 21, 1942. He caught the novice 1st Armoured Division, a recent arrival, with its tanks widely dispersed, and scattered it, trapping and destroying 70 of its tanks in the Antelat area. He then almost succeeded in cutting off Fourth Indian Division in the Benghazi area and it looked as though he was about to repeat his success of the previous spring. Ritchie, however, decided to hold him and hastily constructed defenses between Gazala and Bir Hacheim. The remainder of the Eighth Army withdrew to this line. Rommel followed up, but was now too short of fuel to be able to push the British back any farther.

The port of Benghazi
Axis shipping, damaged by bombing raids, lies in the harbor. Benghazi fell to the British in December 1941, but was retaken by Rommel the following month.

THE WAR IN THE BALKANS AND CRETE

SEPTEMBER 27, 1940–JUNE 1, 1941

War in the Balkans began with Italy's unsuccessful invasion of Greece. Hitler then turned his attention to the region in preparation for his attack on the Soviet Union. The two countries that refused to submit to Hitler's will, Yugoslavia and Greece, were swiftly overrun despite support from Britain.

1940

SEPTEMBER 27
Germany, Italy, and Japan sign Tripartite Pact

OCTOBER 28
Italians invade Greece from Albania

OCTOBER 31
British troops land in Crete

NOVEMBER 4
Italian invasion halted and driven back by Greeks

NOVEMBER 3
Italian 3rd Alpine Division trapped by Greek forces. 5,000 prisoners taken

DECEMBER 4–8
Greek forces advance into Albania

NOVEMBER 20
Hungary joins Tripartite Pact, followed by Romania on the 23rd and Slovakia on the 24th

DECEMBER 28
Mussolini asks for German help in his disastrous campaign against Greece

1941

JANUARY 11
Hitler issues directive pledging support for hard-pressed Italians in Albania

JANUARY 1
Hitler starts to put pressure on Bulgarian government to allow German troops to attack Greece from Bulgaria

FEBRUARY 23
Greek prime minister Alexandros Korizis formally accepts British offer of troops

FEBRUARY 14
Hitler puts diplomatic pressure on Yugoslavia to join Tripartite Pact

MARCH 7
British and Australian troops from Egypt land in Greece

MARCH 1
After much pressure from Germany, Bulgaria signs Tripartite Pact

MARCH 27
Coup in Yugoslavia by officers opposed to Tripartite Pact. Hitler postpones invasion of USSR and calls for immediate attack on Yugoslavia and Greece

MARCH 25
Tripartite Pact signed by Yugoslavia

MARCH 28
Italian naval force defeated by British Mediterranean Fleet at Battle of Cape Matapan northwest of Crete

APRIL 6
German, Italian, and Hungarian troops invade Yugoslavia and Greece. Luftwaffe destroys most of Yugoslav air force while it is still on the ground

APRIL 10
The Ustase, a Fascist Croatian group, proclaims an independent Croatian republic, separate from Yugoslavia

APRIL 17
Surrender of Yugoslavia

APRIL 19
British decide to evacuate troops from Greece. Withdrawal to be covered by rearguard action at Thermopylae

APRIL 20
Greek First Army surrenders to commander of an SS division. This offends Mussolini, who demands second surrender with harsher terms

APRIL 24
Germans break through British positions at Thermopylae

APRIL 27
Athens occupied by Germans

APRIL 30
All Greek mainland in Axis hands

MAY 13
Luftwaffe starts bombing Allied positions on Crete

MAY 20
German airborne invasion of Crete. Paratroops dropped around three airfields on north coast. They capture only one, Maleme, but this allows reinforcements to be flown in

MAY 28
Start of evacuation from port of Sphakia on south coast of Crete

JUNE 1
Evacuation of Crete completed

▓▓ Axis conquest of Greece and Crete Apr 6–Jun 1, 1941
▓▓ Axis conquest of Yugoslavia Apr 6–17, 1941
▓▓ Other events

THE BALKAN CAMPAIGN

Mussolini, jealous of Hitler's territorial acquisitions in Central Europe, had long harbored ambitions of carving out a similar empire in southeast Europe. His first victim was Albania. The country had been under Italian influence for some years, when in March 1939 Mussolini demanded that Albania allow in Italian troops. When King Zog refused, he invaded and, after brief resistance, the monarch fled to neighboring Greece, leaving his country in Italian hands. Greece itself appeared to be Mussolini's next target, but he declared that he had no designs on the country. Unconvinced, Britain and France pledged themselves to uphold Greek and Romanian independence.

On Italy's declaration of war in June 1940, Mussolini again stated that he had no interest in Greece, which declared its neutrality. Even so, that fall he began to make threatening noises, accusing Greece of helping Britain. Mussolini now decided to attack, convinced that it would be an easy victory, even though his generals warned him that it was too late in the year. On October 27, 1940, he informed Hitler of his intention, but rejected his offer of participation by German troops. The following day, two Italian armies invaded from Albania. They advanced a short way into the country, but the Greeks then drove the Italians back across the border and advanced deep into Albania, with only the wintry weather slowing their progress.

DIPLOMATIC MOVES

Churchill, eager to uphold Britain's prewar guarantee, offered the Greeks troops and aircraft, but all they would accept was five RAF squadrons. They did, however, allow a British brigade to garrison Crete so as to release Greek troops to fight on the mainland. The Greek government did not want to antagonize the Germans and they were right to be cautious. Hitler was now turning his eyes toward southeast Europe. His

Ready to invade

German airborne troops prepare to embark in Junkers Ju 52 transport planes prior to the invasion of Yugoslavia. With help from Hungary and Italy, Germany overran Yugoslavia in just 11 days.

mind was firmly set on invading the Soviet Union, but first he needed to secure his southern flank. He therefore launched a diplomatic offensive. Before the end of November Hungary, Romania, and Slovakia—all countries with Fascist-style governments—had agreed to join the Tripartite Pact, the alliance formed by Germany, Italy, and Japan that September.

Hitler, meanwhile, ordered plans to be drawn up for a possible invasion of Greece, but he needed the compliance of Bulgaria so that it could be used as a launching pad. At the beginning of January 1941 Hitler opened negotiations with the Bulgarians, but they decided to play for time. The Italians had managed to halt the Greek advance in Albania, but Mussolini refused a further offer of German troops because he feared that Hitler would take over Albania.

The British now decided to counter Hitler's diplomatic offensive. In February Foreign Secretary Anthony Eden toured the Balkans in an effort to create an anti-Axis pact. Yugoslavia refused to see him, as did Turkey. Aware of their growing isolation, only the Greeks showed any interest. This was largely because General Ioannis Metaxas, the dictator who had resisted a formal alliance with the British, had died at the end of January. The new pro-British government agreed that British troops should be sent to Greece.

On March 1 Bulgaria signed up to the Tripartite Pact and German troops began to move into the country on the following day. German attention now concentrated on Yugoslavia. Hitler demanded rights of passage, offering the port of Salonika and part of Macedonia in recompense. Eventually, on March 25, Yugoslavia succumbed and joined the Pact, although many in the country were unhappy.

British and Commonwealth troops began to land on the Greek mainland on March 7. W Force would eventually consist of the New Zealand Division, two Australian divisions, and a British armored brigade

under the command of General Maitland Wilson. Two days later, the Italians launched an offensive against the Greeks in Albania, but failed to break through. At sea, the Italian Navy attempted to intercept the troop convoys going to Greece. On March 28 it clashed with the Mediterranean Fleet off Cape Matapan, west of the Peloponnese. The battleship *Vittorio Veneto* was badly damaged by a torpedo, while three Italian cruisers and two destroyers fell to the guns of the British ships.

THE INVASION OF YUGOSLAVIA

There was also dramatic news from Yugoslavia. On March 27 a group of air force officers overthrew the regency of Prince Paul in a bloodless coup. They established a government of national unity and made his 17-year-old nephew, Prince Peter, monarch in his place.

The new government then signed a non-aggression pact with the Soviet Union and expressed interest in a pact with Britain.

Operation Punishment

On the first day of the invasion of Yugoslavia, German dive-bombers attacked the airfields of the Yugoslav air force, destroying most of its planes before they could take off.

The invasion of the Balkans

Germany's conquest of Yugoslavia and Greece in spring 1941 was a well-planned, swiftly executed campaign. The Yugoslavs were totally unprepared, while the British and Greek forces in their defensive positions were easily outflanked by the mobile German forces. The airborne invasion of Crete also succeeded, but cost many more lives.

Hitler, furious over what he saw as Yugoslavia's treachery, ordered an immediate invasion of the country—Operation Punishment—with Greece to be attacked at the same time.

Yugoslavia was ill-equipped to face an Axis assault. While its army could call upon over one million men, they were poorly armed and badly trained. The country's long frontiers also did not help. On April 6 the Axis invaded, with Germans and Italians attacking from the north, Germans and Hungarians from the east, and Italians from Albania in the south. Much of the Yugoslav air force was destroyed on the ground at the start of hostilities and within a week Belgrade, the capital, had been occupied. Yugoslav resistance was minimal and a mere 150 German soldiers were killed during the brief campaign, which ended on April 17.

THE CONQUEST OF YUGOSLAVIA AND GREECE
APR 6–JUN 1, 1941

→ Axis advance
⚑ Parachute/glider landing
⚑ Allied defensive position April 6, 1941

THE INVASION OF GREECE

The rapid collapse of Yugoslavia was fatal for Greece. The Greek army's defensive plan was based on two sets of fortifications: the Metaxas Line in eastern Macedonia facing the border with Bulgaria and the Aliakmon Line along the southern boundary of Macedonia. It had been the British understanding that the Greeks would give up Macedonia and concentrate on defending the Aliakmon Line. This was where W Force was deployed, thus leaving their forces considerably less extended. The Greeks, however, planned to do this only if the Yugoslavs offered no resistance to the passage of German troops through their territory. That the Yugoslavs had opposed the Axis, albeit ineffectually, meant that the Greek Second Army remained in the Metaxas Line and was immediately outflanked by a German thrust from southeastern Yugoslavia to the port of Salonika. It was quickly forced to surrender. A thrust through Monastir threatened to do the same to W Force in the Aliakmon Line and the British troops began to withdraw on April 10, although the line itself held for another eight days.

REARGUARD ACTIONS

By now it was clear that little could be done to halt the German blitzkrieg and the Greeks agreed that Wilson could withdraw his troops. Further disaster occurred on April 20, when the Greek First Army was trapped in the west of the country and surrendered. W Force began its evacuation, covered by a rearguard which managed to hold off the Germans at Thermopylae for five days. On April 25 German paratroops seized the port of Corinth and two days later the Germans entered Athens. The British evacuation was completed the following day.

Operation Marita, as the overrunning of the Balkans was code-named, was another devastating demonstration of blitzkrieg and left Churchill's Balkans strategy in tatters, especially since it convinced Turkey to remain neutral. W Force had to leave all its heavy equipment behind along with 900 men killed and some 10,000 taken prisoner. The Greek king and his government fled—first to Crete and from there to Egypt. While some from W Force were taken back to Egypt, the bulk were landed in Crete. The British hoped to use the

Advance through Greece
An infantry column of the German 12th Army marches past Mount Olympus, having broken British and Greek resistance on the Aliakmon Line.

Germans rounding up prisoners
Over 11,000 British and Commonwealth troops were taken prisoner by the Germans on Crete. A few men escaped to the mountains, where they continued to fight alongside the Cretan resistance.

On May 19 the surviving aircraft were withdrawn, leaving Crete with no air cover whatsoever. On the following day the invasion began. Initially it did not go well. Some 2,000 paratroops were killed and none of their objectives captured. All the German commanders, aside from Student, wanted to abort the operation, but he was determined to continue. That night the battalion defending Maleme abandoned the airfield because of misunderstood orders. The Germans captured it the following day and began to land reinforcements. The British mounted a

counterattack, but it failed and the fate of Crete was sealed. Even though the Royal Navy was able to scatter the German seaborne reinforcements, Freyberg decided that it was impossible to hold the island. He had too many problems of command and control, while the Luftwaffe had complete domination of the skies. On May 28 he was given permission to withdraw to the south coast, where the Royal Navy would evacuate his men.

By June 1 Crete was in German hands. The navy managed to rescue some 12,000 men, but at the cost of three cruisers and six destroyers sunk, all victims of the Luftwaffe. Germany's victory in the Balkans and the success of its airborne troops, along with Rommel's victories in North Africa, reinforced the Wehrmacht's growing aura of invincibility. It boded well for Hitler's most momentous undertaking—the invasion of the Soviet Union.

island as a base from which to attack the Romanian oilfields at Ploesti, which were vital to the German war effort. The Royal Navy had also been using Suda Bay in the north of the island as a forward anchorage, although it was now within range of the Luftwaffe in Greece and there were few British aircraft on the island to defend ships using the bay.

AIRBORNE ASSAULT ON CRETE

The Germans also recognized the importance of Crete. On April 21, as the battle for Greece raged, General Karl Student, commander of Germany's paratroops, presented Hitler with a plan for an airborne invasion of the island. Hitler needed some persuasion, but eventually gave his approval and four days later issued a directive for Operation Mercury. German intelligence did not believe that there were more than 5,000 troops on the island, so only two divisions were to be used for the attack. In fact there were some 42,000, although they were poorly equipped after being evacuated from Greece. The 7th Parachute Division, which was deployed from Germany, was to make a series of drops, seize the airfields at Maleme, Rethymno, and Heraklion and also secure the harbor of Suda Bay. The bulk of the other division, 5th Mountain, would be flown in to the airfields once they had been secured, and reinforce the paratroops. Suda Bay was to be used by reinforcements arriving by sea, which would bring in heavy weapons, including tanks.

In command of the British defense of Crete was General Bernard Freyberg, commander of the New Zealand Division in the Middle East and a Victoria Cross winner from World War I. He knew of German intentions from Ultra, but was convinced that the main assault would come from the sea and did not pay sufficient attention to defense of the airfields.

On May 13 the Luftwaffe began to attack Crete. Because of Germany's overwhelming air superiority the RAF refused to reinforce the 25 fighters, most of them obsolete, that they had on the island.

AIRBORNE FORCES

AIRBORNE FORCES USUALLY COMPRISED three elements: paratroops, glider-borne troops, and airlanded troops—those landed by plane on an airfield that had already been secured. Most airborne operations combined at least two of these elements—in the case of Crete all three. Prior to the war only the Soviets and the Germans had created airborne forces, although during 1939–45 the former used theirs only in small-scale operations, the concept falling out of favor during Stalin's purges. The German successes in Norway and the 1940 campaign in the West prompted the British and Americans to create airborne forces of their own. These were first used on a significant scale during the Allied landings in French northwest Africa in November 1942.

Airborne operations are always fraught with risk. On Crete, many German paratroops were shot as they descended to the ground. Operation Mercury also demonstrated the vulnerability of their transport aircraft, which had to fly on a steady course as they approached and flew over the dropping zone. Indeed, so heavy was the loss of Junkers Ju 52 transport planes during the Crete campaign that the Germans never again mounted an airborne operation on this scale. Gliders were likewise prone to being shot down or wrecked on landing. Poor navigation and high winds resulted in a very scattered drop, which created problems once the paratroops had landed. The Allies experienced

German parachute drop over Crete
When they landed in a well-defended area, casualties among paratroops were high. Those who were not shot in the air were likely to be bayoneted as they struggled to get free of their harnesses.

this during the assault on Sicily in July 1943 and again, to some extent, on D-Day, June 6, 1944. Airborne forces were also lightly equipped and could not hold out for long on their own before ground forces linked up with them. The Allies learned this the hard way at Arnhem in September 1944, when much of the British 1st Airborne Division was lost because the ground advance could not reach them in time. The lesson was learned by the time it came to the Rhine crossings in March 1945, where Allied airborne forces played a key role in securing a bridgehead on the east bank.

German column under attack in Serbia
When Axis troops invaded Yugoslavia in April 1941, they met with little opposition. Most resistance came from the Serbs, who, after the conquest, quickly organized guerrilla resistance to the occupying forces.

GERMAN–SOVIET CONFLICT

JUNE 22–DECEMBER 6, 1941

In launching Operation Barbarossa the Germans planned to destroy the Soviet army before it could retreat into the vast Russian interior and extend the campaign into the winter. Initially the German forces achieved considerable success as they advanced toward Leningrad in the north, Moscow in the centre, and into the Ukraine in the south. They failed, however, to secure a quick and total victory, and by December they had come to a halt before Moscow.

JUNE 22
Start of Operation Barbarossa

JUNE 24
Germans occupy Kaunas

JUNE 24
Germans occupy Vilna

JUNE 26
Germans complete encirclement of Soviet troops in Bialystok

JUNE 28
Germans complete encirclement to the west of Minsk

JUNE 30
Germans occupy Lwow

JULY 1
Germans occupy Riga

JULY 9
Germans occupy Vitebsk

JULY 16
Germans take Smolensk

JULY 19
Germans complete encirclement of Soviet forces around Uman

AUGUST 16
Germans occupy Novgorod

AUGUST 17
Germans reach Dnepropetrovsk

SEPTEMBER 1
Leningrad is subjected to artillery fire before being besieged

SEPTEMBER 12
Germans occupy Gomel and Kaluga

SEPTEMBER 8
Leningrad's last overland and rail links from Murmansk are severed

SEPTEMBER 16
Over 600,000 Soviet troops are trapped in pocket east of Kiev

SEPTEMBER 19
Kiev falls to the Germans after more than 40 days of fighting

SEPTEMBER 30
Assault on Moscow–Operation Typhoon–begins

OCTOBER 6
Germans reach Mariupol on the Sea of Azov

OCTOBER 14
Soviet troops in Bryansk pocket surrender, but many break out toward the east

OCTOBER 19
Martial law is imposed in Moscow

OCTOBER 23
End of resistance of Soviet forces trapped in Vyazma pocket

OCTOBER 24
Kharkov is occupied by Germans

NOVEMBER 15
After overcoming resistance at the Tula-Mozhaisk line, Germans resume attack on Moscow

NOVEMBER 16
Germans capture Kerch and begin siege of Sevastopol

NOVEMBER 21
Germans occupy Rostov-on-Don

NOVEMBER 26
Since start of the siege of Leningrad, first trucks with supplies enter the city

NOVEMBER 24
Rostov is abandoned by Germans following Soviet counteroffensive

DECEMBER 4
German forces come to within 15 miles (25 km) of central Moscow

DECEMBER 5
Hitler orders exhausted forces to assume defensive position

DECEMBER 6
Soviet counteroffensive in front of Moscow begins

Operations in the north Jun 22–Nov 26, 1941	Operations in the center Jun 22–Dec 6, 1941	Operations in the south Jun 22–Nov 24, 1941

OPERATION BARBAROSSA

AT 3:30 AM ON JUNE 22, 1941, a total of seven German infantry armies, their advance led by four panzer groups, invaded the Soviet Union. They had opened the greatest land war in the history of military operations. Some 3 million German soldiers, supported by 3,580 tanks, 7,184 guns, and nearly 2,000 aircraft were on the move along a 1,000-mile (1,600-km) front, stretching from Memel on the Baltic to Odessa on the Black Sea.

The operation, which was code-named Barbarossa, had a long period of gestation. A plan for the invasion of the Soviet Union had first been drawn up in August 1940, but it did not emerge in its final form until the spring of 1941.

A call to arms
Following the launch of Operation Barbarossa men from all parts of the Soviet Union were exhorted to defend their "motherland" and avenge the deaths of their wives and children.

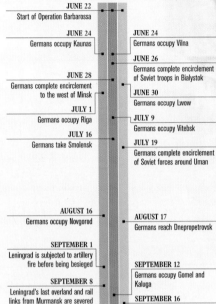

Army Group North, commanded by Field Marshal Ritter von Leeb, was to attack from East Pusssia toward Leningrad, aided by the Finns advancing into the Karelian isthmus. The strongest formation, Army Group Center under Bock, was to drive north of the natural barrier of the freshwater Pripet marshes to Smolensk, the route followed by Napoleon in 1812. To the south of the Pripet marshes, Rundstedt's Army Group South was to advance to the black-earth country of the Ukraine—the Soviet Unions's breadbasket— and the oil-rich industrial areas of the Donetz, the Volga, and the Caucasus. The cream of the German Army was poised to advance into a vast area— about 1,000,000 sq miles (2,600,000 sq km)—of steppe, forest, and swamp.

The invasion of the Soviet Union was the culmination of the twin obsessions that had driven Hitler throughout his career: the seizing of *Lebensraum* ("living space") in the east and, with it, the industry and

Soviet prisoners of war
Soviet troops were totally unprepared for the attack that was unleashed against them on June 22. Many on the frontier were taken prisoner before they had any idea that their country was now at war with Germany.

agricultural land that would ensure Germany's survival as a great power, and his contempt for the "Jewish-Bolshevist" government of the Soviet Union, whose Slav and Asiatic population would be enslaved or expelled into a wasteland beyond the "A-A line" stretching from Archangel to Astrakhan.

THE STATE OF SOVIET DEFENSES

The Soviet Union's Red Army was in no state to resist the German onslaught. Under Marshal Georgi Zhukov, chief of staff since January, a wholesale reorganization had begun, with tank formations that had been disbanded during Stalin's purges of the 1930s being reestablished. It would, however, be some time before the damage inflicted on the army by the purges was fully overcome. The fear engendered by both them and the ever-present NKVD (the Soviet secret service, whose many responsibilities included ensuring the political reliability of the armed forces) had sapped the morale of the army at all levels. Visiting Moscow in October 1941, the British General Ismay noted that when Stalin entered a room, "every Russian froze into silence and the

hunted look in the eyes of the generals showed all too plainly the constant fear in which they lived. It was nauseating to see brave men reduced to such servility." Furthermore, in the spring of 1941 Stalin's complex psychological makeup had resulted in him deeming as "unreliable" the numerous strong intelligence indications he had received of German intentions: from his own networks, from British diplomatic channels, and from Ultra information, which had been laundered to mask its source (see page 82). He had insisted on maintaining compliance with the terms of the Nazi-Soviet Pact of 1939, to the extent that trainloads of minerals and raw materials bound for Germany's war industries continued to rumble across the Soviet frontier until the small hours of June 22, 1941.

Stalin had also insisted on cramming the bulk of the Red Army fronts (army groups) into the incomplete line of fortifications, known as the "Stalin Line," on the Soviet frontier. The shallowest of German penetrations would place these formations at the risk of rapid envelopment.

THE STORM BREAKS

The Luftwaffe prepared the way for Army Group Center's attack. On the morning of June 22 it destroyed 528 Soviet aircraft on the ground and 210 in the air. When darkness fell across the German front on June 22, the Red Air Force had lost approximately 25 percent of its strength, some 1,600 machines. By June 26 Army Group Center was completing encirclements in Brest-Litovsk on the Soviet frontier, and in Bialystok, thus entombing tens of thousands of Soviet troops in what the Germans called "cauldron battles" (see map page 101). By then Army Group Center's two panzer groups had raced 200 miles (300 km) east to launch an encirclement of hard-fighting Soviet troops west of Minsk.

At this stage in the campaign the Soviet Union's primitive roads, and a rail network of a different gauge to that in Germany, posed few problems, although both factors had been underestimated by German military intelligence during the planning of Barbarossa. Racing through flat,

> The bombs were falling with a shriek. The army headquarters building we had just left was shrouded in smoke and dust. The powerful blasts rent the air and made our ears ring. The German bombers dived confidently at the defenseless military settlement. When the raid was over, thick black pillars of smoke billowed up from many places. Part of the headquarters building was in ruins. Somewhere a high-pitched, hysterical female voice was crying out.

AN ENGINEER OFFICER AT SOVIET 4TH ARMY HEADQUARTERS DESCRIBING THE ATTACK BY THE LUFTWAFFE ON JUNE 22

open terrain, whose earth had been baked hard by the scorching sun, the panzer spearheads covered around 50 miles (80 km) a day, halting only to snuff out resistance or take in supplies. Behind them labored the infantry, marching an average of 20 miles (30 km) a day under a pitiless sun while carrying 50 lb (23 kg) of equipment, ammunition, and rations. The landscape through which they passed bore testimony to the savagery of the fighting. One infantryman recalled that "burning villages, staring bodies of fallen Russian soldiers, swollen carcasses of dead horses, rusting, blackened and burnt-out tanks were the signs of the march."

By the end of June the German encirclement west of Minsk had resulted in the capture of 324,00 Red Army soldiers. Army Group

German 240-mm howitzer in action
Soviet defenses came under attack from over 7,000 artillery pieces in the opening phase of Barbarossa. In the seven largest encirclement battles the Germans seized or destroyed over 9,300 tanks and 16,170 guns, as well as taking over 2,250,000 prisoners.

HEINZ GUDERIAN

AFTER SERVICE AS A STAFF OFFICER in World War I, Heinz Guderian (1888-1954) became a specialist in armored warfare. In 1937 he published *Achtung Panzer!*, a book that made him the leading advocate of blitzkrieg warfare, and in 1938 he was appointed Chief of Mobile Forces. In September 1939, at the head of XIX Panzer Corps, he put theory into practice in Poland and eight months later led the same formation in France. His breakthrough at Sedan provided persuasive proof of his prophetic prewar thinking on the employment of armored formations. In Operation Barbarossa, Guderian commanded 2 Panzer Group in a breakneck drive into the heart of the European Soviet Union. On being brought to a halt by the onset of winter and stiffening Soviet resistance, he ordered a tactical withdrawal, and so was dismissed by Hitler in December 1941. He became chief of the army general staff after the bomb plot to kill Hitler in July 1944 failed. Plagued by ill-health, he was a sardonic observer of the collapse of the Third Reich, of which he gave an informative account in his autobiography, *Panzer Leader* (1952).

Center's panzer groups pressed on, crossed the Dnieper on July 10 and closed on Smolensk, beating off determined Red Army counterattacks on both flanks. At Smolensk another 300,000 men of the Red Army surrendered and were marched into captivity. A total of 3,205 tanks and 3,120 guns were also captured. Denied any organized means of transportation to the rear, tens of thousands of Soviet prisoners were to die while marching vast distances or packed like cattle in railroad wagons.

THE SLOWING OF THE ADVANCE

Army Group Center had now penetrated over 400 miles (650 km) into the Soviet Union, but the breakneck pace of the advance was slowing. Although Moscow was only 200 miles (325 km) away, the conditions were beginning to take their toll on the Ostheer (the German Army in the east). An hour or two of heavy rain brought tanks,

Street battle
German infantry fight behind a Panzer Mark III. There were nearly 1,500 in service in 1941, forming the backbone of the panzer divisions in the opening stages of Barbarossa. But they were no match for the Red Army's T-34s.

wheeled vehicles, and horses to a halt in seas of glutinous mud. They remained stuck fast in columns stretching tens of miles until the sun came out. (The Germans' dependence on horses can be gauged from the fact that more than 750,000 were used in the opening phase of Barbarossa, with an average loss of 1,000 animals a day.) Victory also exacted its own price. By the middle of August there were 500,000 German casualties.

After the fall of Smolensk on July 16, Army Group Center halted for several weeks to bring up supplies. Ammunition was running low and tank strength had fallen by nearly half. Meanwhile, there were growing divisions within the German high command that needed to be settled. Field Marshal von Bock wanted to drive on to Moscow

behind a renewed panzer thrust, but on July 19 Hitler intervened. He issued a new directive: one of Bock's two panzer groups was to wheel south to aid Army Group South in another huge encirclement in northern Ukraine. The other was to swing north to reinforce the advance of Army Group North on Leningrad and cut Soviet communications with Moscow. This meant that Bock now had only infantry with which to push toward Moscow.

The ensuing argument over the priorities of the Ostheer lasted a month before Hitler settled matters with an order, issued on August 21, in which he shifted the emphasis to the south and the envelopment of four Soviet armies east of Kiev by Rundstedt's Army Group South. With firm orders from Stalin not to withdraw, the Soviet troops in and around Kiev fought on grimly until September 19, when 665,000 were taken prisoner. After the shock of the German invasion and advance in June and July, Stalin was regaining his grip on the levers of command. He was now supreme commander of the armed forces, and commissar for defense, and sat at the head of the Soviet Supreme High Command, or Stavka as it was known.

ADVANCE TO LENINGRAD

Torn between the competing options of the drive on Moscow, the advance to Leningrad at the head of the Baltic, and the huge maneuver in Kiev, Hitler had opted for the third. However, in the final

Advance through the Soviet Union

The Germans launched Operation Barbarossa along a 1,000-mile (1,600-km) front on June 22. They advanced to Leningrad in the north, to Moscow in the center, and beyond Kiev in the south. By December they were just 15 miles (25 km) from Moscow.

planning stages of Barbarossa he had given priority to the capture of Leningrad as the preliminary to a drive on Moscow from the north. By shuttling his forces up and down a vast front, Hitler was fatally dissipating the early stunning successes of Operation Barbarossa.

By July 20 Leeb's Army Group North had been poised to take Leningrad, but the growing exhaustion of his troops, hardening Soviet resistance, and Hitler's intervention had destroyed the chance of its early capture. At the end of August, as Leeb's armor nosed into the outskirts of the city, the Führer had ordered a halt, possibly fearing heavy losses in a street-by-street battle for the city. Moreover, the Finns had been showing a reluctance to extend their operations beyond the Karelian isthmus once they had succeeded in regaining their 1939 border.

Hitler had ordered Leningrad to be besieged. By September 8 all land communications with the city had been severed, and the only way in which food supplies could be delivered was by using air and river links. These were constantly harassed by the Germans, while Leningrad itself was pounded by German artillery and bombers. In October starvation

Crossing the steppe
Many German soldiers were oppressed by the sheer size and emptiness of the Soviet steppe.

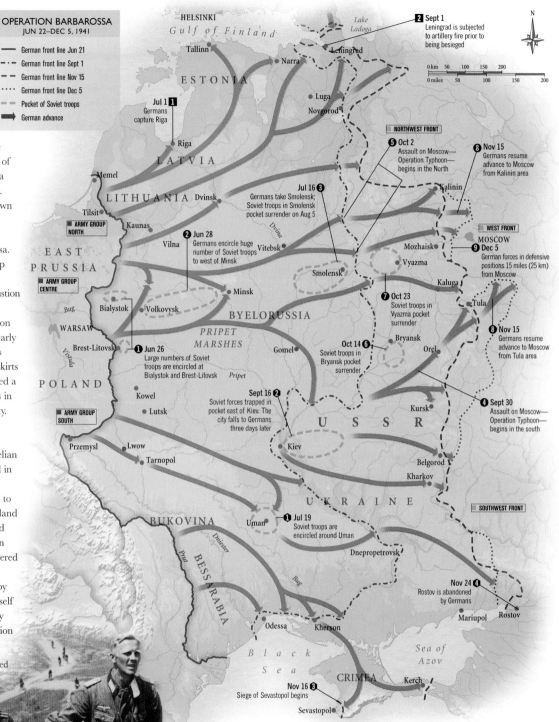

OPERATION BARBAROSSA
JUN 22–DEC 5, 1941

— German front line Jun 21
-- German front line Sept 1
–– German front line Nov 15
···· German front line Dec 5
-- Pocket of Soviet troops
➤ German advance

2 Sept 1
Leningrad is subjected to artillery fire prior to being besieged

HELSINKI
Gulf of Finland
Lake Ladoga
Tallinn
Narra
Leningrad
ESTONIA
Luga
Jul 1 1
Germans capture Riga
Novgorod
NORTHWEST FRONT
Riga
5 Oct 2
Assault on Moscow—Operation Typhoon—begins in the North
8 Nov 15
Germans resume advance to Moscow from Kalinin area
LATVIA
Memel
Dvinsk
Kalinin
LITHUANIA
Jul 16 3
Germans take Smolensk; Soviet troops in Smolensk pocket surrender on Aug 5
ARMY GROUP NORTH
Kaunas
Tilsit
Vilna
Vitebsk
Dvina
WEST FRONT
MOSCOW
Mozhaisk
9 Dec 5
German forces in defensive positions 15 miles (25 km) from Moscow
2 Jun 28
Germans encircle huge number of Soviet troops to west of Minsk
EAST PRUSSIA
ARMY GROUP CENTRE
Smolensk
Vyazma
Bug
Bialystok
Volkovysk
Minsk
Kaluga
WARSAW
BYELORUSSIA
7 Oct 23
Soviet troops in Vyazma pocket surrender
Tula
8 Nov 15
Germans resume advance to Moscow from Tula area
PRIPET MARSHES
Brest-Litovsk
Oct 14 6
Soviet troops in Bryansk pocket surrender
Bryansk
Vistula
Gomel
Pripet
Orel
1 Jun 26
Large numbers of Soviet troops are encircled at Bialystok and Brest-Litovsk
POLAND
Kowel
Lutsk
ARMY GROUP SOUTH
Sept 16 2
Soviet forces trapped in pocket east of Kiev. The city falls to Germans three days later
U S S R
Kursk
4 Sept 30
Assault on Moscow—Operation Typhoon—begins in the south
Przemysl
Lwow
Tarnopol
Kiev
Belgorod
Kharkov
U K R A I N E
SOUTHWEST FRONT
BUKOVINA
Uman
1 Jul 19
Soviet troops are encircled around Uman
Dniester
Prut
Dnepropetrovsk
BESSARABIA
Bug
Nov 24 4
Rostov is abandoned by Germans
Mariupol
Rostov
Odessa
Kherson
Black Sea
Sea of Azov
CRIMEA
Kerch
Nov 16 3
Siege of Sevastopol begins
Sevastopol

0 km 50 100 150 200
0 miles 50 100 150 200

N

and disease began to take a grip, and it was not long before 300 of Leningrad's civilians were dying every day.

By then Hitler's attention had belatedly swung back to Moscow. Buoyed by the encirclement of Kiev, he resisted Rundstedt's cautious advice to call a temporary halt to

operations on the Eastern Front. For the fall drive on the Soviet capital, Army Group North's panzer spearhead was transferred from the Leningrad sector and joined Army Group Center's Fourth Army. To the north of the Fourth Army was the Ninth Army and Panzer Group 3; to the south was the Second Army and Panzer Group 2, commanded by General Heinz Guderian, Germany's leading exponent of armored warfare.

EINSATZGRUPPEN ATROCITIES

DURING THE INVASION OF POLAND in 1939 the German armies were accompanied by special units—*Einsatzgruppen*—charged with the liquidation of priests and members of the Polish intelligentsia. Their successor units, initially comprising 3,000 men and directly responsible to Heinrich Himmler and his deputy Reinhard Heydrich, were tasked with the mass murder of Jews, communists, Romanies, and other non-Aryans in the territories occupied during Barbarossa. Gruppe A was attached to Army Group North and cleared the Baltic states and northeast Russia, Gruppe B followed Army Group Center through Minsk and Smolensk, Gruppe C followed Army Group South through the Ukraine, and Gruppe D tracked the 11th Army to the Crimea. In June 1941 their orders were to eliminate Jewish males aged 17 to 45, but by mid-summer Jewish women and children were also being rounded up, many of them betrayed by anti-Semitic inhabitants of the Baltic states and the Ukraine.

The principal method of the *Einsatzgruppen* was mass shooting, although small numbers of gas trucks were also employed in which the victims were killed by exhaust from the motors. Almost all the victims of these gas experiments were women and

Soviet partisan victims
In a trench they have been forced to dig themselves, Soviet partisans await execution. The Germans did not believe they should apply the laws of war to partisans.

children. The *Einsatzgruppen* were occasionally aided by the Wehrmacht and, more frequently, by local militia groups willing to participate in the massacres. For example, on October 28–29, 1941, in Kaunas in Lithuania, local militia joined *Einsatzgruppe* A in the murder of some 9,200 Jews. The dead were then looted for money, watches, jewelry, and clothing. In Lithuania between July 4 and November 25, 1941, some 130,000 people were killed by *Einsatzgruppe* A. In the Soviet Union between 1941 and 1944 the *Einsatzgruppen* executed between 1.5 million and 2 million people, the great majority of them Jewish.

Execution by shooting
Throughout the *Einsatzgruppen's* reign of terror the great majority of their victims were Jewish, often killed by shooting in the back of the head.

THE DRIVE ON MOSCOW

On September 30, in Operation Typhoon, Guderian opened the drive on Moscow, thrusting toward Orel. To the north, the German attacks went in two days later, and within a week nine Soviet armies had been cut off in pockets west of Vyazma and Bryansk, consigning another 600,000 Red Army soldiers to captivity. Neither Stalin nor the Stavka had anticipated that the Germans would launch an offensive so late in the year. However, the weather came to their aid. At the end of the first week in October, the heavy fall rains—the Russian *rasputitsa*—set in, slowing the German advance in a vast sea of mud.

General Günther von Blumentritt, the German Fourth Army's chief of staff, recalled: "After the Russian forces had been rounded up, we pushed on toward Moscow. There was little opposition for the moment, but the advance was slow—for the mud was awful, and the troops were tired. Moreover, they met a well-prepared defensive position on the Nara River, where they were held up by the arrival of fresh Russian forces. Most of the commanders were now asking, 'where are we going to stop?'"

Snow had fallen as early as the first week in October. By now most of the German front-line units had been in action, without relief, since June 22. Few had warm winter clothing, making it all but impossible for most troops to remain out in the open during the increasingly severe night frosts. Exhaustion exacerbated minor wounds and increased the misery of depleted units with punishing workloads. Hot food seldom arrived in the front line as it froze solid on its short journey forward. Lice thrived and leather boots disintegrated in the musty air of earth dugouts. As the thermometer dropped, the sentries' duty was limited to a maximum of one hour and their goggles froze to the flesh of their faces. Men survived by stripping the clothing from the bodies of the Soviet dead.

A rallying cry
The Russians were rallied to the defense of their country with the slogan: "We will destroy the murderers of our children."

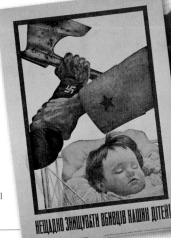

НЕЩАДНО ЗНИЩУВАТИ ВБИВЦІВ НАШИХ ДІТЕЙ!

By the end of October, forward German units were 40 miles (65 km) from the outskirts of Moscow. At night they could see the flash of antiaircraft guns over the Soviet capital. Roads that had been hardened by frost offered a fleeting chance for a final offensive on November 15. However, Zhukov was now in command of the Soviet forces barring the route to Moscow, and these had been reinforced by fresh divisions transferred from Siberia and fully equipped for fighting in winter.

By November 27 the leading panzer units had reached the Volga Canal, within 20 miles (32 km) of Moscow's northern suburbs. Patrols could see the sun glinting on the domes of the Kremlin. But the Germans were unable to advance any farther, and the forward units were pulled back on December 5. The next day, as the Germans considered a tactical withdrawal to a defensive line, Zhukov delivered a crushing counterblow. Hitler's gamble on victory in the Soviet Union by September had failed, and the German people were warned, for the first time, that they should expect a long war. Priority was now to be given to the air raid defense of the Reich.

Trenches outside Moscow
Following the launch on September 30 of the German drive against Moscow, over 500,000 Muscovites responded to the call for help in constructing fortifications outside the city.

The human and material costs of Barbarossa had been on a colossal scale. By the beginning of December the Ostheer had sustained total losses of 743,000 men (not counting the sick) and was short of 340,000 men, approximately 50 percent of the fighting strength of the infantry. In Germany only 33,000 replacements were available. Of the 500,000 trucks that had started the campaign, 150,000 had been written off and nearly 300,000 were in need of repair. It was estimated that it would take at least six months to bring each battered armored division up to full strength again.

These losses paled beside those suffered in the same period by the Red Army. Between June and early December it had lost nearly 3 million killed in action and 3.5 million taken prisoner. The German high command comforted itself with the conviction that this massive bloodletting had exhausted Soviet manpower—but this was by no means the case.

Identifying the dead
Soviet civilians search for their loved ones after a massacre by the Germans. Nazi ideology ensured that the war in the east was fought with unparalleled savagery.

THE WAR BECOMES GLOBAL
1941–42

THE JAPANESE ATTACK ON PEARL HARBOR ON
DECEMBER 7, 1941, WAS ONE OF THE DEFINING MOMENTS
OF 20TH-CENTURY HISTORY. FROM THIS POINT TWO
ALLIED POWERS, THE UNITED STATES AND BRITAIN,
WOULD FIGHT THE WAR IN BOTH THE EUROPEAN AND
THE ASIAN AND PACIFIC THEATERS, UNITING WHAT HAD
BEEN TWO SEPARATE CONFLICTS. WHILE THE ALLIES
MADE COMMON CAUSE TO DEFEAT THEIR ENEMIES, ON
THE AXIS SIDE GERMANY AND JAPAN HAD SEPARATE WAR
GOALS. GERMANY SOUGHT THE DESTRUCTION OF THE
SOVIET UNION AND MASTERY OF EUROPE, JAPAN
POLITICAL AND ECONOMIC PRIMACY IN ASIA.

Spheres of influence
High-ranking German officers and a
Japanese military attaché in Berlin discuss
the progress of the war in March 1941.
Although the two powers regularly shared
intelligence, Hitler did not inform Japan of
his intended invasion of the Soviet Union.

NEW THEATERS OF WAR

IN THE LATE 1930S THE UNITED STATES HAD STOOD ASIDE AS JAPAN'S ARMY SECURED LARGE TRACTS OF NORTHERN AND COASTAL CHINA. WHEN WAR BROKE OUT IN EUROPE IN 1939, THE AMERICAN REACTION WAS AGAIN NOT TO GET INVOLVED. JAPAN, PREOCCUPIED BY THE ONGOING WAR IN CHINA AND SMARTING FROM ITS DEFEAT BY THE SOVIET UNION IN 1938–39, WAS SIMILARLY CAUTIOUS IN ITS RESPONSE TO THE EUROPEAN WAR. ALL THIS CHANGED IN SPRING 1940 WITH GERMANY'S RAPID CONQUEST OF NORTHWEST EUROPE.

THE CHANGED SITUATION in Europe had far-reaching implications, both for the United States and Japan. The defeat of France and the likely defeat of Britain forced the Americans to look to their own defenses. In July 1940 Congress passed the Two-Ocean Naval Expansion Act, which authorized a huge increase over the next few years in the strength of the US fleets in the North Atlantic and the Pacific.

In January 1941 President Roosevelt appealed to Congress to support the nations fighting in defense of what he called the "Four Freedoms": freedom of speech, freedom of religion, freedom from want, and freedom from fear. These were noble sentiments, but what Britain needed was a supply of arms on easier terms than the "cash and carry" basis on which they had been supplied since the outbreak of war.

Roosevelt's answer was the Lend-Lease Act, passed by Congress in March 1941. This allowed Britain to borrow war supplies from the United States against a promise of later repayment. By the end of March, Congress had voted $7 billion to Lend-Lease, the first installment in a program that would eventually total over $50 billion.

In taking "all steps short of war" to sustain the British, Roosevelt was maneuvering indirectly toward war itself. At the end of March 1941 Axis ships in American ports were seized. On May 28, following the torpedoing of the US freighter *Robin Moor* by a U-boat, Roosevelt declared a state of unlimited national emergency. Axis credit in the United States was frozen and Axis consulates closed in June.

On August 9, 1941, Roosevelt and Churchill met in Placentia Bay in Newfoundland to discuss their war goals. They agreed that the defeat of Nazi Germany was the priority and issued the Atlantic Charter, which embodied Roosevelt's Four Freedoms and provided the seed from which the United Nations grew. However, it was also agreed that joint American and British military action could not be undertaken until the United States was at war with Germany. By the end of the year the United States would be at war with Germany, not as a result of a direct confrontation, but through the actions of Japan.

JAPANESE INTENTIONS

For Japan, the defeat of France and the Netherlands in spring 1940 and the apparently impending defeat of Britain presented a golden opportunity. The possessions of the three imperial powers in Southeast Asia had long been coveted by Japan as sources of valuable raw materials, such as rubber and oil. But there remained one important obstacle to a policy of military conquest in Southeast Asia. The Japanese had to decide whether they should risk provoking a war with the United States.

On August 29, 1940, Vichy France bowed to pressure from the Japanese and allowed them to establish bases in northern Indochina. In response, Roosevelt placed an embargo on the export of various raw marterials to Japan. When, in July 1941, the Japanese secured base facilities in southern Indochina, this was a more serious development, posing a threat to the American possession of the Philippines, the British possessions of Malaya and Burma, and the Dutch East Indies. Roosevelt, acting in concert with Britain, froze all Japan's assets in the United States and imposed an oil embargo.

At a stroke Japan was deprived of 90 percent of its oil supplies and 75 percent of its foreign trade. If the Japanese could not secure new supplies of raw materials, they would be forced to accede to American demands that they relinquish all the territory they had gained in China and suffer a humiliating loss of face. In the words of Admiral Osami Nagano, Chief of the Japanese General Staff, Japan was like "a fish in a pond from which the water is gradually being drained away."

Japanese plans for war, begun in earnest in mid-summer 1941, involved two widely separated areas of operation. The seizure of the so-called Southern Resources Area would start with an offensive against the Philippines, accompanied by a simultaneous attack on Malaya. Japan's southern drive was to be coordinated with a preemptive carrier strike on the US Pacific Fleet at its base, Pearl Harbor on the Hawaiian island of Oahu. This part of the plan was the brainchild of Admiral Yamamoto Isoroku, commander-in-chief of the Japanese Combined Fleet since 1939. Yamamoto had suggested this operation as early as January 1941, but it was not until October 1941 that it was given the go-ahead.

The bombing of Pearl Harbor
US servicemen survey Ford Island airbase after the Japanese raid on Pearl Harbor. Contrary to Japanese hopes, the surprise attack did not weaken American fighting spirit, but inflamed the desire for revenge.

"You will not only be unable to make up your losses but will grow weaker as time goes on…we will not only make up our losses but will grow stronger as time goes on. It is inevitable that we shall crush you before we are through with you."

ADMIRAL HAROLD N STARK, CHIEF OF NAVAL OPERATIONS,
TO ADMIRAL NOMURA KICHISABURO, JAPANESE
AMBASSADOR TO THE UNITED STATES

In September 1940 Japan had signed the Tripartite Pact with Germany and Italy. This bound the three nations to mutual support in the event of any one of them being attacked by a country not yet at war. In April 1941 Japan also negotiated a nonaggression pact with the Soviet Union. This would allow the planned Japanese operations in Southeast Asia to go ahead without any fear of a Soviet attack in Mongolia and Manchuria. The harmony of the Tripartite Pact was temporarily disturbed by Hitler's invasion of the Soviet Union in June 1941, of which Japan received no advance warning.

One man who had played a prominent role in negotiating the Tripartite Pact was General Tojo Hideki, the Japanese minister of war. Tojo's view, endorsed by the Japanese Army, was that provoking war with the United States was a risk worth taking. The seizure of Southeast Asia and the resources denied Japan by the Western powers would present them with a *fait accompli*. This would place Japan in a position of great strength in any subsequent peace negotiations. The Americans would surely flinch from the task of fighting across the territories and vast tracts of ocean that would be contained behind Japan's perimeter defense and would come to terms.

The battle for Stalingrad
Red Army soldiers duck and crouch as they advance cautiously across the rubble of Stalingrad. So constant was fighting in the ruined city, troops rarely exposed themselves to enemy fire in this way. They moved around by means of rat runs through the ruins.

On October 17 Tojo succeeded Konoye as prime minister. On November 2 he told Emperor Hirohito that Japan must seize its advantage or become a "third-class nation in two or three years." The war plans were approved by Admiral Nagano on November 3, and Yamamoto's carrier strike force assembled in the Kurile Islands north of Japan. In the meantime diplomatic talks in Washington, ostensibly aimed at averting hostilities, continued on their futile course. By now, the Americans were aware of Japanese intentions since they had been decoding Japanese radio traffic for months, but they remained ignorant of the precise Japanese plans.

REACTIONS TO PEARL HARBOR

The Japanese attack on the US Pacific Fleet at Pearl Harbor on December 7, 1941 transformed the war into a global conflict. The United States immediately declared war on Japan and, on December 11,

Germany declared war on the United States. Hitler addressed the Reichstag, declaring jubilantly that the Japanese had followed the German precept of always striking first. He was now convinced that Germany could not possibly lose the war. The Japanese, after all, were a nation that had not been vanquished in three thousand years. Churchill's reaction was more measured. On being given the news of the attack on Pearl Harbor he reached the same conclusion as Hitler, but from the British perspective, observing, "So we have won after all."

On December 22, 1941, Churchill, Roosevelt, and their respective staffs met in Washington, D.C., at the conference code-named "Arcadia." In formulating a general policy for prosecuting the war, Roosevelt came under intense pressure from his admirals to make the Pacific theater the major priority. However, Roosevelt confirmed the "Germany first" policy agreed in Placentia Bay in August 1941.

"Each position, each yard of Soviet territory must be stubbornly defended to the last drop of blood. We must cling to every inch of Soviet soil and defend it to the end."

JOSEF STALIN IN HIS ORDER TO THE RED ARMY ON JULY 28, 1942

Driven from their homes
Hundreds of families camp in fields on the outskirts of Stalingrad in September 1942 to escape the furious German shelling of the city.

A TRULY GLOBAL WAR

The scale on which the war was being fought in the Soviet Union, along a front of more than 1,500 miles (2,400 km), already dwarfed that of any previous conflict. To this was now added a vast new theater of war in Asia and the Pacific.

To achieve this, both sides agreed that the continent of Europe would have to be invaded and that Britain would be the springboard for this operation. Furthermore, the Soviet Union was to be kept in the war at all costs, and this could best be achieved by extending to Stalin the terms of Lend-Lease.

in perpetuity. This ambitious long-term objective was the background to the German summer campaign of 1942, code-named Operation *Blau* (Blue) and outlined by Hitler in Führer Directive No 41.

In order to wage war, Britain and the United States, until 1945 the only great powers involved in both the German and Japanese wars, needed to move manpower, war material, and food around the globe. In addition to the constant flow of Allied shipping across the Atlantic, American ships now sailed across the Pacific to Australia, and through the Indian Ocean to the Persian Gulf in order to get supplies overland to their Soviet ally.

HITLER'S GRAND DESIGNS

Hitler, meanwhile, was in the grip of his ambitious strategic plans for 1942, encompassing the seizure of the oil fields of the Middle East, which would destroy the basis of British power in the region and provide the fuel to sustain his panzer armies

One of the principal goals of the campaign was to destroy "the entire defense potential remaining to the Soviets and to cut them off, as far as possible, from their most important centers of war industry."

One of the centers of war industry that the invading Germans would attempt to destroy was the city of Stalingrad on the Volga River. From midsummer 1942 Stalingrad was to exercise a morbid hold over Hitler. It would eventually assume an even more terrible significance, when the soldiers of the Red Army demonstrated that they were prepared to sacrifice themselves in their hundreds of thousands to deny the city to the Germans.

For the moment it was hard to predict how the war in the Pacific would develop. By provoking American wrath, the Japanese had awakened a sleeping giant. Through their own choices, both Japan and Germany had brought the United States into the ranks of their enemies. American military and air power in 1941 may have been modest, but in terms of financial, industrial, and demographic resources, the United States was incomparably the greatest power in the world.

EVENTS LEADING TO THE ATTACK ON PEARL HARBOR

MARCH 1940–DECEMBER 1941

US policy in this period was governed by opposition to Japan's war in China and Japanese designs on Southeast Asia, with its rich oil reserves and other natural resources. Japan knew that sooner or later war with the US was inevitable and decided to strike first before the Americans had time to build a larger navy.

1940

MARCH 30
New puppet government established in Nanking to administer region of China under Japanese control

APRIL 17
US warns Japan not to upset status quo in Dutch East Indies

JULY 16
Army brings down moderate government in Japan. New administration formed under Prince Konoye

JULY 18
Under Japanese pressure, Britain closes Burma Road, main supply line for Nationalist Chinese

JULY 20
Two-Ocean Naval Expansion Act passed in US. This convinces Japanese military of need for action before US ready for war

JULY 27
Japan proclaims Greater East Asia Co-Prosperity Sphere

AUGUST 29
Japan granted permission to station troops in northern French Indochina

SEPTEMBER 27
Japan signs Tripartite Pact with Germany and Italy

OCTOBER 16
US government announces 16.4 million men registered for military draft

OCTOBER 18
Britain reopens Burma Road

OCTOBER 29
US government conducts first ever peacetime draft lottery

NOVEMBER 5
Roosevelt elected to third term as president

1941

JANUARY 16
Fighting breaks out between French Indochina and Siam over disputed border regions

JANUARY 31
Japanese arrange truce to end French-Siamese conflict

MARCH 11
Congress passes Lend-Lease Act, giving Roosevelt government power to send military supplies to Britain and China

APRIL 13
Japanese and USSR sign nonaggression pact

MAY 9
Treaty of Tokyo transfers disputed border territory from French Indochina to Siam

JULY 24
Vichy France accedes to Japanese demands for bases in southern French Indochina

JULY 26
US freezes all Japanese assets

AUGUST 17
Roosevelt warns that US will take immediate action to safeguard its interests if Japan starts new military actions

OCTOBER 17
New Japanese government: General Tojo Hideki is both prime minister and minister of war

NOVEMBER 20
Negotiations open between Japan and US in Washington

NOVEMBER 26
Carrier force bound for Pearl Harbor sails from Kurile Islands

NOVEMBER 26
US demands Japanese withdrawal from China and French Indochina

DECEMBER 7
Japanese attack on Pearl Harbor

DECEMBER 8
US and Britain declare war on Japan

DECEMBER 11
Germany and Italy declare war on US

DECEMBER 22
Start of Anglo-US "Arcadia" Conference in Washington

▩ Japanese actions Mar 30, 1940– Dec 22, 1941　　▩ US actions Apr 17, 1940–Dec 22, 1941　　▩ Other events

THE US JOINS THE WAR

WHEN WAR BROKE OUT in Europe in 1939, Japan's high command was understandably cautious. Germany had secretly and treacherously signed a nonaggression pact with the Soviets, whose army had recently inflicted a resounding defeat on Japanese forces in Nomonhan. After agreeing to a cease-fire with the USSR, Japan chose to remain neutral and see how events unfolded.

EFFECTS OF THE FALL OF FRANCE

The German victory in northwest Europe in the spring of 1940 altered Japanese thinking. After the fall of France, the defeat of Britain seemed to be only a matter of time. The European colonies in Southeast Asia—the Dutch East Indies, French Indochina, Burma, and Malaya, the region Japan saw as its Southern Resources Area—lay virtually defenseless. Taking advantage of this situation, the Japanese sought to close supply routes to the Chinese

Nationalists via Indochina and Burma. The French were forced to close the Hanoi-Nanning railroad, and on July 24, 1940, the British closed the Burma Road between Lashio and Chungking (see map page 118).

In July 1940 a new government was formed, headed by Prince Konoye Fumimaro, a former prime minister, who was closely associated with the military. The preconditions of the army and navy for allowing him to form a government were prior acceptance of their demands for a treaty with Germany and Italy, a nonaggression treaty with the USSR, and an expansionist strategy in Southeast Asia.

What seemed an impending German victory in Europe also produced far-reaching policy changes in the United States. Throughout its history, the security of the United States had largely depended on a divided Europe. Faced now with a German victory in Europe and the Japanese threat in the Far East, the United States sought to ensure its security

Aboard an aircraft carrier of the Pacific Fleet
The US response to the Japanese threat in the Pacific was slow, but in May 1940 Roosevelt decided that the Pacific Fleet, which had been conducting exercises off Hawaii, should remain at Pearl Harbor and not return to California.

in both the North Atlantic and the Pacific with the Two-Ocean Naval Expansion Act of July 1940. The act authorized the construction of 11 battleships, 6 battlecruisers, 18 fleet carriers, 27 cruisers, 115 destroyers, and 43 submarines, in addition to the 130 warships already under construction.

Over the next few months the Japanese high command gradually realized the implications of the act. Its provisions would be completed around 1948, but, after 1944, the United States would enjoy an overwhelming advantage in naval strength over Japan. In a way the act presented Japan with a "now or never" dilemma, a window of opportunity around the end of 1941 when Japanese building and mobilization would be complete, but before American construction came on line.

SOUTHEAST ASIA

On September 22, 1940, the French authorities in Saigon were forced to accept Japanese demands for occupation rights in northern Indochina and in the same month Japan concluded the Tripartite Pact with Germany and Italy. From its renewed association with Germany, Japan came into possession of intelligence material obtained from the British steamer *Automedon* by the German raider *Atlantis* off the Nicobar Islands in November 1940. The *Automedon* was carrying mail for Singapore that included the minutes of the British cabinet meeting of August 12, 1940. These revealed that Britain could not oppose any Japanese move against either Indochina or Siam, and would be unable to send a fleet to the Far East in the event of war with Japan. The contents of the papers were sent by signal to Berlin (and were read by British intelligence, though Singapore was not informed) and were then presented by the Germans to the Japanese attachés in Berlin and to representatives of the army and navy staffs in Tokyo.

The revelation of British defenselessness in Southeast Asia was like scales falling from the eyes. The Japanese army now began serious

Battle-hardened troops
Japan's well-trained army had been at war since 1937. Here Japanese infantry and artillery pursue remnants of the Chinese Nationalist army in Honan province north of the Yangtze River in November 1941.

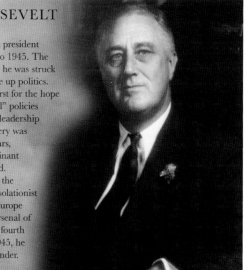

FRANKLIN DELANO ROOSEVELT

FRANKLIN D. ROOSEVELT (1882–1945), the 32nd president of the United States, led his country from 1933 to 1945. The Democratic candidate for vice president in 1920, he was struck down by poliomyelitis in 1921, but refused to give up politics. He is remembered for two great achievements: first for the hope he gave the American people with his "New Deal" policies during the Depression of the 1930s, then for his leadership in World War II. The American economic recovery was completed by the full employment of the war years, allowing the United States to emerge as the dominant political and economic force of the postwar world.

Before his country was drawn into the war by the attack on Pearl Harbor, Roosevelt had faced an isolationist public, although his own feelings on the war in Europe were made clear in his policy of acting as the "arsenal of democracy." In 1944 he was elected to a historic fourth term, but his health declined and on April 12, 1945, he died, less than a month before the German surrender.

training for operations in the south. The troops that were to lead the campaign in Malaya practiced landings on Hainan and training in jungle warfare began on Formosa in February 1941. At the same time Japanese naval staff began to take seriously a suggestion made in October 1940 for a preemptive attack on the US Pacific Fleet at Pearl Harbor.

ECONOMIC WARFARE

Relations between the United States and Japan had been steadily worsening. In January 1940 Washington had refused to agree to a new commercial treaty with Japan. After July 1940 a series of US measures

deprived Japan of aviation fuel, high-grade scrap and, after January 1941, virtually every raw material and metal of any real importance. In March 1941 the Japanese forced the French to accept Japanese occupation of Saigon airport and to turn over the whole of Indochina's rice surplus. Having proclaimed their intention to create a new international order throughout Southeast Asia in February 1941, the Japanese announced what amounted to a claim upon exclusive interest in the resources of the area. Then, in April 1941, came the Japanese conclusion of a nonaggression treaty with the USSR, the essential prerequisite for a move into Southeast Asia.

When Germany attacked the Soviet Union in June 1941, it appeared at first that the Germans were certain to win. On June 25 the two Japanese services met to discuss this new development. They decided to concentrate on the intended takeover of Southeast Asia before dealing with whatever situation existed in the wake of Germany's victory over the Soviet Union. When the imperial conference of July 2 had confirmed this decision, the army called up a million reservists. These were to be deployed in the Home Islands, Manchuria, and China, thus freeing existing divisions for service in Southeast Asia. On July 21 the navy formally declared itself in favor of the occupation of parts of the Southern Resources Area even at the risk of war with the United States and, on July 25, Japanese forces occupied southern

YAMAMOTO ISOROKU

COMMANDER-IN-CHIEF of the Japanese Combined Fleet in 1941, Yamamoto Isoroku (1884–1943), was the originator of the plan for the attack on Pearl Harbor. As a young ensign he fought against the Russians at Tsushima (1905), where he lost two fingers on his left hand. After World War I he spent time in United States, first as a student at Harvard, then as a naval attaché in Washington. He foresaw the importance of airpower in naval warfare and in 1933 was given command of the First Carrier Division. The apparent success of the Pearl Harbor operation made him a national hero, but his Central Pacific offensive in June 1942 resulted in disaster at Midway. Yamamoto retained command of the Combined Fleet, moving his headquarters to Truk. He was killed when the aircraft he was flying in was shot down over Bougainville on April 18, 1943. Yamamoto remains a figure of controversy. He is usually portrayed as one of the more moderate Japanese officers, fearful of American power, but, whatever misgivings he had about war with the United States, these did not prevent him from attaining the highest ranks.

The *West Virginia* sinking in flames
In the attack on Pearl Harbor, the battleship *West Virginia* was hit by six torpedoes and two bombs. After the ship had sunk to the bottom, she continued to burn until the following afternoon.

French Indochina under the terms of a joint Franco-Japanese condominium. Roosevelt immediately froze all Japanese assets and halted US trade with Japan. Britain and the Netherlands followed suit, ending the trade with Southeast Asia on which Japan depended. Japanese attempts to get the American embargo lifted failed because of US insistence that Japan give up all its gains on the Asian mainland. The Japanese therefore decided that the only escape from this deadlock was war.

THE ATTACK ON PEARL HARBOR

In attacking the American fleet at its Hawaiian base at the outset of war the Japanese sought to neutralize the only force that could oppose their planned seizure of Southeast Asia and various island groups in the Pacific. The Japanese plan was to secure these areas and establish a vast perimeter defense around them. The Americans, after fighting to exhaustion against this

This is no drill
This message was sent to all ships in the Hawaii area announcing the air raid on Pearl Harbor minutes after the first bombs and torpedoes had struck.

AIRRAID ON PEARL HARBOR X THIS IS NO DRILL

defensive barrier, would be forced to come to a negotiated settlement. The specific goal of the attack on the fleet at Pearl Harbor was to forestall American countermoves by destroying four battleships. The Japanese calculated that this would limit American offensive capability sufficiently to provide a six-month period in which Japan could complete its planned conquests and prepare for the next phase of war.

The scale of the Japanese raid on the US Pacific Fleet on the morning of Sunday, December 7, 1941, was unprecedented. It was a massed attack involving two waves of aircraft (350 in total) from six fleet carriers. The British air attack on the Italian fleet at Taranto in November 1940 had involved just one carrier and 21 elderly Swordfish biplanes. The thoroughness of the Japanese planning and the successful timing needed to achieve complete surprise were equally impressive. An attack over such a large distance was possible only because of refueling under way, something the units of the carrier force had practiced for the first time in the three weeks before sailing.

THE ATTACK IS LAUNCHED

At 6:05 am on the day of the attack the fleet was 220 miles (350 km) north of Oahu. The Japanese aircraft had to take off in strong winds and heavy seas, the worst conditions the fleet had encountered in its 13-day voyage from the Kurile Islands. In spite of this, the first wave, which consisted of 49 Kate bombers, 40 Kate torpedo-bombers, 51 Val dive-bombers, and 43 Zero fighters, was airborne within 15 minutes, with just two planes lost in the process. The second wave—54 Kate bombers, 78 Vals, and 35 Zeros—was ready for takeoff at 7:15 am.

The air attacks were backed up by five midget submarines launched from their parent submarine close to the entrance to Pearl Harbor during the night. One of the submarines was actually spotted at 3:42 am; another (or the same one) was spotted and sunk shortly before 7:00 am. The second incident was reported but the craft's identity was unknown and no further action was taken. A radar sighting of a large number of aircraft approaching from the north was made at about the same time, but it was assumed these were US planes flying in from the mainland. At any rate, by now, there was hardly any time to take effective action against attack.

THE EXTENT OF THE DAMAGE

The first wave of planes inflicted considerable damage, especially the Kates' attack on "Battleship Row," where seven battleships were moored. The Val dive-bombers and Zero fighters were also extremely effective in neutralizing American air power on Oahu. The second wave, which struck an

JAPANESE AND US CARRIER PLANES

OF ALL THE MAJOR POWERS, Japan was best prepared for a new era in naval warfare dominated by aircraft. In 1941 the Japanese navy had 10 front-line aircraft carriers; the American navy had only three in the Pacific. Both navies agreed on the types of aircraft needed—fighters to gain control of the air, along with dive-bombers and torpedo-bombers to attack enemy ships—but the US planes were markedly inferior to their Japanese counterparts. The Japanese also had better-trained, more experienced crews. Although the Japanese realized the importance of the aircraft carrier, they still believed that battleships—their principal targets at Pearl Harbor—were the key to any major naval action. Both sides soon discovered that this was not the case. Entire naval battles would be fought without any ships coming within range of the other side's guns. Carriers also became launching pads for bombing raids on airfields and other military installations on shore.

Nakajima B5N2 ("Kate")

The B5N2 was Japan's torpedo-bomber. Armed with the advanced Type 95 torpedo, this formidable aircraft enjoyed great success for the first two years of the war. An earlier model, the B5N1, was used as a level-altitude bomber, deployed chiefly in China. Late in the war Kates were used as Kamikaze planes.

Engine 1,115 hp Nakajima Sakae 21 air-cooled 14-cylinder radial	
Wingspan 50 ft 11 in (15.5 m)	Length 33 ft 9 in (10.3 m)
Top speed 235 mph (378 kph)	Crew 3
Armament 2 × 7.7-mm machine-guns, 1 × 7.7-mm machine-gun in rear; 1 × 1,765-lb (800-kg) torpedo	

Radio mast. The Zero was one of the first Japanese carrier aircraft to be equipped with radio

Mitsubishi A6M Reisen ("Zero" or "Zeke")

At the outbreak of war the Japanese Zero was superior to any other carrier fighter and a match for existing shore-based fighters. "Zero" is the translation of the Japanese "Reisen." The lightweight aircraft had unparalleled range for the period. The A6M2 (the model in use at the time of Pearl Harbor) had a mission range of over 1,600 miles (2,500 km). New models of the highly maneuverable Zero continued to be developed—shown here is the A6M5—and by the end of the war a total of almost 11,000 had been built.

Wing-mounted cannon. In earlier models these were concealed within the wing

Three-bladed propellor

On some models the wingtips folded up so the plane could fit into standard carrier elevators

Engine 1,300 hp Nakajimia NK1C Sakae 21 14-cylinder radial	
Wingspan 36 ft 1 in (11 m)	Length 29 ft 11 in (9.1 m)
Top speed 346 mph (557 kph)	Crew 1
Armament 2 × 20-mm cannon in wings, 2 × 7.7-mm machine-guns on fuselage; wing racks carry 2 × 132-lb (60-kg) bombs	

Douglas SBD-3 Dauntless

The US Navy's main dive-bomber at the start of the war, the Dauntless carried a greater bombload than the Japanese Val. Though slow and vulnerable to fighters, it could absorb considerable damage. Dauntlesses were involved in the destruction of six Japanese carriers in 1942. Nearly 6,000 were built.

Engine 1,000 hp Wright R-1820-52 Cyclone 9-cylinder radial	
Wingspan 45 ft 6 in (13.9 m)	Length 33 ft 1 in (10.1 m)
Top speed 250 mph (402 kph)	Crew 2
Armament 2 × 0.5-in machine-guns in nose, 2 × 0.3-in machine-guns in rear cockpit; 1,200-lb (545-kg) bombload	

Aichi D3A ("Val")

A dive-bomber used by the Japanese navy at Pearl Harbor, the Val was feared for its impressive accuracy in the first two years of the war, but after 1943 its lack of armor made it an easy target for US fighters. Its fixed undercarriage made its silhouette easily recognizable.

Engine 1,080 hp Mitsubishi Kinsei 44 air-cooled 14-cylinder radial	
Wingspan 47 ft 1 in (14.4 m)	Length 33 ft 5 in (10.2 m)
Top speed 272 mph (460 kph)	Crew 2
Armament 2 × 7.7-mm machine-guns (1 in nose, 1 in rear); 1 × 550-lb (250-kg), 2 × 66-lb (30-kg) bombs under wings	

MAGIC: CRACKING THE JAPANESE CODES

"MAGIC" WAS THE CODE NAME the Americans gave to deciphered Japanese radio messages, particularly those in the code known as "Purple," used for diplomatic communications. This code was introduced in early 1939, replacing one code-named "Red" that the Americans had already deciphered. The cipher machine that generated the Purple code consisted of two typewriter keyboards connected by a bewildering array of circuits and switches, based on the technology of a telephone switchboard. Not all Japanese embassies were issued with these new machines and they continued to use the "Red" code. This helped

Deciphering Japanese messages

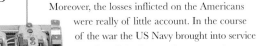

Intelligence analysts work with Purple code machines at the headquarters of the US Army cryptanalysis service in Arlington, Virginia.

Purple machine

The Americans never managed to capture a Japanese Purple encoding machine. Once they had understood how it worked, they simply built their own.

the decryption team at the US Army Signals Intelligence Service, as the same message was sometimes sent out in the two codes. The team of cryptanalysts, headed by William F. Friedman, worked tirelessly for 18 months to crack the code. A vital contribution was made by Harry L. Clark, a naval cryptanalyst, who guessed that the Japanese were not using rotors as on the German Enigma machine, but standard telephone equipment. Success came on September 25, 1940, when the first complete message was deciphered. The team then set about constructing Purple analogue machines.

After the failure of the US intelligence services to foresee the attack on Pearl Harbor, vast resources were devoted to breaking other Japanese codes. The Japanese naval code, JN-25, was never cracked completely, but was understood sufficiently to warn the US Navy of the Japanese attack on Midway in June 1942. Top secret information derived from Japanese coded radio traffic was given the same "Ultra" designation as information gathered from German Enigma communications (see page 82).

through an unrestricted submarine campaign. Moreover, the losses inflicted on the Americans were really of little account. In the course of the war the US Navy brought into service 104 fleet, light fleet, and escort carriers, eight battleships, 46 cruisers, 349 destroyers, 493 destroyer escorts and frigates, and 203 submarines; the aircraft losses incurred at Pearl Harbor represented less than two days' production by March 1944.

WHAT MIGHT HAVE BEEN

Some commentators maintain that Japan's mistake was to leave Pearl Harbor's docks, workshops, power plants, and oil depots virtually intact. Despite the heavy loss of warships, the Americans were left with a more or less functional naval base. Given America's industrial output over the next three years, however, whatever damage might have been inflicted on these facilities would have been repaired very quickly. Others suggest that the Japanese should have conducted not an air strike, but an assault landing with the intention of securing Oahu, yet even this would probably have done little to alter the course of the war.

From the American point of view, commentators have pointed out that by the fall of 1941 signals intelligence had cracked a number of Japanese ciphers and was reading a large amount of radio traffic. But the Japanese Navy in its preparation and training for the attack on Pearl Harbor did not need to use radio and nothing in the signals read by the Americans gave any inkling of a war beginning with an attack on the fleet at its Hawaiian base.

In the build-up to the attack the Japanese Navy had employed a number of deceptive measures. A large number of its sailors had been granted leave in Tokyo over the weekend and wide publicity was given to the sailing of the *Tatsuta Maru* in order to collect Japanese nationals being repatriated from the United States.

hour later, was less successful, largely because smoke from the burning oil spewing from the stricken battleships obscured the attackers' view. In all, the attack accounted for 18 warships either sunk, destroyed, or damaged to some degree, and 198 aircraft destroyed and 174 damaged. A total of 3,748 US service personnel were killed or wounded. American civilian casualties numbered 103.

Of the ships, only three, the battleships *Arizona* and *Oklahoma*, and the target ship *Utah*, were total losses, though the *Oklahoma* was raised in order to clear the anchorage. The *Arizona* was struck by a bomb that penetrated the ship's forward magazine, causing a tremendous explosion and a huge fireball. Nearly 1,000 of its crew were killed and the vessel sank within nine minutes. The battleships *California* and *West Virginia*, and the headquarters ship *Oglala*, were sunk, and the battleship *Nevada*, after suffering extensive damage, was run aground. All four ships, however, were raised, then underwent massive reconstruction and were returned to service. The light cruisers *Helena* and *Raleigh*, and the destroyer *Shaw* were moderately damaged, and were returned to service in 1942; the destroyers *Cassin* and *Downes* were very badly damaged, but were rebuilt and

reentered service in 1944. The damage inflicted on the battleships *Maryland*, *Tennessee*, and *Pennnsyvania*, the light cruiser *Honolulu*, and the auxiliaries *Curtiss* and *Vestal* was minor. Japanese losses numbered 29 aircraft, with at least another 111 damaged.

For all the success registered against the US fleet, the attack was disastrous for Japan. It brought into the war a United States roused in righteous anger and determined to wage war either to total victory or to defeat. The attack forced the US navy to reconstitute its tactical formations around the aircraft carrier rather than the battleship and to carry the war immediately to Japanese shipping

Pearl Harbor

This Japanese aerial photograph of the attack shows Ford Island in the middle of the harbor with the row of US battleships lined up on the far side of the island.

As well as these measures, intended to demonstrate "business as usual," a signals unit in Japan's Inland Sea simulated radio signals from aircraft carrier units, and these, it seems, had the desired effect.

In the aftermath of the attack, the Americans naturally wanted to know what had gone wrong and to find scapegoats on whom to pin the blame. There was little appreciation of the tight security measures taken by the Japanese. Perhaps no more than 100

Assessing the damage
American sailors walk over the wreckage of the destroyers *Downes* (left) and *Cassin* after the Japanese attack on Pearl Harbor. The battleship *Pennsylvania*, flagship of the Pacific fleet, is visible behind the two destroyers.

officers in the Imperial Navy outside the task force earmarked for the operation were aware of the plan. Nor were critics prepared to accept the fact that the United States had no God-given ability to predict the future. The Americans and British had both realized that the Japanese were about to go to war, but in the days immediately before the attack, their attention had been focused on the impending offensives throughout Southeast Asia. This had clouded their appreciation of the strategic picture to the east, in the Central Pacific. The Japanese opening move, spread across nine time zones and over 7,000 miles (11,000 km), was something so utterly without precedent that it could never have been foreseen.

Behind me, a marine lay dead on the deck, his body split in two. I began to realize there were dead men all around me. Some men were burning, wandering aimlessly. The sound of someone shouting "put out the fire" cut through the sound of the battle, but it was obvious the ship was doomed. I made my way to the side of the ship, which by this time was sinking fast, and jumped off the fantail. The shoreline of Ford Island was only a short distance. There was burning oil all around the ship, but the aft was clear. After swimming to shore, I was taken to the naval air station. Every table in the mess hall had a man on it.

GEORGE D. PHRANER, AVIATION MACHINIST'S MATE 1ST CLASS, SURVIVOR OF THE USS *ARIZONA*

BINOCULARS FROM THE BRIDGE OF THE USS *ARIZONA*

The attack on Pearl Harbor was synchronized with the start of Japanese invasions of the American, British, and Dutch colonies in Southeast Asia. For six months the Japanese enjoyed an uninterrupted run of victories, but in June 1942 suffered a serious setback in the carrier battle with the US fleet at Midway.

1941

DECEMBER 8
Japanese bomb Singapore; first landings in Malaya

DECEMBER 8 (7 IN USA)
Japanese attack on Pearl Harbor

DECEMBER 10
Japanese aircraft sink *Prince of Wales* and *Repulse* off coast of Malaya

DECEMBER 14
Siam allies itself with Japan

DECEMBER 16
Japanese forces land in Sarawak in northern Borneo

DECEMBER 18
Japanese invasion force lands on Hong Kong Island

DECEMBER 22
Main Japanese landing on Luzon at Lingayen Gulf

DECEMBER 23
Japanese take Wake Island, having failed at previous attempt on December 11

DECEMBER 25
Hong Kong surrenders

1942

JANUARY 2
Manila falls to Japanese. US and Filipino troops complete withdrawal to Bataan Peninsula

JANUARY 20
Main Japanese invasion force enters Burma

JANUARY 23
Japanese secure Rabaul on New Britain. It remains their main base in Southwest Pacific for the length of the war

JANUARY 23–24
Japanese occupation of Balikpapan, Borneo

JANUARY 31
Withdrawal of Allied troops from Malaya to Singapore completed

FEBRUARY 8
Japanese land on Singapore Island

FEBRUARY 15
Surrender of Singapore

FEBRUARY 19
Japanese carrier raid on Darwin in northern Australia

FEBRUARY 27
Battle of the Java Sea. Squadron of Dutch and other Allied ships defeated

FEBRUARY 28
Japanese invade Java

MARCH 5
Japanese take Batavia

MARCH 8
Japanese take Rangoon, following withdrawal of British troops to the north

MARCH 9
Surrender of Dutch East Indies to Japanese

MARCH 14
US troops start to arrive in Australia in force

MARCH 30
Allies divide Pacific theater into two commands: Southwest Pacific under General MacArthur; Central Pacific under Admiral Nimitz

APRIL 9
US and Filipino forces on Bataan Peninsula surrender. 78,000 captured

APRIL 18
Doolittle Raid. First US carrier raid on Japanese home islands

APRIL 30
Japanese forces take Mandalay, Burma

MAY 4
Japanese invasion force sails from Rabaul for Port Moresby

MAY 6
American forces on Corregidor surrender following Japanese landing on the island

MAY 7–8
Battle of the Coral Sea. Japanese landing at Port Moresby called off

MAY 20
Withdrawal of last Allied troops from Burma into India

JUNE 3
Japanese planes raid Dutch Harbor, US base in the Aleutians

JUNE 4–6
American victory at Battle of Midway. Japan no longer prepared to risk major offensive naval action

JUNE 7
Japanese landings on Kiska and Attu in the Aleutian Islands

■ Japanese conquest of Southeast Asia and Dutch East Indies Dec 1942–Jun 1943

■ Japanese conquest of the Philippines Dec 1942–May 1943

■ Other events

JAPANESE ONSLAUGHT

ON THE SAME DAY as their strike against the US Pacific Fleet—December 7 in the United States and at Pearl Harbor, December 8 in Japan and the Western Pacific—the Japanese unleashed a series of other carefully prepared attacks. In the Pacific, these included a bombardment of the island of Midway and attacks on Wake Island and Guam. Bombers from Formosa launched an air strike against American airfields on the island of Luzon in the Philippines, destroying 103 aircraft, most of them while they were still on the ground. The Japanese then went ahead with preliminary landings on the islands to the north of Luzon. Meanwhile, troops from the Chinese mainland entered the New Territories in order to seize the British colony of Hong Kong. In Southeast Asia, some Japanese troops moved overland into neutral Siam from southern Indochina, while others carried out a series of landings in southern Siam and northern Malaya.

Only at Wake did Japanese plans miscarry. On December 11 the garrison of American Marines managed to repel the invasion force, but the Japanese, with the assistance of two of the carriers returning from the Pearl Harbor operation, were able to secure the island on December 23.

By that date the Japanese had overrun the New Territories, and the garrison on Hong Kong Island surrendered on December 25. In Malaya, the British hoped to put up more substantial resistance. On December 8 they despatched a naval force—the battleship *Prince of Wales*, the battlecruiser *Repulse*, and four destroyers—from Singapore to counter the Japanese landings on the east coast of Malaya and Siam. The ships were spotted and, on the morning of December 10, attacked by land-based torpedo-bombers. In less than three hours both the *Prince of Wales* and the *Repulse* had been sunk.

RAPID ADVANCE

The British fared little better on land. As the Indian, British, and Australian troops retreated south along the Malayan peninsula, they were caught between trying to fight a delaying action and preparing defensive positions. The Japanese, well trained in

Advance into Burma
A column of Japanese troops crosses an improvised bridge in northern Burma. Beside it lie the remains of a metal bridge destroyed by the retreating British forces as they withdrew to the safety of northern India.

jungle fighting, employed light armor on the roads and infantry infiltration through the jungle to get around British defenses. The British abandoned Penang on December 19 and the Japanese were able to bring the nearby airfield in Butterworth into service on the following day to provide air support for their continued advance.

AMERICAN WITHDRAWAL

In the Philippines, the Japanese staged a series of landings by small forces at various points on Luzon and at Davao on southern Mindanao. The main landings took place on December 22 in Lingayen Gulf north of Manila. These were followed by the withdrawal of the main American forces into the Bataan Peninsula, allowing the Japanese to advance to Manila and enter the city on January 2, 1942. In this first phase of the invasion the Americans managed to avoid defeat, but the refuge they had chosen in the Bataan Peninsula would turn out to be a trap. Despite having planned for such an eventuality, they had not prepared or prestocked their defenses. With the Japanese in control of the sea and the air, supplies could only reach the beleaguered forces by submarine. The defensive positions across the mountainous peninsula might prolong resistance, but there was no doubting the outcome of the campaign. For the time being, however, the Japanese command chose to ignore the American sidestep to Bataan. Its main concern at this stage was to free forces from the Philippines for moves against the Indies, and it was not until after the fall of Manila that Japanese attention turned to Bataan, but by then they did not have sufficient forces to overrun the peninsula.

TOJO HIDEKI

PRIME MINISTER OF JAPAN at the outbreak of war, General Tojo (1884–1948) was prominent among the hard-line militarists who came to dominate Japanese politics in the 1930s. He was a founder of the Asian Development Union, which embraced a policy of Japanese conquest and control throughout Asia. Respected both as a staff officer and as a field commander, he became chief of staff of the Kwantung army in Manchuria in 1937 and in the following year vice minister of war in the government of Prince Konoye. When Konoye formed another government in 1941, Tojo was his minister for war. As negotiations with the United States stalled, Tojo ousted Konoye and, in October 1941, established an administration that committed Japan to war. As the tide of war turned against Japan, Tojo took on ever more positions: by February 1944 he was minister of war and army chief of staff as well as prime minister. Tojo and his whole cabinet resigned in July 1944. After the Japanese surrender he made an unsuccessful attempt to kill himself, but was arrested and stood trial as a war criminal. He was hanged in December 1948.

SOUTHEAST ASIA

By this time the Japanese had won resounding victories throughout Southeast Asia. On the Malayan peninsula they continued their drive south to Singapore, advancing sometimes through the jungle, at other times by means of amphibious operations. On the western side of the peninsula they used light craft captured during their advance to outflank British positions with a series of small landings along the coast.

The sinking of the *Prince of Wales*
On December 10, 1942 the *Prince of Wales* was sunk by torpedoes in the South China Sea along with the *Repulse*. About 1,000 men were lost, but 2,081 were picked up by British destroyers.

Japanese conquests

Japan's attack on Pearl Harbor was an extraordinary act of audacious planning and daring execution. The conquest of Hong Kong, the Philippines, Burma, Malaya, and the Dutch East Indies, all accomplished in less than six months, was an even more astonishing achievement. By June 1942 the Japanese had secured the whole of the region they needed to control in order to guarantee their supplies of oil, rubber, and other valuable raw materials.

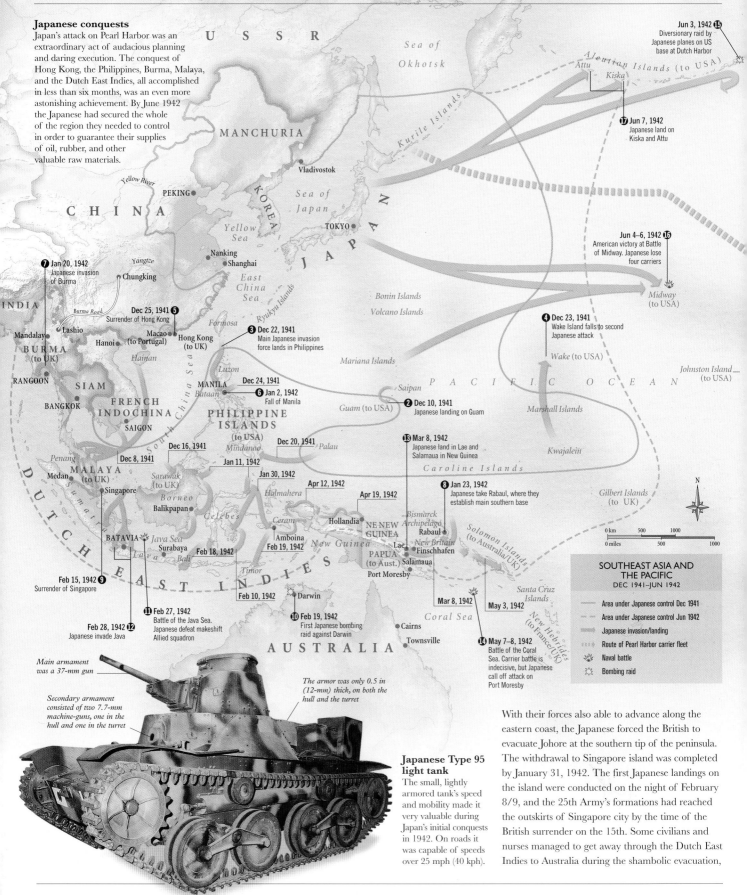

Jun 3, 1942 15
Diversionary raid by Japanese planes on US base at Dutch Harbor

Jun 7, 1942 17
Japanese land on Kiska and Attu

Jun 4–6, 1942 16
American victory at Battle of Midway. Japanese lose four carriers

Jan 20, 1942 7
Japanese invasion of Burma

Dec 25, 1941 5
Surrender of Hong Kong

Dec 22, 1941 3
Main Japanese invasion force lands in Philippines

Dec 23, 1941 4
Wake Island falls to second Japanese attack

Dec 24, 1941

Jan 2, 1942 6
Fall of Manila

Dec 10, 1941 2
Japanese landing on Guam

Dec 16, 1941

Dec 20, 1941

Jan 11, 1942

Jan 30, 1942

Apr 12, 1942

Apr 19, 1942

Mar 8, 1942 13
Japanese land in Lae and Salamaua in New Guinea

Jan 23, 1942 8
Japanese take Rabaul, where they establish main southern base

Dec 8, 1941

Feb 15, 1942 9
Surrender of Singapore

Feb 18, 1942

Feb 19, 1942

Feb 27, 1942 11
Battle of the Java Sea. Japanese defeat makeshift Allied squadron

Feb 28, 1942 12
Japanese invade Java

Feb 10, 1942

Feb 19, 1942 10
First Japanese bombing raid against Darwin

Mar 8, 1942

May 3, 1942

May 7–8, 1942 14
Battle of the Coral Sea. Carrier battle is indecisive, but Japanese call off attack on Port Moresby

SOUTHEAST ASIA AND THE PACIFIC
DEC 1941–JUN 1942

— Area under Japanese control Dec 1941
--- Area under Japanese control Jun 1942
— Japanese invasion/landing
···· Route of Pearl Harbor carrier fleet
Naval battle
Bombing raid

Japanese Type 95 light tank

The small, lightly armored tank's speed and mobility made it very valuable during Japan's initial conquests in 1942. On roads it was capable of speeds over 25 mph (40 kph).

Main armament was a 37-mm gun

Secondary armament consisted of two 7.7-mm machine-guns, one in the hull and one in the turret

The armor was only 0.5 in (12-mm) thick, on both the hull and the turret

With their forces also able to advance along the eastern coast, the Japanese forced the British to evacuate Johore at the southern tip of the peninsula. The withdrawal to Singapore island was completed by January 31, 1942. The first Japanese landings on the island were conducted on the night of February 8/9, and the 25th Army's formations had reached the outskirts of Singapore city by the time of the British surrender on the 15th. Some civilians and nurses managed to get away through the Dutch East Indies to Australia during the shambolic evacuation,

Surrender in Singapore
Japanese troops with fixed bayonets round up a demoralized British unit after the fall of Singapore on February 15, 1942. The humiliating defeat by a despised and underrated enemy was a severe blow to British imperial prestige.

① Dec 7, 1941
Japanese attack on
Pearl Harbor

Hawaiian Islands (to USA)
◤Pearl Harbor

but a large number of troops, including 32,000 Indians, 16,000 Britons, and 14,000 Australians, were made prisoners of war. The Japanese treated the Chinese civilian population of Singapore very differently from the prisoners of war. According to some accounts, the Japanese army killed about 120,000 Chinese in the three months after the surrender.

THE DUTCH EAST INDIES

The security of the Dutch empire in the East Indies had rested upon successive lines of defense—French Indochina, the American Philippines, and British Malaya. Once these had fallen the Dutch empire lay open to defeat and dismemberment. In fact, even before the defeats of the Americans and British were completed, the Japanese made their first moves against the islands, conducting a series of landings along two main axes of advance—one through the Macassar Strait between Borneo and Celebes, the other through the Molucca Sea, which separates Celebes from Halmahera and western New Guinea. The Japanese moves were synchronized and mounted behind a front secured by land-based air power.

As the Japanese moved southward through the Dutch East Indies, their only real losses occurred outside Balikpapan, the main port serving the valuable oil fields of eastern Borneo. On January 24–25, 1942 a group of American destroyers caught four of the transports carrying the Japanese landing force. The night action was fought against a background of flaming oil wells, which had been set alight by the Dutch. Even this reverse, however, did not delay the Japanese. The port was captured and the airfield in Balikpapan was returned to service on January 28.

With the British on the verge of defeat in Singapore, the Japanese mounted a further offensive to the west. Landings were made in southern Sumatra, even as Japanese forces came ashore on Timor and Bali. At the same time Japanese carrier planes raided Darwin in northern Australia. The defense of Java resulted in a vain Allied attempt to meet the Japanese at sea before their forces could come ashore, but this resulted in defeat at the Battle of the Java Sea on February 27–28. The Japanese landings on Java were followed by a naval action in the Sunda Strait and further losses as Allied naval forces abandoned the Indies. The Japanese occupied Batavia (Jakarta) on March 5 and four days later the Dutch East Indies surrendered. Japanese forces had already been operating south of Java, in the Indian Ocean, trying to destroy shipping escaping to Australia. In mid-March Japanese forces from Malaya occupied Medan in northern Sumatra and in early April other forces occupied various small ports on the Vogelkop Peninsula in western New Guinea. From there they advanced along the north coast of the island to Hollandia.

> At first we thought these planes were ours, and then we noticed some silver-looking objects dropping from them. It was not long before we knew what they were as they exploded in smoke and dust on the town and waterfront. More Japanese planes came in from another direction. These were dive-bombers, and they attacked the ships in the harbor... They began strafing us from almost mast height. As the only armament we had against aircraft was a Lewis machine gun, and this had been disabled by a Japanese bullet hitting the magazine pan, the skipper was firing at them with his .45 revolver... Our casualties were nine wounded out of a crew of thirty-six, and one of these died on the hospital ship Manunda on the following day.

CHARLIE UNMACK, STOKER ABOARD THE MINESWEEPER HMAS *GUNBAR*, IN DARWIN HARBOR ON FEBRUARY 19, 1942

NIMITZ AND MACARTHUR

IN 1942 THE UNITED STATES found itself fighting a war along a front stretching from New Guinea to the Aleutians. It also had the problem of supporting and supplying the Nationalist forces in China. A new kind of command structure was needed to implement American strategic goals. The logical solution would have been to put the US Navy in overall command, but the US Army would not agree to this, nor would the navy agree to put the Pacific Fleet under the command of the army. They eventually appointed two commanders, one from the navy, the other from the army, each responsible for one particular theater. Admiral Chester W. Nimitz, commander-in-chief of the US Pacific Fleet since Pearl Harbor, was also made commander-in-chief of the Pacific Ocean Areas. General Douglas A. MacArthur, despite his poor handling of the defense of the Philippines, was made Supreme Allied Commander South West Pacific Command, with his headquarters in Australia. The two were very contrasting characters. Nimitz was a modest man, who deliberately chose able subordinate commanders, while MacArthur was an individualist, obsessed with his own importance and the creation of his own legend.

Joint commanders
MacArthur (with his trademark corncob pipe) and Nimitz study a map. Rivalry between the army and the navy was a constant source of tension between the two, but somehow the job got done.

US troops in Australia
The first American soldiers reached Australia on December 22, 1941. General MacArthur arrived in March 1942, setting up his headquarters in Melbourne.

BURMA

The Japanese victories in Malaya, the Indies, and the Philippines were not the only victories recorded in this period. The Japanese move into Siam at the outbreak of hostilities was the prelude to an invasion of the British colony of Burma. Siam, with very little choice in the matter, allied itself to Japan, allowing its territory to serve as a base for operations against Malaya and Burma.

The Burmese campaign proved a remarkable Japanese success. By the end of April 1942, and at a cost of just over 4,000 dead, the Japanese had captured Lashio and were on the point of occupying

Japanese advance in the Philippines

Once the main American force on the Bataan peninsula had surrendered in April 1942, the Japanese gradually mopped up the other scattered pockets of resistance. Here troops are crossing a river on Type 89 medium tanks.

Japanese propaganda
The Japanese tried to alienate Australians from the Allied cause. This cartoon shows Australians fighting vainly to hold back the Japanese advance, while Roosevelt helps himself to their homeland.

Mandalay. By the end of May the Japanese had secured virtually the whole of Burma. The few British forces that had been in Burma and the Chinese Kuomintang troops that had entered the country in January 1942 were unable to put up any resistance to the Japanese at any point during their advance. The victory was comprehensive, but brought a defensive commitment at the end of a long, vulnerable line of communication. In time, Japan's enemies were certain to launch a counteroffensive.

THE END IN THE PHILIPPINES

The humiliation of the United States was completed by the surrender of its remaining forces in the Philippines. The Americans and Filipinos

on the Bataan Peninsula had resisted Japanese attacks in January and February, but many were struck down by malaria and by February supplies of quinine were running short. Food was an even greater problem , since Japanese air superiority meant that hardly any supplies were reaching the beleaguered troops. There was no fodder at all for the horses and mules, which all had to be killed.

In Washington, Roosevelt accepted that the defense of the Philippines was doomed and on February 23 ordered General MacArthur to leave for Australia to take command of the Allied effort in the Southwest Pacific. On March 11 MacArthur and his family were taken by torpedo boat to Mindanao and from there by Flying Fortress to Australia. Reinforced with fresh troops, the Japanese renewed their attacks on the exhausted defenders of the Bataan Peninsula. On April 9 the American and Filipino forces surrendered. The American forces on Corregidor, off the tip of the peninsula, resisted until the night of May 5, when the Japanese managed to land a battalion on the island. The following day Lieutenant-General Jonathan M. Wainwright, the US commander since

THE BATAAN DEATH MARCH

WHEN THE AMERICAN AND FILIPINO forces on the Bataan Peninsula surrendered on April 9, 1942, the Japanese had a plan for the transportation of the prisoners from Mariveles near the tip of the peninsula to Camp O'Donnell, a trip of about 90 miles (145 km). For some of the way the prisoners would be expected to walk, for other parts of the journey, transportation—either by rail or by truck—would be provided. But Homma Masaharu, the Japanese commander, had imagined there would be no more than 25,000 prisoners. As it turned out, there were 76,000, many already weakened by malaria and months of living on starvation rations. The great majority were Filipinos; about 12,000

were American. For the first day of the march no food was given to the prisoners, who were expected to have their own rations with them, and there was no medical care for the sick and wounded. Random acts of violence were committed against the prisoners: beatings and bayonetings administered by guards and taunts and assaults delivered by Japanese soldiers traveling in the opposite direction. Some prisoners were given water, others were denied it.

The number of prisoners marching grew as they were joined by others who had surrendered at various points along the route. Conditions grew worse as, in baking heat, white dust covered the

marchers as they made their way northward. When the prisoners reached the railroad station, some were packed into freight cars and many died as they stood upright for the journey of 25 miles (40 km). Others were forced to walk the whole way.

Nobody knows how many died on the march, but perhaps 15,000 of those who set out did not reach their destination. A number of these, however, were Filipinos who managed to escape. In 1946 Homma was tried for the actions of his men during the "Death March." He maintained he had been unaware of the conditions endured by the prisoners, but he was convicted and sentenced to death.

Prisoners on the march
American and Filipino soldiers are herded into captivity on the Bataan Peninsula after surrendering to the Japanese on April 9, 1942.

the departure of MacArthur, negotiated terms of surrender for all the forces on the Philippines. It was not until June 9, however, that the process of surrender throughout the islands was completed.

The Japanese victory in Southeast Asia was a triumph. With no overall margin of superiority in terms of military forces available, Japan had totally outfought its three enemies. The American, British, and Dutch troops had all been deployed defensively, but had failed to make any use of this advantage.

The Japanese success was the result of detailed planning and preparation. The United States and Britain had totally underestimated the effectiveness of Japanese air and naval power. Their comprehensive defeat was totally deserved.

AMERICAN FLAME-THROWER

Pressure to propel the flame was provided by compressed nitrogen

Flame-throwers were fuelled with petrol thickened with napalm

Attack on Corregidor
Japanese troops use a flame-thrower to drive American defenders out of a bunker. The island of Corregidor was heavily fortified with an intricate system of underground tunnels.

EXTENDING THE PERIMETER

As the campaign in the Philippines drew to a close, the Japanese were undertaking further landings in the Southwest Pacific. In January they had taken Rabaul in New Britain and from there they set about a series of offensives aimed at giving depth to their position. Their immediate objective was to secure eastern New Guinea and the Solomon Islands in order to develop the airfields needed to fight a defensive battle in this theater. This was to be part of the perimeter along which the Americans would be fought to exhaustion.

Following the outbreak of war the Americans found themselves with defensive commitments throughout the Central and Southwest Pacific. These precluded any serious attempt to interfere with Japanese moves, but in February 1942 they were able to mount a few small-scale carrier raids on Kwajalein, Rabaul, and Wake. The following month, however, on the basis of signals intelligence, the Americans were in a position to counter the Japanese landings at Lae and Salamaua in eastern New Guinea on March 8. Two days later, when Japanese forces came ashore at Finschhafen, American carrier aircraft attacked Japanese shipping off Lae and Salamaua. While losses were modest in terms of numbers, they were serious enough to jeopardize the next moves the Japanese had planned.

Initial Japanese success bred a belief that Japan could not go over to the defensive but should continue with offensive operations, a confidence that came to be known as "Victory Disease." At this stage the Imperial Navy was committed to a carrier operation in the Indian Ocean against British warships and merchantmen, but the main focus of its attention was upon the question of where in the Pacific its next moves should be made.

On April 18, 1942, the Americans carried out a raid on Tokyo and other targets in the Japanese home islands by B-25 medium bombers launched from the aircraft carrier *Hornet*. Led by Lieutenant Colonel James H. Doolittle, the "Doolittle Raid" gave a boost to US morale, but was derisively dismissed by the Japanese as the "Do Nothing Raid." The raid, however, silenced any misgivings about what the next Japanese moves should be. The fleet already had plans in place to extend Japan's defensive perimeter: first by a landing at Port Moresby in New Guinea, then by the occupation of Nauru and Ocean islands by forces from the Solomons. The main effort, however, involved an initial attack on the Aleutian Islands before an assault on Midway.

The Japanese fleet's plan envisaged the Americans having to commit their carrier force in response to the Japanese landings

A telling advantage
Douglas Dauntless dive-bombers stand on the deck of an Essex-class carrier. At the Battle of Midway in June 1942 the Japanese navy lost four of its carriers to American aircraft.

on Midway, but the Japanese carrier force supporting the landings would only be able to stay on station for perhaps ten days. Meanwhile, the aircraft that would subsequently operate from Midway were embarked in the carrier bound for the Aleutians, so it is not exactly clear how the various parts of the operation were to hang together. The Japanese plans envisaged a withdrawal of the fleet—after winning "the decisive battle"—to Truk. Subsequent offensives were already planned against New Caledonia, Fiji, and Samoa in July and against Johnston Island in August, as a prelude to an invasion of the Hawaiian Islands.

BATTLE OF THE CORAL SEA

Japanese plans miscarried from the outset. The operation against Port Moresby required a series of preliminary landings in the lower Solomons and in the islands off the eastern tip of New Guinea. This dispersal of effort allowed the American carrier force to conduct a series of damaging strikes. These succeeded in neutralizing intended air bases and sinking the light carrier *Shoho* on May 7. Aircraft from the Japanese and US carrier forces now sought each other out and on the following day fought what was the first naval battle in which the warships of the two opposing fleets never sighted one another. The Americans lost the carrier *Lexington* and the *Yorktown* suffered considerable damage, as

The Battle of Midway
The US carrier *Yorktown* burns after being hit by Japanese dive-bombers. She was the only US warship to be attacked from the air during the battle.

the attack was unleashed on June 4. As a result they were able to put two carrier groups on station, northeast of Midway.

THE BATTLE OF MIDWAY

After an initial Japanese air strike on the island, the American carriers launched a series of attacks. These caught three of the four Japanese carriers some 30 or so minutes from being able to relaunch their own aircraft. The *Kaga* and *Soryu* sank that evening. The remaining

Japanese carrier was able to inflict heavy damage on the *Yorktown*, but in the last attacks of the day the American carriers caught the *Hiryu* and inflicted such damage that she, along with the *Akagi*, sank the following day. The *Yorktown*, having been abandoned but then reboarded, was under tow when hit by a spread of torpedoes from a submarine, which also accounted for a destroyer alongside. This cumulative damage put an end to attempts to salvage the ship, and the *Yorktown* sank on the morning of June 7.

Victory at the Battle of Midway was seen by the American public as revenge for the attack on the US Pacific Fleet at Pearl Harbor. It was not, as is often claimed, the decisive battle of the Pacific War, but the Coral Sea and Midway were the first in a series of battles over a six-month period, at the end of which the initiative lay clearly in American hands.

did the *Shokaku* on the Japanese side. Japanese aircraft losses, however, were so serious that they could not continue the battle and, as a result, the planned landing in Port Moresby was abandoned.

The Battle of the Coral Sea was the first real check to Japanese intentions. The basis of the setback was the staging of an operation with no margin of superiority over enemy forces known to be in the area. But the damage to the *Shokaku* and the aircraft losses added another dimension to the Japanese reverse. The *Shokaku* and another carrier, the *Zuikaku*, which had lost virtually all its planes, were unable to take part in the operation against Midway. Had these two carriers been present at the Battle of Midway they would have given the Japanese a significant margin of superiority over US forces. The Americans, meanwhile, had broken Japanese signals security and were forewarned of Japanese intentions when

"Pearl Harbor has now been partially avenged. Vengeance will not be complete until Japanese sea power is reduced to impotence."

ADMIRAL NIMITZ, IN A COMMUNIQUÉ
AFTER THE BATTLE OF MIDWAY, JUNE 6, 1942

THE HOME FRONT IN THE UNITED STATES AND JAPAN

NOVEMBER 1941– OCTOBER 1944

The contrast between the American and Japanese home fronts could not have been greater. At the time of Pearl Harbor, Japan's industry was already on a war footing. American industry had just begun to emerge from recession through the supply of war material and food to Britain, but its huge potential lay virtually untapped. By the end of the war the Americans had gained a new prosperity, while the defeated Japanese faced poverty and starvation.

1941

DECEMBER 8
Following attack on Pearl Harbor, US declares war on Japan

NOVEMBER
Coupon system for rice, salt, and sugar rations already in use in major cities is extended to whole of Japan

JANUARY 7 — 1942
Roosevelt announces first war budget. $13,250 million to be spent on defense

JANUARY 31
Private car production suspended to maximize war effort

FEBRUARY 19
Over 100,000 Japanese living on Pacific coast moved to detention camps

FEBRUARY 23
Japanese submarine shells coast of California

APRIL 18
Blackout enforced along eastern seaboard to counter shipping losses to U-boats

APRIL 18
Doolittle Raid launched from carrier *Hornet* on Tokyo and other Japanese cities

APRIL
Japanese junior schools reorganized along militarist, nationalistic principles

MAY 15
Petrol rationing imposed in 17 US Eastern states

AUGUST 28
Japanese seaplane, launched from submarine, bombs forests in Oregon

DECEMBER
Gasoline rationing nationwide

DECEMBER 1
Coffee rationing introduced. Ended in July 1943

1943

JANUARY 11
In budget for second year of war, $100 billion is earmarked for war effort

MARCH 29
Meat ration in the United States set at 28 oz (about 800 g) per week

APRIL 1
Prices and wages frozen in order to put a brake on inflation

MAY 29
First appearance of Norman Rockwell's heroic figure "Rosie the Riveter" on cover of *Saturday Evening Post*

MAY 27
Roosevelt issues executive order forbidding racial discrimination by government contractors

JUNE 22
Race riots in Detroit; 34 killed

JULY 1
Pay-as-you-go income tax introduced in the United States

NOVEMBER
Air Defense Headquarters set up. Makes preparations for air raids, such as public tunnel shelters

1944

FEBRUARY
Mobilization of teenaged students. 1.5 million new recruits conscripted into Japanese armed forces during 1944

MAY 3
Meat rationing ends in the United States, except for certain special cuts

JUNE 15
First American B-29 raid on Japanese Home Islands from China. Parents start evacuating hundreds of thousands of children from cities to rural areas

JUNE 22
Roosevelt signs GI Bill of Rights, entitling all veterans to subsidized education and other benefits after the war

JULY 18
Tojo Hideki resigns as prime minister following US capture of Saipan

OCTOBER 12
Endo case. Detention of Japanese-Americans whose loyalty is not in doubt found unconstitutional

■ US home front   ■ Japanese home front

THE HOME FRONT IN THE US AND JAPAN

PARTICIPATION IN WORLD WAR II had far-reaching political, economic, and social effects on the United States, despite the fact that no enemy ever invaded its shores. Politically, the president and his advisers gained more power to run the country than ever before. Moreover, the Supreme Court helped endorse this new authority by refusing to hear cases that challenged it. During the war the number of federal civilian employees escalated from 1 million in 1940 to nearly 4 million. Many of these new government workers naturally felt a loyalty to President Roosevelt and the Democratic Party. Consequently, the majority party remained the Democrats, the voting constituency staying much the same as that of the 1930s, and Roosevelt won decisive victories in 1940 and 1944.

The Republicans, however, were able to reduce the Democrats' control of Congress and join with conservative Democrats in order to dismantle the social programs of the "New Deal." Military spending caused the administration to slash funding for the Civilian Conservation Corps, the Work Progress Administration, and the National Youth Administration. Because the programs were designed to help the poor and those who faced job discrimination, its demise especially affected blacks, women, and the elderly. There were also changes in the federal bureaucracies, as businessmen who disliked social welfare programs replaced the New Deal's social and economic "brains trust."

THE US ECONOMY

Wartime mobilization affected many aspects of the US economy and effectively ended the Great Depression. The government began to play an increasing role in keeping the economy healthy by "priming the pump" with orders for military goods. Companies with government contracts hired more

Quality control
A young woman checks the cartridge cases of 40-mm artillery shells at an American munitions factory.

Mass production
Production line methods developed in the automobile industry were adopted by aircraft factories. Here fuselages of B-17 Flying Fortress bombers await the next stage of production at the Boeing plant in Seattle, Washington.

people, set longer working hours, and increased production capacity. In 1940 there were 8 million unemployed Americans. By 1943 unemployment was virtually unheard of and there were actually labor shortages in some industries. The average working week in manufacturing durable goods increased from 38 hours in 1939 to 47 hours in 1943. In 1940 steel mills operated at 82 percent capacity, producing 67 million tons; by 1944, they were working at 100 percent capacity producing 89 million tons, half the world's output. From 1940 to 1945, American workers turned out 80,000 landing craft, 100,000 tanks and armored cars, 300,000 aircraft, 15 million guns, and 41 billion rounds of ammunition. The gross national product grew at an unprecedented rate from $91 billion in 1939 to $214 billion in 1945, a 235 percent increase. The national income doubled and consumer spending and savings increased significantly.

WOMEN ON THE US HOME FRONT

THE WAR BROUGHT MAJOR CHANGES to the lives of American women. Before the war, there had been a huge pool of female labor, consisting largely of young, single women. Many jobs were closed to them and they were effectively restricted to working in domestic service and retail businesses. Wartime production requirements, however, combined with the loss of the men who entered the military, provided women with the opportunity to move into a far wider range of jobs.

The response to the US government's request for more women workers was overwhelming and the changes remarkable. In 1941 there were 14.6 million women workers; by 1944 the number had grown to over 19.4 million. At one point during those years, more than 50 percent of American women worked and by 1945 half of all women workers were over 35 years old.

Equipping a bomber
A group of women workers installs interior fixtures in the tail fuselage section of a B-17 Flying Fortress at the Douglas plant, Long Beach, California, in October 1942.

Women were particularly active in the defense industries. Between 1940 and 1944 women working in manufacturing increased by 141 percent. In Detroit in 1943, women made up 91 percent of the new hirings in 185 war plants. Over 10 percent of all shipbuilders were women. Most of these jobs came with a "pink-slip" attached, as women understood they would be dismissed when the men returned from the war. Women were also frustrated by unfair pay differentials; men were paid more money for doing the same job. With the end of the war and demobilization, women were released almost twice as fast as men. In 1945 three-quarters of the women in aircraft and ship-building were let go, and women in the automotive industry decreased from 25 percent to 7 percent. Although women found their work satisfying and liberating, postwar propaganda focused on women's duty to help assimilate the returning veteran into society by "making him the man of the house again." When the war ended, many women left work to take up the duties of homemaking and child rearing.

Rosie the Riveter
The muscular emblem of American women's war work was created by the artist Norman Rockwell in 1943.

Wartime demand also brought new prosperity to farmers as the government kept prices high, provided low interest loans, and helped farmers apply the latest technological advances to increase crop production. Farmers produced all that they could for high prices, with the result that net income soared from $5.3 billion in 1939 to $13.6 billion in 1944. Because the government only provided aid to farmers with large acreages, the number of tenant and small farmers declined drastically. New technologies such as the enhanced grain combine also displaced many farm workers, who moved to urban areas looking for jobs in industry. The rise of the large-acreage farmer supported by government programs and price subsidies ushered in the era of "Big Agriculture."

Rita Hayworth
The Hollywood film star shows she is doing her bit for the war effort by sacrificing her car bumpers for use as scrap metal.

PATRIOTIC DUTY

It was personal sacrifice that lay at the heart of war mobilization and helped to forge a unified society. One of the major goals of the Roosevelt administration was to prepare people for a long, hard effort against Germany and Japan. In addition to military service, which eventually involved some 15 million men and women, those on the home front, through advertisements, magazine stories, films, and radio programs, were encouraged to "do their part." The Office of War Information commissioned a series of movies produced by Major Frank Capra entitled *Why We Fight* to help Americans (especially soldiers) understand why the war began, what was at stake, and why sacrifice was necessary. Stars such as Ronald Reagan, Robert Taylor, and Clark Gable were drafted into the army and then worked in Hollywood on such projects. Public service advertisements attempted to shame Americans into supporting the war effort. One government poster, for instance, showed a dead GI accompanied by the words, "He died today. What did you do?" Others demonstrated how both servicemen and home-front workers were soldiers in the fight for freedom—each making sacrifices for the cause. In all cases, the American GI was shown as a heroic figure, concerned about his family back home, yet dedicated to fighting for freedom and the American Way.

The government encouraged Americans to support their heroes by conserving and recycling materials. They were told that a donated shovel could make four hand grenades or help build a tank; lipstick tubes could be converted into bullet casings, while aluminum foil from gum wrappers would build fast, deadly aircraft. Furthermore, the government rationed certain goods, such as gas, coffee, sugar, and meat, and encouraged citizens to plant "Victory Gardens" to help save on foods needed for the front. Celebrities such as Bob Hope, Frank Sinatra, and Bing Crosby appeared at Savings Bond drives to convince Americans to donate

Recycling metals
This huge site in Brooklyn, New York, was set up for the public to donate cooking pots and pans, and other household objects made of aluminum. The metal was used principally in the manufacture of aircraft.

PLEASE DRIVE CAREFULLY.
MY BUMPERS ARE ON THE SCRAP HEAP

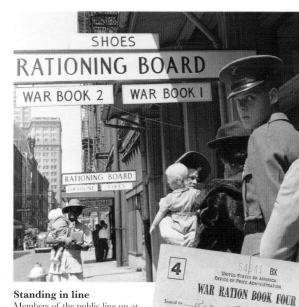

Standing in line
Members of the public line up at the local rationing board in New Orleans in 1943. There they would be issued with ration books, like that of the famous poet Robert Frost (right).

the migration of more than 700,000 blacks to the North and West during the war led to increased racial conflict. Between 1940 and 1946, the black population in urban areas increased significantly. In San Francisco, it grew by some 560 percent compared with a 28 percent increase in the white population. In Los Angeles, the figure was 105 percent compared with 18 percent for whites, in Detroit 47 percent compared to 5.2 percent for whites. Industrial employers discriminated because they paid black workers only a fraction of what they paid whites

doing the same job. Frustration came to a head in the summer of 1943 when race riots broke out in Detroit, Michigan, and Harlem, New York. In the Detroit riot 34 people were killed and 700 injured.

Yet it was during the war years that the Civil Rights movement gained some impetus. Black leaders such as A. Phillip Randolph, head of the Sleeping Car Porters' Union, demanded change. Randolph went as far as threatening President Roosevelt with a million-man march on Washington should he not do something about workplace discrimination. Concerned that the Nazis would humiliate him by making a comparison between discrimination against blacks in the United States and anti-Semitism in Germany, Roosevelt issued Presidential Order 8802, which set up the Fair Employment Practices Committee for federal government hiring procedures.

Building a cargo ship
American shipyards competed to see which could build a new ship in the least time. The Kaiser shipyard in Richmond, California, completed the *Robert E Peary* in just four days, 15 hours, and 29 minutes.

money to the war effort and be repaid with interest later. The government also became involved in the fashion business as it dictated styles that would conserve metal and cloth for the war. Out went three-piece suits and cuffs on pants. Women's skirts became shorter and narrower and the scandalous two-piece swimsuit was introduced to save on cloth and rubber. The new styles were dubbed "Patriotic Chic."

SOCIAL CHANGES
A more unified citizenry and the wartime economy had significant effects on American society. Although people were already moving to the North and West, and to suburban areas of major industrial centers, this trend would accelerate during the war as one in five Americans made a significant move. This helped strengthen the feelings of unity toward the war effort as citizens came into contact with others from different parts of the country, but it also contributed to racial and class conflict.

African-Americans faced continued discrimination and prejudice in the military and in industry. They served in separate units during the war. Some, such as the Tuskegee Airmen, distinguished themselves, but most were restricted to menial jobs such as steward or cook. Many whites refused to salute or take orders from black officers. The secretary of war, Henry Stimson, believed that African-Americans did not have leadership ability. On the home front,

JAPANESE INTERNMENT

AMONG THE INDIRECT VICTIMS of the war were the Japanese who lived in the United States. The majority of these lived in the US territory of Hawaii, which had been bombed by Japan, but they met with much less hostility there than did the Japanese living on the mainland. At the beginning of the war, approximately 120,000 Japanese lived on the West Coast, the majority in California. Despite a lack of credible evidence, Roosevelt succumbed to insistence that the Japanese-Americans should be classified as "enemy aliens." On February 19, 1942, he signed Executive Order No. 9066, which gave the US Army the authority to designate areas from which "any or all persons may be excluded." The military decreed that all people of Japanese descent be removed from the West Coast states of California, Oregon, and Washington, which were declared strategic areas. They were to sell their property, often at ridiculously low prices, abandon their homes, and settle in one of 10 relocation centers.

A number of Japanese-Americans brought cases protesting at this severe violation of their civil liberties, but the courts initially upheld the evacuation and detention orders. However, in the 1944 case Endo v. United States, the Supreme Court found that it was inappropriate in time of war to detain persons whose loyalty was not in question. In late 1944, the authorities began to close some of the camps and families were allowed to return to the West Coast. By this time there were Japanese-American units fighting in Italy and France. In spite of this, discrimination against Americans of Japanese descent continued long after the war.

Forced to sell
A Japanese-owned toy shop in Los Angeles announces it is closing down in 1942.

Evacuation
A young Japanese-American girl sits with her family's belongings, waiting to be transported to an assembly center.

Since the 1970s the record of Japanese-American soldiers and the conscience of a new generation of Americans has reduced levels of prejudice and helped in the assimilation of Japanese immigrants into the American mainstream. Japanese-Americans were not the only Americans placed in detention centers during the war. Conscientious objectors shared a similar fate. They were objects of hatred and ridicule, many calling them cowards, communists, or Nazi sympathizers. The government, unsure of how to deal with an irate public which had lost many sons during the war, built detention centers for them as well. While they were there, conscientious objectors were expected to help the war effort by growing crops or doing light factory work. Those who refused were sent to jail.

Farming at Manzanar
Japanese-American internees farm a field at the Manzanar relocation center in California. In many cases, communities flourished despite the harsh, remote regions they were sent to.

Relocation center
New arrivals survey the bleak interior of their accommodation block at the Manzanar relocation center in eastern California on March 24, 1942.

The committee did very little to stop unfair and discriminatory labor practices, but the very fact that a black leader had succeeded in forcing the president's hand set a precedent for the leaders of the Civil Rights Movement after the war.

Italians, Jews, Japanese, and Mexican-Americans also faced discrimination and prejudice during the war. In 1943 whites targeted Mexican-Americans in the Los Angeles "zoot suit" riots. Japanese-Americans were the most harshly treated when they were forced to give up their homes and relocate into internment camps. Nevertheless, for many other immigrants, especially those from southern and eastern Europe, the war gained them greater social

and economic opportunities as they became more integrated into the fabric of American life. Women also made gains because of wartime demand for industrial workers (see page 125). By 1945, women made up 36 percent of the workforce as they worked in jobs once reserved for men.

With much of the nation on the move, the increasing rates of marriages and births made housing a critical issue. Typically, the housing provided for migrating workers was of inferior quality. A great many of the young women who married in wartime, however, stayed with their parents until their soldier husbands returned from the war. The severe housing shortages inspired a postwar boom,

that would satisfy many people's needs with a plentiful supply of new single-family dwellings. The increasing marriage rate helped to set off a corresponding baby boom that did not abate until the 1960s. Between 1940 and 1943 the rate of first births jumped from 293 to 375 per 10,000 women. The rate of subsequent births also went up—from 506 to 540. With more children, women working, and little housing available, the government was forced to pass legislation establishing daycare centers and providing some social housing. As the war progressed, an increase in juvenile delinquency caused some to blame working mothers and these daycare centers as a major part of the problem.

THE JAPANESE HOME FRONT

When the war started between Japan and China in July 1937, the Japanese government began a propaganda campaign meant to revitalize Japanese culture and instil an attitude of racial superiority. In October 1937, the Japanese prime minister, Konoye Fumimaro, promoted a three-year "National Spiritual Mobilization Movement" to rally the people in support of the war against the Chinese "mongrels." Ceremonies, parades, and a campaign to simplify dress, hairstyles, and diet were all aimed at promoting national pride and spiritual renewal.

By 1940 the state had completed its propaganda efforts by forming the people into local "patriotic" units. Each member worked in a job supporting some aspect of the war, such as national defense, street sweeping, fire watching, or public health. Many of them were run by community leaders, who ensured that people were doing their "duty."

In October 1941, to underline the seriousness of the conflict with China and the bitter diplomatic arguments between Japan and the United States, Konoye initiated a "New Order Movement." This centralized many of the local civil patriotic units. Although it never worked quite as envisioned, the movement did increase the number of units, which began to impose local food and clothing rationing.

THE JAPANESE WAR ECONOMY

With regard to economic planning prior to 1941, most Japanese, including members of the government, believed the war with China would be short. Hence, they saw no need for full-scale mobilization of the country's population. Traditional gender roles prohibited women from working outside the home and this further militated against reorganizing society in order to drive the war economy. Japanese civilians celebrated their country's military victories, but few took a sustained war effort seriously.

In December 1941, when Japan went to war with the United States, the government began a focused effort to gear up the economy for war and the people began to understand the seriousness of their situation. Many people took up jobs in farming or work in arms factories. By 1944 the workforce consisted of more than 33.5 million out of a population of 74 million.

Heroic airman
Japanese propaganda tended simply to extol the might of the army, navy, and air force.

After six months in a barracks at the Santa Anita Racetrack, we were sent to Heart Mountain, Wyoming. We arrived in the middle of a blinding snowstorm, five of us children in our California clothes. When we got to our tar-paper barracks, we found sand coming in through the walls, around the windows, up through the floor. The camp was surrounded by barbed wire... But throughout our ordeal, we cooperated with the government because we felt that in the long run, we could prove our citizenship.

NORMAN MINETA QUOTED BY OTTO FREDERICK IN "A TIME OF AGONY FOR JAPANESE AMERICANS", *TIME* (DEC 2, 1991)

At first women were not required to work because there were enough teenaged boys and older men who volunteered to work. This changed in 1944 when many unmarried women under the age of 25 were conscripted into the workforce.

Food shortages forced many families to enter the black market to find day-to-day living necessities. Obtaining black-market goods was especially difficult for farm workers, who earned about two-thirds the wages of their urban factory counterparts. Rationing became a way of life and had long-term repercussions. By early 1942, every citizen received a daily rice allotment of just 12 oz (330 g). Clothes also were rationed through a points system, with farm workers receiving fewer points than the factory workers. As the war progressed, food became increasingly scarce. Japan normally imported much of its food and by the fall of 1944 its heavy merchant shipping losses were becoming critical.

The "economy of scarcity" caused by the war had an important social-cultural impact on the Japanese people. It was probably as a result of an insufficient diet that younger Japanese men and women were shorter and lighter in 1946 than those a decade earlier. Overcrowded urban areas spawned an outbreak of tuberculosis. Children also received only a modicum of education. Officially, during the war Japanese children went to school for six years. The reality was that, in the latter part of the war, school was shortened to one hour per day in order for older children to work. There was little respite from work and the business of finding food. The government banned most foreign films and music, and closed down bars and amusement parks.

From late November 1944 until the end of the war, American bombers dropped over 160,000 tons of explosives and incendiaries on 66 Japanese cities, destroying about a quarter of all Japanese homes, 42 percent of the industrial areas and killing over half a million civilians. Thus, by mid-1945, the Japanese people knew only the necessity of back-breaking work, little food, mourning for dead relatives, and death from the skies.

A send-off for heroes
Japanese women line the streets of Tokyo in December 1941 as troops leave the country to reinforce the formations that have begun the invasion of Malaya and Singapore.

WARTIME CINEMA

IN WORLD WAR II, films—both features and documentaries—
became powerful instruments of national propaganda, while
continuing to provide escapist entertainment and a relief from
the privations of war. At the start of the war in Europe, US
neutrality made most of the major Hollywood studios reluctant
to adopt a strong anti-Nazi stance. However, after the release of
Warners' *Confessions of a Nazi Spy* (1939) other studios took up
the theme. Among the influential anti-Nazi films made in
America before the attack on Pearl Harbor were Charles Chaplin's
The Great Dictator (1940), Alfred Hitchcock's *Foreign Correspondent*,
and the émigré German director Fritz Lang's *Man Hunt* (1941).

After America's entry into the war in December 1941, some
40,000 of Hollywood's 250,000 technicians, actors, producers, and
directors went into uniform. A number of distinguished directors,
among them John Huston and William Wyler, put their energies
into hard-hitting documentary depictions of war. In 1942, Wyler's
fantasy version of the British home front, *Mrs. Miniver*, won seven
Oscars. After joining the USAF, Wyler forsook the studio for the
skies over Germany, in *Memphis Belle* (1945) and *Thunderbolt* (1945).
Another Hollywood stalwart, John Ford, filmed *The Battle of
Midway* (1942) and later became head
of the Field Photographic Branch of
the OSS. Many Hollywood stars
joined the armed forces, including
Clark Gable, Robert Montgomery, Robert Taylor, and
Douglas Fairbanks, Jr. James Stewart enlisted
in the USAAF, rising to the rank of colonel
and flying 20 bombing missions over Europe.

In the midwar years, some 90 million
Americans went to the movies every week.
The Hollywood production line adapted
all the stock film genres—crime thrillers,
musicals, cartoons, even the B Western—
to accommodate wartime themes. Nazis rode
the range and stalked the streets of Sherlock

The Great Dictator
Charlie Chaplin's 1940 film lampooned
Hitler (Adenoid Hynkel)—and in this
scene, Mussolini (Napaloni)—and sent a
message of hope to the world's oppressed.

Henry V (1944)
This appeal to
British patriotism
was filmed in
neutral Ireland.
Lawrence Olivier
directed and
played the king
in the most heroic
of Shakespeare's
history plays.

Casablanca (1943)
Humphrey Bogart's
character Rick came to
embody the dilemma of
American neutrality.

Betty Grable
The actress was the
most popular pin-up
with US servicemen.

James Stewart
Still in USAAF uniform after his return home
in September 1945, James Stewart talks on
the telephone at his father's hardware store.

Holmes' London. Combat films tended to reinforce the romantic stereotypes of war, and it was not until the end of the conflict that Hollywood came to terms with the reality in feature films such as William Wellman's *The Story of GI Joe*, and John Ford's *They Were Expendable*, both released in 1945.

In Britain the realist school of filmmaking found an outlet in a stream of superb documentaries, among them Harry Watt's *Target for Tonight* (1941) and Humphrey Jennings' *Listen to Britain* (1942) and *Fires Were Started* (1943). These documentaries, and compilations like *Desert Victory* (1942), placed the emphasis firmly on the waging of a "People's War." This had a significant impact on feature films such as *The Foreman Went to France* (1942), *Millions Like Us* (1943), *Waterloo Road* (1944), and *The Way Ahead* (1945), all of which focused on the lives of ordinary soldiers and civilians.

In Germany, the first year of war produced a spate of anti-Semitic films orchestrated by the Nazi minister for propaganda, Josef Goebbels. Three major films of 1940 stigmatized the Jews as racial enemies: the documentary *The Eternal Jew* and two feature films, *The Rothschilds* and *Jew Süss*.

From 1942 Goebbels presided over a nationalized film industry that combined historical epics celebrating the lives of German heroes such as Bismarck and Frederick the Great, with romantic froth and lavish entertainments such as *Münchhausen*, the most expensive film of the Nazi era. Even when facing inevitable defeat, Goebbels devoted huge resources—and the services of much-needed troops as extras—on films such as *Kolberg*, which was premiered in January 1945 and told the tale of the siege of an East Pomeranian town during the Napoleonic Wars. Ironically, by the time *Kolberg* was finished, Nazi Germany was itself under siege.

Wartime line for a movie theater
In September 1939 fear of air raids prompted the British government to shut the nation's movie theaters, but they opened again after two weeks and proved the most popular form of entertainment during the war.

Münchhausen
This spectacular color film was made to show that the German film industry in Babelsberg could compete with Hollywood.

Special prisms divided the light from the lens into its red, blue, and green components

The Eternal Jew
The film was shot in Poland in 1939–40. Its message was one of pure hate, juxtaposing images of Jews with rats to justify their extermination.

A propaganda coup
A German newsreel crew films British war material abandoned in the hasty evacuation from Dunkirk in June 1940.

Technicolor camera
The camera used a complex triple film, so color remained expensive and a relative rarity.

Ohm Kruger
This 1941 German film portrayed the British as villains of the Boer War.

OHM KRUGER
Emil Jannings

GERMAN–SOVIET CONFLICT

DECEMBER 6, 1941–NOVEMBER 12, 1942

In December 1941 the Germans reached a low point in their campaign on the Eastern Front as they were driven back from Moscow. Their fortunes changed from May onward as they went onto the counter-offensive and launched Operation Blue, which took them to the outskirts of Stalingrad.

1941

DECEMBER 6
Soviet forces begin successful attack on German salients north and south of Moscow

DECEMBER 13
German withdrawal ordered; countermanded by Hitler the next day

DECEMBER 13
Soviet Southwest Front begins to attack north of Livny; German 2nd Army begins withdrawal

DECEMBER 15
Soviet forces retake Klin

DECEMBER 23
Germans capture outer ring of forts around Sevastopol, only part of Crimea not yet held by them

DECEMBER 29
Soviet forces land in Feodosiya in Crimea and capture Kerch

JANUARY 1   1942
Soviet forces launch attack south of Kharkov

JANUARY 7
Offensive to relieve blockade of Leningrad is launched

JANUARY 31
Soviet advance from Donets River–crossed on January 24– is brought to a halt

JANUARY 18
German and Romanian forces retake Feodosiya

FEBRUARY 8
90,000 German troops surrounded and cut off by Soviet forces at Demyansk

MARCH 19
Offensive to relieve Leningrad halted as Soviet Second Shock Army cut off

MAY 8
Germans launch offensive in the Crimea

MAY 12
Soviet offensive launched from salient south of Kharkov

MAY 16
Germans gain control of Kerch Peninsula in preparation for offensive in the Caucasus

MAY 18
Germans recapture Kerch

MAY 29
Soviet forces defeated at Kharkov

JUNE 28
German 2nd Army attacks in Kursk area

JUNE 30
German 6th Army launches attack on Soviet Southwest Front

JULY 4
Sevastopol, besieged since November, taken by Germans

JULY 7
German 2nd Army occupies Voronezh in first stage of Operation Blue

JULY 8
German 1st Panzer Army crosses Donets River in advance toward Caucasus

JULY 23
German 1st Panzer Army recaptures Rostov

AUGUST 10
German 6th Army under Paulus crosses Don River to reach outskirts of Stalingrad

AUGUST 19
Paulus launches attack on Stalingrad

AUGUST 24
Zhukov sent to organize Soviet defense of Stalingrad

SEPTEMBER 3
German 4th Panzer Army under Hoth arrives in Stalingrad

SEPTEMBER 13
Paulus renews attempt to capture Stalingrad but progress very slow

NOVEMBER 2
German advance southward in Caucasus ends 5 miles (8 km) west of Ordhonikidze

NOVEMBER 12
In Stalingrad, Germans succeed in breaking through to the Volga River

Soviet attacks in the north and center Dec 6, 1941–Mar 19,1942	Action in the Crimea Dec 23, 1941–Jul 4, 1942
Action in the Ukraine Dec 13, 1941–May 29, 1942	German action in the south Jun 28–Nov 11, 1942

FROM MOSCOW TO STALINGRAD

THE GERMANS HAD BEEN brought to a halt before Moscow in late November 1941. It was only after much heated debate that Hitler had then given permission for a general withdrawal to a secure winter line along the Ugra River, some 200 miles (300 km) to the west of the city. Despite reports from German reconnaissance aircraft of the assembly of large numbers of Soviet troops in the Moscow sector, the German high command was confident that the Red Army had utterly exhausted its reserves of manpower. In fact, when it had become clear that the Japanese would not attack in Siberia, Soviet divisions had been rapidly transferred from the east to reinforce the 59 divisions deliberately withheld from the battle for Moscow. Unlike the Germans, these formations were fully equipped for winter warfare. By early December nearly 720,000 men, 8,000 guns and mortars, and 720 tanks, many of them T-34s, were assembled on the Soviet central front.

COUNTEROFFENSIVE AT MOSCOW

On November 30 Stalin had given Zhukov orders to launch a counteroffensive. The troops moved off, in a violent snowstorm, at 3:00 am on the morning of December 5. Zhukov, who initially had expressed reluctance to go on the attack but had been overruled by Stalin, had devised a characteristically simple plan. Massed artillery was to lead the counterblow before Moscow by delivering an earth-shattering barrage. The two armored German pincers, which were to the north and south of Moscow and threatened to encircle it, would then be driven back to their November start lines.

Zhukov's offensive caught the Ostheer —the German Army on the Eastern Front—at the start of its painfully won withdrawal and immediately prompted a fresh order from the Führer: "The Fourth Army is not to retire a single step." Order and counterorder left the Fourth Army dangerously exposed. Guderian's battered Panzer Group lay beyond the Fourth Army's right wing, around Tula, and was pushed back over the Oka River by the force of the Red Army counteroffensive. On the Fourth Army's left wing, General Erich Höpner's Fourth Panzer Group came under increasing pressure in its forward position and was in danger of being outflanked as a preliminary to the encirclement of the Fourth Army. Soviet cavalry formations, supported by sled-borne infantry, advanced across the frozen rivers to harry

Soviet infantry advance in winter
In the depths of the Soviet winter, temperatures plummet to well below zero. In 1941 Soviet forces were generally better equipped than the Germans to cope with such conditions.

Stuck fast
German motor transportation frequently became trapped in glutinous mud, particularly during the spring and fall. Just 12 hours of rain was enough to produce a morass on the Soviet Union's primitive roads.

GEORGI ZHUKOV

Marshal Zhukov (1896–1974)—one of the very few men with the courage to stand up to Stalin—was indispensable to Soviet victory. He was conscripted into the Russian Army in World War I and later became a specialist in armored warfare. In August 1939 he masterminded the defeat of the Japanese at Khalkin Ghol. In January 1941 he became chief of staff, and later in the year he directed the defense of Leningrad and then of Moscow, before planning the Soviet counterattack at Moscow. In August 1942 he became deputy commissar for defense, effectively Stalin's second-in-command, and directed the defence of Stalingrad. In 1943 he oversaw the defense of the Kursk salient and coordinated the massive Soviet counter-offensive in the Ukraine. Having planned Operation Bagration in 1944, he led the First Byelorussian Front in its advance to Berlin. By Western, though not Soviet, standards, he brought great ruthlessness to the battlefield. In 1945–46 he commanded the Soviet occupation forces in Germany.

the German flanks and rear. In the north, Klin fell on December 15, and to the south the encirclement of Tula was lifted. Within three weeks the German front had been shunted westward by distances of up to 200 miles (300 km).

"HEDGEHOG" TACTICS

The German withdrawal was made in the worst of the winter weather—with night temperatures falling to far below freezing and horses struggling through snow up to their bellies. As the Red Army infiltrated the German lines, local penetrations became breaches. But the piecemeal withdrawal did not degenerate into a total rout. Commanders learned to move back from one hastily prepared defensive position, known as a "hedgehog," to the next. In mid-December a sudden thaw gripped the Red Army in a sea of mud, allowing the hedgehogs to be strengthened before freezing temperatures returned. These strengthened positions gave the German troops the chance to stand fast while reserves were assembled in the rear to plug the gaps in the line.

The rapid development of hedgehog tactics led to the introduction of another feature of the war on the Eastern Front, in which German formations allowed themselves to be encircled. While Red Army cavalry, armor, ski-troops, and great masses of infantry swept around and past them, the hedgehogs' defenders were able to inflict heavy casualties and deny the enemy the road and rail junctions it needed to sustain the momentum of its advance. The German pockets had to be supplied by air, often stretching the resources of the Luftwaffe to the limit. While, for example, sustaining the 90,000 men of II Corps isolated in the large Demyansk pocket south of Lake Ilmen between January and May 1942, the Luftwaffe lost some 250 aircraft.

These tactical developments were taking place against a backdrop of structural upheaval within the German Army's high command. On December 1 Rundstedt had been removed from command of Army Group South, having protested at Hitler's "no withdrawal" order. No fewer than 35 army corps and divisional generals were dismissed, among them Guderian, for

Retreat from Moscow

In December 1941 there was a breakdown in the Ostheer's military cohesion, and morale dropped considerably. It was not until 1942 that steps were taken to equip the troops for winter warfare.

making unauthorized withdrawals. On December 17 the commander-in-chief of the German Army, Field Marshal von Brauchitsch, was relieved of his command, to be succeeded by Hitler himself. From now on, operations in the Soviet Union, down to battalion level, were to be executed according to directives and orders issued by the Führer.

STALIN SEIZES THE INITIATIVE

It seems that in June 1941, during the first days of Operation Barbarossa, Stalin had come close to a mental breakdown and had even briefly considered abandoning Moscow. Once he had recovered, his characteristic reaction had been to consolidate control of the war in his own hands. Thus in June 1941 he had created the State Defense Committee, or GKO, which oversaw all political, military, and economic aspects of the war and whose original members were Stalin, Foreign Minister Molotov, Marshal Voroshilov and Lavrenti Beria, head of the NKVD. The GKO administered military matters through the Stavka, which drew up battle plans and, through the general staff, organized the preparation and execution of strategic operations. In all cases the final decision lay with Stalin, who had appointed himself in the position of supreme commander on August 8. The two dictators and military amateurs, Hitler and Stalin, were now locked in a head-to-head battle for survival on the Eastern Front.

With the entry of the United States into the war in December, Stalin aquired an ally with almost unlimited potential economic power. Emboldened by this change in his fortunes, on January 5, 1942, he ordered a general offensive to drive the Germans back along the entire Eastern Front before the spring rains signaled the onset of the *rasputitsa*: Leningrad was to be relieved, Army Group Center rolled up, and the Ukraine liberated. Only Zhukov dissented, arguing that such an offensive would weaken the critical central counteroffensive and place an intolerable strain on Soviet resources.

A temporary respite for German troops
In the winter of 1941–42 many German commanders forbade the lighting of fires by day to prevent wisps of smoke from betraying positions to the enemy.

THE SOVIET GENERAL OFFENSIVE

One of the principal objectives of Stalin's all-out offensive was to pinch out the distended center of the German line. The Fourth Shock Army attacked from north of Moscow toward Vitebsk and Smolensk with the goal of severing German supply lines, while the Bryansk Front drove west to isolate the German Fourth Army. The fighting along the German salient between these two Red Army drives was exceptionally savage as Soviet forces strove to break through, but were then encircled and cut off.

In February and March, Stalin harried his high command to press home the faltering offensive. But the resistance of the Germans was hardening, and their commanders' more flexible battlefield reflexes were exacting a rising toll on Soviet forces. By the end of March the Red Army had lost some 450,000 dead and the offensive had lost all momentum. German losses were also mounting. In the Ninth Army one regiment that had begun Barbarossa with over 2,000 men now had a strength of just 35.

By early April both sides were in the glutinous grip of the *rasputitsa* and the Red Army offensive slithered to a halt. Since December 1941 the German Army Group Center had lost 265,000 men, while approximately 350,000 had become ill, often suffering from frostbite. Even when they were evacuated by ambulance train, the wounded and frostbitten were not safe: the unheated trains often arrived at their destination carrying a cargo of corpses. Material losses included 1,800 tanks, 55,000 motor vehicles, and 180,000 horses. If the Red Army had displayed a higher degree of tactical competence, the losses would have been far greater.

RED ARMY INFANTRY WEAPONS

BY THE END OF 1942 THE RED ARMY infantryman's standard submachine-gun was the 7.62-mm PPSh-41. By the end of the war some 5 million had been made. In common with all items of Red Army kit, it was simple to manufacture, easy to maintain, and immensely robust and reliable, with a 71-round drum, or 35-round box-type, magazine. It was also one of the few Soviet weapons to be adopted by the Germans in large numbers, and many were adapted to fire German 9-mm ammunition. Up to the summer of 1943, Red Army infantry formations were expected to manage on their initial ammunition allocation, which lasted about 10 days.

Tokarev pistol

Closely modeled on the Colt M1911, and introduced in 1930, the 7.62-mm Tokarev was the standard Red Army sidearm of the war. It had an 8-round magazine.

Hooded foresight

PPS-43 submachine-gun
This variant of the PPSh-41 was manufactured during the siege of Leningrad. The PPSh-41 had a wooden stock.

Ammunition magazine/hand grip

Pistol grip

Metal stock

Grenades

A Soviet infantry-man usually carried three grenades in his pocket or in a linen haversack.

FIGHTING IN THE SOUTH

While the fighting fell away on the central front, it flared again in the south. By early March the Red Army had been thwarted in its attempt to retake Kharkov, but Stalin, champing at the bit, ordered a second offensive to be delivered, in a right hook from Volchansk, in May. Simultaneously, the Germans were preparing to eliminate the Soviet salient around Barvenkovo, which had bitten into the German front 100 miles (160 km) south of Kharkov. On May 12 the Red Army launched offensives from north and south of the city, aiming to take it in a pincer movement, but the Germans contained the thrusts and on May 17 launched their own counterblow. Within a week they had eliminated the threatening salient to the south of Kharkov and driven back the right hook to the north of the city.

At the southern tip of the battle line, 20,000 men of the Soviet 44th and 51st Armies had landed on the Kerch peninsula to relieve Sevastopol, which had been besieged by Manstein's 11th Army. The Red Army force was expanded and redesignated the Crimean Front but was effectively checked by Manstein, who left five divisions at Sevastopol while he launched a counteroffensive with heavy Luftwaffe support. The Soviet forces were routed, losing nearly 200,000 men and all their heavy equipment before the 90,000 survivors were evacuated to the Taman peninsula. Manstein turned back to Sevastopol, sealed it off from the sea, and subjected it to an intense air and artillery bombardment. The battle for the city raged until the end of June, with the German and Soviet forces fighting over ground that had been very hotly contested nearly 100 years before in the Crimean War. Finally, their supplies of ammunition exhausted, the remaining Red Army defenders were evacuated.

Germans advancing in May 1942
From December 1941 to April 1942 the Red Army appeared to be gaining the initiative. However, by May the Germans were again on the offensive, in both Ukraine and the Crimea.

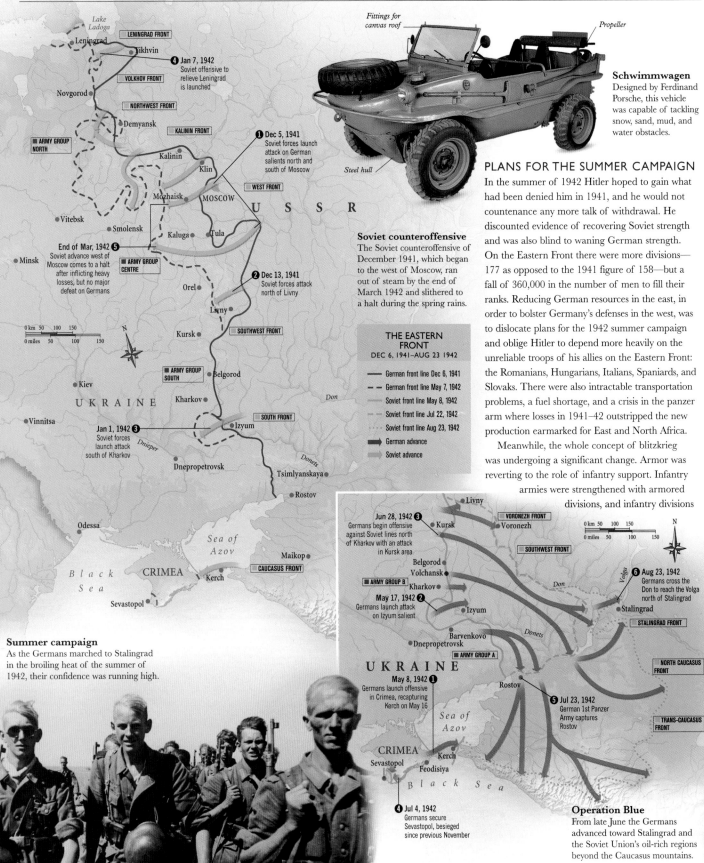

① Dec 5, 1941
Soviet forces launch
attack on German
salients north and
south of Moscow

④ Jan 7, 1942
Soviet offensive to
relieve Leningrad
is launched

End of Mar, 1942 ⑤
Soviet advance west of
Moscow comes to a halt
after inflicting heavy
losses, but no major
defeat on Germans

② Dec 13, 1941
Soviet forces attack
north of Livny

Jan 1, 1942 ③
Soviet forces
launch attack
south of Kharkov

Schwimmwagen
Designed by Ferdinand
Porsche, this vehicle
was capable of tackling
snow, sand, mud, and
water obstacles.

Fittings for
canvas roof

Propeller

Steel hull

Soviet counteroffensive
The Soviet counteroffensive of
December 1941, which began
to the west of Moscow, ran
out of steam by the end of
March 1942 and slithered to
a halt during the spring rains.

THE EASTERN FRONT
DEC 6, 1941–AUG 23 1942

—— German front line Dec 6, 1941
---- German front line May 7, 1942
—— Soviet front line May 8, 1942
---- Soviet front line Jul 22, 1942
······ Soviet front line Aug 23, 1942
➡ German advance
➡ Soviet advance

PLANS FOR THE SUMMER CAMPAIGN

In the summer of 1942 Hitler hoped to gain what
had been denied him in 1941, and he would not
countenance any more talk of withdrawal. He
discounted evidence of recovering Soviet strength
and was also blind to waning German strength.
On the Eastern Front there were more divisions—
177 as opposed to the 1941 figure of 158—but a
fall of 360,000 in the number of men to fill their
ranks. Reducing German resources in the east, in
order to bolster Germany's defenses in the west, was
to dislocate plans for the 1942 summer campaign
and oblige Hitler to depend more heavily on the
unreliable troops of his allies on the Eastern Front:
the Romanians, Hungarians, Italians, Spaniards, and
Slovaks. There were also intractable transportation
problems, a fuel shortage, and a crisis in the panzer
arm where losses in 1941–42 outstripped the new
production earmarked for East and North Africa.

Meanwhile, the whole concept of blitzkrieg
was undergoing a significant change. Armor was
reverting to the role of infantry support. Infantry
armies were strengthened with armored
divisions, and infantry divisions

Summer campaign
As the Germans marched to Stalingrad
in the broiling heat of the summer of
1942, their confidence was running high.

Jun 28, 1942 ③
Germans begin offensive
against Soviet lines north
of Kharkov with an attack
in Kursk area

May 17, 1942 ②
Germans launch attack
on Izyum salient

⑥ Aug 23, 1942
Germans cross the
Don to reach the Volga
north of Stalingrad

May 8, 1942 ①
Germans launch offensive
in Crimea, recapturing
Kerch on May 16

⑤ Jul 23, 1942
German 1st Panzer
Army captures
Rostov

④ Jul 4, 1942
Germans secure
Sevastopol, besieged
since previous November

Operation Blue
From late June the Germans
advanced toward Stalingrad and
the Soviet Union's oil-rich regions
beyond the Caucasus mountains.

assumed a more important role in panzer armies. The production of self-propelled assault guns was stepped up so that by July 1942 they represented almost one-quarter of the Ostheer's armored strength.

Hitler had a grand strategic plan for 1942 which entailed sweeping southward from the Caucasus and northeast from Egypt, in a colossal pincer movement, to seize the oil resources of the Middle East. In fact, the only part of Hitler's plan that was to see the light of day was Operation *Blau* (Blue), a drive aimed east to the city of Stalingrad and south to the mountain passes of the Causcasus and then on to the oilfields on the western shore of the Caspian Sea. British code breakers had gotten wind of the operation and had passed the information to Stalin, who dismissed it as disinformation. He also ignored the hard evidence, retrieved by Soviet troops from a crashed German aircraft on June 19, of the planned order of battle for Operation Blue.

OPERATION BLUE

The German summer offensive began on June 28, 1942. Field Marshal von Bock's Army Group B (the Second, Sixth, and Fourth Panzer Armies) was to advance toward Voronezh and down the grasslands of the Don-Donets corridor toward Stalingrad, while Field Marshal Wilhelm List's Army Group A (the First Panzer and 17th Armies) drove for the Don crossings east of Rostov. As the panzer formations, arrayed in massive squares, advanced, Soviet resistance melted away. By July 6 Army Group B had reached the Don River opposite Voronezh.

Crossing the Don
Tanks of Army Group A ford the Don River east of Rostov in July 1942. In the initial stages of their summer offensive, the German forces appeared to be repeating their success of 1941.

It seemed like a rerun of the summer of 1941, with the front of the Red Army falling apart at the first armored impact. Bock, however, was concerned that Red Army reinforcements might attack Army Group B's left flank from the Voronezh area, and he gained Hitler's permission to secure Voronezh with armor detached from the Sixth Army, commanded by General Friedrich Paulus. Bock was now drawn into a slugging match at Voronezh, which threatened to dislocate Operation Blue's timetable. On July 13 Hitler intervened, replacing Bock with Field Marshal Maximilian von Weichs. Paulus was to wheel east toward Stalingrad, providing further protection for the extended German left flank.

In the Don-Donets corridor the Red Army was now threatened by a series of encirclements on the scale of those executed by the Germans in

Operation Barbarossa. With great difficulty, the recently appointed chief of the Soviet general staff, Marshal Aleksandr Vasilevsky, persuaded Stalin that orders to "stand fast" regardless of the strategic situation invited further catastrophe, and that it was vital for the Soviet forces in the corridor to withdraw. On July 23 Rostov, which the Red Army had lost and then retaken in the winter fighting, fell to Army Group A almost without a fight. Hitler now ordered Army Group A and General Ewald von Kleist's First Panzer Army to drive for the Caucasus oilfields while Army Group B advanced to Stalingrad.

On August 9, just six weeks after the start of Operation Blue, Kleist's forces had reached Maikop, 200 miles (300 km) southeast of Rostov, and captured the Soviet Union's most westerly oilfields. The installations had, however, been wrecked by the retreating Red Army, and the Germans were never to reach the principal sources of oil beyond the Caucasus. Ironically, they had insufficient fuel to maintain the momentum of their advance, and they faced stiffening Soviet resistance from both Red Air Force bombers and locally raised formations.

Red Army logistics
Soviet infantrymen relied heavily on horses and the carts they pulled (*panjes*), which could keep going in a wide range of conditions. *Panjes* were also used extensively by the Germans, despite their vaunted panzer spearheads.

> "It was easily the most desolate and mournful region of the east that came before my eyes. A barren, naked, lifeless steppe without a bush, without a tree, for miles without a village."
>
> A GERMAN SOLDIER DESCRIBING THE LANDSCAPE IN THE DON-DONETS CORRIDOR

ADVANCE TO STALINGRAD

While the First Panzer Army was racing to Maikop, the German Sixth Army—much of whose transportation had been temporarily transferred to Army Group A —was moving slowly down the Don–Donets corridor toward Stalingrad across a wide, treeless, and desolate steppe. By August 19 it was poised to begin its assault on Stalingrad, while the Fourth Panzer Army moved up along a northeast axis. On August 23 a total of 600 aircraft of the Luftwaffe's VIII Air Corps attacked the city, which straggled for some 20 miles (30 km) along the west bank of the Volga, and reduced its center to an inferno. Thousands of Soviet civilians—ordered to remain in Stalingrad so as not to hamper Red

Army movements—were killed in the raid. On the same day German troops entered the outskirts of Stalingrad and also carved out a salient to the north of the city along the western bank of the Volga. At Hitler's forward headquarters in Vinnitsa in the Ukraine, the mood was jubilant. The seizure of Stalingrad was expected within days as the Sixth Army plunged into country cut with gullies and ravines leading to the industrial heart of the city.

On September 5 a Red Army counterattack designed to prise the German grip off the Volga north of Stalingrad was driven off with heavy losses. Stalin was determined that Stalingrad must be held, whatever the cost, and it was only after some argument that he agreed on September 13

> Stalingrad is no longer a town. By day it is an enormous cloud of burning, blinding smoke; it is a vast furnace lit by the reflection of the flames. And when night arrives, one of those scorching, howling, bleeding nights, the dogs plunge into the Volga and swim desperately to gain the other bank. The nights in Stalingrad are a terror for them. Animals flee this hell… only men endure.
>
> **A GERMAN OFFICER OF 24TH PANZER DIVISION, OCTOBER 1942**

German mortar squad
German infantry prepare to move forward in the ruins of Stalingrad. The soldier in the center carries a mortar base plate, and the man to his right, leaning on a grenade, carries a rack of bombs.

to a plan presented to him by Zhukov—now in overall command of the Stalingrad sector—for a wide encirclement of the Axis forces on the Lower Volga and the destruction of Paulus's Sixth Army at Stalingrad. On the same day General Vasili Chuikov was appointed as the new commander of the Soviet 62nd Army in Stalingrad. A no-nonsense fighting officer of peasant stock, Chuikov would prove to be a streetfighter of genius. He set up his headquarters in a bunker on the banks of the Volga, across which a fleet of small boats went back and forth, carrying reinforcements, ammunition, and food to the west bank, and wounded men back to the east bank. From the outset, Chuikov urged his men to fight "as if there is no land across the Volga." At the same time the Stalingrad sector, which had now been redesignated the Stalingrad Front, came under the command of another determined and pugnacious officer of peasant stock, General Andrei Yeremenko.

Stalingrad seen from the east bank
During the battle for the city, some 35,000 wounded Soviet troops were ferried to the east bank, while 65,000 reinforcements crossed to the west.

It was a sniper's paradise, in which all freedom of maneuver and flexibility in the battlefield was lost, and blitzkrieg was replaced by attrition.

The men of the German Sixth Army edged ever closer to the steep banks of the Volga. The giant Univermag department store in Red Square, just under a mile from the ferries, was captured by the Germans after a ferocious fight and became the headquarters of the army's commander, General Paulus. Some 3 miles (5 km) to the south, on the edge of Stalingrad, a massive grain silo became the scene of a grim two-month siege as the city's defenders were slowly pushed back to the water's edge. By November 1 the Germans had chopped Chuikov's command on the western bank into four groups, forcing

Stranded civilian
The civilians stranded in Stalingrad had to endure German bombardment, starvation, and threatened execution by the NKVD if they failed to assist the city's Red Army defenders.

communication between them to be carried out on the east bank. On the 12th the Germans reached the Volga itself on the southern edge of the city, but the battle had now become for them one of the grimmest kind—one whose cost far exceeded its value. It was remorselessly sucking in units essential to sustain the dwindling hopes of a breakthrough being achieved in the Caucasus. This was all too evident to the German high command, but not to Hitler. Stalingrad had become an obsession, its occupation overriding all military sense—and, inevitably, it was the Führer's will that would prevail.

FIGHTING AMONG THE RUINS
In three days of savage fighting from September 13, the Germans inched their way through the shattered city to Stalingrad's main railroad station and Mamayev Kurgan, a vantage point some 5 miles (8 km) to the northwest, which until a few days before had housed the headquarters of the 62nd Army. Both strongholds changed hands repeatedly as Chuikov's men attacked by night and the Germans counterattacked by day, their armor nosing through a nightmare cityscape pitted with shell craters and piled high with the rubble of shattered buildings. As Chuikov's men fell back on the bank of the Volga, reinforcements from 13th Guards Division were rushed up from the interior and fed across the river. They clung to the vital jetties on the western bank but at the cost of almost 100 percent casualties.

Beneath the hulks of burning and collapsed buildings the German attackers and Soviet defenders sheltered and lived in the cellars. They fought from the cover of masonry, scrambling and slithering over dunes of bricks from one position to the next. The front lines were fluid, often no more than a grenade throw apart. Swarms of rats scurried through the carnage, feasting on the dead and dying.

Red Army assault squad
In Stalingrad, fighting raged for days over the possession of the few buildings left standing, which gave the precious advantage of height over the battlefield.

3.5x telescopic sight   MOSIN-NAGANT M91/30 SNIPER RIFLE
Rear sights
5-round fixed box magazine

Soviet sniper's rifle
Adapted with a powerful telescopic sight, the 7.62-mm M91/30 was used by the most famous Soviet sniper at Stalingrad, Vasily Zaitsev. He killed 149 German soldiers.

German tanks near Moscow
The German advance to Moscow halted in November 1941. During the subsequent Soviet counteroffensive, the German formations were pushed back by Soviet troops far better equipped for the winter conditions.

THE INITIATIVE CHANGES HANDS
1942–43

IN NOVEMBER 1942, AS THE GERMAN SIXTH ARMY FOUGHT

FOR THE CITY OF STALINGRAD AND HITLER ORDERED

THE OCCUPATION OF VICHY FRANCE, THE BOUNDARIES

OF THE THIRD REICH REACHED THEIR GREATEST EXTENT.

HOWEVER, THE HIGH TIDE OF NAZI EXPANSIONISM BEGAN

TO RECEDE AS THE INITIATIVE PASSED OVER TO THE ALLIES

ON THREE FRONTS: IN THE SOVIET UNION, NORTH AFRICA,

AND THE ATLANTIC. IN THE PACIFIC THE JAPANESE WERE

ALSO CHECKED, AND THEN DECISIVELY DEFEATED, AT

GUADALCANAL IN THE SOLOMON ISLANDS.

Americans welcomed in Tunis
In November 1942 Vichy French troops at first
resisted the US landings in Algeria and Morocco.
By May 1943, with the Germans and Italians
defeated in Tunisia, the French in North Africa
were firmly on the Allied side.

THE TIDE BEGINS TO TURN

BETWEEN THE FALL OF 1942 AND THE SPRING OF 1943 THE EXTRAVAGANT AMBITIONS THAT HAD FUELED HITLER'S PLANS FOR THE INVASION OF THE SOVIET UNION BEGAN TO DIM. AS THE TIDE OF WAR BEGAN TO TURN AGAINST GERMANY, DEBATE OVER GRAND STRATEGY GAVE WAY TO DEBATE OVER HOW THE THIRD REICH MIGHT RETAIN THE TERRITORY IT HAD WON SINCE SEPTEMBER 1939.

ON THE EASTERN FRONT the German Sixth Army had opened its assault on Stalingrad on August 19. Three months later it was still locked in a ferocious street-by-street battle with the defenders of the city. Hitler was obsessed with securing Stalingrad, while Stalin was equally determined that it should be denied him. Stalin's resolve had been hardened at a meeting with Churchill in August 1942, when he had been informed that there would be no immediate Anglo-American invasion of continental Europe to ease the pressure on the Red Army. He had then agreed to an operation proposed by Zhukov, deputy commissar for defense, in which a holding battle fought in Stalingrad would be followed by an encirclement of the Axis forces on the lower Volga and the destruction of the Sixth Army.

OPERATION URANUS

Code-named Uranus, the operation was launched on November 19, 1942 and by the end of January had secured the surrender of the Sixth Army under Field Marshal Paulus. The Red Army then drove on, threatening Kharkov and the German forces withdrawing from the Caucasus. However, there was to be a major setback for the Soviet Union in February and March 1943, when Field Marshal Manstein's Army Group Don delivered a brilliantly weighted counterblow against the overextended Red Army. When the fighting died down in the spring thaw, there was a huge Soviet salient, centered around the city of Kursk in the heartland of the Ukraine, jutting westward into the German line.

On the surface, it seemed that the rhythms of the Eastern Front would be resumed in the late spring of 1943, when the ground became firm enough to sustain armored operations. But the debacle at

Stalingrad had dealt a heavy blow to the Ostheer, while the Red Army was shrugging off the specter of defeat that had haunted it from June 1941 to the late summer of 1942. One of the reasons for this lay in the stolid figure of Stalin. Unlike Hitler, who grew to despise and mistrust the Prussian military caste that dominated the German high command, Stalin was able to develop a constructive engagement with his high command, the Stavka.

Stalin's gaining of wisdom had, of course, been acquired at the cost of millions of Soviet dead, a price that no other combatant nation could have paid and still remain in the field. Also making it possible for the Soviet Union to continue fighting was the maintenance of supplies of war materiel. In the summer of 1941 the Soviet Union had preserved a crucial part of its industrial infrastructure by shifting much of its war-making plant east, beyond the Urals and out of the reach of the Ostheer and Luftwaffe bombers. The ravages of Operation Barbarossa meant that initially output fell. Even by 1945 coal and steel production had not

"…at the bottom of the trenches there still lay frozen green Germans and frozen gray Russians and frozen fragments of human shape, and there were tin helmets, German and Russian, lying among the brick debris, and the helmets were half-filled with snow."

BRITISH CORRESPONDENT ALEXANDER WERTH DESCRIBING THE SCENE IN STALINGRAD
IN EARLY FEBRUARY 1943 AFTER THE SURRENDER OF THE GERMAN SIXTH ARMY

Marching into captivity
By the end of January 1943 the Red Army
had entombed General Paulus's Sixth Army
in Stalingrad. When Paulus surrendered on the
31st, over 100,000 Axis troops were marched
into a terrible captivity that few would survive.

Meeting in Casablanca
Roosevelt and Churchill
met in January 1943 to plan
the next Allied offensive.
Attempts were also made
to bring together General
Giraud (far left), the French
commander in North Africa,
and the Free French leader
General de Gaulle.

NORTH AFRICA

By the spring of 1943
defeat was also looming
in North Africa. The
German high tide in this
theater had been reached
in August 1942 before
Montgomery checked
Rommel's Afrika Korps
at Alam Halfa. Defeat

These harsh truths bore down heavily on Germany's allies. Europe contained a combination of cowed occupied peoples and increasingly sullen allies. The latter became markedly reluctant to make sacrifices on the Eastern Front, where entire Italian, Hungarian, and Romanian armies had been swept away in Operation Uranus. Finland, Hungary, and Romania began to extend secret peace feelers to the Soviet Union, while between December 1942 and April 1943 Mussolini attempted to persuade Hitler to make a separate political settlement with Stalin in order to free the Axis for the fight against the British and Americans. Hitler, however, had no illusions about the likelihood of dividing the Grand Alliance ranged against him. By the end of March 1943 he was immersed in plans for the summer campaigning season, and his gaze was increasingly fixed on the Soviet-held Kursk salient, swelling menacingly into the German line to the north of Kharkov.

returned to prewar levels, and at first the Soviet war industry survived on prewar stockpiles. When these ran down, the gap was filled by Lend-Lease materiel, supplied by the United States under terms agreed to by Roosevelt and Churchill at the Arcadia Conference of December 1941. By 1945 the Soviet Union had received some 16.4 million tons of Lend-Lease supplies, ranging from 2,000 locomotives to a total of 13 million boots for the Red Army. This crucial aid enabled the Soviet war industry to focus on the output of weaponry for the Eastern Front.

THE WAR AT SEA

Away from the Eastern Front, the tide was to turn abruptly in the Battle of the Atlantic after a period of sustained German success. In March 1943 the struggle for the sea-lanes had reached crisis point for the Western Allies as Grand Admiral Dönitz's U-boat "wolf packs" scored one of their greatest successes, plundering two Allied convoys. That month the number of ships accounted for by U-boats in the North Atlantic was 108, a total that caused almost fatal disruption to the seaborne lifeline between Britain and the United States.

The moment passed. The mid-Atlantic "air gap"—the stretch of ocean in which the U-boats had operated free of interference from Allied long-range patrol aircraft—was closed, and a host of technical developments was introduced, ranging from centimetric radar to the breaking at Bletchley Park of the U-boats' "Shark" code. This was a battle for technological superiority that the German Navy was losing hands down. The "wolf packs" would soon be withdrawn from the Atlantic to go in search of hunting grounds that were less dangerous.

followed at El Alamein in October–November, and on November 8 an Anglo-American army made a number of landings in North Africa in Operation Torch. The response of the Axis was to send reinforcements from Germany. They joined hands with Rommel's retreating army and fierce fighting ensued in the mountains of Tunisia.

By March 1943 the Axis supply situation in Tunisia had become critical. Rommel was brought back to Germany, to be decorated by Hitler but not to return to North Africa. Army Group Africa was less fortunate. By May 12 Axis resistance in North Africa was at an end and, with the fall of Tunis, some 240,000 Axis prisoners, nearly half of them German, passed into Allied captivity. Hitler had gloomily anticipated this defeat but, once again, had been unable to liquidate a front. As a result, he had presided over another debacle.

CASABLANCA CONFERENCE

Allied success made it all the more important to agree on a common strategy. At the Casablanca Conference, held between January 13 and 24, 1943, Roosevelt and Churchill reached several important decisions: to invade Sicily in the Mediterranean; to mount a joint strategic bombing offensive against Germany; to accelerate the build-up of US troops in Britain for an invasion of northwest Europe; and to demand, on Roosevelt's insistence, the unconditional surrender of Germany, Italy, and Japan.

American troops in Operation Torch
On November 8, 1942 Allied troops made landings in northwest Africa as part of a plan to drive out the Axis forces. This was finally achieved in May 1943.

FIGHT-BACK IN THE PACIFIC

In two crucial naval encounters that had taken place in the Pacific—the battles of the Coral Sea (May 1942) and Midway (June 1942)—the Japanese had been decisively defeated. This had left them with the need to defend a vast ocean empire that might be attacked at any point by the Americans. The target chosen by the Americans was the Solomons chain. On August 7, 1942 a force of US Marines stormed ashore on the island of Guadalcanal, where the Japanese were building an airfield. This was quickly secured by the Marines and on August 20 it received its first delivery of aircraft. The Japanese poured reinforcements into the island to retake the airstrip, and launched naval and air offensives against the American beachhead. The fighting continued until early February 1943, when the Japanese evacuated some 10,000 troops. The campaign had provided the Allies with their first large-scale victory over the Japanese.

In driving southward, one of the chief objectives of the Japanese had been Port Moresby, the capital of New Guinea, which was situated on the south coast. Control of the town would have enabled Japan to isolate Australia. However, the check received by the Japanese at the Battle of the Coral Sea had destroyed their hopes of seizing it through a direct landing. Their next move, on June 21–22, 1942, had been to land a force on the northern coast of New Guinea to advance on Port Moresby along the Kokoda Trail, a track leading over the mountains separating the north and south coasts. The Japanese advanced to within 30 miles (50 km) of Port Moresby before being forced back by Australian troops to Buna on New Guinea's north coast. This marked the beginning of one of the most bitter campaigns of the war, fought in possibly the most unforgiving terrain and climate experienced in any theater. It was not until May 1945 that the Allies put an end to active Japanese resistance in New Guinea.

> "We have a new experience. We have victory—a remarkable and definite victory."
>
> WINSTON CHURCHILL ANNOUNCING THE ALLIED VICTORY AT EL ALAMEIN IN NORTH AFRICA, NOVEMBER 1942

FROM STALINGRAD TO KHARKOV

NOVEMBER 19, 1942–MARCH 18, 1943

A major Soviet counteroffensive to drive the Germans back from Stalingrad initially met with great success, leading to the surrender of the Sixth Army. However, in February 1943 it began to falter and the Germans struck an effective counterblow.

1942

NOVEMBER 19
Major Soviet counteroffensive, Operation Uranus, is launched, with Southwest Front striking from north of Stalingrad

NOVEMBER 20
Soviet forces in Don Front launch attack from south of Stalingrad

NOVEMBER 23
The two Soviet attacks meet in the Kalach area, so blocking the supply and exit routes of German 6th Army under Paulus

DECEMBER 2
Soviet forces launch attack on the German 6th Army

DECEMBER 12
Germans launch Operation Winter Storm to relieve the 6th Army

DECEMBER 16
Soviet army launches an offensive in direction of Rostov to cut off German forces in Caucasus

DECEMBER 23
Relief force begins to withdraw after getting to within 30 miles (48 km) of Stalingrad

1943

JANUARY 3, 1943
Germans begin general withdrawal from the Caucasus

JANUARY 10, 1943
Renewed Soviet offensive–Operation Ring–is launched at Stalingrad to push out remnants of German 6th Army

JANUARY 12, 1943
Operation Iskra to break Leningrad blockade is launched

JANUARY 18
Soviet forces relieve Leningrad from the east

JANUARY 24
German 6th Army ordered to break up into small groups

JANUARY 31
Southern pocket of German 6th Army under Paulus surrenders

FEBRUARY 2
Northern pocket of German 6th Army surrenders

FEBRUARY 2
Soviet forces attack from northeast of Kharkov (4th largest Soviet city)

FEBRUARY 8
Soviet forces take Kursk, north of Kharkov and Belgorod

FEBRUARY 8
Soviet forces launch attack on Demyansk salient. Germans succeed in withdrawing

FEBRUARY 14
Soviet forces reoccupy Rostov

FEBRUARY 16
Soviet forces reoccupy Kharkov after it is abandoned by the Germans

FEBRUARY 20
Germans attack Soviet forces between the Donets and Dnieper rivers, forcing Soviet forces to retreat by March 2

MARCH 7
Germans launch attack toward Kharkov with goal of destroying the Soviet forces that are holding the city

MARCH 15
Germans reoccupy Kharkov

MARCH 18
Germans recapture Belgorod

- Soviet counterattack at Stalingrad Nov 19, 1942–Feb 2, 1943
- Action in southern Russia and the Ukraine Feb 2–Mar 18, 1943
- Action in the Caucasus Dec 16, 1942–Feb 14, 1943
- Action in the north Jan 12–Feb 15, 1943

CHANGING FORTUNES ON THE EASTERN FRONT

BY NOVEMBER 12, 1942 THE SIXTH ARMY had exhausted its strength in a final desperate three-day drive to take Stalingrad. Counterattacks by the Red Army began to nibble away at the ground so painfully won by the Germans in weeks of fighting. At the same time, German military intelligence was becoming increasingly aware of a Red Army build-up on the northern and southern flanks of the Stalingrad salient. These flanks were screened by the Third Romanian Army in the north and the Fourth Romanian Army in the south. Both Romanian armies were not at full strength: under pressure from Hitler, their ranks had been bolstered by freed civilian convicts, but desertion was soon thinning their numbers. Belatedly, elements of

RED BANNER

RED STAR

Awards for Red Army soldiers
The Orders of the Red Banner and the Red Star were among the major medals. Stalin also introduced decorations named after 19th-century field marshals.

the German reserve were sent north to bolster the Third Romanian Army. They were spared Stalingrad, but their relief was to be short-lived.

PLANS FOR A COUNTERATTACK

The Soviet build-up to the Stalingrad counterblow, code-named Operation Uranus, was typical of Zhukov's method. He read the enemy's intentions and juggled scant resources in the front line while methodically amassing a powerful reserve in the rear until the time was right to release it against an enemy at the end of its tether. By the beginning of November, Zhukov had assembled a force of over 1 million men, 14,000 heavy guns, nearly 1,000 tanks, and 1,400 aircraft. Throughout the operation the planning had been measured and methodical, in marked contrast with the 1941–42 improvisations. The lives of the defenders of Stalingrad

Fit for battle
Red Army troops in Stalingrad generally had better winter clothing than the Axis troops. Felt boots (*valenki*) and hats made of lamb's wool were often worn by infantrymen.

had been traded for time while the Stavka waited for the arrival of a frost that made the ground hard enough for armor to race across country, and for the Allied landings in North Africa that would tie down German reserves in western Europe.

Stalin raised no objections when presented, on November 13, with the detailed plan for Uranus, and he allowed Zhukov to decide when to launch the attack. The date for the blow on the northern front was November 19, followed within 24 hours by an attack in the south. Chuikov, in command of the forces in Stalingrad, was not informed of this decision until the 18th, to ensure that there was no slackening in the defense of the city.

LAUNCH OF OPERATION URANUS
On the northern flank of the Stalingrad salient were the three Soviet armies of the Southwest Front, while due north of Stalingrad itself was the Don Front's two armies. To the south was the Stalingrad Front, comprising three armies. On November 19 the offensive in the north began with a pulverizing artillery barrage, which was followed by infantry advancing in human waves. Within hours the front of the Third Romanian Army had disintegrated, and Red Army tanks were moving across open country

Romanian and German prisoners
Many of the Romanians at Stalingrad lacked basic winter clothing and suffered very badly from frostbite.

in rapid pursuit of fleeing Romanian and German units. Some 30,000 Axis troops were taken prisoner. In the south, where there was no defensible front, the Fourth Romanian Army was shredded with equal speed. On November 23 the Red Army's northern and southern pincers met south of Kalach, 60 miles (95 km) west of Stalingrad (see map page 150). Paulus's Sixth Army and part of the Fourth Panzer Army—330,000 men —were trapped, separated from the rest of the German front by a corridor 100 miles (160 km) wide that was littered with cairns of frozen corpses and smashed artillery and armor. Inside the Stalingrad pocket, the Sixth Army had rations for only six days and ammunition for just two days.

On November 19 Hitler had been 1,300 miles (2,100 km) from Stalingrad in his mountain retreat at the Berghof in southern Bavaria. His immediate response was to dismiss a proposal that the Sixth Army should break out of Stalingrad. The next day the Führer ordered Paulus to hold firm at all costs. He then ordered a command reshuffle, appointing Manstein commander of Army Group Don, with orders to break through to the Sixth Army.

A Junkers Ju 52 takes to the air
The Germans lost nearly 500 transport aircraft, including many Ju 52s, in their failed attempt to resupply the Sixth Army.

On November 24 Göring promised Hitler that the Luftwaffe would supply the trapped army from the air. This air support was doomed from the outset. Paulus's minimum daily requirement was 550 tons of rations, clothing, equipment, and munitions. But the largest delivery—made on December 7—was only 290 tons. By mid-January the daily average had dipped to 60 tons and the temperature was as low as –22° F (–30° C). Soldiers survived on scant rations of bread, fat or margarine, and horsemeat. The Red Air Force dominated the skies over Stalingrad, and the cost of Göring's airlift to the Luftwaffe was nearly 500 transports, many of them Junkers Ju 52s, the workhorses of the German air force.

On the ground, Manstein's task of breaking through to Paulus was equally compromised. He estimated that he would need a minimum of four armored, four infantry and mountain, and three Luftwaffe field divisions just to make contact with the Sixth Army and restore its freedom of movement. This was the most he could hope to achieve. The strength of the Red Army forces in the corridor around Stalingrad—some 60 divisions and 1,000 tanks—was too great for him to inflict a defeat that would enable the Ostheer to resume the position it had held in early November. Manstein, however, was not granted even this modest capability, the parlous state of the Soviet railroads combining with a thaw in the Caucasus to deny him the formations he needed. His problems were compounded as units were shuffled back and forth on the Don front to plug the cracks radiating from the debacle at Stalingrad.

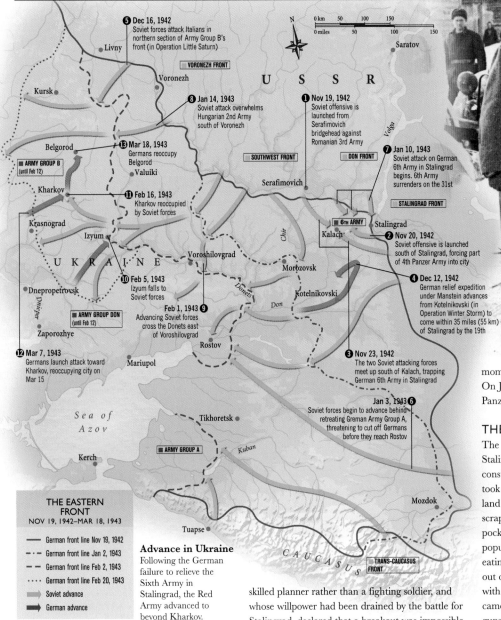

⑤ Dec 16, 1942
Soviet forces attack Italians in northern section of Army Group B's front (in Operation Little Saturn)

VORONEZH FRONT

⑧ Jan 14, 1943
Soviet attack overwhelms Hungarian 2nd Army south of Voronezh

① Nov 19, 1942
Soviet offensive is launched from Serafimovich bridgehead against Romanian 3rd Army

SOUTHWEST FRONT

DON FRONT

⑦ Jan 10, 1943
Soviet attack on German 6th Army in Stalingrad begins. 6th Army surrenders on the 31st

⑬ Mar 18, 1943
Germans reoccupy Belgorod

ARMY GROUP B
(until Feb 12)

STALINGRAD FRONT

⑪ Feb 16, 1943
Kharkov reoccupied by Soviet forces

6TH ARMY

② Nov 20, 1942
Soviet offensive is launched south of Stalingrad, forcing part of 4th Panzer Army into city

⑩ Feb 5, 1943
Izyum falls to Soviet forces

④ Dec 12, 1942
German relief expedition under Manstein advances from Kotelnikovski (in Operation Winter Storm) to come within 35 miles (55 km) of Stalingrad by the 19th

Feb 1, 1943 ⑨
Advancing Soviet forces cross the Donets east of Voroshilovgrad

⑫ Mar 7, 1943
Germans launch attack toward Kharkov, reoccupying city on Mar 15

ARMY GROUP DON
(until Feb 12)

③ Nov 23, 1942
The two Soviet attacking forces meet up south of Kalach, trapping German 6th Army in Stalingrad

Jan 3, 1943 ⑥
Soviet forces begin to advance behind retreating German Army Group A, threatening to cut off Germans before they reach Rostov

ARMY GROUP A

TRANS-CAUCASUS FRONT

THE EASTERN FRONT
NOV 19, 1942–MAR 18, 1943

— German front line Nov 19, 1942
– ⋅ – German front line Jan 2, 1943
– – – German front line Feb 2, 1943
⋅⋅⋅⋅ German front line Feb 20, 1943
➤ Soviet advance
➤ German advance

Advance in Ukraine
Following the German failure to relieve the Sixth Army in Stalingrad, the Red Army advanced to beyond Kharkov.

Paulus surrenders
In addition to Field Marshal Paulus, 22 German generals went into captivity at Stalingrad.

OPERATION WINTER STORM

Manstein finally launched his counterattack, which was code-named Winter Storm, on December 12. At first it made steady progress as the Red Army forces surrounding Stalingrad had turned inward against the city. By December 17 a single corps (LVII) of the Fourth Panzer Army had fought its way to within 35 miles (55 km) of Stalingrad. Manstein requested that the Sixth Army should be allowed to break out of the city. Hitler, however, refused: the Sixth Army was to stay put. Manstein then sent one of his officers to the Stalingrad headquarters of Paulus to make one last plea that the Sixth Army should withdraw. Paulus, a polished and immaculately attired staff officer who was a

skilled planner rather than a fighting soldier, and whose willpower had been drained by the battle for Stalingrad, declared that a breakout was impossible. What was more, a surrender had been expressly forbidden by Hitler, his commander-in-chief.

By December 24 Manstein's relief force was fighting for its own life. It lost an armored division, despatched northeast to reinforce hard-pressed units on the Lower Chir, taking with it all hope of relieving the Sixth Army. For the

Wartime propaganda
The portrayal of events by the magazine *Die Wehrmacht* was in stark contrast with the fate of the Sixth Army survivors, who went into a horrifying captivity.

moment, the initiative had passed to the Red Army. On January 27 the remaining troops in the Fourth Panzer Army began their withdrawal.

THE PLIGHT OF THE SIXTH ARMY

The Sixth Army was now trapped inside the Stalingrad pocket, starving and subjected to constant air and artillery bombardment. Soldiers took desperate risks, venturing into the no-man's-land beyond the defensive perimeter to search for scraps of food and, most precious of all, salt, in the pockets of the Red Army dead. Like the besieged population of Leningrad, they were reduced to eating rats. Transport aircraft were still flying in and out of Stalingrad's airstrips, taking the wounded with them on the return flights, during which they came under constant attack from enemy antiaircraft guns and the Red Air Force fighters that crowded the air space over the city. The most grievously wounded men stood no chance of escape, since stretchers took up too much space.

DIE WEHRMACHT

On January 8 the Red Army offered Paulus the chance to capitulate. He declined, and on the 12th reported to the German high command that there were no reserves and that all his heavy weapons were immobilized. He anticipated that the Sixth Army could hold out only for a few more days. On January 22 he made a personal appeal to Hitler to be allowed to open negotiations with the enemy. The Führer turned a deaf ear, and on the 30th he made Paulus a field marshal. No German field marshal had ever surrendered, and in effect Hitler was pressing a suicide pistol into Paulus's hand. Characteristically, however, Paulus did not pull the trigger. Instead, on the 31st he and 22 German generals stepped into captivity. Two days later the last defenders of Stalingrad laid down their arms.

In the Stalingrad pocket the Ostheer had lost 20 divisions and over 200,000 men. Of the 108,000 who marched into captivity, only 5,000 survived the war. Six German divisions had been destroyed outside the encirclement. Germany's allies on the Eastern Front, the Romanians, Hungarians, and Italians, had lost four armies, upward of 450,000 men, and any lingering desire they might have nursed to play an active part in Hitler's dreams of an empire in the east. For three days, German radio broadcast a continuous program of solemn music.

SOVIET INTELLIGENCE

SOVIET INTELLIGENCE NETWORKS had been active in Europe, the United Sates, and the Far East from the 1920s. In the months leading up to Operation Barbarossa in June 1941, and thereafter, they provided a stream of information which would often have proved vital had not Stalin been repeatedly determined to believe the opposite of what he was told. Among the most important of these sources was Richard Sorge, a German journalist based in Japan who had the ear of the German ambassador and a number of high-ranking Japanese officials. In March 1941 Sorge had sent microfilmed German documents to Moscow indicating a German attack in June and, subsequently, precise details of the German order of battle. They were not believed, but his revelation in

Stalin's spy
A Soviet stamp commemorates spy Richard Sorge, executed by the Japanese in 1944.

November 1941 that Japan was preparing to move south against Britain and the United States was taken at face value, enabling the transfer of divisions from Siberia for the Soviet counteroffensive before Moscow.

High-level Soviet sources in the German high command and civil service in Berlin—the latter part of the network dubbed the "Red Orchestra" by the Germans—also provided valuable information, such as Hitler's plans in the fall of 1941 to besiege Leningrad rather than take it by storm. Elements of the Red Orchestra were based in neutral Switzerland, where the spy Rudolf Rössler was based. A German bookseller, he had sources at a high level within OKW and from 1942 was the lynchpin of the Soviet network known as "Lucy." Rössler provided Moscow with the Ostheer's order of battle for Operation Citadel at Kursk in 1943. John Cairncross, a British army officer, tranferred to Bletchley Park, the home of the British Ultra decoding service, supplied the Luftwaffe's order of battle for Citadel. By the fall of 1943 Stalin would be waging an intelligence war against his allies as well as the Germans.

Harro Shulze-Boysen
A German Air Ministry official and member of the "Red Orchestra" in Berlin, Shulze-Boysen was exposed and executed in 1942.

"The heroism of so many tens of thousands of men, officers and generals is cancelled out by a man like this... He could have freed himself and ascended into eternity and national immortality, but he preferred to go to Moscow."

HITLER ON HEARING THE NEWS OF PAULUS'S SURRENDER

THE SIEGE OF LENINGRAD

ON HITLER'S ORDERS, in September 1941 the German Army Group North and its Finnish allies had pulled back from the outskirts of Leningrad rather than become involved in a costly city battle. On the 25th the Axis forces had begun to besiege the city, subjecting it to constant air and artillery bombardment. The population had already made preparations to defend their city street by street, forming a civilian militia and erecting 17 miles (27 km) of barricades and antitank ditches. Under Marshal Zhukov's direction, mines were laid and guns were taken from ships to strengthen the defenses. Over 600,000 people had been evacuated by the end of August, but by early October the population of some 3.5 million had only enough food to last 20 days. Savage food rationing left up to 500,000 people with no entitlement, and people were driven to eating domestic animals and birds, and making soup from glue and leather.

Starvation and cold weakened even the strongest, and by January 1942 the daily death toll had risen to 5,000. There were incidents of cannibalism. When the city's arms factories ground to a halt, key workers were flown out.

There was one loophole in the blockade. When the large freshwater Lake Ladoga, northwest of Leningrad, froze in November, a road was created over the ice that provided the last link in a 240-mile (380-km) supply route from beyond the German line at Tikhvin. It became known as "The Road of Life." In December the Red Army's capture of Tikhvin, with its railhead, shortened the journey by one-third and enabled the evacuation of over 500,000 civilians. By the spring of 1942 a semblance of normality had returned: industrial production had resumed, and vegetables grown in plots and parks were being supplemented by food aid from the United States, Australia, and New Zealand. In January 1943 Soviet forces succeeded in opening a land corridor south of the lake, enabling trains to reach the city. The siege was to continue until January 27, 1944, when the Germans were driven beyond the distance from which their artillery could fire at the city. It has been estimated that during the 900 days of the siege, about 1 million of Leningrad's citizens died from starvation and other privations, or German bombardment.

A call to patriots
A stern Mother Russia promises death to the German invaders in this propaganda poster.

Digging for water
During the winter of 1941–42 the citizens of Leningrad had to endure not only starvation but a shortage of drinking water when the extreme cold and German shelling combined to interrupt the supply of water to their homes.

Ice road
A Soviet truck creeps forward over a frozen Lake Ladoga. To support the truck's weight, the ice had to be at least 8 in (200 mm) thick.

Garden plot in the cathedral square
By 1943 vegetables were being grown on over 200,000 garden plots. The threat of starvation was lifted by the spring of 1942, but not the German siege, which was to continue until 1944.

The effects of a shell explosion
For month after month, the Germans subjected Leningrad to bombardment by both artillery and aircraft every day between 8:00 am and 10:00 pm.

THE SOVIET ADVANCE CONTINUES

Hitler drew grim satisfaction from the fact that, by condemning the Sixth Army to self-immolation on the Volga, he had prevented an even more disastrous collapse on the Eastern Front. One hundred Soviet divisions had been tied down for a month, so preventing them from rolling up the entire southern wing of the Ostheer between Orel and Rostov.

By the end of the first week in February, the Soviet Southwest Front, under General Nikolai Vatutin, was over the Donets and advancing southeast of Kharkov, while to the north, Colonel General Fillipp Golikov's Voronezh Front was moving on Kharkov itself. On the German side, Manstein's Army Group Don had fallen back on Rostov at the mouth of the Don River. To Manstein's south, Kleist's Army Group A had been forced to withdraw from the Caucasus into the Taman peninsula, on the north coast of the Black Sea, separated from the Crimea by the Kerch Strait and from Army Group Don by 300 miles (500 km).

Manstein, arguably the finest operational commander of the war, had devised a plan to evacuate Rostov and take up a shorter line along the Mius River, which flows into the Sea of Azov 60 miles (90 km) west of Rostov. From here a powerful armored force could strike against the Red Army's counteroffensive. On February 6 Hitler, temporarily unnerved by the disaster at Stalingrad, agreed to the withdrawal. Manstein moved his headquarters west to Zaporozhye, on the Dnieper, and reshuffled Army Group Don in preparation for the planned strike.

SOVIET CAPTURE OF KHARKOV

The situation remained critical for the Germans. On February 8 the Soviet 60th Army had taken the city of Kursk, 120 miles (190 km) north of Kharkov. On February 14 the Germans abandoned Rostov,

A resurgent Red Army
Soviet infantry rush a German outpost, in February 1943, during an attack which saw the retaking of both Kursk and Kharkov before Manstein's brilliant counterblow rocked the Red Army back on its heels.

Panzer Mark III
By 1942 this German tank was obsolescent and, armed with a 75-mm L/24 howitzer, served in a fire support role in panzergrenadier and heavy tank formations.

and on the same day the encirclement of Kharkov itself threatened to bottle up three panzergrenadier divisions. The German high command reacted with another reshuffle. Army Group Don became Army Group South and Army Group B was broken up, with I SS Panzer Corps being absorbed into the forces defending Kharkov. General Paul Hausser, the commander of I SS Panzer Corps, was ordered to defend Kharkov to the last man and last bullet. He did not, however, emulate Paulus. On the 15th he broke out to the southeast, through the one remaining gap in the Soviet ring. Twenty-four hours later, the last of Hausser's rear parties fought their way out of the blazing city to safety. Most of Kharkov's civilian population had fled during the fighting of 1942. Of those who remained, some 250,000 had died during the German occupation, been deported as slave labor, or killed by cold and hunger. When the Red Army took over Kharkov, the Soviet Union's fourth biggest city, they found it almost deserted.

Like Hitler, Stalin wanted everything to happen at once. Both he and the Stavka were convinced that the Ostheer was in full retreat. The race was now on to beat the arrival of the spring *rasputitsa*.

Vatutin was ordered to broaden his offensive, which bulged like a huge sack toward Dnepropetrovsk and threatened to swallow Manstein's headquarters at Zaporozhye. Manstein watched these developments calmly, aware that the Red Army's supply lines were now stretched to breaking point. He proceeded to order his forces to slice into the increasingly exposed northern and southern flanks of the Soviet Sixth Army (part of Vatutin's Southwest Front).

Manstein also had to handle Hitler, who was now eager to overturn the agreement to a withdrawal that he had made on February 6. On February 16 the Führer flew to Zaporozhye to recite a familiar litany —no more withdrawals. Manstein's plan was to be set aside until Kharkov had been retaken by I SS Panzer Corps. Manstein, however, stood firm. The Southwest Front was becoming increasingly exposed to German blows from north and south. Behind it stretched supply lines running across a wasteland left by the withdrawing Germans, who had blown bridges and broken up the few passable roads. Now, before the onset of the *rasputitsa*, was the time to strike at the Sixth Army in the open as the essential preliminary to the retaking of Kharkov. Hitler wavered while the leading elements of the Sixth Army probed to within 40 miles (60 km) of Zaporozhye and the rumble of Red Army guns became audible in the distance. Hitler then flew out, leaving Manstein with a free hand.

MANSTEIN'S COUNTERBLOW

The westward movement of German armored and motorized formations had been noted by Soviet military intelligence but had been interpreted by the Stavka as confirmation of a retreat to the Dnieper. It chose to believe that the significant concentrations of armor it had detected—the First and Fourth

Panzer Armies—were covering a general withdrawal. It came as an unpleasant shock when, on February 20, Manstein's armored shears began chopping away at the right and left flanks of the Sixth Army. Within 24 hours the two Red Army commanders caught by the storm were requesting permission to pull back. They were ordered to press on to cut off the westward German escape routes.

A division of the Sixth Army's XV Tank Corps fought its way to within 10 miles (16 km) of Zaporozhye and then stuck fast, its tanks starved of fuel. Behind it the rest of XV Corps, also short of fuel, was proving to be an easy target for the German tanks on the open, rolling steppe.

Rumbling over the frozen ground at 25 mph (40 kph), the tanks drew alongside trucks packed with infantry and poured machine-gun fire into them at point-blank range. Soviet tank columns, stranded with empty fuel tanks, were shot to pieces. To the south, panzergrenadiers fanned out across the steppe to mop up in a graveyard of burned armor.

At the headquarters of Southwest Front, Vatutin was torn between apprehension of impending disaster and a reluctance to disobey the urgent orders from Stalin to "get that left wing of yours moving." By February 25, however, the greater part

Germans reach Kharkov
The Germans recaptured Kharkov on March 15 after days of savage fighting in which the Soviet defenders used dug-in T-34s and a network of strongpoints in the huge apartment blocks.

of the Soviet Sixth Army was facing encirclement, and Vatutin was obliged to suspend all offensive operations. The Third Tank Army wheeled south from Kharkov to break through to the Sixth Army. Assembling for attack, it was surprised by German armor and dive-bombers and, after four days of heavy fighting, was itself facing encirclement.

The Red Army was saved by the intense cold, which made movement at night all but impossible. The Germans could not seal off the pockets of the badly mauled Soviet forces, who withdrew across the frozen Donets River, leaving behind all their heavy equipment. Manstein now mounted the second phase of his operation, the retaking of Kharkov.

GERMAN RECAPTURE OF KHARKOV

By March 9 the Germans had sealed off Kharkov to the west and north, and after days of savage street fighting the city fell on the 15th. Belgorod, 50 miles (80 km) to the north, was then retaken on the 18th. This brought not only Kursk under threat but also the rear of the Red Army's Central Front, which formed a huge westward bulge in the Soviet line. If Manstein could now coordinate his northward drive with a southward thrust by Field Marshal Günther Hans von Kluge's Army Group Center, the Soviet armies west of Kursk would be trapped and then destroyed. Kluge, however, was of the opinion that his forces were in no shape to launch an offensive. As the Stavka frantically shored up the front around Kursk, and the *rasputitsa* set in, Manstein's chance slipped away. By the end of March the front line had stabilized from the Mius River to Belgorod.

In the course of Manstein's operation against the Southwest Front, the Red Army had lost just over 600 tanks and had left some 23,000 dead on

the battlefield. But significantly, only 9,000 Soviet troops had been taken prisoner. This was not the army that had suffered the huge defeats of 1941 in which hundreds of thousands had been taken prisoner. In 1942 the Red Army had been reshaped from top to bottom. Its officer corps had been invested with new authority—saluting, for example, had been made obligatory—and new decorations invoking the pre-Revolutionary past had been introduced. The granting of privileges had been balanced by a tightening of a military code that was already the most savage of any of the combatants in the western hemisphere. During the battle for Stalingrad, penal battalions, the *strafbats*, had been introduced for both officers and men. The influence of the Communist Party had also been much reduced with the abolition of the "dual command" system in which a formation's political officer, the commissar, shared authority with the commanding officer. With Zhukov at the helm, the Red Army was set to become a far more effective fighting force.

On the German side, Manstein had demonstrated generalship of the highest order in fighting an enemy that outnumbered his own forces by as many as 8 to 1 in vital sectors. The Ostheer had shown that it still had remarkable powers of recovery and tactical superiority in mobile operations over Red Army formations. Contrary to Hitler's unwavering conviction, giving ground was by no means an invitation to certain disaster, but a preconditon for German success on the Eastern Front. Manstein's counterblow had restored the nerve of the Ostheer after the shock of Stalingrad and the initial inroads made by the Red Army counteroffensive. Germany could now plan for the renewal of offensive operations in the summer of 1943.

THE SOVIET HOME FRONT

MORE THAN ANY OTHER COMBATANT in World War II, the Soviet Union was mobilized to fight a "total war." The sacrifices and suffering endured by the Soviet people between 1941 and 1945 were both heroic and horrifying. The brunt of the civilian effort was borne by women. The armed services devoured the male population of the Soviet Union, leaving women to make up 80 percent of the rural workforce by 1944 and over 50 percent of factory workers, much of the balance being met by boys waiting for their call-up. From June 1941 many workers were forced to move eastward, and endure immense hardship, as a program for the relocation of heavy industry was implemented. The program included the transfer of the huge tank plant at Kharkov to the tractor factory at Chelyabinsk, which also housed part of the Kirov plant evacuated from Leningrad. Popularly known as "Tankograd," it was producing T-34s just 10 weeks after the last engineers left the Kharkov works.

In both factories and fields, life was lived at subsistence level and rationing of food was severe: from 1941 children and elderly dependents received just 700 calories a day, factory workers 1,300, and coalminers 4,000. Peasants did not qualify for ration cards but were able to sell food on the flourishing black market. City dwellers sustained themselves with produce from their garden plots, which by 1944 supplied 25 percent of the Soviet potato harvest.

Completely outside this system were the millions of Soviet citizens in labor camps—some 4.6 million in 1942—who were integrated into the Soviet war industry with characteristic ruthlessness. In 1943–44, as the Red Army steadily regained Soviet territory from the Ostheer, it also swept into Stalin's net millions of Soviet citizens—mere contact with the occupiers brought with it the taint of collaboration. Entire populations—the Volga Germans, Chechens, Crimean Tatars, Kalmyks—were uprooted and deported to Soviet Central Asia and Siberia in cattle trucks supervised by the ever-present NKVD or secret police. It has been estimated that at least 1.5 million people were involved in this forced migration, half of whom did not survive the war.

Field workers
This idealized picture of Russian women bringing in the grain harvest belies the fact that, for most women during the war, life was a constant struggle to survive.

Making shells
By November 1941 the Soviet male work force had fallen by 21 million. Their places in factories and on farms were taken by women.

An exhortation to workers
In the names of Lenin and Stalin, civilians were exhorted to work to support the war effort.

Byelorussian refugees
Soviet peasants in the war zones were helpless against German "scorched earth" tactics and anti-partisan operations. Vast numbers of refugees was created as homes were destroyed.

Tank production
Tank factories were among the heavy industries that were moved eastward with as many as 25 million workers and their families in the second half of 1941.

THE HOLOCAUST

THE GERMAN ARMY'S SUCCESSES in the first two years of the war delivered into Hitler's hands the Jewish populations of much of Europe. In the early stages of the conflict the Germans had created numerous ghettos in Poland, the largest in Warsaw, where at least 40,000 Jews died of starvation in 1941. The gains made by Germany in the summer of 1941 in the Soviet Union produced the so-called "Final Solution," a euphemism for the extermination of European Jews.

In January 1942, at a secret conference in Wannsee chaired by Reinhard Heydrich, deputy head of the SS, the Final Solution was systematized. In the east the killing had initially been undertaken by *Einsatzgruppe* units (see page 102) with the help of local auxiliaries and allies. At Odessa in the fall of 1941 up to 80,000 Jews were killed by *Einsatzgruppen* and troops from Romania, into which Odessa had been incorporated. Heydrich industrialized the killing, establishing extermination camps based on the existing concentration camp system. Clusters of camps were built in Poland—among them Treblinka, Belzec, Majdanek, Sobibor, and Auschwitz-Birkenau. Adolf Eichmann and his subordinates organized the transportation to these and other camps of Jews, Slavs, Red Army prisoners-of-war, gypsies, political prisoners, and homosexuals. They came from every part of occupied Europe, and meticulously logged railroad movements later provided much detail for historians of the Final Solution. The camps were sometimes linked to industrial complexes run by the SS, and those deemed capable of work on arrival were given a stay of execution. The rest—the old and the infirm, the children—were gassed. Auschwitz attained a rate of 12,000 victims a day. In April 1943 there was a revolt and mass escape at Treblinka, the destination for many Polish Jews. That same month, the German troops despatched to clear the ghetto in Warsaw met with armed resistance. The fighting, in which some 13,000 Jews died, ended in mid-May 1943, and the survivors were sent to extermination camps.

The Western Allies had learned about the existence of the extermination camps from intelligence sources and refugees by the summer of 1944, when the Red Army reached the abandoned camp in Majdanek in Poland. It overran many more camps in the following months, including Auschwitz, to which 450,000 Hungarian Jews—about 60 percent of the largest surviving Jewish population in Europe—had been delivered from March 1944. The Final Solution caused the death of approximately 5.7 million Jews, some 40 percent of the world's Jewish population, and at least another million more people who were either non-Aryan or deemed undesirable by the Nazis.

Arriving at Auschwitz
Many of the people sent to Auschwitz only learnt on their arrival that it was a death camp.

Distribution of camps
The system of concentration and death camps was extended with each German conquest in Europe.

CENTERS OF PERSECUTION DURING THE WAR

- ◉ Main concentration camp
- ● Extermination camp
- ◻ Site of major mass killing
- ✡ Ghetto
- (8,000) Estimated number of Jews killed
- — Borders Nov 1942
- Greater Germany Nov 1942
- Italy and Axis satellites Nov 1942
- Under German occupation Nov 1942
- Under German and Italian occupation Nov 1942
- Allied territory
- Neutral territory

Crematorium

The bodies of those who had been killed were stripped of all clothes, hair, jewelry, and any gold teeth. They were then placed on stretchers to be pushed into crematoria by fellow prisoners.

I recall a Dutch Jew asking angrily, "Where is my wife? Where are my children?" The Jews in the barracks said to him, "Look at the chimney. They are there. Up there." But the Dutch Jew cursed them. "There are so many camps around," he said. "They promised me we would be kept together." This is the greatest strength of the whole crime, its unbelievability. When we came to Auschwitz, we smelled the sweet smell. They said to us: "There the people are gassed, three kilometers over there." We didn't believe it.

LILLI KOPECKY, DEPORTED FROM SLOVAKIA TO AUSCHWITZ

Corpse pit at Bergen-Belsen

Bergen-Belsen was a concentration, rather than a death, camp. However, as in all other camps, conditions were appalling and disease was rampant. By 1945 mass graves contained the bodies of 40,000 people.

Auschwitz roll-call

Part of the camp complex housed women who were used as a source of forced labor for nearby factories.

Starving prisoners

Food was scarce for camp inmates, who were forced to work until they no longer had the strength to do so and were then killed.

One million pairs of shoes at Lublin camp
As the Red Army advanced into Poland in 1944, it discovered many extermination camps. Among the horrifying evidence of the Holocaust in these camps were piles of the former possessions of murdered Jews.

NORTH AFRICA AND THE MEDITERRANEAN

MARCH 1942–MAY 1943

After two years of inconclusive offensives and retreats across Libya, in November 1942 the British finally won a significant victory over Rommel at El Alamein. In the same month the odds tilted dramatically with the arrival of US forces—the Torch landings—in French northwest Africa. Even so, it took the Allies another six months to drive the Axis from North Africa.

1942

MARCH 20–26
British convoy from Alexandria to Malta fights off Italian ships in Sirte Gulf, but suffers heavy losses as it nears Malta

APRIL 7
2,000-plane raid on Malta

JUNE 11
Two convoys sail for Malta: "Harpoon" from Gibraltar, "Vigorous" from Alexandria. Both suffer heavy losses. "Vigorous" turns back to Alexandria

MAY 26
German offensive begins with march to south of British Gazala Line

JUNE 21
Tobruk falls to Germans

JUNE 30
After Rommel's advance, 8th Army back on El Alamein line. In Cairo British HQ prepares for evacuation to Palestine

JULY 1
Rommel attacks at El Alamein

JULY 7
Rommel halted at El Alamein, but Auchinleck unable to launch effective counteroffensive

AUGUST 11–15
British convoy "Pedestal" sailing for Malta attacked by aircraft, submarines, and torpedo boats

AUGUST 13
Montgomery assumes command of British 8th Army from Auchinleck

AUGUST 30
Rommel launches attack on British 8th Army south of El Alamein

SEPTEMBER 2
Rommel falls back to start line—end of attempt to capture Suez Canal

OCTOBER 18
Germans and Italians halt daylight bombing raids on Malta

OCTOBER 23–24
Start of Second Battle of El Alamein

OCTOBER 27
Axis counterattacks

NOVEMBER 4
Rommel, hopelessly outnumbered in men, tanks, and aircraft, retreats

NOVEMBER 8
Operation Torch. US landings around Casablanca, Oran, and Algiers meet with resistance from Vichy French

NOVEMBER 9
German landings near Tunis

NOVEMBER 10
French end resistance to Allies

NOVEMBER 11
French in Algeria and Morocco sign armistice with Allies

NOVEMBER 13
Tobruk recaptured

DECEMBER 28
Allied advance to Tunis halted

1943

JANUARY 14–25
Casablanca Conference. Churchill and Roosevelt meet to discuss future plans for war

JANUARY 23
British 8th Army enters Tripoli

JANUARY 23
Rommel crosses into Tunisia

FEBRUARY 14–22
Battle of Kasserine Pass. Dual offensive by von Arnim's 5th Army and Rommel's Afrika Korps forces Allied withdrawal

FEBRUARY 22
Axis advance halted; Rommel turns to face British 8th Army advancing from south

MARCH 9
Rommel leaves North Africa on sick leave; replaced by von Arnim

MARCH 20
Montgomery attacks Mareth Line, Axis defensive position in southern Tunisia

MARCH 26–27
Axis troops evacuate Mareth Line after being outflanked by New Zealand Corps

MAY 6
Final Allied offensive opens

MAY 7
Bizerta and Tunis fall

MAY 13
Italian 1st Army surrenders. In all Allies take 240,000 German and Italian prisoners

■ Operations in the Mediterranean Mar 1942–May 1943

■ Egypt and Libya May 6, 1942– Jan 23, 1943

■ Operation Torch and Tunisia Nov 8, 1942– May 13, 1943

THE AXIS DEFEATED IN NORTH AFRICA

AFTER ROMMEL HAD DRIVEN the British back to the Gazala Line in early 1942, a temporary stalemate existed in Libya, with both sides making preparations for renewing the offensive. Malta was still under siege and the Royal Navy was desperately struggling, in the face of Axis air superiority, to keep the island supplied. While the United States had finally joined the war, it would clearly be some time before sufficient US forces were deployed to the European theatre to have any influence on events.

Concerned over Malta, Churchill pressured Auchinleck, the Middle East commander-in-chief, to attack as soon as possible. Auchinleck was not prepared to do so until he was ready and he also wanted to strengthen the Gazala Line so that he could launch his offensive from a secure base. Churchill remained dissatisfied and threatened to remove part of the Desert Air Force to India. This galvanized Auchinleck into agreeing to make an attack on May 1, although he soon postponed this to the middle of June.

British Commonwealth Forces Quad Gun Tractor. Many of these reliable four-wheel drive vehicles were made by Ford, Canada

H5570920

Exhausted German troops
Rommel's German and Italian forces crossed into Egypt and reached the El Alamein line at the end of June 1942, but their fatigue was now such that they were unable to break through the British defensive positions.

AXIS INTENTIONS

There was also disagreement in the Axis camp. While Rommel wanted to push on to the Suez Canal before the British could strengthen their defenses, his superiors remained cautious. By the end of March 1942 they decided that the seizure of Malta must be the priority because of the threat it posed to Axis supply lines across the Mediterranean. After an intensification of the air offensive against the island, a combined airborne and amphibious operation would be launched to capture it.

As far as Libya was concerned, Rommel could expect no more German reinforcements because of the planned offensive on the Eastern Front. His hands were thus tied. Eventually, though, at the beginning of May he was given leave to conduct a limited offensive to recapture Tobruk. Should he achieve this speedily, he would be allowed to advance to the Egyptian frontier, but then his air support would be removed for the assault on Malta. Only once this had taken place and been successful would Rommel be allowed to continue to the Nile Delta.

As far as Rommel was concerned, he had been given the green light and he immediately began his preparations. The Gazala Line had two major weaknesses. Although it stretched some 40 miles (65 km) south to Bir Hacheim, there was open desert beyond this point, which meant that the line could be outflanked. In addition, the defenses consisted of a number of fortified brigade-sized positions, known as "boxes," but some were too far apart to provide mutual supporting fire. Rommel decided to take his armor around the south of the line, while his Italian infantry tied down the defenders. They would then punch a hole through the defenses and establish

British 25-pounder
This gun was the workhorse of the British artillery. It was a multipurpose gun that served primarily as a field gun, but could also be fired at a high elevation like a howitzer. In the desert it was often used in an antitank role.

Camouflaged artillery
The crew prepares to fire a 25-pounder from a gun emplacement in the desert. The British field gun was manned by a crew of six.

a direct resupply route for his tanks. The Gazala Line dispositions had a further weakness, not recognized by Rommel. Although Auchinleck wanted to keep his tanks concentrated so that they could deal with any Axis outflanking move, Ritchie, still commanding Eighth Army, was worried about his supply dumps, which were situated far forward as part of his own attack preparations, and dispersed his armor to protect them.

ROMMEL'S OFFENSIVE

On the evening of May 26, 1942, Rommel began his approach march. Ritchie was convinced that it was a diversion and that the main attack would be against the Gazala Line itself. Next morning, the Axis armor swung around Bir Hacheim and began to advance north to the rear of the British defenses. Caught by surprise, the British tanks became increasing scattered. But Rommel's tanks were now beginning to run out of fuel. It was time to attack the Gazala Line itself, which the Italians did from the west and the Afrika Korps from the east. The particular box selected was soon isolated and Ritchie was unable to concentrate his armor to launch an effective counterattack. By the end of June 2 the Cauldron, as the British called it, had been overrun and an

In the first second we must have received at least four direct hits from armor-piercing shells. The engine was knocked out, a track was broken and one shell hit the barrel of the 75-mm gun and broke it. Then quite a heavy high-explosive shell dropped on the mantlet of my 37-mm gun and pushed it back against the recoil springs... I suffered nothing more than a singing in my ears. But a splinter hit the subaltern in the head and he fell to the floor of the turret dead.

**REA LEAKEY, BRITISH TANK OFFICER,
ON BEING HIT BY GERMAN 88-MM SHELLS**

armored counterattack launched three days later was a disastrous failure, resulting in a heavy loss of tanks. The southern part of the line was now entirely in Axis hands, apart from Bir Hacheim, where the Free French garrison continued to hold out in the face of repeated attacks.

On June 11 the French were ordered to break out, which they successfully did. Rommel, meanwhile, set about destroying the remainder of the British armor to the west of El Adem. In two days' fighting, he largely succeeded and threatened Ritchie's main supply line to the northern part of the Gazala Line.

Accordingly, Ritchie withdrew his forces to prevent them from being totally cut off.

The Eighth Army was now withdrawing to the Egyptian frontier, but Churchill was insistent that Tobruk be held. Unfortunately, the port's perimeter defenses had deteriorated since the long siege of the previous year. The largely South African garrison had little chance to prepare before Rommel's troops had isolated Tobruk and attacked. It fell on June 21.

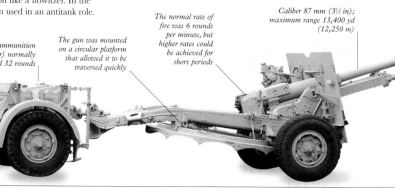

The No 27 ammunition trailer (limber) normally held 32 rounds

The gun was mounted on a circular platform that allowed it to be traversed quickly

The normal rate of fire was 6 rounds per minute, but higher rates could be achieved for short periods

Caliber 87 mm (3½ in); maximum range 13,400 yd (12,250 m)

BERNARD LAW MONTGOMERY

BADLY WOUNDED as a young infantry officer in 1914, Montgomery (1887–1976) served for the remainder of the war as a staff officer on the Western Front. He took Third Infantry Division to France in 1939 and was then made responsible for the defense of the southeast coast of England. It was when he was selected to take over the Eighth Army in Egypt in August 1942 that Monty, as he was generally known, demonstrated his best qualities. His self-confidence, clarity of thought, and insistence on showing himself to his troops and making them believe that each had a key role to play, restored the morale of the army.

Monty's victory at El Alamein made him a household name in Britain. He led his victorious army across Libya into Tunisia, then to Sicily and Italy. His brashness and lack of tact did not go down well with some of his American fellow commanders, but he was appointed to command 21st Army Group for the invasion of Europe. He conducted the Normandy campaign, but was disappointed when Eisenhower subsequently insisted on taking over command.

Two days later, Rommel continued his pursuit of the increasingly disorganized Eighth Army. He signaled Kesselring, his superior in Rome, for permission to keep going into Egypt, pointing out that he had captured large stocks of supplies in Tobruk.

DESPERATE MEASURES

In the British camp, Ritchie wanted to stand and fight at Mersa Matruh, but Auchinleck feared that this would result in the destruction of the Eighth Army. He was starting to construct a new defense line at El Alamein, which had the advantage that its southern end was anchored on the virtually impassable Qattara Depression and hence could not be outflanked. Auchinleck decided to remove Ritchie and take command of the army himself. If the Axis succeeded in penetrating the El Alamein line, he intended to hold them on the Suez Canal or, if need be, in Palestine.

Rommel had already closed up to Mersa Matruh, when he obtained grudging permission to continue his advance. Kesselring had decided that the need to capture Malta was less pressing. He now felt that air assaults and the mining of the waters around the island had effectively neutralized it as a threat to Axis supply lines. Two simultaneous British supply convoys, Harpoon from Gibraltar and Vigorous from Alexandria, had been subjected to ferocious air and sea attacks. Only two supply vessels from Harpoon reached the island, while Vigorous was forced to turn back. It was possible that the island could be starved into submission.

Back in Egypt, Rommel quickly outflanked the defenses at Mersa Matruh, as Auchinleck expected him to do, and by June 30 the Eighth Army was back on the El Alamein Line. On that same day, the Mediterranean Fleet left Alexandria for anchorages farther east, while British headquarters began to burn secret files and prepared to evacuate to Palestine. Rommel was conscious that his troops were now close to exhaustion after five weeks of very intensive combat and that he had to attack immediately to deny the British any opportunity to draw breath. Accordingly, he launched his assault on July 1. Partially thanks to a sandstorm and the

Infantry advance
At El Alamein and other battles in the Desert War Montgomery used his infantry, after an initial artillery bombardment, for what he termed the "crumbling" of Axis defenses.

efforts of the Desert Air Force, it was repulsed. Rommel made further attacks during the next two days, but although these did gain ground he could not achieve the now elusive breakthrough.

Rommel therefore decided to go over to the defensive for the time being. The British tried to dislodge him, but without success. Rommel then launched two further attacks, on July 10 and 12, but again could not break through and finally accepted that he had done all he could. Auchinleck now made further attempts to drive his adversary back, but his troops were also drained and before the end of the month he halted his attacks and a stalemate ensued.

CHANGES IN COMMAND

Disappointed that Auchinleck had failed to drive the Axis back, Churchill flew to Cairo. He decided to replace Auchinleck, appointing Harold Alexander, who had recently overseen the British withdrawal from Burma, in his place. Hardened desert veteran William "Strafer" Gott was selected to take over the Eighth Army, but he was shot down and killed while flying to Cairo to assume command and Bernard Montgomery had to be hastily sent for from Britain. He found an army that was "brave but baffled" and the first action he and Alexander took was to make it clear that there would be no retreat from El Alamein. The Eighth Army's task would be to repulse Rommel's next attack, then go onto the offensive.

Rommel himself had become ill and asked to be relieved of his command, but his request was denied. He knew he had to attack again, but was very short of fuel. Six tankers and ammunition ships were scheduled to cross the Mediterranean during August. Ultra gave the British due warning of their sailing and four were sunk, while the other two did not arrive in time. As a result, Rommel did not have the

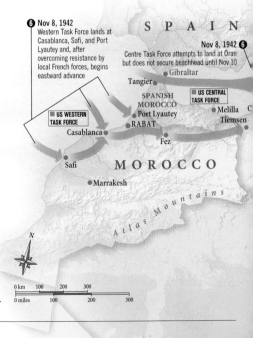

6 Nov 8, 1942
Western Task Force lands at Casablanca, Safi, and Port Lyautey and, after overcoming resistance by local French forces, begins eastward advance

Nov 8, 1942 **6**
Centre Task Force attempts to land at Oran but does not secure beachhead until Nov 10

S P A I N

Tangier • Gibraltar

SPANISH MOROCCO

US CENTRAL TASK FORCE

US WESTERN TASK FORCE

Port Lyautey • Melilla

RABAT • Tiemsen

Casablanca

Fez

Safi

M O R O C C O

Marrakesh

Atlas Mountains

N

0 km 100 200 300
0 miles 100 200 300

fuel to reach the Suez Canal and would have to rely on capturing British dumps. Meanwhile a key convoy to Malta, Pedestal, got through from Gibraltar to reinforce and resupply the island.

Rommel began his attack late on August 30. His plan was to feint in the north, while his tanks broke through in the south and then swung north to cut the Eighth Army's supply lines. Montgomery, partly thanks to Ultra intelligence, had foreseen this and knew that his opponent had to secure the dominant Alam Halfa Ridge, southeast of El Alamein. He was therefore determined to deny Rommel the ridge and, indeed, to use it as bait in order to defeat him. The British had only light screening forces in the extreme south and Rommel hoped to be able to

The Allied victory in North Africa

After US forces landed in Morocco and Algeria in November 1942, the German and Italian forces in this theatre were heavily ounumbered. The Axis sent fresh troops to Tunisia, but they were unable to break out as the Allies closed in from east and west to trap them.

reach the ridge by dawn. Unfortunately, his armor was slowed by two belts of minefields and it was well after daylight when it began to advance toward the Alam Halfa Ridge. While the Desert Air Force attacked from the air, Montgomery's tanks engaged from the ridge itself. After two days of repeated attempts to capture it, Rommel, now desperately short of fuel, was forced to withdraw to his start line.

It was now Montgomery's turn to attack. Churchill wanted him to strike before the end of September, but both Alexander and Montgomery insisted that they would not be ready, especially since the army needed some intensive training. By mid-October the Eighth Army outnumbered the Axis forces by two to one in men and tanks and by almost the same margin in antitank guns, artillery, and aircraft. In addition, Rommel was still beset by fuel problems. Air attacks on the ports along the Egyptian and Libyan coasts had rendered them almost unusable and many of his supplies had to come by road all the way from Tripoli. He himself

German and Italian prisoners

In the aftermath of El Alamein, the Eighth Army took some 30,000 prisoners, about a third of them Germans. Here a large number of Axis troops have been rounded up after the battle by New Zealanders in armored cars.

was ill again and left for Germany for treatment on September 23. Realizing that his forces could no longer fight a maneuver battle, he left instructions for efforts to be concentrated on strengthening the minefields covering his positions.

Montgomery appreciated that there was no means of outflanking the Axis defenses and that he would have to make a frontal assault, opting to do this against the northern part of Rommel's line. Once lanes in the minefields had been cleared, he looked to his infantry to carry out the break-in operation. His armor would then draw the Axis tanks onto it and destroy them prior to the actual breakthrough taking place.

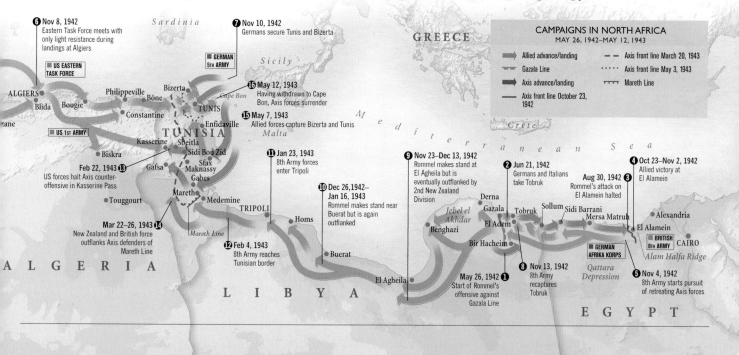

6 Nov 8, 1942
Eastern Task Force meets with only light resistance during landings at Algiers

7 Nov 10, 1942
Germans secure Tunis and Bizerta

GREECE

16 May 12, 1943
Having withdrawn to Cape Bon, Axis forces surrender

15 May 7, 1943
Allied forces capture Bizerta and Tunis

CAMPAIGNS IN NORTH AFRICA
MAY 26, 1942–MAY 12, 1943

- → Allied advance/landing
- ⊔ Gazala Line
- → Axis advance/landing
- — Axis front line October 23, 1942
- – – Axis front line March 20, 1943
- ···· Axis front line May 3, 1943
- ⊤⊤⊤ Mareth Line

US EASTERN TASK FORCE

GERMAN 5TH ARMY

Sardinia

Sicily

Cape Bon

TUNIS

Enfidaville

Malta

Crete

Mediterranean Sea

ALGIERS
Blida
Bougie
Philippeville
Bône
Bizerta
Constantine
US 1ST ARMY
TUNISIA
Kasserine
Sbeitla
Biskra
Sidi Bou Zid
Sfax
Feb 22, 1943 **13**
US forces halt Axis counter-offensive in Kasserine Pass
Gafsa
Maknassy
Gabes
Touggourt
Mareth
Medenine
Mareth Line

11 Jan 23, 1943
8th Army forces enter Tripoli

10 Dec 26,1942–Jan 16, 1943
Rommel makes stand near Buerat but is again outflanked

9 Nov 23–Dec 13, 1942
Rommel makes stand at El Agheila but is eventually outflanked by 2nd New Zealand Division

4 Oct 23–Nov 2, 1942
Allied victory at El Alamein

2 Jun 21, 1942
Germans and Italians take Tobruk

3 Aug 30, 1942
Rommel's attack on El Alamein halted

Mar 22–26, 1943 **14**
New Zealand and British force outflanks Axis defenders of Mareth Line

TRIPOLI
Homs

12 Feb 4, 1943
8th Army reaches Tunisian border

Buerat

Derna
Gazala
Tobruk
Sollum
Sidi Barrani
Mersa Matruh
Alexandria
El Alamein

Jebel el Akhdar
Benghazi
El Adem
Bir Hacheim

GERMAN AFRIKA KORPS

BRITISH 8TH ARMY
CAIRO
Alam Halfa Ridge

8 Nov 13, 1942
8th Army recaptures Tobruk

Qattara Depression

ALGERIA

El Agheila

May 26, 1942 **1**
Start of Rommel's offensive against Gazala Line

5 Nov 4, 1942
8th Army starts pursuit of retreating Axis forces

LIBYA

EGYPT

On the night of October 23/24 the attack began. Nearly 900 British guns fired a preliminary barrage and the mine clearance parties, covered by infantry, began to move forward. The Axis forces were initially taken by surprise and lanes were soon created, but problems of command and control in the darkness, which slowed the passage of the tanks through the lanes, and the sheer depth of the defenses meant that progress was not as quick as was hoped. Rommel's deputy was killed during the day, and Rommel himself returned on October 25. He immediately launched a series of counterattacks against the British lodgements, but these were beaten off. Even so, Montgomery accepted that there was a growing danger that a stalemate might ensue and recast his plans. This meant a pause to reorganize, which agitated Churchill. The new attack was launched on the night of November 1/2. Given his now desperate lack of fuel, Rommel realized that if

The American disembarkation
US troops manhandle a gun up a beach on November 9, the day after the initial Torch landings. Most of the men had no experience of war when they arrived in North Africa, but learned quickly during the Tunisian campaign.

he continued to stand and fight, his army was in danger of being destroyed. He therefore began to withdraw his mobile forces. Hitler ordered him to stay put, but it was too late. By midday on November 4 the Axis forces were in full retreat.

At first Montgomery's armor was slow to take advantage of Rommel's retreat and the arrival of rain on November 6 did not help matters. Even so, El Alamein was a significant victory and a major turning point of the war in the West. It was also the last significant success by British arms alone in the theater. Some 1,800 miles (2,900 km) to the west US forces were about to enter the fray.

THE TORCH LANDINGS

On November 8, 1942 Anglo–US forces landed at points in French northwest Africa. Operation Torch was the upshot of several months of strategic debate between the United States and Britain as to where US forces in Europe could be best employed before the end of 1942. The idea was to secure Morocco, Algeria, and Tunisia quickly so as to threaten the Axis forces facing the British in Egypt and Libya in the rear and help bring about their destruction. The key to the success of the Torch landings was that the Vichy French forces would offer minimum resistance. To this end, Torch's deputy commander, General Mark Clark was taken secretly by submarine for a meeting on the Algerian coast with one of the Vichy French generals, who assured him that they would follow the

Algeria bound
US forces assemble on the deck of a troopship before the landings in Algeria. In all, 39,000 men were landed near Oran, 33,000 around Algiers, and 35,000 in Morocco.

orders of General Henri Giraud, who had been selected as the French figurehead after the Vichy French government in the region had been dissolved.

Three task forces took part in Torch. The Western Task Force under General George S. Patton sailed directly from the United States and landed at points on the Moroccan coast. The other two forces sailed from Scotland. General Lloyd Fredenhall's Center Task Force landed in Oran and General Charles Ryder's Eastern Task Force in Algiers. The latter was the only one to include British forces. These, however, had to be initially disguised as Americans because of Vichy French enmity toward the British since the bombardment of their fleet in July 1940 to prevent it from falling into German hands. There were fears that this would stiffen resistance to the landing. As it happened, the Vichy French did offer some resistance to all three landings. However, Marshal Pétain gave Admiral François Darlan, the Resident-General in North Africa, freedom to negotiate with the Allies and on November 11 an armistice came into force.

GERMAN REACTIONS

The Axis had initially been taken by surprise, especially by the landings in Algeria. Nevertheless, they reacted quickly. On November 9 the Vichy prime minister Pierre Laval gave permission for Axis troops to be deployed to Tunisia and the first of these, German paratroops, landed at an airfield outside Tunis that same day. In revenge for the signing of the armistice with the Allies, the Germans proceeded to occupy Vichy France. The French response was to scuttle their fleet based at Toulon.

The Allies now had to advance into Tunisia as fast as possible to secure it before the Axis forces built up. The forces available, under the command of General Kenneth Anderson's First British Army, were initially slim—two British infantry brigades, an Anglo–US armored task force, together with some Commandos, US Rangers, and paratroops.

ARMOR AND ANTITANK WEAPONS USED IN THE DESERT WAR

ARMOR DOMINATED THE WAR in Egypt and Libya, the desert being ideal terrain for tanks. It was also the scene of intense rivalry between the tank and the antitank gun. Dominant in this respect was the German 88-mm, which totally outranged all the tanks used by the British. The earlier models the British used in the desert were also disadvantaged because they did not have high-explosive shells, a much more effective way of neutralizing antitank guns than solid shot.

Italian CV3/35 flamethrower tankette
The basic CV3, with two machine-guns, entered service in 1933, but was too lightly armed and armored to have any effect in North Africa. The flamethrower version enjoyed virtually no success.

Crew 2	Top speed 26 mph (42 kph)
Range with full fuel tank 100 miles (160 km)	
Maximum armor thickness ½ in (14 mm)	

75-mm gun mounted in side sponson

37-mm secondary armament

British 6-pounder (57-mm) antitank gun
Designed in 1938, the gun did not enter production until 1941 and only began to replace the less effective 2-pounder (40-mm) in the Eighth Army in early 1942.

Weight of gun carriage 2,698 lb (1,224 kg)	Weight of shot 6 lb (2.72 kg)
Armour penetration at 1,000 yd (915 m) 2½ in (65 mm)	
Crew 5	

Side hatch

Muzzle break to reduce smoke visible to enemy on firing

Shield

Trail

US M3 Grant
Used by the British from summer 1942, the Grant was automotively more reliable than British tank types, but its high silhouette was a disadvantage.

Crew 6	Top speed 26 mph (42 kph)
Range with full fuel tank 120 miles (192 km)	
Maximum armor thickness 2¼ in (55 mm)	

90-mm smoke generators

88-mm high-velocity gun

British Humber armored car
Both sides made extensive use of armored cars for reconnaissance and covering their open desert flanks. The Humber was in North Africa from late 1941.

Crew 3	Top speed 45 mph (72 kph)
Range with full fuel tank 250 miles (400 km)	
Maximum armor thickness : ⅗ in (15 mm)	

7.92-mm MG 34 machine-gun

15-mm Besa gun

German PzKpfw VI Tiger heavy tank
The most formidable of all the German tanks, the Tiger made its combat debut in Tunisia. It proved particularly effective in defense, especially in northwest Europe, where its potential as an attacking weapon was limited by the terrain.

Crew 5	Top speed 23 mph (37 kph)
Range with full fuel tank 62 miles (100 km)	
Maximum armor thickness 4 in (100 mm)	

720-mm battle tracks

Recoil chamber

German 88-mm FLAK
Designed as an antiaircraft weapon, it was first used in an antitank role during the Spanish Civil War. It was in North Africa that it really came into its own.

Crew 5	Weight of shot 23 lb (10.4 kg)
Armor penetration at 1,000 yd (915 m) 4 in (103 mm)	
Weight of gun carriage 8,140 lb (3,700 kg)	

German PzKpfw III
There were a number of variants of this tank, with both 37-mm and 50-mm guns. This version is equipped with a 75-mm low velocity gun for firing high explosive.

Crew 5	Top speed 25 mph (40 kph)
Range with full fuel tank 93 miles (150 km)	
Maximum armor thickness 2¾ in (70 mm)	

Sectional interchangeable barrel

Trailer

Breech

Pivoted cruciform carriage

Anderson began by conducting a series of amphibious landings along the Algerian coast and using his paratroops to secure airfields. The two infantry brigades and Blade Force (the armor) then began to advance into Tunisia on separate axes. The first clash with Axis forces came on November 17, when a German battle group turned back the British advance in the north. The following day, however, the Axis suffered a serious blow when French forces in Tunisia declared for the Allies.

THE ALLIED ADVANCE HALTED

Anderson was now facing difficulties. His main supply line from Algiers was a single-track and rather antiquated railroad line and the passage of supplies and reinforcements was slow. Matters were not helped by heavy rain. The Allies were operating largely off grass airfields, which quickly became choked in mud, while the Axis forces had good all-weather airfields in Tunisia itself. As a consequence, they enjoyed air superiority. These problems caused Anderson to order a temporary halt to the advance, which was resumed in the last week of November. Initially it made good progress and the leading elements of his forces reached a point just 20 miles (32 km) from Tunis before the Germans launched a counterattack and drove them back. By the end of the year, both sides had taken up defensive positions and a winter campaign was now inevitable.

There was a political development in Algeria on December 24, when a monarchist French student assassinated Admiral Darlan, Resident-General of French North and West Africa. Eisenhower, as

> "Ike's position just now is something like that of a hen sitting on a batch of eggs. He is waiting for the eggs to hatch, and is in the mental state of wondering if they will ever break the shell."

CAPTAIN HARRY C. BUTCHER, NAVAL AIDE TO GENERAL EISENHOWER (IKE), DIARY ENTRY APRIL 25, 1943, REFERRING TO PREPARATIONS FOR THE FINAL ALLIED OFFENSIVE IN TUNISIA

supreme Allied commander, had retained Darlan in his post as the best way of bringing the French in Algeria and Tunisia firmly on the Allied side. He now appointed Giraud, who had been acting as commander-in-chief of the French forces, in his place. The appointment, however, was not a success. De Gaulle and the Free French did not like Giraud and he also angered Eisenhower by arresting many who had collaborated with the Allies during the Torch landings. These political problems diverted Eisenhower from overseeing the campaign in Tunisia as closely as he would have liked.

GATHERING OF THE FORCES

By January 1943 the Allies in Tunisia were organized in three corps under Anderson's First Army. The British held the north, the French, who were poorly equipped, the center, and the Americans the south. The Axis forces were grouped under Jürgen von Arnim's Fifth Panzer Army. This was now joined by Rommel's Panzer Army Africa, which had been pursued the length of Libya by Montgomery. The two Axis armies now came under the command of

the Italian General Vittorio Ambrosio. Montgomery, meanwhile, paused at Tripoli to reopen the port. He needed to improve the Eighth Army's logistics before starting his advance into Tunisia.

AXIS COUNTERATTACKS

During January von Arnim had managed to seize passes in the French sector. With Rommel now on the scene, they discussed a more ambitious operation to destroy the First Army, but could not agree. Eventually, in mid-February, they launched two separate attacks, both in the US sector. Von Arnim, attacking from the east, took Sidi Bou Zid and Sbeitla, while Rommel, coming from the south, passed through Gafsa. Much to his displeasure, Rommel was now ordered north to cooperate with von Arnim, whereas he wanted to advance farther westward so as to get into the rear of the Allied

American infantry advancing through Tunisia
US troops were deployed mainly in mountainous central Tunisia. They were driven back by fierce counter-offensives led by Rommel and von Arnim, but the terrain prevented the German armor from breaking through.

was, however, nearing its end. German and Italian supply lines to Tunisia across the Mediterranean were being throttled by Allied sea and air action.

AXIS RESISTANCE CRUMBLES

With Montgomery held up at Enfidaville, General Alexander, who had been appointed to command 18th Army Group, which embraced the First and Eighth Armies, decided that the final assault should come from the west. He ordered Montgomery to pass some of his divisions to the First Army, which began its offensive on April 22. Both Tunis and Bizerta fell, to the British and Americans respectively, on May 7 and the remaining Axis forces were trapped in the Cape Bon peninsula. Their resistance finally ended five days later. Two hundred and forty thousand men surrendered to the Allies, a disaster for the Axis comparable to that at Stalingrad. After almost three years the North African campaign was at an end and the Allies could now look northward to Europe.

The battle for the Mareth Line
Exhausted British troops sleep in their trench facing the Mareth Line in March 1943. The fortified line held up Montgomery's advance along the Tunisian coast to link up with the other Allied forces advancing from the west.

defenses. Although between them they dealt the combat-inexperienced Americans a severe blow, notably at the Kasserine Pass, they were now foiled by British reinforcements coming down from the north. Rommel was also aware that Montgomery and the British Eighth Army had finally entered Tunisia and threatened his rear. While he turned to meet his old desert adversary, von Arnim carried out a number of spoiling attacks in the north.

Montgomery had been forewarned by Ultra intelligence that Rommel intended to attack and prepared accordingly. On March 6 the Afrika Korps attacked at Medenine and was repulsed with heavy losses in tanks. Three days later, Rommel left North Africa for good for a spell of sick leave at home.

CLOSING IN

Montgomery now began to advance up eastern Tunisia's narrow coastal plain. As he did so, Patton, who had taken over US II Corps in western Tunisia, regained the territory that had been lost in February and by the end of March had secured the key pass at Maknassy. Montgomery's first obstacle was the Mareth Line, which had originally been built by the French as a defense against an Italian invasion from Libya. A frontal assault, launched on March 20, failed and so he carried out a deep westward outflanking move, which turned the Axis defenses, although it did not prevent them from withdrawing to the next defensive line at Wadi Akarit. He overturned this on April 6 and advanced north to Enfidaville, but was stalemated there by a resolute defense. Meanwhile, in western Tunisia the First Army also began to close in and was undeterred by further spoiling attacks by von Arnim in mid-April. Axis resistance

THE FREE FRENCH

THOSE FEW FRENCHMEN WHO RALLIED to Charles de Gaulle's banner in London in summer 1940 did so realizing that they were regarded as traitors in their own land. De Gaulle decided to concentrate on bringing the French African colonies onto his side, but his first attempt, a landing, with British support, at Dakar in Senegal in September 1940, was a disaster. He did, however, win over other territories in Africa, most importantly Chad. From here Free French elements began to cooperate with the British Long Range Desert Group, whose patrols covered the southern Libyan Desert. Under Philippe de Hautecloque, who took on the pseudonym of Leclerc to protect his familiy in France, a small force began to advance northward from Chad in March 1941.

Meanwhile Free French pilots fought in the Battle of Britain and a French brigade was sent to the Middle East and fought in Eritrea. It was joined in Egypt by further troops. In the hope that they might persuade their fellow Frenchmen to lay down their arms, the Free French took part in the invasion of Vichy French Syria in 1941. In the end, Vichy and Free French fought one another and de Gaulle was furious that he was not consulted over the armistice. Even so, his men continued to fight loyally for the British and their epic stand at Bir Hacheim during the Gazala battle in June 1942 cemented their reputation.

The Allied landings in French northwest Africa in November 1942 brought the French forces in Algeria, Morocco, and Tunisia onto the Allied side. Leclerc's L Force also linked up with the British Eighth Army at the beginning of 1943 and fought with it during the Tunisian campaign. De Gaulle's relations with the US, however, were not good, especially since Washington had maintained diplomatic relations with Vichy France. Roosevelt chose General Henri Giraud, who had escaped from German captivity, to head the new regime in northwest Africa. De Gaulle could not be sidelined completely and was persuaded to join Giraud in a Committee of National Liberation, where he soon became the dominant figure.

Patrol in the Western Desert
A group of French Foreign Legionnaires prepares to set off on a reconnaissance mission in the desert. They are armed with tommy guns and knives.

An invincible alliance
This poster produced in Algeria in 1943 to celebrate victory over the Axis in North Africa shows the united strength of the American, British, and Free French forces.

LA VICTOIRE DES NATIONS UNIES EST MAINTENANT CERTAINE

In the first half of 1942 U-boats sank unprecedented amounts of shipping in the western North Atlantic. When the Americans started regular convoys off the eastern seaboard, the U-boats switched to the central Atlantic. With improved methods of detection, however, the Allies slowly gained the upper hand.

1942

JANUARY 11
Germans begin Operation Drumbeat, directed at shipping along East Coast of US

JANUARY 12
Battleship *Tirpitz* sails to Norway, threatening Arctic convoys

JANUARY 29
Attempt by British bombers to sink *Tirpitz* at anchor in Trondheim fails

FEBRUARY 1
All U-boats start using new Enigma cipher–"Triton"

FEBRUARY 26
RAF raid inflicts severe damage on *Gneisenau* in Kiel

FEBRUARY 10–12
Scharnhorst, *Gneisenau*, and *Prinz Eugen* sail from Brest to home waters via Strait of Dover

APRIL 1
US introduces partial convoy system along eastern seaboard– the "Bucket Brigade"

APRIL 13
US destroyer *Roper* sinks *U 85* off Virginia coast–first such success by US warship

APRIL 18
Blackout imposed along entire eastern seaboard of US to counter heavy shipping losses

APRIL 21
First "milch cow" U-boat, *U 459*, sets sail, carrying fuel, torpedoes, and other supplies for U-boats in Atlantic

JULY 4–10
Arctic convoy PQ-17 ordered to scatter because of threat of attack by German surface force, including *Tirpitz*. Convoy loses 24 ships to aircraft and U-boats

AUGUST 1
Full convoy system introduced along US eastern seaboard and in Gulf of Mexico and Caribbean

SEPTEMBER 18
Convoy PQ-18, first to sail with escort carrier, reaches Murmansk from Scotland. Despite Allied losses, three U-boats are sunk

OCTOBER 30
British boarding party recovers German codebooks from sinking *U 559* in eastern Mediterranean

NOVEMBER
Transfer of many escorts to Torch landings in northwest Africa leads to heaviest monthly losses to U-boats: 729,160 tons

DECEMBER 13
"Triton" deciphered at British decoding center, Bletchley Park

DECEMBER 30–31
Battle of the Barents Sea. Attack by German naval force on British convoy. German ships withdraw

1943

FEBRUARY 4–7
Convoy SC-118 from Halifax attacked in mid-Atlantic by 20 U-boats. 13 merchantmen sunk

JANUARY 29
Dönitz takes over from Raeder as commander-in-chief of German Kriegsmarine

MARCH 12
Hedgehog depth-charge mortars fitted to escorts for first time

MARCH 14–20
37 U-boats employed in attack on five convoys. 21 merchantmen sunk for the loss of one U-boat

MAY 11–23
Nine U-boats sunk in sustained battle in mid-Atlantic involving five convoys and 42 U-boats

MAY
A record total of 41 U-boats lost in course of the month

MAY 24
Dönitz withdraws virtually all U-boats from North Atlantic

▮ Atlantic convoys   ▮ Arctic convoys   ▮ Other events

THE U-BOAT CAMPAIGN IN THE ATLANTIC

THE SECOND HALF of 1941 saw a major improvement in the British position at sea. Sinkings in the North Atlantic fell from 345 ships, totalling 1,800,190 tons in the first half of the year to 151 ships, totalling 621,510 tons, while losses in British waters, the Mediterranean, the South Atlantic, and Indian Ocean fell from 1,082,830 tons to 364,897 tons. These reductions were largely due to the westward extension of the American neutrality zone and greater use of the convoy system. With fewer merchantmen sailing independently, U-boats were increasingly forced to attack convoys. As a result the average number of merchantmen sunk per U-boat lost fell from 21.9 in the first half of the year to 7.3 in the second half.

NEW TARGETS

The German and Italian declaration of war on the United States in December 1941 signaled the start of a new phase in the Battle of the Atlantic. The whole of the western

Canadian recruiting poster
Canada's navy played an important role in the war against the U-boats. By the end of the war it had grown to become the third largest navy in the world.

North Atlantic now became a theater for U-boat operations. The first Type IX long-range U-boats sailed for the coastal waters of the eastern United States as early as mid-December. They carried only 16 torpedoes each, but were under orders to conserve these for large, worthwhile targets, especially tankers. At the start of hostilities the United States was faced with a serious lack of escorts. Lack of organization meant that East Coast shipping was not protected and no blackout was imposed in coastal areas. As a result, in the first six months of 1942 the German submarines enjoyed their second "Happy Time," comparable to their period of success in the second half of 1940.

In the first half of 1942 Allied monthly shipping losses exceeded 650,000 tons on five occasions. U-boats extended their operations into the Caribbean and Gulf of Mexico and in June sank a total of 121 merchantmen in the western North Atlantic. In fact this month, June 1942, saw German operations account for 173 merchantmen of 834,196 tons with U-boats sinking 144 merchantmen of 700,235 tons. The American introduction of

FAITES VITE... FAITES BIEN

LEUR *Victoire* SERA LA VOTRE

U-boat victim
Burning oil engulfs the sinking American tanker *Dixie Arrow*. After being torpedoed by *U 71* off the coast of North Carolina on March 26, 1942, the ship's hull broke in two.

THE U-BOAT WAR

THE CRITICAL PERIOD in the U-boat war in the Atlantic was 1942–43. Sinkings by U-boats reached their monthly peak in November 1942, but thereafter Allied merchant shipping losses, despite the occasional blip, went steadily down. This was in spite of the fact that by 1943 the Germans had four times as many U-boats as at the outbreak of war. It was also the year in which the Allies finally marshaled the aircraft, the escorts, the organization, and the new technology to wage an effective antisubmarine war.

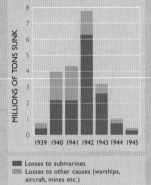

BRITISH, ALLIED, AND NEUTRAL MERCHANT SHIPPING LOSSES

MILLIONS OF TONS SUNK

1939 1940 1941 1942 1943 1944 1945

■ Losses to submarines
■ Losses to other causes (warships, aircraft, mines etc.)

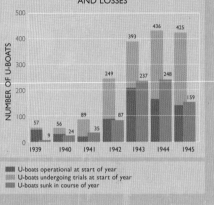

GERMAN U-BOAT BUILDING AND LOSSES

NUMBER OF U-BOATS

1939 1940 1941 1942 1943 1944 1945

■ U-boats operational at start of year
■ U-boats undergoing trials at start of year
■ U-boats sunk in course of year

convoys along the eastern seaboard spelled the end of this period of German success. There was no point in U-boats crossing the North Atlantic if shipping off the eastern seaboard was under escort. The focus of German effort after July 1942 was therefore in the central North Atlantic—in the so-called "air gap." This was the area where Allied shipping was beyond the range of Allied aircraft based in Newfoundland, Iceland, and Britain.

U-BOAT NUMBERS

The rising number of U-boats in service—from a total of 91 in January 1942 to 212 in January 1943—meant that they could be deployed in long patrol lines across the North Atlantic convoy routes. As a result, Allied shipping losses between July and November 1942 were not far short of those recorded in the first half of 1942. At the same time, however, U-boat losses rose steeply—from 22 in the first half of the year to 66 in the second.

Various factors combined to blunt the U-boat offensive. The most important was the increasing number and quality of the warships and aircraft committed to the defense of shipping. This had

been a continuing process since 1940, but in the first two years of the war escort formations had amounted to little more than collections of individual ships. Now formations were being raised on a permanent basis and trained together. Fast new frigates specifically designed for submarine hunting were entering service, and escorts were being equipped with TBS (Talk Between Ships) radio, improved sonar, and hedgehog mortars for throwing salvoes of new more powerful depth charges.

Despite these innovations, Allied shipping continued to suffer losses. These reached their peak when convoys were stripped of their

US Coast Guard cutter *Duane*
On April 17, 1943, along with USCGC *Spencer*, the *Duane* was part of the escort group that located the *U 175*, forcing it to the surface with depth charges, and then firing on it until the crew abandoned the U-boat.

escorts to provide protection for Operation Torch—the US and British landings in French North Africa in November 1942. This month saw the highest number of sinkings by U-boats in the entire war with 729,160 tons of merchantmen sunk.

March 1943 was another bad month for Allied shipping with losses to submarines reaching 627,377 tons. In early March the German change of ciphers meant that the Admiralty temporarily lost its ability to read German naval signals and divert shipping accordingly. Even so, the month's figures were an anomaly and reversed the now established trend.

By this point in the war virtually all the factors that were to contribute to the defeat of the German war against shipping were in place.

Sunderlands on patrol
The British Short Sunderland flying boat was
a very successful reconnaissance aircraft and
submarine destroyer. The Mark III, introduced
in 1942, had a range of about 2,700 miles
(4,340 km). It could carry bombs, torpedoes,
depth charges, and rockets.

RECALL OF THE U-BOATS

In May 1943 Germany's U-boats suffered their worst
monthly losses of the war with 41 sunk or destroyed.
On May 24 the Kriegsmarine recalled its U-boats
from the North Atlantic in what was tantamount to
acknowledgment of defeat. But the German
intention was to refit their boats and return to the
offensive. However, when battle was resumed in
July the losses incurred by the U-boats were still
disastrously heavy. July 1943 saw the destruction
of 37 U-boats and the following month another 25.

The period May–November 1943 effectively
decided the outcome of the campaign against
shipping. The Allied victory was the result of a
number of contributory factors: superior numbers
of escorts and aircraft, improved organization, better
weapons and radar, and more effective intelligence.
In January 1943 the British Navy had realized that
its signals were being read by the Germans. The
situation took months to rectify, but over the course
of the year the Allies acquired a distinct intelligence
advantage over the Germans.

The two most important factors were the
improvement in the quality of escorts and the massive
impact of increased air power, with many more long-
range aircraft available for antisubmarine duties.
Between the start of the war and the end of 1942,
aircraft accounted for just 46 U-boats. In May 1943

U-boat on North Alantic patrol
This propaganda photograph from 1943 shows German
sailors braving bad weather to wage war on enemy shipping.
Despite the diminishing returns of U-boat warfare, captains
and crews remained heroes in the eyes of the public.

they sank 20 and had a hand in the destruction
of five more. This increase in losses was in part the
result of the Kriegsmarine's failure to realize that
the British had developed a form of airborne radar
that U-boat search equipment could not detect.

THE OPPOSING FORCES

The Canadian Navy had grown rapidly and gained
enormous experience over the first three years of the
war. By 1943 escort duties were shared more
or less equally by the British and
Canadians, while US warships in
ordinary convoys to Britain had
all but disappeared. In contrast
to the experience gained by
Allied crews, German U-boat
officers and men were not of the
same overall quality as those of
1940–41. The growing numbers of
U-boats, combined with increased losses,
meant that boats were going to sea with
officers with no more than two operational
missions to their credit.

In addition to accelerating their U-boat
construction program, the Germans had also
developed new weaponry and tactics. They had
high hopes of a new type of acoustic torpedo,

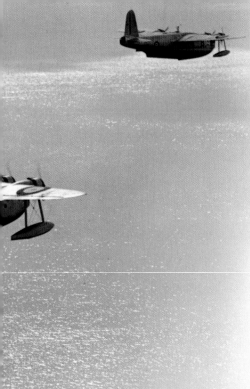

The Allied victory in the Battle of the Atlantic was achieved by limiting shipping losses and maintaining an adequate level of imports into Britain, even though U-boat numbers continued to increase almost to the end of the war. Another factor in this victory was the simple fact that by the third quarter of 1943 American shipyards had replaced all losses incurred to date in the war. The peak of American construction was reached in March 1943 when 130 merchantmen were launched. By the end of the war US yards had built more than 34 million tons of new ships— a total that no campaign against merchant shipping was ever going to overcome.

The Battle of the Atlantic was clearly the most important part of the Allied naval effort. It ensured Britain's survival and role as the base for the liberation of northwest Europe. But the war at sea was not just an economic contest over the defense of trade. Navies were also used to carry the war to enemy territory, and to prevent raids and landings. Over a 16-month period the Allies conducted seven major landings in Europe, starting with the landings on Sicily in July 1943. In every case the German Navy proved ineffective, neither preventing invasion nor inflicting serious losses on enemy naval and amphibious forces.

ARCTIC CONVOYS
The German Navy's most powerful surviving warships, the battleships *Scharnhorst* and *Tirpitz*, were held in Norwegian waters to tie down British naval forces and menace Allied convoys sailing to Soviet ports. In July 1942 the mere threat of an attack by

Aboard an escort on an Arctic convoy
Despite the danger and hardship endured by the crews that sailed to Murmansk and Archangel, this convoy route was not crucial to the Soviet war effort.

the *Tirpitz* led to the near annihilation of a convoy. Acting on intelligence that the *Tirpitz* was about to sail, the Admiralty ordered the commander of convoy PQ-17 to withdraw his escorts and disperse the merchantmen. German aircraft and U-boats then attacked the scattered merchantmen, sinking 24 out of a total of 36. Arctic convoys were always vulnerable, but of the 17,499,861 tons of materiel sent to the Soviet Union during the war, only 3,964,000 tons was sent by this route. The German battleships did not survive to inflict much damage themselves. The *Scharnhorst* was sunk off North Cape on December 26, 1943, during a failed attack on a convoy. The *Tirpitz*, after surviving numerous attacks, was sunk by British bombers off Tromso on November 12, 1944.

which came into service in the fall of 1943, but its success was short-lived. The Allies adopted a simple countermeasure in the form of a noise-making device towed by the escorts to divert the torpedo from its real target. February 1944 saw the appearance of U-boats equipped with the *Schnorchel*, an air tube that would enable the submarine to run at periscope depth using its diesel motors, thus reducing the chances of its being discovered by radar. However, conditions inside the U-boat when the *Schnorchel* was in use were appalling—the limited supply of air was consumed almost entirely by the engines.

German U-boat crew awaiting rescue
Survivors of *U 877* cling to rubber life rafts in freezing Atlantic waters. Their U-boat was sunk northwest of the Azores in December 1944 by the Canadian escort *St. Thomas*.

"There is ground for confident estimate that the enemy's peak effort is passed. Morale and efficiency are delicate and may wither rapidly if no longer nourished by rich success."

FROM A BRITISH ADMIRALTY REPORT ON THE U-BOAT WAR, MAY 1943

ASIA AND THE PACIFIC

JULY 1942–MAY 1943

The second half of 1942 saw the Allies assume a defensive commitment in eastern New Guinea and a limited offensive in the lower Solomons. The Japanese were defeated in both theaters by the turn of the year and the initiative passed clearly to the Americans and their allies.

1942

JULY 7
Australian and Papuan forces start to move from Port Moresby along Kokoda Trail

JULY 22
Japanese landings at Buna and Gona on north coast of New Guinea

JULY 27
First clash between Australians and Japanese on Kokoda Trail

AUGUST 7
US landings on Guadalcanal and Tulagi;. Attackers capture airstrip being constructed by Japanese

AUGUST 8–9
Japanese naval victory off Savo Island but US position on Guadalcanal unaffected

AUGUST 20
Americans fly 21 aircraft to the base on Guadalcanal, now known as Henderson Field

AUGUST 22–25
Drawn naval battle of the Eastern Solomons

AUGUST 25
Japanese landing at Milne Bay; defeated and evacuated September 6

SEPTEMBER 12–14
Battle of Bloody Ridge on Guadalcanal. US Marines repel furious Japanese attack

SEPTEMBER 15
US carrier *Wasp* sunk off Guadalcanal by Japanese submarine

SEPTEMBER 26
Japanese start to withdraw along Kokoda Trail

OCTOBER 21–22, 24–25
Defeat of Japanese assaults on Henderson Field

OCTOBER 26–27
Drawn naval battle off Santa Cruz.; US carrier *Hornet* sunk

NOVEMBER 12–13
First naval battle of Guadalcanal. Japanese battleship *Hiei* sunk and intention to bombard Henderson Field frustrated

NOVEMBER 14–15
Second naval battle of Guadalcanal. Japanese lose battleship *Kirishima*, plus 10 transports and two warships in other operations

DECEMBER 17
Beginning of Allied Arakan offensive in Burma

DECEMBER 31
Formal Japanese decision to evacuate troops on Guadalcanal

1943

JANUARY 22
Last fighting at Buna

FEBRUARY 1–7
Japanese evacuate forces from Guadalcanal

FEBRUARY 9
Guadalcanal in American hands; US landings in Russell Islands on Feb 21

FEBRUARY 18–MARCH 18
First Chindit operation succeeds in interrupting Mandalay-Myitkyina railroad before being forced to withdraw into India

MARCH 2–4
Battle of the Bismarck Sea. Japanese convoy bound for New Guinea loses 12 ships sunk by B-25s

MARCH 24
Japanese counterattack in Arakan

MARCH 26
Japan and US fight drawn naval engagement in the Bering Sea, the Battle of the Komandorski Islands

APRIL 7–18
Japanese air offensive over Solomons and eastern New Guinea decisively defeated

MAY 11
US landings on Attu Island in the Aleutians

MAY 14
British Arakan expedition forced to withdraw

MAY 30
Attu secured by Americans

New Guinea Jul 1942–May 1943	Solomons Aug 1942–May 1943	Burma Dec 1942–May 1943	Aleutians Mar–May 1943

THE PACIFIC WAR IN THE BALANCE

AFTER CORAL SEA and Midway, summer 1942 brought a pause in the Pacific as both sides readied themselves for the next phase of operations. The Japanese reorganized their carrier formations, prepared bases in the lower Solomons, and secured positions in eastern New Guinea. For the United States, the priority given to the European war and the requirements of a North African landing meant that it was possible to undertake only a limited offensive in the lower Solomons. The campaign against the island of Guadalcanal would be the first step in a general offensive in the Southwest Pacific.

STRUGGLE FOR GUADALCANAL

On Guadalcanal the initial American landing was directed against a Japanese airstrip then nearing completion. The US landings on the island and nearby Tulagi were conducted on August 7 with overwhelming force. They were promptly countered by a foray by a Japanese cruiser formation, which at Savo Island (August 8–9) inflicted a comprehensive defeat on Allied naval forces off Guadalcanal. On land, however, the Japanese were not in a position to move immediately and with adequate numbers of troops against the Marines, whose numbers and quality they drastically underestimated. The result was that, while the Americans took the defensive around the captured airfield, which they renamed Henderson Field, the battle for the lower Solomons took place on, off, and above Guadalcanal. During the struggle the Americans developed one highly significant advantage. On August 20 the first US aircraft were ferried into the completed Henderson Field. From that point on American air power was able to control the waters immediately around Guadalcanal throughout the hours of daylight.

Marines with Japanese prisoners
Large numbers of prisoners of war were
not as common in the Pacific as they
were in Europe. The Japanese military
ethos of never surrendering left few
survivors to be taken into captivity.

Over the next four months this would
be a crucial advantage that the Japanese
were simply not able to overcome. In the
wake of their victory off Savo Island, however, the
Japanese did make two further efforts on Guadalcanal:
to put ashore a military force that could overrun
Henderson Field, and to conduct naval operations to
facilitate and support that offensive. But Savo Island
proved to be the first and last clear Japanese victory
of the campaign. Two further carrier actions were
fought—the battles of the Eastern Solomons
(August 22–25) and Santa Cruz (October 26–27)—
and a Japanese submarine sank the aircraft carrier
Wasp off Guadalcanal on September 15. Although
the balance of losses in these exchanges slightly
favored the Japanese, they derived no real advantage.
On the island itself, the Americans fought off the
first major Japanese assault on the defensive perimeter
around Henderson Field, the action for Bloody Ridge
in mid-September. They also launched a number of
spoiling attacks that disrupted Japanese preparations
for a second major effort.

THE CRISIS OF THE CAMPAIGN

As the Japanese commitment in the Solomons
deepened, so their plans began to unravel. On
October 11–12 the Japanese fought and lost the naval
battle of Cape Esperance. On the next night their
battleships bombarded Henderson Field, but a
further night's bombardment by heavy cruisers was
followed by transport losses that the Japanese could
not afford. The army's assaults on Henderson Field
were defeated on October 21–22 and October 24–25,

Rearming on board an aircraft carrier
Deck crew on a US carrier rearm a Douglas SBD
Dauntless dive-bomber. Air superiority was key to
victory in the land and naval battles of Guadalcanal.

and the deployment of a carrier force brought such
aircraft losses in the Battle of Santa Cruz that the
Japanese could not take advantage of their sinking
of the US carrier *Hornet*. The
Japanese made plans for
another assault on
Henderson Field and
a renewal of naval

bombardments of the airfield, but in the middle
of November they suffered two crushing defeats. On
the night of November 12/13, in an action fought
at such close range that the guns of the battleships
could not depress far enough to fire at enemy vessels,
and torpedoes did not have enough range to arm

Marines at Hell's Corner
Marines shelter on Guadalcanal as a US
plane flies above. The area was named Hell's
Corner after concentrated Japanese assaults.

Henderson Field rebuilt
Solomon Islanders work with US engineers to finish
the landing strip at Henderson Field. Interlocking
ready-made metal plates were spread out over cleared
ground to give a firm surface for takeoff and landing.

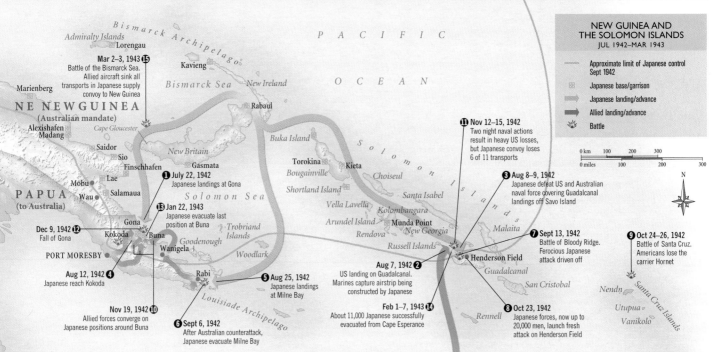

NEW GUINEA AND THE SOLOMON ISLANDS
JUL 1942–MAR 1943

Approximate limit of Japanese control Sept 1942

Japanese base/garrison

Japanese landing/advance

Allied landing/advance

Battle

0 km   100   200   300
0 miles   100   200   300

N

Mar 2–3, 1943 ⑮
Battle of the Bismarck Sea. Allied aircraft sink all transports in Japanese supply convoy to New Guinea

① July 22, 1942
Japanese landings at Gona

⑬ Jan 22, 1943
Japanese evacuate last position at Buna

Dec 9, 1942 ⑫
Fall of Gona

Aug 12, 1942 ④
Japanese reach Kokoda

Nov 19, 1942 ⑩
Allied forces converge on Japanese positions around Buna

⑤ Aug 25, 1942
Japanese landings at Milne Bay

⑥ Sept 6, 1942
After Australian counterattack, Japanese evacuate Milne Bay

⑪ Nov 12–15, 1942
Two night naval actions result in heavy US losses, but Japanese convoy loses 6 of 11 transports

③ Aug 8–9, 1942
Japanese defeat US and Australian naval force covering Guadalcanal landings off Savo Island

⑦ Sept 13, 1942
Battle of Bloody Ridge. Ferocious Japanese attack driven off

⑨ Oct 24–26, 1942
Battle of Santa Cruz. Americans lose the carrier Hornet

Aug 7, 1942 ②
US landing on Guadalcanal. Marines capture airstrip being constructed by Japanese

⑧ Oct 23, 1942
Japanese forces, now up to 20,000 men, launch fresh attack on Henderson Field

Feb 1–7, 1943 ⑭
About 11,000 Japanese successfully evacuated from Cape Esperance

AUSTRALIANS IN NEW GUINEA

FOR THE AUSTRALIAN TROOPS, life on the Kokoda Trail in New Guinea was harsh. They faced an experienced and elite jungle-fighting force, the Japanese South Seas Detachment, which was attempting to take Port Moresby. The young Australian conscripts also faced disease, infection, and starvation with no specialized jungle training and no proper support. The stifling humidity rotted their clothing and made the physical effort needed to move in the Owen Stanley mountains extremely hard. Poor visibility in the dense vegetation often meant that the first sign of the enemy would be an eruption of gunfire. Despite the difficulties, the Australians fought surprisingly well against a force that, at times, outnumbered them by 15 to one.

Short Mark I 25-pounder
The British 25-pounder field gun was shortened and made lighter for use in New Guinea. Nicknamed the "Baby," it could be broken down into 14 mule-loads.

Conical flash shroud

Dial for indirect fire

33-round magazine

Detachable barrel

Owen submachine-gun
The rugged and reliable Australian-made Owen was a favorite weapon among troops facing the exacting conditions of the jungles of the Pacific.

Jungle warfare
Australian soldiers force their way along a difficult jungle track during operations on New Guinea.

Pneumatic tires

The Southwest Pacific
On land, the Allies defeated the Japanese both in eastern New Guinea and on Guadalcanal. In the face of US air superiority, the Japanese abandoned Guadalcanal in order to concentrate their strength in the upper Solomons.

themselves, the Japanese lost the battleship *Hiei* and two destroyers. The Americans lost two light cruisers and four destroyers, with two heavy cruisers and another two destroyers badly damaged. On the night of November 14/15 the Japanese lost the battleship *Kirishima* and a destroyer.

These defeats were accompanied by a failed Japanese attempt to put more formations ashore, in which all but one of 11 transports were lost or ran aground. The Japanese high command now faced crisis on two counts. The fleet losses could not be afforded, but with the services called upon to return shipping to the trade vital to support Japan's Home Islands, neither could the transport losses. About 750,000 tons of shipping had been committed to the operations in the Southwest Pacific. After their losses, the services required another 620,000 tons of shipping in order to continue the campaign. The result was that in December the Japanese high command decided to abandon Guadalcanal in favor of a defensive strategy based on the central and upper Solomons. By February 8, 1943 the orderly withdrawal of 11,706 men from the Cape Esperance area was completed. The Guadalcanal campaign was over. The Japanese now had to face an enemy with a choice of when and where to undertake its next offensive.

NEW GUINEA

The campaign on Guadalcanal was initially separate from, but later influential on, a simultaneous campaign being fought in eastern New Guinea. It had been the Japanese intention after Midway to move by sea and in strength against Port Moresby, the Allied base on the southern coast of eastern New Guinea. With the defeat off Midway, however, the plans were changed. On July 22, 1942 Japanese troops came ashore and secured Buna and Gona on the northern coast, intending to advance on Port Moresby along the Kokoda Trail. Japanese planners believed that this trail was a metaled road. In reality it was a 100-mile (160-km) jungle track across the forbidding Owen Stanley mountain range. For most of its length, it was too narrow for troops to walk two abreast.

The initial Japanese advance swept aside feeble opposition on the part of inexperienced Australian troops, but as Australian units that had recently been withdrawn from the Middle East were fed into the battle, the Japanese encountered mounting

Indigenous allies

A Papuan soldier takes aim with his Bren machine-gun. The local Papuan infantry co-operated with the Australians and Americans against the Japanese in eastern New Guinea, and their knowledge of the island terrain proved a great bonus to the Allies.

resistance. Australian troops lost, retook, and for a second time lost Kokoda. Then Japanese forces, with no supplies and relying on captured enemy stores to sustain themselves, bypassed Australian positions and carried the battle as far as Ioribaiwa, some 30 miles (48 km) from Port Moresby, on September 16. By this time, however, the campaign on Guadalcanal had begun to go badly for the Japanese. Forced to decide between the two efforts, and having seen a secondary landing on New Guinea checked at Milne Bay (August 25–September 7), the Japanese chose to focus their attention on the campaign in Guadalcanal and the lower Solomons.

On September 26, in an attempt to consolidate their position in eastern New Guinea, Japanese troops began a slow withdrawal along the Kokoda Trail.

The Japanese withdrawal from Ioribaiwa was followed by an Australian advance along the Kokoda Trail. Meanwhile American forces were able to

Storming New Guinea

American troops wade ashore on the New Guinea coast. The shallow beaches meant that disembarking troops often had to wade through the surf for some distance.

"I have an idea that the name of the Kokoda Trail is going to live on in the minds of Australians, just as Gallipoli lives on. Every hour is a nightmare."

GEORGE H. JOHNSTON, WAR CORRESPONDENT
SEPTEMBER 1942

undertake an exhausting advance around the Japanese open left flank. Meanwhile, transport aircraft moved forces to occupy Wanigela on the northeast coast and Allied troops were also transported around the coast by sea. This gave the Americans and Australians an overwhelming advantage of numbers and position that enabled them to take the initiative. Japanese forces, who had been wracked by malaria, beri-beri, and dysentery caused by food stores purposely contaminated by the retreating Australian troops, resorted to cannibalism to stay alive. By the end of November they had been penned back into the Gona–Sanananda–Buna beachhead area.

The final Allied offensive against the beachhead stalled several times amid bitter recriminations, and the first Australian move against Gona was beaten back. The Japanese put ashore an extra 1,300 troops during December 1942, and the tough fighting went on in swamps that reached up to armpit level and against fieldworks that could not be seen from more than a few yards away. Still, the Australians took Gona on December 9, American troops, supported by armor, took Buna village five days later, the government building on January 2, 1943, and then Sanananda on the 14th, the day after the Japanese high command made the decision to abandon the struggle. The Allied capture of Giruwa, between Buna and Gona, on January 21 was the last action in a campaign that had cost the Australians 5,698 and the Americans some 2,400 killed and wounded; an additional 38,000 troops were evacuated at various times because of illness. The Japanese ultimately committed about 17,000 troops in eastern New Guinea, and it seems that the survivors of the campaign numbered fewer than 3,000.

JAPANESE WITHDRAWALS

The Japanese evacuation of their surviving troops from Guadalcanal in early February 1943 was soon followed by American landings in the neighboring Russell Islands in the third week of the month. In the first week of March American aicraft secured an overwhelming victory, sinking eight transport vessels and four destroyers in the Battle of the Bismarck Sea (March 2–4). Japanese losses in the course of the week were so heavy that their position south of Finschhafen was severely compromised.

It was not until September 1943, however, that Allied forces moved to secure targets in central New Guinea, including Lae, Salamaua, and Finschhafen. At the end of October, after a series of Japanese attempts to recapture Finschhafen were beaten back, local Japanese forces admitted defeat and began to evacuate the area.

By that time, too, Allied forces were moving into the upper Solomons, but for the most part the

Casualties of Buna
Dead US soldiers lie near a beached landing craft at Buna following the American assault on the Japanese stronghold. Compared with the losses suffered by the beleaguered Japanese defenders, American and Australian casualties in the operation were relatively low.

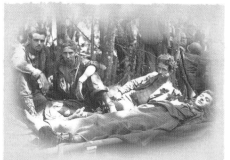

> As the Japs advanced we could hear the bushes rustle. Suddenly all hell broke loose. Grenades exploded everywhere on the ridge nose, followed by shrieks and yells. Then I gave the word to fire. Machine-guns and rifles let go and the whole line seemed to light up. I knocked off two Japs with a rifle. After a few minutes, I couldn't swear how long it was, the blitz became a hand-to-hand battle. All my men were casualties and I was on my own. It was lonely up there.

US SERGEANT MITCHELL PAIGE DESCRIBING THE DEFENSE OF HENDERSON FIELD, GUADALCANAL, OCTOBER 24, 1942

period between February and November 1943 saw very few islands change hands anywhere in the Pacific and very few naval actions. February saw a local Japanese defeat in front of Wau in eastern New Guinea, and April saw a much vaunted—but wholly ineffective—Japanese air offensive in the Southwest Pacific. One damning comment on its failure was the ease with which American fighters shot down a Japanese aircraft carrying the commander of the Combined Fleet, Admiral Yamamoto Isoroku, over Bougainville. June brought a major air battle over the Russells and the annihilation of a Japanese air offensive over Guadalcanal. The same month saw US landings on southern New Georgia and Rendova in the central Solomons, and on Woodlark and the Trobriand Islands off eastern New Guinea. On New Guinea itself, an American force landed in Nassau Bay just to the southeast of Salamaua.

THE ALEUTIANS

In March an indecisive action known as the Battle of the Komandorski Islands was fought in the Northwestern Pacific. On the Aleutian Islands off Alaska, which the Japanese had occupied in June 1942, May brought American landings on Attu, where organized resistance collapsed on the 30th; the island was secured by the following day. Little over a week later the Japanese high command decided to cut its losses and ordered that nearby

Japanese in the Aleutians
Japanese soldiers on Kiska in the Aleutian Islands scour the skies for US aircraft. The Aleutians were a sideshow to the main Pacific conflict, but they witnessed the only time Japan occupied US territory during the war.

Kiska be abandoned. The Japanese evacuation was complete on July 28. With no inkling that the Japanese had already departed, the Americans subjected the island to a full-scale assault in the middle of August. Thereafter the Aleutians were of importance to the wider conflict only as a base for American air and submarine operations against Japan's Home Islands. The first American air raid on the Kurile Islands was an attack by eight B-25 medium bombers staging through Attu on July 10, 1943.

THE BALANCE TILTS
Most of the operations in this period were on a very small scale. Individually they were of little importance, but together they represented notable, if local, gains. More significantly, they were also actions conducted by American forces that were now clearly possessed of the initiative. The Americans had also acquired, by this stage of the war, a clear superiority of numbers and technique.

The extent of that superiority was to be revealed after July 1943. In that month, in the wake of the American landings in the central Solomons, and the simultaneous American and Japanese landings in Kula Gulf at the northern end of New Georgia, two naval actions were fought that were effectively the last battles in the Pacific to pitch two evenly matched sides against one another. The battles of Kula Gulf (July 5–6) and Kolombangara (July 12–13) saw honors more or less shared. By the end of the month, however, the Americans were in a position

to take the tide of war into the upper Solomons in a strength that left the Japanese defenders without an effective response. In around a year and a half of war the Imperial Japanese Navy had in effect fought both the US Navy and itself to a standstill. By the time it had done so, however, it found itself having to face a second US Navy. The new enemy was not a prewar navy but a modern navy that had been built primarily since the attack on Pearl Harbor in December 1941 and was now being gathered in readiness for the next phase of the war.

Captured Japanese flag
American troops proudly display a captured Japanese flag on Guadalcanal. Such items, as well as enemy swords and weapons, were considered prize souvenirs.

THE AXIS ON THE DEFENSIVE
1943–44

DURING THE COURSE OF 1943, THE TABLES WERE

TURNED ON GERMANY AND JAPAN. BOTH NATIONS

HAD MADE SWEEPING TERRITORIAL GAINS

IN THE OPENING PHASES OF THE WAR, IN THE WEST

AND IN SOUTHEAST ASIA AND THE PACIFIC. THESE,

HOWEVER, WERE NOW STARTING TO BE EATEN AWAY

AS THE MANPOWER RESOURCES OF THE SOVIET

UNION AND THE ALMOST LIMITLESS ECONOMIC AND

INDUSTRIAL POTENTIAL OF THE UNITED STATES

WERE BROUGHT FULLY TO BEAR ON THE AXIS.

American landing on Saipan
US troops crouch on a beach under the shelter
of their landing craft. The capture of Saipan,
Tinian, and Guam in the Marianas in June and
July 1944 gave the Americans airbases within
bomber range of the Japanese Home Islands.

THE BEGINNING OF THE END

FROM THE SUMMER OF 1943 THE THIRD REICH FACED A GRIM HOLDING OPERATION ON THE EASTERN FRONT IN THE FACE OF THE INEXORABLE SOVIET ADVANCE. IN ITALY, HOWEVER, THE BRITISH AND AMERICANS MADE SLOWER PROGRESS. IN THE PACIFIC THE AMERICANS BEGAN A DRIVE TOWARD THE JAPANESE HOME ISLANDS, BYPASSING A NUMBER OF JAPANESE BASES AND GARRISONS IN A STRATEGY KNOWN AS "ISLAND HOPPING".

FOLLOWING THE RECAPTURE of Kharkov by the Germans in mid-March 1943, fighting on the Eastern Front subsided as both sides made preparations for further offensives. Hitler calculated that the Red Army was marking time before launching another offensive in the winter of 1943. The aim of the first German offensive would be to eliminate the huge Soviet salient north of Kharkov around the town of Kursk in the Ukraine. This had been created by the success of Manstein's counterblow after Stalingrad.

Opinions differed within the German high command over how to deal with the Kursk salient. Manstein favored what became known as the "backhand solution", waiting for the Red Army to burst out of the salient and then rolling up its advancing columns as the Soviet lines of supply grew ever longer. Hitler and General Kurt Zeitzler, Chief of the Army General Staff, favored a more aggressive strategy. Having rejected a proposal for a frontal attack on the salient, the German high command settled for a pincer attack, delivered on the northern and southern shoulders of the salient with the aim of pinching out the Kursk bulge and trapping the Soviet armies holding it. The operation was codenamed *Zitadelle* (Citadel).

Operation Citadel was based on the dangerous assumption that the Red Army, well dug-in, would crumble at the first impact of German armor. It was also a measure of changing fortunes on the Eastern Front that, for all the massive preparations that preceded it, Citadel's principal objective was limited to a mere straightening of the front line. However, such was the scale of the coming offensive that it was clear to all involved in its preparation that failure would mean the complete collapse of the German strategy on the Eastern Front. Hitler confessed that every time he thought about the operation, his stomach turned over.

Launched on July 4, 1943, Citadel was abandoned within days, after the Red Army had halted both the German northern and southern drives. The advance from the south ended on July 12 at Prokhorovka, scene of the largest tank battle of the war. On the same date the Red Army launched Operation Kutuzov against the Orel salient, a mirror image of the Kursk salient, lying immediately to its north. A series of Soviet counteroffensives to the south of Kursk drove the Ostheer back to the line of the Dnieper River.

Citadel was the last major German offensive on the Eastern Front. The psychological advantage had begun to pass to the Red Army after its victory at Stalingrad. It is clear that, after Kursk, the Red Army not only seized the initiative, but also established an inexorably growing material advantage over the Ostheer that the German mobile forces were no longer able to counter with tactical initiative.

ALLIED PRIORITIES

In the spring of 1941 Hitler had increased the number of fronts on which the British were obliged to fight. Now the roles were about to be reversed. On January 14, 1943 Churchill, Roosevelt, and their chiefs of staff met at Casablanca in Morocco for a conference, codenamed Symbol, to decide their priorities for the war in the West and in the Pacific.

One of the principal fruits of Symbol was an agreement to relieve the pressure on the Soviet Union by opening a "second front" in Europe in the form of a strategic bombing offensive against Germany to be conducted by RAF Bomber Command and the US Eighth Air Force. The objectives of this offensive were twofold: the progressive destruction of the German military, industrial, and economic infrastructures; and the undermining of the will of the German people to a point where "their capacity for armed resistance is fatally weakened". The operational details of the offensive were embodied in a plan codenamed Pointblank, drawn up

"Soldiers of the Reich! This day you are to take part in an offensive of such importance that the whole future of the world may depend on its outcome."

ADOLF HITLER JULY 4, 1943, AT THE BEGINNING OF THE BATTLE OF KURSK

by General Ira C Eaker, commander of the Eighth Air Force, and issued on June 10, 1943. While Bomber Command concentrated on the area bombing of German cities by night, the USAAF flew daylight missions aimed against precise industrial targets. However, with no long-range escort fighters, the USAAF was to suffer heavy losses.

At Casablanca the Americans and British also decided that, once the US and British forces had driven the Germans and Italians out of North Africa, the first Allied objective in the Mediterranean would be the island of Sicily. The Americans argued that it was more important to concentrate on preparations for the planned invasion of northwest Europe, but were persuaded by Churchill that, in the meantime, Sicily was a valuable prize. The Western Allies were also keenly aware of the titanic battles being fought on the Eastern Front and realized that Stalin would resent any reluctance to commit Allied forces in the one theatre of war in which they could now come to grips with the Axis. A cross-Channel assault on Hitler's "Fortress Europe" would have to wait until 1944.

DEFENDING THE MEDITERRANEAN

Hitler was keenly aware of the threat of Italian defection. He observed wryly, "The Italians never lose a war; no matter what happens, they always end up on the winning side." Hitler therefore despatched German troops to mainland Italy and Sicily. Rommel was brought back from North Africa to command a shadow army group in the Alps, to be activated in the event of an Allied landing. Hitler also deemed it necessary to cover Italy by reinforcing German garrisons in Corsica and Sardinia.

To secure Greece and the Balkans against Allied attack, strong garrisons were also needed in Crete and Rhodes and dozens of smaller islands in the eastern Mediterranean. These would deny the British access to the Dardanelles and thus prevent the establishment of a direct seaborne supply route to the Soviet Union, while also deterring Turkey from casting its lot with the Allies.

The Battle of Kursk
German Tiger I tanks move up to their start line at the the launch of Operation Citadel on July 4, 1943. The German offensive rapidly ground to a halt at the Battle of Kursk, where the German armour was outnumbered and outfought by Soviet T-34 tanks.

Occupying forces
British troops patrol the town of Pachino,
captured swiftly on the first day of the
landings in Sicily, July 10, 1943.

In the Mediterranean, as on the Eastern Front,
Hitler's instinct was to defend everything on the
perimeters of the Nazi empire. Although he liked
to compare himself with Frederick the Great, and
carried a portrait of the Prussian king with him to
each of his headquarters, the Führer had forgotten
one of Frederick's most famous dicta—"He who
defends everything defends nothing".

THE ITALIAN ARMISTICE

On July 10, 1943 the British Eighth Army and the
US Seventh Army landed in Sicily, which was secured
by August 17. The Italians' reaction to the invasion
was to rid themselves of Mussolini. This proved
easier than they had anticipated. The dictator was

deposed on July 24 by the Fascist Grand Council and
imprisoned in a mountain hotel on the Gran Sasso
in the Apennines. His successor, Marshal Badoglio,
opened secret negotiations with the Allies and on
September 3 Italy was granted an armistice, to
become effective within five days.

When the terms of the armistice were published
on September 8, the German troops in Italy, under
Field Marshal Albert Kesselring, disarmed their
former allies. Four days later, Mussolini was rescued
from his mountain-top jail in a daring German
airborne raid and brought back behind German lines
to set up a puppet government, the Salò Republic,
in northern Italy. The main Allied landings on the
Italian mainland were made by the US Fifth Army

on September 9 in the Gulf of Salerno, some
40 miles (64 km) southeast of Naples. After ten days
of resistance, the German defenders withdrew.

Churchill had called Italy the "soft underbelly"
of the Third Reich, but its terrain was well suited
to a determined defense. The Germans settled down
behind the successive rivers that flow eastward and
westward out of the Apennines to the sea. Whenever
their line was breached they would fall back to the
next carefully prepared position. In November
1943 the Allied advance was halted by the Gustav
Line, running across the Italian peninsula, north
of Naples, but still south of Rome.

> "Corpses of Polish and German soldiers, sometimes entangled in a deathly embrace, lay everywhere and the air was full of the stench of rotting bodies."
>
> GENERAL WLADYSLAW ANDERS DESCRIBING MONTE CASSINO AFTER ITS FINAL CAPTURE IN MAY 1944

US STRATEGY IN THE PACIFIC

At Casablanca it was decided to extend operations to include the recapture of the Aleutians in Admiral Nimitz's North Pacific command area. In June 1942 the Japanese had occupied two islands, Attu and Kiska, as a diversionary maneuver in the Midway campaign.

In February 1943 the securing of Guadalcanal, in General MacArthur's Southwest Pacific command area, paved the way for the Allied drive across the Central and South Pacific command areas, the latter commanded by Admiral Halsey. In the Southwest Pacific command area, General MacArthur was to outflank the Japanese base at Rabaul, on the northeast tip of the island of New Britain, and approach the Philippines from the south. In the South Pacific Area, Halsey was to cooperate with MacArthur in isolating Rabaul and also push northwest from Guadalcanal along the Solomons. In the Central Pacific Area, Admiral Nimitz was to ensure adequate supplies to MacArthur and Halsey, while simultaneously mounting a drive through the Gilbert, Marshall, Caroline, and Mariana Islands.

The campaign in the central Solomons opened on June 21, 1943 with the assault on New Georgia and the capture of Munda airfield on August 5. At the beginning of November the US 3rd Marine Division went ashore at Empress Augusta Bay on Bougainville. By the end of the year the Americans had secured a defensive perimeter and established a naval base and

operational airstrips on the island. Much of Bougainville still remained in Japanese hands, but the eastern arm of Halsey's advance was now fully extended toward Rabaul. Landings on New Britain and the capture of the Admiralty and St Matthias Islands northwest of New Britain tightened the ring around Rabaul, which was successfully cut off by the end of March 1944. It would remain isolated and impotent until the end of the war.

In the summer and autumn of 1943, Nimitz concentrated an armada of ships, aircraft, and men for his drive in the Central Pacific. The stiffest resistance was encountered on Tarawa Atoll, in the Gilbert Islands. It was secured on November 23 after three days of heavy fighting in which all but 146 of the Japanese garrison of 4,800 were killed. This phase of operations ended on February 21, 1944, with the capture of Eniwetok in the Marshalls.

On June 15, 1944, 69 B-29 bombers flew from eastern India via China to bomb the Imperial Iron and Steel works at Yawata on the Japanese island of Kyushu. It was the first B-29 Superfortress raid on a target in the Japanese Home Islands. The date also marked the start of operations to take the islands of Saipan, Tinian, and Guam in the Marianas. These would serve as bases for a campaign against Japan itself. The capture of Saipan gave the Americans a new airbase for the B-29 1,500 miles (2,400 km) southeast of Tokyo, just within the bomber's range.

The stubborn defense of the Gustav Line throughout December and January forced the Allies to attempt to outflank it with a landing on January 22, 1944 at Anzio, 30 miles (48 km) south of Rome. Through a combination of indecisive Allied generalship and determined German resistance, the plan failed. Heavy fighting continued until May 1944, when Monte Cassino, the lynchpin of the Gustav Line defenses, was finally taken. The way now lay open to Rome, which was liberated on June 5.

The capture of Rome accelerated work on yet another German defense system, the Gothic Line. The German 10th and 14th Armies retired behind this line and awaited the Allied attempts to breach their defenses, which began on August 30, 1944.

The taking of Tarawa
A US Marine prepares to throw a hand grenade at Japanese soldiers entrenched in the ruins of their airbase during the fierce fighting to capture Tarawa in the Gilberts in November 1943.

GERMAN RETREAT ON THE EASTERN FRONT

JULY 5, 1943–MAY 12, 1944

The launch in July, near Kursk, of a major offensive called Operation Citadel was intended to signal the beginning of a German recovery. Instead, the offensive was quickly halted, and by the fall of 1943 Germany had lost the war on the Eastern Front.

1943

JULY 5
Germans launch Operation Citadel in Orel-Belgorod salient near Kursk to destroy Soviet forces

JULY 10
German attack stalls after advance in south of under 20 miles (30 km) and in north of 8 miles (13 km)

JULY 12
Soviet counterattack is launched, leading to "greatest tank battle in history" near Prokhorovka

JULY 13
Hitler calls off Citadel following failure of Germans to break through Soviet defenses at Kursk

AUGUST 3
Soviet attack breaks through toward Kharkov

AUGUST 5
Soviet forces take Belgorod

AUGUST 22
Kharkov is liberated

SEPTEMBER 14
Soviet forces begin drive on Kiev

SEPTEMBER 22
Soviet forces reach Dnieper River south of Dnepropetrovsk

SEPTEMBER 27
Germans begin withdrawal in Ukraine to west bank of the Dnieper

SEPTEMBER 30
Soviet forces cross Dnieper River along 300-mile (500 km) front; 23 bridgeheads are now established

NOVEMBER 8
Germans launch counterattack south of Fastov, forcing Soviet troops onto the defensive from Zhitomir to Dnieper River

NOVEMBER 6
Kiev is liberated

DECEMBER 24
Soviet operations to recover Ukraine west of the Dnieper begin

1944

JANUARY 8
Soviet forces take Kirovograd

JANUARY 14
Soviet Leningrad offensive opens

JANUARY 19
Soviet forces take Novgorod

JANUARY 27
Leningrad relieved at end of almost 890-day siege

FEBRUARY 2
Soviet forces capture Rovno

FEBURARY 12
Soviet forces capture Luga

MARCH 1
Soviet forces reach border of Estonia, marking the end of German threat to Leningrad

MARCH 15
Soviet forces reach Bug River, the starting point for German Operation Barbarossa in June 1941

APRIL 8
Soviet forces launch successful attack on the Crimea from the north and east

APRIL 10
Soviet forces enter Romania

APRIL 17
Soviet forces occupy Tarnopol

MAY 5
Soviet forces launch attack on port of Sevastopol

MAY 9
Sevastopol falls into Soviet hands

MAY 12
25,000 Germans surrender at Cape Khersonessky, near Kherson

■■ Campaigns in Orel-Belgorod salient
Jul 5–Aug 5, 1943

■■ Relief of Leningrad
Jan 14–Mar 1, 1944

■■ Advance through the Ukraine
Aug 3, 1943–Apr 17, 1944

■■ The Crimea
Apr 8, 1943–May 12, 1944

RECAPTURE OF THE WESTERN SOVIET UNION

SINCE MARCH 1943 HITLER and his high command had been planning a major offensive—to be launched after the spring thaw—with the goal of excising the heavily defended salient around Kursk. A concentric attack of the type that had been so effective in the summer of 1941 would trap the Red Army forces inside a large pocket, where they could be destroyed piecemeal and provide a rich haul of prisoners. Moreover, taking Kursk would enable the Ostheer to establish a shorter front line. The operation, code-named *Zitadelle* (Citadel), was to involve two army groups, Center and South. Some 900,000 men, 2,380 tanks and assault guns, 10,000 artillery pieces, and 2,500 aircraft, many of them ruthlessly stripped from other sectors of the Eastern Front, would be sent into action.

Well informed of German intentions by the "Lucy" spy network in Switzerland and a mole inside British intelligence, the Stavka had plenty of time to strengthen the Kursk salient, which was held by the Central Front in the north and the Voronezh Front in the south. By the end of June 1943 it had packed the bulge with 1.3 million men— including 75 infantry divisions, some 40 percent of the Red Army's rifle formations—and had positioned as many as 100 guns nearly a mile along the likely German axes of advance. It had also concentrated some 3,500 tanks and self-propelled guns, of which 2,000 were deployed in the Kursk salient and the bulk of the remainder held in reserve in the Steppe Front's Fifth Guards Tank Army. In the north and south of the salient, a deeply echeloned eight-line defensive network, comprising dense minefields and trench systems linking antitank strongpoints, had been constructed. Some 330,000 civilians had been employed as auxiliaries in the preparation of these killing grounds and in the repair and maintenance of rail links from the Soviet interior.

Semiautomatic vertical sliding wedge breech mechanism

Muzzle break

Shield to protect crew

German 50-mm Pak 38
The standard German antitank gun until late 1942, the Pak 38 could penetrate 3.5 in (90 mm) of armor at a range of 1,000 yd (915 m).

Red Army tank on the move
A T-34, the mainstay of the Red Army, rolls forward with infantry aboard. On July 12, 1943 some 800 T-34s were to confront more than 600 German tanks at Prokhorovka, in the Kursk salient, in the largest tank battle of the war.

The Soviet army commanders went to considerable lengths to conceal from the Germans the depth and scale of the defense they were preparing. Measures included the creation of false troop concentrations and the construction of dummy tanks and air armies. At least 40 false airfields were built, complete with dummy aircraft, runways, and control towers. They were repeatedly bombed by the Luftwaffe in the run-up to the battle. German military intelligence anticipated that Zhukov, now deputy commander-in-chief and in overall command of the Kursk salient, was preparing to fight a grim defensive battle. They were unaware that he was planning to absorb the Ostheer's blows and then launch his own counteroffensive.

OPERATION CITADEL
The German launched a probing attack in driving rain on July 4. After a bombardment on the southern shoulder of the Kursk salient, the Fourth Panzer Army, under General Hermann Hoth, slithered forward through a quagmire to seize the low hills overlooking the German assembly areas. It took some time for Stalin to be convinced that the long-awaited offensive had begun, but eventually,

Despairing German soldier
An artilleryman contemplates captivity after the Soviet counteroffensive that followed the Battle of Kursk. The battle ended any prospect of German victory in the east.

at 10:30 pm, the Soviet artillery opened up with a colossal counterbombardment of the entire area. The following day there was more torrential rain, and massive air battles took place overhead as the Fourth Panzer Army launched its attack on the line held by the Soviet Sixth Guards Army. By nightfall on July 5 the Fourth Panzer Army had made only three small penetrations of the Red Army's line, none of them more than 7 miles (11 km) deep.

The battle on the southern shoulder of the salient was now drawing in significant elements of Zhukov's strategic reserve. On July 7 Hoth's two panzer corps, together with a third on their right flank, began to advance more quickly. For a fleeting moment it seemed as if they might burst through the Red Army's defense zone into open country. However, the armored, artillery, and antitank reinforcements were fed in from flanking sectors on the south face of the salient to meet the threat. By July 9 Hoth was still 55 miles (90 km) from Kursk.

To the north, Army Group Centre under Field Marshal Günther von Kluge had made good progress on July 5 against the Central Front. Its Ninth Army had advanced 6 miles (9 km) on a frontage of 20 miles (30 km). However, on the 7th, Red Army resistance stiffened and in the next two days the Ninth Army sustained some 10,000 casualties as it cleared the villages and wooded country on its front. By July 10 its advance had come to a standstill.

...we found ourselves taking on a seemingly inexhaustible mass of enemy armor—never have I received such an overwhelming impression of Russian strength and numbers as on that day. The clouds of dust made it difficult to get help from the Luftwaffe, and soon many of the T-34s had broken past our screen and were streaming like rats all over the battlefield...

GERMAN SOLDIER DESCRIBING THE BATTLEFIELD AT PROKHOROVKA ON JULY 12

Action in Kursk salient
The German plan at Kursk was to eliminate the massive salient—about half the size of England—with an attack at its northern and southern shoulders. It would then straighten the German line on the Eastern Front.

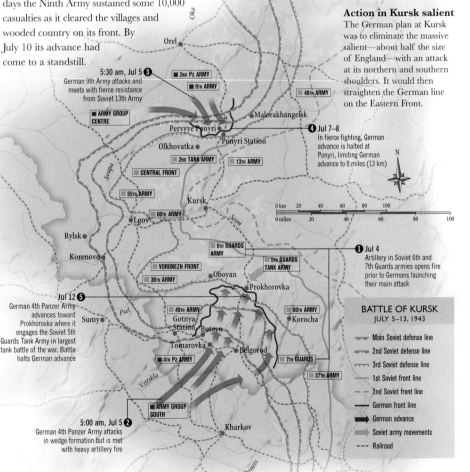

5:30 am, Jul 5 ❸
German 9th Army attacks and meets with fierce resistance from Soviet 13th Army

❹ Jul 7–8
In fierce fighting, German advance is halted at Ponyri, limiting German advance to 8 miles (13 km)

❶ Jul 4
Artillery in Soviet 6th and 7th Guards armies opens fire prior to Germans launching their main attack

Jul 12 ❺
German 4th Panzer Army advances toward Prokhorovka where it engages the Soviet 5th Guards Tank Army in largest tank battle of the war. Battle halts German advance

5:00 am, Jul 5 ❷
German 4th Panzer Army attacks in wedge formation but is met with heavy artillery fire

BATTLE OF KURSK
JULY 5–13, 1943

- Main Soviet defense line
- 2nd Soviet defense line
- 3rd Soviet defense line
- 1st Soviet front line
- 2nd Soviet front line
- German front line
- German advance
- Soviet army movements
- Railroad

Map labels: Oka, Orel, 2ND PZ ARMY, 9TH ARMY, 48TH ARMY, Malorakhangelsk, ARMY GROUP CENTRE, Pervyye Ponyri, Ponyri Station, Olkhovatka, 2ND TANK ARMY, 13TH ARMY, CENTRAL FRONT, 65TH ARMY, 60TH ARMY, Kursk, Lgov, Svapa, Seim, Rylsk, Korenovo, 6TH GUARDS ARMY, VORONEZH FRONT, 38TH ARMY, 5TH GUARDS TANK ARMY, Oboyan, Prokhorovka, 69TH ARMY, Korocha, Sumy, Psel, 40TH ARMY, Gotnya Station, Butovo, Tomarovka, Belgorod, 4TH PZ ARMY, 7TH GUARDS, 57TH ARMY, Vorskla, ARMY GROUP SOUTH, Kharkov, Donets

It was fast becoming apparent to Hitler and his high command that there would be no quick victory. As Anglo-American forces began disembarking in Sicily on July 10, it became clear that Germany would now have to fight in Europe on two fronts.

TANK BATTLE AT PROKHOROVKA

On July 12, at the northernmost point of the Fourth Panzer Army's advance, the German II SS Panzer Corps slammed headlong into the Soviet Fifth Guards Tank Army, which was hastening up from the Steppe Front strategic reserve. In the ensuing armored *mêlée* at Prokhorovka, the largest tank battle of the war in which armoued vehicles clashed at point-blank range, the II SS Panzer Corps was stopped dead in its tracks. It had inflicted heavy losses on the Fifth Guards Tank Army, knocking out or badly damaging at least 400 of a total of 850 vehicles at relatively small cost to itself. However, for

IL2 Sturmovich
This rugged Ilyushin ground-attack aircraft was dubbed the "cement bomber" by the Germans. Some 35,000 were built during the war.

the Fourth Panzer Army's elite units, Prokhorovka must have seemed the last straw. The terrible slog through the Red Army's defenses in which, before the clash at Prokhorovka, it had lost 330 tanks and assault guns, had already sapped morale to the point where the will to press home attacks against continuing strong Soviet resistance was beginning to ebb away.

OPERATION KUTUZOV

The Allied invasion of Sicily had taken the German high command completely by surprise. So, too, did Zhukov's counteroffensive, code-named Kutuzov, which was launched on July 12 against the northern and eastern faces of the Orel salient held by the Second Panzer Army. Kutuzov was conceived as a relieving

Soviet 76-mm antitank gun
Introduced in 1942, this robust antitank weapon had a 14,200-yd (13,000-m) range. Its three-man crew carried personal weapons to engage mechanized infantry.

Double baffle muzzle break

Shield to protect crew

Split carriage trail

attack prior to a major offensive along the entire Eastern Front, but by the evening of July 14 it had achieved an advance of over 10 miles (16 km).

On July 13 Kluge, the commander of Army Group Center, and Manstein, the commander of Army Group South, were summoned to a meeting with Hitler, in which Manstein uncharacteristically urged the Führer to continue the battle of attrition in the Kursk salient. Failure to do so, he argued, would bring powerful Soviet forces crashing down on Army Group South's long salient to the Donets Basin and Black Sea in a rerun of the crisis that had followed Stalingrad. In contrast, Kluge reported that he was making no headway and was being forced to transfer mobile forces northward to check the Red Army's eruption into the Orel salient. Operation Citadel should be abandoned.

Kluge won the day. By July 23 the Fourth Panzer Army was back on the starting line of Operation Citadel and the Red Army counteroffensive was under way.

On July 17 Soviet forces

Retreating from Kharkov
After the failure of Citadel, the Germans fell back from Kharkov, which the Red Army liberated on August 22, 1943.

launched a powerful attack on the German defenses in the south both along the Mius line and across the Donets below Izyum (see map page 192). Meanwhile, north of the Kursk bulge, the Ninth Army was beginning a withdrawal from the Orel salient to escape the expanding Kutuzov drive, which was threatening to surround it. By August 18 it had regained the temporary safety of the Hagen Line, a system of fortifications across the neck of the Orel salient. The commander of the Ninth Army, General Walther Model, was soon to become one of Hitler's most trusted commanders.

FURTHER SOVIET OFFENSIVES

Operation Kutuzov was the first in a series of offensives planned to unroll along the Eastern Front in the wake of Kursk. Initially the success of all other Red Army offensives was subordinated to the objective of taking Belgorod, just below the shoulder of the Kursk salient. Once this had been achieved, on August 5, it was the turn of Kharkov, which was liberated on August 22.

Stalin now began to urge his earlier strategy of striking hammer blows along the entire front, while Hitler, who appeared to be almost completely preoccupied with the situation in the Mediterranean and the Balkans, refused to accept the need for an organized withdrawal. As a result, army group commanders such as Manstein and Kluge were reduced to squabbling with each

other, and with an exhausted and indecisive Hitler, over the allocation of operational reserves. All of this meant little to the officers and men retreating on foot across the baking Ukrainian plains, fighting by day and making forced marches by night, cut off from their headquarters and more fearful of capture by the Red Army than of death itself.

Following the capture of Kharkov, the Red Army advanced into eastern Ukraine with the goal of liberating Kiev and crossing the Dnieper River. Its forces might be under strength after the terrible losses incurred at Kursk, but the Voronezh and

Steppe Fronts now enjoyed an overall superiority over Army Group South of 3:1 in manpower, 4:1 in artillery and tanks, and 3:2 in aircraft. Greatly outnumbered, the German troops defending the Mius Line began to give way. At the end of August, Hitler reluctantly agreed to the strengthening of Army Group South and directed Kluge to assemble a strong force in front of Kiev.

Manstein—previously denied any freedom to maneuver by Hitler—now ordered a retreat to the Dnieper. However, he faced an almost impossible task, for the delays imposed by the Führer meant

Roks-2 flamethrower in action
In the first days of the Battle of Kursk, Soviet forces attacked German tanks at close range, using grenades, gasoline bombs, and flame-throwers, as well as guns.

ERICH VON MANSTEIN

Acknowledged by many as the finest operational commander of World War II, Manstein (1887–1973) fought on the Western Front in World War I. In 1939 he served as Rundstedt's chief of staff in Poland and subsequently developed the Sickle Cut plan, the most significant element of Hitler's 1940 campaign in France. In September 1941 he became commander of the 11th Army and with it conquered the Crimea. Promoted to the rank of field marshal after the fall of Sevastopol, he was given command of Army Group Don in the abortive attempt to relieve the Sixth Army at Stalingrad in late 1942. In the subsequent retreat he prevented the Red Army from crossing the Dnieper and then retook Kharkov in a brilliant counterstroke. In the spring of 1943 Manstein, now in command of Army Group South, was closely involved in the planning of Operation Citadel, about which he entertained the gravest misgivings. After its failure, Manstein again demonstrated generalship of the highest skill in conducting a step-by-step retreat to the Polish frontier. His arguments for taking a long step back were, however, not heeded by Hitler, who replaced him with Model in March 1944. It was the end of Manstein's military career.

SOVIET AND GERMAN ARMOR

By 1943 THE ARMORED BATTLES of the Eastern Front had assumed a new shape. The Red Army now fielded dedicated tank armies, whose mainstay, the T-34, accounted for almost 70 percent of Soviet tank production. In contrast, German tank development focused on the production of a new generation of massively armored vehicles—in particular, so-called "tank destroyers"—which were needed for defensive warfare. Crucially, the tank was no longer the autonomous war-winning weapon it had been in 1940. Rather, it was one, albeit vital, element in the tactics of battlefield attrition. For this new kind of warfare, Soviet armored formations used two standard vehicles—T-34 tanks and US-supplied Dodge trucks.

85-mm primary armament

PzKpfw V Panther main battle tank
The Panther entered production in 1943 as Germany's response to the T-34. It incorporated features of the T-34, including sloped frontal armor and wide tracks.

Crew 5	Max speed 29 mph (47 kph)
Range 110 miles (177 km)	Max armour thickness 4¾ in (120 mm)
Armament 1 × 75-mm gun, 2 × 7.92-mm machine-guns	

T-34/85
The T-34 was the best all-around tank of the war. It fought through the conflict without major modifications, except that in spring 1944 its main armament was upgraded from a 76-mm gun to an 85-mm gun.

Crew 5	Max speed 31mph (50 kph)
Range 186 miles (300 km)	
	Max armor thickness 2⅓ in (60 mm)
	Armament 1 × 85-mm D-5T gun, 2 × 7.62-mm machine-guns

22-in (55-cm) tracks, reducing ground pressure for running cross country

2⅓-in (60-mm) thick sloping front armor

7.62-mm machine-gun

7.92-mm MG34 machine-gun

Long-barrelled 88-mm gun

Jagdpanther heavy tank destroyer
Based on the Panther chassis and armed with an 88-mm gun, which could penetrate the armor of any Allied tank, the Jagdpanther entered service in 1944 but only 382 were produced.

Crew 5	Max speed 45 mph (72 kph)
Frontal armor thickness 3¼ in (80 mm)	
Armament 1 × 88-mm L/71 Pak 43/3 gun, 1 × 7.92-mm machine-gun	

4-in (100-mm) thick Saukopf (pig's head) mantlet

KV-1B heavy tank
The KV-1 entered Red Army service in 1940 and the B version was heavily armored. About 10,500 KVs were built between 1940 and 1943.

Crew 5	Max speed 22 mph (35 kph)
Max armor thickness 3¼ in (82 mm)	
Armament 1 × 76-mm gun, 3 × 7.62-mm machine-guns	

that there was no time to prepare roads, river crossings, demolition charges, or minefields. Manstein's task was to get four armies over five major river crossings and then turn to defend a front of 450 miles (720 km).

The retreating Germans attempted to "sterilize" the rich farmlands and coalfields of the Donets Basin but were thwarted by the haste of the withdrawal. Army Group South had to abandon much of its heavy equipment and nearly 3 million horses and cattle. The Red Army tide rolled on. By the end of September, 23 bridgeheads had been established on the west bank of the Dnieper. For a while Red Army troops struggled to reinforce these bridgeheads, but by October 20 they had successfully built up the position around Lyutezh, and were ferrying tanks over the Dnieper in barges. On November 4 tanks of the Third Guards Army burst out of the bridgehead, headlights blazing and sirens howling. Two days later they were in Kiev.

COUNTING THE COST
By the fall of 1943 Germany had lost the war on the Eastern Front. The premonition of defeat that had stirred at Stalingrad had now become a daily reality for the men of the Ostheer. Hitler had intended Citadel to be a "beacon to the world" and a reaffirmation of German power to his increasingly apprehensive allies. Instead it had led to a series of convulsions which, in two and a half months, had thrown back the Ostheer around 150 miles (240 km) on a front of 650 miles (1,040 km). German manpower losses during the Battle of Kursk and the Red Army counteroffensive had exceeded those at Stalingrad, where some 209,000 "irreplaceable"

German infantryman in Kiev
Lines of exhaustion are etched on the face of a German infantryman during fighting in Kiev in the winter of 1943. The city was liberated by the Red Army on November 6.

Streetfighting in Kiev
Red Army infantrymen, armed with PPSh-41
submachine-guns, engage in house-to-house
fighting in the battle to gain control of the city.

losses (dead, missing, and one-third of the wounded)
had been sustained. Between July and October 1943,
the number of irreplaceable losses in the east, the
greater part inflicted at Kursk and during the retreat
to the Dnieper, had reached 365,000. The Ostheer
could not hope to match the numbers available to
the Red Army. Kursk involved 1.3 million Soviet
troops compared with 900,000 Germans, while
on the Dnieper in October, the Red Army had
2.6 million troops against 1.2 million Germans,
and a 4:1 superiority in tanks and guns.

RELIEF OF LENINGRAD
In January 1943 the Red Army's Volkhov and
Leningrad Fronts had joined hands to carve out a
corridor 7 miles (11 km) wide south of Lake Ladoga

through which trains could pass
to the besieged city of Leningrad.
By the fall a semblance of
normality had returned, though
regular German artillery fire,
and equally regular Soviet
counter-bombardments,
had continued to serve as
permanent reminders that the
battle for the city was not over.
   Relief finally came in
January 1944, when the
Volkhov and Leningrad
Fronts fell on the German
18th Army. The army's commander,
General Lindemann, was forced to give ground, in
spite of the customary orders to the contrary,
leaving the garrison of Novgorod, 90 miles (145 km)
to the south, cut off. Its troops had to abandon the
seriously wounded and fight their way out under

A call to rebuild Leningrad
In 1941 the desperate defense of
Russia's old capital had been vital
to save Moscow, the Soviet Union's
new capital. Pounded by German
artillery throughout an 890-day
siege, its reconstruction from 1944
was to be an immense undertaking.

cover of darkness. By January 27
the railroad between Moscow
and Leningrad had been cleared
and the German Army Group
North had been pushed back to
the eastern shore of Lake
Chuskoye, 160 miles (255 km) to
the southwest. The Germans now
established themselves along a line where Leningrad
lay beyond the range of their artillery. As the 890-
day siege of the city ended, the skies were streaked
with red, white, and blue rockets of celebration.
Leningrad was free, but at a terrible cost.

Red Army storms Sevastopol
The Soviet assault on Sevastopol
opened on May 5, 1944. The
Germans were evacuated on the 9th.

SOVIET ADVANCE IN THE UKRAINE

As the Soviet Leningrad and Volkhov Fronts were
preparing to liberate Leningrad, pressure on the
German Army Group South was mounting. The
Red Army now enjoyed the freedom to attack
where it chose and always in superior numbers. It
also possessed far greater mobility than the Ostheer,
the result of the Lend-Lease conveyor belt that had
provided Stalin with huge quantities of American
four-wheel drive and six-wheel drive trucks that
could operate across country in all but the very
worst weather. In contrast, German motorized
formations were tied to the primitive Soviet road
system. Transportation shortages were now so bad in
German armored formations that they increasingly
relied on Soviet *panjes* (horse-drawn carts).

Systematically, Manstein's front was picked apart,
while in Germany Hitler fought the war from the
map, shuttling formations back and forth and
designating so-called "strongholds"
that must be held at all costs. By
January 28 the First and Second
Ukranian Fronts—the former
General Vatutin's renamed
Voronezh Front—were threatening
to totally encircle two German
corps, about 60,000 men, in the
area of Cherkassy in the center
of Manstein's front. With great
difficulty, and with Hitler interfering
at every turn, about 30,000 men
were extracted from the Cherkassy
pocket, but with none of their

THE EASTERN FRONT
JUL 5, 1943–MAY 9, 1944

― German front line Jul 5, 1943
― German front line Sept 1, 1943
― German front line Nov 30, 1943
⋯ German front line Mar 2, 1944
⋯ German front line Apr 8 and 17, 1944
➡ Soviet advance
➡ German attack
🛡 Major tank battle
● Campaign in Russia and Ukraine
■ Campaign in the Baltic region
● Campaign in the Crimea

① Jan 4, 1944
Soviet forces launch
Leningrad offensive

② Jan 27, 1944
Leningrad is relieved
by Leningrad and
Volkhov Fronts

③ Mar 1, 1944
Soviet forces reach
Estonian border

③ Aug 4, 1943
Soviet forces take Orel

② Jul 12, 1943
Soviet forces defeat
Germans in major tank
battle at Prokhorovka

① Jul 5, 1943
Germans launch
Operation Citadel

④ Aug 22, 1943
Germans evacuate Kharkov

⑥ Nov 6, 1943
Soviet forces
take Kiev

⑧ Jan 28, 1944
Soviet offensive
threaten to encircle
Germans at Cherkassy

Nov 8, 1943 ⑦
Germans counterattack
south of Fastov

Apr 17, 1944 ⑩
Soviet forces
occupy Tarnopol

⑤ Sept 30, 1943
Soviet forces begin to
cross Dnieper River
along 500-mile
(800-km) front

① Apr 8, 1944
Soviet forces launch
offensive on the Crimea

Mar 15, 1944 ⑨
Soviet forces reach
Bug River

② May 9, 1944
Sevastopol's German
garrrison surrenders

Soviet advance
Following the failure of the German
Operation Citadel in July 1943, the
Red Army began a relentless advance
along a front that stretched from the
Baltic region to the Crimea.

heavy equipment. By early March the same fate had befallen the First Panzer Army as it was overhauled by the First Ukrainian Front (now commanded by Zhukov after Vatutin's death at the hands of anti-Soviet partisans) and the Second Ukrainian Front, driving southeast toward the Carpathians.

Manstein was now locked in an argument with Hitler about how best the First Panzer Army might be extracted from imminent encirclement. This time Manstein prevailed and the First Panzer Army was ordered to march northwest 150 miles (240 km)—in effect a moving pocket—living off the land and supplied with ammunition, fuel, and spare parts by air drops flown by night. On April 9 the First

Panzer Army joined hands with the Fourth Panzer Army near Tarnopol, having lost all of its equipment and most of its heavy weapons. By then Manstein had been relieved of his command. His replacement was Model, who had commanded the Ninth Army at Kursk and had become commander of Army Group North in January 1944. He was a favorite of the Führer and was to become his troubleshooter on both the Eastern and Western Fronts.

ACTION IN THE CRIMEA

At this point another lull descended on the Eastern Front, except in the Crimea, where the German 17th Army was now isolated. As the crisis in the

south had deepened, Manstein had shifted north, attempting to close the dangerous gap between Army Groups South and Center. Something had to give, and it was the German 17th Army's front in the Crimea, on the Perekop isthmus, which was breached early in April by the Fourth Ukrainian Front. The Independent Coastal Army then landed on the Kerch peninsula, forcing the Germans to fall back on Sevastopol, which was taken on May 9 after two days of intense fighting.

The victory at Kursk, and its aftermath, had demonstrated the growing confidence of the Red Army. From midsummer 1943 the war in the east would be one of relentless Soviet advance.

SOVIET PARTISANS

IN A RADIO BROADCAST ON JULY 3, 1941, Stalin called for a vast partisan movement to spring up behind the advancing Ostheer. However, it was some time before the partisans became a thorn in the German side. Early resistance by scattered bands of partisans was met with savage German reprisals against the native population: in a single month in Byelorussia, the 707th Division shot nearly 10,500 "partisans" in retaliation for the death of two soldiers. This did more to promote recruitment to the partisan movement than exhortation from Moscow.

A centralized structure was imposed on the partisan movement by Stalin in the spring of 1942, after the Soviet winter offensive, and a semblance of military discipline was imposed by Red Army officers, party officials, and the NKVD. Recalcitrant partisans were summarily shot. Those who toed the line were now well supplied with food, medical supplies, and arms, including tanks and artillery. "Partisan regions" were carved out of areas where there was a limited German presence and where the terrain—dense woods and marshland—lent itself to guerrilla activity. It has been estimated that in the winter of 1942–43 up to 60 percent of Byelorussia was controlled by the partisans. Other partisan regions included the Porkhov region south of Leningrad

Women fighters
Women fought alongside men in Soviet partisan bands. Many became partisans after fleeing from the threat of forced labor.

and the forests around Bryansk, southwest of Moscow. In the Orel region some 18,000 partisans controlled an area containing nearly 500 villages and airstrips used for evacuating the wounded and flying in supplies. The partisans kept this and other occupied areas in touch with Moscow and under a form of communist control.

From the beginning of 1943, partisans waged an effective "rail war" behind German lines. In June 1943 Army Group Center logged 1,092 attacks, with 298 locomotives damaged and 44 bridges blown up. The psychological effect of these attacks on German troops was considerable. Countermeasures included the felling of trees and clearing of undergrowth for distances up to 250 yds (230 m) on either side of the track. Patrols and blockhouses kept the line clear by day, but at night the partisans laid more mines and destroyed ever longer sections of track. The partisan movement was wound up in 1944 as the Red Army liberated the last occupied regions of the European Soviet Union. Many of the partisans were then absorbed into the Red Army.

Poster urging partisan activity
Soviet civilians living in territory that had been occupied by German troops were exhorted to join a partisan group and "Beat the enemy mercilessly."

Partisan ambush
In a staged photograph, partisans lie in wait for a German patrol. The best topography for partisan activity was swampland or forest rather than open steppe.

THE SICILIAN AND ITALIAN CAMPAIGNS

JULY 1943–DECEMBER 1944

After the successful campaign in Tunisia, the Allies decided to strike at Italy by invading Sicily. This led the Italians to seek an armistice, but the Germans rushed troops into Italy and held up Allied progress with a resolute defensive campaign. By the winter of 1944 the Allies had reached northern Italy, but their advance ground to a halt south of Bologna.

1943

JULY 10
Allies land in Sicily

AUGUST 17
Sicilian campaign ends with entry of Americans into Messina

SEPTEMBER 8
Germans begin to disarm Italians

SEPTEMBER 10
Germans occupy Rome

SEPTEMBER 16
British 8th Army links up with US 5th Army southeast of Salerno; Germans withdraw to the north

OCTOBER 1
US troops enter Naples

NOVEMBER 4
Germans establish strong winter position–the Gustav Line

JULY 25
Fascist Grand Council forces Mussolini to resign

SEPTEMBER 3
New Italian government of Marshal Badoglio signs armistice

SEPTEMBER 9
Allies land in Salerno and Taranto

SEPTEMBER 12
German paratroops use gliders to rescue Mussolini

SEPTEMBER 25
Mussolini declares new Italian Republic in Salò in northern Italy

OCTOBER 13
Italy declares war on Germany; US 5th Army crosses Volturno

1944

JANUARY 22
American and British landings at Anzio; beachhead secured, but German soon launch fierce counterattacks

FEBRUARY 29–MARCH 3
Last major German counter-offensive at Anzio

MARCH 18
Unsuccessful tank attack on Monte Cassino by New Zealanders

MAY 11
Operation Diadem to capture Rome launched

MAY 23
Americans break out of Anzio beachhead

JUNE
Germans begin staged withdrawal northward to defensive Gothic Line (completed in fall)

AUGUST 25
Allied Operation Olive opens with attack toward Rimini. Reaches Foglia River to face the Gothic Line

SEPTEMBER 2
Canadians break through Gothic Line

DECEMBER 5
Canadians reach Ravenna

JANUARY 24
Attack by French Expeditionary Corps halted at Monte Cassino

JANUARY 30
US troops renew attack on Monte Cassino

MARCH 15
Allies subject Monte Cassino to massive aerial and artillery bombardment, but troops make little progress

MAY 17–18
Germans finally withdraw from Monte Cassino

JUNE 5
US 5th Army enters Rome

JULY 15
Allies forced to halt at Arno River; French Expeditionary Corps and US VI Corps withdrawn for landings in south of France

AUGUST 31
US 5th Army crosses the Arno

OCTOBER 27
US 5th Army forced to halt operations in mountains south of Bologna

DECEMBER 29
British and Canadian 8th Army's offensive comes to halt at Senio River

Sicilian campaign
Jul 10–Aug 17, 1943

Italian campaign
Sept 9, 1943–
Dec 1944

Other events

THE INVASION OF ITALY

Planning for the landings on Sicily had begun in March 1943, well before the end of the Tunisian campaign. A deception plan to make the Axis believe that Sardinia was the real target was put into effect. It included the planting of a corpse dressed as a British officer, with a briefcase containing misleading documents, on the Spanish coast. As a result, Hitler ordered that Sardinia be reinforced.

Between Tunisia and Sicily lay two small islands—Lampedusa and Pantelleria. If these were not neutralized, aircraft based on them could interfere with the landings. From early May both were subjected to heavy air bombardment. British troops landed on

Pantelleria on June 11 and the Italian garrison surrendered without firing a shot. Lampedusa succumbed in the same way the following day.

THE LANDINGS ON SICILY

The landings on Sicily itself were to be on the south and southeast coasts, with Patton's newly formed US Seventh Army being responsible for the former and Montgomery's British Eighth Army the latter. The plan was that Montgomery would advance up the east coast and cut off the Axis escape route across the Strait of Messina, while Patton protected his left flank. The coastal defenses were manned by low-grade Italian divisions, but there were two well-equipped German mobile divisions on the island. The Allied assault

Wounded in Sicily
An American medical officer administers blood plasma to a wounded US soldier, watched by local Sicilians.

American troops landing in Sicily

The US Seventh Army was opposed by German aircraft and tanks when it landed on the south coast, but supporting fire from warships enabled the troops to get ashore without serious losses.

began on July 10. It was preceded by air-drops to secure airfields and key bridges, but these were badly scattered because of high winds and poor navigation. The landings themselves generally went well and by the end of the day the beachheads had been secured.

Montgomery began to advance up the coast, but soon found his troops held up by stiff German resistance in rugged terrain that favored the defense. Patton took advantage of the fact that the western half of Sicily was held by Italian troops and sent part of his force on a drive to Palermo, the capital. Alexander, whose 15th Army Group was in overall control, wanted him to continue to concentrate on guarding the British left flank, but, after Patton protested, relented. The Seventh Army overran western Sicily and entered Palermo on July 23. Patton then turned east toward Messina, carrying out a number of amphibious landings to outflank Axis defenses. On August 3 Italian troops began to evacuate the island, leaving the Germans to provide the rearguard. By the time the Allies entered Messina on August 17, the Germans had already withdrawn to mainland Italy.

With defeat staring Italy in the face, on July 25 the Fascist Grand Council arrested Mussolini. A new

A spectacular rescue

German gliders crash-landed high in the Apennines to rescue Mussolini from his Italian guards. This part of the operation was conducted by German Special Forces officer, Otto Skorzeny, who had tracked the imprisoned dictator to a mountain hotel.

government was formed under Marshal Pietro Badoglio and this began to make secret overtures to the Allies. Fearing this might be happening, Hitler rushed forces from other theaters to northern Italy, where they came under the command of Rommel's Army Group B. The disgraced Mussolini would be rescued from imprisonment on September 12 by German paratroops.

LANDINGS ON THE MAINLAND

Eisenhower decided that the main landing in Italy should be at Salerno, south of Naples. This was the farthest north that a landing could be supported by Sicily-based fighters. To divert German forces, a preliminary landing would be made across the Strait of Messina by the British Eighth Army. The Salerno landing was to be undertaken by a new formation, the US Fifth Army under General Mark Clark, which contained both US and British troops. Overall operational control would be in the hands of Alexander's 15th Army Group. As for the Seventh Army, Patton was in temporary disgrace for slapping a shell-shocked soldier and he and his HQ were left to administer Sicily.

The hydraulic "horns" absorbed recoil

Maximum elevation of the howitzer was 45°

Gunsight

British 5.5-in howitzer

During the long campaign to conquer Italy, the Allies often found themselves tied down by Germans dug in behind strong defensive lines. To break through the enemy positions required the use of mortars and heavy artillery. The British 5.5-in medium howitzer was introduced in 1942 and remained in service until the 1970s.

Clinometer, for setting elevation of gun

The gun had a 60° traverse

On September 1, the Italian government agreed to the Allied demand that the country lay down it arms and an envoy went to Sicily to sign an armistice agreement. In the event of a surrender, the Germans intended to disarm the Italians themselves and take control of the country. They now had eight divisions in northern Italy under Rommel and 10 in the south under Kesselring. Rommel's strategy was to make the Alpine region impassable to the Allies, whereas Kesselring wanted to fight a delaying action throughout the length of Italy. For the moment Hitler accepted both strategies.

A free man

Mussolini is escorted by his German rescuers to a waiting aircraft. He was flown to Rome, then to Germany for a meeting with Hitler.

On September 3 the British landed in the toe of Italy. They met minimal resistance, but their advance was initially slowed by demolitions. On the same day the Italian armistice was signed. It was due to come into effect on September 8 as the Salerno landings were being mounted. Eisenhower intended to fly the US 82nd Airborne Division into Rome to secure the city, but the Italian authorities said that they could not remove the German threat to its landing grounds and so the operation was cancelled. He also ordered Montgomery to make a landing in Taranto to prevent Italian warships based there from falling into German hands.

Eisenhower broadcast the Italian armistice on the evening of September 8, but the landings at Salerno did not take place until 3:30 am the following morning. This gave the Germans valuable warning and they immediately set about disarming the Italian Army. Kesselring had deduced where the landing would be, and the assault was met by bitter resistance from both troops on the ground and the Luftwaffe. Even so, the attackers did get ashore. The British landing at Taranto was unopposed, on the other hand, and the Italian naval squadron, as well as those based in La Spezia and Genoa, set sail for Malta, where they would formally surrender. The latter two squadrons were, however, attacked by the Luftwaffe, which sank the battleship *Roma*.

At Salerno a fierce counterattack on September 14 was beaten back only with difficulty. Two days later, the Eighth Army linked up with the Fifth Army in the beachhead and Kesselring began to pull his troops back northward. The Allies now began to advance, with the Fifth Army in the west and the Eighth Army in the east. Initially, progress was good, with Clark entering Naples on October 1, while Montgomery secured Foggia on the same day.

On October 4 Hitler ordered Rommel to transfer two of his divisions to Kesselring, who was to delay the US Fifth Army for as long as possible north of the Volturno River. Simultaneously, Kesselring was preparing a formidable defensive position, the Gustav Line, which ran the breadth of Italy and took maximum advantage of the river lines and mountainous terrain. All this was an indication that Hitler now favored Kesselring's forward defense strategy and was not prepared to grant the Allies easy access to Rome. In addition, the fall rains had now arrived and provided a further brake on progress. During October the Fifth Army managed to get across the Volturno, but was then held in the mountainous country to the north. In the Eighth Army sector, Montgomery had been forcing his way over even more river lines and by early November was closing up to the Sangro River. At this time, Hitler finally came off the fence and approved Kesselring's strategy by appointing him commander-in-chief in Italy.

Eisenhower was still eager to capture Rome and obtained the agreement of the Combined Chiefs of Staff to mount an amphibious operation, codenamed Shingle, designed to outflank the Gustav Line. This would mean retaining shipping that should have been sent back to Britain in preparation for the cross-Channel invasion. Simultaneously, and accepting the Fifth Army's problems in breaking through in the south, Alexander ordered Clark to halt his attacks and for Montgomery to break through the Gustav Line in his sector and threaten Rome. The Eighth Army crossed the Sangro on November 20 during a spell of better weather and then managed to penetrate the Gustav Line. Casualties, however, were mounting and the bad weather returned. On December 27 the Canadians managed to seize Ortona. In view

> Monday, September 13, 1943
> Guess I slept until almost 8:00.
> Dead tired. Slept through a hot
> battle. Sgts. Engstrom and
> Swanson were killed. Sgt. Murphy
> was badly wounded; his leg was
> shot off. Our gun position was
> not far away. Had a good
> breakfast of C ration hash mixed
> with genuine Italian onions,
> tomatoes and peppers. Boiled some
> potatoes; made coffee that I got
> from Division. A German soldier
> gave himself up. He got through
> our infantry and got to us.

FROM THE DIARY OF CORPORAL BUD WAGNER, US 151ST ARTILLERY BATTALION AT SALERNO

Bombing German positions on the Volturno
A US B-25 Mitchell bomber drops its bombs on the German artillery positions defending the Volturno River. In the Italian campaign the Allies made use of superior air power to soften up the strong German defenses and to disrupt communications.

Anzio harbour
American and British forces remained trapped in the beachhead around the small port of Anzio for four months between January and May 1944. Allied control of the sea and air allowed the troops to be resupplied regularly.

THE ANZIO BEACHHEAD

The Allies now resumed their efforts to break through the Gustav Line. On January 17 Clark made some territorial gains north of the Garigliano River. Three days later there was a further assault across the Rapido. This was partially successful, but was halted by the German defenses on and around the towering hill of Monte Cassino, a feature that was to dominate the fighting during the next few months. Then, on January 22, came the landings at Anzio. They were conducted by General John P. Lucas's US VI Corps, which contained both American and British troops. They initially caught the Germans by surprise and the attackers got ashore with few problems. Because of lack of clarity in his orders, Lucas did not take advantage of this to advance immediately inland, but contented himself with building up his forces in the beachhead. This gave Kesselring time to deploy forces to Anzio.

The Allies now entered what was to be the grimmest period of the whole Italian campaign. On January 24 the French crossed the Rapido to the north of Monte Cassino, but were halted in their tracks by fierce German counterattacks. Five days later, Lucas began to advance out of the Anzio beachhead. Simultaneously, the Fifth Army made another attack on Monte Cassino, which was again repulsed. On February 3 the Germans launched a counterattack at Anzio and drove the Allies back into the beachhead.

of the growing exhaustion of his troops and the fact that they were now faced with mountainous terrain, Montgomery then halted his attacks.

At the beginning of January 1944 there were major changes in the Allied higher command. Both Eisenhower and Montgomery were summoned back to Britain to prepare for Overlord, the landings in Normandy, and were replaced respectively by Generals Sir Maitland Wilson and Sir Oliver Leese. A number of veteran US and British divisions also left the theater for the same reason. They were replaced by fresh US divisions from the States, Alphonse Juin's French Expeditionary Corps from Northwest Africa and Wladislaw Anders' II Polish Corps, which had been formed in the Middle East from Poles that the Soviets had sent to Siberia and had then released.

German paratroopers
The Germans reacted swiftly to the Allied landings on the Italian mainland, first at Salerno, then at Anzio. Here, motorized units speed south to contain the Allied beachhead at Anzio.

The invasion of Italy
Despite the fact that the Italians soon surrendered and came over to the Allied side, the Italian campaign was a long and bitter struggle. The Germans took over the country and fought a defensive battle, making skilful use of the country's mountains and river valleys to hold up the Allied advance.

Oct 27, 1944 ⑯
Allied advance comes to a halt south of Bologna

Dec 5, 1944 ⑰
8th Army enters Ravenna, as Germans withdraw to Senio River

Aug 25, 1944 ⑮
8th Army storms Gothic line, the German defensive position

Aug 3–4, 1944 ⑭
Retreating Germans blow up all bridges across the Arno in Florence (except the Ponte Vecchio)

Sept 12, 1943 ⑧
German paratroopers use gliders to rescue Mussolini from hotel in the Appenines where he is being held

Jun 5, 1944 ⑬
General Clark enjoys triumphal entry into Rome

Jan 22, 1944 ⑪
Allied landings at Anzio. Troops pinned down in narrow beachhead until May

May 17, 1944 ⑫
Germans finally abandon Monte Cassino after four months of fighting

Oct 6, 1943 ⑩
Germans withdraw to line of Volturno

Sept 20, 1943 ⑨
British 8th Army links up with Salerno forces

Sept 9, 1943 ⑥
US and British landings at Salerno meet with strong resistance

Sept 9, 1943 ⑦
Diversionary landing at Italian port of Taranto

Jul 23, 1943 ②
US troops enter Palermo

Sept 3, 1943 ⑤
Two divisions of British 8th Army cross to Italian mainland

Aug 11–17, 1943 ③
Germans successfully evacuate troops across Strait of Messina

Sept 3, 1943 ④
New Italian government of Marshal Badoglio secretly signs armistice with Allies

Jul 10, 1943 ①
Operation Husky: US 7th Army and British 8th Army land in southern Sicily

THE ALLIED INVASION OF ITALY
JUL 10, 1943–DEC 31, 1944

— German front line Sept 25, 1943
–·– German front line Mar 31, 1944
– – German front line Jun 5, 1944
····· German front line Dec 31, 1944
⊥⊤⊥ Gothic line
➡ Allied landing/advance

ARMY GROUP SOUTHWEST
10TH ARMY
14TH ARMY
BRITISH 8TH ARMY
US 5TH ARMY
15TH ARMY GROUP
US VI CORPS
US 7TH ARMY
BRITISH 8TH ARMY
15TH ARMY GROUP

Alexander was still determined to seize Cassino. He transferred British, Indian, and New Zealand formations from the Eighth Army for another attack. On the very top of the mountain stood a monastery, which the Allies were convinced the Germans were using as an observation post, although in practice they were not. On February 15, Allied bombers attacked the monastery and virtually destroyed it. German paratroops occupied the ruins and turned them into a formidable bastion. On the following day the Indians and New Zealanders attacked, but could make little headway. At the same time, the Germans mounted another assault at Anzio. Only massive Allied air and artillery support prevented them from splitting the beachhead in two.

ATTACKS ON CASSINO

Realizing that he was getting nowhere, Alexander drew up a fresh plan. He now intended to deploy the bulk of the Eighth Army to the Cassino sector for an all-out assault. Simultaneously, while the Fifth Army created a diversion to tie down German

British gun emplacement at Cassino
The barrel of a Bofors antiaircraft gun projects from the ruins of Cassino. The versatile Bofors was often used for shelling defensive positions. On the hilltop above stand the bombed-out remains of the monastery of Monte Cassino.

Rome in Allied hands
American troops walk past the Colosseum. The Fifth Army's triumphal entry into Rome on June 5,1944, was somewhat overshadowed by the news of the D-Day landings in Normandy on the following day.

troops, the Anzio force would break out and sever the German supply lines from Rome to the Gustav Line. To prepare the way, Alexander intended to mount an air campaign against German communications throughout Italy. He would not be ready to put his plan into effect until late April and wanted to retain the troops earmarked for Operation Anvil, the landings in southern France, which were scheduled to take place at the same time as those in Normandy. The Combined Chiefs of Staff eventually consented to this and Anvil was postponed until July.

On March 15 the Indians and New Zealanders also assaulted Cassino once more. They managed to enter what remained of Cassino town at the base of the mountain, but the German defenses otherwise remained impregnable and Alexander halted the attack after six days' fighting. There was now a comparative lull, while the Allied air forces launched their campaign against German communications, which was largely aimed at road and railroad bridges. Not until the night of May 11/12 did Alexander mount his all-out offensive. This time it was the turn of

the Poles to attack at Cassino, but again they were unable to make much progress. There was, however, a development in the Fifth Army sector. Juin's French troops managed to break through in the mountains to the south and by May 14 were in a position to outflank Cassino. Realizing this, Kesselring ordered the withdrawal from the Gustav Line to begin. On May 17 the Poles attacked Monte Cassino once more and hoisted their flag on top of the monastery.

On May 23 the break-out from Anzio began, while the Germans started to fall back to a fresh defensive line, which ran through the Alban hills, south of Rome. Two days later the Fifth Army linked up with the Anzio force. The goal now was to cut off the German 10th Army's withdrawal from the Gustav Line by cutting Highway 7, the main route to Rome. Clark, however, now became mesmerized by the prize of Rome itself and directed the majority of his forces in the direction of the capital. Not only did this mean a stiff fight to break through the German defenses in the Alban hills, but it enabled the bulk of the 10th Army to escape the planned trap. Even so, Kesselring accepted that Rome could not be held. By June 4 the last of his troops had withdrawn north of the city, enabling Clark to enter it in triumph the following day.

THE GOTHIC LINE

The Allied advance came to a halt in mid-July along the line of the Arno River. To the north, Kesselring was once more taking advantage of mountainous terrain to construct another defensive barrier across the width of Italy—the Gothic Line. Alexander was determined to resume the offensive, but had to pause while the French Expeditionary

The end of the battle
Allied troops search the ruins of Cassino in May 1944 following the German withdrawal from the monastery above the town.

Corps and US VI Corps, which were required for Anvil, were replaced by the untried Brazilian Expeditionary Corps and a new US division. The new plan called for the Eighth Army to advance east of the Apennines, draw the Germans toward the Adriatic coast, and then for the Fifth Army to punch through the center of the Gothic Line and advance toward Bologna.

The new offensive opened on August 25 and by the end of the month the Eighth Army was across the Foglia River and hammering at the Gothic Line. As expected, Kesselring began to switch his forces to the east to counter this threat, which grew as the Allies broke through the German defenses and reached the Conca River before heavy rain caused a temporary halt. Then, on September 12, the Fifth Army crossed the Arno and aimed for the boundary between the German 10th and 14th Armies. Simultaneously, the Eighth Army resumed its advance. It now faced a succession of river lines, much as it had the previous fall. The American attack

Hilltop defense
A German paratrooper armed with an MP40 submachine-gun takes aim from an almost impregnable position among the ruins of Monte Cassino.

initially made good progress. Breaking through the Gothic Line, Clark headed for Bologna. If he could seize the city, the 10th Army, facing Leese in the east, would be cut off. But the fall rains, combined with the mountains, slowed his momentum and Kesselring was able to fill the gaps in his defenses. The Eighth Army continued to push forward, Leese

being replaced by General Sir Richard McCreery at the beginning of October. On the 27th of the month Clark, still in the mountains south of Bologna, was forced to halt, his casualty rate becoming unsupportable. The increasingly tired Eighth Army continued its endless river crossings, but the chances of achieving a decisive breakthrough were receding.

On November 24, Alexander succeeded Wilson as supreme theater commander, with Clark taking over 15th Army Group. The Eighth Army was still advancing, with the Canadians capturing Ravenna at the beginning of December. By the middle of the month it had reached the Senio River. More river lines lay between this and Bologna and the troops were exhausted. Alexander therefore closed down the offensive. He would wait until the spring before resuming the offensive.

German MP40 submachine-gun
Originally intended principally for use by paratroops and vehicle crews, the weapon was widely used by German infantry.

Lightweight metal stock

Butt and stock could be folded alongside the gun

Hooded foresight

pistol grip

Stick magazine holding 32 rounds of 9-mm ammunition

The underside of the barrel was designed so the gun could be fired from an armored vehicle

ENTERTAINING THE TROOPS

USO (UNITED SERVICES ORGANIZATIONS) was founded in February 1941. By 1944, USO was run by nearly 750,000 volunteers who operated over 3,000 clubs across the United States and overseas, providing rest, recreation, and entertainment for the troops. Many Hollywood stars served in theaters of war. Bob Hope began the first of his five decades of USO service in 1942. Marlene Dietrich, a USO stalwart, was entertaining near the front line in Belgium in December 1944 when the Germans launched the Ardennes offensive. The most famous USO casualty of the war was bandleader Glenn Miller, who disappeared on December 14, 1944 on a cross-Channel flight to Paris to join his orchestra, a mystery which has never been satisfactorily solved. Between 1941 and 1947 over 7,000 "soldiers in greasepaint" put on nearly 430,000 shows for the troops, and USO continues to this day as USO Celebrity Entertainments.

The British equivalent was the Entertainments National Service Association, or ENSA. Initially, the quality of ENSA shows was extremely variable and the organization earned the nickname "Every Night Something Awful." Nevertheless, by the end of November 1939 ENSA had some 700 artistes on its books and had given nearly 1,500 shows which had been seen by some 600,000 people. ENSA crossed the Channel to entertain British troops in France, where in the winter of 1939–40 comedian George

Marlene Dietrich
Marlene poses on top of a piano with a group of admiring GIs at an evacuation hospital in Italy in May 1944.

The Forces' Sweetheart
Vera Lynn sings to a group of British servicemen, raising morale during the Blitz.

Formby kept the troops laughing and Gracie Fields sang to huge audiences. ENSA was gradually expanded to include more highbrow entertainment, and its Good Music section staged concerts by Yehudi Menuhin, Sir Adrian Boult and the BBC Symphony Orchestra. ENSA performed wonders overseas, often in the most grueling and hazardous conditions, entertaining troops from North Africa to Burma. In the spring of 1944, Vera Lynn, the "Forces' Sweetheart," toured Burma, entertaining troops in the jungle. ENSA followed the Allies into Normandy and there was even an ENSA concert party on Lüneburg Heath when on May 5, 1945, the German forces in the West surrendered to Field Marshal Montgomery. The show was lit by the headlights of six jeeps. ENSA was disbanded in 1947; at its wartime peak it was mounting 500 shows a week at home and abroad, showcasing some 4,000 artists.

Bob Hope on stage in New Georgia
Hope was one of USO's most indefatigable entertainers. Here he is playing to a vast audience on the island of New Georgia in the Solomons.

Bombing raid on Cassino
A formation of US Mitchell B-25s flies toward
Cassino. Despite persistent bombardment by artillery
and from the air, the German defenses in Cassino
held up the Allied advance in Italy for six months.

THE ALLIED BOMBING OF GERMANY

FEBRUARY 1942– DECEMBER 1943

In spring 1942 RAF Bomber Command decided to concentrate on night raids over German cities. When the US Air Force joined the campaign later in the year, it used its heavily armed bombers for daylight raids on specific targets. Without long-range fighter escorts, both air forces suffered heavy losses.

1942

MARCH 3
Lancaster heavy bomber enters service, laying mines off Brest in northwest France

MARCH 8
New system of marking targets with flares used in raid on Essen, but with little success

APRIL 17
Daylight raid on diesel engine factory in Augsburg by 14 Lancasters. 7 planes lost

MAY 30/31
First 1,000-bomber raid by RAF. Target switched from Hamburg to Cologne because of bad weather

AUGUST 18
First mission of RAF's Pathfinder Force–whose job is to find and mark target for main force– against Flensburg

FEBRUARY 23
Arthur (Bomber) Harris takes over Bomber Command. He is a fervent proponent of saturation area bombing of Germany

MARCH 28
RAF incendiary raid devastates medieval city of Lübeck

APRIL 24
In retaliation for Lübeck, Luftwaffe bombs Exeter, first in series of attacks on historic cities of Britain– the "Baedeker raids"

AUGUST 17
First all-American bombing mission over France. 12 Flying Fortresses bomb Rouen marshaling yards

DECEMBER 20
Navigation device "Oboe" used for first time on small raid on power plant in Holland

1943

JANUARY 16/17
First raid on Berlin for 14 months. Despite failure of German air-raid warning system, bombers inflict limited damage

JANUARY 30/31
Raid on Hamburg, first to use H2S radar system for locating targets

MAY 16/17
Dambusters raid. "Bouncing bombs" used against Ruhr dams. Two dams breached

JULY 24/25
791-bomber raid on Hamburg. First use of "Window," strips of aluminum foil dropped to confuse German radar

AUGUST 17/18
RAF bomb "V" weapon installations in Peenemünde on Baltic coast

AUGUST 23/24
1,700 tons of bombs dropped on Berlin. 56 aircraft lost

OCTOBER 14
More heavy losses in American raid on Schweinfurt. Decision to concentrate on closer targets within range of fighter escorts

NOVEMBER 18/19
Start of a sustained bombing campaign against Berlin

JANUARY 27
First American raid on Germany. Daylight raid on Emden and Wihelmshaven

JUNE 10
Decision made for Americans to bomb Germany by day, British by night

JULY 27/28
Follow-up raid on Hamburg causes violent firestorm that engulfs large area of the city. 40,000 killed

AUGUST 17
60 American bombers lost in raids on Messerschmidt factory in Regensburg and ball-bearing plant in Schweinfurt

SEPTEMBER 6
338 American heavy bombers attack Stuttgart. Heavy losses and disappointing results

NOVEMBER 3
US 400-bomber daylight raid on Wilhelmshaven accompanied by 600-strong fighter escort

DECEMBER
First P-51 Mustangs delivered to Europe. With external fuel tanks, Mustangs can escort US bombers deep into Germany

British bombing raids Feb 1942– Dec 1943 US bombing raids Aug 1942–Dec 1943 Other events

WAR IN THE AIR

The BUTT REPORT, published in August 1941, examined the performance over three months of British bombers against targets in France and Germany. Butt, a member of the War Cabinet Secretariat, had examined hundreds of photographs taken at the moment of bomb release and concluded that, in the summer of 1941, only a third of Bomber Command aircraft had succeeded in placing their bombs within 5 miles (8 km) of the aiming point.

AREA BOMBING

In February 1942, Bomber Command received a new directive. The main weight of its operations was to be thrown into "area" attacks on German cities. The aiming points were to be built-up areas rather than specific industrial plants and facilities. Precision raids continued, but from this point to May 1945, 75 percent of the total tonnage of bombs dropped fell on area targets.

In the spring of 1942, Bomber Command was better placed to execute the new policy. Its twin-engined Wellington, Whitley, Blenheim, and

Hampden bombers were gradually giving way to a generation of four-engined bombers capable of delivering bigger payloads—the Short Stirling, Handley Page Halifax, and Avro Lancaster.

Simultaneously, the Butt report was bearing fruit. Late in 1941, the first of a series of navigational aids, "Gee," was introduced. By February 1942, 200 aircraft had been equipped with Gee, a modification that led to the introduction of specialized bomb aimers. The job had previously been handled by the navigator. As Gee was going into service, a new commander arrived at Bomber Command's headquarters in High Wycombe, outside London.

The appointment of Air Chief Marshal Sir Arthur Harris was the single most important factor in the systematic organization of the bombing offensive.

Harris never abandoned the belief that the progressive destruction of the urban areas of Germany would, by itself, bring the war to

Mission accomplished
The crew of a Lancaster bomber walks away from the aircraft after a flight in April 1943, while the ground crew checks it over.

Avro Lancaster bombers
The Lancaster was the principal aircraft used on British night raids over Germany. A total of 3,345 out of 7,373 were lost on operations.

an end. His intention was to mount increasingly heavy raids compressed into progressively shorter periods of time, thus overwhelming German civil defenses on the ground.

On the night of March 3/4, 235 aircraft attacked the Renault factory in Billancourt in occupied France. The concentration achieved on this raid was about 120 aircraft an hour, a first step toward the saturation raids of the later war years. Production at the Billancourt factory was not resumed for three months.

Harris now turned his attention to the Baltic cities of Lübeck and Rostock. The latter was the site of the Heinkel aircraft factory, but the main reason for their choice as targets was their vulnerability to incendiary attack. The densely packed streets of the medieval cities were like tinderboxes. Lübeck was bombed on March 28/29, 1942, and a month later Rostock was subjected to four raids in quick succession.

THE 1,000-BOMBER RAID
Harris had a flair for publicity, which he exploited to the fullest in the 1,000-bomber raid flown against Cologne on May, 30/31, 1942. In Operation Millennium, Harris planned to throw the whole of his front-line strength, and his entire reserve, into a massive raid on a major German city. It was a tremendous gamble, but the prize was the survival of the strategic bombing offensive. Of the 1,047 aircraft that took off that night, 367 were from training units. During the attack, which lasted just under two and a half hours, some 870 bombers dropped 1,445 tons of bombs. The fires the bombers left behind burned for several days. Some 50,000 people were "dehoused." Harris launched two more "1,000" raids, against Essen (June 1) and Bremen (June 25). Neither matched the success of the Cologne raid and both operations suffered mounting losses to the Luftwaffe's night fighters.

The man responsible for the improving German night fighter defenses was General Josef Kammhuber, who established the so-called "Kammhuber Line," a system of closely controlled fighter-defended areas covering every approach to Germany from Denmark to France. The Kammhuber Line consisted of "boxes," each of which was controlled by a small radar station deploying both long-range early-warning radar and narrow-beam systems. The latter

The bombing of Cologne
Cologne suffered many raids during the war, but none was as terrifying as the first 1,000-bomber raid. Aircrews reported seeing the framework of white-hot building joists glowing in the immense fire raging below.

could pick up and hold a bomber at a range of 30 miles (48 km) and then direct a night fighter onto the target. The major drawback of this system was that only one fighter could operate in a box at any given time. By concentrating its bombers in a "stream," Bomber Command could pass through as few as four boxes on an inward flight, although there was a tendency to spread out on the way home, bringing more night fighters into play.

COMBINED BOMBING OFFENSIVE
Even before the United States entered the war, Anglo-American strategic discussions had resulted in the decision to direct the main weight of the Allied effort against Germany. To defeat Germany, the United States pledged complete land, sea, and air participation in the Anglo-American effort. The United States Army Air Force (USAAF) was confident that, given a sufficient number of aircraft, it could conduct a strategic bombing offensive that would bring Germany to its knees. At the core of the USAAF's philosophy were two firmly held beliefs: first, that high-level daylight precision bombing could be employed to break down the key elements in the German war economy; and second, that, in the absence of a satisfactory long-range escort fighter, the heavily armed USAAF Flying Fortress and Liberator bombers could fight their way to and from their targets without suffering unacceptable losses.

> "There are a lot of people who say that bombing cannot win the war. My reply is that it has never been tried yet. We shall see…"

AIR CHIEF MARSHAL SIR ARTHUR HARRIS, AOC-IN-C, BOMBER COMMAND, FEBRUARY 1942

Assessing the damage
Air Chief Marshal Harris and his staff study aerial photographs and reports of the latest air raids over Germany at Bomber Command headquarters in High Wycombe.

The bombers of the US Eighth Air Force began to arrive in England in July 1942 and, on August 17, twelve B-17s raided the rail yards in Rouen. The Americans spent the next five months acclimatizing and training. While the Eighth Air Force grappled with the huge logistical task of establishing bases in Britain, only 30 raids were flown—against targets in the Netherlands, Belgium, and northern France.

THE US BOMBING CAMPAIGN

The bedrock of USAAF tactics was formation flying, the success of which depended on the concentration of defensive firepower. By spring 1943, the so-called "tucked-in" wing had been introduced, which comprised three 18-aircraft squadrons stacked closely together with one squadron flying lead, one high, and one low. It could take up to three hours to assemble 300 or more bombers in combat wings of this kind before they flew on to their target. This enabled German radar and listening stations in northwest Europe, the latter counting radio sets as they were switched on, to estimate with some accuracy the strength of the force flying against them.

B-24 Liberator

Although more vulnerable than the Flying Fortress, the Liberator proved its worth as a bomber both in Europe and in the Pacific.

B-17 bombers over Germany

A squadron of B-17 Flying Fortresses maintains its tight formation on its way to bomb Stuttgart on September 6, 1943.

Early in 1943, following the Casablanca conference, the British and Americans outlined their plan for the air offensive in Europe. Its goal was "the progressive destruction and dislocation of the German military, industrial, and economic system." This strategy was embodied in the Pointblank Directive of June 1943. The USAAF's confidence ran high, but it was to be tested almost to the point of destruction in the skies over Germany.

The USAAF had begun to make shallow penetrations into Germany in January 1943, and from February losses began to mount steadily. The Luftwaffe's day fighters were as well armed as the American bombers and by fall 1943 they were equipped with 30-mm heavy cannon and 210-mm rockets. The latter were not particularly accurate but were effective in loosening up the bomber formations.

By spring 1943, heavy losses were the norm over Germany. On June 22 the Eighth Air Force mounted its first large-scale raid on the Ruhr, attacking the synthetic rubber plants in Hüls.

Only 16 bombers were lost out of 235, but of those that returned no fewer than 170 had been damaged. Operations were often handicapped by poor weather conditions. Crew who had trained for high-altitude bombing with the excellent Norden bombsight could achieve pinpoint accuracy in the clear blue skies of the Nevada desert in the United States. Bombing targets in Germany through dense cloud, smoke screens, or industrial haze was another matter, particularly with the Luftwaffe in close attendance.

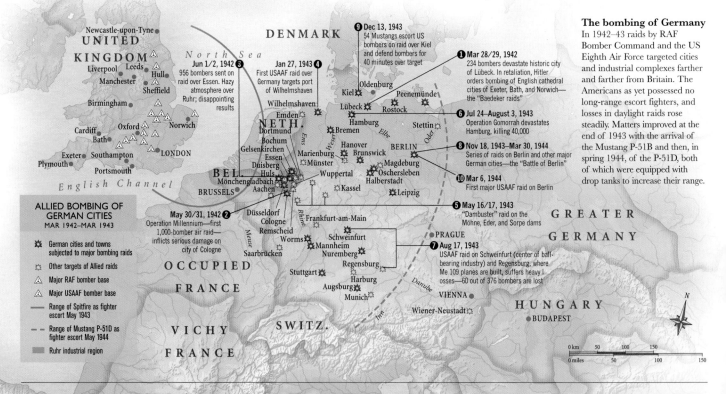

The bombing of Germany

In 1942–43 raids by RAF Bomber Command and the US Eighth Air Force targeted cities and industrial complexes farther and farther from Britain. The Americans as yet possessed no long-range escort fighters, and losses in daylight raids rose steadily. Matters improved at the end of 1943 with the arrival of the Mustang P-51B and then, in spring 1944, of the P-51D, both of which were equipped with drop tanks to increase their range.

❾ Dec 13, 1943
54 Mustangs escort US bombers on raid over Kiel and defend bombers for 40 minutes over target

❹ Jan 27, 1943
First USAAF raid over Germany targets port of Wilhelmshaven

❸ Jun 1/2, 1942
956 bombers sent on raid over Essen. Hazy atmosphere over Ruhr; disappointing results

❶ Mar 28/29, 1942
234 bombers devastate historic city of Lübeck. In retaliation, Hitler orders bombing of English cathedral cities of Exeter, Bath, and Norwich—the "Baedeker raids"

❻ Jul 24–August 3, 1943
Operation Gomorrah devastates Hamburg, killing 40,000

❽ Nov 18, 1943–Mar 30, 1944
Series of raids on Berlin and other major German cities—the "Battle of Berlin"

❿ Mar 6, 1944
First major USAAF raid on Berlin

❺ May 16/17, 1943
"Dambuster" raid on the Möhne, Eder, and Sorpe dams

❷ May 30/31, 1942
Operation Millennium—first 1,000-bomber air raid—inflicts serious damage on city of Cologne

❼ Aug 17, 1943
USAAF raid on Schweinfurt (center of ball-bearing industry) and Regensburg, where Me 109 planes are built, suffers heavy losses—60 out of 376 bombers are lost

ALLIED BOMBING OF GERMAN CITIES
MAR 1942–MAR 1943

☼ German cities and towns subjected to major bombing raids

☼ Other targets of Allied raids

△ Major RAF bomber base

△ Major USAAF bomber base

— Range of Spitfire as fighter escort May 1943

-- Range of Mustang P-51 as fighter escort May 1944

▪ Ruhr industrial region

UNITED KINGDOM
Newcastle-upon-Tyne
Liverpool Leeds Hull
Manchester Sheffield
Birmingham
Cardiff Oxford Norwich
Bath
Exeter Southampton LONDON
Plymouth Portsmouth

North Sea
DENMARK
English Channel
BRUSSELS
BEL.
NETH.
Wilhelmshaven
Emden Bremen
Hamburg
Oldenburg Kiel Peenemünde
Lübeck Rostock
Stettin
Hanover BERLIN
Dortmund Brunswick
Bochum Marienburg Magdeburg
Gelsenkirchen Münster Oschersleben
Essen Halberstadt
Duisberg Wuppertal Kassel Leipzig
Mönchengladbach Huls
Aachen
Düsseldorf
Cologne
Remscheid Frankfurt-am-Main PRAGUE
Worms Schweinfurt
Saarbrücken Mannheim
Nuremberg
Regensburg
Stuttgart Harburg
Augsburg VIENNA
Munich Wiener-Neustadt

Rhine Meuse Ems Weser Elbe Oder Danube Inn

OCCUPIED FRANCE
VICHY FRANCE
SWITZ.
GREATER GERMANY
HUNGARY
BUDAPEST

0 km 50 100 150
0 miles 50 100 150

FINDING THE TARGET

FROM THE BLITZ ONWARD, the war in the air became an electronic battle of measures and countermeasures between Allied and German scientists, technicians, and aircrews. "Gee," a British target-finding system introduced in late 1941, consisted of a master and two "slave" transmitter stations positioned on a base line some 200 miles (320 km) long. A receiver in the aircraft picked up a complex sequence of pulses sent in a predetermined order across Europe. Much depended on the skill of the navigator, who applied the time differences between pulses to a special grid chart and thus calculated the aircraft's position. The Germans, however, began to jam Gee successfully in the fall of 1942.

"Oboe," introduced in December 1942 was a blind-bombing system that depended on an aircraft flying on an arc at a constant range from a radio beam transmitted from a station in England to pass over the target. A signal conveyed by a second intersecting beam cut the arc at the correct point for bomb release. Because it could only handle one aircraft at a time, Oboe was restricted to Pathfinder Mosquitos. H2S, which went into service early in 1943, was a downward-looking radar, housed in a blister in the bomber's belly. The returning echoes, displayed on a cathode ray tube known as the Plan Position Indicator (PPI), gave a continuous picture of the terrain over which the aircraft was flying. From 1944, German night fighters equipped with Naxos radars could home in on H2S radiations, forcing bombers to switch on their H2S equipment only for very short periods.

In November 1943, Bomber Command formed 100 Group whose sole purpose was to use radar and radio countermeasures. Toward the end of the war, in a big operation, it could put up as many as 90 jamming aircraft.

Bombs away
Bombs from a USAAF bomber fall toward their target during an air raid on the docks of Bremen in December 1943.

H2S radar
First used in January 1943, H2S radar scanned the ground beneath the aircraft. The echoes were strongest from built-up areas and weaker from open country and water, The navigator compared the image created by the returning echoes with a map.

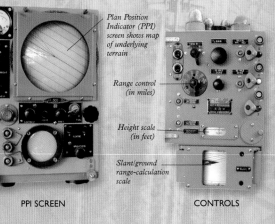

Plan Position Indicator (PPI) screen shows map of underlying terrain

Range control (in miles)

Height scale (in feet)

Slant/ground range-calculation scale

PPI SCREEN

CONTROLS

At the end of July 1943, predominantly cloudless skies over Europe enabled the Eighth Air Force to mount a series of raids, during which 100 aircraft were either destroyed or written off. The attrition reached its peak on August 17 when the Eighth Air Force made its deepest penetration into the Reich, attacking the Me 109 assembly plant at Regensburg and the ball-bearing factories in Schweinfurt. Of the 376 aircraft despatched on the Schweinfurt and Regensburg raids, 60 were lost and many more written off. A second raid on Schweinfurt in October cost the Americans 77 aircraft lost and another 133 damaged out of 291 despatched. Average losses were now running at an unacceptable 10 percent and by the fall of 1943 morale had fallen. After the second Schweinfurt raid, bombing operations were temporarily suspended. Schweinfurt was hit again on February 24, 1944. Some 266 USAAF bombers attacked by day and 734 Bomber Command aircraft by night. This raid was part of Operation Argument ("Big Week"), a concerted attempt to cripple the German aircraft industry. The USAAF flew 3,300 sorties in Big Week, losing 224 bombers and 41 fighters. Help, however, was at hand. The spring of 1944 saw the introduction of the P-51D Mustang. Equipped with drop tanks, the Mustang had a range of 1,500 miles (2,400 km), enabling it to fly escort to any target in Germany, including Berlin. Thanks

Nose gun
The nose blister of a B-17 bomber housed one of a total of 13 machine-guns defending the Flying Fortress.

principally to the P-51D, the Luftwaffe lost over 1,000 day fighter pilots between January and April 1944, a rate of attrition it could not sustain.

PATHFINDERS

By the spring of 1943, RAF Bomber Command had the weapons and navigational aids to proceed with the Pointblank directive. Gee now had only limited usefulness, as the Germans had learned how to jam it, but two new radar devices, H2S and "Oboe," were now operational. The first aircraft to receive Oboe were six Mosquitos of 109 Squadron, which took it on a calibration raid against a power plant in the Netherlands on December 20/21, 1942. In the twin-engined Mosquito, Bomber Command possessed a fighter-bomber that was fast enough to outrun all the Luftwaffe's prejet fighters. 109 Squadron was part of 8 Group, known as the Pathfinder Force (PFF), which was formed in August 1942 to exploit the new radar devices in locating and marking targets.

By the end of February 1943, the Pathfinders had progressed from being a target-finding force to being a target-marking force, introducing and constantly refining systems of groundmarking and skymarking. On March 5, 1943 Bomber Command delivered the first blow in the so-called Battle of the Ruhr when a Main Force of 442 aircraft led by 36 PFF crews flew to Essen. Summer 1943 saw the introduction of a Master Bomber who remained over the target throughout the raid, instructing the Main Force where to aim its bombs.

THE AIR WAR OVER GERMANY

FROM 1942, BRITAIN AND THE UNITED STATES fielded powerful strategic bombing forces in the European theater. By the end of 1944, RAF Bomber Command's heavy bomber force was dominated by the Avro Lancaster. The duties of the US Eighth Air Force's strategic day-bombing campaign were shared by the Consolidated B-24 Liberator and the Boeing B-17 Flying Fortress. The Allied bomber chiefs' belief that strategic bombing could win the war was sorely tested in 1943–44 when both the Eighth Air Force and Bomber Command suffered heavy losses over Germany at the hands of the Luftwaffe's day and night fighters. During this period only about 35 percent of the Eighth Air Force's bomber crews could expect to complete a tour of 25 operational missions.

De Havilland Mosquito

Designed as an all-wooden unarmed day bomber, capable of outrunning any fighter, the versatile Mosquito also appeared in reconnaissance, ground-attack, night-fighter, and precision night-bomber versions. Some 6,700 were built during the war.

Engines 2 × 1,290 hp Rolls Royce Merlin	
Wingspan 54 ft (16.45 m)	Length 40 ft 6 in (12.34 m)
Top speed 408 mph (656 kph)	Crew 2
Armament 4 × 500-lb (225-kg) bombs internally plus 2 × 500-lb (225-kg) bombs underwing; or 1 × 4,000-lb (1,800-kg) bomb	

P-51D Mustang

With its ability to escort US bombers all the way to any target in continental Europe, the bubble-canopied Mustang, fitted with extra fuel tanks, changed the face of the air war in the spring of 1944. It was not only used for close escort duty, but also flew fighting patrols to seek out and destroy enemy day fighters.

Engine 1 × 1,490 hp Rolls Royce/Packard Merlin	
Wingspan 37 ft (11.27m)	Length 32 ft 3 in (9.83 m)
Top Speed 437 mph (437 mph)	Crew 1
Armament 6 × .50-in machine-guns plus 2 × 1,000-lb (450-kg) bombs or 6 × 5-in rockets on underwing racks	

Waist gunner position. In the G model (introduced autumn 1943) this was often glazed

Rear turret

Ball turret

Chin turret

Boeing B-17G Flying Fortress

The bomber's heavy defensive armament not only compromised its bombload but also, without long-range fighter escort, was not enough to ward off enemy fighters. By the end of the war some 13,000 B-17s had been built.

Engines 4 × 1,200 hp Wright Cyclone radials	
Wingspan 103 ft 9in (31. 6 m)	Length 74 ft 9 in (22.8 m)
Top speed 302 mph (486 kph)	Crew 10
Armament 13 × .50-in machine-guns; maximum bombload 12,800 lb (5, 800kg)	

Consolidated B-24J Liberator

Ease of manufacture led to the production of some 18,500 Liberators during the war, many of which served in the Pacific theater. Its cruising range was the highest of any land aircraft of World War II, but it was a poor formation keeper and, when damaged, it tended to catch fire or blow up very quickly.

Engines 4 × 1,200 hp Pratt and Whitney Twin Wasp radial	
Wingspan 110 ft (33.5 m)	Length 67 ft 2 in (20.5 m)
Top speed 300 mph (483 kph)	Crew 10
Armament 10 × .50-in machine-guns; maximum bombload 12,800 lb (5,800 kg)	

Captain, navigator, 1st wireless operator, flight engineer

Mid-upper gun turret

Rear gun turret

2nd wireless operator/air gunner

H2S downward-looking radar blister below fuselage

Avro Lancaster

Introduced to operations in March 1942, Lancasters of RAF Bomber Command flew some 156,000 sorties in World War II, dropping 609,000 tons of bombs. Originally designed to carry 4,000 lb (1,800 kg) of bombs, the Lancaster was adapted to carry much larger loads, culminating in the 22,000-lb (9,980-kg) Grand Slam bomb. Primarily a night bomber, the Lancaster flew some daring daylight operations, including a raid on Augsburg in which two Victoria Crosses were won. By 1945, Lancasters were routinely flying by day in loose formations, or "gaggles".

Engines 4 × 1,460 hp Rolls Royce Merlin	
Wingspan 102 ft (31.09 m)	Length 69 ft 6 in (21.18 m)
Top speed 275 mph (442 kph)	Crew 7
Armament 10 × .303-in machine-guns; maximum normal bombload 14,000 lb (6,350 kg)	

Messerschmitt Bf 110C-4

The Me 110 failed as an escort fighter in the Battle of Britain but proved successful as a night fighter over the Reich, particularly when equipped with radar and twin upward-firing "Schrage Musik" (Jazz Music) cannon mounted behind the cockpit. Some 6,000 Me 110s were produced by 1945.

Engines 2 × 1,475 hp Daimler Benz	
Wingspan 53 ft 4 in (16.25 m)	Length 39 ft 7 in (12.07 m)
Top speed 349 mph (560 kph)	Crew 3
Armament 2 × 30-mm cannon, 2 × 20-mm cannon 2 × 7.92-mm machine-guns	

Focke Wulf 190A-8

One of the great fighters of the war, the radial-engined FW 190 made its combat debut in the late summer of 1941, easily outclassing the Spitfire V. It was successfully adapted as a fighter-bomber and as a heavily armoured ground attack aircraft and in this role could carry up to 1,100 lb (500 kg) of bombs.

Engine 1 × 1,700 hp BMW radial	
Wingspan 34 ft 6 in (10.5 m)	Length 29 ft 5in (9 m)
Top speed 408 mph (656 kph)	Crew 1
Armament 2 × 13-mm machine-guns, 4 × 20-mm cannon	

"The sight approaching Hamburg was fantastic. It was as if a black swathe had been cut through a sea of light and flashes."

FLIGHT LIEUTENANT V WOOD, 12 SQUADRON, ON THE HAMBURG RAID OF JULY 24/25, 1943

The area bombing campaign reached its climax at the end of July 1943. The target was Hamburg, Germany's second city. For this operation, Bomber Command deployed a new weapon, codenamed "Window". More than a million metallized strips (the USAAF called the strips "Chaff") were dropped to jam German radar. On the night of July 24/25, Window achieved complete tactical surprise, disabling the Kammhuber Line and Hamburg's defenses. The raid overwhelmed the city's firefighting forces, dislocating communications and blocking streets.

Bomber Command struck Hamburg in force again on July 27/28. Over 700 aircraft set off a fire storm in eastern Hamburg. It reached its height in the small hours of the morning amid scenes of horror which were to be repeated in Dresden and Tokyo in 1945. A million of Hamburg's citizens fled into the countryside. Some 215,000 homes were destroyed, along with 600 factories and countless smaller workshops. There were two more raids on Hamburg, the last flown by 730 aircraft on August 2/3. The raids caused two months' lost industrial production, but many of Hamburg's aircraft plants,

Aftermath of the Hamburg air raids

In the four big raids of July and August 1943, 8,334 tons of bombs were dropped on Hamburg. Despite the unprecedented devastation, the city recovered with remarkable speed.

which lay at the heart of the Pointblank Directive, were quickly dispersed across the Reich by armaments minister, Albert Speer. Nor was the city's production of U-boats seriously hampered.

THE BATTLE OF BERLIN

Although Harris was happy to pay lipservice to Pointblank, he remained a fierce advocate of the area bombing of Germany's cities. On November 3, 1943 he told Churchill, "We can wreck Berlin from end to end if the US Army Air Force come in on it. It will cost us between 400 and 500 aircraft. It will cost Germany the war." The Battle of Berlin began on November 18 with a raid by 440 Lancasters. It was the first of 16 major raids on Berlin, combined with 19 attacks on other German cities. It was the last great drive to win the war by area bombing.

Berlin was too distant a target, perpetually cloud-covered and too big and well-defended. After the raids of August, the Germans had adopted new night-fighter tactics, in which twin-engined fighters were directed into the bomber streams by ground controllers. These tactics proved highly effective, particularly when the fighters were fitted with SN-2 radar, which was not affected by Window.

I set off in the direction of Hammerbrook because everything was still burning in the direction of the school where our post was. The air was hardly breathable and my injuries hurt hellishly. Dead lay everywhere. Most were naked because their clothes had been burnt away. All had become shrunken, really small, because of the heat.

HERBERT BRECHT, A TEENAGED FIREFIGHTER, ON THE HAMBURG FIRESTORM OF 27/28 JULY, 1943

On the night of March 30/31, 1944 Bomber Command mounted a raid on Nuremberg in which 95 out of 795 aircraft failed to return. This was the end of the Battle of Berlin, in which overall losses had now reached nearly 600 aircraft. Even Harris had to accept that such losses could not be sustained. In April 1944 he considered providing his bombers with escort fighters. Even under cover of darkness, Bomber Command was discovering what the USAAF had learned by day: before it could strike at the heart of the Third Reich, it had first to defeat the Luftwaffe.

OPERATIONS IN ASIA AND THE PACIFIC

JUNE 1943–JUNE 1944

From June to October 1943 the Allies recorded minimal gains in the Pacific. In November, however, the American offensive on the Gilberts heralded the start of a drive across the Central and Southwest Pacific. It produced in June 1944 an overwhelming victory in the greatest carrier battle in history.

1943

JUNE 21–22 US landings on New Georgia	**JUNE 22** US landings on Woodlark and Kiriwana, off eastern New Guinea
JULY 2–6 American landings on New Georgia; drawn surface action in Kula Gulf	**JUNE 29–30** US and Australian landings at Nassau Bay, near Salamaua, New Guinea
JULY 13 Surface action off Kolombangara; drawn	**JULY 22** Start of Japanese evacuation of garrison on Kiska in the Aleutians
AUGUST 25 New Georgia cleared of Japanese	**AUGUST 6–27** US victory in surface action in Vella Gulf, and landings on Vella Lavella and Arundel, central Solomons
SEPTEMBER 3–16 US landings at Nadzab and occupation of Salamaua; Allied capture of Lae	
OCTOBER 2 Finschhafen captured by Australians	**OCTOBER 6** US landings on Kolombangara, central Solomons; drawn surface action off Vella Lavella. Start of air campaign to neutralize Rabaul
NOVEMBER 1–2 Allied landings on Bougainville	
NOVEMBER 5–11 Raids by US carrier- and land-based bombers on Rabaul	**NOVEMBER 10** Operation Galvanic, aimed at Gilbert Islands: start of US drive across Central Pacific
NOVEMBER 10–28 Landings on Tarawa and Makin in the Gilberts. Makin secured on Nov 23, Tarawa on Nov 28	
DECEMBER 15–30 Allied landings in western New Britain. Airfield at Cape Gloucester secured by Dec 30	

1944

	JANUARY 31 US launches Operation Flintlock against Marshall Islands. US occupation of Majuro and landings on Kwajalein.
FEBRUARY 6 Japanese diversionary offensive in the Arakan	
FEBRUARY 15 New Zealand troops land on Green Island	**FEBRUARY 17–18** Following US carrier raid, Japanese forces withdraw from naval base at Truk to Singapore
FEBRUARY 17–23 US landings in the Marshalls and occupation of Eniwetok Atoll	**MARCH 30–31** Operation Desecrate: US carrier raid on Palaus
MARCH 4–6 Start of Japanese offensive into northeast India	**APRIL 3** Start of Japanese siege of Kohima; broken Apr 18–20
APRIL 2 Start of Japanese siege of Imphal	**APRIL 17** Start of first phase of Japanese Ichi-Go offensive in China
APRIL 22 American landings at Aitape and Hollandia in Dutch New Guinea	**MAY 17** US-Chinese forces take Myitkyina airfield
	MAY 27 Japanese troops cross Yangtze below Ichang to launch second phase of Ichi-Go offensive
JUNE 15 First combat mission flown by B-29 Superfortresses, from bases in India against Bangkok	**JUNE 15** American landings on Saipan in the Marianas
JUNE 19–20 Battle of the Philippine Sea. Japanese lose over 400 aircraft in attack on task force supporting landings in Marianas	**JUNE 22** British relief of Imphal

▓ The Solomon Islands and New Guinea	▓ Campaigns in China, Burma, and India	▓ Other theaters in the Pacific War

AMERICAN OFFENSIVES IN THE PACIFIC

IN THE FIFTEEN MONTHS after the defeats in the Coral Sea in May and off Midway in June 1942, the Japanese suffered a series of reverses in eastern New Guinea, in the lower and central Solomons, and on Attu Island in the Aleutians. Still, the Japanese high command could take comfort from the fact that these defeats were local and in distant, remote theaters. None of the islands or places that had been lost possessed any real strategic significance. In addition, the Americans' very slow advances in the central Solomons and their lack of any real

Taking the airfield at Tarawa
US Marines move out from a beachhead to assault the Japanese airstrip at Tarawa. The battle for Tarawa cost 1,000 American lives and had a profound effect on public opinion at home.

progress in front of Lae and Salamaua in eastern New Guinea after February 1943 seemed to augur well for continuing Japanese resistance (see map page 176). After nearly two years of conflict they still held the Americans at arm's length from areas of political, economic, or military importance.

In reality, however, in the last quarter of 1943 the situation in the Pacific was transformed in two ways. First, in the Southwest Pacific the Americans adopted the island-hopping technique for the first time when they landed on Vella Lavella and

Attacking Japanese shipping
A B-25 Mitchell bomber attacks a Japanese freighter in Rabaul Harbour, New Britain. US strategy effectively isolated and neutralized the Japanese base there.

of six raids between November 5, 1943, and January 4, 1944. The raids effectively neutralized Rabaul, and thereafter the Americans completed the isolation of the base. In February 1944 they landed on Green Island and in the Admiralties, after which they also moved against central New Guinea. Rabaul itself remained in Japanese hands until September 1945, but the forces left there were helpless.

THE CENTRAL PACIFIC

In any case, by February 1944 the main focus of strategic attention had shifted northward. The raids on Rabaul in November 1943 were part of a series of attacks that paved the way for the main American effort in the Central Pacific. No fewer than six fleet, five light, and eight escort carriers of the Fifth Fleet were concentrated in support of landings on Makin and Tarawa in the Gilbert Islands on November 20. Both islands were secured within three days.

Tarawa came to acquire a certain notoriety in American folklore as a symbol of the supposed costliness of such amphibious landings. Photographs published in the press of corpses floating in the sea reinforced the image of what were dubbed the "bloody beaches of Tarawa." Despite the shocked public reaction in the United States to the cost of the landing, the casualty list—1,009 dead and 2,101 wounded—pales into insignificance when compared with the average of 19,014 dead incurred by the Soviet Union every day of the Great Patriotic War.

thereby bypassed the Japanese garrisons on New Georgia and the island of Kolombangara. The development marked a change in American policy: their goal was no longer the recapture of the Japanese base at Rabaul in New Britain. Instead, they would side-step and isolate what should have been the keystone of Japanese defense. Second, during 1943 the US Navy commissioned into service a tonnage of warships equivalent to the size of the entire Japanese fleet in December 1941. The acquisition of carriers in such numbers as virtually to ensure victory allowed the Americans to launch Operation Galvanic, an offensive in the Gilbert Islands, in November 1943. This was the first operation in a drive across the Central Pacific (see map page 255).

The policy of island-hopping and the American superiority in carrier numbers came together in November 1943, when Rabaul

was reinforced by Japanese carrier air groups and cruiser formations detached from the fleet anchorage at Truk to the north. Warned by signals intelligence, the Americans used carrier task groups to savage both the carrier groups and the cruisers in a series

Aftermath of Tarawa
Dead US Marines lie among the wreckage of vehicles on the beach at Tarawa, November 22, 1943. The Japanese defenders were well dug in and fiercely resisted the US assault.

Attack on Nadzab, September 5, 1943
The first airborne assault of the Pacific War on Nadzab was key to the Allied campaign to seize Lae and central New Guinea. Paratroops from the US 503rd Parachute Infantry descend from C-47 planes, while in the distance another battalion descends against a smokescreen.

"The enemy received all his supplies from the air, while we had to swallow our tears and throw away strategic positions because of supply difficulties."

LIEUTENANT COLONEL YOSHIHARA TSUTOMU, CHIEF OF STAFF, JAPANESE 18TH ARMY, ON THE FIGHTING AT LAE

AMERICANS GAIN THE UPPER HAND

On New Guinea, meanwhile, the Allies were helping to complete the isolation of Rabaul. With American forces having secured Lae in central New Guinea during September 1943 and the Australians having taken Finschhafen the following month, December saw American forces landing at Cape Gloucester on New Britain, at the opposite end of the island from Rabaul.

In January 1944 the Americans moved against the Marshall Islands in the Western Pacific. When the island of Kwajalein had been taken, an American carrier force—with four fleet and six light carriers, plus six new battleships—launched an offensive throughout the Western Pacific. With contributions from both submarines and surface units, the attack on the Japanese anchorage at Truk in the Carolines on February 17 resulted in the destruction of three light cruisers, three destroyers, and three minor warships,

Bombs over New Guinea
Bombs from aircraft of the Fifth US Air Force fall on Hollandia in New Guinea. Some Japanese units on New Guinea stubbornly refused to surrender, even after defeat.

along with 32 service auxiliaries, merchantmen, and oilers. The shipping sunk—almost 200,000 tons—made this the most costly single day in naval history.

After the collapse of Japanese resistance in the Marshalls, it was clear that the fleet could not sustain itself at Truk. The fleet abandoned the anchorage, and its shipping, and established itself at Singapore. The new base was close to supplies of oil and gave the Japanese carriers the chance to train groups to replace those lost at Rabaul. Placing a safe distance between the fleet and American carrier formations, however, was achieved only at the cost of giving the Americans a free hand in the Western Pacific.

The result was devastating. On March 30, 1944, an American carrier raid on Koror in the Palaus destroyed 11 minor warships and no fewer than 22 service auxiliaries, oilers, and merchantmen, a total

of almost 130,000 tons. Meanwhile, Liberators from the Fifth Air Force struck Hollandia on the north coast of Dutch New Guinea. Repeated raids in the first half of April destroyed the Japanese 6th Air Division, and paved the way for American landings at Hollandia and Aitape on April 22.

WESTERN NEW GUINEA

The ease with which the Japanese air and ground forces were overwhelmed in these exchanges provided encouragement for the Americans to look west. They recast their plans to provide for landings on Wakde Island and in the Arare–Toem area of western New Guinea on May 17 and on Biak 10 days later. At the same time the Japanese, in the middle of enforced command changes, recognized that they could no longer defend their intended centers of resistance. A plan to fall back to new positions was compromised, however, by the loss of the equivalent of a division when US submarines sank transport vessels at sea. The Japanese were forced instead to base their resistance on Sorong and Halmahera. In just 17 days after American forces had landed at Hollandia, the Japanese high command had in effect drawn back its proposed front line a distance of over 1,000 miles (1,600 km).

AMPHIBIOUS LANDINGS

AMPHIBIOUS WARFARE has been used since the time of the Ancient Greeks. The American armed forces developed the technique in the interwar years, learning much from the mistakes made by the British during their disastrous 1915 landings at Gallipoli in World War I. By 1941 the Americans were well rehearsed in getting thousands of soldiers and their equipment from sea to shore, often under intense enemy fire. Such landings were complex, however, and sometimes did go wrong, as they did at Guadacanal, where men were separated from their units and units from their supplies.

The US forces were formidably well equipped. In the course of World War II the Americans produced 23,398 units of the 36-ft (11-m) Landing Craft, Vehicle Personnel (LCVP), the standard assault vessel that could carry 36 combat-equipped soldiers or 3.5 tons of cargo. They also built 11,392 of the 50-ft (15.24-m) Landing Craft, Mechanized (LCM), which was designed to carry tanks and other armored vehicles, and more than 1,000 of the Landing Craft, Infantry (LCI)—158-ft (48.15-m) sea-going amphibious vessels capable of carrying as many as 200 men. Landing craft were also used as fighting vessels, and many were equipped to provide fire support with rockets, machine-guns, mortars, and even large deck guns.

Amphibious landings were always risky, despite intense preparation. At Tarawa, for example, despite the "softening up" of the landing zone with extensive shellfire, the landing craft ran aground on reefs and the Marines were forced to wade hundreds of yards through the surf across razor-sharp coral.

American amphibious operations increased in size and complexity throughout the Pacific war. The final assault, on the Japanese island of Okinawa, in April 1945, involved 318 US combat ships, 1,139 auxiliary vessels, 1,000 amphibious vehicles, and 500,000 men.

Landing Vehicle, Tank (LVT)
The LVT was an amphibious armored vehicle designed to carry troops into combat. Tracked like a tank, it also provided fire support. Some were equipped with flame-throwers.

Crew/cargo compartment could carry a load of 2.5 tons

76 YP 61

Six-wheel drive — *Tyre pressure could be controlled by the driver from the dashboard*

DUKW
This US amphibious vehicle was capable of carrying 25 soldiers and their equipment. At sea it could maintain a speed of 5 knots.

Disembarkation
US troops storm ashore in the Pacific. The skills of amphibious operations became better honed as more were launched. Despite rigorous training, there was no substitute for experience.

Until this stage of the conflict Japanese policy had defined a perimeter that ran from Saipan through Truk to Timor as the line on which they would make their main defensive effort. Now they established a new defensive line stretching from Saipan through the Carolines to the Vogelkop Peninsula in New Guinea. The Japanese high command ordered forces east of the line to resist American advances in order to buy time for the preparation of defenses to the west.

The Japanese Navy now had five fleet and four light carriers and some 450 carrier aircraft being readied for battle. It was hoped that land-based and carrier-borne aircraft would be able to complement one another and compensate for their separate numerical inferiority to any American carrier force that moved into the Western Pacific. The Japanese also hoped that the next American move might take enemy ships in the direction of the Palau Islands, where they could be attacked by land-based aircraft from the Marianas, the Carolines, the Philippines, and western New Guinea. This second hope proved to be self-delusion.

In New Guinea, American forces came ashore as planned at Arare and Wakde on May 17–18 and on Biak on May 27. Despite having abandoned their former defensive line, the Japanese chose to give battle in defense of Biak. The island's garrison continued to offer serious resistance until July 22, and it was not until August 20 that the Americans declared the island secured. But this resistance, during which Japanese defenders had to resort to cannibalism to survive, was isolated and could not be supported. The Japanese, meanwhile, moved about 170 aircraft to airstrips in the western Carolines and on the Vogelkop Peninsula in readiness for operations, and a battle force sailed from the Philippines on June 10. But malaria swept through the aircrews sent to the south and Japanese land-based air power was neutralized without battle.

At the same time as the Japanese battle force arrived in Batjan on June 11, American carriers struck at Guam, Saipan, and Tinian in the Mariana Islands. The Japanese at once recognized that they would have to fight in defense of the Marianas. On June 12 they suspended the defense of Biak and ordered their forces to regroup in readiness for the imminent sortie into the Philippine Sea.

THE BATTLE FOR SAIPAN

American formations came ashore on Saipan on June 15. On the same day 47 B-29 Superfortresses, operating from India via the Chengtu airfield in southern Hunan in China, bombed the steel factory in Yawata on Kyushu. Aside from raids on the Kuriles, this marked the first raid on the Japanese Home Islands since the Doolittle Raid of April 1942. The coincidence of timing was appropriate: once in American possession, the Marianas would become home to the strategic Allied bombing campaign that would begin in November 1944 and that would result in widespread devastation throughout the Japanese Home Islands after March 1945.

The campaigns on the various islands in the Marianas proved very short. Saipan was declared secure on July 9, but in fact the Americans had cleared all but the rugged northern tip of the island within seven days of the landings. The campaign was effectively over after June 30, with the exception of a final *banzai* charge—named for a Japanese war cry—around Makunsha on July 7. The 32,000-strong Japanese garrison died almost to the last man. Over the previous two years the Americans had become familiar with the practice of Japanese defenders fighting to the death. The situation on Saipan, however, was different in one crucial respect. It was the first place visited by the Pacific war that was home to a sizable civilian population. More than 22,000 of these civilians chose to join the service personnel in death rather than allow themselves to be taken prisoner. Whole families perished, with parents killing their children before killing themselves. Most of the suicides took place on two high bluffs: the 1,000-ft (305-m) Suicide Cliff, over which hundreds of people threw themselves onto the jagged rocks below, and the 80-ft (24-m) drop into the ocean near Marpi Point. There the dead and dying lay so thick in the water that they fouled the propellers of destroyers trying to rescue survivors. In spite of this, hundreds of civilians were plucked to safety.

GREAT MARIANAS TURKEY SHOOT

The first days of the campaign on Saipan saw the covering American carrier task group assault various Japanese bases in the southern Bonins and on Guam and Rota. The Japanese had mustered five fleet and four light carriers, in the hope that their carrier-borne and land-based air formations would complement one another and ensure a rough numerical balance with US carrier aircraft. But by destroying more than 150 aircraft on various islands before June 16, the American carriers had broken the effectiveness of Japanese land-based aviation three days before

ANTIBIOTICS

THE USE OF ANTIBIOTICS—SUBSTANCES DERIVED from living organisms, usually bacteria or molds, that kill microorganisms or inhibit their growth—dramatically reduced the number of wounded who died in World War II. The most important of these substances was penicillin, discovered in 1929 by Scottish biologist Alexander Fleming. During the early years of the war Britain's laboratories could not cope with the demand for penicillin, so the United States agreed to produce it on behalf of the British. It was a timely decision, since only six months later the United States was dragged into the war by the Japanese attack on Pearl Harbor and needed penicillin for its own wounded service personnel. The first batches of American antibiotics were administered in 1943 to men of the US Eighth Air Force stationed in Britain.

Penicillin was rationed at first, but by 1944–45 plentiful stocks became available. Although it is impossible to say how many lives were saved by antibiotics—improved surgical techniques also played a part—only 4 percent of the wounded died, the lowest figure in military history until that point.

A rare drug
An early ampule of penicillin produced at the Squibb Plant in New Brunswick, New Jersey. Because of its rarity, penicillin was restricted to military uses.

Saving lives
American medics treat casualties in a portable surgical unit in Burma. Penicillin counters bacteria that cause infections such as pneumonia and diphtheria.

Making penicillin, the "wonder drug"
Bottles of liquid media are planted with penicillin seed by means of a spray gun under sterile conditions. There are several hundred different species of mold, but only one was suitable for yielding the powerful substance that combatted bacterial infection.

Casualty on the beach
A US Marine doubles up as a Japanese sniper's bullet strikes its target during the American landings on Saipan in June 1944.

Physical conditions of many were pitiful. Most of them were skeleton thin, as they had no nourishment for many days. Many were suffering from shock caused by the shelling and bombing, and fright because they did not have the vaguest idea as to what we would do to them. Civilians caught in a war that was not of their making.

ROBERT F. GRAF, MARINE PRIVATE, ON TAKING CIVILIAN JAPANESE PRISONERS ON SAIPAN

the Battle of the Philippine Sea was even joined. The damage caused by the attacks wrecked the Japanese intention to defend the Marianas. Moreover, by choosing to stand off the Marianas and to fight defensively, US admiral Raymond Spruance was able to concentrate a massive superiority of numbers, specifically fighters. This allowed him to give battle in front

of and above the five formations that made up Task Force 58. What made the American tactics possible was radar and radio facilities, which meant that they were able to locate and report the position of enemy forces. The Japanese did not realize the effectiveness of such technology, and had no answer to it.

The Japanese carrier force, having refueled the previous day, found the American carrier force some 200 miles (320 km) west of the Marianas late on June 18. It was too late to launch a strike operation, partly because of the hazards of landing on carriers in the dark. The next day, however, the Japanese had not managed to get their aircraft into the air before they had lost two fleet carriers, both torpedoed by submarines. Those attacks that were mounted fared disastrously. Only the first and third strike missions managed to make proper contact with American groups, and they had little effect. In the course of the day just two American carriers and one battleship incurred only minor damage. Meanwhile American aircraft accounted for some 80 Japanese land-based

aircraft on or over the southern Marianas and about 360 of the 450 carrier aircraft with which the Japanese had opened proceedings. The Americans themselves lost just 18 fighters and 12 other aircraft. So one-sided were the air battles of June 19, 1944, that they came to be dubbed "the Great Marianas Turkey Shoot." The following day saw the Americans sink a third carrier, and the Japanese fleet was reduced to just 35 aircraft. The battle was a defeat from which Japanese carrier aviation never recovered. For the Americans, victory opened the route across the Pacific to the Philippines and Formosa.

THE ALLIES' GREAT OFFENSIVES

1944

THE SECOND HALF OF 1944 WITNESSED DRAMATIC DEVELOPMENTS IN EVERY THEATER OF WAR. FOLLOWING THE SEIZURE OF THE MARIANAS, THE AMERICANS LANDED IN THE PHILIPPINES AND FINALLY CRUSHED THE JAPANESE FLEET. A MAJOR SOVIET OFFENSIVE ALMOST DESTROYED THE GERMAN ARMY GROUP CENTER AND REACHED POLAND'S VISTULA RIVER. IN ITALY THE WESTERN ALLIES ENTERED ROME AND ADVANCED NORTHWARD. FINALLY THE LONG-AWAITED SECOND FRONT IN CONTINENTAL EUROPE WAS OPENED WITH THE ALLIED LANDINGS IN NORMANDY, FRANCE, ON JUNE 6.

7

US troops landing on Leyte
A long campaign to drive the Japanese out of the Philippines began with the landings on Leyte in October 1944. The Japanese reaction to the landings led to the last major naval battle in the Pacific, in which the Japanese fleet was totally crippled.

THE AXIS IN RETREAT

IT WAS CLEAR BY LATE 1943 THAT THERE COULD BE ONLY ONE OUTCOME OF THE WAR AGAINST NAZI GERMANY AND JAPAN. MUCH, HOWEVER, STILL NEEDED TO BE DONE, AND TOUGH CHALLENGES AND HARD FIGHTING LAY AHEAD FOR THE ALLIES. WHILE THE PACIFIC WAS VERY MUCH THE PROVINCE OF THE AMERICANS, THE WAR IN EUROPE REQUIRED EVER MORE CAREFUL COORDINATION BETWEEN THE SOVIET UNION AND ITS WESTERN ALLIES.

BY THE MIDDLE OF 1944 Japan's situation was growing increasingly parlous with, in particular, the lack of raw materials beginning to make itself very much felt. The passage of rubber, tin, oil, and other vital items from Southeast Asia had all but dried up as a result of a campaign waged by US submarines—a campaign so successful that a lack of targets would result in the withdrawal of some submarines from the Pacific. Massive B-29 bombers, flying from airfields in China, were also beginning to bomb Japan itself. Admiral Chester Nimitz's advance across the Central Pacific had reached the Marianas, which were secured by early August. He had also broken the back of Japanese naval airpower at the Battle of the Philippine Sea in June 1944. General Douglas MacArthur had isolated Rabaul, the main Japanese base in the Southwest Pacific and had almost completed the clearance of New Guinea. He was now planning to liberate the Philippines, beginning with the island of Leyte.

US OPERATIONS IN THE PACIFIC

Nimitz had been ordered to prepare an assault on Formosa (Taiwan). However, during the summer of 1944 it became apparent that the Japanese were reinforcing Formosa. They had also launched an offensive in China that was beginning to threaten the US air bases there. In view of this, the US planners decided that operations would have to be accelerated. They even considered bypassing the Philippines and Formosa and launching a direct assault on the Japanese Home Islands. Both Nimitz and MacArthur objected to this, arguing that it would be impossible without securing the southern and central Philippines first. MacArthur also believed that if the northern and main island in

the Philippines, Luzon, could be seized, a landing on Formosa would be unnecessary. Nimitz disagreed, arguing that an attack on Formosa would remove the need to occupy Luzon. In early October 1944 it was decided that after securing Leyte, MacArthur was to liberate Luzon, while Nimitz prepared to attack Iwo Jima, followed by Okinawa. The projected Formosa operation was left in abeyance.

MacArthur's landing on Leyte on October 20 provoked an immediate Japanese response. The Combined Fleet set sail, its object the destruction of the US Third and Seventh Fleets, and the amphibious shipping in Leyte Gulf. It was to prove a disaster. The Japanese lost 28 warships, including four carriers. The battle also witnessed a further indication of growing Japanese desperation—the extensive use of suicide aircraft to destroy Allied ships. It was a tactic that was to be used increasingly, but it had little effect on the American advance. MacArthur succeeded in securing Leyte before the end of December and prepared to land on Luzon.

The other active theater of war in the Far East was Burma, which was essentially run by the British. After the gloom of 1942, the first Chindit expedition deep behind the Japanese lines in Burma had at least shown that British troops could match their opponents in the jungle. The time had now come to begin

> "…there will come moments in which the tension between the Allies will become so great that the break will happen…We must only wait for the moment…"

ADOLF HITLER IN A MILITARY CONFERENCE AT RASTENBERG, EAST PRUSSIA, AUGUST 31, 1944

driving the Japanese out. Lord Louis Mountbatten, the Allied commander, explained his strategy at the conference convened by Churchill and Roosevelt at Cairo in late November 1943. The Chinese premier, Chiang Kai-shek, was also present. Mountbatten envisaged an offensive in Burma's coastal region, the Arakan, a further Chindit operation in central Burma, and an assault by the Chinese into northern Burma. However, Chiang Kai-shek would only agree to the last if there was a major amphibious operation in the Bay of Bengal to capture a port and so improve the supply of equipment to his forces. It was also decided at the conference to maintain the offensive in Italy, even if it meant delaying the planned cross-Channel invasion of Normandy—Operation Overlord—and to give more help to the partisans in the Balkans.

CONFERENCE AT TEHRAN

Churchill and Roosevelt then left for Tehran, in Iran, to meet Stalin. Overlord was foremost on Stalin's mind, and he made it clear that he would accept no postponement to the agreed date of May 1944. While he liked the idea of a simultaneous landing in the south of France, he dismissed the Western Allies' Italian and Balkan strategy. Churchill and Roosevelt therefore confirmed Overlord for May 1944, and, in return, Stalin agreed to mount a simultaneous major offensive on the Eastern Front to prevent the Germans from switching troops to the west. The Western

Allies remained eager for the early capture of Rome. This included mounting an amphibious landing south of the city, which meant that it was impossible to provide sufficient amphibious shipping for a major operation in the Bay of Bengal. This had to be postponed, to the displeasure of the Chinese premier.

Even so, the British began to advance into the Arakan in January 1944. They were aware that the Japanese had been planning an invasion of India, and although they were ready for it, there were four months of bitter fighting before the Japanese finally halted their attacks in July 1944. From this point, the British embarked on an offensive against the Japanese. The Chinese began to advance into northern Burma, while other US-led Chinese forces built a road from India to connect with China.

EASTERN FRONT OFFENSIVES

On the Eastern Front the Soviet Union launched a massive offensive—Operation Bagration—in Byelorussia on June 22. Thrusting into Poland, the Red Army tore the heart out of the German Army Group Center. As Soviet forces closed on Warsaw, the Polish Home Army staged an uprising against the German garrison, but the Red Army now halted its offensive, leaving the Poles to their fate. Farther south, the Red Army advanced into Romania and Bulgaria, forcing them to change sides. It also crossed the border into Hungary, Hitler's last remaining ally in southeast Europe.

PLANNING FOR D-DAY

For the Western Allies the high point of 1944 was undoubtedly D-Day, June 6, when they launched their invasion of Normandy in France. Their attention had been firmly focused on such an invasion from the end of 1943, but it was an operation that had taken almost four years to plan and prepare. Even while Britain had faced invasion in the summer and fall of 1940, Churchill had

The invasion of Normandy
A British-manned six-wheel amphibious vehicle sets out for the shore during the Allied landings on beaches in Normandy in June 1944. While the landings themselves met with limited German opposition, it was to take many weeks for the Allied forces to break out of Normandy.

been looking for ways to strike back at Hitler. On October 5, 1940, he had issued a directive calling for plans to be drawn up for an assault on continental Europe, culminating in an advance to the Ruhr in Germany. At the time Britain had lacked the resources, especially in amphibious capability, to make this possible in the short term.

Late in 1941 the Combined Commanders committee was set up. Consisting of senior naval, army, and air force officers, it became the focus for planning an invasion of continental Europe. It began to gather intelligence on the German defenses in western Europe and to consider where an assault force might be landed. Soviet calls for the opening of a "second front" and US insistence that a cross-Channel invasion should be the

Allied priority concentrated minds still further on the problem. The British, however, were certain that an early invasion was not possible. This was seemingly reinforced by the abortive raid by a largely Canadian force on the French port of Dieppe in August 1942. Few troops managed to get off the beach and casualties were very heavy. But the lessons learned were to prove invaluable.

The Allies now pursued their Mediterranean strategy and the numerous landing operations which took place served to develop the amphibious warfare techniques that were an essential prerequisite for a successful invasion. The decision at the Trident

Conference in Washington, D.C., in May 1943 that a cross-Channel invasion would be mounted in May 1944 accelerated planning. The Combined Commanders committee had concluded that Normandy provided the best option, and an Anglo–US team drew up a detailed plan on this basis.

GERMAN DEFENSES IN THE WEST

On the German side, work had begun in 1940 to build what Hitler was to call the Atlantic Wall—a series of coastal batteries and strongpoints stretching from northern Norway to the Pyrenees. Aside from this, German attention was fixed firmly on the

Hungarian Jews rounded up by SS
In June 1944 the Third Reich was under increasing pressure from all sides, and many of its extermination camps were being liberated by the Red Army. Yet the policy of eradicating the Jews continued, with some 450,000 Hungarian Jews being rounded up between March and July to be sent to their deaths in the camps.

Eastern Front and its forces in western Europe were generally low grade. Indeed, France itself became a sanatorium for divisions decimated in the Soviet Union. Once they had been rebuilt, they returned to the east. Not until the late fall of 1943 was the growing threat of a cross-Channel invasion recognized. Hitler sent Rommel on a tour of the Atlantic Wall and the German forces in France and the Low Countries began to be strengthened.

By the end of 1943 the Allied command team for the invasion of Normandy, Operation Overlord, was in place. Eisenhower, the overall commander, and Montgomery, the groundforce commander, enlarged the existing plan by insisting on an initial assault by five, rather than three, divisions. But much still needed to be done. First, the Allies had to be sure of air supremacy over the landing area. To this end, their air forces set about a systematic degradation of the Luftwaffe in France and the Low Countries. They then switched their attention to the goal of sealing off Normandy —by attacking roads and railroads—in order to prevent the rapid deployment of German reinforcements. They had to be careful, though, to scatter their attacks so as not to draw the attention of the Germans to the assault area.

This itself was part of an elaborate deception plan code-named Bodyguard. One element of this was to pose a threat to Norway, which was partially achieved by stationing a mythical British army in Scotland. Similarly, the equally make-believe US First Army Group was stationed in southeast England to make the Germans believe that the attack would come across the Pas de Calais, the narrowest part of the English Channel. These parts of Bodyguard were remarkably successful in encouraging the Germans to maintain an unnecessarily large garrison in Norway and in believing that the Pas de Calais was the most likely point of attack by the Allies. Among the lessons learned from Dieppe was that to land at a port was to court disaster, since it was likely to be heavily fortified. Open beaches would have to be used, but this would create resupply problems. Two massive artificial harbors, called

Stalin, Roosevelt, and Churchill at Tehran
During their conference in Tehran, in November 1943, the three Allied leaders confirmed that there would be simultaneous assaults on Germany from east and west in the summer of 1944. Stalin also agreed to declare war on Japan once Germany had been vanquished.

Mulberries, were constructed, to deal with this problem. Positioned off the beaches, they would enable ships to land supplies and reinforcements. Fuel was taken care of through the construction of an underwater pipeline, PLUTO (Pipeline Under The Ocean). Another Dieppe lesson was the need for modified tanks that could get ashore with the leading assault troops and enable them to overcome obstacles on the beaches and beyond. A range of specialized armor was developed, among which were swimming tanks, bridge-layers, and tanks for clearing mines.

D-DAY POSTPONED

Because of the need to bring amphibious shipping back from the Mediterranean, D-Day was postponed until June 5. After the final invasion rehearsals on beaches in Britain, which resembled those in Normandy, the assault troops were deployed to sealed camps close to their embarkation ports. On May 31 the loading of the ships began and messages began to be broadcast to the French Resistance, which had an important role to play in helping to seal off Normandy from the Germans. All now depended on the uncertain weather.

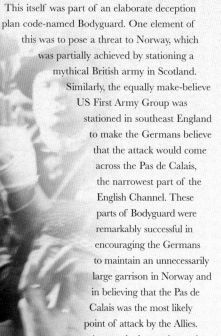

"He told me that if Overlord failed, the United States would have lost a battle, but for the British it would be the end of their military capability."

US PRESIDENTIAL ENVOY AVERELL HARRIMAN
ON A MEETING WITH CHURCHILL, MAY 4, 1944

THE WESTERN FRONT

JUNE 6, 1944–JANUARY 8, 1945

After six weeks of grim fighting in Normandy, the Allies broke out and it seemed that the war might be won before the end of 1944. Supply problems and a rejuvenated German defense, culminating in a major counteroffensive in December, put paid to this hope.

1944

JUNE 6
Allied forces make "D-Day" landings on beaches of Normandy

JUNE 10
British attempt to isolate and capture Caen begins

JUNE 13
German V-I flying bombs fired against Britain for first time

JUNE 27
Cherbourg is captured by US forces

JULY 18
Operation Goodwood–third British attempt to take Caen–is launched; Americans take St. Lô

JULY 20
Attempt made by group of German officers to take Hitler's life

JULY 25
American Operation Cobra–which is to lead to break-out from Normandy–is launched

AUGUST 1
US 3rd Army under Patton begins advance into Brittany and south toward Loire

AUGUST 15
Allied forces land in southern France between Toulon and Cannes

AUGUST 19
Uprising begins in Paris

AUGUST 25
French and US troops enter Paris

AUGUST 28
Toulon and Marseilles are liberated by Free French troops

AUGUST 31
British capture Amiens and cross Somme River

SEPTEMBER 1
Eisenhower assumes control from Montgomery of Allied ground operations in northwest Europe

SEPTEMBER 3
British liberate Brussels

SEPTEMBER 8
German V-2 rockets are fired against Britain for first time

SEPTEMBER 14
Hodges' US 1st Army reaches German border

SEPTEMBER 17
Operation Market Garden is launched by the British at Arnhem in Netherlands

SEPTEMBER 26
The failed Operation Market Garden comes to an end

SEPTEMBER 30
Boulogne and Calais fall to Allied troops

OCTOBER 18
Germans call up every able-bodied man aged 16–60 to the *Volkssturm* (Home Guard)

OCTOBER 21
Aachen, on German border, is taken by US forces

NOVEMBER 8
US 3rd Army begins offensive in Saarland in Germany

DECEMBER 4
US 3rd Army establishes bridgeheads over Saar River

DECEMBER 9
US 9th Army secures west bank of Roer in Germany between Brachelen and Altdorf

DECEMBER 15
Attempt by Americans to advance to Roer dams is halted

DECEMBER 16
Germans begin offensive in Ardennes in Belgium

DECEMBER 22
German offensive grinds to a halt. Bastogne is surrounded

DECEMBER 26
Bastogne is relieved by US forces

1945

JANUARY 3
Major Allied counterattack is launched

JANUARY 8
German 6th Panzer Army withdraws

▓ Allied advance through France Jun 6–Dec 15, 1944

▓ Allied advance through the Low Countries Sept 3–Dec 15, 1944

▓ Offensive and counteroffensive in the Ardennes Dec 16, 1944–Jan 8, 1945

▒ Other events

ADVANCE INTO NORTHWEST EUROPE

B Y THE END OF MAY the Allies were ready to launch Operation Overlord, their long-planned invasion of Normandy. It was intended to begin with landings on five beaches to the east of the Cotentin peninsula on June 5. However, by the 3rd it was clear that a depression was *en route* from the Atlantic, making conditions unfavorable for a landing. When it was predicted that the weather would be slightly better on the 6th, Eisenhower decided to postpone D-Day by 24 hours. He knew that he was taking a gamble and realized only too well that if disaster struck it might be many months before the invasion could be remounted.

Soon after dusk fell on June 5, 1944, two RAF bomber squadrons flew over the Straits of Dover and Boulogne, dropping strips of aluminum foil. This was intended to produce a picture on German radar screens of an invasion fleet heading for the Pas de Calais. Other bombers flew over the base of the Cotentin peninsula dropping dummy parachutes and devices to simulate small-arms fire to the south of where two US airborne divisions were to land.

AIRBORNE LANDINGS

Preceded by pathfinders to mark the drop zones on the ground, the US 82nd and 101st Airborne Divisions began to jump from their aircraft at 1:30 am on June 6. Their task was to secure the area west of Utah beach to the Merderet River and block German reinforcements moving to the beach. High winds, coupled with the fact that many of the pathfinders' indicators on the ground failed to work, resulted in very scattered drops. Once they landed,

Gliders taking part in the D-Day landings
Follow-up waves of the two US airborne divisions were brought in by glider. The operation was, however, fraught with risk, since crashes, collisions, and landings in the wrong place were frequently associated with gliders.

Beach landings at Omaha
Pinned down on the beach by enemy fire, US troops desperately seek cover behind German obstacles. Of the five beaches on which Allied troops landed on June 6, Omaha proved to be by far the most difficult to secure.

their fire onto the coastal batteries. The Germans opened fire first, engaging two destroyers off Utah at 5:05 am. The bombardment groups then set about pulverizing the defenses.

The assault troops now began to scramble down the netting on the sides of their transport vessels and into the flat-bottomed landing craft that pitched in the rough seas alongside. Many men had been seasick during the crossing and few had had much sleep. Patrol boats, equipped with radar and radio, guided in the landing craft, which were supported by other amphibious vessels armed with rocket batteries and guns.

LANDINGS AT UTAH AND OMAHA

Utah beach was the responsibility of General Lawton Collins' US VII Corps. The beach itself—1.5 miles (2.4 km) long—was backed by a sea wall. Behind lay a partially flooded area traversed by causeways, some of which were being secured by the 101st Airborne Division. Just one German battalion defended the beach, with one other in support. It had been intended to launch Sherman DD swimming tanks with the leading US troops 5 miles (8 km) out from the beach, but because of the conditions this was reduced to 1 mile (1.6 km).

D-Day "crickets"
Making a noise like crickets, these devices were used by paratroops to find each other.

the paratroops were disoriented and it took time for parties to gather. Luckily, the Germans, who believed the weather was too poor for the invasion to take place, were initially caught by surprise. This enabled the 101st to secure some of the exits from Utah and for the 82nd to capture Ste. Mère-Eglise, which would prove critical during the next 48 hours, but it was unable to seize crossings over the Merderet (see map page 222).

At the eastern end of the Allied landing area, the British 6th Airborne Division had a similar task. It was to land between the Dives and Orne Rivers, secure bridges over both, and provide a shoulder for the troops landing on Sword beach. The British paratroops experienced the same problems as the Americans over scattered drops. However, five out of six gliders full of infantry landed in precisely the right spot—close by bridges over the Orne River and Caen Canal, which were then captured intact. A coastal battery at Merville, which threatened the eastern flank of Sword beach, was also captured.

While the Allied airborne forces had been in action, aircraft from RAF Bomber Command had been attacking the coastal batteries. Low cloud, however, made accurate bombing difficult. With the coming of daylight, American bombers made similar attacks. Now came the turn of the Allied navies. Their first task was to clear the water of mines, and by 2:00 am minesweepers were hard at work. Each

of the five beaches had a naval bombardment force allocated to it, consisting of larger warships—battleships, monitors, cruisers—11,000 yd (10,000 m) offshore, and destroyers 5,500 yd (5,000 m) from the coast. Bombers laid a smokescreen to help protect the ships, and spotter planes were used to direct

DWIGHT D EISENHOWER

BETWEEN THE TWO WORLD WARS General Dwight D. Eisenhower (1890–1969) proved himself to be one of the most able officers of his generation. In December 1941 he was appointed deputy chief of the War Plans Division and then headed the Operations Branch in Washington, D.C. In June 1942 he took command of the US Army's European Theater of Operations and commanded the Allied forces in French northwest Africa that November. In February 1943 he became commander of the Allied forces in the Mediterranean. His easy charm and determination to weld the Allies into a unified force made him the natural choice to command the Allied Expeditionary Forces for the Normandy landings and the campaign in northwest Europe. He insisted on conducting the ground campaign himself, although he allowed Montgomery to exercise command in Normandy. This put him in conflict with the British general, who criticized his broad front approach. Eisenhower, however, stuck to his strategy. After the war he was US Army Chief of Staff and the first supreme allied commander of NATO. His career culminated in two terms as US President.

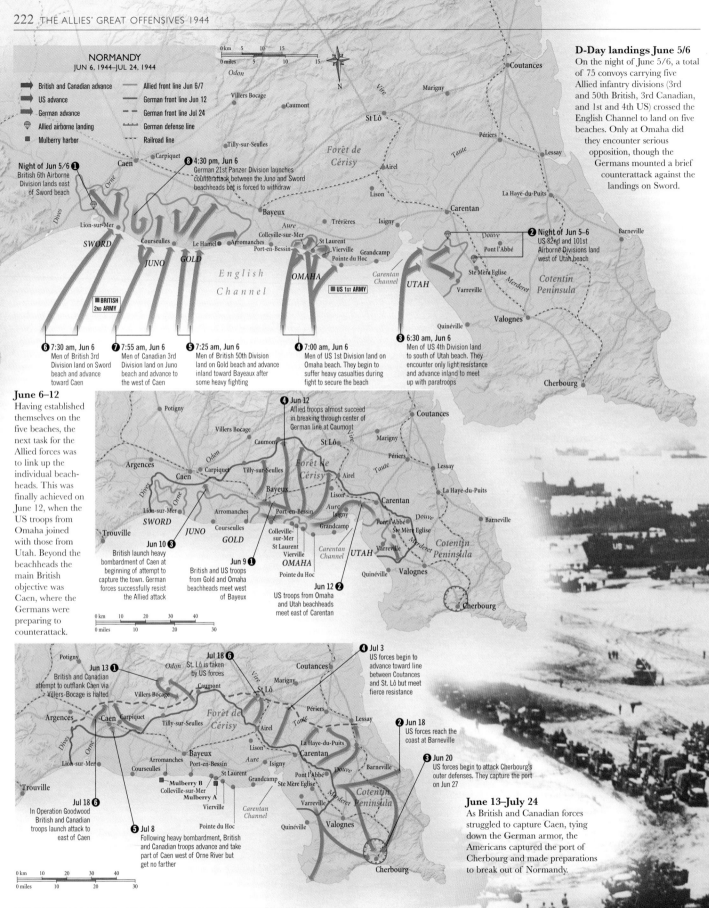

NORMANDY
JUN 6, 1944–JUL 24, 1944

- British and Canadian advance
- US advance
- German advance
- Allied airborne landing
- Mulberry harbor
- Allied front line Jun 6/7
- German front line Jun 12
- German front line Jul 24
- German defense line
- Railroad line

0 km 5 10 15
0 miles 5 10 15

N

D-Day landings June 5/6
On the night of June 5/6, a total of 75 convoys carrying five Allied infantry divisions (3rd and 50th British, 3rd Canadian, and 1st and 4th US) crossed the English Channel to land on five beaches. Only at Omaha did they encounter serious opposition, though the Germans mounted a brief counterattack against the landings on Sword.

Night of Jun 5/6 ❶
British 6th Airborne Division lands east of Sword beach

4:30 pm, Jun 6 ❽
German 21st Panzer Division launches counterattack between the Juno and Sword beachheads but is forced to withdraw

Night of Jun 5–6 ❷
US 82nd and 101st Airborne Divisions land west of Utah beach

7:30 am, Jun 6 ❻
Men of British 3rd Division land on Sword beach and advance toward Caen

7:55 am, Jun 6 ❼
Men of Canadian 3rd Division land on Juno beach and advance to the west of Caen

7:25 am, Jun 6 ❺
Men of British 50th Division land on Gold beach and advance inland toward Bayeux after some heavy fighting

7:00 am, Jun 6 ❹
Men of US 1st Division land on Omaha beach. They begin to suffer heavy casualties during fight to secure the beach

6:30 am, Jun 6 ❸
Men of US 4th Division land to south of Utah beach. They encounter only light resistance and advance inland to meet up with paratroops

BRITISH 2ND ARMY
US 1ST ARMY

English Channel

Caen, Carpiquet, Lion-sur-Mer, SWORD, Courseulles, JUNO, GOLD, Le Hamel, Arromanches, Port-en-Bessin, Colleville-sur-Mer, St Laurent, Vierville, Pointe du Hoc, OMAHA, Grandcamp, Carentan Channel, UTAH, Ste Mère Eglise, Varreville, Quinéville, Valognes, Cotentin Peninsula, Barneville, Cherbourg

Villers Bocage, Caumont, St Lô, Forêt de Cérisy, Airel, Lison, Bayeux, Trévières, Isigny, Carentan, Périers, Lessay, La Haye-du-Puits, Pont l'Abbé, Douve, Merderet, Taute, Vire

Coutances, Marigny, Odon, Orne, Dives, Aure

June 6–12
Having established themselves on the five beaches, the next task for the Allied forces was to link up the individual beach-heads. This was finally achieved on June 12, when the US troops from Omaha joined with those from Utah. Beyond the beachheads the main British objective was Caen, where the Germans were preparing to counterattack.

Jun 12 ❹
Allied troops almost succeed in breaking through center of German line at Caumont

Jun 10 ❸
British launch heavy bombardment of Caen at beginning of attempt to capture the town. German forces successfully resist the Allied attack

Jun 9 ❶
British and US troops from Gold and Omaha beachheads meet west of Bayeux

Jun 12 ❷
US troops from Omaha and Utah beachheads meet east of Carentan

0 km 10 20 30 40
0 miles 10 20 30

Potigny, Villers Bocage, Argences, Caen, Carpiquet, Tilly-sur-Seulles, Lion-sur-Mer, SWORD, Trouville, Arromanches, JUNO, Courseulles, GOLD, Colleville-sur-Mer, St Laurent, Vierville, OMAHA, Pointe du Hoc, Bayeux, Port-en-Bessin, Caumont, St Lô, Forêt de Cérisy, Airel, Lison, Isigny, Grandcamp, Carentan Channel, UTAH, Varreville, Quinéville, Valognes, Cotentin Peninsula, Cherbourg, Périers, Lessay, La Haye-du-Puits, Pont l'Abbé, Ste Mère Eglise, Barneville, Coutances, Marigny, Taute, Douve, Merderet, Odon, Orne, Dives, Vire

Jun 13 ❶
British and Canadian attempt to outflank Caen via Villers-Bocage is halted

Jul 18 ❻
St. Lô is taken by US forces

Jul 3 ❹
US forces begin to advance toward line between Coutances and St. Lô but meet fierce resistance

Jun 18 ❷
US forces reach the coast at Barneville

Jun 20 ❸
US forces begin to attack Cherbourg's outer defenses. They capture the port on Jun 27

Jul 18 ❻
In Operation Goodwood British and Canadian troops launch attack to east of Caen

Jul 8 ❺
Following heavy bombardment, British and Canadian troops advance and take part of Caen west of Orne River but get no farther

June 13–July 24
As British and Canadian forces struggled to capture Caen, tying down the German armor, the Americans captured the port of Cherbourg and made preparations to break out of Normandy.

Potigny, Villers Bocage, Caen, Carpiquet, Argences, Caumont, St Lô, Forêt de Cérisy, Airel, Lison, Tilly-sur-Seulles, Lion-sur-Mer, Trouville, Arromanches, Courseulles, Bayeux, Port-en-Bessin, St Laurent, Grandcamp, Mulberry B, Colleville-sur-Mer, Mulberry A, Vierville, Pointe du Hoc, Carentan Channel, Isigny, Carentan, Ste Mère Eglise, Varreville, Quinéville, Valognes, Cotentin Peninsula, Cherbourg, Pont l'Abbé, Douve, Barneville, La Haye-du-Puits, Lessay, Périers, Coutances, Marigny, Merderet, Taute, Vire, Odon, Orne, Dives

0 km 10 20 30 40
0 miles 10 20 30

"Two kinds of people are staying on this beach, the dead and those who are going to die. Now let's get the hell out of here."

US COLONEL GEORGE TAYLOR ON OMAHA BEACH

Wounded US troops
Nearly 3,000 men were killed or wounded during the landings on Omaha beach. Many were forced to huddle against the sea wall, on a narrow strip of shingle, as the tide came in.

The initial bombardment dazed the German defenders and cut their communications to the rear. It was just as well, since the US troops found themselves having to wade through 100 yd (100 m) of water before they reached dry land. They then found that, because of a combination of current and smoke, they had landed 2,000 yd (2,000 m) to the south of Utah. They were ordered inland and northward to secure the correct beach, and they soon made contact with the paratroops. A German gun line on a low but dominant ridge caused some difficulties, but even so, Utah was secure at the end of the day at a cost of just 200 US casualties.

The other American beach—the 6-mile (10-km) long Omaha—would prove to be a very different proposition. At high tide it consisted of a narrow strip of shingle backed by a sea wall, behind which was a 200-yd (200-m) wide plateau with an antitank ditch. To the rear there were cliffs with numerous strongpoints on top. It was the strongest held of all the beaches, with two German regiments deployed. Just 3 miles (5 km) to the west of Omaha there was a battery on Pointe du Hoc, which covered the beach from the flank.

Omaha was the target of the US 1st Infantry Division, which intended to land with two regimental combat teams (RCTs) abreast. Almost all the swimming tanks supporting the RCT on the right were drowned in the heavy swell. Those supporting the RCT on the left only made it to the shore because the skippers of the landing craft carrying them took them right to the beach. Many landing craft were wrecked by underwater obstacles and others were swamped, with the result that most of the supporting artillery never made it to the beach. As for the infantry, many found themselves shoulder-deep in water. Weighed down by their equipment, some drowned, while others fell to the murderous fire from the strongpoints on the cliffs to the rear of the beach. Those who did get ashore often landed in the wrong place and sought shelter at the foot of the sea wall. Many officers trying to gather their men were shot, and few radios worked because they had been impregnated with seawater. Soon, the incoming tide restricted the survivors to a narrow strip of shingle. Meanwhile, 150 Rangers had succeeded in climbing the cliffs that led up to

Arrival of follow-up forces
Following D-Day, it was essential that the Allies reinforce their troops on the Normandy beachhead more rapidly than the Germans.

The explosions were very near now, and one threw spray over us. 'Going in to land.' We touched, bumped, slewed around. 'Ramp down,' the boat began to empty. At the stern, my men and I were the last to leave. I heaved on my rucksack and seized a stretcher. ... and flopped into the water. It came up about midthigh. I struggled desperately for the shore. There was a thick fog of smoke all over the beach. The tide was flooding. There were many bodies in the water... As I got nearer the shore, I saw wounded among the dead, pinned down by the weight of their equipment.

BRITISH CAPTAIN PATTERSON OF 4 COMMANDO ON LANDING AT SWORD BEACH IN A LANDING CRAFT

Pointe du Hoc, only to discover that the guns had beeen removed. They were then subjected to several German counterattacks for 48 hours. On the beach itself, some semblance of order was eventually established, and groups managed to get off it to infiltrate the cliffs behind. Even so, by nightfall the beachhead was still only some 1,000 yd (1,000 yd) deep and very vulnerable to counterattack.

BRITISH AND CANADIAN LANDINGS

Men of the British 50th (Northumbrian) Division began to land on Gold beach at 7:25 am, five minutes before the stipulated time. The defenses

Mulberry harbor
Two artificial harbors were erected to maintain the flow of supplies.

within the village of Le Hamel were the main problem and it took most of the day to reduce them. Nevertheless, by the end of the day the division had succeeded in almost reaching the town of Bayeux.

Juno beach was the target of the Canadian Third Division. Offshore reefs restricted the landing places and the swell slowed the approach to the shore. In this case, the tanks landed well before the infantry, who were 25 minutes late. As on other beaches, while the air and naval bombardments had largely silenced the coastal batteries, they had not had much effect on the strongpoints and there were fierce battles to subdue these. The landing of follow-up waves of troops caused congestion on the beach, but by early afternoon the Canadians were moving inland toward their ultimate D-Day objective, the airfield in Carpiquet, west of Caen. By dusk they had reached a point 1.5 miles (2.4 km) short of it and had linked up with 50th Division on their right.

The final beach, Sword, was to be assaulted by the British Third Infantry Division, whose ultimate D-Day objective was the city of Caen. In spite of heavy German fire, the leading waves of troops got ashore and by 8:30 am were off the beaches. A Commando force moved swiftly to relieve the glider-borne troops holding the bridge over the

Caen Canal. The main body was held up by beach congestion, which delayed the arrival of its supporting tanks. Matters were not helped by the obstinate resistance of a German strongpoint that lay on the route to Caen. Even so, the troops reached a village 2.5 miles (4 km) north of the city by 4:00 pm. Thirty minutes later the Germans launched their only significant counterattack of D-Day.

GERMAN COUNTERATTACK

There was only one German mobile formation in Normandy on D-Day. The 21st Panzer Division was deployed in the Caen area, but was widely scattered. Rundstedt, the German commander-in-chief, had a reserve of three other panzer divisions, but Hitler had insisted that they could not be deployed without his permission, and not until the afternoon of D-Day was this forthcoming. Meanwhile, the 21st Panzer Division, which had initially been deployed between the Orne and the Dives, was ordered to counter the landings on Sword. The attack, which did not begin until 4:30 pm, was repulsed, except for one Panzergrenadier battalion that managed to advance through the gap between the Canadian Third and British Third divisions. It withdrew only through fear of being cut off by reinforcements for the Sixth Airborne Division. Meanwhile, the deployment to the beachhead of the reserve panzer divisions was badly hampered by Allied airpower, and the leading elements only began to arrive, too late, on the night of D-Day.

Thus, by the end of D-Day the Allies had landed 150,000 men at a cost of 9,000 casualties, far fewer than they had feared. The Germans had been caught by surprise and had failed to prevent any of the landings from taking place. They were also still not convinced that there would be no landings elsewhere, especially in the Pas de Calais.

BEACHHEAD BATTLES

After the success of D-Day, the Allies' first priority was to link up the individual beachheads. They finally achieved this on June 12, when Utah was joined with Omaha. In the British sector the main

Advancing from Sword beach
British forces move inland to join the battle for the capture of Caen. The city was a D-Day objective, but the Germans fought grimly to prevent its capture. It took six weeks for British and Canadian forces to secure Caen.

ALWAYS RUTH

The destruction of Valognes
The inhabitants of Normandy often paid a heavy price for their liberation. It was not so much the ground fighting which caused destruction and civilian deaths, but the Allied use of carpet bombing from the air.

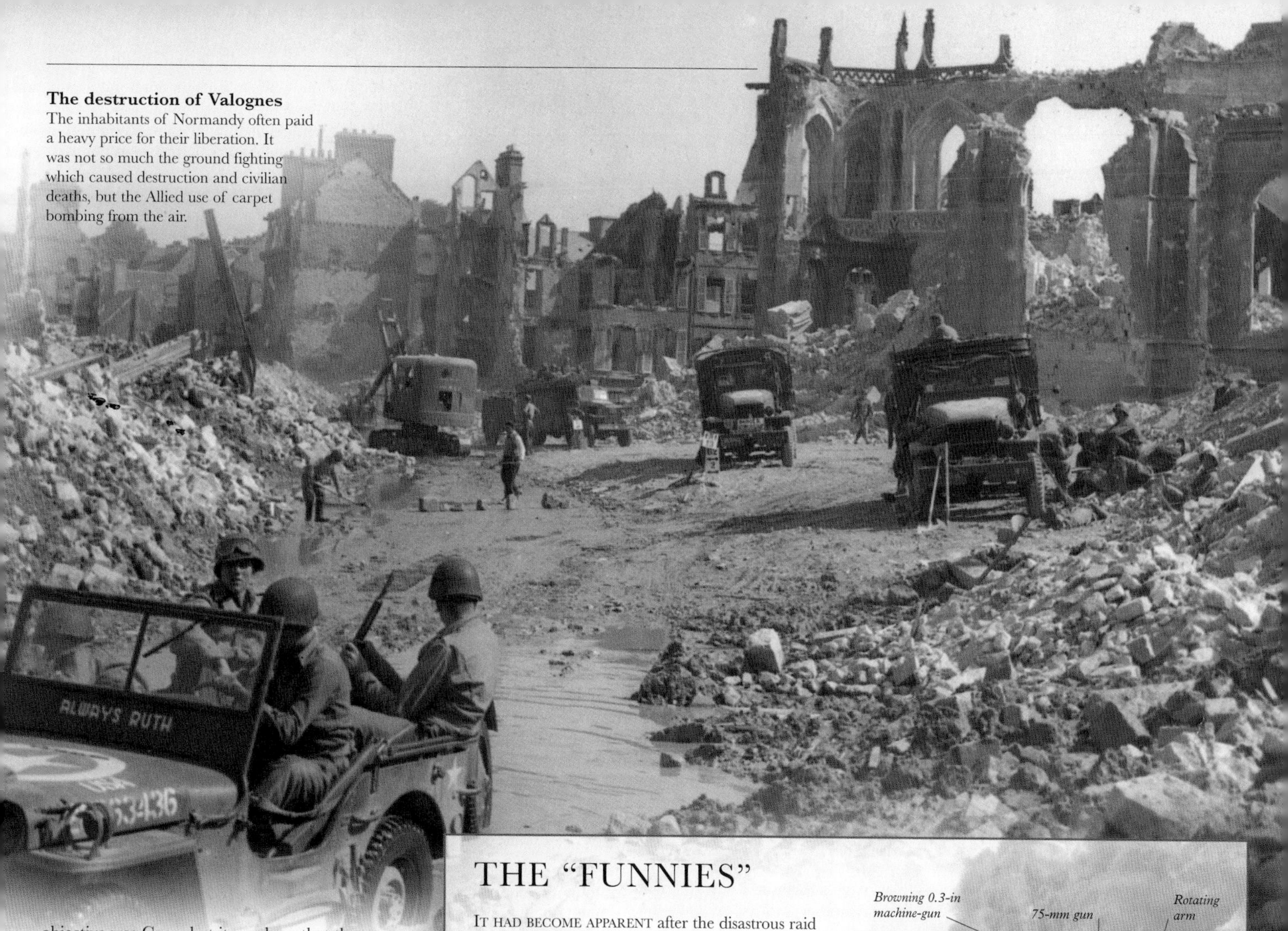

objective was Caen, but it was here that the Germans were attempting to concentrate their armor for a major counterattack. The 12th SS Panzer Division had joined the 21st Panzer and was able to foil Canadian attempts to capture the city from the west. A British thrust south and then east of Bayeux during June 11–14 proved abortive for the same reason. But while more panzer divisions were arriving, their progress was slowed by destroyed bridges and the constant Allied air threat. At the same time, pressure on the ground meant that they had to concentrate on holding the line rather than mounting a significant attack.

ADVANCE TO CHERBOURG

Once they had secured the beaches the Allies had set about assembling two Mulberry harbors, one in the US sector and the other in the British. The former began to operate on June 16, but three days later it was virtually destroyed by a violent storm. This made it all the more important for the Americans to capture Cherbourg so that it could be used as a resupply port. To this end, they first cut off the Cotentin peninsula by advancing across its base before turning north toward Cherbourg. Hitler had

THE "FUNNIES"

IT HAD BECOME APPARENT after the disastrous raid on Dieppe in August 1942 that tanks should have the capability to overcome beach obstacles and surmount sea walls. There was also the problem of getting the tanks to the beach. Work began on specialized types based on existing tanks, especially the American Sherman and British Churchill.

One of the most important was the Sherman DD (Duplex Drive), which could swim through the sea. It had a collapsible canvas screen and a propellor attached to the main engine to provide propulsion. Once ashore, the gear could be removed and it became a normal tank. Sherman DDs landed with the initial assault troops on all the D-Day beaches, although some did sink, especially off Omaha. On the beaches themselves, a plethora of "funnies," as they became known, were needed. Tanks with bulldozer blades were used to clear beach obstacles. The carpet-layer Churchill laid trackway on soft sand to enable wheeled vehicles to cross it, while the turretless Churchill Ark was used to ram a sea wall and then become a surface over which other tanks could drive. To deal with antitank ditches, various types of bridging tank were developed. A new method of clearing a lane through a minefield was the Conger explosive hose, which fired from a trailer behind a tank. To deal with strongpoints there was the Churchill Crocodile flamethrower and the Churchill AVRE (Armoured Vehicle Royal Engineers). This had a short-barreled mortar that fired a projectile filled with 26 lb (11.8 kg) of explosive charge.

With the exception of the Sherman DD tank, the Americans usually took little interest in the "funnies," which were very much the province of the British.

Browning 0.3-in machine-gun
75-mm gun
Rotating arm
Flail of metal chains for clearing mines

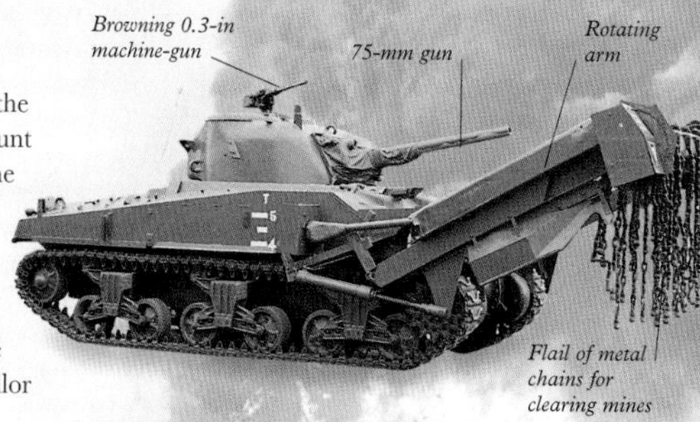

SHERMAN V (M4A4) CRAB FLAIL TANK

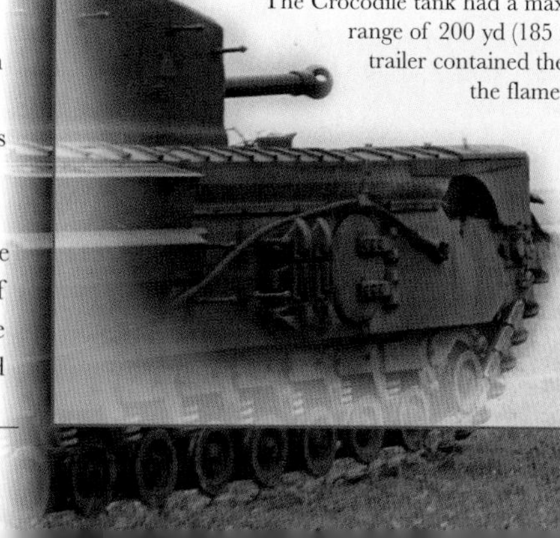

Churchill Crocodile flamethrower
The Crocodile tank had a maximum range of 200 yd (185 m). A trailer contained the fuel for the flame-thrower.

INFANTRY WEAPONS ON THE WESTERN FRONT

THE INFANTRY OF BOTH the Allied and the German armies on the Western Front had a wide variety of weapons. They ranged from pistols and grenades, to rifles, submachine-guns, and light and medium machine-guns, as well as mortars and antitank weapons. The rifle, however, remained the basic infantry weapon. On the Allied side, the ammunition for British and American small arms was generally of different calibers and so could not be used in each other's weapons.

3 lb (1.4 kg) projectile

Monopod support

Spring-loaded launch tube

PIAT rocket launcher
The British PIAT ("Projector, Infantry, Anti-Tank") came into service in late 1942. A hollow-charge bomb was launched by means of a powerful spring. It was awkward to handle, but effective up to 90 yd (100 m).

| Length 39 in (99 cm) | Weight 32 lb (14.5 kg) |

Aperture-style rear sights

Hand-operated breechbolt

Spike-type bayonet

Detachable 10-round box magazine

British Lee Enfield no. 4 rifle
The British Army's standard rifle from 1941 to 1959, the Lee Enfield no. 4 was caliber 0.303 in (7.69 mm). It was cheaper to manufacture than its predecessor, the Short Muzzle Lee Enfield (SMLE).

| Length 44¼ in (113 cm) | Weight 9 lb (4.1 kg) |

Colt .45 automatic pistol
Adopted by the US Army in 1911, the Colt .45 was used in both world wars. It had a 7-round magazine, used large-caliber bullets, and had a reputation for being a "man-stopper."

| Length 8½ in (21.6 cm) | Weight 2½ lb (1.14 kg) |

British M36 or Mills hand grenade
The Mills grenade entered British Army service in 1915 and is still used today. It can be set with a 4- or 7-second delay fuse.

| Length 3¾ in (9.53 cm) | Weight 1¾ lb (0.77 kg) |

"Leaf with aperture" type foresight

Wooden forward grip

20- or 30- round ammunition magazine

Removable wooden buttstock

Thompson M1928A1 "Tommy Gun"
Beloved of American gangsters in the 1920s, the Thompson became the standard US submachine-gun of World War II. It was also much used by British commandos. It could fire 800 rounds of 0.45-in caliber per minute and used a 20- or 30-round box magazine, or a 50- or 100-round drum magazine.

| Length 33¼ in (84.5 cm) | Weight 10 lb 2 oz (4.6 kg) |

Thin sheet steel canister enclosing powder charge

German Steilhandgranate 39
Dating from World War I, the StG 39 contained 7 oz (2.78 gm) of TNT and had a 4.5-second delay.

| Length 16 in (40.6 cm) | Weight 1 lb 6 oz (0.63 kg) |

Threaded safety cap

Pistole Parabellum 1908
Usually known as the Luger, this pistol had an 8-round magazine and used 9 mm ammunition. It was prized as a souvenir by Allied soldiers.

| Length 8¼ in (22.2 cm) | Weight 1 lb 15 oz (0.85 kg) |

German Karabiner 98K
The last of a long line of bolt-action Mausers, which served the German Army well. It was based on a rifle designed as early as 1898 and became standard issue in 1935. It used 7.92 mm (0.312 in) ammunition and had a 5-round magazine.

| Length 43⅜ in (110.7 cm) | Weight 8½ lb (3.89 kg) |

Bayonet

Bolt

---

ordered the garrison to defend the port to the last. It fell on June 27, but only after the Germans had destroyed the dock facilities. It would be some weeks before the port was operational. In the British sector there was another attempt to outflank Caen from the west toward the end of June, but again there was no decisive breakthrough.

Much of the Allied lack of progress, aside from the capture of Cherbourg, lay in the nature of the Normandy terrain known as the "*bocage*." It was hilly and often wooded country, with twisting roads bordered by banks topped with hedges, and small enclosed fields. It had a claustrophobic atmosphere, which favored defense, and the Allied troops took time to acclimatize. The Germans had the problem of manpower. In spite of pleas by Rundstedt and Rommel for more men, and even for permission to withdraw from Normandy, Hitler was adamant that the Allies be driven back into the sea. So disgusted was Rundstedt that Hitler replaced him with Hans Guenther von Kluge at the beginning of July.

Searching among the ruins of Caen
Armed with Sten guns, two Allied soldiers search for German snipers in a city that had taken a pounding in successive Allied attacks. The last part to remain in German hands was captured by the Canadians on July 18.

PARIS
ROUEN
LE MANS
LAVA

ATTEMPTS ON ST. LÔ AND CAEN

Montgomery, who was *de facto* still in overall control of the Allied ground operations, was now concerned to tie down the maximum amount of German armor in the east to enable the Americans to get into a position from which they could break out. On July 3 the US First Army began to attack southward toward St. Lô, a key communications center, which it was essential for the Americans to secure if their eventual break-out were to be successful. It was to be a slow and costly business in the face of continuing bitter German resistance. The next day, the Canadians made another attempt to seize Carpiquet airfield, only to be frustrated by the fanatical defense of the 12th SS Panzer Division. Preceded by a massive air attack that destroyed much of Caen, and with naval gunfire and heavy artillery fire in support, British and Canadian troops attacked the city once more on July 8. They managed to break into it and secure the area north of the Odon River, but the Germans held firm on the southern bank.

Although St. Lô was not yet in Allied hands, Montgomery's plan for the break-out was issued on July 10. The Americans were simultaneously to thrust eastward into Brittany to secure its ports and westward toward the line of Alençon–Le Mans.

BOMB PLOT AGAINST HITLER

THERE HAD BEEN A NUMBER of plots against Hitler's life, but the one implemented on July 20, 1944, was the closest to being successful. The plotters were a mixture of middle- and high-ranking army officers and civil servants, many of whom believed that Germany must make peace if it was not to be totally destroyed.

The plot was centered on the Reserve Army, which had its HQ in Berlin, one of whose staff officers, Colonel Claus von Stauffenburg, regularly attended conferences at Hitler's headquarters in Rastenberg in East Prussia. The plan was for him to take a bomb hidden in a briefcase into such a conference and then leave before it exploded. Once Hitler was dead, elements of the Home Army would seize government buildings in Berlin. The same would happen in Paris, whose military governor was involved in the plot.

Stauffenburg duly flew to Rastenberg and attended the conference. Placing the briefcase under the table, he announced that he had to make a

telephone call and left. The bomb detonated and Stauffenburg reported this to HQ Reserve Army. In Paris there were wholesale arrests of SS, Gestapo, and other Nazis, but in Berlin the plot leaders hesitated before ordering the occupation of the key buildings. Government officials in Berlin then learned that Hitler was shaken but had survived. The Berlin plotters were arrested with some, including Stauffenburg, being summarily shot. In Paris the governor was forced to release his captives.

Hitler instituted a massive witch hunt. Hundreds were arrested. After torture, some were subjected to show trials and then hanged with piano wire in Berlin's Plottensee prison. Others, including Rommel and Kluge, who were aware of the plot but not involved, were forced to commit suicide to protect their families.

Bomb damage
Mussolini, who arrived at Hitler's HQ in Rastenberg—the "Wolf's Lair"—later on July 20, is shown the bomb damage.

Eisenhower, however, was beginning to believe that the terrain in the British sector was more suitable for a break-out than that in the US sector.

OPERATION GOODWOOD

As it happened, Montgomery had been planning an attack just to the east of Caen, with the purpose of keeping the German armor tied down, but he let Eisenhower believe that a breakthrough was intended. Rommel sensed what was about to happen and personally briefed his subordinate commanders. On July 17, while returning from a visit to one of these commanders, his car was hit by a marauding fighter-bomber and he was badly injured. Rommel was evacuated back to Germany, and Kluge took over direct command of his Army Group B, as well as continuing to be commander-in-chief west.

Montgomery's assault, Operation Goodwood, opened on July 18. Again, RAF Bomber Command prepared the way. A shortage of approach routes

meant that only one armored division could deploy at a time, but the air bombardment had dazed the defenders and initially there was good progress. The Germans, however, quickly recovered. Antitank guns in villages on the flank of the advance suddenly came to life. Worse, German tanks took up position on a dominant ridge, which marked the first major objective. They brought the British armor to a halt. Attempts to resume the attack on the following day failed and thunderstorms on July 20 brought Goodwood to an end with a loss of 400 tanks. The Canadians had, however, secured the remainder of Caen.

General Omar Bradley, commanding the US First Army, had intended to launch his break-out from St. Lô, which had finally been secured, on July 20. However, he also wanted US bombers to prepare the way, and

Exhausted German prisoners
Over 50,000 German prisoners had been taken by the end of June. They were put in temporary "cages" prior to being shipped back to Britain.

THE RESISTANCE AND THE SOE

FORCES
FRANÇAISES
DE L'INTÉRIEUR
ARMBAND

THE COUNTRIES OF EUROPE OCCUPIED by Germany and Italy were not totally cowed, as the development of resistance movements testified. For these movements to flourish, their members had to believe that liberation would eventually take place. It was also necessary for the bulk of the population to continue normal life as best it could, since this provided essential cover for Resistance activities. Inevitably, this meant passive collaboration with the occupiers. Furthermore, outside support was vital, and it was to provide this that Churchill established the Special Operations Executive (SOE) in the summer of 1940. This was followed in May 1942 by the founding of the US equivalent to SOE, the Office of Strategic Services (OSS).

The SOE and OSS saw the Resistance as fulfilling two main roles—sabotage and intelligence gathering. The first not only helped to tie down Axis troops, but also hampered the utilization of indigenous industry for the Axis war effort. Intelligence produced by the Resistance was often vital, the progress of heavy water production in Norway for the German atomic bomb program and the development of V-weapons being but two examples. To coordinate the activities of the various groups, the SOE and OSS deployed agents to act as a link and arrange for the necessary weapons, explosives, and other equipment to be delivered to the Resistance.

The Resistance often faced great difficulties. Countries with mountainous terrain provided an easier environment in which to operate than the flatlands of the Low Countries or Denmark, where more effort had to go into establishing places to hide. Another problem was that the groups themselves often held very different political beliefs and it was difficult to get them to work together. In France, for example, there were groups that supported de Gaulle, and others that were communist, with a very different postwar agenda. There was the constant danger of betrayal. Fascist sympathizers often infiltrated the Resistance networks, as did those who were

prepared to betray their fellow countrymen for money. The German *Abwehr* was also highly skilled in identifying Resistance members and calling them out. In March 1942 they succeeded in "turning" an SOE radio operator in the Netherlands. For 18 months he continued to transmit to London without the SOE being aware that he was in German hands. As a result, many agents were captured and the Dutch Resistance network was virtually destroyed for a time.

In spite of such difficulties, the Resistance played its part in winning the war for the Allies. On D-Day, for example, the French Resistance succeeded in virtually isolating Brittany from Normandy and thus prevented the movement of German reinforcements. It also helped to delay the movement of German divisions from other parts of France through its attacks on the transportation system.

Sabotaged railroad track
Resistance groups excelled in acts of sabotage that disrupted the movement of supplies.

Concealed weapons
These were designed for SOE operatives by the SOE's highly secret Station IX.

Suppressor (silencer)

Ejection port

WELROD SILENCED PISTOL

Cocking wheel

Combined magazine and pistol grip

Sheath attached to armband worn under clothing

Blade

THUMB KNIFE

Cartridge

Button pulled back to fire

PENCIL PISTOL

End unscrewed for loading

Weapons demonstration
French Resistance members examine weapons dropped by parachute. They include a Sten gun with a skeleton butt—an earlier model than the Mk 5.

SOE camouflage suit
Many agents wore a camouflage suit when being dropped into occupied Europe by parachute to reduce the high risk of capture.

Padded flying helmet

Sten gun Mk 5
Firing 550 rounds per minute, the Mk 5 Sten gun was used by the Resistance from the summer of 1944.

Magazine containing 32 9-mm rounds

British Mk 111 suitcase radio
This radio was the SOE agent's main means of communication.

Morse key

Tuning coil

Waveband selector

Battery leads

Headset

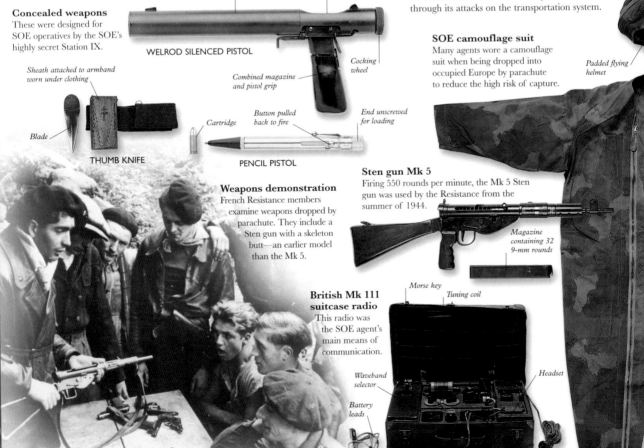

the bad weather prevented this. As a result there was an awkward pause, which led to yet further recrimination between Eisenhower and Montgomery over the failure of Goodwood. News of the failed assassination attempt against Hitler did, however, give the Allies some comfort, for it indicated that cracks were appearing in the Nazi regime.

ALLIED BREAK-OUT

Operation Cobra, General Bradley's break-out from St. Lô, was now scheduled for July 24 (see map page 231). The weather was still doubtful and it was decided to recall the bombers after they had taken off. Some did not receive the message and dropped their bombs as planned, inflicting 130 casualties on their own troops. A better weather forecast encouraged Bradley to try again the following day. Inaccurate bombing again inflicted casualties on the attackers, but the attack went ahead and made progress. Further attacks by the Canadians in the Caen area prevented Kluge from switching panzer divisions to counter the threat.

On July 30 the Americans entered Avranches. On the same day the British mounted Operation Bluecoat, with the goal of preventing the German armor from attacking the US flank from the east. Despite a lack of suitable routes, this was largely achieved. The moment to exploit the break-out now arrived. On August 1 Patton's US Third Army came into being and Bradley ordered him to clear Brittany as a priority. He sent two armored divisions to seize Brest and Lorient, but Hitler declared both to be *Festungen* (fortresses) which were to hold out to the bitter end. Brest was to fall in mid-September, but the garrison at Lorient did not surrender until the end of the war. Thus the Allies were denied early use of the Brittany ports.

COUNTERATTACK AT MORTAIN

Some of Patton's forces had begun to advance south and were threatening the German left flank. Kluge wanted to withdraw to the Seine, but Hitler insisted that he mount a counterstroke against Patton's eastern flank. Because of British pressure, Kluge was only able, with great difficulty, to assemble four panzer divisions for the attack, and these attacked in the Mortain area shortly after midnight on August 7. The Americans were initially caught off-balance, and by daylight the Germans had penetrated up to

German POWs near Falaise
On August 20 the remnants from two German armies streamed back toward the Seine, leaving 10,000 dead and 50,000 to be taken prisoner.

6 miles (10 km). With the coming of daylight, the situation changed dramatically as hoards of Allied fighter-bombers took to the skies and engaged the German armor with rockets. The attack was stopped in its tracks and troops on the ground now threatened the flanks of the penetrating forces.

The Canadians now launched an attack south of Caen, Operation Totalize, which was designed to block the withdrawal of the German forces in front of the British Second Army. While it did not reach its final objective of Falaise, the attack further restricted Kluge's options. Worse, the counterattack at Mortain had not inhibited Patton, who had both thrust into Brittany and advanced south to the Loire River. He was now turning east, threatening the main German supply base at Alençon.

Realizing that the German forces in Normandy were being squeezed, Montgomery decided to trap them. The Canadians were to press on to Falaise and then to Argentan, with the British on their left advancing to the Flers-Argentan road. Meanwhile, Patton was to thrust toward the southeast of Argentan. In this way, Montgomery hoped to create a pocket with no decent escape routes to the east. Patton's troops entered Alençon on August 12 and headed for Argentan, to which the Germans hastily redeployed tanks from Mortain. Bradley now ordered Patton to halt at Argentan rather than press on to Falaise as he feared a clash with the Canadians. They had resumed their attacks toward Falaise on

August 14. The 12th SS Panzer Division, held them for a time on the last ridge before Falaise, but by the end of August 17 they had secured almost the whole town. The gap between them and the Americans at Argentan was now a mere 12 miles (19 km).

In spite of Kluge's pleas, Hitler continued to insist on further counterattacks at Mortain as late as August 16. He would not accept that a withdrawal might be necessary, and appointed Model in place of Kluge, who was ordered back to Germany. Fearing arrest on suspicion of being involved in the July bomb plot, Kluge committed suicide *en route*.

TRAPPED IN THE FALAISE POCKET

Immediately grasping how desperate the situation was, on August 17 Model ordered the Seventh and Fifth Panzer Armies to withdraw to the Dives River and take up a new defensive position. However, events were moving too fast for him. The Canadians attacked across the river and by the evening of August 18 had reached Chambois. With the Americans also closing up, there was now a mere 6-mile (10-km) gap through which the German forces were beginning the pour. Just 24 hours later the pocket was finally closed and the Germans still inside it were being hammered from the air. On August 20 desperate attacks by the Germans opened a gap in the mouth of the pocket for a few hours, but by the evening it had been closed again. The battle for Normandy was at an end.

"The scenes in the Falaise pocket…were horrendous. The various German divisions had taken a terrible pounding in the Normandy battle. Panzer Lehr, for instance, had lost all its tanks and infantry units."

STUART HILLS, BRITISH SHERMAN TANK COMMANDER
DURING THE ALLIED ADVANCE THROUGH NORMANDY

LANDINGS IN SOUTHERN FRANCE

On August 15, while the Allies were setting about creating the pocket at Falaise, landings took place far to the south on France's Mediterranean coast. The original intention had been for these to be mounted at the same time as those in Normandy, but developments in Italy and the lack of sufficient amphibious shipping had made it necessary to postpone them. Preceded by an airborne drop, General Alexander Patch's US Seventh Army came

Paris liberation celebrations
German snipers were still active even as Parisians celebrated, and several people died in an outbreak of shooting in the Place de la Concorde on August 26.

Searching for Germans
After the Allied landings in southern France, members of the Resistance go into action. The woman has a Schmeisser MP40 submachine-gun.

ashore without the degree of German resistance that the Allies had met on D-Day. The southern half of France contained a mere ten German divisions and the coastal defences were not as strong as in Normandy. Overwhelming Allied air supremacy and powerful naval support also contributed.

Eisenhower's prime objective was to secure Marseilles so that it could be used as a resupply port, a task given to General Jean-Marie de Lattre de Tassigny's *Armée B*, soon to be renamed the French First Army. This consisted of the French Expeditionary Corps, which had fought in Italy, and further troops from North Africa. Hitler had designated both Marseilles and the former French naval base Toulon *Festungen*, but the French ensured that both were secured by August 28. In the meantime, the Americans had begun to advance rapidly northward up the Rhône valley, much assisted by the *Forces Françaises de l'Intérieur* (FFI). This had been formed in February 1944 as an umbrella for all the French Resistance groups, including the *Maquis*, which consisted largely of young men evading compulsory

labor in Germany, who had sought refuge in the forested and mountainous area around the Massif Central. Many would be incorporated into the French First Army. The Allies were helped, too, by the fact that Hitler, appreciating that the situation in northern France was fast disintegrating, allowed the German forces in the south to withdraw.

US ADVANCE TO PARIS

In northern France, Model had hoped to form a new defense line based on the Seine River, but the Allies moved too quickly for him. Patton, frustrated by Bradley's refusal to allow him to advance north of Argentan, had been allowed to continue to advance eastward. Montgomery's intention was that he should strike toward the port of Le Havre so as to create an outer cordon to trap the forces that had escaped from the Falaise pocket. In fact, Patton sent only one corps in this direction, while two others headed for Chartres and Orléans. Once these two

A triumphant General de Gaulle in Paris
On August 26 over 1 million people flocked to the center of Paris to cheer the city's liberation as de Gaulle walked up the Champs Elysées, followed by members of the FFI.

A vibrant crowd surrounds the French tanks draped in flags and covered in bouquets of flowers. On each tank, on each armored car, next to crew members in khaki mechanics' overalls and little caps, there are clusters of girls, women, boys, and fifis (FFI members) wearing armbands. People lining the street applaud, blow kisses, raise clenched fist salutes, call out to the victors their joy at liberation.

BOOKSELLER JEAN GALTIER-BOISSIÈRE DESCRIBING THE SCENE IN PARIS ON AUGUST 25, THE DAY OF LIBERATION

towns had been liberated, Bradley ordered Patton to halt for two days for fear that his advance would become overextended. However, on August 18 he allowed the Third Army to resume its thrust eastward. Late on the following day, Patton's leading elements found an intact footbridge over the Seine west of Paris. They immediately established a bridgehead and then secured another to the east of Paris on August 23. Thus, Model's hopes were crushed and his battered troops were forced to continue their withdrawal eastward.

In Paris itself there had been momentous events. Eisenhower's original intention had been to bypass the city, fearing that to attack it directly would result in unnecessary casualties and collateral damage. Actions within the city caused a change of plan. On August 10, sensing that liberation was close, public sector workers went on strike. The reaction of the Resistance groups in Paris was mixed. Gaullist elements, having been warned that Allied forces would not enter for some time to come, considered it prudent to stand by and wait for events to unfold. The communists, on the other hand, wanted an immediate uprising. Fearing that if this happened the communists would seize the machinery of government, the Gaullists preempted them and on August 19 the insurrection began.

The military governor of Paris, General Dietrich von Choltitz, was known by the Allies to have been involved in the destruction of Rotterdam in May

1940 and the Soviet Black Sea port of Sevastopol in 1942. There was also the knowledge that the Poles in Warsaw were at that very time fighting a desperate battle against their German oppressors.

As it turned out, thanks to the efforts of the Swedish consul-general in Paris, Raoul Nordling, Choltitz agreed to a truce and undertook not to inflict on Paris the terrible punishment that Warsaw was receiving. This was despite a direct order from Hitler that the French capital be defended to the last. The skirmishing continued, however, and on August 22 the FFI commander in Paris called for every street to be barricaded. Finally, on August 23, Eisenhower relented and gave the go-ahead for General Philippe Leclerc's French Second Armored Division and a US infantry division, both part of Patton's Third Army, to dash to the capital. The race was won by Leclerc, who used local knowledge to reach the center via the back streets. Choltitz ordered his troops to withdraw east of the Seine and next day, August 25, surrendered to Leclerc. The next day de Gaulle walked triumphantly up the Champs Elysées.

SPLITS IN THE ALLIED CAMP
Splits now began to appear in the Allied camp. On August 21 Eisenhower had held a meeting at his Advanced HQ in Normandy. He announced that he was taking personal control of the ground forces from September 1 and gave instructions that Bradley's 12th Army Group was to aim for the Franco-German border, while Montgomery's 21st Army Group advanced into Belgium. Montgomery protested, on the grounds that either he or Bradley should continue to conduct the ground campaign and that the Allies should concentrate on a single thrust to the Ruhr, Germany's main industrial region in the west. Eisenhower was adamant that his Broad Front strategy should prevail and that he would take charge. There matters rested.

Advance through France and Belgium
By the time the Allied forces in the south of France linked up with those advancing from Normandy, progress had slowed because of overstretched supply lines. This gave the Germans time to recover and there was to be some hard fighting as the Allies gradually closed on the Rhine.

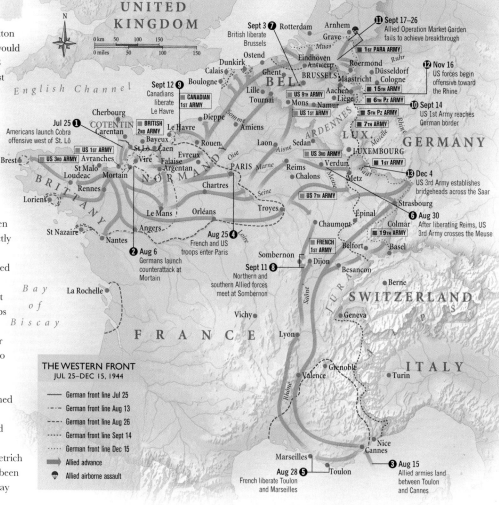

Paratroops in the Netherlands
Three airborne divisions took part in Operation Market Garden, Montgomery's gamble to break the growing deadlock in the west.

By August 29 the Allies had reached the Seine River, although Patton was already advancing farther east and had reached the Marne. While the Canadians advanced along the Channel coast to secure its ports, the British Second Army launched a lightning thrust, with the US First Army covering its right flank, and succeeded in reaching the Belgian border on September 2. Patton, too, was now across the Marne and heading for the Meuse.

There was a penalty to be paid for these rapid advances. The Allied armies were still being largely supplied from Cherbourg, and the supply lines were becoming dangerously overstretched. The railroads were too badly damaged to be used, and resupply by air was limited by the fact that much of the transport fleet was allocated to the airborne forces. Every available truck had been pressed into service to bring fuel up to the forward supply depots, but the farther the Allies advanced the more fuel was consumed and the less there was for the forward divisions. The Canadians were unable to capture the Channel ports quickly because Hitler had declared them *Festungen*, and the dock facilities of those they did liberate had been largely destroyed.

Montgomery believed that if he could quickly capture Antwerp the problem would be solved. His tanks achieved this on September 4, the day after the Belgian capital, Brussels, had been liberated. So surprised were the German defenders that they had no time to sabotage the docks. Unfortunately, Antwerp as a port was useless unless the Scheldt River, which linked it to the sea, was secured. Montgomery was looking eastward rather than westward and the opportunity was missed. Thus, by the end of the first week of September, Allied fuel tanks were almost dry and the advance ground to a virtual halt.

The slowing of the Allied advance allowed the Germans a vital breathing space in which to regroup. Meanwhile, Montgomery was conceiving an ambitious plan for maintaining the Allied momentum and perhaps ending the war in 1944.

British paratroops in Oosterbeek
Aside from the battle for the bridge in Arnhem, the most intense fighting in Operation Market Garden was in Oosterbeek, a suburb of the town.

OPERATION MARKET GARDEN

The main obstacle barring the Western Allies' way into Germany was the Rhine River. Consequently, Montgomery proposed that airborne troops should seize bridges over the Lower Rhine and other rivers in the southern Netherlands, so allowing ground forces to advance rapidly into Germany. Eisenhower sanctioned Montgomery's plan on September 10 and a week later Operation Market Garden was mounted. The US 101st Airborne Division was to be dropped in the area around Eindhoven, and the US 82nd Airborne Division around Grave, while the British 1st Airborne Division was to seize the bridge over the Lower Rhine in Arnhem. At the same time, a British ground force was to advance north and relieve the airborne divisions in turn.

There were problems from the outset. First, the British paratroops were dropped too far—6 miles (10 km)—from the bridge in Arnhem. There were also two SS panzer divisions reequipping in the area. A US officer was captured with a copy of the operational orders, and the ground force made slow progress, in places being restricted to a single route that was repeatedly attacked. It did eventually link up with the US divisions, but Arnhem proved too ambitious an objective. The British paratroops, reinforced by the Polish Parachute Brigade, were subjected to relentless pressure by the two SS divisions and eventually forced to surrender, with only a fifth of their number escaping back to Allied lines. Thus, the chance to end the war in 1944 had been lost.

A STEP-BY-STEP ADVANCE

In the American sector General Courtney Hodges' First Army had begun to penetrate the Siegfried Line, while Patton's Third Army had reached the Moselle and linked up with the US Seventh and First French Armies, now under General Jacob Devers' US Sixth Army Group. Everywhere the Germans were recovering and the Allies were only achieving a step-by-step advance. The Canadian First Army had besieged several Channel ports, all of which, aside from Dunkirk, eventually fell. Montgomery now ordered the Canadians to clear the Scheldt estuary so that Antwerp could be opened. Meanwhile, the British Second Army set about enlarging the salient into the Netherlands that had been created by Market Garden.

In mid-October Eisenhower issued new orders. Montgomery was to continue to clear the Scheldt and, once Antwerp had been opened, advance from

The gun fired 6 rounds per minute and had a maximum range of 9,760 yd (8,930 m)

At 14.6 lb (6.63 kg), the shell was ineffective against solid defenses

The trail was holed to save weight

Airborne howitzer
The US M1AI 75-mm pack howitzer was used by both American and British airborne troops. It weighed 2,160 lb (980 kg) and could be carried in a glider.

V-WEAPONS

V-WEAPONS OR *VERGELTUNGSWAFFEN* (revenge weapons) were one category of Hitler's so-called "miracle" weapons that were designed to turn the tide of war. The three types that entered service were the V-1 flying bomb, the V-2 rocket, and the V-3 long-range, smooth-bore gun, of which only two were actually completed and used.

Development work on the V-1 and V-2 was centered in Peenemünde on Germany's Baltic coast. It was subjected to heavy bombing by the RAF in August 1943, putting back the development program. The V-1 had a preset guidance system and a maximum range of 125 miles (200 km).

V-2 ROCKET

It flew at a top speed of 420 mph (670 kph) and had a 1,875-lb (850-kg) warhead. The Germans launched their V-1 offensive against Britain on June 13, 1944. Initially, it was successful and caused many to evacuate London. The British then installed antiaircraft guns along the south coast and these, combined with fighters, meant that fewer got through. The Allies also overran the launch sites once they broke out of Normandy. A longer-range version was then developed to be launched from the Netherlands, but many continued to be shot down.

By this time the V-2 was in service. This was a very different proposition to the V-1. Flying at speeds as high as 2,500 mph (4,000 kph), it could not be intercepted. It also operated from a mobile launcher, which could withdraw within 30 minutes of firing. The first two were fired on September 8, one hitting Paris and the other London. A steady stream was then launched from the Netherlands, the last on March 27, 1945. The final V-1 against Britain was launched the following day. By this time, Allied air attacks on German oil and transportation targets were starving the V-weapons of fuel. They had in fact come into service too late to affect the course of the war.

V-1 FLYING BOMB

Explosive warhead of 1,875 lb (850 kg)

Pulse jet engine

Damage resulting from a V-2 attack
About 2,000 V-2s were fired at Britain, causing 9,000 casualties. About 16,000 V-1s were fired, some at northern France and the Netherlands, causing 45,000 casualties.

---

the Maas to the Rhine. Bradley's mission was to advance to the Rhine at Cologne, while Devers in the south closed up to the Rhine via the Belfort gap. The Americans advancing toward Cologne found themselves involved in tough fighting, initially to capture the first German town of any significance, Aachen, and then in the Huertgen Forest. In the south Patton reached the Saar River, while Devers reached the Rhine, although he failed to clear an obstinate German pocket based on Colmar. In the north the Canadians continued to clear both sides of the Scheldt. On November 1 amphibious landings took place on the Walcheren, the island guarding the Scheldt's mouth, and one week later it was secured. The river was then swept of mines and the first supply ships entered the port of Antwerp on November 26, thus easing the supply situation.

While these grim fall battles were being fought, Hitler had been secretly preparing to mount a major counteroffensive. Divisions had been withdrawn from the line and reequipped, all of this unbeknown to the Allies. Hitler planned to attack

US camouflaged Shermans outside Aachen
The tanks carry infantry who are ready to jump off on coming under fire. The fighting for the first significant German town captured by the Allies was very bitter.

GEORGE S PATTON

THE EMBODIMENT OF AGGRESSION, and dubbed by his troops "Old Blood and Guts," General George S. Patton (1885–1945) was one of the few senior American officers to have seen service in tanks in World War I. Following success as commander of the US II Corps in Tunisia in March 1943, he led the US Seventh Army in its invasion of Sicily. A notorious incident in which he struck a US soldier suffering from combat fatigue cost him his position, but he was reemployed as commander of the US Third Army in the build-up to D-Day. In July 1944 he led the Third Army in a race across France from Normandy, but he became embroiled in a battle of attrition on the German frontier before playing a crucial role in the relief of Bastogne during the Battle of the Bulge. Patton crossed the Rhine at Oppenheim on March 22, 1945, ending the war deep in Czechoslovakia. A brilliant exponent of armored warfare, he was one of the few Allied tank commanders who was respected by his German opposite numbers. He was killed in a traffic accident in Germany.

through the Ardennes, his ultimate objective being Antwerp. In this way he hoped to split the British 21st Army Group from the Americans. It was an audacious scheme and, although his generals were not optimistic, he was determined that the offensive should go ahead in mid-December.

BATTLE OF THE BULGE

Hitler's counteroffensive in the west, Operation Watch on the Rhine, was to be spearheaded by two panzer armies, Sepp Dietrich's Sixth, consisting largely of SS divisions, in the north, and Erich von Manteuffel's Fifth in the south. Manteuffel's southern flank would be protected by Erich Brandenburger's Seventh Army. Facing them in the Ardennes were elements of the US First Army. The sector was considered a quiet one and was held by formations recovering from the bitter fighting in the Huertgen Forest and others which had recently arrived from the United States. There were intelligence indicators that the Germans were preparing an attack, but the Allies did not believe that they were capable of mounting a major offensive, especially in the hilly and wooded Ardennes in winter.

On December 16, after a sharp predawn artillery barrage and in thick fog which grounded Allied airpower, the Germans attacked. In the north they found that the narrow winding roads slowed their advance, but one armored battle group did manage to break through the American lines and began to head for bridges over the Meuse. Manteuffel had more

Advancing in the Ardennes
German troops pass an ambushed US convoy in the opening days of their assault. Their initial success made them believe that they could deal the Allies a crippling blow.

favorable terrain and made better progress. The Germans also infiltrated men dressed in US uniforms, who changed signposts around and caused much confusion, including confining Eisenhower in his HQ in Versailles for fear that he might be assassinated. Total confusion reigned in the battle area, with many US units overrun and forced to surrender or caught while on the move. Not until the afternoon did the Allied high command accept

"The present situation is to be regarded as one of opportunity for us and not of disaster."

GENERAL EISENHOWER SPEAKING TO HIS STAFF ON DECEMBER 19, 1944

that this was a major attack. The fog persisted, but in the north Dietrich's progress remained slow, with enterprising US engineers frustrating the SS battle groups by blocking their advance with blown bridges. Manteuffel, however, continued to thrust eastward and was soon approaching Bastogne, a vital center of communications.

ACTION AROUND BASTOGNE

Eisenhower agreed that Montgomery should take over the northern part of the growing salient and take the US First and Ninth Armies temporarily under command. Montgomery also deployed British troops to guard the bridges over the Meuse River, which the Germans had to seize before advancing to Antwerp. Eisenhower ordered Patton to halt his advance eastward, but Patton had already anticipated this and was swinging his army northward to strike the Germans in their southern flank. Simultaneously, the US 101st Airborne Division was rushed in by truck to reinforce Bastogne, which troops of Manteuffel's Fifth Panzer Army now surrounded.

By December 22 Dietrich's advance had come to a grinding halt and he was ordered to pass divisions to Manteuffel, whose spearheads were continuing to advance toward the Meuse. Two days later they reached it in Dinant, but the Bastogne garrison still

Offensive in the Ardennes

According to Hitler's plan, the German Fifth and Sixth Panzer and Seventh Armies would drive through the Ardennes forests and sweep on to Antwerp. In fact, they did not even succeed in crossing the Meuse and only caused a short interruption in the Allied advance.

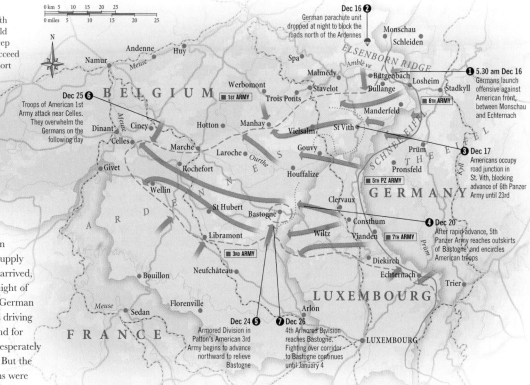

Dec 16 ❷ German parachute unit dropped at night to block the roads north of the Ardennes

❶ 5.30 am Dec 16 Germans launch offensive against American front, between Monschau and Echternach

❸ Dec 17 Americans occupy road junction in St. Vith, blocking advance of 6th Panzer Army until 23rd

❹ Dec 20 After rapid advance, 5th Panzer Army reaches outskirts of Bastogne and encircles American troops

Dec 25 ❻ Troops of American 1st Army attack near Celles. They overwhelm the Germans on the following day

Dec 24 ❺ Armored Division in Patton's American 3rd Army begins to advance northward to relieve Bastogne

❼ Dec 26 4th Armored Division reaches Bastogne. Fighting over corridor to Bastogne continues until January 4

BATTLE OF THE BULGE
DEC 16–26, 1944

— US front line Dec 16
⋯ US front line Dec 20
– – US front line Dec 25
⛳ Area of German parachute drop Dec 16/17
➤ German advance
➡ US counterattacks from Dec 25
– – – Major railroad

held out. The failure to secure the town presented Manteuffel with growing resupply difficulties. Worse, although snow had arrived, the skies had begun to clear and the might of Allied airpower was unleashed on the German forces. On December 26 Patton's forces driving up from the south relieved Bastogne and for the next few days Manteuffel battled desperately to drive them back and take the town. But the momentum had gone and the Germans were increasingly forced on to the defensive.

OPERATION NORTH WIND

On the night December 31/January 1 Hermann Balck's Army Group launched a fresh offensive, Operation North Wind. It was designed to destroy the Allied forces in Alsace, but they were ready. Eisenhower did order Devers' Sixth Army Group to withdraw in order to shorten its line, but the French refused to give up the recently liberated Strasbourg.

In any case, North Wind soon ran out of momentum. In the meantime, on New Year's Day itself, the Luftwaffe launched a major air assault against Allied airfields to destroy as many aircraft as possible. Approximately 900 aircraft took part and they managed to knock out some 300 planes, but lost the same number themselves. More serious was the fact that many of their more experienced pilots were killed, a loss that would be deeply felt during the final air defense of the Third Reich.

Realizing that his offensive had failed, Hitler turned his attention to the east, where the Red Army was about to attack across the Vistula. His attack in the west had temporarily knocked the Allies off balance, but they had recovered quickly and, while the two sides had suffered the same number of casualties, the German loss of 80,000 men and much weaponry was one they could ill afford. The offensive had delayed the Allied advance, but it would not affect the inevitable final outcome.

American wounded soldiers helped ashore
During the Allied landings in Normandy in June
1944, specially converted landing craft were used
to carry the wounded back to Britain. A continuous
service ensured speedy evacuation from the beaches.

PARTISAN RESISTANCE IN THE BALKANS

SEPTEMBER 1943–FEBRUARY 1945

Under Axis occupation, resistance movements sprang up in Yugoslavia, Greece, and Albania. The most successful campaign was waged by Tito's partisans in Yugoslavia. In all three countries there was bitter rivalry between communist and anti-communist forces and, when the Germans withdrew, these divisions had a lasting effect on postwar Europe.

1943

SEPTEMBER 8
Following Italian surrender, Tito disarms many Italian troops

SEPTEMBER 3
New Italian government signs secret armistice with Allies

SEPTEMBER
ELAS, Greek communist partisan movement, seizes Italian weapons

SEPTEMBER 9
Germans move to disarm Italian troops in Yugoslavia, Albania, and Greece

NOVEMBER 3
Germans occupy island of Kos

SEPTEMBER 16
British force occupies island of Leros in move to take over Dodecanese

NOVEMBER 12–16
German invasion and capture of Leros

DECEMBER 22
Allies grant Tito status of full Allied commander. His partisans now estimated at over 200,000 men and women under arms

DECEMBER 4
Provisional government established by Tito's partisans

1944

JANUARY
Tito agrees to British raiding forces being based on island of Vis

FEBRUARY
Truce between ELAS and EDES puts end to period of civil war

MARCH 26
ELAS sets up committee of liberation

APRIL 22
Tito's partisans take Adriatic Island of Korcula and capture 800 Germans

APRIL 26
Greek prime minister resigns. Social Democrat Papandreou forms new government

MAY 25
SS parachute battalion raids Tito's headquarters in Drvar. Tito escapes to Italy

MAY 31–JUNE 2
Joint British-partisan operation against island of Brac

JUNE 13
Tito sets up headquarters on island of Vis

AUGUST 1
Papandreou asks for British help in uniting Greek resistance against Germans

SEPTEMBER 9
Bulgaria changes sides

SEPTEMBER 17
British Foxforce lands on island of Cerigo

OCTOBER 4
Operation Manna launched; British troops land in Patras on northern coast of Peloponnese

OCTOBER 12
Germans evacuate Athens

OCTOBER 16
Papandreou's government arrives in Athens

OCTOBER 20
Tito links up with invading Russians to liberate Belgrade

OCTOBER 28
Germans begin to abandon Albania

NOVEMBER
By middle of month Germans have withdrawn north of Yugoslav border; Bulgarian forces have also withdrawn

NOVEMBER 21
Albanians free Tirana

DECEMBER 3
Civil war breaks out in Athens. Communist units start to march on the capital. British troops ordered to restore order

DECEMBER 25
Churchill flies to Athens

1945

FEBRUARY 12
Peace of Varzika. Temporary solution to Greek problem. Communists withdraw to mountains in north

JANUARY 4
New Greek government installed with Archbishop Damaskinos regent in place of King George

▓ Greece   ▓ Yugoslavia   ▓ Other events

BALKAN RESISTANCE

AFTER THE AXIS overran the Balkans in April 1941, Yugoslavia was virtually dismembered. Some parts were given to neighboring members of the Tripartite Pact, and others occupied by German or Italian forces. The rump became the puppet state of Croatia. Likewise, the easternmost part of Greece was given to Bulgaria, Macedonia occupied by the Germans, and the remainder of the country by the Italians. The monarchs of both countries established governments-in-exile, that of the Yugoslavs in London and the Greeks in Egypt. Albania remained under Italian occupation.

Resistance movements sprang up in all three countries, but they were initially disparate in nature. Albania saw a split between those who lived in the mountains in the north, who were loyal to King Zog, and the more urban communist-leaning population of the south. The latter eventually became dominant, but looked to Moscow for support and remained deeply suspicious of the Western Allies.

In Greece the main groupings were the Communist National Liberation Front (EAM), with its military arm, the National People's Liberation Army (ELAS), which also absorbed noncommunists. In the summer of 1942 ELAS began to take to the mountains, where it was joined by the noncommunist but also antimonarchist National Republican Greek League (EDES). There were a few small monarchist groups, but of little significance. SOE Middle East, based in Cairo, sent in agents, but its intelligence on the Resistance was virtually nil. Even so, they managed to get ELAS and EDES to combine in the destruction of a bridge carrying the main railroad to the port of Piraeus and an important Axis supply route to North Africa. Thereafter the two groups were mutually suspicious, especially after the British persuaded EDES to declare its support for the monarchy.

In Yugoslavia the situation was even more complicated. The two principal resistance groups were Tito's communists and Colonel Draza

OPERATIONS IN THE DODECANESE

IN THE AFTERMATH of the Italian surrender in September 1943, British Special Forces landed in the Dodecanese, Aegean islands lying close to the Turkish coast, to secure their Italian garrisons before the Germans could react. They succeeded on a number of the islands, but on the largest, Rhodes, there was also a sizeable German force, which preempted the British. Even so, Churchill was sufficiently encouraged that he ordered a brigade to be sent from the Middle East to occupy the other islands. In this way he hoped he could finally persuade Turkey to enter the war, especially since it claimed the Dodecanese, which had been an Italian possession since 1912.

Occupied Leros
A small German occupying force remained on Leros until 1945.

The Americans, who had long been suspicious of British designs on the Balkans, refused to back the operation, stating that the priority was the campaign in Italy. In particular, they would not allow any aircraft under Allied command to be used. In addition, while the British enjoyed naval superiority in the area, the air situation was very different. The Dodecanese were within easy flying range of Luftwaffe units in Greece, while the nearest British aircraft that could be used were based in Libya.

On October 3 the Germans landed on the island of Cos and secured it the following day. They then turned their attention to Leros, which contained the bulk of the British troops. The original intention was to attack on October 9, but that night the Royal Navy intercepted one of the amphibious forces approaching the island and virtually destroyed it. The operation was therefore postponed while the Luftwaffe sank or damaged a number of warships, restricting the remainder to operating by night. Finally, on November 12 the attack went in. The British, helped by the former Italian garrison, repulsed some of the landings, but the use of German paratroops proved decisive. After four days the British were forced to surrender. The remaining British troops on the islands were then evacuated. It was an embarrassing reverse for Churchill, which did little for his standing in US eyes.

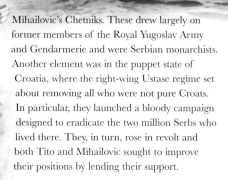

Germans come ashore
The amphibious landings on Leros in November 1943 were accompanied by air drops.

The liberation of Yugoslavia
A well-disciplined group of partisans marches through a Yugoslavian village. The young men wear uniforms and carry weapons from many different countries, a good number of them captured from Germans and Italians.

Mihailovic's Chetniks. These drew largely on former members of the Royal Yugoslav Army and Gendarmerie and were Serbian monarchists. Another element was in the puppet state of Croatia, where the right-wing Ustase regime set about removing all who were not pure Croats. In particular, they launched a bloody campaign designed to eradicate the two million Serbs who lived there. They, in turn, rose in revolt and both Tito and Mihailovic sought to improve their positions by lending their support.

CHETNIK STRATEGY

The Germans joined in the persecution of the Serbs and Mihailovic began to accept that the uprisings had been premature and threatened to destroy the Resistance movement. On the other hand, he had scant regard for the communists and became increasingly content to let the Axis

Italian soldier searching suspected partisan
An Italian of the Alpine Corps searches a Yugoslavian for weapons. In September 1943 many of the Italian occupying troops were disarmed by Tito's partisans.

occupiers operate against them. Indeed, some of his followers began to give active help to the Italians. The upshot of this was that Tito and his partisans were driven out of Serbia into Bosnia at the end of 1941.

TITO'S PARTISAN MOVEMENT

The British initially supported the Chetniks, even when it began to become apparent that Mihailovic was largely content to await the liberation of Yugoslavia. In the meantime, Tito's partisans were being relentlessly harried by a series of drives by Axis troops against them. Forced marches in the inhospitable mountains, and with little food, were frequent and tested their endurance to the limit. Yet, they maintained their discipline and continued to grow in number, especially after Tito formed the Anti-Fascist Council for the National Liberation of Yugoslavia in November 1942. He was, however, now at war with the Chetniks and during a German offensive against the partisans in early 1943, succeeded in destroying a force of 12,000 of them. The result was that Mihailovic was no longer able to muster significant forces in the field.

The British now began to take note of Tito and in July 1943 Churchill sent a personal representative to establish a system through which the Allies could give Tito active support. The British, however, still maintained contact with Mihailovic, which made Tito suspicious. On the other hand, the Soviets were not in a position to supply him with munitions, while the British and Americans were.

THE SURRENDER OF ITALY

When the Italians surrendered in September, the Germans moved quickly to disarm their garrisons in Greece and Yugoslavia. Tito partly forestalled them, taking the surrender of 10 Italian divisions, adding greatly to his stock of weapons. He was also able to liberate parts of Dalmatia, Croatia, and Slovenia.

In April 1944, the Germans launched their seventh and final offensive against the partisans. Tito was very nearly captured when a German airborne unit was dropped close to his HQ, and he had to be flown to Italy. He then established himself on Vis, which was being used as a base for joint Anglo-partisan raids on German-occupied islands.

Anti-Tito partisans
Many anticommunist Yugoslavians were armed by the Germans to fight Tito's forces. In spite of this, Tito managed to gain control of large parts of the country.

TITO (JOSIP BROZ)

TITO (1892–1980) was born Josip Broz in Croatia. From the early 1920s he was a clandestine revolutionary communist, using a number of pseudonyms, one of which, Tito, he adopted permanently. In the late 1930s he spent time in Moscow, then took over as Secretary of the Yugoslav Communist Party. When Germany invaded in April 1941, the communists stood by, since the USSR was still an ally of the Third Reich. The June 1941 invasion of the Soviet Union changed this, but Tito and his followers were initially more concerned with eradicating rival groups so as to ensure a postwar communist government. When he realized that this could not happen until the Axis occupiers had been driven out, he began to recruit partisans from all sectors. Tito's leadership ensured that he gained the support of the Western Allies to add to that of the Soviet Union. After the liberation of Belgrade in November 1944, he was able to bring the monarchists onto his side and became head of the new federal Yugoslav government in March 1945. Later that year he established a dictatorship, which he maintained until his death. It was marked by his ability to preserve the unity of the state, with its very disparate population, and to steer a neutral line between Moscow and the West.

At about the same time the British finally abandoned their support for Mihailovic. In August 1944 Tito met Churchill in Italy and the following month, with Soviet forces advancing toward Yugoslavia, he flew to Moscow in order to coordinate operations with them.

ALBANIA AND GREECE

The effect of the Italian surrender on Albania was somewhat different. The resistance groups immediately combined and succeeded in capturing much of the Italian equipment in the country and quickly liberated large areas. The Germans reacted by sending troops into the capital Tirana and then went on to place an iron grip on Albania, with harsh reprisals on the population. Enver Hoxha, the communist leader, decided that Germany would lose the war, and split with King Zog's supporters. The latter were now inveigled by the Germans into operating against the communists, thus starting a virtual civil war.

In Greece SOE worked hard to try to create a combined ELAS/EDES resistance movement, even to the extent of establishing a joint HQ, with ELAS members being allowed the majority of the key positions in it. This recognized the fact it was now

the more powerful of the two groups. In August 1943 a resistance delegation was taken to Cairo to negotiate with the Greek government-in-exile and the British. The delegation demanded that King George should not return to Greece until there had been a plebiscite on the future of the monarchy. This was refused and the delegation returned to Greece convinced that the British meant to enforce a return of the monarchy. Fighting broke out between ELAS and EDES, although a truce was arranged and each group was given its own operational area, which meant that EDES was now confined to northwestern Greece.

The fall of Romania to the Soviets at the end of August 1944 and Bulgaria's change of sides a week later dramatically transformed the situation in the Balkans. The Germans immediately began to pull their troops out of the Greek islands in preparation for a withdrawal northward. In October the Soviets thrust into Yugoslavia and, in conjunction with Tito's partisans, liberated Belgrade on the 20th of the month. The Red Army then advanced north into Hungary. Simultaneously, the Germans were withdrawing from Greece.

Ultra had forewarned the British of this. It was also clear to them that ELAS was bent on seizing power as soon as the Germans left. Under pressure from Greek army officers in Egypt, the king formed a new government, which would represent all political parties. Once the German withdrawal

The Soviets reach Belgrade
Following the capture of the city on October 20, 1944, a Soviet soldier with a mine detector makes the streets safe for the passage of vehicles.

Marching into Corinth
Headed by a detachment of ELAS partisans, British troops enter Corinth in October 1944.

"In the midst of our task of... maintaining the rudiments of order... we have become involved in a furious, although not as yet very bloody struggle."

CHURCHILL ON THE SITUATION IN GREECE, IN A TELEGRAM TO ROOSEVELT, DECEMBER 17, 1944

began in earnest, Churchill ordered British troops to be landed in southern Greece. Then, as soon as the Germans evacuated Athens, a parachute brigade was landed at a nearby airfield, while the Royal Navy occupied the port of Piraeus. In the meantime, Churchill obtained Stalin's agreement that he would not interfere in Greece provided he was given a free hand in the rest of the Balkans. On October 16 the reformed Greek government established itself in Athens. The British warned that it must move quickly to disarm the guerrillas, recreate an army, introduce a new currency, and set up the necessary machinery for international aid agencies to feed the population.

The government did its best, but it was not good enough. On December 3 communist demonstrators clashed with police in

Athens and ELAS units began to march on the capital. British reinforcements were quickly sent to Greece, but the fighting spread rapidly through the country. On Christmas Day Churchill arrived in Athens and a peace conference was set up, presided over by the respected Archbishop Damaskinos. Churchill pleaded with the delegates to resolve their differences and to continue helping in the defeat of Germany. He then persuaded King George, who was still in the Middle East, to accept the archbishop as Regent. A new government was formed at the beginning of January and a truce was signed by the warring factions. This was enshrined in the Peace of Varkiza of February 12, 1945. The communists agreed to disband their forces and support the formation of a national army. In fact, ELAS was determined on another bid to seize power once the war had ended and many ELAS members returned to the mountains.

Civil war
Steel-helmeted ELAS troops use a corner building as a shelter as they fire at police headquarters during the fighting in Athens in December 1944.

A number of massive Soviet offensives along the entire Eastern Front began with the launch of Operation Bagration on June 23 in Byelorussia. By the end of July the Red Army had reached the Vistula River and Warsaw. In subsequent months it advanced in the north through the Baltic states, and in the south through the Ukraine into southern Poland, Romania, Bulgaria, Yugoslavia, and Hungary.

JUNE 10
Soviet troops launch attack on Finland in direction of Viipuri

JUNE 20
Viipuri falls

JUNE 23
Soviet offensive in Byelorussia–Operation Bagration–begins along 450-mile (700-km) front

JUNE 26
Soviet forces take Vitebsk, one of cities that Hitler has given orders to be held to the last man

JULY 3
Minsk, capital of Byelorussia, is liberated by Soviet troops

JULY 13
Soviet offensive is launched south of Pripet Marshes

JULY 17
Soviet forces reach Bug River, the 1939 Polish border

JULY 23
Extermination camp at Majdanek, east of Lublin, is liberated

AUGUST 1
Soviet forces take Kaunas, capital of Lithuania

AUGUST 1
Poles in Warsaw begin uprising against Germans

AUGUST 20
Soviet forces land at mouth of Danube River and launch attack into Romania

AUGUST 23
King of Romania declares war to be at an end

AUGUST 30
Germans withdraw from Bulgaria

AUGUST 31
Soviet forces enter Bucharest

SEPTEMBER 5
Soviet Union signs armistice with Bulgaria

SEPTEMBER 8
Soviet forces enter Bulgaria

SEPTEMBER 19
Armistice is signed with Finland

SEPTEMBER 14
Soviet forces enter suburbs of Warsaw

SEPTEMBER 22
Soviet forces occupy Estonian capital, Tallinn

OCTOBER 1
Soviet forces cross border from Romania into Yugoslavia

OCTOBER 11
Hungarians sign armistice

OCTOBER 15
Riga is captured; Germans retreat across Finnish border to Kirkenes in Norway

OCTOBER 20
Belgrade falls to Soviet forces after week-long battle

OCTOBER 29
Soviet forces begin last stage of advance against Budapest, crossing Tisza River

NOVEMBER 4
Soviet forces reach southern and eastern suburbs of Budapest but fail to break through

DECEMBER 5
Soviet forces launch third attempt to capture Budapest, which Hitler has ordered to be defended to the last man

DECEMBER 26
Soviet forces begin siege of Budapest, in which two Hungarian and four German divisions have become trapped

■ Advance in the Baltic region
Jun 10–Oct 15, 1944

■ Advance through Eastern Europe
Jun 22–Dec 27, 1944

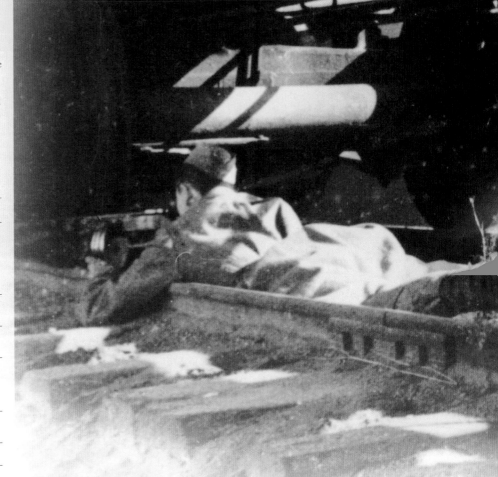

ADVANCE INTO POLAND

THE GERMAN ABANDONMENT of Sevastopol in early May 1944 had resulted in the loss of some 65,000 men. By the end of the month, total German casualties on the Eastern Front stood at approximately 1.25 million dead, over 3 million wounded or sick, and over 500,000 missing.

Casualties had remorselessly eaten away at the Ostheer's morale and fighting efficiency, particularly among the infantry. Since 1943 a growing number of troops had been conscripted from ethnic Germans in eastern Europe, and they now made up nearly one-third of Army Group Center's new intake. Senior commanders doubted both their commitment to the Third Reich and their ability to withstand the shock of their first battlefield encounter with the Red Army. At the same time, the Luftwaffe was becoming alarmed at the transfer of large numbers of day fighters and pilots to the west to defend the Reich against American bombers and at the toll being taken by constant combat.

As the spring rains fell, both sides made plans for their summer campaigns. The Stavka planned a westward drive, of which the largest element—

Operation Bagration—would be launched north and south of the Pripet Marshes, with the goal of expelling the Germans from Byelorussia, trapping and destroying Army Group Center, and then advancing through central Poland, toward Warsaw and Lublin. To the south, another offensive—the Lwow-Sandomiercz operation—was to roll through Ukrainian Galicia into southern Poland.

OPERATION BAGRATION

Operation Bagration envisaged a vast envelopment of Army Group Center along a 450-mile (700-km) front. A northern pincer, spearheaded by the Third Byelorussian Front and supported by the Second Byelorussian Front, was to drive 200 miles (320 km) westward to Minsk, where it was to link with the southern pincer formed by the northern wing of the First Byelorussian Front (see map page 247). Carrying out this encirclement would be 1.7 million troops, over twice the number in Army Group Center. Initially, they would have the support of 2,715 tanks and 1,355 assault guns, approximately six times the number available to the Germans.

Close combat in Lwow
Red Army infantry advance cautiously through the rail yards in Lwow in the Ukraine. The city was abandoned by the Germans and liberated on July 27, 1944, by troops of the First Ukrainian Front.

Bagration was preceded by a closely meshed web of deception measures and, from June 19, by concerted partisan operations against rail communications in occupied Byelorussia. By the summer of 1944 some 270,000 partisans in the region were cooperating closely with deep reconnaissance units of the Red Army and tying down up to 15 percent of Army Group Center's combat strength.

On June 22 a "reconnaissance in force" was launched by the Red Army to probe Army Group Center's defenses. In the early hours of June 23, after a crushing artillery barrage, the blow fell as

the Third Byelorussian Fronts burst on the Third Panzer Army in the area of Vitebsk. Commanded by General G. H. Reinhardt, this was a panzer army in name only, consisting of nine infantry divisions forward and two in reserve. Four of Reinhardt's divisions, comprising LIII Corps, were, on Hitler's insistence, committed to the static defense of Vitebsk. By the evening of the 23rd, Reinhardt was making demands that the commander of Army Group Center, Field Marshal Ernst Busch, allow him to evacuate Vitebsk immediately. Busch relayed this to Hitler, who eventually agreed that three divisions could fight their way out, leaving one behind to hold Vitebsk.

It mattered little, since all four divisions of LIII Corps were lost,

wiped from the map without a trace. Those who escaped the clutches of the Red Army fell into the hands of Soviet partisans, who had little enthusiasm for taking prisoners. As Army Group Center splintered under the ferocity of Bagration, Reinhardt lost a second corps and was now left with only two of his 11 divisions. To the south, around Bobruisk, the greater part of the Ninth Army was encircled. In the center of the German line the Fourth Army was forced to give ground to the Second Byelorussian Front and was threatened with isolation as the Red Army drove on toward Minsk.

On June 26 Hitler demanded that Orsha and Mogilev, which lay in the path of, respectively, the Third and Second Byelorussian Fronts, should be held to the last man, so condemning another two German divisions to destruction. He then tore himself away from the situation in Normandy to take personal control of plugging the gaping holes that had been torn in Army Group Center's front.

FALL OF MINSK

By June 28 Red Army tanks had already crossed the Berezina River and were racing westward. Busch, completely out of his depth, was replaced by Model, who immediately grasped that the Red Army's

The road to Minsk
A smashed German artillery battery is left in the wake of the drive by the Second Byelorussian Front on Minsk—part of Operation Bagration — in early July 1944.

Majdanek discovered
A pile of human remains bears grim testimony to the horrors of the extermination camp in Majdanek, near Lublin in Poland, discovered by Soviet troops on July 23, 1944.

objectives lay far beyond the rear of Army Group Center. Minsk fell on July 3, having been cut off by the Third and First Byelorussian Fronts. The envelopment left large numbers of troops of the German Fourth and Ninth Armies trapped in a giant cauldron east of the city. Between July 5 and 11 the Red Army and partisans began methodically to slice up these pockets while the Soviet armor continued to roll westward, reaching Vilna on July 13 and Bialystok on the 27th.

The scale of German losses in Bagration can only be estimated, but in the course of a month the Red Army had destroyed the equivalent of 25 divisions of the Ostheer—some 350,000 men. This number included 150,000 taken prisoner, of whom at least half would die during transportation to the camps, or from malnutrition and disease after they reached their destinations. The few survivors would not see Germany again until the middle of the next decade. The Red Army lost some 179,000 men.

LWOW–SANDOMIERCZ OPERATION

As the Red Army approached Vilna, preparations were completed for the Lwow-Sandomiercz operation, to be undertaken by Marshal I S Konev's First Ukrainian Front. A mighty force of around 1 million men, 1,600 tanks, 14,000 guns and mortars, and 2,800 combat aircraft was now ready to attack the German Army Group North Ukraine. In early summer the army group's strength on the ground had

nearly matched that fielded by Konev, but it had been much weakened as units had been withdrawn to stem the Soviet floodtide in Byelorussia.

Konev attacked on July 13. After two days of fierce fighting, the center of the German line was breached near Koltov, enabling infantry and two Soviet tank armies to pour through on July 16 and 17. The German XIII Corps and part of the First Panzer Army were encircled and then overwhelmed within a week, while the Red Army tanks advanced westward, bypassing Lwow to the north. By July 30 Konev had crossed the Vistula, having advanced 130 miles (210 km) in 17 days, and gained a lodgment on the western bank in Sandomiercz, later expanded into the Baranow bridgehead.

ADVANCE TO WARSAW

At the end of July, troops of the First Byelorussian Front reached the Vistula and by August 2 they were pushing into the outskirts of Warsaw. The capture of the Polish capital had not played a major role in the Stavka's planning for the summer of 1944. Furthermore, the situation on the ground was complicated by a rising within the city by the Polish Home Army, an armed demonstration of Polish nationalism unwelcome to Stalin. The advance to Warsaw was halted, leaving the German garrison in the city to put down the uprising ruthlessly.

As the major fighting initiated by Bagration came to an end, the Ostheer set about reinforcing the line along the Vistula while the Red Army turned to the task of rebuilding and reequipping its exhausted formations. Offensive operations in Poland were not to resume until January 1945.

OPERATIONS IN THE BALTIC

The Stavka's operational focus now shifted north to the Baltic and south to Romania. In the Baltic the German Army Group North faced four Red Army fronts whose goal was to liberate Estonia, Latvia, and Lithuania. By the end of July the Leningrad Front had captured Narva on the Baltic coast, the Third Baltic Front had driven deep into Latvia and Estonia, and the Second and First Baltic Fronts had thrust toward Riga and Memel, so severing land communications between Army Groups North and Center. On August 16 the Germans launched a counterattack which briefly reestablished a land link between the two army groups and offered Army Group North an opportunity to pull out of the Baltic states with all its heavy equipment.

Confrontation of tanks in Poland
A T-34 noses its way past a damaged German Mk VI Tiger I heavy tank. It usually took about six medium tanks to knock out a massively armored Tiger.

Red Army troops in Poland
Infantrymen race through a blazing street during Operation Bagration. Because Red Army soldiers were not issued with blankets, greatcoats were worn even in the summer.

THE WARSAW UPRISING

FROM 1939 THE POLES had organized an underground resistance movement. Its armed wing was the Polish Home Army, whose members were loyal to the Polish government-in-exile in London. However, in July 1944 the Soviet Union had established its own communist government in waiting in the liberated Polish city of Lublin. On August 1, 1944, with the Red Army only 12 miles (19 km) from Warsaw, 20,000 members of the Polish Home Army, commanded by General Tadeusz Bor Komorowski, rose up against the German garrison. In four days they succeeded in taking control of about three-fifths of Warsaw, but no strategic points.

The First Byelorussian Front did not come to the aid of the Home Army, instead halting to the south and east of Warsaw. Warsaw had never been an objective of Bagration, and if the Red Army entered the city, it would face an army of citizens who were also hostile to the Soviet Union. Stalin prevaricated, even refusing a British and American request to land on Soviet soil to provide the Home Army with arms and medical supplies. When Home Army detachments from outside Warsaw attempted to aid the uprising, they were surrounded and disarmed by Red Army troops.

Freed of pressure from the Red Army, SS troops quashed the uprising with utter ruthlessness. Captured Polish fighters were summarily executed by squads of released convicts, as were doctors and nurses attending the wounded. Civilians were marched in front of tanks as human shields. Gas was used to flush out those who attempted to flee through the sewers.

On September 10 the First Byelorussian Front finally moved on Warsaw, but did not break into the city. On October 2 Komorowski surrendered. In the uprising some 15,000 members of the Home Army and approximately 225,000 civilians had lost their lives. Those who had survived were deported to German camps while the Germans set about the total demolition of what remained of the ancient city.

Injured resistance fighter
Few members of the Polish Home Army managed to escape the terrible vengeance wreaked by the Germans as they suppressed the uprising. Even hospitals, with staff and patients inside, were burned down.

German staff car captured by insurgents
In the early days of the uprising the rebels overwhelmed parts of the German garrison. They failed, however, to capture the railroad stations or the bridges over the Vistula.

Hitler, however, spurned the opportunity. The Red Army went on the offensive again in mid-September. Tallinn, the Estonian capital, was taken on September 22, and Riga fell on October 15. By mid-October the coast around Memel had been secured, but the city itself was to hold out until January 1945. Twenty-six divisions of Army Group North withdrew to the Courland peninsula, where they remained until the end of the war in order to provide the German Navy with continuing access to Baltic waters for the training of U-boat crews.

WAR WITH FINLAND

After the failure of Operation Citadel, Finland had sought to make peace with the Soviet Union, but the negotiations had broken down. In the fall of 1943 Finland had a highly skilled and durable army of 350,00 men who faced just 180,000 Red Army troops of poor quality. In northern Lapland the German 20th

> ## "…in the final analysis, what can we expect of a front… if one now sees that in the rear the most important posts were occupied by downright destructionists, not defeatists, but destructionists?"

HITLER IN A REVIEW OF THE MILITARY SITUATION ON THE EASTERN FRONT, JULY 31, 1944

Mountain Army was some 180,000 strong, more than a match for the Soviet troops on the Karelian Front. The Finns, however, had no illusions about the likely outcome of the war. While their president, Risto Ryti, pledged to the Germans not to sign a separate peace with the Soviet Union, they were determined to sit out the conflict.

For his part, Stalin was eager to settle with Finland before Bagration. Having reinforced the Red Army's Karelian and Leningrad Fronts, Stalin ordered them to go on the offensive in June 1944 against the vulnerable southeast flank of the Finnish army. The Finns clung on throughout the summer. On August 4 Marshal Carl Gustaf Mannerheim, the hero of the Winter War of 1939–40 and the Finnish commander-in-chief, succeeded Ryti as head of state and repudiated the latter's pledge. Moscow then agreed to resume negotiations with Finland on the condition that Mannerheim broke off relations with

Germany and the 20th Mountain Army left Finnish territory by September 15. The Finns were able to demand this withdrawal following a German attempt on September 15 to seize the Finnish naval base of Suursaari, which was beaten off with heavy German losses. An armistice was signed with the Soviet Union on September 19 as the German withdrawal continued, and by the end of October the 20th Mountain Army was in Norway, bringing an end to Finnish participation in World War II.

BALKAN STALINGRAD

By the end of July 1944 relations between Germany and Romania had badly deteriorated. The Romanian dictator, Marshal Ion Antonescu, insisted on equality

Celebrations in Bulgaria
Bulgarians celebrated their country's signing of an armistice with the Soviet Union on September 5, 1944. Three days later Bulgaria declared war on Germany.

Jewish man mourns in Budapest
Over 60 percent of Hungary's 750,000 Jews were sent to Auschwitz in 1944. Some, however, were still living in Budapest when it came under siege in December.

Advance from the Baltic to the Balkans

With the opening, on June 23, of Operation Bagration along a 450-mile (700-km) front in Byelorussia, the relentless Soviet advance through eastern Europe got under way. Along the entire Eastern Front, from the Baltic states in the north to Romania, Bulgaria, and Yugoslavia in the south, the Germans were steadily pushed back.

2 Jun 20 Soviet forces take Viipuri

3 Jun 21 Soviet forces attack Finns east of Lake Ladoga

KARELIAN FRONT

1 Jun 10 Soviet forces launch offensive against Finns

Sept 22 4 Soviet forces occupy Tallinn

LENINGRAD FRONT

3RD BALTIC FRONT

Oct 15 5 Riga is captured from Germans

2ND BALTIC FRONT

ARMY GROUP NORTH

1ST BALTIC FRONT

3RD BYELORUSSIAN FRONT

Aug 1 7 Poles in Warsaw launch uprising against Germans

ARMY GROUP CENTRE

2 Jul 3 Minsk is liberated

2ND BYELORUSSIAN FRONT

5 Jul 20 Brest-Litovsk is taken by Soviet forces

1 Jun 23 Operation Bagration is launched in Byelorussia

1ST BYELORUSSIAN FRONT

Sept 14 8 Soviet forces reach outskirts of Warsaw

ARMY GROUP NORTH UKRAINE

4 Jul 13 Soviet offensive is launched south of Pripet Marshes

Jul 23 6 Soviet forces liberate Majdanek extermination camp

3 Jul 20 Soviet forces reach Bug River west of Kowel

1ST UKRAINIAN FRONT

Nov 4 6 Soviet forces reach outskirts of Budapest. Siege of city begins Dec 26

4TH UKRAINIAN FRONT

ARMY GROUP SOUTH UKRAINE

2ND UKRAINIAN FRONT

Oct 6 4 2nd Ukranian Front launches operation to conquer Hungary

3RD UKRAINIAN FRONT

Oct 20 5 Belgrade falls to Soviet forces at end of week-long battle

ARMY GROUP F

1 Aug 20 Soviet forces land at mouth of Danube and advance into Romania

Aug 31 2 Soviet forces enter Bucharest

BULGARIAN ARMY

ARMY GROUP E

3 Sept 8 Soviet forces enter Bulgaria

THE EASTERN FRONT
JUN 10–DEC 26, 1944

— German front line Jun 22
–·– German front line Jul 25
–– German front line Sept 15
···· German front line Dec 15
⟹ Soviet advance
⟹ Bulgarian advance

0 km 50 100 150 200
0 miles 50 100 150 200

of command, and the Germans were forced to accept it despite their deep misgivings about the evident inefficiency and corruption of their Romanian allies. In May Antonescu had also opened secret but short-lived negotiations with the Soviet Union. The new German commander of Army Group South Ukraine, General Johannes Friessner, was well aware of the unreliability of his Romanian allies and the possible dangers of shared command. His warnings were ignored by Hitler.

Army Group South Ukraine consisted of two German armies and two Romanian armies, all of which were short of experience, armor, air support, and motor transportation. On August 20 the Soviet Second and Third Ukrainian Fronts fell on Friessner's forces. Within 24 hours the German Sixth Army had been cut off, and—as it became apparent to Friessner that the Romanians were surrendering without a fight—it quickly found itself trapped in a cauldron between the Dniester and the Pruth.

Antonescu was arrested on August 23 and King Carol of Romania then appealed to his troops to lay down their arms. Two days later, Hitler ordered 150 aircraft to bomb the Romanian capital Bucharest, giving the Romanians the pretext to declare war on Germany. Meanwhile, under constant attack from the Red Air Force, the Sixth Army tried to fight its way westward. Another 200,000 German troops were consumed in nine days, a disaster to rank alongside Stalingrad, though the end came more swiftly and in stifling summer heat.

On August 30 the Red Army seized the oilfields in Ploesti, Germany's last major source of crude oil, and on the following day took Bucharest. Romania was rapidly occupied by Soviet troops, together with Bulgaria, which declared war on Germany on September 8. The 500,000-strong Bulgarian Army joined the Red Army as it entered Yugoslavia.

To the north, the Red Army had overextended itself as it pushed into southeast Hungary against more resolute opposition than it had encountered in

Romania. Its leading forces reached Debrecen, just 70 miles (110 km) from Budapest, on October 8. But then, as panic rose in the Hungarian capital, two German panzer divisions attacked the Soviet spearhead to cut off and destroy three corps. The Second and Third Ukrainian Fronts made further attempts in November and December to advance

to Budapest, but it was not until December 26 that they succeeded in encircling the city. The four German and two Hungarian divisions inside the city were ordered to hold out until relieved. This relief, however, was never to come, and when 30,000 troops attempted to break out on February 11, 1945, fewer than 700 reached the lines to the west.

ASIA AND THE PACIFIC

JUNE–DECEMBER 1944

After victory at the Battle of the Philippine Sea in June 1944, the Americans took the tide of war to the Philippines and thus cut Japan's lines of communication with the Southern Resources Area. With complementary victories in western New Guinea and Burma, by the end of 1944 Japan's defeat was assured.

JUNE 2
Start of Japanese withdrawal from the Kohima area. British relief of Imphal by June 22

JUNE 5
First B-29 combat operation; directed at railroad yards in Bangkok, Siam

JUNE 15
B-29 raid on Japan from China

JUNE 15
American marines land on Saipan

JUNE 20
Japanese start retreat from Imphal toward Burma

JUNE 19–20
Battle of the Philippine Sea. Japanese lose three carriers and more than 400 aircraft

JUNE 22
British reopen Kohima-Imphal road

JULY 9
US declaration that Saipan had been secured. Japanese mass suicides following collapse of resistance at the end of June

JULY 21
US landings on Guam; island declared secure August 8

JULY 24
US landings on Tinian; island declared secure August 1

AUGUST 3
Allies capture town of Myitkyina

JULY 30
American landings on the Vogelkop Peninsula at western end of New Guinea

AUGUST 10–17
Japanese defeated in series of actions around Aitape on northern coast of central New Guinea

SEPTEMBER 9–14
American carrier raids on the southern and central Philippines

SEPTEMBER 15
American landings on island of Morotai in Dutch East Indies. Airbase established to support upcoming Philippines campaign

SEPTEMBER 15
American landings on Peleliu in the Palau Islands; island declared secure October 12

OCTOBER 10–17
US carrier offensive over the Ryukyus, Formosa, and the Philippines

OCTOBER 15
Chinese and British start offensive from Myitkyina

OCTOBER 20
Virtually unopposed landings on Leyte by 60,000 US troops

OCTOBER 23
First Japanese reinforcements arrive on Leyte. Main Japanese effort ended after shattering of troop convoy by US aircraft on November 11

OCTOBER 23–26
Battle of Leyte Gulf. Japanese navy crippled by loss of four carriers and three battleships. First use of kamikaze suicide aircraft

NOVEMBER 24
First raid on the Japanese mainland by B-29s from Saipan

DECEMBER 6–7
Japanese counterattack against US airbases on Leyte

DECEMBER 7–25
US landings near and capture of Ormoc. Japanese high command writes off forces on Leyte

DECEMBER 15
Chinese enter Bhamo in northern Burma. US landings on Mindoro

DECEMBER 26
Americans declare Leyte and Samar secure

| India and Burma Jun–Dec 1944 | Central Pacific Jun–Sept, 1944 | Invasion of the Philippines Oct 20, 1944 | Other events |

JAPAN NEAR THE BRINK

THE JAPANESE CONQUEST of the British possession of Burma between December 1941 and May 1942 cost the victors few casualties and achieved three objectives: the closing of the Burma Road and the main supply route into Kuomintang (Nationalist) China; the possession of a country rich in resources, such as rice; and defense in depth for Southeast Asia. Burma became part of the perimeter on which Japan planned to fight its enemies to exhaustion.

The mountains, valleys, and jungle of the India–Burma border did indeed serve as a line

Aerial resupply of the Chindits
The Chindits—Allied troops commanded by Orde Wingate who fought behind the Japanese lines in Burma—depended on efficient aerial resupply missions.

of mutual exhaustion in spring 1942, but events after the monsoon ended in November 1942 changed the attitudes of the Japanese. For the British, the defeat in Burma had to be reversed and, at the insistence of the Americans, the overland route to China had to be reopened. The British began two offensives, one from the Chittagong area on the Indian coast of the Bay of Bengal into the Arakan, and another by a force known as the Chindits, which were infiltrated across the border area. A Japanese division comprehensively and embarrassingly outfought the

The high ground
Sikh machine-gunners look out from Pagoda Hill during the recapture of Mandalay in March 1945, while the battle rages below around Fort Dufferin.

British corps in the Arakan, while the only real achievement registered by the Chindits was measured in column inches in British newspapers rather than on the ground. But the Japanese read the signs correctly: the 1942–43 effort was only a foretaste of what would come as soon as the British recovered their strength in northeast India and the Allies sought to clear Burma in order to reopen overland communications with the Chinese Nationalists. In 1943–44 the situation on the line of mutual exhaustion, which a year earlier had been convenient to both sides, threatened to change, posing new problems for the Japanese. Accordingly the imperial high command undertook the so-called "March on Delhi," a spoiling offensive into northeast India that would secure the border towns of Imphal and Kohima at the end of the dry season. The onset of the monsoon would prevent any Allied counteroffensive to recover the towns.

SETBACKS FOR THE JAPANESE
Before the Japanese offensive began, however, a Sino-American force in northeast India began to advance down the Hukawng valley in the direction of Myitkyina. A Japanese diversionary attack in the Arakan was quickly halted, and while Japanese formations crossed the Chindwin to move against Imphal and Kohima, a second Chindit operation, with units moved by transport aircraft, began in the Japanese rear areas. Again, the Chindits achieved little in real terms. By the time that Myitkyina fell in August 1944, however, disaster had overwhelmed the Japanese at Imphal and Kohima.

The Japanese move through the mountains failed either to encircle British formations or to capture the two towns. The British were therefore able to withdraw in good order to strong new defensive positions, in which they were kept supplied by transport aircraft drawn from as far away as the Mediterranean theater. Although the siege of Kohima was very quickly broken, the Japanese still refused to abandon the offensive. Their supply lines were wholly inadequate, however, and, in effect, the besiegers became the besieged. After Imphal had been relieved on June 22 by Allied forces coming forward from Kohima, the Japanese 15th Army was destroyed piecemeal. The loss of some 50,000 men killed and wounded was to compromise the army's ability to conduct an effective defensive campaign in northern Burma in 1944–45.

Chindit insignia
The Chindit badge portrays a Chinthe, the mythical beast that guards Burmese temples. It was from the word Chinthe that the Chindits derived their name.

The main Allied offensive effort in northern Burma was undertaken by the British. The capture of Ramree Island in December 1944 was the first in a series of operations in the Arakan that ended with the capture of strategic targets. Meanwhile, the main British effort was directed against Meiktila—which was captured on March 4—while the attention of the Japanese was focused on Mandalay. With Chinese forces breaking down resistance on the Myitkyina and Salween sectors, the Japanese hoped to retain Mandalay and retake Meiktila. By the end of March, however, they were pulling back through the lower Salween valley in order to defend Tennasserim and Siam, while the British

Marauders in the Burmese jungle
In 1944 a detachment of "Merrill's Marauders," a US commando force, patrols the Burmese jungle on the lookout for snipers during the advance on Myitkyina.

THE INDIAN NATIONAL ARMY

NOT ALL INDIANS supported the Allies in World War II. The most prominent of those who sided with the Axis powers was Subhas Chandra Bose, who was elected president of the Indian National Congress Party in 1938. Imprisoned by the British, he escaped in 1941 and went first to Germany for talks with Nazi leaders and then to Japanese-held Singapore. With the help of the Japanese, Bose led the 40,000 strong Indian National Army (INA), which advanced across Burma but was defeated in India in 1944. When Japan surrendered in August 1945, Bose fled India and died after a plane crash in Taiwan. Reviled by some, Bose is praised by others for fostering anticolonial sentiment in the subcontinent.

Indian Nationalist
Subhas Chandra Bose was the founding father of the Indian National Army and a fierce advocate of Indian independence from Britain.

Hitler's Indian allies
Before taking over the Japanese-formed INA, Bose created an Indian Legion in the German Army. Some 3,000-strong, it became part of the Waffen-SS in 1944.

advanced down the Irrawaddy and Sittang valleys. The British took Rangoon unopposed on May 3, just ahead of the monsoon. By then the rationale for much of the Allied effort in Burma had been overtaken by events. Although the first convoys to Nationalist China reached Kunming in January 1945, their importance had been reduced by air supply routes. Throughout the next eight months overland communications never accounted for more than a twelfth of the materials supplied to the Chinese. Despite its local significance, the clearing of Burma contributed little to victory over Japan.

THE JAPANESE IN CHINA

In 1937–38 the Japanese overran virtually the whole of China that was worth occupying. Thereafter, aside from some minor operations in the south of the country in 1941, they adopted a primarily defensive stance. Saddled with a crippling manpower and financial commitment, without the military means

Japanese prayer flag
Many Japanese soldiers carried flags inside their combat jackets during World War II. The flags were often decorated with prayers and family names, and were designed to bring good luck on the battlefield.

to defeat the Kuomintang, and unwilling to sponsor a credible alternative to the Chungking regime, the Japanese faced a war that could not be won.

In the north the Japanese devastated considerable areas and neutralized communist resistance in the so-called "Three-All" offensives—"Kill All," "Burn All," and "Loot All." However, between 1938 and 1944 there existed in many areas a "special undeclared peace," despite occasional "rice raids" by the occupying troops. Nationalists, communists, and Japanese effectively observed an unofficial truce, broken by clashes between Chinese factions and local Japanese operations. The Nationalists were unwilling to fight because they felt that Japan's defeat was assured and would come without any major contribution from the Chinese. Their policy was therefore to preserve their strength in readiness for a resumption of the civil war with the communists. The latter naturally reasoned along very much the same lines as the Nationalists.

Chinese infantry
Chinese infantrymen ford a stream in southern Yunnan province on their way to reinforce troops fighting the Japanese on the Salween River front.

After the start of the Pacific war in 1941, however, the United States sought a full Chinese military contribution to Japan's defeat. It undertook to provide supplies for an army of 90 divisions that would undertake major offensive operations. The Americans also planned to use airfields in China from which to bomb the Japanese Home Islands. The first 14th Air Force raid on Formosa, on November 25, 1943—launched from within China—was by common consent the spur for the Japanese high command to consider a general offensive in China. Its aim was to secure the Peking–Hankow, Canton–Hankow, and Hunan–Kwangsi railroad lines and the airfields at Hengyang, Kweilin, Ling Ling, and Liuchow.

The offensive, code-named Ichi-Go, involved some 620,000 troops and began in April 1944 with the conquest of Hunan province. The main effort was made south of the Yangtze, below Ichang, in May. The Japanese secured Liuyang on June 14, Changsa four days later, and Hengyang on August 8. The next phase of operations saw simultaneous offensives from Hengyang toward Kweilin and Liuchow, and from Canton (Guangzhou) toward Wuchow and Nanning. So great was Japanese success that by December they had secured unbroken communications over land from Malaya to Korea. The Japanese occupied Tushan and Tuyün in December 1944 and Sichuan in

The temples, cellars, and mysterious chambers covering Mandalay Hill were made of reinforced concrete. No Japanese was alive and visible; but scores of them were alive, invisible, in the subterranean chambers. A gruesome campaign of extermination began, among the temples of one of the most sacred places of the Buddhist faith. Sikh machine-gunners sat all day on the flat roofs, their guns aimed down the hill on either side of the covered stairway. Every now and then a Japanese put out his head and fired a quick upward shot. A Sikh got a bullet through his brain five yards from me.

JOHN MASTERS OF THE GURKHA RIFLES ON THE BRITISH RECAPTURE OF MANDALAY, MARCH 20, 1945

January 1945, but spring saw the start of a general reduction and withdrawal of the Japanese forces in southern China in readiness for transfer north to Manchoutikuo (Manchuria).

POLITICAL CONSEQUENCES

The Ichi-Go offensive was of dubious military relevance, but it was significant in two other ways. First, the failure of the Kuomintang to offer any kind of coherent or successful resistance to Japanese aggression provoked a full-blown crisis between the regime and the United States. Washington, tiring of Kuomintang ineffectiveness, sought to place its local commander, Joseph Stilwell, in charge of all operations in the region. Without any viable political alternative to the regime led by Chiang Kai-shek, however, the effort miscarried. When the Americans threatened to choke his regime to death, Chiang simply threatened to die. In October 1944 Washington was forced to recall Stilwell and further underwrite the Nationalist regime in Chungking.

Second, and more importantly, the Kuomintang failure to resist the Ichi-Go offensives had a profound effect on the the Chinese public. Hunan province was overrun at the cost of just 869 Japanese dead. The collapse of Kuomintang resistance, or more accurately its failure to materialize at all, enraged local

Flying Tigers
US pilots in China were known as "Flying Tigers." After July 1942 they were part of the US China Air Task Force. They painted sharks' mouths on their planes to cause alarm among the shark-fearing Japanese.

populations which for years had lived under Nationalist misrule. Angry civilians launched widespread massacres of Kuomintang troops as they tried to desert the people they should have protected. This was Ichi-Go's real significance: it demonstrated clearly the direction in which opinion was moving within China. By this time it was clear that the Kuomintang was too weak to rule, but too strong to be overthrown. The confirmation of its military weakness and incompetence, together

Vinegar Joe
Joseph Stilwell, commander of US and Chinese forces in Burma, takes a break beside the Tani River. Stilwell, whose brusque manner earned him the nickname "Vinegar Joe," led the attack on Myitkyina.

with its long record of corruption and violence toward its opponents, were crucial in the protracted process whereby the political and moral initiatives in China were secured by the communists, who would eventually take power in 1949.

A PLACE TO DIE

Defeat in the carrier battle off the Marianas in June 1944 left Japan in an impossible situation. It was saddled with defensive commitments that reached from the Home Islands to the Indies, but

The assault on Leyte
Rockets from a US Navy landing craft streak toward the beachhead in support of troops assaulting the Philippine island of Leyte in October 1944.

had no carrier force worthy of the name to meet them. The high command also saw that any American move into the Philippines, and thus across Japanese lines of communication with the vital Southern Resources Area, would represent a defeat as comprehensive as an invasion and conquest of the Home Islands. It prepared for a battle that might check or even turn back the American tide. Within the navy, there was a further consideration: as a service it simply could not envisage surviving national defeat.

In seeking a final battle with the enemy it wished to be afforded "a fitting place to die," and "the chance to bloom as flowers of death."

For the Americans in this same period a series of carrier operations revealed a previously unsuspected Japanese weakness in the Philippines. The revelation came at the same time as the possibility of landings on Formosa was set aside in favor of landings in the Philippines, and encouraged an acceleration of the planned schedule of operations. Bypassing the island of Mindanao, troops would land on Leyte in the third week of October. A planned landing in the Palau Islands in the West Pacific, meanwhile, went ahead because it was too late to cancel it.

Defending the invasion fleet
US ships in Leyte Gulf launch antiaircraft fire on a scale that illustrates the overwhelming firepower US forces enjoyed during the Pacific campaign.

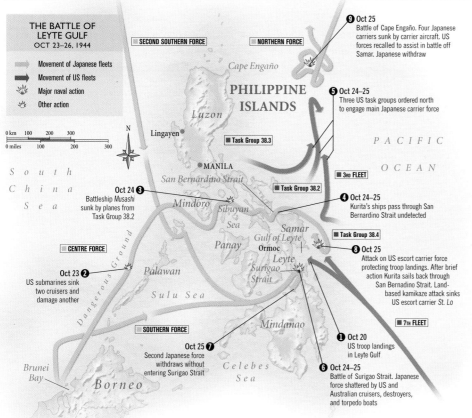

THE BATTLE OF LEYTE GULF
OCT 23–26, 1944

Movement of Japanese fleets
Movement of US fleets
Major naval action
Other action

PHILIPPINE ISLANDS

Cape Engaño

SECOND SOUTHERN FORCE   **NORTHERN FORCE**

9 Oct 25
Battle of Cape Engaño. Four Japanese carriers sunk by carrier aircraft. US forces recalled to assist in battle off Samar. Japanese withdraw

5 Oct 24–25
Three US task groups ordered north to engage main Japanese carrier force

Luzon

Lingayen

Task Group 38.3

MANILA

San Bernardino Strait

Mindoro   *Sibuyan Sea*   *Panay*

Oct 24 3
Battleship *Musashi* sunk by planes from Task Group 38.2

CENTRE FORCE

Task Group 38.2

3RD FLEET

4 Oct 24–25
Kurita's ships pass through San Bernardino Strait undetected

P A C I F I C   O C E A N

Samar   *Gulf of Leyte*   *Leyte*   Ormoc   *Surigao Strait*

Task Group 38.4

8 Oct 25
Attack on US escort carrier force protecting troop landings. After brief action Kurita sails back through San Bernardino Strait. Land-based kamikaze attack sinks US escort carrier *St. Lo*

Oct 23 2
US submarines sink two cruisers and damage another

Palawan   *Sulu Sea*

Dangerous Ground

SOUTHERN FORCE

Oct 25 7
Second Japanese force withdraws without entering Surigao Strait

Mindanao

7TH FLEET

1 Oct 20
US troop landings in Leyte Gulf

6 Oct 24–25
Battle of Surigao Strait. Japanese force shattered by US and Australian cruisers, destroyers, and torpedo boats

Brunei Bay   *Borneo*   *Celebes Sea*

South China Sea

Rallying to the cause
This US propaganda poster was designed to raise morale among Filipino soldiers and recruit more Filipinos for the fight against Japan.

THE FIGHTING FILIPINOS WE WILL ALWAYS FIGHT FOR *FREEDOM!*

safely through the San Bernardino Strait and emerged off Samar early on October 25. There it engaged the American escort carrier groups in a confused and, on the Japanese side, badly conducted action. The Japanese lost three heavy cruisers in accounting for one escort carrier, two destroyers, and one destroyer escort. The Japanese ships turned away and kamikaze aircraft took up the offensive for the rest of the action, sinking one escort carrier and damaging four more.

Despite the fact that the American force that sailed north succeeded in sinking four aircraft carriers and two destroyers, leaving the San Bernardino Strait unguarded was an undoubted error. The Americans were lucky to escape from the engagement off Samar with only light losses. In the course of the whole battle American ships, aircraft, and submarines accounted for one fleet and three light carriers, three battleships, six heavy and four light cruisers, and 11 destroyers—28 ships of 318,667 tons—plus two submarines and three landing ships.

The full measure of the victory soon became apparent. American carrier aircraft ranged over the Philippines and preyed upon Japanese shipping stripped of any air cover. From October 29 to November 30, the Americans sank 49 warships of

Taking cover
US soldiers are forced to crouch low as the enemy fires rounds overhead on the east coast of Leyte Island, just after the initial landings on October 20, 1944.

After aircraft from American carriers had bombed airfields and other targets on first Formosa and then the Philippines, the initial landings were made on October 17 on the tiny islands that guarded the approach to Leyte. The main landings on Leyte came three days later, by which time no fewer than four Japanese fleet formations were making their way to the Philippines. The Japanese planned to use their single carrier formation as bait to lure the US carrier force away from the Philippines. They then hoped to use land-based aircraft from the islands to strike against the US carrier formations. The main battle force, without any close air support because of the limited availability of Japanese aircraft and aircrew, was meanwhile to make its way through the San Bernardino Strait. As it turned out, however, this force was divided. One formation was ordered to make its way into Leyte Gulf through the Surigao Strait. It would be joined by another independent force coming from the north.

Leyte Gulf
Although its focus lay in the waters to the east of the Philippine Islands, the naval battle was fought over a vast area of 450,000 sq miles (1,165,500 sq km).

The Japanese lost two heavy cruisers to American submarines even before the main action was joined on October 24. On the first day of the battle US carrier aircraft attacked the main Japanese force moving through the Sibuyan Sea and sank the giant battleship *Musashi*. With the Japanese turning away under repeated attacks, the Americans belatedly discovered the Japanese carrier force to the northeast. The US carrier force—which lost the light carrier *Princeton* to a lone Judy dive-bomber – turned to the north. This left the San Bernardino Strait open. Although the Japanese formation that had been sent to the south lost all but one of its ships in the Battle of the Surigao Strait, the main formation passed

> "People of the Philippines: I have returned. By the grace of Almighty God our forces stand again on Philippine soil—soil consecrated in the blood of our two peoples…. Rally to me."

GENERAL DOUGLAS MACARTHUR, OCTOBER 20, 1944

JAPANESE SHIPPING LOSSES

THESE GRAPHS SHOW CLEARLY the devastation suffered by Japanese shipping during World War II. As an island nation that was always dependent on imports of food and raw materials, Japan found such losses unendurable. In the second half of 1944 merchant shipping losses were so heavy that in the final year of the war much of the population of Japan came perilously close to starvation. The figures in parentheses in the right-hand table give the number of warships lost in each period.

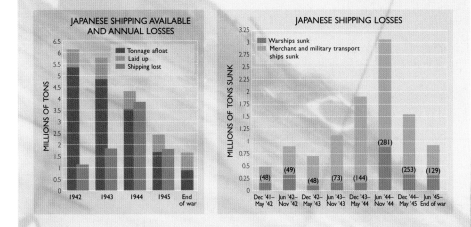

JAPANESE SHIPPING AVAILABLE AND ANNUAL LOSSES

Tonnage afloat
Laid up
Shipping lost

MILLIONS OF TONS

1942 1943 1944 1945 End of war

JAPANESE SHIPPING LOSSES

Warships sunk
Merchant and military transport ships sunk

MILLIONS OF TONS SUNK

Dec '41–May '42 (48)
Jun '42–Nov '42 (49)
Dec '42–May '43 (48)
Jun '43–Nov '43 (73)
Dec '43–May '44 (144)
Jun '44–Nov '44 (281)
Dec '44–May '45 (253)
Jun '45–End of war (129)

119,655 tons and 48 service auxiliaries, oilers, and merchantmen—a further 212,476 tons—around the Philippines. Such was the finale to a battle fought over some 450,000 sq miles (1,165,500 sq km). The Imperial Navy had found its "fitting place to die." From now on it was reduced to coastguard status.

JAPAN'S SUPPLY CRISIS

The defeat in the Battle of Leyte Gulf left Japanese merchant shipping in crisis. In terms of shipping losses, the three-month period from September to November 1944 was the worst quarter-year of the war for Japan. In reality, however, the country's position with regard to shipping and trade had been little more than a disaster waiting to happen since the very start of the conflict. Even before hostilities began, Japan lacked both sufficient resources at home to maintain its own population and enough merchant shipping to import what it needed. Once war did break out, there were not enough shipyards and building facilities to build fleet units, escorts, and merchantmen at the same time. Military and trade considerations competed against one another, to the detriment of both. Japan also lacked adequate numbers of high-quality escorts that could protect merchant vessels and the organization to manage shipping requirements.

In 1941 Japan had imported a total of some 48,700,000 tons of food, raw materials, and other goods. Maintaining such a volume of trade required 10 million tons of shipping. On March 31, 1942, however, Japan had under its own flag no more than 6,150,000 tons of shipping, of which over a tenth was laid up. By the end of the war, when Japan possessed just 1,620,000 tons of shipping, more than two-fifths of the total was laid up. By 1944 Japan's imports had fallen to 17,150,000 tons. The following year they fell again, to a disastrous 7,100,000 tons. Some estimates suggest that, had the war continued into 1946, the lack of food imports would have led to perhaps 7 million deaths in Japan as a direct result of malnutrition-related disease.

Rearming the fleet

US sailors supervise the loading of a torpedo into an attack submarine. Each weapon was loaded manually and it could take a number of hours to rearm fully.

The basic lack of merchant shipping was compounded by the low priority given to protecting trade—the Imperial Navy was overwhelmingly concerned with battle. When an escort command was belatedly organized in November 1943, it had just 32 escorts of dubious quality. They lacked adequate radio, radar, sonar, and depth charges, while escort aircraft lacked any weapon other than bombs.

The elements of defeat began to come together with the start of the American drive across the Central Pacific. During the first two years of war it was American submarines that carried the burden of the campaign against shipping; by 1944 their effectiveness was increased by the ability to read enemy signals and thus calculate Japanese shipping

US air supremacy

A Japanese destroyer is struck amidships during an aerial attack by a squadron of B-25 Mitchells, the powerful twin-engined bombers that helped to maintain US air supremacy over the Pacific Ocean.

0 km 400 800 1200
0 miles 400 800 1200

ASIA AND THE PACIFIC
APR 1944–DEC 1944

——— Approximate extent of Japanese control Jun 1, 1944

Japanese advance

Allied advance/landing

Naval battle

Area of operation of US submarines

❶ Apr–Dec 1944
Large areas of southern and central China seized by Japanese in Ichi-Go offensive

❺ Jul 8, 1944
Japanese 15th Army retreats from Imphal pursued by British

❼ Jul 24, 1944
US forces land on Tinian and gain control of island eight days later

❹ Jun 19, 1944
Battle of the Philippine Sea commences when Japanese launch a series of unsuccessful air attacks on US Task Force 58

❸ Jun 15, 1944
US Marines launch amphibious assault on Saipan. Despite fierce Japanese resistance island is secured on Jul 9

❻ Jul 21, 1944
US troops invade Guam and defeat Japanese on Aug 10

Eniwetok (taken by USA Feb 17, 1944)

Kwajalein (taken by USA Jan 31, 1944)

Gilbert Islands (taken by USA Nov 21, 1943)

❶❶ Oct 23–26, 1944
Battle of Leyte Gulf

❶❷ Dec 15, 1944
US landings on Mindoro

❾ Sept 15, 1944
III Amphibious Corps lands on Peleliu in the Palau Islands. US troops also take Morotai

❶⓪ Oct 20, 1944
US landings on Leyte

❽ Jul 30, 1944
US forces land in western New Guinea

❷ May 27, 1944
US landings on Biak

Hollandia (US landing Apr 22, 1944)

Offensives in Asia and the Pacific

Allied advances in 1944—in Burma, New Guinea, and the Marianas—and the start of the reconquest of the Philippines pushed Japan's defensive perimeter closer to the Home Islands. Japan's defeat was virtually assured—the only real question was how long it would take.

Searching for shipping

An officer of the watch peers through the periscope in the control room of a US submarine as it patrols the waters of the Pacific.

movements. From 1944, too, the carriers and shore-based aircraft reached into the Western Pacific. Between December 1941 and June 1944 carrier aircraft, their attention fixed elsewhere, sank just three merchantmen of 4,375 tons; between July 1944 and March 1945, carrier aircraft accounted for 327,173 tons of merchant shipping.

US submarines remained the main agency of destruction at sea, but in the war's final months the Americans also undertook a devastating mining campaign—Operation Starvation—against the Home Islands. The peculiarities of Japan's geography and its inadequate cross-country rail communications meant that ports on the sheltered Sea of Japan were not able to handle any great volume of trade. The ports on the exposed east coast and in the Inland Sea, however, were hopelessly vulnerable to mining. The American effort only exacerbated Japan's shipping crisis. By August 1945 shipping had fallen to only one-quarter of May levels—themselves already low—and Japan's economic collapse was all but complete.

THE FINAL
BATTLES
1945

THE YEAR THAT FINALLY BROUGHT WORLD WAR II TO AN
END BEGAN WITH A MASSIVE RED ARMY OFFENSIVE
THROUGH POLAND INTO GERMANY. THE WESTERN
ALLIES FOUGHT THEIR WAY TO THE RHINE AND THEN
SWEPT ON TO THE ELBE AS SOVIET FORCES PREPARED
TO ATTACK BERLIN. IN ITALY, TOO, ALLIED PRESSURE
BROUGHT ABOUT THE SURRENDER OF THE AXIS FORCES.
JAPAN STILL FOUGHT ON, AND AFTER GRIM BATTLES
TO SECURE THE PACIFIC ISLANDS OF IWO JIMA AND
OKINAWA, THE ALLIES WERE FACED WITH THE
POTENTIALLY COSTLY INVASION OF THE JAPANESE HOME
ISLANDS. THE DEPLOYMENT OF A NEW AND TERRIBLE
WEAPON WAS TO MAKE THIS UNNECESSARY.

8

Americans crossing the Rhine
US troops huddle down to avoid enemy
fire as they cross the Rhine in March.
The river was the last major obstacle
the Allies had to overcome during their
advance into Germany.

THE DEFEAT OF THE AXIS

IN JANUARY 1945, WITH THE FAILURE OF THE ARDENNES COUNTER-OFFENSIVE AND THE SOVIET UNION ABOUT TO MOUNT A MAJOR ASSAULT ACROSS THE VISTULA, TIME WAS RUNNING OUT FOR THE THIRD REICH. ITS PROBLEMS WERE COMPOUNDED BY THE RENEWED ALLIED BOMBING OFFENSIVE. JAPAN FACED SIMILAR DIFFICULTIES AS THE AMERICAN-LED OFFENSIVE CREPT EVER CLOSER TO THE MAINLAND, WHICH WAS NOW SUBJECTED TO INTENSIVE AIR ATTACK.

THE SOVIET PLAN FOR 1945 called for a continuation of the assaults on East Prussia and Hungary. The main blow, however, would be an offensive across the Vistula River in Poland, its target Berlin. German intelligence became aware of the plan and warned Hitler. Heinz Guderian, the army chief of staff, recommended evacuating Army Group North, now cut off in the Courland peninsula, and thinning out the forces in Norway so as to strengthen the Vistula defenses. But Hitler would have none of it. Apart from the now failing Ardennes offensive, his primary concern was Budapest, which – with its large German garrison – was under siege by the Red Army. An attempt to lift the siege during January 1945 failed, and the city fell in mid-February.

SOVIET ADVANCE FROM THE VISTULA

The main Soviet assault across the Vistula River was launched on January 12 and soon gained momentum, cutting off further German forces in East Prussia and reaching the Oder River at the end of the month. The Soviet troops had been inflamed by propaganda calling on them to exact revenge for the sufferings that their country had endured at the hands of the Germans. Soon, streams of German refugees were heading westward, bringing with them grisly tales of rape, murder, and pillage. This served to heighten the realization that the Third Reich was now facing its Armageddon.

In the west, the Allies soon recovered the ground they had lost during the German counteroffensive in the Ardennes and were now advancing on a wide front toward the Rhine. But wintry weather and often resolute German resistance meant that progress was slow. The Allies' strategic bombing forces were now concentrating on transportation and oil targets, but, to aid the Soviet offensive, they also attacked cities in the eastern part of Germany, notably Dresden, where at least 25,000 people were killed in a single night.

YALTA CONFERENCE

In early February 1945 Stalin, Roosevelt, and Churchill met at Yalta in the Crimea. Roosevelt, now a terminally sick man, was prepared to make concessions to Stalin in return for confirmation that the Soviet Union would enter the war against Japan as soon as the fighting in Europe came to an end. Churchill, worried over Stalin's intentions in eastern Europe, especially Poland, wanted his firm guarantee that its peoples would be allowed to determine their own future. The postconference communiqué, however, contained little of substance, and Churchill was forced to accept that Roosevelt and Stalin had united against him. In truth, Britain's voice no longer counted for much.

After establishing two bridgeheads over the Oder, the Soviets halted their offensive, while they cleared Pomerania and pushed back the remnants of Army Group North in East Prussia toward the Baltic. In the far south, Hitler launched a final offensive to recapture the Hungarian oilfields in the Lake Balaton area. It was soon halted and the Red Army renewed its own offensive in the region, this time aiming at Vienna, which would fall on April 13. The Western Allies eventually reached the Rhine, and were across it before the end of March. The Broad Front versus Narrow Front controversy that had dogged the northwest Europe campaign now resurfaced. With the Soviet Union not yet ready to launch its final assault on Berlin, the British wanted to advance quickly and secure the German capital. Eisenhower, not wishing to provoke clashes with his eastern ally and concerned that the Germans were planning to make a final stand in the Alps, informed Stalin that he would leave Berlin to the Red Army.

CROSSING THE RHINE AND ODER

The final act began with the Anglo–US forces breaking out of their Rhine bridgeheads and advancing rapidly eastward. In Italy, after a winter of preparation, the Allied forces broke through the German defenses and were soon advancing toward the Alps. The German forces, realizing they were on the brink of defeat, were able to negotiate their own surrender. Mussolini, however, did not fall into Allied hands alive. He was caught by Italian partisans while fleeing northward and was executed.

Meanwhile, the long-awaited Soviet offensive across the Oder opened on April 16. The previous day, Hitler, now entombed in his underground headquarters near the Reichstag in the center of Berlin and buoyed by the death of Roosevelt on April 12, issued a defiant message to his people. "Berlin stays German," he declared. "Vienna will be German again and Europe will never be Russian." However, within a few days the Red Army was not only across the Oder but had encircled the German capital. On April 25 it had also met up with the Western Allies, who had halted on the Elbe. Now began the break-in battle, as the Soviet forces fought their way toward the center of Berlin. On April 29 they threatened the heart of the Third Reich: the Reichstag and Chancellery. Hitler committed suicide, naming Grand Admiral Karl Dönitz his successor. Forty-eight hours later the last remnants of the German garrison surrendered and the Soviet flag was hoisted over the Reichstag.

GERMANY SURRENDERS

A series of overall German surrenders now took place. The German forces in northern Germany and Denmark surrendered to Montgomery. There followed a capitulation ceremony at Eisenhower's headquarters in Reims and another in Berlin. May 8 was decreed Victory in Europe Day, although hostilities did not formally end until the following day. Even so, fighting continued in Czechoslovakia, Austria, and Croatia until May 14, when the German Army Group E surrendered to Tito's forces in Yugoslavia. Dönitz was allowed to function long enough to ensure that the U-boats at sea had received orders to put into Allied ports to surrender. He was then arrested on May 23. This marked the end of the Third Reich. The Allies were now faced with a range of new problems in Europe, most notably those of governing Austria, Germany, and Italy, the reconstruction of the continent as a whole, and coping with the vast numbers of people who had been displaced by the ravages of war.

Dawn in Berlin on May 2, 1945.
A Soviet soldier waves his country's flag on the roof of the Reichstag building, home of Germany's parliament. This act symbolized not just the end of the 48 hours of fighting required to overcome the defenders of the building, but also the end of the bitter Battle of Berlin.

"We ask you to cease fire. At 05:00 hours Berlin time we are sending envoys to parley at the Potsdamer Bridge. The recognition sign is a white square with a red light. We await your reply."

RADIO MESSAGE FROM THE GERMAN LVI PANZER CORPS PICKED UP BY
THE SOVIET 79TH GUARDS DIVISION, 22:40 HOURS MAY 1, 1945

CLOSING IN ON JAPAN

While the Allies began to grapple with the problems that came in the wake of their victory in Europe, the conflict against Japan continued. In early January 1945 General MacArthur's forces landed on the main Philippine island of Luzon, but it took a month just to liberate the capital, Manila, such was the bitterness of the Japanese resistance. In February 1945, after a lengthy preliminary air bombardment, Admiral Nimitz launched an assault on the island of Iwo Jima. Much of the island was subdued after three weeks of bitter combat, but there were pockets of resistance until late March.

The significance of Iwo Jima was that long-range fighters could reach the Japanese mainland from it. B-29s had been attacking Japan from bases in China since June 1944, but the Japanese offensive had put these under threat. The B-29s had then been transferred to the newly captured Marianas and had begun to bomb Japan from here in November. But the results were disappointing and the loss rate rose, mainly because they lacked escort fighters. In March 1945, both B-29s and P-51 Mustang fighters began to deploy to Iwo Jima. At the same time they launched a new type of offensive based on low-level incendiary attacks by night. The effect on the largely wooden-built Japanese cities was devastating. At the same time, daylight raids were carried out using the P-51s as escorts. The steady destruction of cities combined with the increasingly desperate shortage of raw materials meant that the Japanese war effort was in rapid decline. However, the resolve to continue fighting showed no sign of weakening.

FIRST CRACKS IN THE JAPANESE WILL

The next Allied objective was Okinawa, which represented the last stepping-stone on the route to Japan itself. The initial landings took place on April 1. They were supported by nearly 1,500 ships, including those of the recently arrived British Pacific Fleet. It would take until late June to secure the island in a campaign characterized by fanatical Japanese defense. There were frequent kamikaze attacks, and many civilians committed suicide rather than fall into Americans hands. Yet, for the first time a number of Japanese soldiers did surrender voluntarily—a sign of cracks in the Japanese will.

A further sign came after the Soviet Union renounced its 1941 nonaggression pact with Japan in April 1945. The following month the Japanese Supreme Council discussed peace for the first time and looked to using the Soviet Union as a go-between, believing that Moscow would want a strong postwar Japan to act as a buffer between itself and the US. Yet, on June 6 the Japanese Supreme Council passed a resolution that the country would fight on until the end.

The Allies had begun their planning for the final assault on Japan, which they knew was likely to be costly. However, a new weapon—the atomic bomb—was reaching the end of its development, and by early July the Americans and British had agreed on the possibility of employing it against Japan. On July 17 the Allies met at Potsdam for the last of their great wartime strategic conferences. It soon became apparent that there was an ominous divergence of views between Moscow and the West over Europe. After a recession for the British general election, in which Clement Attlee's Labour Party decisively defeated Winston Churchill's Conservative Party, the Conference turned to Japan.

On July 26 the Allies issued an ultimatum to Japan. It was to surrender unconditionally or face "prompt and utter destruction." Two days later, the Japanese rejected the demand on the grounds that it made no mention of the future of the Emperor and that they were still awaiting a Soviet response to a proposal to send a peace envoy to Moscow. The Americans took the Japanese reply to be an outright rejection and issued orders for two atomic bombs that were on their way to the Marianas to be dropped on Japan. The terrible scenes that ensued were immediately followed by a massive Soviet invasion of Manchuria. Emperor Hirohito now stepped in and on August 15 took the unprecedented step of broadcasting acceptance of the Allied terms on Japanese radio. Japan's formal surrender took place on September 2. It was followed ten days later by the surrender of the Japanese forces in Southeast Asia. World War II had finally come to an end.

Unloading supplies at Iwo Jima
Initially, Japanese resistance to the US landings on the island of Iwo Jima, on February 19, 1945, was light. But the US Marines then came under heavy fire and they suffered many casualties as 30,000 men landed over the course of the day.

Emperor Hirohito inspects Tokyo bomb damage
Tokyo was the first Japanese city to be subjected to an incendiary attack. On the night of March 9/10 a raid by American B-29s caused destruction on a massive scale.

"When the capture of an enemy position is necessary to winning a war, it is not within our province to evaluate the cost in money, time, equipment, or, most of all, human life. We are told what our objective is to be and we prepare to do the job."

GENERAL HOLLAND M. "HOWLIN' MAD" SMITH,
COMMANDING GENERAL OF THE US FLEET MARINE FORCE PACIFIC

ADVANCE INTO GERMANY AND HUNGARY

JANUARY 1–MARCH 31, 1945

On the Eastern Front the year began with a massive Red Army offensive in Poland, which took it from the Vistula to the Oder River. To the north, Soviet forces drove into East Prussia, while to the south they quickly overcame Hitler's last offensive in Hungary. On the Western Front, the Allied forces pushed on to the Rhine and crossed it in mid-March.

JANUARY 1
4th SS Panzer Corps advances to within 15 miles (25 km) of Budapest, but is forced to withdraw

JANUARY 12
Vistula-Oder offensive is launched in Poland. Konev's 1st Ukrainian Front attacks toward Cracow

JANUARY 13
Soviet forces begin advance into East Prussia

JANUARY 14
1st Byelorussian Front under Zhukov attacks in direction of Warsaw and Poznan

JANUARY 16
British launch Operation Blackcock to clear Roermond triangle

JANUARY 17
4th SS Panzer Corps launches another unsuccessful operation to relieve Budapest

JANUARY 17
Warsaw falls to Soviet forces

JANUARY 19
Soviet forces take Cracow and Lodz in Poland

JANUARY 20
French begin campaign to clear Colmar pocket west of Rhine River; this achieved February 5

JANUARY 28
Ardennes salient finally cleared

JANUARY 31
Soviet forces under Zhukov establish bridgehead across Oder River south of Küstrin

FEBRUARY 2
Vistula-Oder operation ends with Zhukov and Konev poised to advance on Berlin

FEBRUARY 8
Konev renews offensive around Breslau, southeast of Berlin

FEBRUARY 8
Canadian and British Operation Veritable launched southeast of Nijmegen toward the Rhine

FEBRUARY 13
Soviet forces overcome stiff resistance from German garrison to take Budapest

FEBRUARY 13–15
British and Americans bomb Dresden as part of effort to help Soviet advance through Germany

FEBRUARY 23
US Operation Grenade–the advance to Düsseldorf–begins

FEBRUARY 24
Fresh Soviet offensive into Pomerania, west of East Prussia, is launched

MARCH 1
Zhukov joins Pomerania offensive and the Soviet advance to the Baltic coast

MARCH 1
Troops in the US 1st Army seize intact bridge across the Rhine at Remagen

MARCH 2
Americans reach Rhine opposite Düsseldorf, but bridges blown up

MARCH 5/6
Hitler's planned offensive in Hungary–Spring Awakening–is launched south of Lake Balaton

MARCH 15
Spring Awakening is halted by Soviet counterattack

MARCH 19
Hitler issues scorched earth order but Speer persuades industrialists not to implement it

MARCH 21
US and British troops are ready to cross the Rhine

MARCH 22
Leading troops of US 3rd Army under Patton cross the Rhine at Oppenheim

MARCH 23/24
Leading troops in Montgomery's 21st Army Group cross the Rhine in Operation Plunder

MARCH 30
Soviet forces capture Danzig

MARCH 31
French cross the Rhine near Germersheim

▨ Action in Hungary Jan 1–Mar 15, 1945

▨ Soviet advance through Poland and Germany Jan 12–Mar 21, 1945

▨ Allied advance to the Rhine Jan 16–Mar 21, 1945

THE ROAD TO BERLIN

AT THE BEGINNING OF JANUARY 1945 the Allies were fighting to regain the ground they had lost on the Western Front during the German offensive in the Ardennes, while on the Eastern Front preparations were being made for a further massive offensive in central Poland. Here, in the late summer of 1944, the Red Army had established three bridgeheads on the western bank of the Vistula. The southernmost and most substantial bridgehead was at Baranow in the sector controlled by Konev's First Ukrainian Front; the smaller Pulawy and Magnuszew bridgeheads in the sector of the First Byelorussian Front lay some 70 miles 110 km() to the north at the junction of the Vistula and the Pilica, 25 miles (40 km) from Warsaw (see map page 271). These bridgeheads were to provide the springboards for the Red Army's drive to Berlin, which would be spearheaded by the First Byelorusssian Front, placed under the direct command of Zhukov in November 1944.

THE VISTULA–ODER OPERATION

The scale of the preparations for the coming offensive was massive. Along a front of nearly 400 miles (650 km), the Stavka was to launch four major breakthrough operations aimed at Danzig, Königsberg, Poznan, and Breslau with 30 rifle armies, five tank armies, and four air armies, supported by mobile operational groups and artillery breakthrough

divisions. Packed into Zhukov's Magnuszew bridgehead alone—15 miles (24 km) deep and 8 miles (13 km) wide—were some 400,000 infantry and nearly 2,000 tanks. Zhukov and Konev had under their command approximately 2.25 million men, including one-third of all Red Army infantry formations and 40 percent of all the Soviet armor deployed on the Eastern Front.

These massive concentrations made it all the more important for the Stavka to mislead the Germans as to where the main blows would fall and to blur the enemy's assessment of their size. Complex deception measures included a dummy army of 600 tanks and self-propelled guns, serviced by a network of new roads, on the southern wing of the First Ukrainian Front. This, combined with German intelligence appraisals, helped

Volkssturm prisoners
A form of home guard made up of boys and elderly men, the *Volkssturm* was ill-equipped to face the Red Army. From January 1945 its members were integrated with regular formations whenever possible.

Fighting in Frankfurt an der Oder
The Red Army reached the Oder at the end of January. In the following weeks it fought to secure east German towns as preparations were made for the final assault on Berlin.

while he was slipping armor, infantry, and artillery across the Vistula by night into the area opposite Kielce, 40 miles (65 km) to the north.

Hitler could not be persuaded that a Soviet offensive was imminent. He was convinced that the Eastern Front would remain quiet while Stalin continued to wrangle with the Western Allies over the status of the puppet Polish government. Stalin was in fact reluctant to go on the offensive in conditions of heavy mud and poor visibility. He was waiting for the rivers and canals to freeze over and the ground to become iron-hard, under a thin covering of snow, which would allow the T-34s to forge across the flat, open plains of western Poland to Silesia with its rich prize of heavy industry.

In the Soviet bridgeheads the final briefings were made on January 11. The ground was now hard, but visibility was poor, eliminating the possibility of close support for the impending attack from Ilyushin IL2 Sturmovich attack aircraft, the "flying artillery" which accounted for about 25 percent of all Soviet combat missions flown on the Eastern Front.

THE ATTACK IS LAUNCHED

Inside the Baranow bridgehead the artillery was ranged wheel-to-wheel in concentrations of up to 500 guns per mile (300 per kilometer) of front.

At 4:35 am on January 12, Konev's artillery attack began, obliterating the German front line, churning the frozen earth and collapsing command posts and bunkers. Half an hour later, Soviet reconnaissance battalions, stiffened by punishment battalions (*strafblats*), stormed the first line of enemy trenches. They then pushed forward to identify the individual strong points between the first and second lines that had survived the initial bombardment. At around 10:00 am the Germans who had survived Konev's first bombardment were subjected to a second pulverizing barrage. For just under two hours it worked its way back and forth across the full depth of the German defenses. The headquarters of the Fourth Panzer Army was destroyed, and the German mobile reserves—deployed close to the main battle line—were broken up.

By midafternoon Konev's Fourth Tank Army had advanced 12 miles (19 km) toward Kielce, crashing through dense forests, crisscrossed with river valleys, which the Germans had thought "untankable." The capture of Kielce secured Konev's right flank, spilling his armor into open country and rolling over the uncoordinated counterattacks launched by General Josef Harpe, the commander of Army Group A. By the evening of January 17, Konev's left flank was encircling

the Stavka to persuade OKH that Konev was planning to launch a major assault heading southwest from the left flank of his bridgehead at Baranow. As a result, the German Army Group A, deployed opposite the Soviet bridgeheads, shifted two infantry divisions south to the Tarnow sector to cover Konev's phantom preparations

Wooden stock

Bolt

Rear sight

Fore sight

Air-cooled barrel

Ammunition magazine

Soviet Tokarev 40 7.62-mm rifle
Often issued to Red Army marksmen, the self-loading Tokarev rifle influenced the German MP43 submachine-gun and was the precursor of the postwar Soviet AK 47 range.

Cracow, which was evacuated by its German garrison without a fight on January 19. The way now lay open for Konev's rifle armies to secure the heavy industrial treasure trove in Silesia.

Zhukov's First Byelorussian Front had gone onto the attack against Army Group Center early on the morning of January 14 after a crushing 25-minute artillery bombardment which raked the German lines up to a depth of 5 miles (8 km). By nightfall a bridge had been seized over the lower Pilica, and tanks of the Second Guards Tank Army were pouring over it to swing northwest toward Sochaczew, a rail and road junction 30 miles (50 km) west of Warsaw, whose capture would block the German retreat.

ADVANCE TO THE ODER

By nightfall on the 15th, Konev and Zhukov's forces had torn three gaping holes in the German tactical defense zone. They then joined up to hold a continuous 300-mile (480-km) stretch on the west bank of the Vistula, while tanks and mechanized infantry moved rapidly across open country up to 70 miles (110 km) from their start lines. On Zhukov's right flank, north of Warsaw, the Soviet 47th Army set about clearing the area between the Vistula and the Bug River. Warsaw was liberated on January 17 by the Red Army and Polish troops. They entered a silent city whose prewar population had been reduced to 160,000 famished survivors.

On the 19th, the day Konev took Cracow, units of the Third Guards Tank Army crossed the German frontier east of Breslau. Around 100 miles (160 km) to the northeast, Zhukov's armour was fanning out across western Poland. Simultaneously, Konev was launching a skillfully handled envelopment of the Silesian industrial heartland. By January 27 he was in a position to close off all the Ostheer's escape routes, but mindful of his instructions to seize the region's war industries intact, he left a "golden bridge" for the remnants of Army Group A, now commanded

Soviet attack on Sopot, near Danzig
Troops of the Second Byelorussian Front reached the Gulf of Danzig at the end of March. They attacked the seaside resort of Sopot prior to capturing Danzig on March 30, 1945.

by Field Marshal Ferdinand Schörner, a diehard Nazi. Schörner seized his chance but sensibly delayed telling Hitler that he was withdrawing to make a stand on the Oder until the movement was well under way. Meanwhile, Hitler once again reshuffled his command pack. On January 26 the surrounded Army Group North became Army Group Courland. Army Group Center, also cut off from the Reich, became Army Group North, while Army Group A became Army Group Center. A new formation, Army Group Vistula, under the nominal command of Himmler, was created to cover Danzig and Pomerania.

The Oder was now within the Red Army's sights, but the speed of Zhukov and Konev's advance was outrunning the Soviet supply lines. The situation was further complicated by the fact that the two commanders were vying with each other in a race to reach Berlin. While the Stavka wrestled with this problem, Zhukov's dash to the Oder was delayed by the city of Poznan, located at the junction of six railroads and seven roads, massively fortified and garrisoned by 60,000 determined troops. The city was besieged by six Red Army divisions but held out until February 22. Zhukov pressed on, leaving Poznan in his rear, to reach the Oder and launch a crossing at the beginning of February.

To the south of Küstrin, Chuikov's Eighth Guards Army established a number of bridgeheads on the western bank of the Oder. These were rapidly linked together, although the bulk of the army's artillery and armor remained on the eastern bank. The pontoons needed to bring them over were still deep in the rear of the Red Army. Although the Ostheer was to hold bridgeheads east of the Oder until March 20, Zhukov and Konev had reached the middle Oder along almost its entire length and had gained firm footholds on its western bank. On February 2 the Stavka declared a formal end to the Vistula–Oder operation. The final assault on Berlin would not be made until mid-April.

GERMAN OPERATION SOLSTICE
Zhukov's advance to the Oder had left the flanks of his First Byelorussian Front exposed to a German counterblow, a fact that had not escaped the attention of Heinz Guderian, chief of the army general staff. In Operation *Sonnenwende* (Solstice), Guderian planned to slice off the nose of the huge Soviet salient that had been driven into Germany by Zhukov as far as Küstrin. A pincer attack would be executed in the north by Army Group Vistula and in the south by Army Group Centre, its jaws closing behind the troops of Zhukov in the area of Küstrin. Guderian's plan was undermined by Hitler's refusal to reinforce either of the army groups involved and,

Soviet infantry on a T-70
As Soviet troops advanced across Germany they sometimes rode aboard T-70 light tanks. These were used for reconnaissance duties or direct infantry support.

after making a small dent in Zhukov's right flank, Operation Solstice had petered out by February 19. Guderian was dismissed on March 28.

DRIVE INTO EAST PRUSSIA

On Zhukov's right flank at the beginning of January 1945 was the Second Byelorussian Front under Marshal Konstantin Rokossovsky. Between Rokossovsky and the Baltic were two more fronts, the Third Byelorussian and First Baltic. Rokossovsky's principal task was to protect Zhukov's flank during the Vistula–Oder operation and that of the other two fronts securing the Baltic coast. In this northern sector the going was much tougher for the Red Army, depriving Zhukov of effective flank protection and causing much anxiety in the Stavka. However, by early February German forces had been pinned back into a few pockets of resistance on the Bay of Danzig, and East Prussia had been cut off from the rest of the Reich.

The Red Army drive had sent a tide of refugees pouring both westward and to the Baltic coast, ending 800 years of German resettlement in the east. At the northeastern tip of this vast forced migration, tens of thousands of refugees were trapped in the city of Memel, the port which had been ceded to Germany in March 1939, Hitler's last peaceful conquest. Now it was besieged by troops of the First Baltic Front, into whose hands the refugees were terrified of falling. Red Army troops were all too aware of the barbarity with which the Germans had treated the Soviet people and many were now determined to wreak their revenge. They had acted with great savagery during their advance through East Prussia and Silesia, torturing and killing villagers, and shelling and bombing refugees.

THE BOMBING OF DRESDEN

By THE FALL OF 1944 the British Bomber Command's target-marking techniques had reached new levels of sophistication, ensuring that the destruction caused by bombing was spread in an unfolding V-shape across the target—the so-called "Death Fan." Such raids were the prelude to Operation Thunderclap, the triple blow delivered to the historic city of Dresden between February 13 and 15, 1945, by the RAF Bomber Command and the US Eighth Air Force. Having largely escaped the attention of Allied bombers, the city lacked an adequate system of civil defense and had been stripped of its antiaircraft guns. In February 1945 it was crammed with at least one million refugees.

Bomb victims
An estimated 60,000 people lost their lives in the Allied bombing raids on Dresden.

Operation Thunderclap had originally envisaged Berlin, 110 miles (70 km) to the north, as the main target, but during the runup to the Yalta Conference the British were eager to help the Red Army in its westward drive by reducing the importance of Dresden as a railhead for reinforcing the Ostheer. On the night of February 13–14, two waves of Lancasters, a total of 773 aircraft, dropped 2,600 tons of high-explosive and incendiary bombs on Dresden with no interference from night-fighters. They caused the worst firestorms of the war, in which jets of flame 50 ft (15 m) high belched across streets and squares, and temperatures rose to 1,800°F (1,000°C). The dead and dying lay where they fell in the melting asphalt of the streets, their clothes burned away, their bodies shriveled like mummies. Hundreds who sought refuge in the tunnels and passageways of the main railroad station were asphyxiated where they sat. Approximately 12 sq miles (31 sq km) of Dresden were devastated in one night. During February 14 and 15 there were daylight raids by a combined total of 516 bombers of the USAAF's Eighth Air Force.

The destruction of Dresden was followed by a propaganda battle waged by both sides. Churchill distanced himself from the operation, and the finger of blame rested on Air Chief Marshal Harris, commander-in-chief of Bomber Command and an unrepentant advocate of area bombing. He was, however, carrying out decisions made by the combined US, Soviet, and British chiefs of staff, fully supported by Roosevelt, Stalin, and Churchill. Thunderclap was the logical climax of the policy of area bombing that the British had been pursuing since 1942.

> "Our pilots report that…a terrific concentration of fires was started in the center of the city."

FROM A BBC NEWS BULLETIN AT 6 PM ON
FEBRUARY 14, 1945

Devastation in Dresden
Dresden's fate sparked a fierce debate about the morality of the Allied bombing offensive in Germany that continues to this day.

THE SINKING OF THE *WILHELM GUSTLOFF*

THE ERUPTION OF THE SECOND BYELORUSSIAN FRONT into East Prussia triggered a torrent of German refugees pouring westward in search of safety from the Red Army. By the end of January an estimated 3.5 million German civilians were on the move in the east, all under no illusions about the treatment they could expect from Soviet troops. Over a million headed for Danzig and other Baltic ports in the hope that they would be evacuated. On January 30 the liner *Wilhelm Gustloff* sailed from the Polish port of Gdynia (which Hitler had renamed Gothenburg) with 8,000 refugees crammed on board. With no warships present to escort her, and only 12 lifeboats swinging from her davits, the ship steamed slowly into the Baltic, an easy target for Soviet submarines. At 11:08 pm on the 31st, one of them, S13, fired three torpedoes into her side. The *Wilhelm Gustloff* capsized, immediately drowning 2,000 refugees on the lower promenade deck. Just over an hour later, the liner sank, her siren wailing eerily across the Baltic ice floes. German warships picked up 960 survivors, many of whom later died of exposure. At least 7,000 people perished in the disaster, five times more than the number who went down with the Titanic. A further 23 vessels would be sunk by Soviet submarines before the war's end in May

Some 90 miles (145 km) to the south of Memel, at the base of the Samland peninsula, the fortified Prussian city of Königsberg had also been cut off by the Red Army. Overseen by Marshal Vasilevsky, a plan was now devised to storm the city. Four armies were concentrated in the Königsberg sector, plus an air strike force of 870 fighters, 470 attack aircraft, and 1,124 bombers drawn from the massive Stavka reserve. The storming of Königsberg began on April 2 with a four-day artillery barrage. On the 7th, when the weather lifted, the aircraft flew in to bomb and strafe. By April 8, Königsberg was cut off from the rest of the German forces fighting in the Samland peninsula, and two days later General Lasch, commander of Königsberg's garrison, surrendered. Red Army forces entered the captured city and took their revenge against the Germans amid scenes of almost medieval barbarity.

POMERANIA AND SILESIA

Although it had been a failure, Guderian's Solstice offensive had a disproportionate effect on the Stavka, confirming its fears that Zhukov's right flank was dangerously exposed. He now received the instruction to clear East Pomerania, the result of which was the destruction of Army Group Vistula. Rokossovsky started the ball rolling on February 24, while Zhukov was still reshuffling the forces on his right wing. Zhukov went on the offensive a week later,

Defenders of Königsberg
In East Prussia the resistance of the German defenders was sometimes suicidal. Königsberg, ringed by three defense lines and incorporating 15 forts, was taken after fighting in which some 42,000 of its defenders were killed.

sending three armies on a northward drive to the Baltic, fanning out across East Pomerania and slicing Army Group Vistula into isolated fragments. On March 4 the First Guards Tank Army reached the Baltic at Kolberg, on the boundary between the First and Second Byelorussian Fronts, cutting off the German Second Army to the east and forcing it to fall back on the fortresses of Gdynia, which fell on the 28th, and Danzig, which followed two days later. Hitler immediately declared Kolberg, which was packed with refugees, another "fortress."

By March 16 the German Navy, operating a shuttle service from Swinemünde, had evacuated Kolberg's civilian population. Two days later the last of Kolberg's defenders slipped away. Within 48 hours, Heinrich Himmler had relinquished his command of what was left of Army Group Vistula and had taken refuge in a sanatorium.

SIEGE OF BRESLAU

Some 250 miles (400 km) to the south of Kolberg, on the banks of the Oder, lay the city of Breslau, the capital of Lower Silesia, covered by Army Group Center. Breslau lay directly in the path of a renewed offensive launched by Konev on February 8 with the goal of clearing Silesia west of the Oder. By closing up on the line of the Neisse River in Brandenburg, Konev would bring himself alongside Zhukov in readiness for the assault on Berlin. Breslau was cut off on February 15 by the Soviet Sixth Army and the Fifth Guards Army. The encirclement was completed when the Third Guards Tank Army positioned itself to the west of the city. Trapped inside Breslau were some 35,000 regular German troops, 15,000 *Volkssturm* and 80,000 civilians. By the end of February, Konev's front had reached a 60-mile (90-km) stretch of the Neisse running south from its junction with the Oder, 60 miles (90 km) southeast of Berlin. Breslau, isolated and lacking the defensive features of the fortress cities of Poznan and Königsberg, was vainly waiting for relief by Army Group Center.

For 77 days, the defenders of Breslau occupied the attentions of some 13 Red Army divisions. Inside the improvised fortress, a semblance of normal life, including regular classical concerts, was maintained. Throughout the siege the Aviatik factory turned out half a million cigarettes a day, ensuring that no one went without a smoke. Berlin had already fallen when, on May 6, with about 80 percent of the city in ruins, the commandant

of Breslau surrendered. Of Breslau's garrison of 50,000 troops, 29,000 had become casualties. About half of the city's population of 80,000 had lost their lives in the siege.

HITLER'S LAST OFFENSIVE

At the beginning of January 1945, four German divisions had been trapped in Budapest. A rescue attempt made by IV SS Panzer Corps, called down from Army Group Center, fought its way to within 12 miles (19 km) of the city but was forced to withdraw by the end of the month. The fall of Budapest on February 13 had served only to stoke Hitler's obsession with the Hungarian oilfields at Nagykanisza, 50 miles (80 km) southwest of Lake Balaton, which produced well over half of the oil remaining to Germany. A plan was drawn up, code-named *Frühlingserwachen* (Spring Awakening), in which Army Group South was to trap and destroy the Red Army's Third Ukrainian Front between Lake Balaton and the Danube. The major thrust

Panzer Mark VI Tiger II
Introduced in 1944, the "King Tiger" was the heaviest and best-protected tank of the war. Some 485 were produced. Since it had a maximum speed of just 24 mph (38 kph), there was always the danger that it would be stranded in a fast-moving battle. However, it could fight against heavy odds while sustaining minimal damage.

88-mm KwK 43 L71 tank gun with 68-mile (109-km) range

12-cylinder Maybach HL 230 P30 engine mounted at rear

Armor 1–4½ in (26–110 mm) thick

7.92-mm machine-gun

Combat tracks 31½ in (800-mm) wide

was to be launched by the Sixth SS Panzer Army attacking southeast from the northern end of Lake Balaton to a line on the Danube between Budapest and Baja, around 90 miles (150 km) south of the Hungarian capital. South of Balaton, the Second Panzer Army was to drive east while a supporting attack was to be launched northward from the Yugoslavian border by Army Group E in the direction of Mohacs. Budapest would be retaken, the oilfields retained, and an entire Red Army front struck off Stalin's order of battle.

Preparations for the operation were made in the greatest secrecy and the approach to the start lines was conducted in driving rain and deep mud. The attack went in on March 5. In the vanguard was the Sixth SS Panzer Army, desperate to redeem itself after its recent failure in the Ardennes in Belgium. Among the 600 tanks available to it were a number of Mark VI "King Tiger" heavy battle tanks, armored on a massive scale and each mounting an 88-mm gun.

At the limit of the German advance—a salient driven some 20 miles (30 km) into the Third Ukrainian Front's line—more than 600 tanks and self-propelled guns tried to batter their way through the Soviet line south of Lake Velencze (northeast of Lake Balaton). By March 15 the offensive was all over. Hundreds of tanks were left stranded in the waterlogged Hungarian plains, their fuel tanks empty, to be pounded by Soviet artillery and attack aircraft. The Red Army counteroffensive swept past the gutted hulks of the tanks, smashed through the Hungarian Third Army, covering the Sixth Panzer Army's left flank, and rolled on toward Vienna.

Spoils of war
Some 25,000 civilians died in the siege of Königsberg, which was later incorporated into the Soviet Union and renamed Kaliningrad.

Wir halten Königsberg.

GERMANY IN 1945

GERMANY IN THE EARLY MONTHS OF 1945 was an increasingly grim place. Its already battered towns and cities were receiving further punishment from the Allied strategic air forces by day and by night. Systematic air attacks on oil and transportation targets were making movement ever more difficult. The Luftwaffe was becoming grounded through lack of fuel and was powerless to defend the skies over Germany. Industry, in particular, was suffering. While production actually peaked in 1944, it was now rapidly disintegrating. Earlier bombing had forced much industry to be dispersed to the countryside in the form of satellite factories, but now it was creating enormous difficulties in moving material around the country.

In terms of manpower, Josef Goebbels had declared "total war" in the immediate aftermath of the January 1943 disaster in Stalingrad. All males between 16 and 65 were registered for labor, and members of the Hitler Youth were drafted to help the farmers. Women, too, were gradually conscripted, although never to the same extent as in Britain or the Soviet Union. Some 100,000 of them were called up in September 1944 for duty in air defense. In that same month the *Volkssturm* was created. This was a form of home guard for which all those not yet in uniform and aged 16–60 were liable. Because the vast majority were in reserved occupations in industry, their training was restricted to four hours on Sunday. With the Soviets now close to Berlin, they were to be mobilized for the final defense of the Reich.

Women at war
German women had played an essential part in their country's war effort since the beginning of the war. By 1945 many were being employed in jobs that provided direct support to the armed services. These included the refueling of planes—provided the fuel was available.

As for the mood of the German people as a whole, it was now one of resignation as the majority were completely caught up in the sheer struggle to survive. With his enemies approaching from both east and west, Hitler tried to inspire the country by drawing parallels with Frederick the Great of Prussia, but with little success. In truth, people were largely cowed through draconian measures that had been instituted after the July 1944 bomb plot. These included tribunals that came down heavily on any suspicion of defeatist talk. They were also well aware of the Allies' demand for unconditional surrender, which appeared to mean that they had little to lose by continuing the fight. Some may have pinned their hopes on the promise of "miracle weapons" that would turn the tide. Others dreamed that the Western Allies would wake up to the real threat to Europe and help turn back the communist hordes that were now engulfing the east of the country. There were, too, the fanatics, notably the SS, who were determined not to surrender. For all these reasons, the war would continue until there was nothing left.

Lining up for food
Ration cards became irrelevant as food shortages in urban areas grew because of the disruption of road and rail communications by Allied bombing.

***Volkssturm* conscripts**
Uniforms were often not available for *Volkssturm* conscripts. Most were armed with the Panzerfaust anti-tank rocket projector.

Destroyed street in Bremen
By early 1945 many of Germany's cities had become virtual shells, but the inhabitants still tried to lead normal lives.

ALLIED ADVANCE TO THE RUHR

During January 1945 the Western Allies regained all the ground they had lost during the recent German offensive. Their main objective now was to get across the Rhine. In the middle of the month, and conscious that the Soviet Union had launched its long-awaited offensive across the Vistula in Poland, Eisenhower issued his orders. In essence, the Ruhr was to be the primary target. To this end, the 21st Army Group under Montgomery was to cross the Rhine to its north, while Bradley's 12th Army Group did so to the south. They would then cut off the Ruhr. In the south, Devers' 6th Army Group would clear the Saarland and reduce an obstinate German pocket around Colmar before advancing to the Rhine. No attempt would be made to liberate the northern Netherlands—a strategy that would result in the Dutch people coming close to starvation.

On the German side, Rundstedt, who had been reappointed Commander-in-Chief West the previous September, wanted to withdraw his forces across the Rhine so as to conserve them for the defense of the Ruhr. Hitler, however, was insistent that Rundstedt hold the West Wall, the German equivalent of the Maginot Line, at all costs. It meant that the Allies would face some very tough fighting.

While the US First and Third Armies continued to regain ground lost in December and the US Seventh and French First Armies set about dealing with the eight German divisions in the Colmar pocket, Montgomery began his approach to the

Action in the Reichswald
Canadian troops played a major part in the grim fighting in the Reichswald, a heavily wooded area close to the Lower Rhine.

Rhine. The first phase was for the German salient in the Roermond area to be eradicated— a task begun by the British Second Army on January 16. Up to this point the ground had been frozen hard, but there was now a sudden thaw which reduced it to mud. This, coupled with resistance by the Germans, meant that it took ten days to clear the Roermond triangle. It was a portent of things to come.

On January 28 the Ardennes salient was finally eliminated and the next task for the US First and Third Armies was to penetrate the West Wall. Their first concern was the dams on the Roer River. If the Germans opened the sluices, much of the surrounding countryside would be flooded and so become a major obstacle. The Americans began their advance on January 31, but they experienced much the same problems as the British had to the north. As a result, they failed to reach the dams in time to prevent the Germans from flooding the whole Roer Valley. A further advance toward the Rhine in the Cologne-Düsseldorf area could not take place until the waters subsided. The one consolation was that the Colmar pocket was finally reduced on February 5, enabling the French and Americans to close up to the Rhine south of Strasbourg. The US Seventh Army then began to clear the Saarland, while the US Third Army began to advance across the Moselle River.

Advance to the Rhine
Men of the US Ninth Army shelter from shellfire during the battle for the German town of Jülich, on the Roer River. They crossed the river on February 23, 1945.

OPERATION VERITABLE

It was now the turn of the Canadians. They were to clear the region that stretched from southeast of Nijmegen to the Lower Rhine between Emmerich and Wesel. Operation Veritable was launched on February 8. Preceded by the fire of over 1,000 guns in the largest artillery bombardment that the 21st Army Group had staged during the campaign, the Canadians quickly broke through the initial German lines. Then, however, they came up against Eugen Meindl's First Parachute Army, which consisted of a significant number of hardened veterans, and the picture changed. The fighting became intense, especially in the wooded area of the Reichswald, where the Germans had constructed five lines of defenses. The situation was not helped by a further thaw, which caused much flooding and restricted the advance to a very narrow front. Even assistance from RAF Bomber Command did not help much, and casualties were heavy.

By February 23 the floods in the Roer Valley had subsided sufficiently for the Americans to resume their advance. General William Simpson's US Ninth Army, which was under Montgomery's command, began to attack toward Düsseldorf. Simpson had the advantage in that German troops had been drawn north to block the Canadians. Once his forces had crossed the Ruhr and advanced farther toward the Rhine, one part turned northeast to link up with the Canadians, while the remainder continued toward Düsseldorf. Simultaneously, the US First Army began to approach the Rhine between Cologne and Coblenz. Meanwhile, Patton's spearheads reached the river at Neuwied on March 7. The US Third and Seventh Armies now set about clearing the remainder of the German forces between the Moselle and the Rhine.

Rundstedt accepted that he could not hold ground west of the Rhine for much longer and embarked on a delaying action designed to buy sufficient time to get the bulk of his forces back over the river. He was, however, particularly concerned that the Allies would capture an intact bridge and consequently organized matters so that there was a phased demolition of all crossings over the Rhine. Thus, when, on March 2, the Ninth Army reached the river at Düsseldorf, the bridges had been blown. It was the same when the US First Army arrived at Cologne two days later, just after the Canadians had finally cleared the Reichswald. Then, on March 7, Rundstedt's worst fear was realized.

CROSSING THE RHINE AT REMAGEN

That afternoon the leading elements of a US First Army task force reached the high ground that overlooked the small town of Remagen. To their surprise, they could see that the Ludendorff railroad bridge spanning the Rhine at this point was still intact. Fighting their way through the town, they reached the bridge, which was defended on the west bank. At this point the Germans attempted to demolish it, but the charges failed to explode. With artillery support, the Americans overcame the defenders and rushed the bridge itself. The Germans now made another attempt to blow it, but this was

Pontoon bridge over the Rhine
By the time they reached the Rhine, virtually all of whose bridges had had been partially or totally destroyed, the Allied engineers were well-practiced in building pontoon bridges.

Fighting in Cologne
US troops reached the heavily bombed city on March 5. They took the Germans by surprise, but the Hohenzollern bridge over the Rhine had already been destroyed.

only partially successful. The attackers charged across the bridge, cutting demolition cables as they did so, and reached the other side. The Western Allies had crossed the Rhine at last.

Rundstedt gave orders that the bridge should be destroyed from the air or by divers. Hitler was furious and immediately sacked the field marshal for the third and final time, summoning Kesselring from Italy to replace him. As for those responsible on the ground for demolishing the bridge, an SS flying tribunal summarily executed five of them. Neither air attack nor divers were able to destroy the bridge, and even V-2 rockets were fired at it, also without success, such was the desperation of the Germans. The Americans quickly reinforced their bridgehead, and soon it contained some four

divisions. However, they feared that if they advanced too far eastward they would lay themselves open to being cut off. In any event, a single thrust from here did not accord with Eisenhower's Broad Front strategy. Hence the US First Army did not exploit this success, although it did cut the Cologne-Frankfurt *autobahn*. The bridge itself collapsed on March 17, but by this time the Americans had constructed two pontoon bridges upstream.

FURTHER ALLIED CROSSINGS

By now the Allies were everywhere closing up to the Rhine and preparing to make other crossings. At this juncture Hitler issued a draconian order. Everything that might be of possible value to the Allies was to be destroyed—communications, industry, and even food supplies. "If the war is lost, the nation will also perish," he declared. Albert Speer, his armaments minister, was horrified, believing that it was the duty of the leadership to ensure that the German people had some means of reconstructing their lives once the war was over. He succeeded in persuading the

YOU ARE NOW
CROSSING THE
RHINE RIVER
THROUGH COURTESY
OF E CO. 17 ARMD.
ENGR. BN. AND
C CO. 202
ENGR. C. BN.

commanders in the west not to carry out the order. The next Allied crossing over the Rhine was in the US Third Army's sector. On the night of March 22/23 Patton's men achieved a "bounce" crossing over the river at Oppenheim, in which they reached the west bank and crossed to the other side without any pause for preparation. They thus caught most of the defenders asleep. The following night the British and Canadians made three crossings. In marked contrast to the hasty action at Oppenheim,

these were deliberate operations, which had been under preparation for the past two weeks. Assault boats, amphibious vehicles, and bridging equipment had been carefully deployed. In addition, a massive weight of artillery had been massed, and RAF Bomber Command had launched two attacks, by day and by night, on the town of Wesel, where the main concentration of German troops in the area was located. Once the assault troops had established themselves on the far bank, the final airborne operation of the war in the west took place. The British 6th and US 17th Airborne divisions dropped by parachute and landed by glider to the east of Wesel in order to provide instant depth to the bridgehead that had been created there. They

actually landed among the German artillery positions, and thus prevented any possibility of a counterattack.

The US Third Army achieved two further crossings on the night of March 24/25 and the Seventh Army was also across the Rhine in two places by the end of the 26th. Finally, the French made a crossing at Germersheim on March 31. It meant that the Allies were now on the east bank of the Rhine on a 200-mile (320-km) front and were still shoulder-to-shoulder, in line with Eisenhower's strategy. During the campaign the Germans had suffered 60,000 casualties, but a further 250,000 had been made prisoner and vast amounts of equipment had been lost. The German forces in the west were crumbling, and the overall picture was very different from that in January, when it appeared that the Soviet offensive across the Vistula would reach Berlin within weeks. Now the Red Army was halted on the Oder and there was every chance that the Western Allies would get to the city first—a prospect that was to trigger the final squabble among them.

German prisoners
As the Allies advanced to the Rhine, many German soldiers were trapped on the west bank and consequently fell into Allied hands.

Closing in on the Third Reich
By the end of March the Red Army was on the Oder River, only 50 miles (80 km) from Berlin, and had virtually overrun Hungary. The Western Allies were about to fan out across Germany. Only in Italy were the Allies yet to resume their assault on the Third Reich.

THE ALLIED ADVANCE
INTO GERMANY
DEC 15, 1944–MAR 31, 1945

- ᵀᵀᵀ Siegfried Line
- ── German front line Dec 15, 1944
- ── German front line Mar 31, 1945
- ☼ Major bombing raid
- ➤ Western Allied advance
- ➤ Soviet advance
- ── German operations

0 km   100   200   300
0 miles   200   400

3 Feb 8
Canadians and British launch Operation Veritable

8 Mar 23–24
21st Army Group begins to cross the Rhine

5 Mar 2
US troops reach the Rhine near Düsseldorf

7 Mar 22
Troops of Patton's 3rd Army cross the Rhine at Oppenheim

1 Jan 16
British launch Operation Blackcock to clear Roermond triangle

6 Mar 7
US troops cross the Rhine at Remagen. By March 21 they have established a 12-mile (19-km) deep bridgehead

2 Feb 5
Allied campaign to clear Colmar pocket is completed

9 Mar 31
French cross the Rhine at Germersheim

Feb 13/14
British and Americans bomb Dresden

4 Jan 22
Germans evacuate Memel

8 Mar 30
Soviet forces capture Danzig

2 Jan 13
Soviet forces begin advance into East Prussia

3 Jan 17
Warsaw falls to Soviet forces

1 Jan 12
Soviet forces launch offensive in Poland

5 Feb 13
Soviet forces capture Budapest from Germans following failure of German relief operations in January

7 Mar 15
Spring Awakening is halted by Soviet counterattack

6 Mar 5
German offensive, Spring Awakening, is launched south of Lake Balaton

ARMY GROUP NORTH (COURLAND)
ARMY GROUP CENTRE (NORTH)
ARMY GROUP VISTULA
ARMY GROUP A (CENTRE)
ARMY GROUP SOUTH
ARMY GROUP E
ARMY GROUP F

2ND BALTIC FRONT
1ST BALTIC FRONT
3RD BYELORUSSIAN FRONT
2ND BYELORUSSIAN FRONT
1ST BYELORUSSIAN FRONT
1ST UKRAINIAN FRONT
4TH UKRAINIAN FRONT
2ND UKRAINIAN FRONT
3RD UKRAINIAN FRONT

1ST PARA ARMY
CANADIAN 1ST ARMY
BRITISH 2ND ARMY
15TH ARMY
US 9TH ARMY
US 1ST ARMY
5TH ARMY
US 3RD ARMY
US 7TH ARMY
1ST ARMY
19TH ARMY
FRENCH 1ST ARMY
10TH ARMY
14TH ARMY
US 5TH ARMY
BRITISH 8TH ARMY

LATVIA · RIGA
COURLAND
SWEDEN
Baltic Sea
LITHUANIA
Memel
Königsberg · Gdynia
Danzig
Kolberg
Kolobrzeg
EAST PRUSSIA
POMERANIA
Hamburg
Stettin
Torun
Vistula
BERLIN · Küstrin · Poznan
Frankfurt an der Oder
Oder
WARSAW
Bug
NETH.
AMSTERDAM
Nijmegen · Arnhem
Rotterdam
Emmerich
Wesel
BEL.
Roermond
Düsseldorf
BRUSSELS
Aachen
Cologne
Bonn
Remagen
Coblenz
LUX.
Frankfurt
Oppenheim
Mannheim
Germersheim
Strasbourg
Colmar
Basel
FRANCE
SWITZERLAND
Milan
Po
Genoa
Bologna · Ravenna
ITALY
Moselle
Rhine
Danube
GERMANY
AUSTRIA
Dresden
PRAGUE
Breslau
SILESIA
Cracow
Lodz
Kielce
Baranow
POLAND
Dniester
CARPATHIANS
SLOVAKIA
VIENNA
BUDAPEST
Lake Balaton
HUNGARY
Drava
Zagreb
Trieste
Venice
BELGRADE
YUGOSLAVIA
Adriatic Sea
Elbe
N

THE FINAL PUSH IN EUROPE

APRIL 1–MAY 11, 1945

The last few weeks of the war witnessed dramatic events on every front as Germany was squeezed from the west, east, and south, and split in two by the Western Allies and the Soviet Union. The fall of Berlin to the Red Army at the beginning of May was followed by the signing of four separate surrenders. German troops, however, continued to fight in Czechoslovakia for three days after hostilities ended.

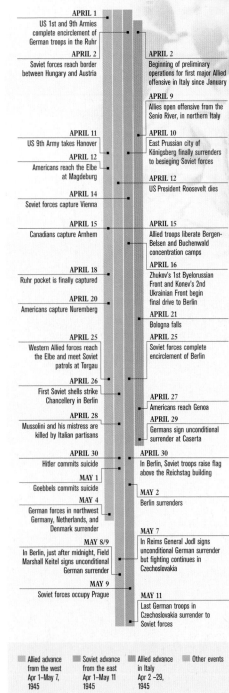

APRIL 1
US 1st and 9th Armies complete encirclement of German troops in the Ruhr

APRIL 2
Soviet forces reach border between Hungary and Austria

APRIL 2
Beginning of preliminary operations for first major Allied offensive in Italy since January

APRIL 9
Allies open offensive from the Senio River, in northern Italy

APRIL 11
US 9th Army takes Hanover

APRIL 10
East Prussian city of Königsberg finally surrenders to besieging Soviet forces

APRIL 12
Americans reach the Elbe at Magdeburg

APRIL 12
US President Roosevelt dies

APRIL 14
Soviet forces capture Vienna

APRIL 15
Canadians capture Arnhem

APRIL 15
Allied troops liberate Bergen-Belsen and Buchenwald concentration camps

APRIL 16
Zhukov's 1st Byelorussian Front and Konev's 2nd Ukrainian Front begin final drive to Berlin

APRIL 18
Ruhr pocket is finally captured

APRIL 20
Americans capture Nuremberg

APRIL 21
Bologna falls

APRIL 25
Western Allied forces reach the Elbe and meet Soviet patrols at Torgau

APRIL 25
Soviet forces complete encirclement of Berlin

APRIL 26
First Soviet shells strike Chancellery in Berlin

APRIL 27
Americans reach Genoa

APRIL 28
Mussolini and his mistress are killed by Italian partisans

APRIL 29
Germans sign unconditional surrender at Caserta

APRIL 30
Hitler commits suicide

APRIL 30
In Berlin, Soviet troops raise flag above the Reichstag building

MAY 1
Goebbels commits suicide

MAY 4
German forces in northwest Germany, Netherlands, and Denmark surrender

MAY 2
Berlin surrenders

MAY 7
In Reims General Jodl signs unconditional German surrender but fighting continues in Czechoslovakia

MAY 8/9
In Berlin, just after midnight, Field Marshall Keitel signs unconditional German surrender

MAY 9
Soviet forces occupy Prague

MAY 11
Last German troops in Czechoslovakia surrender to Soviet forces

■ Allied advance from the west Apr 1–May 7, 1945	■ Soviet advance from the east Apr 1–May 11 1945	■ Allied advance in Italy Apr 2 –29, 1945	■ Other events

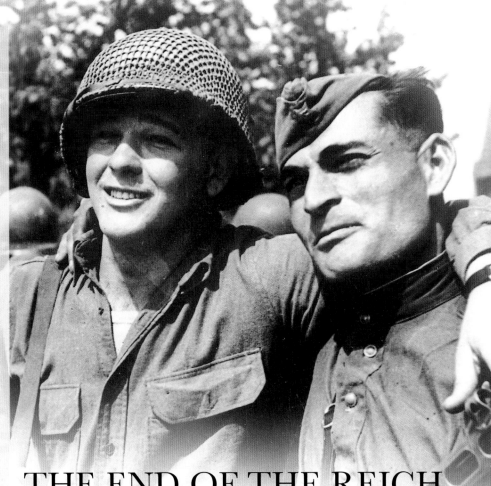

THE END OF THE REICH

O N MARCH 28, 1945 Eisenhower had drafted a message to Stalin to reassure him that he did not intend to make Berlin an objective for his forces. He would leave the German capital to the Soviets, and advance instead to the Erfurt-Leipzig-Dresden line, an area to which he believed the Germans were moving their organs of government. The British were aghast at this. Churchill believed that to wait for the Soviets to capture Berlin would merely prolong the war and enable them to reap the main fruits of victory. Montgomery, too, considered that this was the ideal opportunity for the single-thrust strategy to be used. However, the US chiefs of staff supported Eisenhower, and the British climbed

down after he assured them that his decision was not irreversible. Furthermore, Allied intelligence had been warning of the Nazi intention to establish a final bastion in the Alps and he needed to forestall this. Stalin, however, was convinced that Eisenhower was bluffing and took this as a signal to accelerate preparations for the final assault on Berlin.

ADVANCE FROM THE RHINE

Eisenhower's plan for the advance from the Rhine was that Bradley's 12th Army Group was to make the main thrust toward Dresden, taking back the US Ninth Army under command once the Ruhr had been encircled. Montgomery, to his fury, was given the supporting role of covering Bradley's northern flank. Devers' Sixth Army Group was to advance southeastward toward the Bavarian Alps to prevent the establishment of the so-called National Redoubt, where a last-ditch stand might be made.

The various armies were already breaking out of their bridgeheads before the end of March, and the US First and Ninth Armies had the Ruhr encircled

American war correspondent and prisoners
Fred Ramage, one of the many journalists who reported on the advance of the Western Allies, brings in two German air force men on his press jeep.

US and Soviet troops meet at Torgau

On April 25 members of a US reconnaissance patrol crossed the Elbe at Torgau to meet Soviet troops and celebrate the fact that Germany was now divided in two.

on April 1 (see map page 276). Trapped inside was a large part of Army Group B, still commanded by Model. Hitler ordered him to defend the Ruhr to the last and so his troops did not attempt to escape the encirclement. This left a yawning gap in the German defenses. Bradley was quick to take advantage of this and his forces were soon racing to the Elbe. Elements of the Ninth Army entered Hanover on April 11 and reached Magdeburg the following day. Those forces allocated to reducing the Ruhr pocket steadily squeezed it and by April 18 it was no more. Some 325,000 German troops surrendered, but Model chose to commit suicide. To the south, progress was equally rapid. Patton found stiff resistance in Franfurt-am-Main. He left his infantry to deal with this, bypassing the city with his armor, and quickly linked up with the First Army to his north. Kassel was in his army's hands on April 4. While the French First Army headed for the Swiss border, clearing the Black Forest *en route*, the US Seventh Army advanced quickly to the Main River, reaching Würzburg

... orders from the Supreme Command were still couched in the most rigorous terms, enjoining us to "hold" and "fight" under threats of court martial. But I no longer insisted on these orders being carried out. It was a nerve-racking time we experienced—outwardly putting a bold face on the matter ... while we secretly allowed things to go their own way. On my own responsibility I gave orders for lines to be prepared in the rear ready for a retreat.

GENERAL BLUMENTRITT OF THE GERMAN FIRST PARACHUTE ARMY, DESCRIBING THE SITUATION AT THE END OF MARCH

on April 5 and Schweinfurt six days later. German resistance was patchy. Many towns displayed white flags and offered no resistance at all. In others, especially if SS troops were in the vicinity, there was bitter fighting. There was virtually no movement of refugees since there was really nowhere they could go. Civilians stayed in their homes and hoped that the fighting would quickly move on.

The main focus of attention continued to be the Elbe. By mid-April the US First and Ninth Armies had closed up to it. Indeed, Simpson's Ninth Army already had a bridgehead at Magdeburg and he pleaded with Eisenhower to be allowed to go on

to Berlin, just 70 miles (110 km) away. Eisenhower, however, was concerned that US troops were already inside the agreed Soviet postwar zone of occupation. He insisted that there was to be no further advance east of the river or across the Mulde to its south. Instead, Bradley was to turn southeast to the Danube valley and link up with the Red Army so as to isolate the National Redoubt, which did not, in fact, exist. The US Seventh Army captured Nuremberg on April 20 after a fierce battle against SS troops and continued south to the Danube. Meanwhile, Patton led the US Third Army into the Danube valley and into Czechoslovakia, reaching Pilsen before he was halted by Eisenhower.

The burning question was when the Soviet forces would appear. The US First Army on the west bank of the Mulde had sent reconnaissance patrols eastward to a limit of 5 miles (8 km) from the river. On April 25 one of these could not resist going farther and met Soviet troops at Torgau on the Elbe. Germany was now physically split in two.

ADVANCE IN THE NORTH

In the north, Montgomery had also made good progress. The Canadian First Army had the initial task of liberating the northeast Netherlands. In spite of coming across much flooding, it made a rapid

US troops enter Nuremberg

The city—a symbol of National Socialism—was defended fanatically by SS troops. It was finally captured by the Americans on April 20.

THE DISCOVERY OF BERGEN-BELSEN

JUST AS THE SOVIETS had come across extermination camps during their advance through Poland in 1944, so the Western Allies stumbled across similar horrific sites as they overran the western and southern parts of Germany in April 1945. One of these camps was Bergen-Belsen, which lay between Hanover and Hamburg.

On April 12 forward elements of the British 11th Armoured Division on the Aller River received a German officer bearing a flag of truce. He asked that the area around the camp at Belsen be declared neutral, since there had been an outbreak of typhus there and the Germans did not want it to spread. The British agreed and three days later sent a party to inspect the camp. They discovered that there were, in fact, two camps—one for men and the other for women. In both, there were thousands of unburied corpses, as well as mass graves containing another 40,000 bodies. While not an extermination camp, Bergen-Belsen had been crammed with some 60,000 inmates and disease had become rampant. Worse, the administrative system had totally broken down and there was virtually no food for the prisoners, although the British discovered a building crammed with rations for the SS guards. Some troops were assigned to doing what they could for the 38,000 survivors, many of whom were dying. However, with the advance to Hamburg continuing, the division could not spare any food or medical support and it was to be a few days before this could be provided in sufficient quantities. The local inhabitants, who denied all knowledge of the existence of the camp, were made to help with the burial of the dead so that they could see what had been done in their name. The SS staff of the camp initially had to be protected from inmates determined on revenge. Eventually, they were tried for war crimes and a number, including the commandant, were hanged. The camp of Bergen-Belsen remains to this day a memorial site and a stark reminder of the inhumanity of which people are capable.

Belsen inmates
Around 38,000 people were found alive in the camp on April 15, but as many as 28,000 died in the weeks that followed.

Burying the dead
Guards were made to help with burials in some camps. In others, they were shot by Allied troops.

Corpses in an open pit
In addition to the 40,000 corpses in mass graves, there were 10,000 unburied corpses of inmates who had died from starvation and disease.

advance and reached Groningen on April 16. The German 25th Army was thus finally cut off, but it showed no sign of surrendering. The plight of the starving Dutch was now of very real concern and so agreement was reached with the 25th Army's commander that the Allies could deliver foodstuffs by air. The strategic bombing forces were given the task—code-named Operation Manna—and dropped supplies from a very low height with no interference from the Germans. Meanwhile, the Canadians began to clear the German North Sea coast.

The British Second Army continued its advance in a northeastward direction, capturing Osnabrück on April 4 and reaching the Weser River the next day. Montgomery's orders were to secure Hamburg and the naval base at Kiel, cut off Schleswig-Holstein, and prepare to liberate Denmark. As the Americans

were finding to the south, some German forces were still prepared to fight and there were some bitter encounters. The fiercest resistance was in Bremen, where the German commander and 6,000 men only surrendered after nine days of fighting. The British were concerned that Hamburg might prove to be an even tougher battle.

Eisenhower was becoming worried about Soviet intentions in the north of Germany. The speed of the

Occupying Bremen
German resistance was fierce on the many river lines in the north of the country. It was particularly obstinate at the port of Bremen, which was finally captured by the British Second Army on April 26.

Soviets' advance north of Berlin created a danger that they might enter Schleswig-Holstein themselves. If this happened, it could be they rather than the Western Allies who liberated Denmark. He therefore ordered Montgomery to cross the Elbe and secure Lübeck. With the support of the US XVIII Airborne Corps, the river was crossed on April 29. The British reached Lübeck on May 2, the day on which Berlin surrendered and two days after the suicide of Hitler (see page 279). The Americans went farther east to Wismar, where they met the Red Army. Meanwhile, the commander of the Hamburg garrison was persuaded to surrender.

By this time many German troops were making their way westward to avoid falling into Soviet hands. This was particularly the case in the British 21st Army Group sector. At the instigation of Grand Admiral

Liberation of Milan
Troops of the US Fifth Army enter Milan, already liberated by Italian partisans, on April 29.

Dönitz, who in Hitler's will had been appointed as the Führer's successor and was now in Schleswig-Holstein, a delegation went to Montgomery's tactical HQ on Lüneberg Heath on May 3. They asked him to accept the surrender of Army Group Vistula, which was facing the Second Byelorussian Front, but also requested that he shape his operations so that as many civilians as possible be given the chance to escape falling into Soviet hands. Montgomery replied that Army Group Vistula was a Soviet concern, but that he would accept the surrender of all German forces in northwest Germany, the Netherlands, and Denmark. Dönitz agreed to this, and on the following day the delegation returned and signed the document of surrender. It was a major consolation for the frustration that Montgomery had suffered over the last nine months, but it was not the first German surrender in a major theater.

CAMPAIGN IN ITALY

In Italy the Allies had spent the first three months of 1945 planning their final offensive. The lull had, however, enabled the Germans to send four divisions to assist in the defense of western Germany, not that this had made any difference. The remaining Canadian corps in Italy had also departed, and their place had been taken by a number of Italian partisan brigades. During March 1945 several peace overtures were made to the Allies by the German military governor of northern Italy. He was an SS officer

and his overall boss, Heinrich Himmler, who was also trying to make a deal with the Allies, eventually stepped in and, in the fear of being upstaged, ordered that no more contact be made.

The eventual Allied plan for bringing the war in Italy to an end was to destroy the German forces by trapping them between the US Fifth and British Eighth Armies. The Americans were to attack northward to the west of Bologna, while the British struck through a narrow strip of land, known as the Argenta Gap, that lay between Lake Comacchio,

close to the Adriatic coast, and the Reno River. Throughout the winter months there had been an air campaign to throttle German communications and by the spring the Germans' ability to redeploy their troops quickly no longer existed.

After some preliminary operations to tie down the German left flank on Lake Comacchio, the Eighth Army attacked on April 9. The fighting was initially tough, not helped by the numerous waterways, but gradually the defenses crumbled. Delayed by two days because of bad weather, the Americans joined in on the 14th. Argenta fell to the British four days later, and then the Fifth and Eighth Armies jointly seized Bologna. General Heinrich von Vietinghoff, the German commander, realized that his defenses had disintegrated and ordered a withdrawal northward. The Fifth Army then advanced toward Milan, while the Eighth struck northeastward toward Venice.

On April 23 the Germans made further peace overtures and six days later a delegation from Vietinghoff signed a surrender document with the Allies, who included a Soviet representative, at Caserta in southern Italy. It was done without reference to Berlin and came into effect on May 2. By this time the US Fifth Army had reached Milan—already occupied by Italian partisans—and was simultaneously advancing through the Alps toward Austria, eventually meeting up with the US Seventh Army in the Brenner Pass on May 6. At the same time, the British had reached Trieste, where they came face to face with Tito's Yugoslav partisans, who had designs on the port. The arduous campaign in Italy was finally at an end, but Trieste was to create an immediate postwar problem.

THE DEATH OF MUSSOLINI

IN THE AFTERMATH OF HIS RESCUE by the Germans in September 1943, Benito Mussolini established himself as head of an Italian Social Republic in Salò in northern Italy, but he had little power. When the German forces began to disintegrate in April 1945, Mussolini declared that he would make a last stand with his German allies in the Alps. Accordingly, on April 25 he left Milan for Lake Como, where he expected to meet a force of 3,000 Blackshirts. On arrival he discovered that the force consisted of just 12 men, and he joined a German convoy heading northward. At 7:00 am the following morning the convoy was stopped at a partisan roadblock. The partisans agreed to let the Germans pass, but not the Italians. Mussolini and his mistress Clara Petacci were then kept prisoner until the afternoon of April 28, when a communist partisan, Walter Audisio arrived to drive them away in his car. After a short way, he ordered them out and shot them. Audisio took the bodies to Milan, where they were strung up by their ankles in a main square. It was a grisly end to Mussolini's dream of creating a new Roman empire.

Fallen Duce
The citizens of Milan threw filth on the corpses of the former dictator and his mistress.

Mussolini and Petacci
The bodies were hung in a square where partisans had been executed.

ADVANCE TO VIENNA

While the Western Allies were crossing the Rhine to advance farther into Germany, on the Eastern Front the Soviet Third Ukrainian Front was overwhelming the German Army Group South in Hungary and Austria. By April 4 it had smashed its way through the Vertes mountains to cut off Vienna on three sides and join hands with the Second Ukrainian Front. A torrent of armor, over which flew fleets of attack aircraft, was followed up by waves of infantry, who poured through every gap that was torn in the Army Group South's lines. There was then a fierce nine-day struggle for Vienna, in which the city's defenders were relentlessly pushed back, and savage hand-to-hand fighting raged in the sewers. By April 14 Vienna had fallen into Red Army hands.

PLANNING THE BERLIN BATTLE

On April 1 Stalin informed his generals that he intended to "take Berlin before the Western Allies did" and launch an offensive into Brandenburg by April 16. Three days earlier he had informed the Western Allies that the coming Red Army offensive would be launched against Dresden and Leipzig, probably in mid-May, and it was not until mid-April that the British and Americans became aware that the offensive was imminent. Stalin calmly reassured them that the principal thrust was to be made on Leipzig. Meanwhile, Hitler had convinced himself that the offensive would be made toward Prague rather than Berlin. Confident that the line on the Oder would hold, and convinced that the Red Army was at breaking point, at the end of the first week in April he transferred three panzergrenadier divisions of Army Group Vistula to the south.

THE ALLIED ADVANCE THROUGH GERMANY
APR 1–MAY 7, 1945

— German front line Apr 1
--- German front line Apr 19
— Western Allied front line May 7
— Soviet front line May 7
➤ Western Allied advance
➤ Soviet advance
▫ Borders Sept 1939

❷ Apr 16
Northern Soviet armies restart their advance from the Oder-Neisse Rivers and drive toward Berlin

Apr 1 ❶
Forces in US 1st and 9th armies meet at Lippstadt, so encircling the Ruhr

❸ Apr 10
US 9th Army takes Hanover

❹ Apr 11
Americans reach the Elbe at Magdeburg

❸ Apr 20
Soviet forces begin to shell central Berlin, which surrenders on May 2

❷ Apr 2
US 3rd Army takes Kassel

❻ Apr 25
Western and Soviet forces meet at Torgau

❺ Apr 20
Americans capture Nuremberg

❹ May 9
Prague is occupied by Soviet forces

Apr 14 ❶
Soviet forces take control of Vienna

Apr 25 ❸
Americans take Parma and Verona

Apr 27 ❹
Americans reach Genoa

Apr 21 ❷
Bologna falls

❶ Apr 9
Allies open offensive from the Senio River

2ND BYELORUSSIAN FRONT
1ST BYELORUSSIAN FRONT
1ST UKRAINIAN FRONT
4TH UKRAINIAN FRONT
2ND UKRAINIAN FRONT
3RD UKRAINIAN FRONT
CANADIAN 1ST ARMY
BRITISH 2ND ARMY
US 9TH ARMY
US 1ST ARMY
US 3RD ARMY
US 7TH ARMY
FRENCH 1ST ARMY
BRITISH 8TH ARMY
US 5TH ARMY
YUGOSLAV ARMY OF NATIONAL LIBERATION

Advance to the Elbe
The Western Allies advanced from the Rhine on a broad front, with the Americans making the main thrust toward Dresden and the British pushing north. An Allied offensive in Italy made rapid progress, while in the east the Red Army advanced from the Oder and captured Berlin.

0 km 50 100 150 200
0 miles 50 100 150 200

The last battle
The Red Army broke into Berlin using assault groups cooperating closely with armor, artillery, and antitank teams. Security detachments mopped up behind.

Meanwhile, Stalin was exploiting to the hilt the simmering rivalry between Zhukov and Konev over who should take Berlin. At a meeting on April 3 it was decided that Zhukov's First Byelorussian Front was to drive to Berlin and seize the city. Konev's First Ukrainian Front was to provide support by attacking the German forces south of Berlin, thus isolating the principal formations of Army Group Center from the units defending the city. However, in the event of stiff enemy resistance on the eastern approaches to Berlin, Konev should also be ready to deliver a blow from south of the city. The Second Byelorussian Front, under Rokossovsky, which had only just completed operations in Gdynia and Danzig, was to join the offensive four days after Zhukov and Konev had gone onto the attack.

A total of 23 Soviet armies set about regrouping on the Oder. On Zhukov's front 7 million shells were brought up by rail and road for 9,000 guns. Meanwhile, 27 engineer battalions kept open damaged bridges on the Oder and built 25 new ones, linking the Küstrin bridgehead with the east bank of the river. No fewer than 120 engineer and 13 bridging battalions on Konev's front worked on bridges over the Oder and Neisse. Four air armies, deploying 7,500 aircraft, were to support the ground forces. On Zhukov's front, the 16th Air Army had assembled 3,200 aircraft, and was augmented by the 800 long-range bombers of the 18th Air Army.

GERMAN PREPARATIONS

Between the Baltic coast and Görlitz, around 100 miles (160 km) southeast of Berlin, there were some 50 German field divisions, five of them armored, supplemented by a patchwork of makeshift battle groups and approximately 100 *Volkssturm* battalions. According to postwar Soviet figures, against them were ranged approximately 190 Red Army divisions, although many of these were very run down, averaging between 2,500 and 5,500 men. For the assault on Berlin, the Red Army was relying on its massive superiority in artillery, aircraft, and armor. On the German side, there was a grim determination to fight on in the east, despite almost universal recognition of impending defeat.

Between November 1943 and March 1944 RAF Bomber Command had tried, and failed, to "wreck Berlin from end to end." By the early spring of 1945, British and American bombers were flying almost at will over the German capital by day and night, forcing Hitler to retreat to his bunker in the Chancellery garden and reducing swathes of the city to rubble. Also in the air over the German capital were Red Air Force reconnaissance aircraft gathering information that was then combined with captured documents and prisoner interrogations to produce detailed assault maps. Zhukov was well aware that a modern city could devour an army committed to a house-to-house battle, as had happened in Stalingrad. He was determined that Berlin would be taken in an all-out power drive, in which specially chosen assault groups would be supported by armor and massed artillery laying down a path of destruction all the way to the center.

The Germans did not give any serious thought to the defense of Berlin until March, when a makeshift "obstacle belt" was thrown up in a ring some 30 miles (50 km) outside the capital. A second ring was improvised around Berlin's rail system, whose cuttings, culverts, and overhead lines provided good cover and a formidable barrier to Soviet armor. The last-ditch defense ring—code-named Citadel and containing eight wedge-shaped command sectors—lay at the heart of the city and contained nearly all the government buildings.

To defend the German capital, its commander General Helmuth Reymann initially had at his disposal some 60,000 *Volkssturm* and a collection of Hitler Youth, engineer, police, and antiaircraft units. The only unit of any operational value was the Berlin Guard Battalion. In Berlin's streets

> "Even the last soldier was now aware that the war was lost. He was aiming to survive, and the only sense he could see was to protect the front in the east to save as many refugees as possible."
>
> GERMAN OFFICER ON THE SITUATION IN GERMANY IN THE LAST WEEKS OF THE WAR

Escaping destruction
Berlin was ravaged by Allied bombers and Red Army artillery. The battle in the streets produced strange contrasts, with a delirium of fighting in some districts and an eerie calm in others.

the erection of flimsy barricades prompted the sour joke that it would take the Red Army two hours and 15 minutes to break them down—two hours laughing their heads off and 15 minutes smashing them up.

THE RED ARMY'S POWER DRIVE

The terrain facing Zhukov's bridgehead at Küstrin was unsuitable for armored operations—a 10-mile (16-km)-wide valley, heavily mined and crisscrossed with streams, ditches, and canals, and overlooked by the heavily defended Seelow Heights. Zhukov decided to commit his armor to the attack's first phase only when the 200-ft (60-m) Heights had been seized.

The initial thrust was made on April 16, but it met with unexpectedly fierce resistance, and at noon Zhukov sent in his armor—1,300 tanks and self-propelled guns—a full 24 hours before he had thought it would be necessary. The Seelow Heights

were taken after ferocious fighting on the 17th and on the following day the second German defensive line was breached. By April 19 Zhukov had prised open the Oder line on a 45-mile (70-km) front, but was now at least two days behind schedule. On April 20 Berlin's northeast perimeter was breached, and shortly before 2:00 pm the heavy guns of the Third Shock Army opened fire on the city.

To the south, Konev had made rapid progress, clearing the Neisse River by the 17th, and driving a wedge between Army Group Vistula and Army Group Center before swinging north toward Berlin

on the 20th. Hitler, swooping wildly between drug-induced euphoria and deep depression, continued to marshal phantom armies on the map in his bunker. Only on April 22 did he admit the the war was lost.

Berlin was now cut off on three sides. On April 23 Stalin issued the order that decided who was to win the race to Berlin. Konev's troops were placed a crucial 150 yd (140 m) to the west of the Reichstag, the preeminent symbolic objective in the assault on the city. Zhukov had been given the prize. Now the Soviet armies that had encircled Berlin— 464,000 men, supported by 12,700 guns, 21,000 rocket launchers, and 1,500 tanks—drove relentlessly forward. Berlin's S-bahn ring was breached on April 26 and by nightfall on the 27th "Fortress Berlin" had been squeezed down to an east–west belt 10 miles (16 km) long and 3 miles (5 km) wide.

On the night of the 26th the first shells struck the Chancellery, sending vibrations through the *Führerbunker* as tons of masonry toppled into the street. Two days later the Red Army had fought its way to within a 1 mile (1.5 km) of the hideout. On April 30 Zhukov's 150th and 171st Rifle Divisions launched their final assault on the Reichstag, which

Arch of defeat
German soldiers march into captivity by the Brandenburg Gate. The Red Army claimed to have taken 134,000 prisoners on May 2, 1945, but this included able-bodied civilians destined for labor camps.

HITLER'S LAST DAYS

ON JANUARY 16, 1945, Hitler descended from the Reich Chancellery into the 13th and last of his headquarters, the *Führerbunker*. With the exception of two excursions, on February 25 and March 16, and occasional brief visits to the Chancellery, the bunker was to remain the center of the shrinking Third Reich until its leader's death. Built in 1944, the *Führerbunker* was contained within a complex of shelters, one of which housed the staff of Martin Bormann, Hitler's secretary, and another a field hospital. Buried 55 ft (17 m) below the Chancellery garden, the main *Führerbunker* was built in two stories. In the bunker's upper level were a kitchen and living quarters, latterly occupied by Josef Goebbels and his family. Below was the *Führerbunker* proper, a series of small rooms that included a telephone exchange, a map room, and Hitler's spartan living quarters.

In the bunker, night merged into day, with the last military conferences often ending at 6:00 am. On April 15 Hitler was joined by his mistress, Eva Braun, who had lived in the Chancellery since mid-March. On April 20, Hitler's 56th birthday, there was a final melancholy reunion of the Nazi paladin in the Chancellery and then the bunker. In the small hours

Hitler's grave
Allied troops view the shell crater in the Chancellery garden where the bodies of Hitler and Eva Braun were buried after being burned.

of April 29 Hitler dictated his final testament and married Eva Braun. At about 3:30 pm on the 30th he and Braun committed suicide together, Hitler biting on a cyanide capsule and shooting himself with his Walther 7.65-mm revolver. Their bodies were partially burned in the Chancellery garden, and discovered by an NKVD officer on May 5. Also in the garden were the bodies of Goebbels and his wife Magda, who had poisoned their six children before committing suicide. Bormann, it seems, committed suicide after escaping.

Bunker entrance
The bunker remained intact, even as the Reich Chancellery was being heavily shelled.

Last public appearance
On his 56th birthday, on April 20, 1945, the Führer appeared in public for the last time when he met young defenders of the Third Reich in the garden of the Chancellery.

was defended by over 5,000 SS men, Hitler Youth, and *Volkssturm*. In the early afternoon, as a Red banner was attached to a column at the building's entrance, Hitler prepared to commit suicide.

While fighting continued, the Germans opened negotiations with General Chuikov about a new successor German government and a ceasefire. At 10 am on May 2 General Weidling, Berlin's recently appointed battle commandant, ordered a general surrender. As a chilling drizzle fell on Berlin, its defenders began to lay down their arms. In the battle for the city, the Soviet fronts under Zhukov, Konev, and Rokossovsky had sustained losses of 305,000 men killed, wounded, and missing. They were the heaviest casualties suffered by the Red Army in any battle of the war with the exception of the great encirclements of 1941. In Berlin itself up to 100,000 German soldiers and civilians had lost their lives, while in the fighting since April 16 some 480,000 German officers and men had become prisoners-of-war.

The surrender in Berlin did not end the fighting in the one remaining pocket of German resistance, in Czechoslovakia, where on May 4 the citizens of Prague took to the streets, emboldened by the approach of the US Third Army. However, on May 7 the Americans were ordered to withdraw by US President

Fallen eagle
This massive eagle was captured by the Red Army in the Reich Chancellery.

Truman, who was determined that no American lives were to be risked in so volatile a situation. Murderous confusion had reigned in Prague between May 4 and 8 as Czechs clashed with SS units. In the wee hours of May 9, Soviet tanks reached the outer suburbs of Prague, while its German garrison streamed westward to escape the Red Army. Later that day the Soviet armor rolled into Prague. Just two days before, the Germans had surrendered unconditionally to the Allies. A formal ceremony took place on May 7 in Reims and—as millions of people celebrated in Europe, the US, and elsewhere—on May 8 in Berlin.

Fleeing from the Red Army in Germany
Refugees cross the Elbe River at Tangermünde, to the west of Berlin, on a bridge blown up by the Germans. As the Red Army advanced westward in 1945, vast numbers of German civilians fled in fear for their lives.

ASIA AND THE PACIFIC

JANUARY–SEPTEMBER 1945

The final months of the Pacific war saw frenetic action across the entire region. Landings took place on Iwo Jima and the Philippines, while the British forced the Japanese out of Burma. The infamous fire bombing of Tokyo started in March, and Japanese surrender followed shortly after the dropping of the atom bombs on Hiroshima and Nagasaki.

JANUARY 9
US landings on Luzon. Secondary landings Jan 29 and Jan 31

JANUARY 14–16
First two bridgeheads across Irrawaddy River established by Indian divisions. Main crossings in February

JANUARY 27
Chinese Y Force advances down Burma Road after Burma and Ledo Roads joined at Mongyu

FEBRUARY 10–18
US carrier raids on Honshu, including first on Tokyo

FEBRUARY 19
US landings on Iwo Jima

FEBRUARY 21 – MARCH 4
Battle for Meiktila. Taken Mar 4

MARCH 16
Iwo Jima declared secure

MARCH 9/10
Firestorm raid on Tokyo. 1 million killed, wounded, or homeless

MARCH 21
Mandalay cleared, marking overall Japanese defeat in Burma

APRIL 1
US landings on Okinawa

APRIL 7
First fighter escorts, from Iwo Jima, for B-29 raids on Japan

APRIL 6–7
Massive kamikaze attacks on US invasion fleet at Okinawa. Japanese battleship *Yamato* sunk by US carrier aircraft

APRIL 23
Japanese start to evacuate Rangoon, Burma

MAY 3
British occupy Rangoon

MAY 2
"Dracula" landings by 26th Indian Division as preliminary to securing Rangoon

MAY 23
Firestorm raid on Tokyo is largest B-29 raid of the war

MAY 11–14
Australian landings at Wewak, New Guinea. Organized resistance in area ended by 23rd

MAY 27
Naha, capital of Okinawa, secured

JUNE 10
Allied landings in Brunei Bay

JUNE 17
On Okinawa, Japanese resistance collapses and troops begin to surrender voluntarily. Okinawa declared secure by June 22

JUNE 22
Emperor Hirohito tells Supreme Council that steps toward peace must be taken

JULY 22–23
Korean port of Najin is mined in the longest duration bomber mission of World War II

JULY 24
Kure naval base attacked by 1,747 US carrier aircraft

AUGUST 1/2
Largest single-day B-29 effort of the war. 836 B-29s dispatched

AUGUST 6
Atomic bomb dropped on Hiroshima. 78,000 killed outright

AUGUST 9
Atomic bomb dropped on Nagasaki. 35,000 killed in the initial blast

AUGUST 9
Soviets invade Manchuria

AUGUST 15
Emperor Hirohito broadcasts surrender to his people, but some fighting continues

AUGUST 28
First US forces reach Japan

SEPTEMBER 2
Formal surrender of Japan aboard USS *Missouri* in Tokyo Bay. Local surrenders continue

SEPTEMBER 12
Formal surrender of Japanese forces in Southeast Asia at Singapore

■ Philippines, Western Pacific, and Japan
■ Burma and Southeast Asia
■ Other events

JAPAN SURRENDERS

T HE SETTING OF AMERICAN policy for the war in the Pacific was beset by rivalries between the army and navy. These were compounded by personal differences, specifically between Admiral Ernest King, chief of naval operations, and General MacArthur, commander in the Southwest Pacific theater.

In summer 1944 King wanted the US Navy to advance across the Pacific to Formosa (Taiwan) and on to Okinawa, but MacArthur contended that America should concentrate on the Philippines instead. MacArthur's motives were partly personal— he had made a public pledge to return to the islands after the Japanese invasion in 1942—but he also argued that the Philippines would provide the best base for the next phase of operations and that an attempt to recapture them would be less costly than an attack on Formosa. King's views commanded little support even among his colleagues within the navy, so it was MacArthur's view that prevailed.

RETAKING THE PHILIPPINES

The capture of the Philippines would become the longest and largest US action of the Pacific War thanks to protracted Japanese resistance, first on Leyte and then on Luzon. Seasonal rains, the forced withdrawal of US carriers for replenishment, and the success of kamikaze raids enabled the Japanese to assemble 75,200 troops to defend Leyte. It took until December 1944 to break the defense, by which time the Americans had 200,000 men on the island.

American naval power
US Task Group 38.3 sails to its anchorage at Ulithi, in the Caroline Islands: the light carrier *Langley*, fleet carrier *Ticonderoga*, and three battleships were accompanied by four cruisers and 18 destroyers.

The Japanese Army finally abandoned Leyte on December 19, 1944, although scattered resistance continued into May 1945. Meanwhile US forces had landed on Mindoro on December 15, 1944. They met little resistance there and easily secured useful airfields from which to support landings on Luzon.

The main US assault on Luzon began on January 9, 1945, with landings at Lingayen Gulf, about 100 miles (160 km) northwest of the capital,

Manila. Facing 200,000 US troops were 275,000 men of the Japanese 14th Area Army under the command of Lieutenant General Yamashita Tomoyuki. With much of the Japanese Navy lying at the bottom of the Pacific after Leyte Gulf, and only 200 aircraft available, Yamashita had no prospect of supply or reinforcement. He split his forces into three groups and dispersed them to fight delaying actions in key strategic positions, where they dug themselves into cave complexes.

The US Sixth Army's advance to the Philippine capital, Manila, involved two thrusts: XIV Corps under Major General Oscar Griswold proceeded straight to the city across the central plain, taking Clark Field airbase and the town of Calumpit, while I Corps secured the left flank against a Japanese counterattack. Further US forces came ashore at Nasugbu, southwest of Manila, on January 31 and moved north to meet Griswold. Cheering Filipinos welcomed the Sixth Army as it entered the capital on February 4, but the Battle of Manila continued until March 3. Although Yamashita had withdrawn into the mountains, 17,000 naval troops under Rear Admiral Iwabuchi Sanji fought for the city in vicious hand-to-hand fighting. More than 100,000 Filipinos died, along with 1,000 Americans and 16,000

Raising the flag on Iwo Jima
In one of the most evocative images of World War II, US Marines raised the Stars and Stripes on Mount Suribachi. This photograph was not taken in the heat of the battle but specially posed shortly after the island's capture.

Japanese. By March 1945 the city was liberated but lay largely in ruins.

During the battle for Manila the Americans also captured Corregidor, the small rock island located in the entrance to Manila Bay. It was occupied by some 5,000 well-provisioned troops, but after the assault landing on February 15 and a parachute drop the next day, in the words of the official US Navy history, "the defense showed neither spirit nor cohesion." In an action lasting 10 days, the Americans lost some 225 killed and 405 wounded. The Japanese dead numbered over 4,500. Some 500 of these were buried alive, sealed in the caves from which they had been fighting by US bulldozers or demolition charges. Only 20 were taken prisoner.

THE WAR AT SEA

While US land forces were making inroads on Leyte and Luzon, American carrier task groups were operating off the Philippines. In November 1944 the US Navy destroyed 38 Japanese warships and

Manila in ruins
The fighting for the Philippine capital left thousands dead and reduced the old Spanish walled city, Intramuros, to rubble. After Warsaw, Manila was the most heavily damaged of all the Allied capitals during the war.

KAMIKAZE PILOTS

TOWARD THE END OF WORLD WAR II some Japanese pilots undertook suicide missions in which they deliberately flew their aircraft, laden with bombs, into enemy targets such as ships. The pilots had no means of escaping. Both the tactics themselves and the fliers were known as kamikaze, meaning "divine wind." Kamikaze squadrons sank or damaged beyond repair more than 70 American vessels, damaged hundreds of others, and took many lives at Leyte in 1944 and Okinawa in the following year. To some extent kamikaze tactics were adopted through force of circumstance—Japanese aircraft were no match for American aircraft. However, the practice was rooted in the ancient traditions of the Japanese samurai warriors, whose code of honor demanded death before surrender. The name itself is derived from that of a typhoon—the divine wind—which in 1281 destroyed a massive Mongol armada that had been preparing to attack and invade Japan. Kamikaze pilots would go through a ritual ceremony in which they would honor the emperor and drink a cup of sake before taking off on their final mission.

Kamikaze pilots
Kamikaze pilots pose for a last photo before a suicide mission. Around 2,550 kamikaze missions were flown, but their effectiveness lessened as US defenses against the attacks improved.

Kamikaze attack
A Japanese pilot tries to maneuver his Zero fighter into a US warship. In response to kamikaze attacks, the Americans increased their anti-aircraft guns and added fighters to their carrier air groups.

service and merchant ships, while US submarines sank the 64,800-ton carrier *Shinano* and the escort carrier *Shinyo*. During December 1944 and January 1945 Japanese kamikaze attacks sank or damaged 79 US warships, amphibious vessels, and service ships. In early January the US carrier force entered the South China Sea and raided Japanese-held ports in Indochina. On January 12 it destroyed 11 warships and 29 service and merchant ships totaling 115,000 tons. On January 21–22 another two warships and 17 service and merchant ships of 58,000 tons were sunk off Formosa. The relatively small tonnages reflected the lack of any large Japanese ships to sink. However, compelling evidence of American naval power came on February 17, when the carrier force, totaling 119 warships, raided the Japanese Home Islands for the first time since April 1942. Of the

Approaching Okinawa
Sailors on the battleship *West Virginia* keep watch for Japanese aircraft off the coast of Okinawa in late March 1945. On April 1 the ship was hit in a kamikaze attack, which killed four and wounded seven sailors.

ships deployed in this raid, only six—two carriers, two battleships, and two heavy cruisers—had been in service at the time of Pearl Harbor; the others had all been commissioned and built since.

IWO JIMA AND OKINAWA

The capture of two islands south of Japan— Iwo Jima in the Volcano Islands and Okinawa in the Ryukyus—was authorized by the American high command in October 1944 (see map page 290). Once the Americans had decided to launch a strategic air offensive against Japan from the southern Marianas, the small island of Iwo Jima assumed obvious importance as a base from which fighters could escort B-29 bombers on their missions. Similarly, once the decision to retake the Philippines had been made, then Okinawa presented itself as a potential forward base for land, air, and naval formations in the invasion of the Japanese Home Islands.

The campaigns for possession of these two islands are synonymous with the final phase of the Pacific War. Iwo Jima and Okinawa were of critical importance in the final closing of the ring around

Japan. Both also entered the US popular imagination through potent symbolism, such as the famous image of the capture of Mount Suribachi on Iwo Jima.

The campaign on Iwo Jima began on February 19, 1945, that on Okinawa on April 1. The islands were declared secure on March 26 and June 30, respectively. On the 8 sq miles (20 sq km) of Iwo Jima, where the Japanese had deployed about 25,000 troops, some 2,400 further Japanese were killed or captured after the island was declared secure, and resistance continued into June. Just 216 Japanese were taken prisoner. The island cost 6,821 Americans killed and nearly 18,000 wounded, but its value was revealed as early as March 11, when fighters began operations from the first of the airfield complexes that ultimately covered half the island.

The value of Okinawa was somewhat different from that of Iwo Jima. It would also provide airfields to support the campaign against the Home Islands, but its real value lay in the forward anchorage it would provide for the navy and its strategic position astride Japan's lines of communication with Southeast Asia. No tanker reached Japan from the Southern Resources Area after March 1945.

THE STRUGGLE FOR OKINAWA

On Okinawa the Japanese 32nd Army, with some 131,000 troops, ceded the central and northern part of the island in order to concentrate on a defensive campaign on the Shuri Line. The Japanese policy was to force the Americans to fight a protracted campaign within range of aircraft concentrated in the Home Islands. The air campaign was the most important part of the final despairing Japanese attempt to influence events to their advantage by reducing US resources. Suicide aircraft struck at American warships throughout the first four months of the campaign in the Philippines, but the greatest kamikaze effort came in the battle for Okinawa. Its failure demonstrated that there was no effective substitute for conventional air power. In the course of the Philippines campaign as a whole the Japanese armed forces lost an estimated 3,000 aircraft, and in the Okinawa campaign some 7,000 aircraft. In both campaigns, however, the Allies proved able to absorb their losses. Ten American fleet carriers were driven from the battle in the course of 1945, but, with one exception, all were returned to service before the end of the war.

The scene became wild and terrible. More Japs rushed screaming from the caves. They tumbled over the rocks, their clothes and bodies burning fiercely. Soon the flame-throwers paused. There were no shots from the caves. A Jap with his clothes in rags hunched himself out of one hole, his arms upraised. The Marines behind the rocks waved to him to come out. The Jap indicated that there were more who would like to surrender.

ANONYMOUS US MARINE CORPS CORRESPONDENT, IWO JIMA

The Okinawa campaign cost the Allies 48,193 service personnel killed, wounded, and missing. They lost 34 ships of all types sunk and another 25 damaged beyond economic repair; 343 more were damaged to varying degrees. The reality underlying these results was two-fold. First, given their shortages of aircraft, fuel, and personnel, the Japanese could not simultaneously prepare for a conventional air battle and undertake kamikaze offensives. Even the most effective use of suicide missions in the battles for the Philippines and Okinawa could only have one outcome. Second, while the shock created by the employment of suicide forces was very real when they were first employed, it was one that lessened as the attacks themselves became less effective. By the end of the Okinawa campaign the Americans, by adopting new tactics and deployment, had gotten the better of the kamikazes.

In terms of an invasion of the Home Islands, the Americans had moved into a position of strength that ensured victory in the air battle. Sixty fleet, light, and escort carriers saw action off the Ryukyu Islands, and 90,662 missions were flown by US carriers during the Okinawa campaign. Of this total 53,077 missions were flown by the fleet and light fleet carriers between March 14 and June 8, while the rest were flown by escort carriers prior to the end of June. Against such numbers even self-sacrifice was largely ineffective. Tacit acknowledgment of this reality was provided by the fact that 10,755 prisoners were taken on Okinawa, the first occasion on which Japanese soldiers surrendered in any appreciable numbers.

BOMBING RAIDS ON JAPAN

In the American advance across the Pacific the carriers paved the way for landings, and the forces put ashore captured or built airfields from which aircraft were in turn

able to support the fleet against the next objective. The naval, land, and air efforts were mutually supporting, and the capture of the Marianas added another dimension to American strategy. The islands provided the airfields from which a strategic bombing campaign could

Tokyo destroyed by bombing
Little remains standing in this part of Tokyo after waves of incendiary bomb attacks by US aircraft in 1945. More people perished in the Tokyo fire bomb raids than in the atomic bomb attack on Nagasaki.

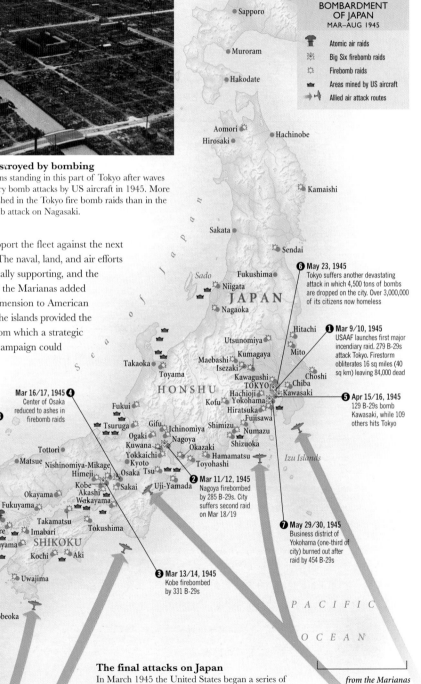

BOMBARDMENT OF JAPAN
MAR–AUG 1945

- Atomic air raids
- Big Six firebomb raids
- Firebomb raids
- Areas mined by US aircraft
- Allied air attack routes

6 May 23, 1945
Tokyo suffers another devastating attack in which 4,500 tons of bombs are dropped on the city. Over 3,000,000 of its citizens now homeless

1 Mar 9/10, 1945
USAAF launches first major incendiary raid. 279 B-29s attack Tokyo. Firestorm obliterates 16 sq miles (40 sq km) leaving 84,000 dead

5 Apr 15/16, 1945
129 B-29s bomb Kawasaki, while 109 others hits Tokyo

8 Aug 6, 1945
First atomic bomb dropped on Hiroshima, exploding 2,000 ft (600 m) above ground, devastating the city and killing 78,000 people instantly

4 Mar 16/17, 1945
Center of Osaka reduced to ashes in firebomb raids

2 Mar 11/12, 1945
Nagoya firebombed by 285 B-29s. City suffers second raid on Mar 18/19

7 May 29/30, 1945
Business district of Yokohama (one-third of city) burned out after raid by 454 B-29s

3 Mar 13/14, 1945
Kobe firebombed by 331 B-29s

9 Aug 9, 1945
Second atomic bomb explodes over Nagasaki, destroying over 40 percent of the city and killing 35,000 people outright

HOKKAIDO
Sapporo
Muroram
Hakodate
Aomori
Hirosaki
Hachinobe
Kamaishi
Sakata
Sendai
Fukushima
Niigata
JAPAN
Nagaoka
Hitachi
Mito
Utsunomiya
Kumagaya
Maebashi
Isezaki
Takaoka
Toyama
Kawagushi
TOKYO
Choshi
Chiba
Kofu
Hachioji
Yokohama
Kawasaki
Hiratsuka
Fujisawa
HONSHU
Fukui
Shimizu
Numazu
Tsuruga
Gifu
Ichinomiya
Nagoya
Okazaki
Shizuoka
Ogaki
Kuwana
Yokkaichi
Hamamatsu
Kyoto
Toyohashi
Tottori
Matsue
Nishinomiya-Mikage
Himeji
Osaka
Tsu
Uji-Yamada
Okayama
Kobe
Akashi
Wakayama
Sakai
Fukuyama
Hiroshima
Takamatsu
Kure
Imabari
Tokushima
Tsushima
Matsuyama
SHIKOKU
Shimonoseki
Ube
Kochi
Aki
Yawata
Kita-Kyushu Moji
Fukuoka
Saga
Oita
Uwajima
Sasebo
Omuta
Kumamoto
Nobeoka
Nagasaki
KYUSHU
Kagoshima

Sado
Sea of Japan
Izu Islands
PACIFIC OCEAN
East China Sea

from China
from Carrier Task Force 38
from the Marianas

The final attacks on Japan
In March 1945 the United States began a series of devastating firebomb attacks on major Japanese cities. In August US commanders took the historic decision to drop atomic bombs on Hiroshima and Nagasaki.

Superior payload
A B-29 drops its massive payload over mainland Japan. Its gigantic internal bomb bays could hold 20,000 lb (9,072 kg) of bombs.

Superfortress in flight
With a wingspan of over 140 ft (43 m) and an unladen weight of over 140,000 lb (63,640 kg), the American B-29 Superfortress was the largest bomber to see action during World War II. Its sheer size presented engineering problems previously unencountered in aviation history, but it was a hugely successful aircraft nonetheless.

be staged against the Japanese Home Islands. The bombing campaign began in November 1944, but for its first three months it proved singularly ineffective.

The Americans faced a number of problems. They had insufficient combat aircraft and bombers with which to launch massed attacks. Meanwhile heavy cloud, strong winds at high altitude, and the difficulty of identifying targets reduced the accuracy of their raids. In addition, the B-29 Superfortress still had technical problems. Above all, precision bombing failed to make a significant impact on Japanese industry, much of which was local and small-scale. Consequently, when Major-General Curtis LeMay took over XXI Bomber Command on January 20, 1945, he ordered that its B-29s be stripped of their armor and guns in order to increase their flying range and load capacity in readiness for an area-bombing campaign against Japanese cities. This would be conducted from low altitude at night.

Most Japanese cities were composed of densely packed wooden buildings and had little firefighting capability. They thus became death traps for their citizens during incendiary attacks. On March 9/10, 279 Superfortresses attacked Tokyo and caused greater destruction than the subsequent atom bomb on Hiroshima. Over 2,000 tons of incendiary bombs created a massive firestorm whose glow could be seen 150 miles (240 km) away. The inferno destroyed 16 sq miles (40 square km) of the city, killed or wounded 124,711 people, and left a million homeless. The raid on Tokyo was the first of 18 against Japan's six largest cities in spring 1945.

Both the frequency and the intensity of the raids rose as aircraft were released from commitments in China and Southeast Asia. The raid on Tokyo by 562 Superfortresses on May 23/24 was the largest single B-29 raid of the war, while the greatest number of B-29s committed to a single series of

raids was on August 1/2, when 627 Superfortresses attacked Hachioji, Mito, Nagaoka, and Toyama. By the war's end large areas of 66 major cities had been laid to waste, 13 million civilians were homeless, and a further 8 million had been evacuated. Over 40 percent of Japan's industrial capacity had been destroyed. Such devastation, inflicted in just under seven months, rivaled that inflicted on Germany in the entire last three years of the European war.

With US carrier aircraft flying combat air patrols over Japanese airfields, fighters escorting the bombers, and air groups providing electronic countermeasure operations and night harassing attacks, US air superiority was so great that the Americans were able to announce their targets in advance. The effects on Japanese morale were clear. Rates of absenteeism rose as high as 80 percent in some industrial centers, and touched 40 percent even in

"If you're going to use military force, then you ought to use overwhelming military force…. All war is immoral, and if you let that bother you, you're not a good soldier."

MAJOR-GENERAL CURTIS LEMAY
QUOTED BY ROBERT S. MCNAMARA, *LOS ANGELES TIMES*

Kyoto, which was never bombed. The bombing campaign and the inability of the Imperial armed forces to oppose it were crucial in convincing many ordinary Japanese that the war was lost.

By summer 1945 Japan's situation was hopeless. Its people were on the brink of starvation. Food shortages were so bad that the average adult had lost a minimum of 10 lb (4.5 kg) in weight, and two-thirds of all adults had lost 20 lb (9 kg). Diet deficiency contributed to an increase in tuberculosis, and some estimates suggest that, had the war lasted into 1946, some 7 million Japanese would have died of malnutrition-related disease or starvation. State price controls were ineffective and rationing was haphazard. The average price of black-market goods in July 1945 was 42 times that of official prices; sugar could cost as much as 240 times its official value. Clothing was scarce or unobtainable. It had made up 9 percent of Japanese expenditure in 1936 but accounted for just 1.3 percent in 1944. Taxes, meanwhile, had risen by over a fifth to 61.4 percent of income during the same period.

Industrially, Japan was coming to a standstill. By summer 1945 the country was producing twice as much electricity as it needed. This was because industry was falling idle for want of raw materials. The level of productivity in those industries that were still working was low and falling, as a

Mother and child
A Japanese mother bathes her starving child in 1945. The Japanese turned over any available land to growing food, but shortages remained crippling.

Rifle practice
Members of Japan's National Defecse Women's Association perform rifle drill as part of their military training. All Japanese civilians were encouraged to take up arms in readiness for the expected US invasion of their Home Islands.

direct result of conscription policies, which made no provision for reserved occupations. Output per worker in the oil industries fell by half from 1941 to 1945, and the few ships that remained in service had crews some 20 percent greater than in 1941 because of the loss of high-quality personnel.

At sea, summer 1945 was disastrous. One indication of the totality of the defeat now engulfing Japan was the fact that in July 1945 the Allies sank 139 merchantmen, service transports, and auxiliaries— 298,223 tons of shipping. Of these, only three merchantmen—just 2,820 tons—were sunk outside home waters. All semblance of strategic mobility had been lost by this stage of proceedings, and, as Japan faced the certainty of

invasion, even its defensive intentions were confounded by reality. The 1945 class of recruits who would be called upon to defend the Home Islands was basically untrained and the 1944 class was little better. Even if the Japanese army could work out where Allied forces would be obliged to land, it faced an impossible dilemma. Formations held back from beaches would be subjected to overwhelming air attack as they tried to move forward. It was highly unlikely that they would be able to get into the battle in an effective way. If they were held in forward positions, however, they would doubtless be subjected to equally overwhelming fire from amphibious and support forces. Even the good-quality Japanese divisions that were available lacked the armor, motor transports, and radios essential to the effective conduct of the defensive battle.

A PREMONITION OF DEFEAT

After the war some Japanese authorities claimed that the most effective course the Allies could have adopted in summer 1945 would have been simply to suspend all offensive operations. This would have made it clear to the Japanese that there was absolutely nothing they could do to redeem the situation. As it was, in what proved to be the last weeks of the war American and British warships bombarded factories and installations on Honshu on five nights during the second half of July and again on August 9. The bombardment of the Hamamatsu aircraft factory on July 29 was the last occasion when a British battleship fired her guns in anger in the conflict.

These final operations of the war are notable for providing a fascinating perspective on the Japanese attack on Pearl Harbor in December 1941. One of the little-known and often overlooked facts of the war was a report received by the Japanese cabinet on August 27, 1941, over three

JAPANESE PRISONERS OF WAR

ONE OF THE MOST DISTASTEFUL realities of World War II was the manner in which the Imperial Japanese Army treated its prisoners of war. Although by no means all their captives were treated with intolerable cruelty, life as a Japanese prisoner was invariably harsh. Chinese POWs were usually regarded as subhuman and treated barbarically, while Western POWs were treated a little better. Although the Geneva Convention laid down rules for the humane treatment of prisoners, combatants in Japanese custody were routinely beaten, tortured, and killed. They were also used as labor, for which they received a token payment. The construction of the Burma–Siam railroad was a notorious project in which malnourished British and Australian POWs were forced to work under the most extreme conditions. When Allied troops liberated the POW camps they were shocked at the physical and mental state of many of the surviving prisoners, and this galvanized their resolve to continue the fight against the Japanese.

Since the end of the war there has been much speculation about the reasons for Japan's cruelty to its captives. Many Japanese saw themselves as ethnically superior to other races, and believed that surrender was humiliation. One theory is that some of their contempt for their prisoners may have been inspired by the feeling that, if their enemies had been honorable, they would not have allowed themselves to be captured in the first place.

Death railroad
Clearly showing the effects of malnutrition, Australian POWs lay a section of the railroad from Burma to Siam. Its construction cost the lives of around 16,000 Allied POWs.

Canvas straps

Homemade sandals
When their boots wore away or were stolen by other POWs they made their own sandals from screws, tires, and scraps of canvas.

Rubber sole for grip

Hand-carved spoon

Inmate number

Eating equipment
Inmates made their own eating utensils from spare pieces of wood or whatever they could find. They had to purchase their food with the token wages they earned by laboring for the Japanese.

Liberated POWs
American prisoners of war pose in Bilibid Prison, Manila, in April 1945. Their emaciated bodies show the privations they had suffered during three years' Japanese captivity.

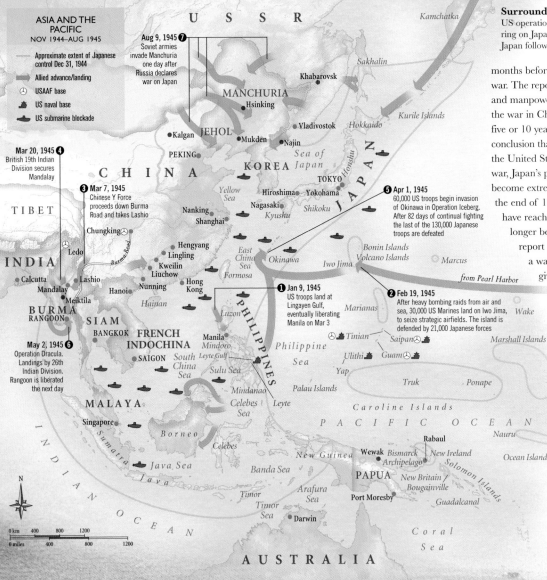

ASIA AND THE PACIFIC
NOV 1944–AUG 1945

— Approximate extent of Japanese control Dec 31, 1944

➤ Allied advance/landing

✈ USAAF base

⚓ US naval base

🛥 US submarine blockade

Aug 9, 1945 ❼
Soviet armies invade Manchuria one day after Russia declares war on Japan

Mar 20, 1945 ❹
British 19th Indian Division secures Mandalay

Mar 7, 1945 ❸
Chinese Y Force proceeds down Burma Road and takes Lashio

Apr 1, 1945 ❺
60,000 US troops begin invasion of Okinawa in Operation Iceberg. After 82 days of continual fighting the last of the 130,000 Japanese troops are defeated

Jan 9, 1945 ❶
US troops land at Lingayen Gulf, eventually liberating Manila on Mar 3

Feb 19, 1945 ❷
After heavy bombing raids from air and sea, 30,000 US Marines land on Iwo Jima, to seize strategic airfields. The island is defended by 21,000 Japanese forces

from Pearl Harbor

May 2, 1945 ❻
Operation Dracula. Landings by 26th Indian Division. Rangoon is liberated the next day

Map labels: U S S R, Kamchatka, Sakhalin, Kurile Islands, Khabarovsk, MANCHURIA, Hsinking, Hokkaido, Vladivostok, Najin, Kalgan, JEHOL, Mukden, PEKING, KOREA, Sea of Japan, TOKYO, Yokohama, Hiroshima, Honshu, CHINA, Yellow Sea, Nanking, Nagasaki, Shikoku, Shanghai, Kyushu, TIBET, Chungking, Hengyang, Lingling, East China Sea, Okinawa, Bonin Islands, Volcano Islands, Marcus, Iwo Jima, INDIA, Ledo, Kweilin, Liuchow, Formosa, Calcutta, Lashio, Nunning, Hong Kong, Mandalay, Hanoi, Hainan, Marianas, Wake, Meiktila, Luzon, Philippines, Saipan, Marshall Islands, BURMA, SIAM, Manila, Mindoro, Tinian, Guam, RANGOON, BANGKOK, FRENCH INDOCHINA, Philippine Sea, Ulithi, SAIGON, Leyte Gulf, Yap, South China Sea, Sulu Sea, Leyte, Truk, Ponape, MALAYA, Mindanao, Celebes Sea, Caroline Islands, PACIFIC OCEAN, Singapore, Borneo, Nauru, Sumatra, Celebes, New Guinea, Wewak, Rabaul, Bismarck Archipelago, New Ireland, Ocean Island, Java Sea, Banda Sea, PAPUA, New Britain, Bougainville, Solomon Islands, Java, Timor, Arafura Sea, Port Moresby, Guadalcanal, Timor Sea, Darwin, Coral Sea, AUSTRALIA, INDIAN OCEAN

Scale: 0 km 400 800 1200 / 0 miles 400 800 1200

Surrounding Japan
US operations in the Pacific aimed to close the ring on Japan; the Soviets joined the war against Japan following the dropping of the atomic bombs.

months before the Japanese initiated the Pacific war. The report concluded that Japan's economy and manpower could not sustain the burden of the war in China, should it continue for another five or 10 years. The report also came to the conclusion that Japan could never win a war with the United States. It predicted that, in such a war, Japan's position in terms of shipping would become extremely difficult after late 1943. By the end of 1944, it concluded, Japan would have reached the point at which it would no longer be able to wage war effectively. The report also predicted a Soviet entry into a war against Japan. States are seldom given such a warning of defeat. As it turned out, the report proved to be accurate in almost all respects.

THE FINAL ACT
On July 26, 1945, Allied leaders meeting at Potsdam, Germany,, warned Japan to surrender immediately and unconditionally on pain of utter destruction. Unknown to the Japanese command, on July 16 the US Manhattan Project had achieved the first successful detonation of an atomic bomb in Alamogordo, New Mexico. Equivalent to 20,000 tons of TNT, the explosion coud be seen from 125 miles (200 km) away.

Armored might
A Soviet armored column moves through a pass in the Great Khingan Mountains into Manchuria in August 1945. The Soviet action routed the Japanese defenders.

Bolt *Rear sight* *Foresight*

Japanese Arisaka Type 99 rifle
This bolt-action rifle was adopted by the Japanese Army
in 1939. It fired a 7.7-mm bullet and the magazine held
a total of five rounds.

Preparing for the assault
Soviet infantry watch a preliminary bombardment
before advancing on a Japanese position in northern
China during the invasion of summer 1945.

In fact, since the dismissal of Tojo Hideki as prime
minister in July 1944, Japanese leaders had been
looking for a way to end a war that they knew was
lost. In spring 1945 Japan had made contact with the
Soviet Union in the hope that it might mediate an
acceptable surrender. The Soviet Union, however,
had given an undertaking to Britain and the United
States at the Tehran Conference in November 1943
that it would enter the war against Japan once the
European conflict was over. On April 5, 1945, the
Soviet Union announced that it would not renew
its 1941 nonaggression treaty with Japan. Although
the Soviets did not tell their allies that Japan had
made peace overtures, successful codebreaking of
Japanese diplomatic signals meant that the American
high command was already aware of Japan's search
for a possible end to the war.

Privately, Japan's leaders feared that any attempt
to surrender would provoke mutiny on the part of
an ultranationalist military. The army was not
convinced by the reality of defeat but was in any case

certain that a final battle would have to be fought
in order to uphold the honor of the nation and of
the services. The absence of any Allied guarantee to
preserve the emperor and the imperial system in the
event of a surrender only compounded the difficulties
facing the leadership. On July 28 the Japanese high
command issued its response to the Potsdam
Declaration. It chose to do this in an unfortunately
worded statement that seemed to reject Allied
demands in a preemptory and dismissive manner.

THE ATOMIC BOMBS

Japan's apparent rejection of the Potsdam demands
invited the obvious conclusion on the part of the
Allies that it intended to fight on. The American high
command naturally sought to bring about Japan's
surrender without the daunting prospect of assault
landings and a final campaign in the Home Islands.
The possession of atomic weapons provided an
alternative to invasion, but the decision to use the
bombs was underwritten by other considerations.

The prime minister asked me:
"Is the Kwantung Army capable
of repulsing the Soviet Army?"
I replied: "The Kwantung Army
is hopeless. Within two weeks
Hsinking will be occupied."
The premier sighed upon hearing
my words and said: "Is the
Kwantung Army that weak? Then
the game is up."

ACCOUNT BY S. IKEDA, CHIEF OF THE JAPANESE CABINET
PLANNING BUREAU, OF A MEETING WITH PRIME MINISTER
ADMIRAL SUZUKI KANTARO

The Americans had previously sought a Soviet involvement in the Japanese war, but now that the conflict was clearly in its final stage, that necessity had declined. Instead, there was in Washington an awareness that a demonstration of the possession and use of these new weapons would strengthen the American hand in dealings with the Soviet Union in the aftermath of the war. The Potsdam conference had suggested that relations between the two countries were already becoming difficult.

Accordingly, in the first days of August 1945 the only two atomic bombs that the Americans had so far produced arrived in the Marianas. There they would be loaded aboard specially-modified B-29s. On the morning of Monday, August 6, Colonel Paul W. Tibbetts flew a Superfortress known as *Enola Gay* to drop the first bomb, "Little Boy," on Hiroshima. At 8:15 am three-quarters of the city was destroyed, and more than 78,000 of its citizens were killed instantly in the blast. Many thousands more were condemned to suffer a slow lingering death. Three days later Major Charles W. Sweeney, at the controls of the *Boshcar*, dropped the second atomic bomb, "Fat Man," on Nagasaki. This time two-fifths of the city was destroyed, and more than 35,000 people were killed.

The attack on Nagasaki heralded the Soviet entry into the war. Inside a week the outclassed Japanese forces in Manchuria had been brought to the brink of total defeat. Soviet formations crossed the Greater Khingan Range and the Gobi to reach Hsinking, Mukden, Jehol, and Kalgan, while forces from the

The shock of defeat
Three schoolgirls join other shocked Japanese weeping in front of Emperor Hirohito's palace in Tokyo in August 1945. For many Japanese, defeat in the war was a cause of deep personal shame as well as a national humiliation.

Soviet Union's Maritime Provinces overran northeast Manchuria and were later involved in landings in southern Sakhalin. The Japanese surrender in Manchuria came on August 19 at Khabarovsk. The Soviets then used airborne detachments to secure airfields, towns, and communications centers ahead of their main advance. There was sporadic resistance, but the Soviet occupation of Manchuria and northern Korea was largely unopposed. In the Kuriles, however, there was bitter fighting between August 17 and 23, after which Soviet forces proceeded to occupy the entire chain of islands.

The atom bomb attacks on Hiroshima and Nagasaki and the Soviet entry into the war only served to worsen the divisions that already existed

within the Japanese high command. Fear of occupation by Soviet forces, and the parallel fear of social revolution that might come in the wake of defeat, were major influences in Japan's attempts to search for a way to end the war while the United States still held the power of decision. Within the army, however, there remained a determination to fight a last battle of annihilation that would atone for the military defeat. It took the emperor himself, at a meeting on August 9–10, to indicate that it was time for considerations of his own personal safety and position to be subordinated to national needs. For the sake of Japan, the war had to be ended immediately.

THE SURRENDER

The emperor's decision was considered binding by all the members of the Japanese cabinet and war council. However, when the Japanese attempted to ensure that the Potsdam Declaration did not comprise any demand which prejudiced "the prerogatives of His Majesty as sovereign ruler," the American reply was that "the authority of the Emperor and Japanese government to rule the state shall be subject to that of the supreme commander of the Allied powers." This provoked a second crisis, and Hirohito was obliged to reaffirm his previous

decision. Some junior ranks inside Tokyo, claiming that the emperor had been wrongly advised, attempted a coup, but army discipline, backed by royal princes, who were sent to various commands, ensured compliance with the Imperial decision.

What most ensured an orderly path to national surrender was the emperor's radio broadcast to the people of Japan on August 15. It was the first he had ever made. Using a phrase infamous in Japanese history, he said that it was time "to bear the unbearable," although he did not use the word "surrender." Even after this there were isolated incidents, including an appeal to the people to rise and create a "Government of Resistance," but by the end of August dissent had been stifled.

On August 28 Allied warships entered Sagami Bay; next day they entered Tokyo Bay. There the instrument of surrender "by command and on behalf of Imperial General Headquarters" was signed on September 2 on the battleship *Missouri*. The actual process of surrender throughout East Asia, the Western Pacific, and Southeast Asia was not complete until spring 1946. It would not be until 1974 that the last surviving Japanese not to have surrendered finally emerged from his hiding place on Lubang in the Philippines. Some Japanese in Malaya deserted after August 1945 and joined the communists. Two survivors did not lay down their arms in southern Thailand until 1991. For some, it seemed, there was no end to World War II.

Hiroshima after the bomb
This panorama of the devastation in Hiroshima was taken in March 1946, more than six months after the city had been subjected to the first atomic bomb attack.

INTO THE NUCLEAR AGE

CODE-NAMED THE MANHATTAN PROJECT, the US and British development of the atomic bomb during World War II was kept secret even from their allies, including the Soviet Union. Based on theoretical work by Enrico Fermi and Albert Enstein, nuclear fission—on which Britain and Germany had been working independently in the 1930s— offered unprecedented levels of destructive capability. The US nuclear fission project began in 1939 and was allocated a budget of $6,000. By 1945, when the first bomb was ready, the government had spent $2 million. The man behind the development of the bombs was J. Robert Oppenheimer, who was based at the Los Alamos Laboratory in New Mexico. Although widely regarded as the father of the atomic bomb, he actually built on foundations laid by scientists at laboratories across America, each working on different aspects of the new technologies and materials needed. The first atomic bomb was tested successfully at Alamogordo air base in New Mexico on July 16, 1945. Three weeks later, the first bomb was dropped on Hiroshima.

Robert Oppenheimer
The man behind the Manhattan Project, Julius Robert Oppenheimer. A brilliant theoretical physicist, he developed the bombs that were dropped on Japan.

Einstein's letter
The first page of a letter dated August 2, 1939, from Albert Einstein to Franklin D. Roosevelt in which the scientist outlines to the US president his concerns about the implications of nuclear research.

Radio antennae

Contact fuse

Latches

Fat Man
A replica of "Fat Man," the atomic bomb dropped on Nagasaki on August 9, 1945. The bomb was 3 m (9 ft 4 in) long and weighed 545 kg (10,000 lb). Its fission source was plutonium, which gave it an explosive power equivalent to 21,000 tons of TNT.

Fins to stabilize freefall

A NEW WORLD
1945–49

IN THE AFTERMATH OF THE CONFLICT BOTH VICTORS AND
VANQUISHED TOOK STOCK OF THE NEW WORLD THAT
HAD BEEN CREATED. EUROPE'S AGE-OLD PRIMACY IN
INTERNATIONAL AFFAIRS WAS OVER, BROUGHT TO AN
END BY THE DESTRUCTION OF WAR, DEBT, AND THE
GROWTH OF TWO SUPERPOWERS, THE UNITED STATES
AND THE SOVIET UNION. WHILE SHATTERED COUNTRIES
IN THE WEST ATTEMPTED TO REBUILD, IN THE EAST THE
ECLIPSE OF JAPAN AND EUROPE PAVED THE WAY FOR NEW
STRUGGLES AS COLONIES TOOK THE OPPORTUNITY TO
FIGHT FOR INDEPENDENCE. IN SOUTHEAST ASIA, INDIA,
AND ELSEWHERE, THE END OF WORLD WAR II MARKED
ONLY THE BEGINNING OF A NEW ROUND OF BLOODSHED.

It's over
New Yorkers gather in
Times Square on August 17,
1945, to celebrate the
Japanese surrender.

REBUILDING A SHATTERED WORLD

THE IMPACT OF WORLD WAR II WAS FELT IN ALMOST EVERY PART OF THE GLOBE. WHILE VICTORS AND VANQUISHED ALIKE BEGAN TO REBUILD THEIR ECONOMIES, POLITICIANS AND CIVILIANS FACED A CHANGED WORLD IN WHICH FEW CERTAINTIES SURVIVED FROM THE YEARS BEFORE 1939.

BEFORE WORLD WAR II there were many "Great Powers"; by the end of the conflict the United States and the Soviet Union dominated global diplomacy and economics. Europe, the strongest and wealthiest continent at the beginning of the 20th century, was devastated. Many of its nations were on the verge of bankruptcy or communism, while those that had empires were struggling to hold on to their colonies.

ONE WAR IN TWO PHASES

In many ways, World War II was a continuation of World War I. The settlements that had ended the Great War had failed to deal with its causes—mainly nationalism, imperialism, and the balance of power. These matters would not be resolved until the defeat of the Axis powers in 1945.

Just as in World War I, when war broke out in 1939 the European empires called on their colonial subjects for manpower and material aid. In the first war the soldiers and materials had been shipped to Europe; in the second conflagration the war came to them, as European powers fought not only at home but also in their dependencies. What began as French and British resistance to German attempts to dominate Europe became, by the end of 1941, a truly global conflict that involved the United States, North Africa, the Middle East, the Soviet Union, India, China, Japan, and many other parts of Asia.

There were other differences between the two world wars. In the first, the fighting had reached a stalemate by the end of 1914. The Western Front barely moved for four years. Even in the east, where fighting was more fluid, the most significant alteration of the front line came with Lenin's territorial concessions to Germany in 1918 as the price for Russia leaving the war. Mindful of the debilitating effects of another war of attrition, politicians and planners in World War II were determined not to repeat earlier mistakes. Strategists on all sides prepared for a war of movement: in this they were aided by the development of highly maneuverable weapons, in particular, tanks and aircraft, that lent themselves to offensive warfare in a way that trenches and machine-guns in 1914–18 had not.

CIVILIAN INVOLVEMENT

The use of tanks and aircraft also ensured that many more civilians came under direct attack than in the first war—the air bombardment of entire cities had a particularly harrowing effect. Even though World War I is described as the first total war in the sense that civilians were mobilized to work in domestic industries, noncombatants were rarely directly involved in conflict. In World War II, civilians in many parts of the world faced death and destruction.

For many civilians, tanks and bombs were not the main enemy. For the Jews of Europe, war came in the form of the "Final Solution"—the attempt by the Nazis to exterminate them. World War I had had its own racially motivated atrocities—the massacre of Armenian civilians by Turkish forces being perhaps the most hideous example—but the Holocaust was different in form and substance: it was premeditated and systematic.

SHAPING THE FUTURE

Throughout World War II the leaders of the "Big Three" Allied nations—Roosevelt from the United States, Stalin from the Soviet Union, and Churchill from Great Britain—communicated frequently with one another. They also met to hold discussions about war strategy in Tehran in November 1943 and at Yalta in February 1945. Unlike World War I, in which military officers had largely taken the lead, the overall direction of World War II was always under the command of politicians. Just as civilians defined the shape of the war on the Allied side, so they would define the peace. In July–August 1945, the Big Three met again in Potsdam, just outside Berlin.

A nation's guilt
Civilians from Nuremberg help rebury victims of the SS, whose bodies had been dumped in a pit. Throughout the country, the Allies forced ordinary Germans to face up to the atrocities committed in the name of the Third Reich.

"If leaders are called to account and condemned, very well, but you cannot punish the German people at the same time. The German people are free of guilt."

NAZI LEADER HERMANN GÖRING IN A CLOSING STATEMENT
TO THE NUREMBERG WAR CRIMES TRIBUNAL, AUGUST 31, 1946

There were new faces around the table: Harry S. Truman, who had become US president on the death of Roosevelt in April, and newly elected British prime minister Clement Attlee. No longer united by their common goal, and facing the task of reconstructing war-torn Europe along with the coming final assault on Japan, the Allied leaders were more tense at this final meeting than they had ever been before.

Potsdam was successful in certain key areas, principally those concerning the temporary control of Germany. The nation was to be divided into four zones and placed under the supervision of an Allied Control Commission consisting of representatives from the Big Three and France, which was included at British insistence as a counterweight to Soviet power. Berlin, the German capital, was also to be divided between the four powers. Furthermore, all territories conquered by the Nazis were to be returned to their former owners. The talks further provided for the conclusion of separate peace treaties with all the defeated combatants, including Austria. The Potsdam Conference also introduced the concept of war crimes so that the Nazi leaders could be tried by an international court. Finally, Stalin, Truman, and Attlee agreed on the creation of a Council of Foreign Ministers. These ministers would meet regularly in an attempt to smooth as much as possible the transition from war to peace.

Despite these manifest successes, a pall hung over the conference. Truman had arrived in Potsdam determined to enforce the Declaration on Liberated Europe, which had been agreed to at Yalta. Under its provisions, all countries conquered by Germany were to be reconstituted and allowed free elections. When it came to the thorny issue of the future of Poland, however, Stalin had already demonstrated that he would take any measures necessary to ensure that the Poles elected a government that was "friendly" to the Soviet Union—in other words, a communist

regime. The British and the Americans feared that if Stalin had his way over Poland, the rest of eastern Europe would also become communist. For their part, Soviet delegates insisted that, since the Soviet Union had been attacked twice by Germany in 25 years, it was only right that they be allowed to establish a western buffer zone.

The Western Allies left Potsdam with grave concerns about Soviet expansionism. Days later the suspicions became mutual as the United States dropped atomic bombs on Hiroshima and Nagasaki to end the war against Japan. The lack of trust between the United States and its allies on the one hand, and the Soviet Union and its communist allies on the other, would soon lead to a new kind of conflict—the Cold War — which was to dominate international politics until the end of the 1980s.

RISINGS IN THE EAST

The total capitulation of Japan was followed by American occupation of the country on August 28, 1945. Commanded by the powerful figure of General Douglas MacArthur, US forces in Japan were given *carte blanche* by Truman. Like Germany, Japan needed almost total political and economic reconstruction; it also needed psychological rehabilitation. In a nation not previously defeated in war, with a strong code of personal and national honor and an emperor who was seen as a god, surrender was regarded as a disgrace.

The United States faced the task of demilitarizing not only Japan's economy and state, but also the attitudes of the people. It reformed the education system to encourage individualism, banned Shinto as the state religion, reduced the prominence of politicians and military leaders, and took control of the press. A new 1947 constitution, drawn up under US influence, created an independent judiciary, guarantees of civil liberty, universal suffrage, and equal land rights. Significantly, Article 9

The Nationalists' last stand
Watched by Nationalist troops, a policeman executes a suspected communist in Shanghai moments after killing another, on May 16, 1949. Shortly after, China's civil war ended when the Nationalists fled to Formosa (Taiwan).

Empty hope?
Eleanor Roosevelt studies a copy of the Universal Declaration of Human Rights, which was adopted by the United Nations on December 10, 1948. Roosevelt was a prime mover in drafting the document which, for all its bold intent, changed little.

"Every segment of the population has united in obedience, to stand behind the great leader Sukarno, to await whatever commands or obligations are put before them. It is our firm conviction that this struggle is a sacred struggle...."

INDONESIAN FREEDOM MOVEMENT REPRESENTATIVE ON GROWING OPPOSITION TO DUTCH COLONIAL RULE, OCTOBER 15, 1945

of the constitution stated Japan's intention of "forever renouncing war." Many Japanese military and political leaders were tried for war crimes; most were imprisoned, but some were sentenced to death. They included former prime minister Tojo Hideki, who was hanged in December 1948.

Throughout the reform process, the Americans took pains to make it seem as if it were the Japanese themselves who were driving the changes and administering justice, even though the majority of the orders actually came from MacArthur and Washington, D.C. Ensuring that the Japanese were able to maintain their dignity did much to expedite the nation's postwar recovery.

DECLINE OF EMPIRE

In other parts of Asia the future looked less certain. In China, civil war, which had been put on hold during the world conflict, immediately erupted again. The United States backed Chiang Kai-shek's Nationalists as the only force that could resist the spread of communism, but they failed to prevent the victory of Mao Zedong's Red Army in 1949. Chiang's Nationalists fled to Formosa (Taiwan), and Mao created the People's Republic of China.

The end of World War II also hastened the decline of European influence in Asia. Britain granted independence to India in 1947, Burma and Ceylon (Sri Lanka) in 1948, and—after a protracted guerrilla war—the Malay states in February 1948. World War II also reduced British influence in Australia and New Zealand. Elsewhere a four-year guerrilla campaign freed Indonesia from rule by the Netherlands in 1949. French influence in Indochina was also weakened, and in the early 1950s Vietnamese nationalism erupted into a war that would eventually also involve the United States, which was now the main force in the region. Just as in Europe, postcolonial Asia would be dragged into the Cold War.

EFFECTS OF THE WAR

SEPTEMBER 1945–DECEMBER 1949

The end of the war saw the emergence of the United States and the Soviet Union as ideologically opposed superpowers. As tensions mounted, the two powers reached a standoff known as the Cold War. Meanwhile, many colonies of European countries began to seek independence from their imperial rulers.

1945

OCTOBER 31
Beginning of attacks by Jews on British in Palestine

OCTOBER 24
UN Charter comes into force

NOVEMBER 20
Nuremberg International War Crimes Trials begin

1946

MARCH 5
Churchill makes speech in which he refers to the "Iron Curtain" descending across Europe

MARCH 16
French troops occupy Hanoi in northern Vietnam

JUNE 3
Tokyo International War Crimes Trial begins

JULY 4
Philippines gain independence from US

OCTOBER 1
Sentences passed on defendants at Nuremberg War Crimes Trials; 12 are sentenced to death

DECEMBER 20
Open conflict between French and Viet Minh (Vietnamese communists) breaks out in Hanoi

1947

FEBRUARY 14
UN takes over responsibility for Palestine from Britain

MARCH 12
The Truman Doctrine, stating that the US will oppose any further expansion of communist territory, is announced by US

AUGUST 15
Britain grants independence to India and Pakistan, formed from partition of India

JUNE 5
European Recovery Program (ERP or Marshall Plan) is announced by US, providing economic aid to friendly war-devastated countries. Aid does not go to communist eastern European states

NOVEMBER 29
UN recommends partition of Palestine to form Israel

1948

JANUARY 4
Burma becomes independent

MAY 15
Arab states invade newly created Jewish state of Israel

JUNE 16
Beginning of communist uprising in Malaya, which British will fight to suppress until 1960

JUNE 24
Soviet Union imposes blockade round Berlin in attempt to drive the US, the UK, and France out of western half of city

NOVEMBER 4
Sentences passed on defendants at Tokyo International War Crimes Trial: seven are sentenced to death

1949

APRIL 4
North Atlantic Treaty Organization (NATO) is set up

MAY 12
Berlin blockade ends

AUGUST 29
Soviet Union produces its first atomic bomb; arms race begins

OCTOBER 1
People's Republic of China founded following victory of the communists in Chinese Civil War

NOVEMBER 2
Indonesia becomes independent

Breakdown of colonial empires
Oct 1945–Nov 1949

Developments in the Cold War
Mar 1946–Oct 1949

Other events

THE LEGACY OF THE WAR

IN TERMS OF LIVES LOST, World War II was the most costly conflict in history. Estimates of the total number of deaths vary, but there may have been around 55 to 60 million, including 25.5 million Soviet citizens, 13.5 million Chinese, 5.25 million Germans, 2.6 million Japanese, around 290,000 Americans, and 300,000 Britons. Unlike the casualties in World War I, many were civilians, and the loss of manpower had a devastating effect on the recovery of the countries involved. Massive bombardment had reduced many cities to rubble. This was particularly true in Germany, which had suffered intense air attacks by British and US forces, and the Soviet Union, which had lost 70 to 80 percent of its industrial capacity in its bitterly fought campaign to expel the Nazi invaders. Much of the rest of Europe was at a virtual standstill.

The mass destruction of homes, schools, offices, and factories meant that large numbers of people were on the move, looking for new places to live. Some removed themselves voluntarily; others were

Civvy street
Carrying their new civilian clothes in cardboard suitcases, demobilized British troops leave a depot in Olympia in west London. By the end of the conflict, some soldiers had not seen their families for as long as five or six years.

A country in ruins

Three years after the end of hostilities, women in Berlin clear rubble from a destroyed factory. With so many men lost in the war, and German infrastructure in ruins, women were responsible for much of the reconstruction work.

forced to leave. These refugees, officially termed Displaced Persons (DPs), became one of the most distressing features of the immediate postwar era. To care for them, the United Nations (UN)—the world peacekeeping body founded in 1945—set up DP camps throughout Europe. By 1947 there were 700 such camps operated by the United Nations Relief and Rehabilitation Administration (UNRRA). Among the DPs were those who had been brought to German-occupied territory as forced labor, ex-prisoners-of-war, Jews, and other survivors of the concentration camps.

In the immediate aftermath of the war there were as many as seven million DPs. This figure grew alarmingly as a number of newly formed governments began to expel various minority groups. In 1947 the creation by the UN of the International Refugee Organization (IRO) was very much opposed by the Soviet Union, which saw the IRO as a Western attempt to assist the flight of refugees from the communist states of eastern Europe. While it would be many years before the refugee problem was finally resolved, substantial numbers of DPs did find new homes relatively quickly. There were several countries that faced severe labor shortages after the war came to an end, particularly in skilled occupations. Britain was among the nations that actively encouraged immigration, offering the inducement of immediate resettlement to qualified foreign nationals as part of its drive to replace skilled workers who had been killed or incapacitated during the war.

REDRAWING THE MAP OF EUROPE

After the war much of Europe was restructured politically and many of its frontiers were altered. The Red Army had entered Germany from the east, and the countries through which it had passed *en route*—Bulgaria, Czechoslovakia, Hungary, Poland, Romania, and, for a while, Yugoslavia—became Soviet satellites in the postwar world. Britain and the United States had launched their assault on the Axis powers from the south and west, and consequently brought Austria, Greece, and Italy into their sphere of influence. Germany

itself, meanwhile, was divided into four zones by the victors: the east of the country was dominated by the Soviet Union, while the west was shared among the Americans, the British, and the French.

The American, British, and Soviet leaders were united in their determination to de-Nazify Germany, and this policy was carried through with notable success. The main public manifestation of their resolve was a series of war crimes trials held under international law. The most famous of these involved Hitler's top surviving henchmen and were held in 1945–46 in Nuremberg. The location was chosen deliberately by the Allies because it had been the

site of the spectacular Nazi Party rallies of the 1930s and was widely regarded as the symbolic cradle of the National Socialist movement.

While a number of leading Nazis faced the legal consequences of their wartime deeds, Allied civilian administrators in western Germany were mindful of the need to feed, clothe, and find shelter for those worst affected by postwar privations. In the eastern zone, however, Soviet leaders were determined to recover as much industrial capacity as possible. To this end they dismantled many industrial plants and factories in their sector of Germany and shipped the components back to the Soviet Union.

THE NUREMBERG TRIALS

As EARLY AS 1943 Britain, the United States, and the Soviet Union agreed that, if they won the war, they would put the German leaders on trial. As victory approached and the worst atrocities came to light, the Allies created new international laws enabling them to prosecute Nazis for waging aggressive war and for crimes against humanity.

On November 20, 1945, an International Military Tribunal convened for the trials of 23 leading Nazis, including Hermann Göring, Rudolf Hess, and, in absentia, Martin Bormann. The Tribunal delivered its verdicts on October 1, 1946. It rejected the defense that the accused had had no alternative but to follow Adolf Hitler's orders. Twelve of the defendants were sentenced to death, seven were given various terms of imprisonment, and four were acquitted. Bormann was sentenced to death in his absence, and Hermann Göring committed suicide with a cyanide pill hours before he was due to be executed. On October 16, 1946, ten of the leading figures from the Third Reich were executed by hanging in Nuremberg Prison.

Right-hand man
Hitler's former deputy, Hermann Göring, prepares to give evidence to the court. Göring was the most senior Nazi to stand trial. His request to be shot rather than hanged was refused, and he committed suicide by taking poison.

Nazis in the dock
In the courtroom some of the main Nazi war criminals are guarded by Allied military personnel. Separate trials dealt with Nazis accused of war crimes in specific places.

The Soviet Union turned eastern Germany into a communist society by closing every private bank and confiscating all negotiable gold and silver, foreign currency, and other valuables. As a general rule, Soviet administrators were much more interested in obtaining reparations—direct compensation for the damage caused by the war—than in the well-being of those people who were now under their control.

Acknowledging the victors
A Japanese prisoner bows his head as he passes his American jailer. For many Japanese such humiliations were a devastating blow to national pride.

POSTWAR JAPAN

The war against Japan ended with the dropping of atomic bombs on Hiroshima and Nagasaki in early August 1945. On September 2 the government of Japan signed a formal surrender aboard the USS *Missouri*, anchored in Yokohama Bay. World War II was now officially over, and the victorious Allies set about the arduous task of reconstruction in Japan. In comparison with Germany, which it had been agreed to divide into four zones of occupation, Japan was treated as a single political and economic entity under American supervision.

> "The war situation has developed not necessarily to Japan's advantage. We have resolved to pave the way for a grand peace for all the generations to come by enduring the unendurable and suffering what is unsufferable."
>
> EMPEROR HIROHITO BROADCASTS TO HIS PEOPLE ON THE JAPANESE SURRENDER, AUGUST 15, 1945.

Since the Americans had borne the brunt of the fighting against Japan, they demanded the lion's share of involvement in the peacemaking. American leaders made it clear that, while they welcomed aid from their wartime allies, British and Soviet plans for Japan's future would be subordinate to their own. Truman and his cabinet decided that unconditional Japanese surrender did not necessarily mean the dethronement of Emperor Hirohito. They felt that the Japanese would accept defeat more easily if Hirohito kept his position, albeit with powers that were considerably reduced. One of the conditions imposed by the United States on Japan was that the emperor would no longer be regarded as a deity; Hirohito's public acknowledgment of his own mortality was a central part of the price of peace.

General Douglas MacArthur, the Supreme Allied Commander in the Pacific, was placed in charge of Japanese reconstruction, and Truman left him very much to his own devices in the running of the country. In an effort to ensure that militarism would have no place in the future Japan, MacArthur and his advisers decided that those who had led the nation into war would be tried as war criminals, with the important exception of the emperor himself. The postwar Japanese constitution drawn up by the Supreme Allied Commander was intended to rid Japan of the worst excesses of its reliance on tradition while at the same time preserving an emphasis on obedience to authority. Under MacArthur's autocratic leadership, Japan began a transformation from a rigid, hierarchical society into a modern, pluralistic nation. Land reform was introduced, trade unions were established, the role of women in society was vastly expanded, and provision for a parliamentary democracy was written into the new Japanese constitution. These innovations made a significant contribution to Japan's remarkable postwar recovery.

RECOVERY BEGINS

While negotiations continued on a final peace treaty with Japan (it was not finally signed until September 1951), MacArthur concentrated on ensuring that Japan would emerge as an economically vibrant US ally in the Far East. The need to rebuild the Japanese economy became all the more pressing as US–Soviet relations began to deteriorate. US leaders realized that Japan would have to be self-sufficient if it were to serve as a bulwark

The final verdict
Flanked by military police, General Tojo Hideki, Japan's prime minister during the war, listens to the Allied court's sentence of death. He was hanged on December 23, 1948.

By the time MacArthur was recalled from Tokyo to focus on the US response to the Korean War, Japan was well on the way to becoming exactly what American leaders had envisioned: a politically stable, economically powerful, Asian ally of the United States. As the Cold War intensified, the leaders of the Western nations appreciated the presence of a democratic, anticommunist bastion in the Far East.

JAPANESE WAR CRIMINALS

Unlike the Nuremberg trials, which were organized by the Allied Control Council, the trials of Japanese war criminals were held under the auspices of one man—MacArthur. In January 1946 he set up in Tokyo an International Military Tribunal for the Far East to bring to justice those responsible for such horrific events as the Rape of Nanking, the Bataan Death March, and the attack on Pearl Harbor. The Tribunal divided the accused into three categories:

Japan's leaders on trial
All 25 defendants in the Tokyo war trials were found guilty. Seven were sentenced to hang; all 16 sentenced to life imprisonment were paroled within 10 years.

against potential communist incursion in the Pacific. MacArthur's efforts to rebuild Japan's economy were aided by the fact that the nation had not been the scene of close combat. Japan had endured heavy bombing from 1944 onward, suffered severe damage to its industrial base, and undergone the physical and psychological trauma of having two atomic bombs dropped on home soil. Yet, in contrast with many Europeans, Japanese civilians had not suffered

the consequences of having huge numbers of troops rampage through their villages and towns. There was also still a semblance of infrastructure in Japan that US planners could harness, along with a central administrative organization that was accustomed to obeying orders. The available workforce was greatly increased as soldiers returned home. When the Cold War flared into military conflict in the Korean War (1950–53), fought between communist China and North Korea on the one hand and South Korea and the United Nations on the other, the huge boost to the Japanese economy from supplying the United States and its allies cemented its recovery.

WAR LOSSES

ALL THE FIGURES IN the table below are estimates. Historians particularly dispute figures for Chinese and Soviet casualties. Many killings in China took place in rural communities that kept poor or no records during wartime. Soviet dead were often buried in unmarked mass graves; government attempts to establish the number of war dead were based on an unreliable system of interviews with families.

	Troops mobilized	Military dead	Civilian dead
ALLIED POWERS			
Soviet Union	20,000,000	8,700,000	16,900,000
United States	16,400,000	292,000	N/A
France	5,000,000	250,000	170,000
Britain	4,700,000	240,000	65,000
Yugoslavia	3,700,000	300,000	1,400,000
China (Communist)	1,200,000	1,100,000	4,000,000
China (Nationalist)	3,800,000	2,400,000	6,000,000
India	2,400,000	48,000	N/A
Poland	1,000,000	600,000	6,000,000
Belgium	800,000	10,000	90,000
Canada	780,000	40,000	N/A
Australia	680,000	34,000	N/A
Netherlands	500,000	10,000	240,000
Finland	250,000	80,000	10,000

	Troops mobilized	Military dead	Civilian dead
Czechoslovakia	180,000	7,000	310,000
Greece	150,000	17,000	400,000
New Zealand	150,000	12,000	N/A
South Africa	140,000	9,000	N/A
Norway	25,000	5,000	8,000
Denmark	15,000	4,000	3,000
Spain	40,000	12,000	1,000
AXIS POWERS			
Germany	10,800,000	3,250,000	2,000,000
Japan	7,400,000	1,700,000	500,000
Italy	4,500,000	380,000	180,000
Romania	600,000	200,000	460,000
Bulgaria	450,000	10,000	7,000
Hungary	350,000	140,000	610,000

April 1945, President Truman took up the policy of seeking to create the conditions necessary to ensure that the nations of central and eastern Europe would enjoy self-determination.

At the Potsdam Conference (July 17–August 2, 1945), Truman insisted that the Soviet Union establish truly democratic nations in this region. For Stalin, however, the priority was domestic security, not global political freedom. At the end of World War II there were a million Red Army troops in the countries of eastern Europe. This military presence was largely maintained throughout the Cold War: for the next 40 years Poland, Bulgaria, Czechoslovakia, Hungary, and, to a lesser

Before the curtain falls
A US border guard talks to his Soviet counterparts on the German–Czech border on August 1, 1946. The Soviets' advance to Berlin left much of eastern Europe under their control, and the nations of the region remained under communist rule for the next 40 years.

those who had planned and waged an aggressive war, those under whose command atrocities were committed, and those who carried out the atrocities.

For almost three years the tribunal heard evidence of atrocities carried out on a routine basis by Japanese soldiers of all ranks; the testimonies of eyewitnesses to the brutality made for harrowing sessions in court. Finally in November 1948 the Tribunal returned its verdicts. Unlike the outcome in Nuremberg, every one of the accused was found guilty as charged. The major criminals, those found guilty of having prepared and planned Japanese aggression over two decades, were sentenced to death. Among those to suffer this fate was former prime minister Tojo Hideki, who had approved the attack on Pearl Harbor and was widely regarded as the personification of Japanese militarism. The executions of Tojo and his senior cohorts were intended as a message to the world that such acts of inhumanity would not be tolerated in the future.

INTO THE COLD WAR
At the Yalta Conference of February 4–11, 1945, US president Roosevelt and British prime minister Churchill appear to have decided, in private at least, that there was nothing they could do, short of war, to remove the Soviet Red Army from the territories it had occupied in central and eastern Europe during its advance into Germany. Despite this, both leaders signed with Stalin the Declaration on Liberated Europe. This document provided for the restoration of democracy in the countries overrun by Nazi Germany. On the death of Roosevelt in

BERLIN BLOCKADE

ONE OF THE EARLIEST FLASHPOINTS in the Cold War was Berlin, Germany. By the end of World War II the Soviet Red Army had reached the banks of the Elbe River, nearly 60 miles (100 km) west of the capital. Although Berlin was thus within the Soviet sphere of influence, the Allies shared the administration of the old German capital, dividing it into American, British, French, and Soviet zones.

In 1948 the Western powers announced plans to unify their zones of occupation in western Germany. This alarmed the Soviets, who imposed a blockade on road and rail transportation into and out of Berlin. Western leaders saw this as a challenge to their commitment to the independence of western Europe. Berlin became a test case of their desire to check Soviet aggression. They set about supplying West Berlin by air. The Berlin Airlift began in June 1948 and lasted until September 1949, when the Soviets lifted the blockade. With its commitment to remain in Germany now manifest, the next step for the West was clear: the creation of West Germany. In September 1949 the Federal Republic of West Germany was established. The Soviet response was the creation of the German Democratic Republic in East Germany the following month.

Keeping the planes aloft
Giant wheels for transport planes are loaded onto a Dakota freighter during a nightshift at a British airfield in November 1948. During the airlift, Allied planes carried 2.3 million tons of supplies to Berlin.

Airborne lifeline
On July 1, 1948, near the beginning of the Berlin Airlift, a group of Berliners watch from the ruins at the edge of Tempelhof Airfield as a C-47 cargo plane prepares to land with a cargo of food.

extent, Romania would be independent only insofar as they adhered to the Soviet party line. These countries were to form Stalin's buffer zone against the threat of a renewed German invasion. The Allies' failure in Potsdam to agree on a solution to these problems caused a lingering atmosphere of mistrust, fear, and suspicion on both sides. This uneasy situation eventually hardened into a Cold War between East and West. Although it would sometimes erupt into overt but limited confrontation, the Cold War was more often fought with weapons of propaganda, psychology, economics, and subversive undercover operations as the competing ideologies of Western capitalism and Soviet communism vied to win over the people of the world.

THE IRON CURTAIN

In March 1946 Winston Churchill, now out of office, coined a phrase that came to epitomize the Western perception of the Cold War. In a speech in Fulton, Missouri, the former British premier spoke of an "Iron Curtain" that was falling across the middle of Europe, to the east of which lay totalitarian states controlled by Moscow. Churchill's provocative speech was initially viewed by many people as dangerous warmongering—a terrible conflict had just ended, and there was great fear of causing another one. However, as relations between East and West deteriorated, a consensus began to emerge in what became known as "the Free World" that Churchill had been correct in his prognosis.

The deteriorating relations became evident in Greece in 1947. In a secret meeting held in Moscow in October 1944, Stalin and Churchill had agreed that following the war, Greece—which had been occupied by Germany and Italy—should fall within the British sphere of influence. To the surprise of some British officials, Stalin kept to the agreement once the war was over. Thus, when hostilities ended, the British installed a pro-Western monarchist government in Greece.

However, the National Liberation Front (EAM)— a communist group in northern Greece—had a different vision of the country's future. It began a series of military attacks on the government in Athens. The country was soon engulfed in civil war. Britain provided financing and troops in support of the regime in Athens. The civil war ended in early 1945 but flared up again in 1946. Britain then decided that it could no longer afford to maintain its presence in the

Saving Europe
This poster of the late 1940s was intended to encourage the German people to realize the benefits of the US-funded Marshall Plan for postwar economic regeneration.

The "Iron Curtain"
The position of the "Iron Curtain," dividing Soviet-dominated communist regimes from the rest of Europe, was to change after 1948. Yugoslavia was not a Soviet ally in the Cold War.

THE DIVISION OF POSTWAR EUROPE
1945–49

- Territory under Soviet occupation 1945-55
- Soviet-dominated communist states by 1948
- Members of NATO in 1949
- Iron Curtain in 1948
- ⊗ Cities divided into zones of occupation

Symbol of division
A workman paints a line across Potsdammer Strasse in Berlin to mark the border between the British and Soviet zones of occupation in August 1948. In 1961 the painted line was replaced by a fortified wall across the city that would remain standing until 1989.

country. In response, President Truman took it upon himself in March 1947 to commit the United States to going to the aid of the Greek government in its struggle against the rebels. The Americans supplied military equipment and advice that contributed to the eventual defeat of the rebels in the summer of 1949. In applying to Congress for the necessary funds, Truman asserted that it must now be the policy of the United States to aid free peoples anywhere in the world in their struggle against communism. The Truman Doctrine, as the statement became known, was received badly in Moscow and served as a key catalyst in the intensification of the Cold War.

Another came in 1947, when the US government made public a telegram sent to Washington, D.C., during World War II by George Kennan, the American attaché in Moscow. In it he had warned that the Soviet leadership was intent on expansion and should not be trusted. Kennan had advised that the best way of stopping the Soviet Union was by confining it to the regions in which it already held sway. Within a year of the letter's release, containment of the perceived threat of communism had become the cornerstone of Western foreign policy.

CHINESE CIVIL WAR

In China during World War II the Kuomintang government of Chiang Kai-shek and the communists led by Mao Zedong maintained an uneasy truce as they united against Japanese invasion. When the war ended, however, they resumed hostilities despite the efforts of the Soviet Union and the United States to broker a deal. Fearing a takeover of China by the communists, President Truman sent George Marshall to persuade the two sides to share power, but the mission failed and fighting was resumed in March 1946.

Chiang's forces had access to US military supplies and enjoyed territorial advantage, while the communists were confined to northern areas of the country and received little aid from the Soviet Union. Nevertheless, the Kuomintang soon lost support among Chinese peasants. Whereas Mao's forces instituted land reform in the areas under their control, the nationalists backed corrupt landowners. Mao's forces became an organized, disciplined movement for revolution, while Chiang's forces lost the will to fight. In January 1949 the civil war ended with the victory of the communists under Mao. Chiang withdrew to Formosa (Taiwan) and set up a dictatorship. In communist China the Soviet Union now had a prospective ally in the Cold War.

Mao's warriors
Victorious troops of the Communist People's Liberation Army assemble in Shanghai on July 9, 1949, after the Nationalists had fled to Taiwan. The soldiers are wearing US combat helmets taken from Nationalist troops.

A landowner's fate
A communist soldier prepares to execute a landowner in the aftermath of Mao's victory. Property ownership was banned in Red China.

Chairman Mao
In Tiananmen Square, Peking (Beijing), on October 1, 1949, Mao Zedong proclaims the foundation of the People's Republic of China.

THE MARSHALL PLAN

Having adopted the policy of containment, the US government began to fear that the rubble of western Europe might provide a fertile breeding ground for communism. In the words of Secretary of State George Marshall, "Europe must have substantial additional help or face economic, social, and political deterioration of a very grave character." As a result, the United States provided 16 countries with enormous financial and material aid to help them rebuild. The European Recovery Program, or Marshall Plan as it became known, was established in June 1947. Under the program, the United States set aside $17 billion to aid the countries of western European—outright grants accounted for seven-eighths of the amount, the rest was in loans. The regeneration of Europe began almost immediately.

As European countries began to recover, Western leaders became concerned that the Soviet Union might strike against them before they could build up their defenses. To forestall such an attack they formed, in April 1949, the North Atlantic Treaty Organization (NATO), a military alliance of western European nations, the United States, and Canada, which guaranteed mutual assistance in the event of Soviet aggression. More pertinently, NATO placed western Europe under the nuclear protection of the United States. The Soviet Union and its allies countered NATO by forming first the Council for Mutual Economic Assistance (COMECON) in 1949, and then in 1955 the Warsaw Pact, a military alliance. Europe was now divided into two armed camps. At the time the NATO alliance was signed, the United States was the world's only atomic power.

Within months, however, the Soviet Union had successfully tested its own nuclear weaponry. The news was greeted by dismay in the West, and set off an arms race with the East.

THE WIDER WORLD

Even before World War II it was clear that the independence movements emerging in Asia would force Western governments to confront the issue of colonial imperialism. Britain, for example, was facing mass nonviolent revolt in India, while France recognized that it would soon have to deal with an increasingly militant nationalist movement in Southeast Asia.

The United States was committed to making the Philippines independent. When war began, Japan invaded many Western colonies in Asia. For a time many local nationalist and independence movements allied themselves to the Japanese cause against the European and American empires in the mistaken belief that Japan planned to establish an Asia of equals. When this did not happen, Asian nationalists found themselves in a dilemma: they did not want to further the cause of Japanese aggression, but neither did they want to bolster the hold of the Western powers on their colonies. In the end, the nationalists came to see the defeat of Japan as their best hope of achieving independence.

After the war, the Philippines gained its promised independence, but with the proviso that the United States retain its military presence there. Elsewhere, the end of empire was less well ordered. Most European countries tried to hold on to their Asian possessions or retake them after Japan's defeat. The exception was Britain, which relinquished control in India. However, there was to be violence, which

Celebrating independence in India
Crowds greet the British governor general of India, Lord Mountbatten, on August 15, 1947. Mountbatten and his wife were in New Delhi to proclaim India's independence.

resulted in at least 1 million deaths in the years following independence. During the war, Churchill had insisted that Britain would never give up India, despite the urgings of Roosevelt and the mass campaign of nonviolent civil disobedience led by Mahatma Gandhi. The British perspective changed, however, with the election of a Labour government in 1945. The new prime minister, Attlee, was determined that India should become independent, and this was achieved in 1947. The transfer of power did not go smoothly. As India approached independence, violence broke out between its Hindu and Muslim communities, and the British decided that the country should be partitioned. A separate Muslim state—Pakistan—was created, but the violence grew worse as millions of Hindu and Muslim refugees sought safety in the two new states. A dispute between the two countries over the border state of Kashmir is still unresolved.

Unlike Britain in India, France made desperate efforts to regain control of its colonies in Indochina. Nationalists in the region had fought long and hard.

"Persecution of the revolutionary people only serves to accelerate the people's revolutions on a broader and more intense scale."

MAO ZEDONG, MOSCOW, NOVEMBER 6, 1957

Last flames of empire
Dutch Marines patrol a burning village in Indonesia in 1947 during their ultimately futile campaign to suppress revolutionaries. The insurgents were determined to reinforce independence from the Netherlands, declared in August 1945 by nationalist leader Sukarno.

The people's uncle
A founder of the Vietnamese Communist Party, and later president of Vietnam, Ho Chi Minh led the nationalist struggle against the French from 1945 to 1954.

against the Japanese Army. At the end of the war Vietnamese nationalists, led by Ho Chi Minh, fully expected to be rewarded for their efforts with independence. The French had other ideas. They were adamant that France be allowed to retake its place in Vietnam and the rest of Indochina. Initially, the United States condemned this French reversion to imperialism—after all, the United States had itself been founded after the expulsion of a colonial power in the 18th century. Before long, however, the emerging Cold War forced a rethink. As the United States began to implement the policy of containment of communism, so the Truman administration perceived the need for a stable ally in Southeast Asia, particularly since its main Asian ally, China, was at the time engaged in a civil war between the Nationalist government and communist rebels. The United States supported French efforts to regain control in Vietnam, and nationalist forces now found themselves engaged in another war against imperialists. The direct French involvement in the war against Vietnamese nationalists lasted until 1954; direct American involvement in Vietnam's political conflict began soon after.

The move toward decolonization spread throughout Asia as European powers struggled to recover from the ravages of war. The colonies of the Dutch East Indies were able to re-form themselves as the independent country of Indonesia only after four years of struggle against the Dutch; Burma and Ceylon managed to force the British out, with the latter colony renaming itself Sri Lanka. World War II had played a major

Nowhere to hide
Three generations of a Vietnamese family flee from Hanoi in February 1947, during fighting between Vietnamese revolutionaries and their French rulers.

role in these developments. During the conflict European nations had called on their Asian (and to some extent North African) possessions to help them in their battle against the Axis powers. Most colonies responded positively, but their wartime experience had taught them the techniques and tactics of guerrilla warfare and increased their sense of national identity. By 1945 they not only wanted independence; they now also knew how to use force in pursuit of their objective. World War II made the decolonization of Asia and North Africa inevitable.

THE CONTINUING WAR

As East–West relations deteriorated, both sides began casting about for fresh allies. By the end of the Cold War in 1990, most of the world's nations were regarded as "Eastern" or "Western" on the basis of their political allegiance. The terms had little to do with geography: Cuba, for example, belonged to the "Eastern bloc," while Hong Kong was a "Western" foothold on the edge of Red China.

Having worked so closely together during World War II, Britain and the United States were obvious candidates to head the Western alliance against the Soviet Union. These two democracies did share common interests—largely revolving around the desire to prevent the spread of communism—but nothing about cooperation between them could be taken for

Ship of hope
Illegal Jewish refugees arrive in Haifa, Palestine, on June 17, 1946. Many European Jews made their way to the Holy Land in the years immediately after the end of World War II. The banner in Hebrew bears the legend: "Keep the gates open, we are not the last."

granted. Although Britain was eager to stress its "special relationship" with the United States, American policymakers tended to view Britain as simply a useful ally which was no longer as great a power as it had been at the start of the century, or even at the start of World War II. Nevertheless, the two countries worked well after the war: their similarities generally outweighed their differences, although the United States was clearly the senior partner in the relationship.

The United States supported French resistance to Vietnamese nationalism because it feared that an independent Vietnam would gravitate into the Soviet orbit. The Americans also backed Britain in 1948, when it started to fight communist insurgents in Malaya, because the United States believed that a rebel victory in Malaya would represent a victory for Stalin. In fact, the ideology of the Malayan

rebels was closer to that of China than that of the Soviet Union, but during the Cold War, Western leaders often did not differentiate between forms of communism, even in cases where communist and nationalist ideology were interlinked.

THE FOUNDATION OF ISRAEL

The Cold War also provided the backdrop to the creation of Israel. After World War I (1914–18) the mandate to administer Palestine had been granted by the League of Nations to Britain, which, in the Balfour Declaration of 1917, had committed itself to establishing a homeland for the Jewish people. However, by the end of World War II the issue had not been resolved, and Zionists (Jewish nationalists) waged an increasingly violent terrorist campaign against the British in Palestine. As the details of the Holocaust began to emerge, the Zionist case became even more urgent. When in 1946 Britain refused to allow an influx of 100,000 Jewish refugees from Europe into Palestine, the violence escalated uncontrollably, and Britain handed the matter over to the United Nations in late 1947.

In early 1948 the UN partitioned Palestine into two states—a solution that satisfied neither the Jews nor the Arabs with whom they shared the territory. On May 14 Zionists declared the state of Israel, and both the United States— spurred in part by

Taking the land
Jewish settlers prepare to defend their new Israeli homes from their previous Arab inhabitants after the creation of Israel on May 14, 1948. The new state managed to survive war with its neighbors.

sympathy for Jewish wartime suffering—and the Soviet Union recognized it the following day.

The surrounding Arab states of Egypt, Iraq, Transjordan (now Jordan), Syria, and Lebanon went to war with Israel, but the infant state defeated them all and expanded the borders allotted to it by the UN. Almost overnight, more than a million Palestinian Arabs were forced out of Israel and condemned to live as refugees. The resentment felt by the displaced Palestinians festered for years and undermined subsequent attempts at Jewish–Arab negotiation.

Both the United States and the Soviet Union sought to increase their influence in the region, with varying degrees of success. Thus the Middle East was drawn into the Cold War.

The pattern was repeated around the world. When colonies sought independence they asked for, or had to accept, intervention from either the United States or the Soviet Union. As far as possible, however, the two superpowers avoided direct confrontation, which might escalate to the use of atomic weapons.

World War I had been dubbed the "war to end all wars." In the aftermath of World War II, few harbored such illusions. Fascism had been beaten, but communism remained. Militarism had been defeated, but at the cost of splitting the world into armed camps. German expansion had been replaced by Soviet expansion. There were also reasons for hope, however, such as the optimistic internationalism that inspired the UN and that organization's key role in settling East-West disputes. Most significantly, perhaps, the democracies of the West had survived one of their moments of gravest crisis. That victory stood democracy in good stead for its ongoing struggle against totalitarianism, and helped encourage its eventual triumph in the Cold War.

By the end of the 1948 war, hundreds of entire villages had not only been depopulated but obliterated, their houses blown up or bulldozed. To this day the observant traveler of Israeli roads can see traces of their presence: now and then a few crumbled houses are left standing, a neglected mosque or church, collapsing walls along the ghost of a village lane, but in the vast majority of cases all that remains is a scattering of stones and rubble across a forgotten landscape.

PALESTINIAN EYEWITNESS W. KHALDI DESCRIBES THE SCENE AFTER THE 1948 ARAB–ISRAELI WAR

Ruins of the Reich
Watched by German civilians, Soviet troops ride on a truck through a ruined square in Berlin in July 1945. The two-week long battle for the city had left most of its industrial, commercial, and residential buildings in ruins.

GLOSSARY

ACRONYMS AND ABBREVIATIONS

ASDIC Acronym for the Anglo-French Allied Submarine Detection Investigation Committee, applied to a method of detecting submarines by echo-location. Also referred to as sonar.

DAK Deutsches Afrika Korps

DUKW US 6 x 6 truck fitted with buoyancy tanks. Used to ferry stores from ships lying offshore to beachheads.

Gestapo (*Geheime Staatspolizei*) Secret state police, formed in 1933 by Hermann Göring to replace existing political police. From 1934 it came under the control of Heinrich Himmler, evolving into an independent executive arm of the Nazi Party, with sweeping powers to deal with anyone it considered an enemy of the Third Reich. In 1939 it merged with the criminal police to form the *Sicherheitspolizei* (State Security Police or "Sipo"), commanded by SS General Reinhard Heydrich.

GKO The Soviet State Defense Committee created in June 1941. Oversaw all political, military, and economic aspects of the war.

NKVD (*Narodny Kommissariat Vnutrennikh Del*) People's Commissariat for Domestic Affairs. Soviet secret service, headed by Lavrenti Beria, created in 1934 to control all espionage and counterintelligence activities. Its principal instrument was terror.

OKH (*Oberkommado des Heeres*) The German Army's designated high command for operations on the Eastern Front.

OKW (*Oberkommando der Wehrmacht*) The German armed forces high command which, in theory, was the supreme German joint services high command. It did not have control over the Navy and Luftwaffe high commands, OKM and OKL, whose chiefs reported directly to Hitler.

SAS Acronym for British Special Air Service, formed in Egypt in 1941. It came into its own following D-Day (June 6, 1944), coordinating Resistance activities and carrying out sabotage.

SOE The Special Operation Executive was established in July 1940 to gather intelligence, carry out sabotage, and support Resistance movements in Axis-occupied territories. The American equivalent, established in 1942 was the Office of Strategic Services (OSS).

SS The *Shutzstaffeln*, or Protection Squads, started as Hitler's personal bodyguard and evolved into the most powerful arm of the Nazi administration under Heinrich Himmler. The *Allgemeine* (General) SS staffed the concentration camps and imposed Nazi rule throughout Europe, while the *Waffen* (Armed) SS consisted of military formations dedicated to Hitler.

FORMATIONS AND UNITS

army Two or more corps.

army group Two or more armies.

battalion Usually consisted in the infantry of three to four companies and a heavy weapons company. The total strength was approximately 600–900 men. A tank battalion had three to four companies, with a total of some 50 tanks, while an artillery battalion usually had three batteries.

battery Four to eight artillery guns.

battle group An *ad hoc* German unit formed to meet a particular tactical situation and usually based on an infantry battalion or regiment with tanks and artillery.

brigade Three infantry or tank battalions.

company Usually three to four infantry or tank platoons.

corps A military formation made up of two to three divisions.

division This consisted of two to three infantry/tank regiments or brigades and three to four artillery battalions, a reconnaissance battalion and other supporting arms and army services. Its total strength was 10,000–18,000 men. Divisions were designated infantry ("rifle" in the Soviet Army) or armored ("tank" in the Soviet Army), but mountain and airborne divisions also existed, as well as other types.

platoon In the infantry usually made up of three rifle sections and a HQ section (total 35–40 men). A tank platoon consisted of three to four tanks.

regiment Usually consisted of three battalions, except in British and Commonwealth forces, where it equated to an armored or artillery battalion.

section/squad The smallest subunit in the infantry, consisting of roughly ten men. Squad was the US term.

squadron The equivalent of a tank company in British and Commonwealth forces.

troop The equivalent of a tank platoon in British and Commonwealth forces.

MILITARY ORGANIZATIONS

Kampfgruppe 100 An elite Luftwaffe formation established to exploit the X-Verfahren and Y-Verfahren blind bombing systems, both of which were used against British cities in the Blitz in 1940–41.

Luftwaffe The German air arm.

Ostheer The German Army in the East.

Red Army Front The Soviet high command's term for a distinct operational organization of armed forces. A "front" usually consisted of five to seven armies, with one or two tactical air armies and special armored and infantry formations in support. A "front" could total one million men.

Stavka *Stavka Glavnogo Komandovaniia*, the Red Army's Main Headquarters, formed in June 1941. The Stavka drew up battle plans and through its adjunct, the General Staff, directly organized the preparation and execution of strategic operations.

Wehrmacht The regular armed ground forces of the Third Reich.

WARSHIPS AND LANDING CRAFT

amphibious shipping Vessels designed to support landings from the sea, with the ability to either beach themselves or carry landing craft into which troops transfer when nearing the shore.

battlecruiser A heavily armed ship, built for speed. By 1939 the concept was obsolescent.

destroyer A high-speed, lightly armoured vessel armed with guns, torpedoes, and anti-submarine weapons.

escort carrier A converted merchant ship, it was designed to provide air cover for convoys. It carried 6–35 aircraft.

fleet carrier These large ships provided air protection for the fleet and the means of launching air strikes against opposing fleets. The usual complement of aircraft was 30–95.

heavy cruiser Smaller than a battleship, its main armament was usually 8-in (203-mm) guns. It fulfilled a variety of roles from fleet actions to shore bombardments.

light cruiser More lightly armed than heavy cruisers, normally having 6-in (152-mm) guns, light cruisers were used for reconnaissance and patrolling the sea lanes.

LCT Landing Craft, Tank. An amphibious vehicle designed to carry troops into combat.

LST Landing Ship, Tank. An assault ship designed to beach, and fitted with an opening bow, enabling tanks and other vehicles to drive ashore across a lowered ramp.

pocket battleship Designed by the Germans to circumvent the limit on warship size imposed by the Treaty of Versailles. Officially termed an "armored ship", but reclassified as a cruiser in 1940. Exceptionally fast, with six 11-in (280-mm) guns, its principal role was commerce raiding.

MILITARY TECHNOLOGY

Chain Home British early warning radar system established on south and east coasts of the United Kingdom by the outbreak of war in 1939.

Grand Slam bomb A 22,000-lb (10,000-kg) bomb designed by Barnes Wallis. On March 14, 1945 14 specially modified Lancaster bombers used these bombs to destroy the massive Bielefeld viaduct linking Hamm and Hanover.

Gee A British navigational and blind bombing system which entered service in 1941. First used in raid on Lübeck in March 1942, but thereafter effectively jammed by the Germans.

H2S Downward-looking radar fitted in a blister beneath British bomber aircraft, which gave a clearly defined differentiation between water and land. Radar-equipped German night-fighters were able to home in on H2S emissions, forcing the equipment to be used only in short bursts. The equivalent US system was designated H2X.

Hedgehog An antisubmarine weapon used in conjunction with ASDIC. Hedgehog was a multi-barrel spigot mortar, which threw out a pattern of up to 24 contact-fused bombs.

Knickebein (crooked leg) German blind bombing aid, based on intersecting radio beams, employed in the Blitz. It gave a bomber crew about a 50 percent chance of placing their bombs within 1,100-yd (1-km) diameter circle.

Oboe British radio blind bombing system in use from 1942 and installed in the Mosquito aircraft of Pathfinder squadrons.

Pathfinder Role was to find and mark targets with an increasingly sophisticated range of target markers. The first effective pathfinding unit was the Luftwaffe's Kampfgruppe 100, which used the X-Verfahren and Y-Verfahren to find and mark targets with incendiary bombs and flares for the following main force.

window Codename for lightweight strips of foil dropped from British bombers to form reflectors of German radar signals. The strips were 10 in (26.5 cm). They jammed radar by cluttering its tubes with thousands of false returns. The Germans developed a similar system codenamed "Duppel".

X-Verfahren A German blind bombing system used in the Blitz. A director beam was transmitted from the continent over a target in England. Three other beams, directed from other ground stations, intersected the director beam.

The distance between the two final intersecting beams gave an accurate indication of the aircraft's speed, enabling an onboard computer to calculate the optimum bomb release point.

CODES AND CODEBREAKING

Enigma The commercial name for the encoding machine used in World War II by the German armed forces and civilian organizations such as the railroad system. To the end of the war, the Germans believed that Enigma's encoded messages generated by its system of gears, electric wiring, and drums, were unbreakable.

Magic US codename for decryptions of the Japanese "Purple" cipher and their JN25b naval code. It played a key role in the Battle of Midway in June 1942.

Purple US codename for a Japanese diplomatic cipher system generated on a machine similar to the German Enigma typewriter. The cipher was broken on September 25, 1940, enabling the Americans to read all Japan's diplomatic traffic.

Ultra British codename for intercepts and decrypts of German Enigma coded signal traffic. The name Ultra indicates its security grading and importance. Ultra was arguably the outstanding British scientific-technical achievement of the war.

TERMINOLOGY AND TACTICS

beachhead The initial area captured as a result of an amphibious landing, which provided a base from which subsequent operations inland could be launched.

Big Wing In the Battle of Britain Air Vice-Marshal Trafford Leigh Mallory, commander of 12 Group, advocated that large formations of up to five Fighter Command squadrons be used to fight offensively rather than purely defensively.

bounce crossing Assault across a river, without pausing for preparation on the home bank.

bridgehead Territory seized on the enemy side of a river from which subsequent operations could be launched.

Festung (fortress) From 1944–45, as the Allies advanced in the west and east, Hitler designated cities under threat as "fortresses" to be held to the last man.

Happy Time The period between July and October 1940 in the Battle of the Atlantic when German U-boats sank 217 ships with the loss of only one submarine.

Lebensraum The "living space" in Soviet European Russia which Hitler intended to conquer and seed with German settlements, expelling the Slav population beyond a line drawn from Archangel to Astrakhan (the "A-A" line).

lodgement Bridgehead established in enemy territory by an amphibious landing operation or a river crossing.

open flank A position that is exposed on one side, enabling the enemy to pass round behind it.

rasputitsa The Russian spring and autumn rainy seasons which reduced the countryside to a morass and closed down offensive operations.

screen A lightly armed body of troops deployed in front of the main force to detect the enemy's approach and monitor his progress.

scuttle To sink a ship to prevent it from falling into enemy hands.

INDEX 313

INDEX

Note: page numbers in **bold** indicate biographies and features; those in *italics* refer to illustrations. Battles and offensives are indicated by dates in parentheses.

A

Aachen 233
Abraham Lincoln Brigade 30
Abyssinia (Ethiopia) 84, 86–7
  Italy invades (1935) 12, 28, 29, 31
Achilles, HMNZS 81
Addis Ababa 86, 87
Admiral Scheer (German battleship) 82
Admiralty Islands 185, 209
African-Americans 127–8
Afrika Korps 77, 87, 89, 91, 146, 161, 167
Agordat, Battle of 86
air war
  air forces in 1939 44
  Allied bombing of Germany 202–7
  Allied bombing of Japan 179, 185, 212, 216, 251
  atomic bombs 260, 291–2
  Battle of Britain and the Blitz 58–63, **61**
  see also aircraft; Luftwaffe; RAF; Red Air Force
air-raid shelters 48, 67
airborne forces **95**
aircraft
  air war over Germany **206**
  Battle of Britain **61**
  Japanese and US carrier planes **113**
  British
    Boulton Paul Defiant *61*
    Cierva C-30 autogiro *59*
    Fairey Swordfish *85*, 113
    Hurricane I *61*
    Lancaster 202, *202*, *206*, 265
    Mosquito 205, *206*
    Spitfire 60, *61*
    Sunderland Mark III *170–1*
  German
    Dornier 17Z-2 *61*, 62
    Focke Wulf 190A-8 *206*
    Heinkel He 111 *58*, 60, *61*, 62, 63
    Junker Ju 52 *92*, *95*, *149*
    Junker Ju 87 (Stuka) *55*, 60
    Junker Ju 88 *60*, *61*
    Messerschmitt Me 109 60, *61*
    Messerschmitt Me 110 60, *206*
  Japanese
    Aichi D3A (Val) *113*
    Mitsubishi A6M Reisen (Zero) *113*
    Nakajima B5N2 (Kate) *113*
  Soviet
    Ilyushin IL2 Sturmovich *188*, 263
  US
    B-17 Flying Fortress *203*, *204–5*, *206*
    B-24 Liberator 203, *204*, *206*
    B-25 Mitchell *196*, *200–1*, *208–9*, *254–5*
    B-29 Superfortress *124–5*, 185, 212, 219, 260, *287*, 292
    C-47 cargo planes *304*
    Douglas SBD-3 Dauntless *113*, *122–3*, *175*
    Mustang P-51B/D 204, 205, *206*, 260
aircraft carriers 41, 110, 113, *122–3*, 175, 253, 282
Aitape 210
Akagi (Japanese carrier) 123
Alam Halfa 146, 163
Albania 76, 92, 93, 238, 240
Alençon 229
Aleutians 122, 179, 185, 208
Alexander, General Harold 162, 163, 167, 195, 196, 198, 199
Alexandria 84, 85
Algeria 164, 166, 167
Aliakmon Line 94
Alsace 235
Altmark (German ship) 50
Ambrosio, General Vittorio 166
amphibious warfare 41, 171, **211**, *216–17*, 218, 219, 220–4

B

Anders, Wladislaw 185, 197
Anderson, General Kenneth 164, 166
Anschluss (1938) *8–9*, 13
Anti-Comintern Pact (1936) 13, 24
anti-Semitism *see* Jews, persecution of
antibiotics **212**
Antonescu, Marshal Ion 246–7
Antwerp 232–3
Anvil, Operation (1944) 198
Anzio 185, *196*, 197–8
Aosta, Duke d' 87
appeasement 13, 29, 31, 32
Arab–Israeli War (1948) 309
Arakan 217, 248, 249
Arcadia Conference (1941) 108, 146
Arctic convoys 171, *171*
Ardennes offensive (1944–45) 233–5, 258, 269
Argenta Gap 275
Argentan 229, 230
Argument, Operation (1944) 205
Arizona (US battleship) 114, *115*
Ark Royal (British carrier) 83, *85*
Armenia 296
armoured cars *165*
Arnhem 95, 232
Arnim, Jürgen von 166, 167
Arno River 198, 199
ARP wardens 68
Artillery *see* guns
ASDIC 81
Asian Development Union 117
Asmara 86
Athenia (liner) 40
Athens *78*, 94, 241, 305
Atlantic Charter 106
Atlantic Wall 218–19
Atlantic, war in the 40, 80–3, 168–71
  Allied shipping losses 81, 82, 83, 168, 169
Atlantis (German raider) 111
atomic bombs 260, 290, 291–2, **293**, *293*
Attlee, Clement 260, 296, 307
Attu Island 179, 185, 208
Auchinleck, General Sir Claude 89–91, 160, 161–2
Audisio, Walter 275
Auschwitz-Birkenau 156, *156–7*, 157
Australia and Australian forces
  Balkans 93
  casualties 178, 303
  Malaya 116
  New Guinea 147, *176*, **176**, 177, 210
  North Africa 85–6, 87, 88
  post-war 299
  Syria 89
Austria 259
  Anschluss *8–9*, 13, 31
  failed Nazi coup (1934) 29
  post-war 301
Automedon (British steamer) 111
Avranches 229

Badoglio, Marshal Pietro 184, 195
Bagration, Operation (1944) 133, 217, 242–4
Balaton, Lake 258, 267
Baldwin, Stanley 67
Balfour Declaration (1917) 309
Balikpapan 119
Balkans 76, 78, 92–5, *96–7*, 183
  partisan resistance 238–41
  see also Albania; Bosnia; Bulgaria; Croatia; Greece; Macedonia; Romania; Serbia; Slovenia; Yugoslavia
Baltic, operations in 244, 246
Baltic States 102, 244, 246
Baranow 262, 263
Barbarossa, Operation (1941) 79, 98–103, 134, 137, 144, 151
Bardia 85, 91
Barvenkovo 135
Bastogne 234–5
Bataan Peninsula 117, 120
  Baatan Death March **121**, 303

C

Batavia 119
Battleaxe, Operation (1941) 89
Bayeux 224
BBC 70
Beck, General Ludwig 32
Beda Fomm, Battle of (1941) 86
BEF *see* British Expeditionary Force
Beijing *see* Peking
Belgium 49, 231, 232
  Allied advance through (1944) 231–2
  army 54, 55
  casualties 303
  German occupation 69
  invasion of 38, 48, 52–5
  see also Ardennes
Belgorod 154, 189
Belgrade 93, 240, 240
Benes, Edouard 32
Benghazi 85, 86, 87, 91
Bergen-Belsen 156, *157*, *274*, **274**
Beria, Lavrenti 134
Berlin 258, *278*, *300–1*, *310–11*
  advance on (1945) 272, 273
  airlift 304
  blockade **304**
  communist movements in *14*
  division of (1945) 298, 304
Berlin, Battle of (bombing campaign) 207
Berlin, Battle of (1945) *258–9*, 276–9, *276–7*
Bessarabia 78
Biak 210, 211–12
Bialystok 99, 244
Big Wing tactics 60
Biggin Hill 60
Billancourt 203
Billotte, General Pierre 48
Bir Hacheim 91, 161, 167
Bismarck (German battleship) 82, *83*, **83**
Bismarck Sea, Battle of the 178
Bizerta 167
Bizerte 166
Black, Hermann 235
black market
  Germany 73
  Japan 129
blackout
  Britain 68
  Germany *73*
Blackshirts 15
Bletchley Park 82, 146, 151
Blitz, the 62–3, *64–5*, 66
blitzkrieg 38, 45, **55**, 100, 136–7
Blücher (German cruiser) 51
Blue, Operation (1942) 109, 136, 137
Bluecoat, Operation (1944) 229
Blumentritt, General Günther 102, 273
Bock, General Fedor von 42
  advance in the Low Countries 52, 53
  Soviet campaigns 98, 100, 137
Bodyguard plan 219
Bogart, Humphrey 130
Bologna 199, 275
Bolshevism 10
bombers *see* aircraft
bombing
  atomic bombs 260, 290, 291–2, *293*, **293**
  the Blitz 62–3
  of Germany 182–3, 202–7, 216, **265**, 277
  of Japan 179, 185, 212, 251, 286–8
  Malta 85
  V-weapons *233*, **233**
book-burning *11*, 19
Bormann, Martin 279, 301
Borneo 119
Boschcar (US aircraft) 292
Bose, Subhas Chandra 249
Bosnia 239
Boult, Sir Adrian 199
Boulogne 54, 220
Bradley, General Omar 227, 229, 231, 269, 272–3
Brandenburg 267, 276
Brandenburger, Erich 234
Brauchitsch, Field Marshal Walther von 78, 134
Braun, Eva 279
Brazilian Expeditionary Corps 199
Brecht, Herbert 207
Bremen 203, *268*, 274, *274*

Breslau 262, 264, 266–7
Brest 229
Brest-Litovsk 44, 99
Brevity, Operation (1941) 89
Briand, Aristide 16–17
Britain and British forces
  Anglo-Polish Alliance (1939) 43
  appeasement 13, 29, 31, 32
  Atlantic 40, 80–3, 168–71
  Balkans 92–5, 239–41
  the Blitz 62–3, *64–5*
  bombing of Germany 202–7
  Burma 120, 216–17, 248–50
  casualties 300, **303**
  D-Day landings 220–4
  declares war on Germany (1939) 13, 33
  Greece 78, 87, **239**
  home front 66–8
  Hong Kong 116
  ill-prepared 38, 49
  and Indian independence 307
  invades Syria 89
  invasion threat 41
  and invasion of the West 52–7
  Italy and Sicily 183–5, 194–9, 275
  Malaya 116–17
  Mediterranean 84–5
  Middle East 88–9
  military strength (1939) 29, 44
  Normandy 220–9
  North Africa 78, 84–91, 160–7
  Norway 50–1
  preparations for war 48–9
  relations with United States 308–9
  Singapore 117–19
  Western Front 220–35, 269–75
  see also RAF; Royal Navy
Britain, Battle of (1940) 58–62
British Empire 41, 299, 307, 309
British Expeditionary Force 48, 49, 52, 54, 55, 56, 57, 74
Brittany 229
Brownshirts 17, 19
Brussels 53
Bryansk 102, 134, 193
Bucharest 247
Budapest 247, *247*, 258, 267
Bug River 44, 45, 264
Bukovina 78
Bulgaria 78, 93, 217, 238, 240, *246*, 247, 301, 304
  casualties 303
Bulge, Battle of the (1944) 234–5
Buna 147, 177, 178, *178*
Burma 106, 110, *117*, 120, 216–17, 248
  independence (1948) 299, 308
Burma Road 110, 248
Burma–Siam railroad 289, *289*
Busch, Field Marshal Ernst 243
Butcher, Captain Harry C 166
Butt Report 202
Byelorussia 193, 242–4

C

Caen 221, 224, 225, 226, *226–7*, 227, 229
Cairncross, John 151
Cairo Conference (1943) 217
Calais 54, 56, 219, 220
California (US battleship) 114
Canada and Canadian forces
  Atlantic 168, 170
  casualties 303
  D-Day landings 224
  Dieppe raid (1942) 218
  France 225, 227, 229, 232
  Italy 196–7, 199, 275
  Western Front 225, 227, 229, 232, 269–70, 273–4
Canton 251
Cape Esperance, Battle of 175
Cape Gloucester 210
Cape Verde 76
Capra, Frank 126

Capuzzo 89, 91
Carol, King of Romania 247
Caroline Islands 185, 211, 212
Carpiquet 224
Casablanca (film) 30
Casablanca Conference (1943) 146, *146*, 182–3, 185, 204
Caserta 275
Caspian Sea 137
Cassin (US destroyer) 114, 115
casualties 300, **303**
    atomic bombs 292
    the Blitz 66
    civilian 66, 67, 265, 287, 292, 300
    war in the air 204–5, 207
    see also individual countries by name
Caucasus 137, 144, 149
cauldron battles 99
cavalry, Polish *42*
censorship *11*, 19
Ceylon (Sri Lanka) 299, 308
Chad 167
Chaff 207, 220
Chamberlain, Neville 13, 32, 33
Chambois 229
Changchun 292
Changsa 251
Chaplin, Charlie 130, *130*
Chartres 230
Chasseurs Alpins *51*
Cherbourg 57, 225, 226, 232
Cherkassy 192
Chetniks 239
Chiang Kai-shek 23, 24–5, 26, 217, 251, 299, 306
children, evacuation of 67
China and Chinese forces
    casualties 300, 303
    civil wars 22, **23**, 299, **306**, 308
    Ichi-Go offensive against (1944) 251
    Korean War (1950–53) 303
    Nationalist misrule 251–2
    Rape of Nanking **25**, 26
    Sino–Japanese War (1937–45) 13, 25–7, 106, 112, 129, 217, 248, 249, 250–1
Chindits 216, 217, 248–9, *249*
Chindwin River 249
Chittagong 248
Choltitz, General Dietrich von 231
Chou En Lai see Zhou Enlai 3
Chuikov, General Vasili 138, 139, 149, 264, 279
Chungking *20–1*, 250, 251
Churchill, Winston Spencer *53*, **53**
    Balkans strategy 94
    Cairo Conference (1943) 217
    Casablanca Conference (1943) 146, *146*, 182
    on Dunkirk 39
    election defeat (1945) 260
    Greece 92, 241
    Iron Curtain 305
    Mediterranean strategy 84–5, 183–4
    mobilizes British forces 32
    North Africa campaigns 89, 160, 161, 162, 163
    Operation Overlord (1944) 217–18
    Pearl Harbor 108
    Placentia Bay 106, 108
    Tehran Conference (1943) 217, *219*
    Yalta Conference (1945) 258, 296, 304
cinema, wartime **130–1**
Citadel, Operation (1943) 151, 182, *182–3*, 186, 187–8, 190
civil defence 67–8
Civil Rights movement 127–8
Clark, General Mark 164, 195, 196, 197, 198, 199
Clark, Harry L. 114
Clemenceau, Georges 10
Coblenz 269
Cobra, Operation (1944) 229
codes
    German **82**
    Japanese **114**
Cold War 298, 299, 303, 304–5, 308, 309
collaborators 69, 70
Collins, General Lawton 221
Colmar 233, 269
Cologne 203, *203*, 233, 269, 270
colonial rule
    disintegration of 296, 299, 306, 309
Comacchio, Lake 275

COMECON
    see Council for Mutual Economic Assistance
communism 14, 69, 102, 296, 308
    Berlin *14*
    China 250, 299, 306
Communist People's Liberation Army 306
concentration camps 156–7, *156–7*, *158–9*
    for political prisoners 19
    see also individual camps by name
conscientious objectors 128
convoys
    Arctic 171, *171*
    Atlantic 76, 80–3, 168, 169, 170
Coral Sea, Battle of the (1942) 122–3, 147, 174, 208
Corinth *241*
Corregidor 120, *121*, 283
Cotentin peninsula 220, 225
Council for Mutual Economic Assistance 306
Courageous (British carrier) 40, 81
Courland peninsula 246, 258
Coventry *62–3*, 63, 67
Cracow 264
Crete 76, 78, 89, 92, 94
    invasion of 95, *95*
Crimea 102, 135, 193
Croatia 238, 239, 240, 259
Crosby, Bing 126
Crusader, Operation (1941) 77, 90–1
Cuba 308
Cunningham, Admiral Sir Andrew 85
Cunningham, General Alan 86, 90, 91
Cyrenaica 86, 87, 90, 91
Czechoslovakia 259, 273, 279
    after Treaty of Versailles 10
    casualties 303
    cedes Sudetenland (1938) 13, 31–2
    invasion (1939) 13, 32–3
    postwar 301, 304

D-Day (1944) 95, 217–18, 220–4
Dakar 167
Daladier, Edouard 32, 33
Dalmatia 240
Dali, Salvador 30
Damaskinos, Archbishop 241
Danube River 267, 273
Danzig *33*, **33**, 43, 262, 264, 277
Dardanelles 183
Darlan, Admiral François 164, 166
Davao 117
Dawes Plan (1924) 16
Debra Markos 86
Debrecen 247
Declaration on Liberated Europe (1945) 298, 304
decolonization 296, 299, 306–9
Delhi 249
demobilization *300*
Denmark 259, 274
    attitude to Jews in 72
    casualties 303
    invasion 50–1
    neutrality 46
    occupation 69
Desert Air Force 162, 163
Desert War *76–7*, 78, 84–91, 160–7
    armour and antitank weapons in *165*, **165**
Devers, General Jacob 232, 235, 269, 272
Dieppe 218, 219, 225
Dietrich, General Sepp 234
Dietrich, Marlene *199*
Dinant 234
Displaced Persons 301
Dives River 221
Dixie Arrow (US tanker) *168–9*
Dnieper River 153, 182, 189, 190, 191
Dodecanese **239**
Dolfuss, Engelbert 29
Don River 137, 138, 149, 153
Donets River 137, 138, 153, 154, 189
Dönitz, Admiral Karl 76, 146, 259, 274–5
Doolittle, Lieutenant Colonel James 122
Doolittle Raid (1942) 122, 212
Dorsetshire (British cruiser) 83
Dowding, Sir Hugh 53, 57, 58
Downes (US destroyer) 114, *115*

Dresden 207, 258, *265*, **265**, 272, 276
Duane (US Coast Guard cutter) *169*
Dunkirk 38–9, *38–9*, 55, *56*, **56**, 57, *131*
Düsseldorf 269, 270
Dutch East Indies 106, 110, 118, 119, 308
Dutoit, Henri-Edouard, Bishop of Arras 69
Dyle Line 52, 53
Dynamo, Operation (1940) 56
Dzhugashvili, Josef Vissarionovich
    see Stalin, Josef

E

Eagle Day 59
Eaker, General Ira C 183
EAM (Communist National Liberation Front) 238
East Germany 302, 304
East Prussia 258, 265–6
Eastern Front 98–103, 132–9, 144–6, 148–54, 182, 186–93, 217, 242–7, 262–7, 276–9
Eastern Solomons, Battle of (1942) 175
Eben Emael 52
Eden, Anthony 93
EDES (National Republican Greek League) 238, 240
Egypt 76, 84–5, 87, 88, 137, 162, 163, 164, 167, 309
Ehrhardt Brigade *17*
Eichmann, Adolf 156
Eindhoven 231
Einsatzgruppen atrocities 102, **102**, 156
Einstein, Albert 293, *293*
Eisenhower, General Dwight D *221*, **221**
    North Africa 166
    Sicilian and Italian campaign 195, 196, 197
    Western Front 219, 220, 227, 229, 230, 231, 232, 234, 235, 258, 259, 269–71, 272–3
El Agheila 87, 91
El Alamein, Battle of (1942) 85, 89, 146, 147, 162, *162*, 163–4
El Duda 91
ELAS (National People's Liberation Army) 238, 240, 241
Elbe River 259, 273, 274
Enfidaville 167
Enigma **82**, *82*, 83
Eniwetok 185
Enola Gay (Superfortress) 292
ENSA 199
entertaining the troops *199*, **199**
Entertainments National Service Association
    see ENSA
Eritrea 31, 84, 86, 167
Ernst Thälmann Bridgade 30
escort vessels 83, 169, 170
Essen 203, 205
Estonia 78, 244, 246
Eternal Jew, The (film) 131, *131*
Ethiopia *see* Abyssinia
European Recovery Program *see* Marshall Plan
evacuations
    civilian 38, **67**
    see also Dunkirk

F

Facta, Luigi 15
Fairbanks, Douglas, Jr 130
Fairey Swordfish *85*, 113
Falaise 229, 230
Falkenhorst, Niklaus von 50
Fasari 178
fascism
    in Italy **15**
    rise of 11–12
    in Spain 30
    see also Nazi Party
"Fat Man" (atomic bomb) 292, 293, *293*
Federal Republic of West Germany
    see West Germany
Felix Plan 76
Fengtien 23
Fermi, Enrico 293
Fiji 122
Final Solution 18, 156, 296

Finland 33, 78, 146, 246
    casualties 48, 303
    invasion of 46–8
Finschhafen 121, 178, 210
flamethrowers 121
    Churchill Crocodile 225
    Roks-2 188–9
Fleming, Alexander 212
Flying Tigers 251
Foggia 196
food 41, 66, 71, 73, 129, 155, 268
Forces Françaises de l'Intérieur (FFI) 228, 230
Ford, John 130, 131
Formby, George 199
Formosa (Taiwan) 216, 251, 252, 253, 282, 284, 299, 306
Four Freedoms 106
France and French forces
    advance into Saarland (1939) 44, 48
    Allied landings in southern 230
    Army **44**, 54, 55, 230
    casualties 303
    colonial rule 307–8
    Czechs appeal to 32
    declares war on Germany (1939) 13, 33
    French-German armistice (1940) 57
    French North Africa 164–7
    home front 69–70, 71, 73
    imperialism 299, 307–8, 309
    invasion 52–7
    Jews in 72
    Locarno Pact (1925) 17
    military strength (1939) 29, 44, 48
    Norway 51
    occupation 69–70
    occupies Ruhr (1923) 16
    preparations for war 38, 48–9
    resistance 219, **228**, *228*, 230
    women in 71
    see also D-Day; Dunkirk; Normandy; Paris; Vichy government
France, Battle of (1940) 52–7, 76
Franco, General Francisco 13, 30, 76
Frankfurt an der Oder *262–3*
Frankfurt-am-Main 273
Fredenhall, General Lloyd 164
Frederick the Great 168, 184
Free French 161, 166, **167**
Freikorps units 14–15, 17
French Expeditionary Corps 197, 198, 230
French Foreign Legion *167*
French Resistance 219, **228**, *228*, 230
Freyberg, General Bernard 95
Friedman, William F 114
Friessner, General Johannes 247
Frost, Robert *127*
"Funnies", the, *225*, **225**
Fuso (Japanese battleship) *12–13*

G

Gable, Clark 126, 130
Gafsa 166
Gallipoli 41
Galtier-Boissière, Jean 231
Galvanic, Operation (1943) 209
Gamelin, General Maurice 48, 53, 55
Gandhi, Mahatma 307
gas masks *24*, 38, *48*, 68
Gaulle, Charles de 53, 166
    appointed deputy war minister 55
    Casablanca Conference (1943) 146, *146*
    and Free French 57, **167**
    liberation of Paris 230, 231
    and Resistance 228
Gazala, Battle of (1942) 91, 167
Gazala Line 160, 161
Gdynia 266, 277
Gee 202, 205
Geneva Convention 289
George Cross *85*
George, King of Greece 240
George VI, King 85
George Washington Brigade 30
Georges, General Alphonse 48
German Democratic Republic
    see East Germany
Germany and German forces
    in 1945 **268**

Germany (cont.)
African colonies 10
air war 38, 45, 58–65, 202–7
Allied strategic bombing of 182–3, 202–7
annexes Austria (Anschluss) 9, 13, 31
Anti-Comintern Pact (1936) 13, 24
Ardennes counteroffensive (1944–45) 233–5, 258
atomic bomb program 228
Balkans 76, 78, 92–5, 96–7, 183, 238–41
Battle of Britain (1940) 58–62
the Blitz 62–5
blitzkrieg tactics 38
casualties 45, 51, 55, 67, 78, 103, 134, 151, 190–1, 235, 242, 244, 247, 271, 300, **303**
D-Day counterattack (1944) 224
declares war on United States 108
division into four zones (1945) 298, 301
Eastern Front 98–103, 132–9, 144–6, 148–54, 182, 186–93, 217, 242–7, 262–7, 276–9
economic crisis 12
Einsatzgruppen atrocities 100, 100
foreign workforce in 41, 69, 71
French-German armistice 57
home front 70–1, 73, **268**
humiliated at Versailles 10, 14, 33
invasion of Belgium 38, 48, 52–5
invasion of Czechoslovakia (1939) 13, 32–3
invasion of France 52–7
invasion of Greece 93, 94–5
invasion of Netherlands 38, 49, 52–3
invasion of Norway 49–51
invasion of Poland (1939) 13, 33, 42–6, 102
invasion of Soviet Union 63, 78–9, 98–103
invasion of Yugoslavia 93, 96
Italy 184–5, 194–9
Jews in 11, 18, **18**, 19, 131
life under occupation by 68–70
Locarno Pact (1925) 17
Middle East campaigns 88–9
military strength 29, 44, 186
naval war 29, 40, 44, 80–3, 146, 168–71
Nazi-Soviet Non-Aggression Pact (1939) 13, 33, 78, 99, 110
North Africa 77, 78, 87–91, 146, 160–7
path to war 10–15, 16–17, 28–33
payment of reparations 10, 14, 16–17
postwar 301, 304–6
Potsdam Conference 298
propaganda 18, 33, 45, 131, 131, 150
Rapallo Treaty (1922) 16
rearmament 12, 28, 29
rise of fascism 11–12, 14–15
Rome–Berlin Axis (1936) 13, 30
surrenders 259, 275, 279
Tripartite Pact (Sept 1940) 93, 108, 111
war aims 105
war crimes tribunal 297, 301
war economy 73
Western Front 217–35, 259, 269–75
women in 70–1, 268
see also Luftwaffe; U-boats
Germersheim 271
ghettos, creation of 41, 72, 72, 156
Gibraltar 76, 78, 84
Gideon Force 86, 86
Gilbert Islands 185, 209
Giraud, General Henri 146, 164, 166, 167
GKO (State Defence Committee) 134
glider-borne troops 95, 220, 271
Gneisenau (German battleship) 82
Goebbels, Josef 18, 19, 70, 131, 268, 279
Goebbels, Magda 279
Gold beach 224
Golikov, General Fillipp 153
Gona 177, 178
Gondar 87
Good Hope, Cape of 82, 85
Goodwood, Operation (1944) 227–9
Göring, Reichsmarschall Hermann 55, 58, 59, 76, 149, 297, 301, 301
Görlitz 277
Gort, Lord 55
Gothic Line 185, 198–9
Gott, William "Strafer" 162
Grable, Betty 130
Graf, Robert F 213
Graf Spee (German battleship) 40, 50, 81
Graziani, Marshal Rodolfo 78
Great Depression 14, 21, 22, 124
Great Dictator, The (film) 130

Greater Khingan Range 290, 292
Greece
casualties 303
civil war 241, 305
Dodecanese operations **239**
German conquest 78, 82, 94–5
government-in-exile 238
Italian invasion of 76, 78, 92
postwar 301, 305
resistance movements 238, 240–1
Green Island 209
grenades 226
Griswold, Major Oscar 283
Groningen 274
Guadalcanal campaign 147, 174–9, 175, 185, 211
Guam 116, 185, 212
Guderian, Heinz 100, **100**, 101, 132, 133, 264, 266
Guernica 30, 30, 38, 44
guns (artillery and small arms)
Australian
Owen submachine-gun 176
Short Mark I 25-pounder 176
British
25-pounder 161
5.5-in howitzer 195
6-pounder (57-mm) antitank gun 165
Lee Enfield no. 4 226
Sten gun Mk 5 228
Welrod silenced pistol 228
Finnish
anti-tank rifle 46
German
50-mm Pak 38 186
88-mm FLAK 165
240-mm howitzer 99
Luger (Pistole Parabellum 1908) 226
MP40 submachine-gun 199
Japanese
Arisaka Type 99 rifle 291
Soviet
76-mm anti-tank gun 188
M91/30 sniper's rifle 139
PPS-1943 submachine-gun 135
PPSh-41 submachine-gun 135
Tokarev 40 7.62-mm rifle 263
Tokarev pistol 135
US
Colt .45 automatic pistol 226
Karabiner 98K 226
M1A1 75-mm airborne howitzer 232
Thompson M1928A1 "Tommy Gun" 226
Gustav Line 184–5, 196, 197, 198

H
H2S radar 205, 205
Haakon, King of Norway 51
Hacha, Emil 32
Hachioji 287
Hagen Line 189
Haile Selassie, Emperor 31, 86, **86**
Halder, General Franz 78, 79
Halfaya Pass 89
Halmahera 210
Halsey, Admiral 185
Hamburg 67, 274
area bombing of 207, 207
Hanoi 308
Hanoi-Nanning railway 110
Hanover 273
Harbin 292
Harker, Jack 81
Harpe, General Josef 263
Harriman, Averell 219
Harris, Air Chief Marshal Sir Arthur 202–3, 203, 207, 265
Hausser, General Paul 153
Hautecloque, Philippe de (Leclerc) 167, 231
Haw-Haw, Lord 70
Hawaiian Islands 122, 128
see also Pearl Harbor
Hayworth, Rita 126
health 71, 129, 155
"hedgehog" tactics 133, 169
Heilungkiang 23
Heinlein, Konrad 31
Helena (US cruiser) 114

Henderson Field 174–5, 175, 179
Hengyang 251
Henry V (film) 130
Hersh, Arek 72
Hess, Rudolf 16, 301
Heydrich, Reinhard 102, 156
Hiei (Japanese battleship) 176
Hills, Stuart 229
Himmler, Heinrich 102, 264, 266, 275
Hirohito, Emperor 21, 108, 260, 260, 292–3, 298, 302
Hiroshima 292, 292–3, 293, 298
Hirota 24
Hiryu (Japanese carrier) 123
Hitchcock, Alfred 130
Hitler, Adolf 17, **17**, 28–9
appeals to Britain for peace (1940) 76
attitude to women 70–1
Balkans Offensive 78
becomes chancellor (1933) 17–18
becomes Führer 17
bomb plot (Jul 1944) 89, 100, 227, 229
fall of Warsaw 45
founds Nazi Party 12
and Franco 13, 30
invasion of Belgium 48
invasion of Britain, plans for 46, 58
invasion of Czechoslovakia 32
invasion of France 54–5
invasion of Greece 93
invasion of Norway 50
invasion of Poland 33
invasion of Soviet Union 78–9, 98–9, 101, 103
invasion of Yugoslavia 93
Italian campaigns 195, 196
last days 277–8, 279, **279**
Lebensraum 11, 31, 33, 268, 277, 279
Middle East oil fields 109, 137
Munich Beer-Hall putsch (1923) 16, 17
and Mussolini 31, 87–9
Night of the Long Knives (1934) 17, 19
obsession with Stalingrad 139, 144, 149, 150, 151
opinion of US military power 76
orders no retreat at Moscow 132
and Pearl Harbor 108
persecution of the Jews 41
rearmament programme 12, 28, 29
reoccupies Rhineland 13, 31
restructures Army high command 133–4
rise to power 17
speeches 11, 31, 182, 246
suicide 259, 274, **279**
Hitler Youth 18–19, 31, 33, 268, 277, 279
HMS Bittern (British destroyer) 49
Ho Chi Minh 308, 308
Hodges, General Courtney 232
Hollandia 119, 210, 210
Hollywood 130–1
Holocaust, the 156–7, **156–7**, 158–9, 218–19, 247, 296
home front 66–73, 124–31
Britain 66–8
France 69–70, 71, 73
Germany 70–1, 73, 268
Japan 129
Soviet Union 155
United States 124–8
Home Guard 66, 68
Homma Masaharu 121
Hong Kong 116, 308
Honshu 288
Hood (British battlecruiser) 83
Hope, Bob 126, 199
Höpner, General Erich 132
Hornet (US carrier) 122, 175
Hoth, General Hermann 187
howitzers see guns
Hoxha, Enver 240
Hsinking 292
Huertgen Forest 233, 234
Hukawng Valley 249
Hunan province 251
Hungary 44, 93, 217, 240, 267
after Treaty of Versailles 10
casualties 303
Eastern Front 136, 146, 151
post-war 301, 304
Hupei province 23
Huston, John 130
hyperinflation, German 16, 16

I
Iceland 83
Ikeda, S 291
Illustrious (British carrier) 87
immigration, postwar 301
Imphal 249
India 217, 248, 249
casualties 303
independence (1947) 299, 306, 307
Italian campaigns 198
Malayan campaign 116
Middle East and North Africa 88–9, 91
Indian National Army **249**
Indian Ocean 40, 81, 122
Indochina 110, 299, 307–8
Japanese bases in 106, 111, 112, 116, 284
Indonesia 299, 307, 308
see also Dutch East Indies
Inner Mongolia, Japanese offensive in 23
intelligence 82, 83, 114, 146
Allied 146, 170
Enigma and Ultra 82, 83
Resistance 228
Soviet 151, 186
United States 114
International Brigade 30
International Military Tribunal for the Far East 303
internment 68, 128
Inukai Tsuyoshi 24
Ioribaiwa 177
Iran 89
Iraq 84, 88–9, 309
Iron Curtain, the 305
Irrawaddy River 250
Ishihara Kanji 26–7
Ismay, General 99
Israel 309
Italy and Italian forces
Allied invasion of 183–5, 194–201, 275
armistice (1943) 184, 195, 196, 240
attacks Malta 85
casualties 303
enters war (1940) 40, 49, 54, 57, 84
fleet 85, 113, 196
invades Abyssinia (1935) 12, 28, 29, 31, 86
invades Albania 92
invades Egypt 85
invades Greece 76, 92–3
military strength 44, 84
North Africa 76, 78, 84–6
post-war 301
rise of fascism 11–12, 15–16
Rome–Berlin Axis (1936) 13, 30
Tripartite Pact (Sept 1940) 93, 108, 111
troops on Eastern Front 136, 146, 151
Versailles 13
Iwabuchi Sanji, Rear Admiral 283
Iwo Jima 216, 260, 260–1, 283, 284–5
Izyum 189

J
Japan and Japanese forces
air power 113
Allied bombing of 179, 185, 212, 216, 251, 286–8, 288, 289
Anti-Comintern Pact (1936) 13, 24
army 22, 111, 112
atomic bombs dropped on 260, 291–2, 292–3
atrocities 19
casualties 114, 178, 210, 212, 213, 253–4, 292, 300, 303
codes 114
defeat at Nomonhan (1939) 27, 106, 110
economic collapse 129, 216, 254–5, 288
expansion into China 20–5
Guadalcanal campaign 147, 174–6, 177
home front 129
Ichi-Go offensive (1944) 251
imperialism 20–7
Inner Mongolian campaign 23
invasion of Burma 120, 248–50
invasion of China (1937) 13
invasion of Malaya 116–17
Japanese society 21

Japan (cont.)
Lansing–Ishii agreement (1917) 21
Manchurian campaign 12, 23
militarism 22–3, 22
nationalist government seizes power (1930) 12
Naval Limitation Treaty (1922) 21–2
New Guinea 147, 176–9
non-aggression pact with Soviet Union (Apr 1941) 108, 111, 260, 291
occupies Indochina 106, 111, 112
Pacific and Asia 116–23, 147, 174–9, 185, 208–13, 216–17, 248–55, 260, 282–93
path to war 20–7
Pearl Harbor 106–8, 106–7, 111, 112–15, 114
Philippines 116, 117, 120–1, 252–4
post-war 298–9, 302–4
prepares for war (1941) 106, 129
prisoners of war **289**
rejects Potsdam demands (1945) 291
shipping losses **254**
Sino–Japanese War (1937–45) 13, 25–7, 106, 112, 129, 217, 248, 249, 250–1
Southern Resources Area 106, 110, 111, 112, 248, 252, 285
surrender 260, 292–3, 298, 302
Tripartite Pact (Sept 1940) 93, 108, 111
US declares war on 108
US economic warfare on 106, 111, 112
war aims 105, 106, 108, 110–11
war crimes tribunal 303–4
and World War I 10, 12, 20–1
Japanese-Americans **128**, 128, 129
Java Sea, Battle of the (1942) 119
Jebel el Akhdar 86, 87, 90
Jehol 22, 23, 292
Jennings, Humphrey 131
Jews, persecution of 41, 72, **72**, 156–9, 156–7, 158–9, 296
in Danzig 33
in Germany 11, 18, **18**, 19, 131
in Hungary 218–19, 247
in Poland 41, 45, 102, 156
in Soviet Union 102
Jodl, General Alfred 41
Johnston, George H 177
Johnston Island 122
Johore 118
Jordan 309
Joyce, William see Haw-Haw, Lord
Juin, Alphonse 197, 198
Jülich 269
Juno beach 224

K

Kaga (Japanese carrier) 123
Kalgan 292
kamikaze 216, 253, 260, 284, **284**, 285, 286
Kammhuber, General Josef 203
Kammhuber Line 203, 207
K'ang-te, Emperor see P'u Yi
Kapp, Wolfgang 14, 17
Karelia 46, 47, 246
Kashmir 307
Kasserine Pass 167
Katyn massacre 45
Kaunus 102
Kellogg-Briand Pact (1928) 17
Kennan, George 305
Kenya 84
Kerch Peninsula 135
Keren, Battle of (1941) 86, 86–7
Kesselring, Marshal Albert 85, 91, 162, 184, 195, 196, 197, 198, 199, 270
Khabarovsk 292
Khaldi, W 309
Kharkov 135, 144, 146, 153
Germans recapture 154, 154, 182
liberation of 189
Soviet capture of 153
Kichisaburo, Admiral Nomura 107
Kiel 274
Kielce 263
Kiev 100, 101, 189, 190, 190–1
King, Admiral Ernest 282
King George V (British battleship) 83

Kirin 23
Kirishima (Japanese battleship) 176
Kiska 179, 185
Kleist, General Ewald von 137, 153
Kluge, Field Marshal Günther Hans von 154, 187, 188, 189, 226, 227, 229
Knickebein 62
Koa Domei (Agency for Developing Asia) 27
Kohima 249
Kokoda Trail 147, 176, 177
Kolberg 266
Kolombangara 209
Battle of (1942) 179
Komandorski Islands, Battle of the (1942) 179
Komorowski, General Tadeusz 245
Konev, Marshal I S 244, 262–4, 267, 277 9
Königsberg 262, 266, 266–7, 267
Konoye Fumimaro, Prince 108, 117, 129
Kopecky, Lily 157
Korean War (1950–53) 303
Koror 210
Kriegsmarine 170
Kristallnacht (Crystal Night) 18
Kula Gulf, Battle of (1942) 179
Kunashiri 292
Kunming 250
Kuomintang 23, 24–5, 26, 120, 248, 249, 250, 251, 306
Kurile Islands 179, 212, 292
Kursk 144, 146, 153, 154, 182
Battle of (1943) 186–7, 189, 190, 191
Küstrin 264, 277, 278
Kutno 43
Kutuzov, Operation (1943) 182, 188–9
Kwajalein 121, 210
Kwantung Army 23–4, 27, 291
Kweilin 251
Kyoto 288
Kyushu 212

L

La Spezia 196
Lacey, J H "Ginger" 60
Ladoga, Lake 152, 191
Lae 121, 178, 208, 210
Lampedusa 194
land girls 70
landing craft 41, 211
Lang, Fritz 130
Langley (US carrier) 282–3
Lansing–Ishii agreement (1917) 21
Lasch, General 266
Lashio 120
Lattre de Tassigny, General Jean-Marie de 230
Latvia 78, 244, 246
Laval, Pierre 164
Le Hamel 224
Le Havre 230
League of Nations
establishment of 10, 14
expels Soviet Union 46
fails to preserve peace 12–13
Germany enters (1926) 17
Germany walks out of (1933) 28, 29
and invasion of Abyssinia (1935) 31
Leakey, Rea 161
Lebanon 309
Lebensraum 31, 32, 78, 98
Leclerc see Hautecloque, Philippe de
Leeb, Field Marshal Ritter von 98, 101
Leese, Sir Oliver 197, 199
Leigh-Mallory, Air Vice-Marshal Trafford 58, 60
Leipzig 276
LeMay, Major-General Curtis 287
Lemnos 76
Lend-Lease Act 106, 109, 146, 192
Lenin, V I 43, 296
Leningrad 79, 100
relief of 191
siege of 101, 150, 152, **152**
Leros 239, 239
Lexington (US carrier) 122
Leyte Gulf, Battle of (1944) 214–15, 216, 252–4, 252, 282–3
Libya 76–8, 77, 84–7, 89, 91, 160–1, 163–4, 166
Liebknecht, Karl 14
lightning war see blitzkrieg

Lindemann, General 191
List, Field Marshal Wilhelm 137
Lithuania 78, 102, 244
Liuchow 251
Liuyang 251
Lloyd George, David 10
Locarno Pact (1925) 17
Lodz 43
Loire River 229
London, bombing of 63, 63, 64–5, 67
London Treaty (1930) 24
Long March 23, 23
Lorient 229
Low Countries see Belgium; Netherlands
Lubang 293
Lübeck 203, 274
Lublin 158–9, 245
Lucas, General John P 197
Luftwaffe 29, 202–7
attacks refugees 38, 53
Battle of Britain 58–62
the Blitz 41, 62–3
Dunkirk 56
Leningrad 152
losses on Eastern Front 133
Malta 85
and naval operations 80, 82
Netherlands, Belgium and France 52
Poland 43
Soviet Union 99
Stalingrad 149
Warsaw and Rotterdam 38
see also aircraft
Lüneberg Heath 275
Luxemburg, Rosa 14
Luzon 116, 117, 216, 260, 282–3
Lwow 242–3, 244
Lynn, Vera 199
Lyutezh 190

M

Maas River 233
Maastricht 53
MacArthur, General Douglas 119, 119, 120–1, 185, 216, 253, 260, 282
post-war Japan 298–9, 302–3
McCreery, General Sir Richard 199
Macedonia 93, 94, 238
machine-guns see guns
Madrid 30
Magdeburg 273
Maginot, André 49
Maginot Line 31, 38, 44, 48, 49, **49**, 57
Mahnuszew 262
Maikop 137, 138
Main River 273
Majdanek 156, 244
Makin 209
Makunsha 212
Malaya 106, 110, 111, 116–17, 119, 299, 309
Maleme 95
Malta 78, 85, 85, 87, 90, 160, 161, 163
Manchukuo 23
see also Manchuria
Manchuria 108, 112, 251, 260, 292
seized by Japan (1931) 12, 23, 27
Mandalay 120, 249, 251
Manhattan Project 290, **293**
Manila 117, 260, 283, 283
Manna, Operation (1945) 274
Mannerheim Line 46, 47
Mannerheim, Marshal Carl Gustaf 246
Manstein, Erich von 48, 135, 144, 149, 182, 188, 189, **189**
Kharkov 153–4
Operation Winter Storm (1942) 150
retreat in Soviet Union 189–90, 192–3
Manteuffel, Erich von 234, 235
Mao Zedong 13, 23, 299, 306, 306, 307
maps
Allied advance into Germany (Dec 1944–Mar 1945) 271
Allied advance through Germany (Apr–May 1945) 276
Allied bombing of German cities (Mar 1942–Mar 1943) 204
Allied invasion of Italy (Jul 1943–Dec 1944) 197

maps (cont.)
Asia and the Pacific (Dec 1941–Jun 1942) 118
Asia and the Pacific (Apr–Dec 1944) 255
Asia and the Pacific (Nov 1944–Aug 1945) 290
Battle of the Bulge (1944) 235
Battle of Kursk (July 5–13, 1943) 187
Battle of Leyte Gulf (1944) 253
bombardment of Japan (Mar–Aug 1945) 286
campaigns in North Africa (May 1942–May 1943) 162–3
campaigns in Poland and Scandinavia 47
centres of persecution 156
conquest of Yugoslavia and Greece (Apr–Jun 1941) 93
division of post-war Europe 305
Eastern Front (Dec 1941–Aug 1942) 136
Eastern Front (Nov 1942–Dec 1943) 150
Eastern Front (Jul 1943–May 1944) 192
Eastern Front (Jun–Dec 1944) 247
Europe after Versailles 15
expansion of Nazi Germany (Mar 1935–Mar 1939) 32
German bombing of British cities 62
invasion of the Low Countries and France 54
Japanese expansion (1930–39) 27
New Guinea and the Solomon Islands (Jul 1942–Mar 1943) 176
Normandy (Jun–Jul 1944) 222
offensives in Libya and Egypt (Sept 1940–Feb 1942) 91
Operation Barbarossa (Jun –Dec 1941) 101
Western Front (Jul–Dec 1944) 231
Maquis 230
Marco Polo Bridge incident (1937) 25
Mareth Line 167
Mariana Islands 185, 211, 212–13, 216, 252, 260, 286, 292
Marita, Operation (1941) 78, 94
Market Garden, Operation (1944) 232
Marne River 232
Marseilles 230
Marshall, George 306
Marshall Islands 185, 210
Marshall Plan 305, 306
Massawa 86
Masters, John 251
Matapan, Cape 93
Matsui Iwane, General 25
Medan 119
Medenine 167
Mediterranean 40, 82, 84–5, 160–1, 164, 183–4
convoys 78, 85, 90
Meiktila 249
Mein Kampf (Hitler) 16, 17, 19
Meindl, Eugen 269
Memel 244, 246, 265–6
Menuhin, Yehudi 199
merchant shipping 40, 168, 169
Japanese 254–5
Mercury, Operation (1941) 95
Merderet River 220, 221
Merrill's Marauders 249
Mersa Brega 87
Mersa Matruh 162
Messina 195
Metaxas, General Ioannis 93
Metaxas Line 94
Meuse River 52, 53, 232, 234
Mexican-Americans 128
Middle East 88–9
and Cold War 309
Hitler's designs on oil fields 84–5, 109, 137
Midway, Battle of (1942) 116, 122, 123, 147, 174, 177, 208
migration, Soviet forced 155
Mihailovic, Colonel Draza 238–9, 240
Milan 275, 275
Millennium, Operation (1942) 203
Miller, Glenn 199
Mills grenades 226
Milne Bay 177
Mindanao 252
Mindoro 283
mines 81, 85, 221, 255
Mineta, Norman 129
minority populations 10
Minsk 99, 102, 243
Missouri (US battleship) 293, 302
Mius River 153, 154, 189
Model, General Walther 189, 193, 229, 230–1, 243, 273

Modlin 43, 45
Mogadishu 86
Mogilev, V M 243
Molotov 78, 134
Monastir 94
Mongolia 108
Monte Cassino 185, 197, 198, *198*, *200–1*
Montevideo 81
Montgomery, Field Marshal Bernard Law *162*, **162**
  North Africa 85, 146, 163–7
  Sicilian and Italian campaigns 194–7
  Western Front 219, 227–9, 231, 232, 234, 259, 269, 272, 274
Montgomery, Robert 130
Morocco 164, 167
Mortain 229
Moscow 79, 100, 101, 102–3, 132, 191
Moselle River 232, 269
Mountbatten, Lord Louis 217, 307
Mukden 292
Mulberry harbours 219, *224*, 225
Mulde River 273
Münchhausen (film) 131, *131*
Munich Beer-Hall *putsch* (1923) 16, 17
Munich Pact (1938) 13, 38
Musashi (Japanese battleship) 253
Mussolini, Benito *15*, **15**, 29, 92
  arrest and escape (1943) 184, 195, *195*
  creates modern navy 44
  declares war on Britain and France 57, 84
  execution 259, *275*, **275**
  founds Italian Fascist Party 12, 15
  and Hitler *31*, 43, 49, 146, *227*
  invades Abyssinia (1935) 31
  invades Greece 76
  Libya 76, 78
  seizes power 12, 15–16
  support for Franco 13, 30
Myitkyina 249

N

Nadzab *210*
Nagano, Admiral Osami 106, 108
Nagaoka 287
Nagasaki 292, 298
Nagykanisza 267
Namsos 51
Nanking, Rape of *25*, **25**, 26, 303
Nanning 251
Naples 196
Napoleon 79
Narva 244
Narvik 49, *50*, 51
National Liberation Front (EAM) 305
National Redoubt 272, 273
National Socialist German Workers' Party *see* Nazi Party
NATO 306
Naval Limitation Treaty (1922) 21–2
naval war *see* Atlantic; Baltic; Mediterranean; North Sea; Pacific; South Atlantic
Nazi Party
  life under 18–19
  racial policy 72
  rise of 12, 16, **17**
  war crimes 301
Nazi-Soviet Non-Aggression Pact (1939) 13, 78, 99, 110
Neame, General Philip 88
Neisse River 267, 277, 278
Netherlands 232
  casualties 303
  Dutch East Indies 119, 121, 299, 307
  German occupatiof 68–9
  invasion of 38, 49, 52–3
  Jews in 72
  liberation 273–4
  resistance 228
Neuwied 269
Nevada (US battleship) 114
New Britain 121, 185, 209
New Caledonia 122
New Deal, the 111, 124
New Georgia 179, 185, 209
New Guinea 119, 121–2, 147, 174, 176–9, *177*, 208–11, 216
  Australians in *176*, **176**

New Territories 116
New York *294–5*
New Zealand and New Zealand forces
  Balkans 93
  British influence reduced in 299
  casualties 303
  Italy 198
  North Africa and Middle East 91, 95
Night of the Long Knives (1934) 17, 19
Nimitz, Admiral Chester W *119*, **119**, 123, 185, 216, 260
Nixon, Barbara 63
NKVD (Soviet Secret Service) 99, 134, 155, 193
Nomonhan, Battle of (1939) 27, 27, 110
Nordling, Raoul 231
Normandy 89, *216–17*, 217–19, 220–7, 229
North Africa *76–7*, 78, 84–91, 160–7
  French territories 76, 164
North Atlantic Treaty Organization *see* NATO
North Korea 303
North Sea 40, 49–51
North Wind, Operation (1944-45) 235
Norway
  Bodyguard plan 219
  casualties 51, 303
  invasion 41, 49–51, 82, 95
  neutrality 46, 50
  orders partial mobilization 51
Novgorod 191
Nuremberg 207, 273, 273
Nuremberg War Crimes Tribunal 297, *301*, **301**
Nuremberg Laws 18

O

Oahu 106, 113, 114
Oboe 205
Ocean Island 122
O'Connor, General Sir Richard 78, 86, 88
Oder River 258, 259, 264, 266, 267, 271, 276, 277
Odessa 156
Odon River 227
Office of Strategic Services *see* OSS
Oglala (US headquarters ship) 114
Ohm Kruger (film) 131
Oka River 132
OKH 78
Okinawa 211, 216, 260, 282, 284–6
Oklahoma (US battleship) 114
OKW 78
Olivier, Lawrence 130
Omaha beach *220–1*, 223, *223*, 224
Oosterbeek 232
Oppenheim 271
Oppenheimer, J Robert 293, 293
Oran 164
Orel 182, 188–9, 193
Orléans 230
Orne River 221
Orsha 243
Osnabrück 274
OSS 228
Ostheer 98–103, 132–9, 144–6, 148–54, 182, 186–93, 217, 242–7, 262–7, 276–9
Overlord, Operation (1944) 197, 217–19, 220–4

P

Pacific, war in the 116–23, 147, 174–9, 185, 208–13, 216–17, 248–55, 260, 282–93
Paige, Sergeant Mitchell 179
Pakistan 307
Palau Islands 210, 211, 252
Palermo 195
Palestine 84, 89, 162, 309
Pangani 178
Panjes 137, 192
Pantelleria 194
Papen, Franz von 17
Papua 177
paratroops 38, *50*, 95, *232*
Paris
  German Military Administration in 69
  Germans enter (June 1940) 57, *57*
  liberation 230–1, *230*

Park, Air Vice-Marshal Keith 58, 60
partisans *see* resistance movements
Patch, General Alexander 230
Pathfinder Force (PPF) 205
Patterson, Captain 224
Patton, General George S *234*, **234**
  North Africa 164, 167
  Sicilian and Italian campaigns 194–5
  Western Front 229, 230–2, 234, 235, 269, 271, 273
Paul, Prince Regent of Yugoslavia 78, 93
Paulus, General Friedrich 137–9, 144–5, 149, *150*, 151
peace treaties
  with Japan 302
  Potsdam Conference (1945) 296, 298
  Versailles (1919) 10, 14, 29
Pearl Harbor 106–8, *106–7*, 111, 112–15, *114*, 303
Peenemünde 233
Peking (Beijing) 25, 26
Penang 117
penicillin **212**
Pennsylvania (US battleship) 115
Petacci, Clara 275
Pétain, Marshal Henri 53, 57, 69, *69*, 76, 164
Peter, Prince of Yugoslavia 93
Petsamo 46, 47
Philippine Sea, Battle of the (1944) 213, 216, 248
Philippines 21, 106, 211, 212, 216, 248, 252–4
  postwar 303
  US retake (1945) 282–6
  US surrender in 120–1
Phoney War (1939) 40, 48, 68
Phraner, George D 115
Pilica River 262, 264
Pilsen 273
Piraeus 241
Placentia Bay 106, 108
Plan Position Indicator (PPI) 205, *205*
planes *see* aircraft
Platt, General William 86
Ploesti 95, 247
Pointblank Directive (1943) 182, 204, 205, 207
Pointe du Hoc 223, 224
Poland and Polish forces
  after Versailles 10
  Anglo-Polish Alliance (1939) 43
  casualties 45, 303
  government-in-exile 245
  Home Army 46, 245, 245
  invasion (1939) 13, 33, *36–7*, 38, 42, 43–6, 102
  Jewish ghettos in 41, 45, 72, 156
  military strength (1939) 44
  postwar 298, 301, 304
  Soviet advance into 217, 242–5, 258, 262
  troops in Italy 197, 198
Polish Corridor 33
Pomerania 258, 264, 266
pontoon bridges *270*
Popular Front, French 31
Porkhov region 193
Porsche, Ferdinand 136
Port Arthur 292
Port Moresby 122, 123, 147, 176, 177
Potsdam Conference (1945) 260, 291, 292, 296, 298, 304
Poznan 43, 262, 264, 267
Prague 276, 279
Prince of Wales (British battleship) 83, 116, *117*
Princeton (US carrier) 253
Prinz Eugen (German cruiser) 83
prisoners 57
  Bataan Death March *121*, **121**
  British and Commonwealth *95*, 119, 289
  Chinese 289
  Filipino 121
  German *144–5*, 146, 149, 151, *163*, 244, *271*
  Italian *163*
  Japanese *174*, 286, *302*
  Japanese internment in USA *128*, **128**
  Japanese POWs *289*, **289**
  Soviet *98–9*, 154
  United States 121, *289*
Prokhorovka 182, 187, 188
propaganda
  Allied 48
  Cold War 305
  German *18*, *33*, 45, 131, *131*, *150*
  Italian *15*

propaganda (cont.)
  Japanese *120*, 129, *129*
  radio **70**
  Soviet *29*, *152*
  Spanish *30*
  United States 126, *253*
  Vichy 70
  wartime cinema *130–1*, **130–1**
P'u Yi, Emperor 23, *25*
Pulawy 262
Punishment, Operation (1941) 93
Purple code *114*, 114

Q

Quisling, Vidkun 51

R

Rabaul 121, 185, *208–9*, 209, 210, 216
radar **59**, 63, 170, 203, **205**, 207, 213
radio **70**, 169, 213, 228
Raeder, Grand Admiral Erich 29, 76
RAF
  air offensive in Europe 202–7
  Battle of Britain 58–62
  Berlin 277
  Dresden *265*, **265**
  Normandy landings 221
  Operation Goodwood 227
  Rhine crossings 271
  strategic bombing offensive 182–3
Raleigh (US cruiser) 114
Ramage, Fred 272
Randolph, A Phillip 127–8
Rangoon 250
Rapallo Treaty (1922) 16
Rashid Ali 88–9
Rastenberg 227
rationing 41, 66, 71, 73, 127, 129, 268
Ravenna 199
Reagan, Ronald 126
rearmament, European **29**
Red Air Force 99, 137, 149, 150, 247, 277
Red Army 44, 46, 51, 79, 99–100, 103, 109, 132–9, 144–6, 148–54, 186–93, 262–7, 276–9
  infantry weapons *135*, **135**
  medals *148*
"Red Orchestra" 151
refugees *40–1*, 300–1
  French *40*, 57
  German 266, *266*
  Jewish 309, *309*
  Luftwaffe attacks on 38, 53
  Soviet 155
Regensburg 205
Reichstag fire (1933) 18
Reichswald 269–70, *269*
Reims 279
Reinhardt, General G H 243
Remagen 270
Rendova 179
Reno River 275
reparations 10, 14, 16
Repulse (British battlecruiser) 116
resistance movements 57, **228**
  Balkans 238–41
  Cretan 95
  French 219, *230*
  Italian 275
  Poland 46, 245
  role of women in 71
  Serb 96
  Soviet *78–9*, *102*, *193*, 193
  Yugoslav 238–40, *238–9*, 275
Reymann, General Hermann 277
Reynaud, Paul 57
Rhine River 95, 232, 233, *256–7*, 258, 259, 269
  Allied crossings 270–1, *270*
Rhineland, Hitler reoccupies 13, 31
Rhodes 239
Ribbentrop, Joachim von 33
rifles *see* guns
Riga 244, 246
Ritchie, Neil 91, 161

River Plate, Battle of the (1939) 81
Robert E. Peary (US cargo ship) *127*
Robin Moor (US freighter) 106
rockets 233
Rockwell, Norman *125*
Rodney (British battleship) 83
Roer River 269
Roermond 269
Röhm, Erich 19
Rokossovsky, Marshal Konstantin 265, 266, 277, 279
Roma (Italian battleship) 196
Romania 44, 76, 78, 87, 93, 217
   casualties 303
   falls to Soviets 240, 246–7
   post-war 301, 305
   troops on Eastern Front 136, 146, 148, 149, 151
Romanies 102
Rome 185, 196, *198*, 217
Rome–Berlin Axis (1936) 13, 30
Rommel, Field Marshal Erwin *89*, **89**
   invasion of France and the Low Countries 54, 57
   Italy 183, 195, 196
   North Africa 77, 78, 87–8, 90–1, 95, 146, 160–4, 166–7
   Western Front 219, 226, 227
Roosevelt, Eleanor 298
Roosevelt, Franklin D 106, **111**, 124, 127, 128, 167, 293, 298, 307
   Cairo Conference (1943) 217
   Casablanca Conference (1943) 146, *146*, 182
   Churchill woos 41
   death of 259
   Pearl Harbor 108
   and Philippines surrender 120
   Tehran Conference (1943) 217, *219*
   Yalta Conference (1945) 258, 296, 304
Rössler, Rudolf 151
Rostock 203
Rostov 137, 153
Rota 212
Rotterdam 38, 52, 66, 231
Rouen 204
Royal Navy 40, 49–51, 80–3, 84–5, 116, 160–1, 164, 168–71
Royal Oak (British battleship) 40, 81
Ruhr 16, 16, 204, 205, 231, 269, 272–3
Rundstedt, Gerd von
   Eastern Front 98, 100, 101, 133
   invasion of Low Countries and France 48, 52, 53, 54
   invasion of Poland 42
   Western Front 226, 269, 270
Russell Islands 178, 179
Russia *see* Soviet Union
Russian Civil War 22
Ryder, General Charles 164
Ryti, Risto 246
Ryuku Island 286

S

Saarland 44, 48, 269
sabotage 228
Saigon 111
St Lô 227
Saipan *180–1*, 185, 211, 212–13, *212–13*
Salamaua 121, 178, 208
Salerno 184, 195, 196
Salò Republic 184, 275
Salonika 93
Salween 249
Salzburg *8–9*
Samar 253
Samland peninsula 266
Samoa 122
San Bernardino Strait 253
Sandomiercz 244
Santa Cruz, Battle of 175
Sardinia 183, 194
Savo Island 174, 175
Sbeitla 166
Scandinavia
   invasion 46–8, 49–51
   occupation 68–9
   see also Denmark; Finland; Norway; Sweden
Scharnhorst (German battleship) 29, *82*, 171

Scheldt River 232, 233
Schleicher, Kurt von 17
Schleswig-Holstein 274–5
Schleswig-Holstein (German battleship) 43
Schnorchel 171
Schörner, Field Marshal Ferdinand 264
Schuschnigg, Kurt von 31
Schweinfurt 205, 273
Schwimmwagen 136
Sealion, Operation (1940) 58, 62
Seelow Heights 278
Seine River 229, 230, 232
seinengakko 22
Senegal 167
Serbia *96–7*, 239
Sevastopol *192*, 193, 231
   Battle for (1942) 135, 242
Shaibah 89
Shanghai 23, 25, 26, 26, *298–9*
Shansi province 23
Shantung province 23
"Shark" code 146
Shaw (US destroyer) 114
Shikotan 292
Shimushu 292
Shinano (Japanese carrier) 284
Shinto 298
Shinyo (Japanese escort carrier) 284
Shoho (Japanese carrier) 122
Shokaku (Japanese carrier) 122, 123
Shulze-Boysen, Harro 151
Siam (Thailand) 116, 120, 249
Sian Incident (1936) 23, 25
Siberia 132
Sichuan 251
Sicily 85, 87, 95, 183, 188
   Allied landings on 183, *184–5*, 188, 194–5, *194*
Sidi Bou Zid 166
Sidi Rezegh 77, 91
Siegfried Line 232
Sikorski, General Wladyslaw 46
Silesia 263, 264, 265, 266
Sinatra, Frank 126
Singapore 117–19, *119*, 210
Sino-Japanese War (1937–45) 13, 25–7, 106, 112, 129, 217, 248, 249, 250–1
Sirte 87
Sittang River 250
ski troops *46–7*, *51*
Skorzeny, Otto 195
Slovakia 42, 93, 136, 279
Slovenia 240
Smith, General Holland M "Howlin' Mad" 261
Smolensk 100, 102, 134
Sobibor 156
Sochaczew 264
Soddu 87
SOE **228**, 238, 240
Sollum 89
Solomon Islands 121, 122, 147, 174–9, 185, 208
Solstice, Operation (1945) 264–5, 266
Somaliland 31, 84, 86
Somme River 53, 55
sonar 169
Sopot *264*
Sorge, Richard 151, *151*
Sorong 210
Soryu (Japanese carrier) 123
South Africa 303
South Atlantic 40, 81
South Korea 303
Southern Resources Area 106, 110, 111, 112
Soviet Union and Soviet forces
   advance on Berlin 258–9, 262–7
   Battle of Nomonhan (1939) 27, 106, 110
   Bolshevik Revolution (1917) 10, 43
   casualties 45, 47, 103, 134, 144, 154, 209, 244, 300, **303**
   enters war with Japan (1945) 292
   expelled by League of Nations 46
   German–Soviet conflict 98–103, 132–9, 144–6, 148–54, 182, 186–93, 217, 242–7, 262–7, 276–9
   home front **155**
   invasion 63, 78–9, 98–103
   invasion of Finland 46–8, 246
   invasion of Poland 42, 44
   Katyn massacre 45
   Lend-Lease 109
   military strength 44, 99, 148

Soviet Union and Soviet forces (cont.)
   Moscow counter-offensive 132
   Nazi-Soviet Non-Agression Pact (1939) 13, 33, 78, 99, 110
   non-aggression pact with Japan (Apr 1941) 108, 111, 260, 291
   Operation Bagration (1944) 217
   Operation Kutuzov (1943) 188–9
   Operation Uranus (1942–43) 144, 146, 148–9
   partisans **193**
   post-war 296, 298, 300, 301–2, 304–6, 308–9
   Rapallo Treaty (1922) 16
   recapture of Western 186–93
   satellite states 298, 301, 304–6
   war with Finland (1944) 246
   see also Leningrad; Moscow; Red Air Force; Red Army; Stalingrad
Spain
   casualties 303
   Civil War (1936–39) 13, **30**, 38, 44
   rise of fascism 12, 30
   troops on Eastern Front 136
Spartacist movement 14
Special Air Service 90
Special Operations Executive *see* SOE
Speer, Albert 73, 207, 270
Spencer (US coast guard cutter) *172–3*
Spring Awakening, Operation (1945) 267
Spruance, Admiral Raymond 213
Sri Lanka *see* Ceylon
SS
   and final solution 18, 156
   Night of the Long Knives (1934) 19
Staffenburg, Colonel Claus von 227
Stalin, Josef *43*, **43**
   and German invasion 99, 100, 102, 108
   Greece 305
   ignores intelligence 137, 151
   invasion of Finland 46
   Moscow counter-offensive (1941) 132, 134
   Nazi-Soviet Non-Aggression Pact (1939) 13
   Operation Uranus (1942-43) 144, 149
   purges 95, 99
   race for Berlin 272, 276, 278
   and Spanish Civil War 30
   Tehran Conference (1943) 217, *219*
   Yalta Conference (1945) 258, 296, 304
Stalingrad 137
   Battle of *108–9*, 109, *138–9*, 138–9, 144, 148–51
Stark, Admiral Harold N. 107
Starvation, Operation (1945) 255
Ste Mère-Eglise 221
Stewart, James 130, *130*
Stilwell, Joseph 251, *251*
Strasbourg 235, 269
Strength through Joy movement 19
Stresa Front 29
Streseman, Gustav 16–17
Student, General Karl 95
submarines
   Soviet 266
   United States 216, 255, 284
   see also U-boats
Suchow 26
Suda Bay 95
Sudan 84, 85, 86
Sudetenland 13, 31–2
Suez Canal 84, 85, 88, 161, 163
Sukarno 299, 307
Sumatra 119
Suomussalmi 46
Surigao Strait, Battle of the (1944) 253
Suzuki Kantaro, Admiral 291
Sweden, neutrality 46
Sweeney, Major Charles W 292
Swinemünde 266
Sword beach 221, 224
Syria 89, 167, 309

T

Taiwan *see* Formosa
Talinn 246
Taman Peninsula 135
tanks
   in Desert War 165
   the "Funnies" 225, 225
   Soviet and German armour 190

tanks (cont.)
   British
      M3 Grant 165
      Matilda II 88
   German
      Jagdpanther heavy tank destroyer *190*
      Panzer PzKpfw II *55*
      Panzer PzKpfw III *100*, *153*, *165*
      Panzer PzKpfw V Panther *190*
      Panzer PzKpfw VI Tiger I *165*, *182–3*, *244*
      Panzer PzKpfw VI Tiger II *267*
   Italian
      CV3/35 flamethrower tankette 165
   Japanese
      Type 89 120
      Type 95 light tank 118
   US
      Sherman DD swimming tank 221, 225
      Sherman V (M4A4) crab flail tank 225
   Soviet
      KV-1B heavy tank *190*
      T-34 100, 155, 186, 190, 244
      T-34/85 190
      T-70 264–5
Tao Remmei (East Asian League) 27
Taranto 85, 113, 196
Tarawa, battle for 185, *185*, *208*, 209, *209*
target-finding systems 205
Tatsuta Maru 114
Tawitawi 212
Taylor, Colonel George 223
Taylor, Robert 126, 130
Tehran 89
Tehran Conference (1943) 217, *219*, 291, 296
Thermopylae 94
Thunderclap, Operation (1945) 265
Tibbetts, Colonel Paul W 292
Ticonderoga (US carrier) *282–3*
Tikhvin 152
Timor 119
Timoshenko, General Semyon 46–7
Tinian 185, 212
Tirana 240
Tirpitz (German battleship) 83, 171
Tito, Marshal (Josip Broz) 238–9, *240*, **240**, 259, 275
Tobruk 161, 162
   siege of 77, 85, 88, 89–90, *90*, 91
Tojo Hideki, General 27, 108, *117*, **117**, 291, 299, 303, 304
Tokubetsu Koto Keisatsu (Special High Police) 23
Tokyo 122
   bombing of 207, *260*, *286*, 287
   war crimes trials *303*
Torch, Operation (1942) 146, *146–7*, 164, 169
Torgau 272, 273
torpedoes *81*, 170–1
total war 10, 38, 41, 296
Totalize, Operation (1944) 229
Toulon 164, 230
Treblinka 156
trench warfare 45, *103*
Trident Conference (1943) 218
Trieste 275
Tripartite Pact (Sept 1940) 93, 108, 238
Tripoli 87, 166
Trondheim 49, 51
Truk 209, 210, 211
Truman, Harry S 279, 298, 302, 304, 305
Tube, the *66–7*
Tukhachevsky, Marshal 43
Tunis *142–3*, 146, 167
Tunisia 89, 146, 164, 166–7
Turkey 93, 94, 183, 239, 296
Two-Ocean Naval Expansion Act (1940) 106, 111
Typhoon, Operation (1941) 102

U

U-boats 40, 76, 80–3, *82*, *83*, 146, 259
   Class II coastal *80*
   Sinkings by U-boats **169**
   U-boat losses **169**
Ugra River 132
Ukraine 102, 134, 135, 138, 144, 150, 189, 192–3, 244
Ultra *82*, 95, 99, 151, 162, 163

United Kingdom *see* Britain
United Nations 106, 309
   International Refugee Organization (IRO) 301
   Relief and Rehabilitation Administration (UNRAA) 301
United Services Organizations *see* USO
United States and US forces
   air force 179, 185, 202–7, 212, 216, 251, 260 291–2
   air offensive in Europe 202–7
   bombs Japanese Home Islands 179, 185, 212, 216, 251, 286–8
   Burma *249*
   casualties 114, 178, 209, 213, 223, 300, **303**
   D-Day landings 220–4
   declares war on Japan 108
   economic warfare against Japan 106, 111, 112
   economy 124–6
   enters the war (1941) 108, 109, 110–11
   Germany declares war on 108
   home front 124–8
   intelligence 114
   isolationism 12, 13, 21
   Italy and Sicily 183–5, 194–9, 275
   Japanese internment in *128*, **128**
   Lansing–Ishii agreement (1917) 21
   military strength 76, 106, 109, 111, 114
   Naval Limitation Treaty (1922) 21–2
   navy 21–2, 113–14, 119, 171, 179, 209
   New Guinea 177, 178, 210–11
   Normandy 220–9
   North Africa 164, 166–7, *166*
   Pacific and Asia 116–23, 147, 174–9, 185, 208–13, 216–17, 248–55, 260, 282–93
   Pearl Harbor 106–8, *106–7*, 110, 111, 112–15, *114*
   Philippines 117, 120–1, 216, 248, 252–4, 282–6
   postwar domination 296, 298–9, 301–9
   reconstruction of Japan 298–9, 302
   relations with Britain 308–9
   relations with Nationalist China 251
   Western Front 220–35, 269–75
   women in **125**, *125*, 128
Universal Declaration of Human Rights *298*
Uranus, Operation (1942–43) 144, 146
USO 199
USSR see Soviet Union 199
Utah beach 220–1, 223, 224
Utah (US battleship) 114

V
V-1 flying bomb *233*, **233**
V-2 rocket *233*, **233**
V-weapons 67, *233*, **233**
Valletta 85
Valognes 225
Varkiza, Peace of (1945) 241
Vasilevsky, Marshal Aleksandr 137, 266
Vatutin, General Nikolai 153, 154, 192, 193
VE Day (May 8 1945) 259, 279
vehicles
   amphibious *211*, **211**
   Humber armoured car *165*
   Quad Gun Tractor *160*
   Schwimmwagen *136*
   Sd Kfz 251 half-track vehicle *55*
   Zündapp KS750 motorcycle *55*
   see also landing craft; tanks
Vella Lavella 208
Venice 275
Veritable, Operation (1945) 269–70
Versailles, Treaty of (1919) 10, 14, 29
Vichy government 57, 69–70, 71, 76, 167
   allows Japanese bases in Indochina 106, 111, 112
   anti-Semitic laws 72
   in North Africa 164
   relations with Germans 89
Victor Emmanuel III, King of Italy 15
Victorious (British carrier) 83
Vienna 258, 259, 267, 276
Vietinghoff, General Heinrich von 275
Vietnam War 299, 308, 309
Viipuri Bay 46, 47
Vilna 244

Vinnitsa 138
Vistula River 33, 42, 43, 235, 244, 258, 262–4
Vitebsk 134, 243
Vittorio Veneto (Italian battleship) 93
Vogelkop 119, 211, 212
Volchanksk 135
Volga Canal 103
Volga River 109, 138, 139
Volkhov 191
Volkssturm 262–3, *268*, 277, 279
Volturno River 196
Voronezh 137, 153, 186, 189, 192
Voroshilov, Marshal K E 134
Vyazma 102

W
WAAF *59*
Wagner, Bud 196
Wainwright, Jonathan M 120
Wakatsuki Reijiro 24
Wakde Island 210, 211
Wake Island 116, 121
Wall Street Crash 14, 17
Wanigela 178
war crimes 298, 299
   German *301*, **301**
   Japanese 303–4, *303*
Warsaw 217, 231, 244
   bombing 38, 66
   Jewish ghetto *72*, 156
   liberation 264
   siege of 43–5
   surrender *36–7*, *42–3*
   uprising **245**
Warsaw Pact 306
Wasp (US aircraft carrier) 175
Watch on the Rhine, Operation (1944) 234
Watt, Harry 131
Wau 179
Wavell, General Sir Archibald 85, 86, 87, 88, 89
weapons
   Desert War antitank **165**
   Red Army infantry **135**
   Resistance and SOE *228*
   V-weapons **233**, *233*
   Western Front infantry **226**
   see also flamethrowers; grenades; guns; mines; rockets; tanks; vehicles
Weichs, Maximilian von 137
Weidling, General 279
Weimar Republic 10, 12, 14, 16
Wellman, William 131
Werth, Alexander 144
Wesel 271
Weser Exercise 50–1
Weser River 274
West Africa, British 76
West Germany 304
West Virginia (US battleship) *112*, 114, *284–5*
West Wall 269
Western Front 217–35, 259, 269–75
Westerplatte 43
Weygand, Maxime 53, 55
Wilhelm Gustloff (German liner) **266**, *266*
Wilhelm II, Kaiser 14
Williamson, W E 57
Wilson, General Maitland 93, 94, 197, 199
Wilson, Woodrow 10, 21
Window 207, 220
Wingate, Orde 86, 248
Winter Storm, Operation (1942) 150
winter warfare **51**, *51*, 102, 132–3, *132–3*, *148, 149*
Wismar 274
women
   in Britain 68
   in Germany 70–1
   in Japan 129, *288*
   in Soviet Union 155, 193
   in Spanish Civil War *30*
   under the Nazis 19, *19*
   in United States *125*, **125**, 128
Woodlark Island 179
World War I 9, 10, 45, 296
Wuchow 251
Würzburg 273
Wyler, William 130

X
X-Verfahren 62

Y
Yalta Conference (1945) 258, 296, 298, 304
Yamamoto Isoroku, Admiral 106, 108, *112*, **112**, 179
Yamashiro (Japanese battleship) 20
Yamashita Tomoyuki, Lieutenant General 183
Yawata 185, 212
Yeremenko, General Andrei 138
Yorktown (US carrier) 122, 123, *123*
Youden, Private John 88
Young Plan (1929) 17
Yugoslavia 78, 259, 275
   after Treaty of Versailles 10
   casualties 303
   invasion 93, 96, 238
   postwar 301
   resistance 238–40

Z
Zaitsev, Vasily 139
Zaporozhye 153
Zeitler, General Kurt 182
Zhou Enlai *23*
Zhukov, Marshal Georgi 99, *133*, **133**, 134, 154, 193
   Battle of Kursk (1943) 187
   drive to Berlin 262, 264–5, 266–7, 277–9
   Moscow counteroffensive (1941) 103, 132
   Operation Kutuzov (1943) 188
   Operation Uranus (1942–43) 144, 148–9
   Stalingrad 138
Zionists 309
Zog, King of Albania 92, 238, 240
Zuikaku (Japanese carrier) 123

ACKNOWLEDGEMENTS

The publisher would like to thank the following for their kind permission to reproduce their photographs:

Firepower, The Royal Artillery Museum, Royal Artillery Historical Trust

Imperial War Museum, Duxford

ABBREVIATIONS KEY:
t=top, b=bottom, r=right, l=left, c=center, a=above, bg=background

akg: akg-images
BPK: Bildarchiv Preußischer Kulturbesitz, Berlin
DK: DK Images
Hulton/Getty Images: Hulton Archive/Getty Images
RHL: Robert Hunt Library
IWM: Imperial War Museum

Endpapers Hulton/Getty Images **1** DK/Andrew L Chernack, Springfields, Pennsylvania (cr), popperfoto.com (b); **2-3** Magnum/Soviet Group; **4-5** National Archives and Records Administration, USA (26-G-4122); **6-7** Corbis; **8-9** Topfoto.co.uk/Keystone; **10-11** Topfoto.co.uk; **12-13** Corbis/Bettmann, **13** Hulton/Getty Images (tr); **14** RHL; **15** Mary Evans Picture Library (br), Hulton/Getty Images (cl), Topfoto.co.uk (bl); **16** Corbis/Bettmann (bl), (t), Topfoto.co.uk (bc); **17** Corbis/Bettmann (c), Hulton/Getty Images (tr), RHL (b); **18** Hulton/Getty Images (t), (b), RHL (cr); **18-19** RHL; **19** Corbis Bettmann (b), RHL/US Library of Congress (cr); **20** Corbis/Bettmann (b); **20-21** Hulton/Getty Images; **21** Corbis/ Bettmann (br), Corbis/Underwood&Underwood (cr), RHL (cl); **22** Corbis/Bettmann (b), (t); **23** Corbis/Hulton-Deutsch Collection (cl), Hulton/Getty Images (cr), TRH Pictures (tr); **24** RHL (t), TRH Pictures (cl); **25** Corbis/ Bettmann (bl), (br), Hulton/Getty Images (t); **26** Corbis/Bettmann (b), Corbis/Hulton-Deutsch Collection (c); **27** Novosti (London); **28** akg (t), Corbis/Bettmann (b); **29** RHL (c), Peter Newark's Military Pictures (br), popperfoto.com (b); **30** Corbis/Bettmann (bl), (br), Mary Evans Picture Library (cl), Hulton/Getty Images (tr); **31** RHL (br), Topfoto.co.uk (t); **32-33** Corbis/ Hulton-Deutsch Collection; **33** Corbis/Bettmann (b), Peter Newark's Military Pictures (cl); **34-35** Getty Images/Time Life Pictures; **36-37** Corbis; **38-39** IWM (C1748); **40** popperfoto.com (bl); **41** Rex Features Roger-Viollet (cr); **41-42** Hulton/Getty Images; **42-43** Hulton/Getty Images (b); **43** Corbis/Bettmann (br), Corbis/SYGMA (bl); **44** akg (bl), Corbis (t bg); **44-45** Getty Images /Time Life Pictures/ Hugo Jaeger; **45** Getty Images/Time Life Pictures/Hugo Jaeger (t); **46** DK/MOD Pattern Room, Nottingham (br), Getty Images/Time Life Pictures (cl); **46-47** Hulton/Getty Images; **48** Eden Camp Modern History Theme Museum, Malton (tr), Hulton/Getty Images (b), Rex Features/Roger Viollet (tl); **49** IWM (N65) (b), Peter Newark's Military Pictures (cr), Rex Features/Roger Viollet (tc); **50** Bundesarchiv, Koblenz (183-LO4481) (tl), Mary Evans Picture Library; **51** akg (cl), Bundesarchiv, Koblenz (183-LO3926) (tr), Getty Images/Time Life Pictures/Carl Mydans/Stringer (b); **52-53** BPK/Kriegsberichter Ege; **53** Peter Newark's Military Pictures (tr), popperfoto.com (b); **54** Hulton/Getty Images (br); **55** akg (b), Peter Newark's Military Pictures (cr), (t); **56** IWM (c), Hulton/Getty Images (t), IWM (HU2287) (br), Getty Images/Time Life Pictures (bl); **57** Corbis (t), Getty Images/Time Life Pictures (b); **58** BPK; **58-59** Corbis/Hulton-Deutsch Collection; **59** IWM (CH3680) (t); **60** Aviation Picture Library/John Stroud Collection (c), BPK (t); **61** Aviation Picture Library/Austin J Brown (tl), Aviation Picture Library/Austin J Brown (br), Aviation Picture Library/John Stroud Collection (bl), BPK/Ruge (bg), The Art Archive (c), Hulton/Getty Images (tr), (cl); **62-63** IWM (HU36229); **63** Getty Images/Time Life Pictures (t); **64-65** popperfoto.com; **66** Peter Newark's

Military Pictures (b); **66-67** IWM (HU44272); **67** Peter Newark's Military Pictures (cl), Rex Features (cr); **68** Hulton/Getty Images (bl), IWM (L103) (t); **68-69** popperfoto.com; **69** Peter Newark's Military Pictures (c), Rex Features/Roger-Viollet (t); **70** BPK/Lauros-Giraudon (t), DK/IWM (br), Hulton/Getty Images (b); **70-71** Corbis/ Bettmann; **72** akg (tl), BPK (b), DK/IWM (crb), Hulton/Getty Images (tr); **72-73** IWM (IA 37578); **73** BPK (b), Hulton/Getty Images (c); **74-75** Ullstein Bild; **76-77** The Art Archive; **78** Bundesarchiv, Koblenz (101I-164-0349-20) (bl); **78-79** akg; **80** Mary Evans Picture Library (b); **80-81** akg; **81** akg (br), Hulton/Getty Images (tr); **82** akg (br), Corbis (c), DK/IWM (t), Courtesy of The Museum of World War II, Natick, Massachusetts (bl); **83** The Art Archive (tr), (cr), RHL (b); **84** Corbis/Hulton-Deutsch Collection; **85** DK/IWM (cr), Hulton/Getty Images (tr), Rex Features/Roger-Viollet (bg); **86** Corbis/Bettmann (b); **86-87** RHL; **87** akg (tr), The RHL (b); **88-89** akg; **89** Corbis/Bettmann (t); **90** Corbis/Bettmann (b), RHL (tr); **91** Corbis/Bettmann (t); **92** akg; **93** RHL (bl); **94** akg; **95** akg (b), RHL (tl); **96-97** Ullstein Bild/Wolff&Tritschler; **98** Corbis (b); **98-99** akg; **99** RHL (b); **100** akg (b), BPK (t); **101** akg (b); **102** akg (tr), (b), Ullstein Bild (tl); **102-103** Novosti (London); **103** Novosti (London) (t); **104-105** Corbis; **106-107** akg; **108-109** Hulton/Getty Images; **109** Hulton/Getty Images (t); **110** Aviation Picture Library/John Stroud Collection; **111** Corbis/Bettmann (b), Corbis/Oscar White (c); **112** Corbis (tr), Peter Newark's Military Pictures (bl), Courtesy of The Museum of World War II, Natick, Massachusetts (br); **113** Corbis/Hulton-Deutsch Collection (bg); Museum of Flight (c), Hugh Cowin (br), IWM (HU 63027) (t), National Air and Space Museum, Smithsonian Institution (RAC 1074) (bc); **114** Associated Press AP/U.S. Defense (cl), Courtesy of the National Security Agency (t); **114-115** Hulton/Getty Images/Archive Photos; **115** Courtesy of The Museum of World War II, Natick, Massachusetts (c); **116** BPK; **117** Hulton/Getty Images (t), IWM (HU2675) (b); **118** Bovington Tank Museum/Roland Groom (b); **119** Alamy Images (t), Corbis/Bettmann (b), Hulton-Deutsch Collection (cr); **120** Corbis/Bettmann (b), Courtesy of The Museum of World War II, Natick, Massachusetts (t); **121** RHL (b), (t), Courtesy of The Museum of World War II, Natick, Massachusetts (c); **122-123** The Art Archive/National Archives; **123** Corbis (t); **124-125** RHL; **125** akg (tr), The Art Archive/National Archives Washington DC (cr), Peter Newark's Military Pictures (bl); **126** Corbis (t), RHL (b); **127** Corbis (t), RHL (b), Courtesy of The Museum of World War II, Natick, Massachusetts (cl); **128** Corbis (c bg), Corbis/Bettmann (ctl), Corbis/Hulton-Deutsch Collection (tr); The Art Archive/National Archives Washington DC (ca); **129** BPK (br), Peter Newark's Military Pictures (bl); **130** Kobal Collection/United Artists (tl), Kobal Collection/Warner Bros (tr), (ca), Getty Images/Time Life Pictures (c), Corbis/John Springer Collection (cl) **130-131** Corbis/Hulton-Deutsch Collection (bl); **131** akg (tr), Mary Evans Picture Library (cl), Kobal Collection/DFG (tr); Kobal Collection/Tobis (crb); **132** Ullstein Bild (t); **133** Novosti (London) (b), (t); **134** Ullstein Bild/Grimm (b); **134-135** Novosti (London); **135** DK/IWM (tr), (ca), (cra), Hulton/Getty Images (cr), Ullstein Bild (b); **136** Bundesarchiv, Koblenz (Bild101/217/465/32A) (bl); **137** akg (b), Hulton/Getty Images (t) **138** The Art Archive (b); **138-139** Novosti (London); **139** akg (tr), DK/IWM (c), IWM (NYP38410) (br); **140-141** Ullstein Bild; **142-143** Hulton/Getty Images; **144-145** Corbis; **146** Hulton/Getty Images (tl); **146-147** Getty Images/Time Life Pictures; **148** DK/IWM (bc), Hulton/Getty Images (t); **149** Bundesarchiv, Koblenz (101I-700-0256-38) (t), IWM (FLM1476) (b); **150** Hulton/Getty Images (t), Peter Newark's Military Pictures (b); **150-151** Ullstein Bild/AP; **151** akg (c), Peter Newark's Military Pictures (tr); **152** akg (tl), (cl), Mary Evans Picture Library (cr),

Novosti (London) (crb), (b); **153** Hulton/Getty Images (t), IWM (FLM 1474 XF) (b); **154** Ullstein Bild; **155** Hulton/Getty Images (bl), Peter Newark's Military Pictures (cl), Novosti (London) (bg), Getty Images/Time Life Pictures (tr), (c); **156** akg (tr); **157** akg (tr), (bl), akg/Michael Teller (t), Hulton/Getty Images (b), (br); **158-159** Corbis/Bettmann; **160** RHL (t); **161** The Art Archive/IWM (tr); **162** Alamy Images (t), TRH Pictures (b); **163** RHL (t); **164** akg (b), RHL (c); **165** Bovington Tank Museum (tl), (tr), (c), (cr), Hulton/Getty Images (br), popperfoto.com (bg); **166** RHL; **167** The Art Archive/Musée des 2 Guerres Mondiales Paris/Dagli Orti, RHL (tl), (br); **168** The Art Archive/National Archives Washington DC (b); **168-169** Hulton/Getty Images; **169** RHL (tr), (tr bg); **170** akg (bl); **170-171** RHL; **171** Hulton/Getty Images (b), RHL (tr); **172-173** akg; **174** RHL (tl), (tr), Getty Images/Time Life Pictures (b); **175** Corbis/ Bettmann (br), Hulton/Getty Images (bl), RHL (t); **176** RHL (b); **177** Corbis/ Bettmann (b), Hulton/Getty Images (t); **178** akg (t); **179** RHL (tl), (tr), Getty Images/Time Life Pictures (b); **180-181** Hulton/ Getty Images; **182-183** akg; **184-185** Hulton/Getty Images; **185** Hulton/Getty Images (b); **186** Nik Cornish/Stavka (t); **187** Hulton/Getty Images (bl), RHL (tr); **188** Nik Cornish/Stavka (tr); **189** akg (b), Hulton/Getty Images (t); **190** Bovington Tank Museum (c), DK/IWM (b), Hulton/Getty Images (br), Ullstein Bild/Scherl-SV-Bilderdienst (bl), Ullstein Bild (bg), Ullstein Bild (t); **191** akg (b), Nik Cornish/Stavka; **192** akg (t); **193** akg (b), Corbis (cr), DK/IWM (cl); **194** akg (t), Hulton/ Getty Images (b); **195** RHL (cr), (b); **196-197** RHL; **197** RHL (tl), (tr); **198** Hulton/Getty Images (t), RHL (br), National Archives and Records Administration, USA/US Army ((C-1710) 111-CPF Box 15 and 34) (bl); **199** Corbis/Bettmann (br), The Art Archive/National Archives Washington DC (bl), RHL (t), popperfoto.com (cb); **200-201** RHL; **202** Hulton/Getty Images (b), RHL (t); **203** akg (b), Corbis/Bettmann (t); **204** RHL (c); **204-205** Corbis; **205** Corbis/Jeff Albertson (b), Hulton/Getty Images (tr), Courtesy of Norman Groom (cr); **206** Aviation Picture Library/Austin J Brown (br), aviation-images.com/John Dibbs (b), DK/Gary Ombler (cra), Hulton/Getty Images (crb), RHL (bg), National Air and Space Museum, Smithsonian Institution (SI 71-338) (b), National Air and Space Museum US Air Force, courtesy (SI 98-15407) (tl), TRH Pictures (tr); **207** akg (t), Hulton/Getty Images (b); **208** RHL (b); **208-209** Corbis; **209** RHL (b); **210** Corbis/Hulton-Deutsch Collection (b); **210-211** RHL, Bovington Tank Museum/Roland Groom (c), Corbis (t), TRH Pictures (b); **212** Corbis (bl), Corbis/Bettmann (c), (t); **212-213** RHL, RHL/US National Archives (144) (b); **214-215** Corbis/Hulton-Deutsch Collection; **216-217** RHL; **218-219** akg; **219** popperfoto.com (t); **220** popperfoto.com (b); **220-221** Magnum/Robert Capa R; **221** Corbis/Bettmann (b); **222-223** akg; **223** Hulton/Getty Images (t); **224** Hulton/Getty Images (t), IWM (BS266) (b); **225** Bovington Tank Museum (cr), Hulton/Getty Images (b), RHL (t); **226** DK/ Courtesy of Firepower, The Royal Artillery Museum, Royal Artillery Historical Trust (cbl), DK/IWM (cr), Courtesy of The Museum of World War II, Natick, Massachusetts (t); **226-227** Hulton/Getty Images (bg); **227** akg (t); Hulton/Getty Images (b); **228** DK/HK Melton (clb), DK/IWM (t), (cb), (br), DK/MOD Pattern Room, Nottingham (c), Hulton/Getty Images (bl), Rue des Archives (Photo Agency)/Jean Louis Mondange (cr); **229** akg; **230** Hulton/Getty Images (cr), RHL (tl), Getty Images/Time Life Pictures (b); **231** Corbis/Bettmann (tl); **232** The Art Archive (c), Hulton/Getty Images (t); **233** Hulton/Getty Images (t), RHL (b), Ullstein Bild/Frentz (tl); **234** Corbis/Bettmann (t); **234-235** TRH Pictures; **236-237** Hulton/Getty Images; **238-239** RHL; **239** RHL (bl), Ullstein Bild (tr), (c); **240** akg (br), RHL (bl); Getty Images/Time Life Pictures (t); **241** Hulton/Getty Images (b), RHL (t); **242-243** RHL; **243** RHL (b); **244** Nik Cornish/Stavka (tl), (b); **244-245** Hulton/Getty Images (t);

245 Hulton/Getty Images (bl), (br); **246** akg; **247** akg (tl); **248** IWM (KY471207) (b), popperfoto.com (t); **249** RHL (b), Topfoto.co.uk (tr), (t); **250** RHL (b); **251** Hulton/Getty Images (b), RHL (b); **252** IWM (NYF55918) (b); TRH Pictures (t); **253** RHL (tr), (b); **254** TRH Pictures (b); **254-255** RHL (t bg); **255** RHL/US National Archives (58) (b); **256-257** RHL; **258-259** Magnum/ Soviet Group; **260** Hulton/Getty Images (b); **260-261** Corbis/Bettmann; **262** akg; **263** Mary Evans Picture Library/Meledin Collection (b); **264-265** akg (b); **265** akg (t), (t); **266** Ullstein Bild (c); **266-267** akg (t); **267** akg (c), Bovington Tank Museum/Roland Groom (tr); **268** akg (bl), (t), DK/IWM (cl), (cr), Hulton/Getty Images (c), (br), Ullstein Bild (t); **269** RHL (b), akg (t); **270** RHL (b), (t); **271** RHL (cl); **272** akg (t); Hulton/Getty Images (b); **273** Corbis/Hulton-Deutsch Collection; **274** akg (c), Corbis/Bettmann (t), RHL (cl); Hulton/Getty Images; **275** Hulton/Getty Images (br), RHL (bc); **276-277** akg (t); **278** akg (t); **278-279** Hulton/Getty Images; **279** DK/IWM (c), RHL (tl), (tc), (bg); **280-281** Hulton/Getty Images; **282** Corbis/Bettmann; **283** RHL (b); US National Archives (156)/Joe Rosenthal, Associated Press (t); **284** RHL (t), Topfoto.co.uk (b); **284-285** US Naval Institute; **285** Associated Press AP (tr); **286** Corbis (t); **287** Corbis/Bettmann (cr), (t); **288** Corbis/Hulton-Deutsch Collection (b), The Mainichi Newspaper (t); **289** Australian War Memorial (P00406.027) (tr), Corbis/Bettmann (b); **290** Topfoto.co.uk/Novosti (b); **291** Corbis/Yevgeny Khaldei (b), Novosti (London) (t); **292** Associated Press AP (t); **292-293** RHL; **293** Corbis (t), Corbis/Bettmann (b); DK/Bradbury Science Museum, Los Alamos (c); **294-295** Corbis; **296-297** RHL; **298** Topfoto.co.uk/UN (bl); **298-299** Corbis/Bettmann; **300** Corbis/Bettmann (t), Topfoto.co.uk (b); **301** RHL (b), Topfoto.co.uk (t); **302** Hulton/Getty Images; **303** Corbis/Bettmann (tl), Corbis/Dave Bartruff (b); RHL (tr); **304** Hulton/Getty Images (cr), Getty Images/Time Life Pictures (b), (tl); **305** Hulton/Getty Images (b), Topfoto.co.uk (bl); **306** Corbis/Bettmann (cr), (t), Hulton/Getty Images (c); **307** Corbis/Bettmann (t), TRH Pictures (b); **308** Hulton/Getty Images (tl), Topfoto.co.uk (b); **309** Hulton/Getty Images (t), TRH Pictures (b); **310-311** Corbis/Bettmann.

Every effort has been made to gain permission from the relevant copyright holders to reproduce the extracts that appear in this book.

p.283: *US Marines on Iwo Jima*, The Dial Press, Inc., 1945, reprinted by Battery Press.
p.179: *The Old Breed*, Infantry Journal Press, 1949, reprinted by Battery Press. Used by permission of Mrs. Cecily McMillan.
p.208: Southern Cross account of the New Guinea Campaigns, translated by Doris Heath. Australia-Japan Research Project at the Australian War Memorial Research Center
p.211: US Marine Corps Reserve, Public Domain.
p.249: *The Road Past Mandalay*, Michael Joseph, 1961, reprinted by Orion Books. Used by permission of the Estate of John Masters.
p.289: Marine Corps Association, Quantico, Virginia, USA.
p.309: *All That Remains: The Palestinian Villages Occupies and Depopulated by Israel in 1948*, Walid Khalidi, Ed., 1992, Institute for Palestine Studies.

DORLING KINDERSLEY WOULD LIKE TO THANK: Les Smith and the staff at Firepower, the Royal Artillery Museum. Natalie Finnigan and staff at the Imperial War Museum, Duxford. Alex Reay at Advanced Illustration. Neale Chamberlain, DK Picture Library. Helen Peters for the index. Neil Grant for additional contributions. Catherine Day for proofreading.